P9-CDR-892

YALE JUDAICA SERIES

EDITOR

LEON NEMOY

ASSOCIATE EDITORS

JUDAH GOLDIN ISADORE TWERSKY

VOLUME XXIV

SIFRE ON DEUTERONOMY

Sifre
A Tannaitic Commentary on the Book of Deuteronomy

TRANSLATED FROM THE HEBREW
WITH INTRODUCTION AND NOTES BY

REUVEN HAMMER

Assistant Professor of Rabbinic Literature
Jewish Theological Seminary of America
Jerusalem Branch

YALE UNIVERSITY PRESS NEW HAVEN AND LONDON

BM
517
.S75
A3
1986

Copyright © 1986 by Yale University.
All rights reserved.
This book may not be reproduced, in whole
or in part, in any form (beyond that
copying permitted by Sections 107 and 108
of the U.S. Copyright Law and except by
reviewers for the public press), without
written permission from the publishers.

Set in Garamond #3 type by Brevis Press,
Bethany, Connecticut.
Printed in the United States of America by
Vail-Ballou Press, Binghamton, New York.

Library of Congress Cataloging-in-Publication Data

Sifrei. Deuteronomy. English.
Sifre: a Tannaitic commentary on the book of Deuteronomy.
(Yale Judaica series; v. 24)
Includes index.
1. Bible. O.T. Deuteronomy—Commentaries.
I. Hammer, Reuven. II. Title. III. Series: Yale
Judaica series; 24.
BM517.S75A3 1986 222'.1507 85–29556
ISBN 0–300–03345–1

The paper in this book meets the guidelines for permanence and durability of the Committee on Production Guidelines for Book Longevity of the Council on Library Resources.

10 9 8 7 6 5 4 3 2 1

Editor's Note

Professor Saul Lieberman, of the Jewish Theological Seminary of America, died in his sleep on March 23, 1983, in an airplane taking him to Israel.

Although his tenure as associate editor of the Yale Judaica Series was comparatively brief (1976–83), his interest in the series was aroused many years earlier, and both the editors of, and the contributors to, the series were frequent recipients of his wise counsel, and benefited greatly from his immense erudition in rabbinics as well in Greco-Roman antiquities.

He will be sorely missed.

Philadelphia
January 30, 1984

L. N.

To my father, David Hammer, of blessed memory,
who lived a blameless life and did what was right

Contents

Acknowledgments xi

A Note on the Text and Translation xiii

Introduction 1

Torah Lessons 22

SIFRE: A TANNAITIC COMMENTARY ON THE BOOK OF DEUTERONOMY

Piska̦s 1–357 23

Abbreviations 384

Notes 385

Biblical Passages Cited 515

Rabbinic Sources 533

Rabbinic Authorities 551

General Index 555

Acknowledgments

The task of translating and explaining Sifre on Deuteronomy, which is basically the task of understanding it, has occupied me now for almost a decade. My interest in the work led me to teach it at the Jewish Theological Seminary of America in Jerusalem and finally to undertake this task for the Yale Judaica Series. As the Rabbis have remarked, one's feet go where one's heart leads. I would never have done it had I not been fascinated by the book itself. The ancient aggadah is a source of inspiration, the ancient halaḵah is a constant illumination.

The more I have studied and investigated Sifre D., the more it has become obvious that there is no way in which I could exhaust its meaning or the references to which it leads. This work is, therefore, not really finished, but then it never could be. I hope that it has at least reached the point where what I have learned can be helpful to others.

This book would not have been possible without the tremendous erudition displayed in Professor Finkelstein's notes to his edition. It also owes a great deal to my students, whose questions and suggestions sharpened the meaning of so many passages, and to many of my colleagues, who generously shared their time and ideas when consulted. My deepest appreciation is to Dr. Leon Nemoy for his editorial advice.

I am indebted to the Abbell Research Fund of the Jewish Theological Seminary of America and to the Memorial Foundation for Jewish Culture for support which helped in the work, and especially to the National Endowment for the Humanities whose support enabled me to devote a concentrated period of time to it and complete it.

Most of all, I am indebted to my wife and children for their encouragement, which enabled me to go on even when the task seemed too difficult.

A Note on the Text and the Translation

The text of Sifre on Deuteronomy (henceforth Sifre D.) has come down to us in several manuscripts, the best of which is Vatican 32, stemming from the tenth century. The first edition of the work was printed in Venice in 1545. Another edition was issued by M. Friedmann in Vienna in 1864. H. S. Horovitz, who had previously prepared the critical edition of Sifre on Numbers, had partially completed a similar work on Sifre D. before he died. This was used by L. Finkelstein in preparing his own edition which was issued in Germany in 1939, was virtually destroyed by the Nazis, and was reprinted in New York in 1969.

While any of those editions could have served as the basis for this translation, each having its own advantages and disadvantages, the decision to choose the Finkelstein edition was based upon the fact that although it represents an eclectic text containing certain emendations, it is nevertheless the closest that we have to a critical edition and contains notes, parallel sources, and a critical apparatus. It was also felt that the text chosen should be the one which is most readily available for study and upon which other references and resources have been based. In this regard it is especially important to note that B. Kosovsky's *Concordance to the Sifre* (Jerusalem, 1970) also uses the Finkelstein edition.

This translation is therefore an attempt to represent faithfully that edition of Sifre D. Wherever significant differences affecting meaning and interpretation exist between the Finkelstein edition and the Vatican manuscript, this fact is mentioned in the notes. However, since these notes are intended primarily to cite important parallel sources with some indication of the basic issues involved, and to enable the general reader to read and understand Sifre D., they are by no means a complete set of critical notes exhausting all of the issues involved in establishing a definitive text. Such an endeavor is impossible within the confines of this work.

Since the scope of the notes is thus limited, it was deemed necessary to consult manuscripts and to check thoroughly Vatican 32 and Berlin 382 (listed in Finkelstein's edition as 328). Although the nature of the notes in this volume does not permit listing every departure from these manuscripts (which do not always agree with one another), I have noted what I felt were significant differences, and especially instances where Professor Finkelstein emended the text on a basis other than the manuscript readings. In his edition he included many sections which he felt were not part of the original text of Sifre D. This decision was frequently subjective, since many of these sections do appear in the better manuscripts. In this translation these doubtful sections are enclosed within brackets. When I felt that it was important, I have commented on the reason for the differentiation.

This translation is, therefore, a rendering of the Finkelstein edition. Where the translation departs from the Finkelstein edition, this fact is clearly indicated in the notes. Finkelstein's notes to that edition have been consulted and are frequently quoted in my notes, but they are not the exclusive basis for my interpretation. I have also used traditional commentaries as well as modern discussions whenever available.[1]

Explanatory words to clarify the meaning of the often concisely worded text are enclosed within parentheses. Restored lacunae and extended Biblical quotations are placed within square brackets.

Introduction

1. Sifre on Deuteronomy (Sifre D.) as Part of the Genre of Tannaitic Midrash

Sifre D. is one of a small group of books of classical interpretation of Scripture stemming from the formative period of normative Judaism in the first centuries of the Common Era. During that time the understanding of Scripture which had continuously developed since the time of Ezra was formulated and organized, each generation adding to the work of the former generations, to create an interpretation which reflected the various opinions of the Sages, known as Tannaim, concerning the meaning of Scripture.

The term *Midrash* derives from the root *drš* which is frequently found in the Bible, referring to inquiring or seeking out the word of God, usually through a prophet. In Tannaitic literature it came to signifiy seeking the meaning of a Scriptural verse, in a sense seeking the word of God through the interpretation of Scripture, the received written word.[1] Since the basic constitution, the Torah, had been established and accepted, there was no place for seeking God's will through additional personal revelation.[2] In the Book of Ezra (7:10) *drš* is used in the sense of interpreting a text,[3] but even earlier it meant to check or investigate what had been written.[4] Midrash, then, means enquiry in the sense of investigating the true meaning of a text. The early Scribes were both strict guardians of the Sacred Text and conveyors of its meaning.[5] Eventually the term came to mean that learning which is text-connected as opposed to laws which are stated without any such connection and are termed *halaḵah* or *mishnah.*[6]

Throughout the centuries material had accumulated from the early explanations of the Scribes, from the laws enacted by the Sages, and from the legal interpretations made by the use of "a complicated system of interpretation"[7] expanded by the various generations of teachers. This material was organized and edited by the two great schools of the second century, the School of R. ʿAḳiba and the School of R. Ishmael, into the various collections which, in a form augmented during the following century, have come down to us as Tannaitic Midrash.[8]

It is likely that the works which we now have on hand are only part of the deliberations which actually took place.[9] Aside from Sifre D., those extant are Mek̲ilta de-R. Ishmael to Exodus and Sifre on Numbers, from the School of R. Ishmael, and Sifre (or Torat Kohanim) to Leviticus from the School of R. ʿAḳiba.[10] In addition we now have reconstructions of two more works from R. ʿAḳiba's School, the Mek̲ilta of R. Simeon ben Yoḥai to Exodus[11] and Sifre Zuṭa to Numbers,[12] as well as Genizah fragments of a Mek̲ilta to Deuteronomy, and Midrash Tannaim to Deuteronomy from the School of R. Ishmael.[13]

Since the early days of critical Jewish scholarship the term "Midrash-halak̲ah," i.e., interpretation of legal matters, has been used to describe these works, in order to differentiate them from "Midrash-aggad̲ah," narrative interpretations, even the earliest of which was edited at a later period, and which are concerned with legends and lore rather than law.[14]

In view of the nature of these works, however, the term "Midrash-halak̲ah," with its implied limitation, may well have been an unfortunate choice, even a misnomer, since all of them include interpretations of narrative Biblical verses, sometimes of specific words,[15] legends concerning Biblical persons, stories from the lives of the Sages themselves, theological concepts and parables which illuminate the ideas presented, as well as legal matters. In some areas we have almost word by word or verse by verse explanations,[16] in others lengthier discourses which are connected to a verse but are actually complex discussions of specific topics.[17] For Biblical verses which are legal in nature, the halak̲ic implications are drawn, and discussions based on the *middot̲* (principles of interpretation) are recorded, together with differences of opinion and copious citations from the Mishnah itself. The organization of the material differs widely from place to place. Since the essence of Midrash is the explanation of the meaning of Scripture, it is not surprising that the contents of the Midrash reflect the diversity of Scripture itself. Although it is true that we do not have a work from this period based on the Book of Genesis,[18] which contains almost no legal material, the narrative portions of the other four Books of the Pentateuch are by no means stinted. In Sifre D., for example, the same verse by verse treatment given the legal sections of Deuteronomy is accorded also to the poetry of Deut. 32, while in the Mekilta the Song at the Sea (Exod. 15) is accorded an interpretation as elaborate as that given the code of law in Exod. 21. In view of this, it would be preferable to speak of Tannaitic Midrashim, reflecting the period of their origin and authorship rather than their content.[19]

In regard to the legal sections of these Tannaitic Midrashim, ever since the inception of the historical study of Judaism the question of their relationship to apodictic laws (Mishnah), laws without discussion, without explanations, without a specific connection to Biblical verses, has been debated. Which form developed first, Mishnah or Midrash?[20] And what does this mean in regard to the antiquity of the legal sections of the Tannaitic Midrashim?

Urbach[21] has traced the various points of view concerning the relationship of the two forms from the time of Krochmal on. Two definite schools may be seen: one which believes that independent apodictic laws came first, later to be strengthened by connecting them to Scripture by means of Midrash; and the other which maintains that Midrash, i.e., inquiry into the Biblical text to determine specific laws and applications, was the original way of study, from which laws emerged which were only later separated from their Biblical context and assumed the form of Mishnah. Rather than adopting either view, Urbach urges us to consider the differences in the circumstances of the times, which would account for both forms appearing at different periods. Thus the situation was not one of simple development from one form to another.[22] In addition, he notes that Midrash—inquiry—originated with the early Scribes, who were keepers of the Scriptural text, while the Sages, a different group, were enacting independent laws. Only later was exegetical learning recognized as a legitimate source of law. The antiquity of a particular law cannot therefore be determined by its form, but only by an analysis of all the relevant sources; nor can the antiquity of a passage be fixed by its form alone.[23]

It seems unlikely that each and every law that we have and which developed over the years did so as a result of Midrash, i.e., exposition of the Scriptural text. Unwritten laws have always existed and were recognized by the literature itself as laws "given to Moses at Sinai" and ascribed to the "Oral Torah," considered of equal antiquity to the written one.[24]

At the same time it is equally obvious that any written work requires explanation, and the more important and sacred the text, the more likely it is to be interpreted. Thus we find that at the very moment when the sanctity and authority of the Torah was publicly proclaimed, the process of explanation, Midrash, took place, as described in the ceremony held after the return from the Babylonian exile, when Ezra gathered all the people before the Water Gate and read them the Teaching of Moses, *from early morning until midday . . . and they read . . . distinctly, and they gave the sense* (Neh. 8.3–8). Some laws developed independently, while others sprang from interpretation of the Scriptural text.

The collections of legal Midrash which we have in these Tannaitic Midrashim contain several layers of material, incorporating traditions from the early days as well as those of the latest Tannaim, and reflecting a final redaction completed after the formulation of the Mishnah by R. Judah the Prince (ca. 200 C.E.).

Within them may be found:

1. simple Midrashim, the original formulation of which may be quite ancient;[25]

2. complex Midrashim utilizing hermeneutical rules which originated at the time of Hillel or later;[26]

3. Midrashim which connected an established ruling with a Biblical text;[27]

4. legal expositions, explaining the halaḵic meaning of a text.

Similarly, the narrative Midrash is also multi-layered and many-faceted, containing explanations of words, stories about the Biblical characters, theological expositions, parables, and stories about, and sayings of, the Rabbis.

These few books, then, represent as close an approximation as we can form of an "official" Rabbinic interpretation of Scripture. These classical expositions are invaluable documents for the understanding of the Rabbinic approach to the Bible as well as of the thinking and values of the Rabbis themselves.[28]

2. *Sifre on Deuteronomy—Origin and Structure*

The Tannaitic Midrash to Deuteronomy is known as *Sifre,* which is the plural of the Aramaic *Sifra,* "writing" or "book." The plural form is used because the Midrashim on both Numbers and Deuteronomy appear together as one work, Sifre, i.e., Books concerning Numbers and Deuteronomy."[1]

Sifre is referred to several times in the Talmud,[2] and is also referred to by R. Sherira Gaon as the way in which, through oral transmission of Scriptural interpretation, the laws were passed on.[3]

The work has been traditionally referred to as Sifre de-be Rab (see B. Ber 11b, 18b), either because, as Maimonides says in his introduction to his Code, it was thought to have been transmitted together with Sifre on Numbers and Sifra by Rab (R. Abba), the pupil of R. Judah the Prince, who founded the Sura academy in Babylonia in the 3rd century, or because, as Rashi comments (on B. Ḥul 66a), it was taught in the general academy of study, *Be Rab̲,* as distinguished from those Midrashim which were studied only by R. Ishmael's pupils.[4] A parallel exists in D. Hoffmann's collection known as Midrash Tannaim, which he formed out of Genizah fragments and those sections of the Yemenite work entitled Midrash hag-Gadol to Deuteronomy which he judged to have originated in the School of R. Ishmael.[5]

The text is divided into 357 sections, called *Pisḳaʾot,*[6] of varying lengths, and covers a major portion of the Book of Deuteronomy, but not all of it. The legal sections receive comprehensive treatment, the opening narrative portions are treated selectively, and the concluding narrative portions are given full commentary. Interpretations are found of the following verses: 1:1–30 (Dĕb̲arim), 3:23–4:1, 6:4–9 (Wa-ʾet̲ḥannan), 11:10–25 (ʿEḳeb̲), 11:26–16:16 (Rĕʾeh), 16:18–21:9 (Šofṭim), 21:10–25:19 (Ki t̲eṣeʾ), 26:1–15 (Ki t̲ab̲oʾ), 31:14 (Niṣṣab̲im), 32:1–52 (Haʾăzinu), 33:1–34:11 (Wĕ-zoʾt̲ hab-Beraḵ̲ah).

The opening verses of the first two Torah lessons, the conclusion of the third lesson and the sections found in the recitation of the *Shemaʿ,* the entire legal portion, the command that Moses must die and that Joshua will replace him,[7] and the conclusion of Deuteronomy—the poetry of chapters 32 and 33 (Haʾăzinu) and the verses concerning the death of Moses—are expounded.

The fragmentary nature of some of the comments, in contrast with the extensive treatment of other sections of Deuteronomy, has, along with other problems, given rise to speculation concerning the origin and unity of the work.[8]

This matter has been discussed at great length and in detail by Abraham Goldberg, who, in disagreement with the widely held opinion that Sifre D. is a composite work combining legal sections from the School of R. ʿAḳiba with aggadic material from the School of R. Ishmael,[9] demonstrates that the aggadic part is also from the School of R. ʿAḳiba.[10] Teachings of R. Ishmael are quoted because it was the common practice of each school to quote the other as an alternate opinion.[11] Goldberg's argument is based upon a careful analysis of both the terminology and the names of authorities in Pisḳas 1–30 which are overwhelmingly from the School of R. ʿAḳiba.[12] The legal material of the first section of Sifre D., Pisḳas 31–44, connected to the recitation of the *Shemaʿ*, is, however, that of R. Ishmael. Goldberg notes that this opening section, which is fragmentary and deals only with selected portions, unlike the rest of Sifre D., resembles in its structure the Meḵilta, and he concludes that it also is of the School of R. Ishmael, and is indeed a continuation of Sifre on Numbers. The aggadic sections, however, even if transmitted in a work of R. Ishmael's School, reflect the School of R. ʿAḳiba, as do the aggadic sections of all of the Tannaitic Midrashim.[13] Sifre D., then, may better be seen as a two-part work, the first part being basically the continuation of Sifre on Numbers, stemming from R. Ishmael's School, while the rest is directly from R. ʿAḳiba's.[14]

Sifre D. contains many statements, especially parables, taught by R. Simeon which he transmitted together with material taught by his master R. ʿAḳiba,[15] so that his influence is seen intensely in the work.

According to the Talmud, Sifre D. is the product of the School of R. ʿAḳiba as transmitted by his pupil R. Simeon ben Yoḥai, who lived in the Land of Israel during the early second century:

> R. Johanan said: the author of an anonymous Mishnah is R. Meir; of an anonymous Tosefta, R. Nehemiah; of an anonymous dictum in the Sifra, R. Judah; in the Sifre, R. Simeon; and all are taught according to the views of R. ʿAḳiba (B. Sanh 86a).

Assuming that Sifre refers to Sifre D., we have here a complete list of those Tannaitic works which have survived from the School of R. ʿAḳiba. The legal sections of Meḵilta on Exodus and Sifre on Numbers are products of the School of R. Ishmael.[16] Although we have no assurance that the Sifre, or for that matter also the other works, are the same as those mentioned by the Talmud, it seems reasonable to assume that what we have includes those works. If collections existed of Midrash to the Biblical Books, the editors surely utilized them. What we have is later versions, edited, added to, or changed in ways we cannot know, into which even later marginal notes were incorporated.[17]

Targum Onkelos, the Aramaic translation of the Pentateuch dating from the end of the 4th or the beginning of the 5th century, relies heavily on the Sifre in both the legal and the narrative sections.[18]

Sifre D. is quoted extensively by most of the classical medieval Biblical commentators, especially Rashi, who uses it with great regularity.

As in the other Tannaitic Midrashim, laws found in the Mishnah are often quoted, usually introduced with the term *mik-kan ᵓomru,* literally "from this they said," which indicates that the verse in question supports the teaching of the Mishnah and thus vindicates the Mishnaic ruling. The quotations do not cite the entire Mishnah, but only the first few words, indicating that the reader is to fill in the rest from his own memory, much as the Midrash cites Biblical verses only in part. Thus although Sifre D. is an independent work which stands in its own right as a Rabbinic explanation and interpretation of Deuteronomy, in the final redaction, which we have, it is also concerned to support the Mishnah by citing the Scriptural basis for the Mishnaic ruling wherever possible.[19]

Although the final redaction of the work was executed after the publication of the Mishnah,[20] so that Mishnaic passages are quoted and connected with Biblical verses and their interpretation, there are signs that earlier versions were independent of the Mishnah, reflecting sources which the Mishnah itself may have used, or citing laws which differ from the Mishnah and thus represent either earlier laws later changed or different laws rejected by the Mishnah's codifier.

Sifre's view that the *Shemaᶜ* must be recited aloud (Pisḳa 31) does not reflect the Mishnah, which says this is not necessary (Ber 2:3). This law preceded the Mishnah, as both Finkelstein and Lieberman have shown.[21] Finkelstein has cited other cases as well which indicate that sometimes the later redaction, for whatever reason, did not change all early material to make it conform with the Mishnah.[22] In his study of Bik 1:1, D. Halivni has shown that Sifre has used different verses from those cited in the Mishnah for the same laws, indicating that both drew upon more ancient laws and found appropriate verses. At a later stage, however, the Mishnah's wording was added to that of Sifre.[23]

As do all other classical Rabbinic works, Sifre D. contains several literary layers.[24] The earliest redactions are those from the Schools of R. ʿAḳiba and R. Ishmael, which form the basic matter of the work and contain material from earlier times, followed by the main portion which was that of R. ʿAḳiba's pupils. Sifre has further material from the time of R. Judah the Prince and a post-Mishnaic layer in which the latest authorities quoted are R. Judah's disciples of the third century, such as R. Benaiah. Lieberman has pointed to sections containing quotations from actual speeches used in the pagan world, and concludes that "the date of the text is not later than the beginning of the third century."[25] It thus seems quite certain that the basic work was edited by the pupils of the pupils of R. Judah in the third century and was compiled in the Land of Israel,[26] as was all of the Tannaitic literature.

3. *Interpretive Methods and Formulas*

The essence of Midrash, as the name itself implies, is the elucidation of the Biblical text. In the case of a legal text, this implies a discussion of the legal practices involved and the connection of the Biblical text to the accepted halaḵah as formulated in an authoritative Mishnah. This includes argumentation citing the various conclusions that one might reach and formulation of the correct interpretation. For the most part, the Tannaitic Midrashim are marked by the use of standard formulas of interpretation, including those that form part of the accepted hermeneutical rules utilized by Hillel the Elder and later elaborated and formalized into the thirteen principles of R. Ishmael.[1] Since Sifre D. is basically from the School of R. ʿAḳiba, however, his methods are those most often encountered. While R. Ishmael approached the text by the use of highly formalized and technical methods of interpretation and did not assume that the interpretations could be based on peculiarities of language ("Scripture uses normal language"), R. ʿAḳiba used methods which included interpretation of every word, including "only" and *ʾeṯ,* a particle indicating the definite predicate ("words are amplifications"), as well as using the traditional reading of Scripture (*ḳĕri*) and not only the written consonantal spelling (*kĕṯiḇ*). In addition, R. ʿAḳiba used the more inclusive interpretive principle of *ribbuy u-miʿuṭ,* "the general followed by the particular subsumes everything which is like the particular."[2] These hermeneutics appear in Sifre D. as we see in the following examples:

Gĕzerah šawah, the inference drawn from the similarity of words in two verses:[3]

> Just as the abominable thing spoken of in the latter verse refers to consecrated animals that have become unfit, so does the abominable thing spoken of in the former verse refer to consecrated animals that have become unfit. (Piska 99)

Heḳḳeš, the drawing of analogy or comparison:

> Why then does Scripture say, *Thou shalt set the blessing on Mount Gerizim* (11:29)? . . . To indicate the analogy between curses and blessings: just as the curses were pronounced by the Levites, so were the blessings pronounced by the Levites; just as the curses were pronounced aloud, so were the blessings pronounced aloud; just as the curses were spoken in the holy tongue, so were the blessings spoken in the holy tongue; just as the curses were general or particular, so were the blessings general or particular; just as both groups answered Amen to the curses, so did they answer Amen to the blessings, turning toward Mount Gerizim for the blessings and toward Mount Ebal for the curses. (Piska 55)

Ḳal wa-ḥomer, logical inference from minor to major or from major to minor:

> This is a matter of logical inference from the minor to the major: if Hebron, the refuse of the Land of Israel, is superior to the best place in Egypt—which is the best of all the other lands—it follows that the verse speaks in praise of the Land of Israel. (Piska 37)

Ribbuy u-miʿuṭ, the general followed by the particular subsumes everything which is like the particular:

> I might at this point exclude also sin and guilt offerings; hence the verse says, *thy holy things* (12:26). Who then tells you to include sin and guilt offerings but exclude the first-born and the tithes? (The fact that) after the verse includes, it proceeds to exclude: I include the sin and guilt offerings, which have no remedy except in their own place, and I exclude the first-born and the tithes, which have a remedy anywhere. (Piska 77)

Sifre D., like other early Midrashim, transmits interpretations of words and phrases in the Biblical verses under consideration which serve to help the reader understand the text, changing classical Biblical Hebrew into current usage or demonstrating the connection of one stitch of a verse to another:

> *Thou shalt not be afraid of them; for the Lord thy God is with thee, who brought thee out of the land of Egypt* (20:1): He who had brought you out of the land of Egypt is with you in time of trouble. (Piska 190)

Some of these seem to be little more than translations of terms which were not well understood, either because of their difficulty or because they reflected realia no longer current.[4] Thus we find the formula *ʾen . . . ʾellaʾ* (literally "it is nothing other than . . .") utilized as a philological Midrash.[5] Here a word in one Biblical verse is explained on the basis of its use in another verse:

> *Hand* means a place, as it is said, *Behold, he is setting himself up a hand* (1 Sam. 15:12). (Piska 257)

> Enticement always implies acting in error, as it is said, *Whom Jezebel his wife enticed* (1 Kings 21:25). (Piska 87)

Formulaic Words and Phrases

In order to understand these interpretations, it is helpful to note the more commonly used phrases and words which appear as technical terms connecting Biblical verses and their interpretations.

The prefix *šĕ*, "that," appears as an introduction to an interpretation, in the sense of "this indicates that . . ." or "so that . . ." At times it need not be translated at all, since it may do little more than indicate that an interpretation follows:

> *And known to your tribes* (1:13): (*šĕ*) they should be known to you, for when such a man wraps himself up in his cloak and comes to sit before me, I do not know what tribe he belongs to, but you know him, because you grew up with them. Hence *known to your tribes,* meaning (*šĕ*) they should be known to you. (Piska 13)

> *To observe to do all this commandment* (15:5)—meaning (*šĕ*) that a lesser commandment should be as precious to you as a weighty commandment. (Piska 115)

> What does Scripture mean by saying, *Asher, one portion . . . Reuben, one portion . . . Judah, one portion* (Ezek. 48:2, 6, 7)? That (*šĕ*) in the

future Israel will encompass an area stretching (all the way) from east to west in length, and twenty-five thousand rods, or seventy-five miles, in width. *And there shall be no strange god with Him* (32:12): There (*šĕ*) will be no idolaters among you. (Piska 315)

Both *maggid,* "informs us," and *melammed,* "teaches us," appear in Sifre D. with Scripture as the unspoken subject: "(Scripture) teaches us," "(Scripture) informs us." The intent of the verse is to teach us something, either an idea or a specific course of conduct.[6] *Melammed* is usually used by the School of R. ʿAḳiba, and *maggid* by that of R. Ishmael, but the texts as edited and transmitted are not always consistent in this respect:[7]

That are within thy gates (14:29): Hence (*melammed*) we learn that the poor man may not be taken outside of the (Holy) Land. (Piska 110)

And this shall be the priests' due (18:3): Hence (*melammed*) we learn that these dues may be claimed through the judges. (Piska 165)

For the Lord will surely bless thee in the land (15:4)—This indicates (*maggid*) that blessing is dependent upon the land alone. (Piska 114)

Through his ear and into the door (15:17), That is (*maggid*), put the awl through the ear until it reaches the door. (Piska 122)[8]

A similarly used interrogative form is introduced by the word *minayin,* "from whence?" The question is asked, what is the Scriptural source of a known practice? The verse which teaches it is then cited:

Seven weeks shalt thou number unto thee (16:9): (The counting to be done) by the court. Whence (*minayin*) do we learn that each person must also count? From the verse, *And ye shall count unto you from the morrow after the day of rest* (Lev. 23:15)—each person (must count) individually. (Piska 136)

A more complicated formula utilizing *minayin* is *ʾen li ʾellaʾ . . . minayin . . . talmud lomar,* "so far my understanding of Scripture indicates . . . ; what is there that teaches . . . as well? The verse states . . ." This formula cautions against limiting one's interpretation of a verse to too narrow a focus. It insists that by returning to the verse one may find that more was included than a superficial reading might indicate. Sometimes this is accomplished by citing various phrases in the verse and interpreting them:

Now this obviously refers only (*ʾen li ʾellaʾ*) to long duration; but

> what about (*minayin*) short duration (of travel)? The answer (*talmud lomar*) is supplied by the phrase in the same verse, *So that thou art not able to carry it.* Now this obviously refers only (*ʾen li ʾellaʾ*) to a poor man; whence (*minayin*) do we learn the rule for a rich man? From (*talmud lomar*) another phrase in the same verse, *When the Lord thy God shall bless thee.* (Piska 107)

This is not always the case, however, and it is not always clear whether the additional meaning is gained by the repetition of a root-word, by some peculiarity in the verse, some seemingly needless addition, or simply by taking a word in its broader rather than its most constricted meaning. For example, *ʾiš* may mean a male, but it could also mean mankind:

> *There shall no man be able to stand against you* (11:25): This refers to (*ʾen li ʾellaʾ*) a single man: what about (*minayin*) a nation, a family, or even a woman plying her witchcraft? Hence (*talmud lomar*) the verse says, *There shall no man be able to stand*—in any combination. If so, why does Scripture say *man*? To include even (a man) like Og king of Bashan, of whom it is said, *For only Og king of Bashan remained of the remnant of the Rephaim* (3:11). (Piska 52)

The term *yakol . . . talmud lomar,* "you might think . . . , hence . . . ," appears frequently and almost without exception introduces a proposition which is to be negated: this is what we might have thought, but Scripture specifically indicates otherwise:

> You might (*yakol*) think that you must wait until a prophet tells you, hence the verse goes on to say, *Even unto His habitation shall ye seek and thither thou shalt come* (12:5)—search for and find a place, then the prophet will tell you. (Piska 62)

> *Because the Lord thy God shall bless thee* (16:15): One might (*yakol*) think that this means only in the same kind; therefore the verse goes on to say, *in all thine increase.* (Piska 142)

In general this is part of the tendency of Tannaitic Midrashim to demonstrate the dependence of the halakah upon the written word, both positively and negatively. Every phrase of a verse, sometimes every word, is useful in teaching what is to be done, every verse is needed in order to prevent misinterpretations. Logic alone could lead to incorrect halakic conclusions, and thus requires the specific limitations and expansions which Scripture specifies. See Piskas 34, 36, 101, and 107 for examples of this.

Similar to *yaḵol* is the phrase *ʾo ʾeno ʾellaʾ . . . talmuḏ lomar.* An interpretation is offered which is rhetorically challenged by another possible interpretation. Another phrase or verse is cited which indicates that the first meaning is the correct one. Were it not for the Scriptural verse, we might have been misled into accepting an incorrect interpretation:

> *And I will give grass in thy fields for thy cattle* (11:15): So that you will not be troubled to go into the wildernesses. You might say, "Is it as you explain it, so that you will not be troubled to go into the wildernesses, or (*ʾo ʾeno ʾellaʾ*) does *And I will give grass in thy fields for thy cattle* mean literally just what it says?" Therefore the verse goes on to say, *And thou shalt eat and be satisfied.* How then am I to understand *And I will give grass in thy fields for thy cattle?* That you will not be troubled to go into the wildernesses. (Pisḳa 43)

There are two formulaic phrases which deal with the question of seemingly superfluous verses. One, *lammah neʾĕmar . . . lĕ-fi šĕneʾĕmar . . . šomeʿa ʾani,*[9] "Why is this said? . . . Since another verse states . . . , which I might have wrongly understood to mean . . . ," discusses a verse whose purpose seems unclear. The comment then demonstrates that the verse is needed in order to correct a possible misunderstanding of another verse:

> Another interpretation: *That thou mayest gather in thy corn*—why is this said? Because elsewhere it is said, *This Book of the Law shall not depart out of thy mouth* (Josh. 1:8)—I might think that this is to be taken literally; therefore the other verse says, *That thou mayest gather in,* etc., for the Torah usually speaks of normal things in life. (Pisḳa 42)

The other phrase, *wĕha-loʾ ḳĕḇar neʾĕmar,* "does it not state elsewhere," is concerned with a verse which seems to be only a repetition of another verse. Why, then, is this one stated at all? The answer is that it indicates something additional not found in the other verse:

> Another interpretation: What does (the repetition of) *with all your heart and with all your soul* mean? Does not Scripture say elsewhere (*wĕha-loʾ ḳĕḇar neʾĕmar*), *With all thy heart and with all thy soul* (6:5)? (The answer is,) the latter refers to the individual, while the former refers to the entire community; the latter refers to study, while the former refers to performance. (Pisḳa 41)

Another introductory term, found in aggadic sections connecting verses to commentary, which should be mentioned is *šĕ-neʾĕmar,* "as it is said," in which a thought is presented and then verses are cited which illustrate the idea (see, for example, the end of Piska 38).

Rejection of the Simple Meaning

One of the prominent literary characteristics of the work is the search for a deeper meaning following the rejection of the more obvious surface meaning of a Scriptural verse or tale. Sifre D. begins with an overall view of a personality, for example, and then decides that in view of what we know about that person's entire life and work a particular recorded incident contradicts logical expectation and therefore cannot mean what it seems to mean. A different interpretation of the text is then sought and offered. For example, we read in Piska 9:

> *I am not able to bear you myself alone* (1:9): Is it possible that Moses could not sit in judgment over Israel, this man who had brought them out of Egypt, who had split the sea asunder for them, who had brought down the manna for them, who had fetched the quails for them, and had performed other signs and miracles for them? Such a man could not sit in judgment over them? Rather, he spoke to them thus: *The Lord your God hath multiplied you* (1:10) upon the backs of your judges.

In view of our overall knowledge of Moses, such a thing is not possible, therefore the meaning must be otherwise, since it must make sense. See Piska 31 for several other examples of this.

Similarly, a statement cannot be taken at face value if it contradicts other facts. The entire work, for example, begins with the question, how can we take the first verse of Deuteronomy literally, with its implication that what follows is the record of all that Moses spoke, when we know that he also said many other things? Obviously the real meaning must be something else:

> *These are the words which Moses spoke* (1:1): Did Moses prophesy nothing but these words? Did he not write the entire Torah, as it is said, *And Moses wrote this Torah* (31:9)? Why then does the verse state, *These are the words which Moses spoke?* Hence we learn that they were words of rebuke, as it is said, *But Jeshurun waxed fat, and kicked* (32:15). (Piska 1)

It is therefore taken to mean that we are dealing with harsh words alone, with rebuke.

Similarly, when Scripture says "take men" when commanding the appointment of judges, the question is asked, why did Scripture say this, seeing that no one would even think of appointing women to such a post? The words must therefore imply something else:

> *Men* (1:13): Would we ever think of appointing women? Why then does the verse say *men*? To indicate men that are as multifaceted as a mosaic, that is to say, men who are trustworthy and suitable. (Piska 13)

Many such sections begin with the phrase "Would we ever think . . . ?," indicating a quest for the logical and consistent meaning in the face of the "impossible" surface meaning—impossible either because it contradicts other facts or givens or because it is too obvious for Scripture to have even bothered to state it.

Other examples may be found in Piskas 153, 298, and 342.

Repetition of the Interpretation

Finally we should note that it is characteristic of Sifre D. that particular interpretive phrases are connected to a specific word or phrase and are then repeated whenever that word appears. The appropriateness of the interpretation is questionable in some cases; the comment may have been meaningful in its original place, but is either meaningless or inappropriate when repeated elsewhere. It is impossible to know whether these repetitions are ancient or reflect the work of some later editor who simply copied the explanation of a phrase whenever the phrase recurred. Being cognizant of the latter possibility, however, helps one to avoid a great deal of needless interpretation and search after some deeper intent on the part of the interpreter when none may have existed.[10] See, for example, the case of the clause *So shalt thou put away the evil from the midst of thee* (Deut. 13:6), which, whenever it occurs in Sifre D., is followed by the comment "remove the evildoer from Israel" (Piska 86, 151, 155, 186, 240, etc.).

4. *Basic Homiletic Themes and Ideas*

R. Simlai remarked that the Torah begins and ends with acts of loving-kindness (B. Soṭa 14a). One might say that Sifre D. begins with rebuke and ends with reconciliation. The Book of Deuteronomy itself is a similar mixture, with its significant stretches of denunciation and predictions of dire punishment tempered with words of comfort and Moses' blessing his people.

Deuteronomy predicts national disaster but also national revival and ultimate triumph. It was written before the exile, possibly in the hope of preventing it by urging fidelity to God's word which would bring His favor. Sifre D., on the other hand, came into being hundreds of years later, when there had been not one but two destructions of the nation and of the Temple, when the political structure and independence of the nation had been dissolved and the challenges to the legitimacy of Judaism were at their height. It was important, therefore, to strengthen the authority of Rabbinic law and to demonstrate the divine nature of Scripture by interpreting the legal portions of Deuteronomy in such a way as to integrate the halaḵah with Scriptural verses and highlight the relevance of each verse, indeed each word, of the Bible. By the time of the final editing of the Sifre in the third century C.E. the problem was not how to avert disaster by inculcating obedience, threatening punishment, or promising reward, but how to sustain Jewish life through hope for the future by reaffirmation of the basis of Judaism: the eternal relationship between God and Israel.

Thus, although Sifre begins with a famous section which goes even further than Deuteronomy itself in chastising the people for their sins from the time of the Exodus onward and in emphasizing the fact that this is a work of rebuke, other sections tend to soften the punishment and accentuate the eventual comfort and restoration. This may be illustrated by the following passage, which appears toward the end of the work:

> *Happy art thou, O Israel, who is like unto thee?* (33:29): Israel says, *Who is like unto thee, O Lord, among the mighty?* (Exod. 15:11), and the holy spirit responds, *Happy art thou, O Israel. Happy art thou, O Israel*: All Israel gathered together before Moses and said to him, "Our master Moses, tell us what good things the Holy One, blessed be He, has in store for us in the future." He replied, "I do not know what to tell you. Happy are you with that which is prepared for you." (Piska 356)

Although it is undoubtedly true that the argument from silence is no argument, one may wonder whether the fact that the harsh passages in Deut. 27 and 28—the curses—which are so crucial to the Biblical text, do not receive any Midrashic attention in Sifre D., is totally accidental.

Indeed the concluding aggadic sections of the work, especially Haʾăzinu, which is the major portion, display a didactic tendency which would be appropriate to the period of time following the failure of the Bar Kokhba rebellion. The element of punishment is softened for Israel but not for the nations:

> *Babylonia hath been a golden cup in the Lord's hand, that made all the earth drunken* (Jer. 51:7): Just as broken (vessels of) gold can be restored, so after the punishment of the nations ceases, it will be brought upon them once more. But concerning Israel's punishment what does Scripture say? *Thou shalt even drink it and drain it, and thou shalt crunch the sherds thereof* (Ezek. 23:34): Just as broken vessels of clay cannot be restored, so after the punishment of Israel ceases, it will never be reimposed. (Piṣka 324)

The element of comfort is heightened:

> Once again, on the morrow, she (Israel) will say before Him: "Master of the universe, Thou hast already written down, *saying: If a man put away his wife, and she go from him, and become another man's wife, may he return unto her again?* (Jer. 3:1)." God replies: "Did I not specifically write *a man*? And has it not already been said, *For I am God, and not man* (Hos. 11:9)?" Another version (of God's reply): "Have you been divorced from Me, O house of Israel? Has it not already been said, *Thus saith the Lord: Where is the bill of your mother's divorcement, wherewith I have put her away? Or which of My creditors is it to whom I have sold you?* (Isa. 50:1). (Piṣka 306)

And the overall effect is to lead the reader to a feeling of anticipation of *ʿaṯiḏ la-ḇoʾ*, the great Messianic future with the vindication of Israel.

Prominent in Sifre D. are the following themes:

1. The importance of the people of Israel. Although the sections on rebuke are replete with condemnation of Israel, which must be seen not only as a reflection of historical events but also as a comment on current affairs (see Piṣkas 12, 14, 20, 24, and numerous sections in Haʾăzinu), Sifre misses no opportunity to praise the people and to stress God's positive relationship to them, emphasizing the unbroken nature of this relationship. To reassure the Jewish people in the hour of tragedy and depression and to refute those who held

otherwise, the Sages and editors of Sifre stress that Israel is the favored of God (Piska 15), that love and intimacy remain intact between God and Israel (Piskas 355, 356). God is indeed the Master of the universe, but His relationship with Israel is special and unique (Piska 31). Regardless of what they may have misdone, God forgives His people (Piska 30) and feels no hatred toward them (Piska 24).

2. If Israel is beloved and will be redeemed, the nations who have dealt cruelly with her are condemned and will suffer the consequences of their cruelty. Reflecting the bitterness of the post-destruction era, Sifre, especially in its latter sections, describes the nations in harsh terms and sees them as doomed to repeated destruction.

3. Closely allied to the preceding themes is Sifre's attitude toward Jacob, the prototype of Israel, and his children. The theme of Jacob's special merit and of the superiority of his entire family appears in several places in the work, such as Piska 312, and is dwelt upon at great length in the complex composition found in Piska 31. As has been discussed in detail by E. Mihaly,[1] this may be a response to Christian claims and certainly strengthens Israel's claim to the position of the exclusive people of the covenant. Only those who are descended from Jacob can claim to be part of this relationship, for the others who sprang from Abraham or Isaac are mere refuse. Only conversion to Judaism will bring one not descended from Jacob into this special relationship (Piska 354). In this connection one should also note the heavily critical attitude toward the nations of the world, including a different attitude toward the seven Noachide commandments than that usually taken (see B. Sanh 56a; it is echoed in a similar aggadic section, B. AZ, beginning). These laws were not observed by the other nations, and were therefore taken from them and given as additional commandments to Israel.

4. In contrast to Jacob, Abraham appears in quite a different capacity. He brings about a revolutionary change in the world and in God's relationship to it, but it is in his role as an individual that he does this, and the covenant relationship is not emphasized.

Abraham's major merit is seen in the fact that he brought knowledge of God into the world (Piska 354). It was Abraham who changed God's relationship to the world, moving Him from emphasis upon justice (or even severity) to mercy through the sufferings of love imposed upon Abraham which continued upon the Israelites (Piska 311). The Christian claim that redemptive suffering came first and exclusively through Jesus is countered here by the Jewish claim that it had existed before and has always been the role of the people of Israel.

In addition to the places where Abraham and Jacob are compared in respect to the merits of their progeny, they are also compared once (Piska 336) in respect to their observance of God's commands. Here, too, the emphasis is upon Jacob, for Abraham is said to have observed only one command, whereas Jacob is anachronistically credited with observing the entire Torah!

5. The personality of Moses is dealt with extensively, as was to be expected, since Deuteronomy is couched in the form of a speech given by Moses, and his plea to let him enter Israel and the story of his death are also contained in this book. Sifre D. describes his unhappiness with the conduct of the people (Piskas 1–2) and their attitude toward him (Piska 14), his concern for the people (Piska 342) and for the leader who is to follow him (Piskas 304–05). His death is depicted in a particularly artistic story which combines humor and great poignancy (Piska 326).

6. Just as the merit of the people of Israel is stressed, so is the merit and worth of the Land of Israel. Using the slightest of pretexts, the editors have included a highly sophisticated section on the merits of the Land. Its beauty, its fruitfulness, its uniqueness are all commented upon at great length in what can only be described as a rhapsodic paean to a land which realistically speaking was suffering a decline (Piskas 37–40;[2] see also Piskas 316 and 354). To a people suffering destruction, economic problems, and foreign subjugation, these words served to reaffirm the Biblical promises and the centrality of the Land to Judaism.[3]

7. Questions of God's nature and judgment of peoples and individuals are discussed. As Kadushin has shown in his studies of Rabbinic thinking and of Tannaitic texts,[4] the two qualities of God, mercy and justice, encompass the tension in the world and the various ways in which God is experienced according to Rabbinic doctrine (see Piskas 49, 311, 306).

This also results in an interesting attitude toward human merit. Basing itself upon the merits of such great men as Moses and David, the text adopts a posture which became normative for Judaism in the liturgy of the High Holy Days: God's graciousness to man, who can never be truly deserving of the mercy that he is shown (Piska 26).

Without denying the existence of human merit, we are taught that merit is never used in a plea to God, but only His graciousness, which is given *ḥinnam,* "unearned," to man.

8. On the other hand, in human relationships, justice must be the rule. The need for a good system of justice and for the seriousness with which the work of the judge should be treated is emphasized time and time again (Pisḳas 9, 17, 29).

9. The Torah and its glory is an obvious theme which is taken up in Sifre as well. It is the antidote to the evil Inclination (Pisḳa 45). Methods for its study are discussed in detail (Pisḳa 48). It is Israel's exclusive property (Pisḳa 345).

10. An interesting point is the problem of the observance of the commandments outside of the Land (Pisḳas 25, 43). Since the problem of exile was a real one, Israel-centered Sifre went out of its way to indicate that such observance outside of the Land was no more than practice for the true observance, which can be practiced only in the Land itself.

Taken as a whole, then, the aggadic sections of this work reflect the basic value scheme of Pharisaic Judaism, and take a stance intended to strengthen the Jews' resolve in the face of adversity. The historical background is that of a time of trouble, suffering, even disaster: the situation of the Jewish people in the Land of Israel during and after the Hadrianic persecution and the failure of the Bar Kokhba revolt. There are, of course, stories, legends, and interpretations which originated long before that time. Not missing either are pointed, though indirect, answers to the challenges of the newly emerging Christian group.

In spite of all this Sifre does not conceal the faults of the Jewish people, their rebelliousness, and their unfaithfulness. In reviewing the stern admonitions of Moses, it thus also criticizes the contemporary scene. On the other hand, it stoutly affirms the status of the people, both from the events in the lives of the Patriarchs and from Scriptural promises, as God's peculiar treasure with a unique relationship to Him. It denounces the claims of the nations or of Christianity to have displaced them. It draws a picture of the Land of Israel as the Promised Land and the land of promise, and reaffirms the Torah as the supreme object of value. The people of Israel, the Land of Israel, and the Torah of Israel are placed squarely in the center of the values to be taught.

As for God, He is the God of Israel while being also the universal God of all nations. He is God of mercy and God of righteousness, whose mercy far exceeds His justice, who expects obedience and moral conduct from Israel, but grants His favor to men out of His grace and not because of their deeds.

The work, especially in the later sections, is permeated by Messianic expectation. This is what will happen in the future—tomorrow—in the renewed world. Then Israel, His people, will be revealed and restored in all their glory. The failures and punishments of the past will be forgotten and obliterated. The nations will be seen for what they are and will be punished.

Torah Lessons

Lesson	*Piska*
Debarim	1–25
Wa-ʾethannan	26–36
ʿEkeb	37–52
Reʾeh	53–143
Šofṭim	144–210
Ki teṣeʾ	211–296
Ki taboʾ	297–303
Niṣṣabim	304–305
Haʾăzinu	306–341
Wĕ-zoʾt hab-berakah	342–357

Piska 1

These are the words which Moses spoke (1:1*): Did Moses prophesy nothing but these words? Did he not write the entire Torah, as it is said, *And Moses wrote this Torah* (31:9)?[1] Why then does the verse state, *These are the words which Moses spoke?*[2] Hence we learn that they were words of rebuke, as it is said, *But Jeshurun waxed fat, and kicked* (32:15). Similarly Scripture states, *The words of Amos, who was among the herdmen of Tekoa, which he saw concerning Israel in the days of Uzziah king of Judah, and in the days of Jeroboam the son of Joash king of Israel, two years before the earthquake* (Amos 1:1). Did Amos prophesy concerning none but these kings? Did he not prophesy about more (rulers) than any one of his fellows? Why then does the verse state, *The words of Amos,* etc.? Hence we learn that they were words of rebuke. Where is it stated that they were words of rebuke? In the verse, *Hear this word, ye kine of Bashan that are in the mountain of Samaria, that oppress the poor, that crush the needy, that say unto their lords: 'Bring, that we may feast'* (Amos 4:1). This refers to their courts. Similarly Scripture states, *And these are the words that the Lord spoke concerning Israel and concerning Judah* (Jer. 30:4). Did Jeremiah prophesy nothing but these words? Did not Jeremiah write two scrolls, as it is said, *Thus far are the words of Jeremiah* (Jer. 51:64)?[3] Why then does the verse state, *And these are the words?* Hence we learn that they were words of rebuke. Where is it stated that they were words of rebuke? In the verse, *For thus saith the Lord: We have heard a voice of trembling, of fear and not of peace. Ask ye now, and see whether a man doth travail with child: wherefore do I see every man with his hands on his loins, as a woman in travail, and all faces are turned into paleness? Alas! for that day is great, so that none is like it; and it is a time of trouble unto Jacob, but out of it shall he be saved* (Jer. 30:5–7). Similarly Scripture states, *Now these are the last words of David* (2 Sam. 23:1). Did David prophesy nothing but these words? Does not Scripture state also, *The spirit of the Lord spoke by me, and His word was upon my tongue* (2 Sam. 23:2)? Why then does it say here, *Now these are the last words of David?* Hence we learn that they were words of rebuke. Where is it stated that they were words of rebuke? In the verse, *But the ungodly, they are as thorns thrust away, all of them, for they cannot be taken with the hand* (2 Sam. 23:6). Similarly Scripture states, *The words of Koheleth, the son of David, king in Jerusalem*

*For references to the Book of Deuteronomy only chapter and verse are given.

(Eccl. 1:1). Did Solomon prophesy nothing but these words? Did he not write three scrolls and half of his wisdom in proverbs?[4] Why then does the verse state, *The words of Koheleth*? Hence we learn that they were words of rebuke. Where is it stated that they were words of rebuke? In the verse, *The sun also ariseth, and the sun goeth down . . . (the wind) goeth toward the south, and turneth about unto the north; it turneth about continually in its circuit, and the wind returneth again*—meaning east and west—(*to its circuits*). *All the rivers run into the sea* (Eccl. 1:5–7). Solomon uses here the sun, the moon, and the sea to represent the wicked, for they will receive no reward.[5]

Unto all Israel (1:1): Had he rebuked only some of them, those who were in the market place might have said, "You heard this from the son of Amram, and you did not answer him back? By God, had we been there, we would have had four or five retorts to him for every one of his words!"[6]

Another interpretation: *Unto all Israel*: Hence we learn that Moses had gathered them all together, from the oldest to the youngest, and said to them, "I am about to rebuke you. If anyone has anything to say in a rebuttal, let him come forth and speak."

Another interpretation: *Unto all Israel*: Hence we learn that all of them were deserving of rebuke and able to stand up under rebuke.[7] R. Tarfon said: "I swear by the Temple service, I doubt if there is anyone in this generation who is fit to rebuke others."[8] R. Eleazar ben Azariah said: "I swear by the Temple service, I doubt if there is anyone in this generation who is able to receive rebuke." R. ʿAḳiba said: "I swear by the Temple service, I doubt if there is anyone in this generation who knows how to rebuke."[9] R. Johanan ben Nuri[10] said: "I call heaven and earth to witness for me that R. ʿAḳiba was rebuked through me more than five times before R. Gamaliel in Jabneh, when I would complain about him, and R. Gamaliel would rebuke him, yet I am certain that he loved me more each time." This bears out what Scripture has said, *Reprove not a scorner, lest he hate thee; reprove a wise man, and he will love thee* (Prov. 9:8).[11]

Beyond the Jordan (1:1):[12] Hence we learn that he rebuked them for what they had done beyond the Jordan.[13]

In the wilderness (1:1): Hence we learn that he rebuked them for what they had done in the wilderness.

Another interpretation: *In the wilderness*: Hence we learn that they seized their infant sons and daughters and hurled them into Moses' bosom, saying to him, "Son of Amram, what ration or sustenance do you intend to provide for them?" R. Judah says: Hence Scripture states, *And the children of Israel said unto them: Would that we had died by the hand of the Lord in the land of Egypt, (when we sat by the flesh-pots, when we did eat bread to the full; for ye have brought us forth into this wilderness, to kill this whole assembly with hunger)* (Exod. 16:3).

Another interpretation: *In the wilderness*: This applies to everything they had done in the wilderness.

In the Arabah (Plain) (1:1): Hence we learn that Moses rebuked them for what they had done in the Plains of Moab, as it is said, *And Israel abode in Shittim, (and the people began to commit harlotry with the daughters of Moab)* (Num. 25:1).

Over against Suph (1:1): Hence we learn that Moses rebuked them for what they had done at the sea,[14] for they rebelled at the sea and turned their backs on Moses for the space of three journeys.[15] R. Judah says: They rebelled at the sea, and they rebelled also in the midst of the sea, hence Scripture says, *They were rebellious at the sea, even in the Red Sea* (Ps. 106:7).[16]

One might think that he rebuked them only at the beginning of a journey. Whence do we learn that (he rebuked them also) between one journey and another? From the statement *between Paran and Tophel* (1:1).[17]

[*And Tophel, and Laban*] (1:1): This refers to the disparaging words[18] that they spoke concerning the manna, as it is said, *And our soul loathed this light bread* (Num. 21:5). He[19] said to them: Fools! Even kings choose light bread for themselves in order to avoid vomiting or diarrhea, but you—you use the favor that I have bestowed upon you to complain before Me. It seems that you are following the foolish ways of your father,[20] for I had said, *I will make him a help meet for him* (Gen. 2:18), and he said, *The woman whom Thou gavest to be with me, she gave me of the tree and I did eat* (Gen. 3:12).

And Hazeroth (1:1): He said to them: Should you not have learned from what I did to Miriam in Hazeroth?[21] If I showed no partiality in judgment toward the righteous Miriam, how much more so toward other persons.

Another interpretation: If Miriam, who spoke only about her younger brother, was punished thus, how much more so will this happen to a person who speaks thus of one who is older than himself.

Another interpretation: If Miriam, who spoke in such a way as to be heard by no one save God alone,[22] was punished thus, how much more so will this happen to one who speaks disparagingly of his fellow in public.

And Di-Zahab (1:1):[23] He said to them: I would have overlooked[24] everything that you have done, but the incident of the (golden) calf is to Me worse than all the rest put together. R. Judah used to say: A parable: to what may this be likened? To A who had caused a great deal of trouble to B. Finally, A troubled him once more, whereat B said, "I could have overlooked everything that you had done to me, but this is worse for me than all the rest put together." Even so God said to Israel, "I could have overlooked everything that you had done to Me, but the incident of the calf is worse for Me than all the rest put together."

R. Simeon says: A parable: to what may this be likened? To one who used to entertain scholars and students, and everyone praised him. Heathen came, and he entertained them; robbers, and he entertained them also. Finally people said, "It is his nature to entertain anyone at all." Even so Moses said to Israel, "Enough gold[25] for the Tabernacle, and enough gold for the calf!" R. Benaiah says: Since Israel have worshiped idols, they are liable to extinction. Let the gold of the Tabernacle therefore atone for the gold of the calf.[26] R. Jose ben Ḥaninah says: *And thou shalt make an Ark cover of pure gold* (Exod. 25:17)—let the gold of the Ark cover atone for the gold of the calf.[27] R. Judah says: Scripture says, *In the wilderness, in the Arabah,* etc.—this refers to the ten occasions when our ancestors tried God in the wilderness, to wit: two concerning the sea, two concerning water, two concerning manna, two concerning quails, one concerning the calf, and one concerning the spies in the wilderness of Paran.[28] R. Jose ben Dormaskit[29] said to him: Judah son of Rabbi,[30] why do you distort Scripture for us? I call heaven and earth to witness for me that we have examined all these place-names, and they are all actual places named after some event.[31] Similarly Scripture says, *(And the herdmen of Gerar strove with Isaac's herdmen, saying, "The water is ours"). And he called the name of the well Esek, because they contended with him* (Gen. 26:29), and *And he called it Shibah* (Gen. 26:33).

In a similar manner R. Judah interpreted the verse, *The burden of the word of the Lord. In the land of Hadrach, and in Damascus, shall be His resting-place; for the Lord's is the eye of man and all the tribes of Israel* (Zech. 9:1). This refers to the Messiah, who is sharp (*ḥaḏ*) toward the nations and soft (*rak*) toward Israel.[32] R. Jose ben Dormaskit said to him: Judah son of Rabbi, why do you distort Scripture for us? I call heaven and earth to witness for me that I come from Damascus, and there is indeed a place there called Hadrach. He replied: How then do you explain *and in Damascus shall be His resting-place?*[33] (R. Jose replied:) Whence do we learn that in the future Jerusalem will expand as far as Damascus? From *and in Damascus shall be His resting-place*; "resting-place" always means Jerusalem, as it is said, *This is My resting-place forever* (Ps. 132:14).[34] (R. Judah) said to him: How then do you explain the verse, *And the city shall be builded upon her own mound* (Jer. 30:18)?[35] He replied: In the future Jerusalem will not move from its location, for how do I explain the verse, *And the side-chambers were broader as they wound about higher and higher; for the winding about of the house went higher and higher round about the house; therefore the breadth of the house continued upward* (Ezek. 41:7)? That in the future the Land of Israel will expand on all sides like a fig that is narrow below and broadens upwards, so that in the future the gates of Jerusalem will reach as far as Damascus.[36] Hence Scripture says, *Thy nose is like the tower of Lebanon which looketh toward Damascus* (Song 7:5), and the returning exiles will come and settle therein, as it is said, *And in Damascus shall be His resting-place* (Zech. 9:1), *And it shall come to pass in the end of the days, that the mountain of the Lord's House shall be established at the top of the mountains, and shall be exalted above the hills, and all nations shall flow into it; and many peoples shall go and say,* etc. (Isa. 2:2–3).

In a similar manner R. Judah interpreted the verse, *And he made him to ride in the second chariot which he had, and they cried before him "Abrech"* (Gen. 41:43). This refers to Joseph, who was a father (*ʾab*) in wisdom and young (*rak*) in years. R. Jose ben Dormaskit said to him: Judah son of Rabbi, why do you distort Scripture for us? I call heaven and earth to witness for me that *Abrech* means "I will make them bend their knees (*birkayim*)," for everyone had to come and go under his authority, as it is said, *And they set him over all of Egypt* (Gen. 41:43).

Piska 2

It is eleven days' journey from Horeb unto Kadesh-barnea by the way of Mount Seir (1:2): Is it really eleven days from Horeb to Kibroth-hattaavah, and from Kibroth-hattaavah to Hazeroth, and from Hazeroth to the wilderness of Paran?[1] Is it not rather a journey of only three days, as it is said, *And they set forward from the Mount of the Lord three days' journey (and the Ark of the Covenant of the Lord went before them three days' journey, to seek out a resting-place for them)*[2] (Num. 10:33)? R. Judah says: Could Israel have made eleven journeys[3] in three days' time? Is it not rather a journey of forty days, as in the matter of Elijah, of whom it is said, *And he arose, and did eat and drink, and went in the strength of that meal forty days and forty nights (unto Horeb, the Mount of God)* (1 Kings 19:8)?[4] Seeing how impossible this is, go back to the first matter, that of the *eleven days' journey*: had Israel been meritorious for eleven days, they would have entered the land immediately, but since they had acted corruptly, God imposed upon them forty years for the forty days, as it is said, *After the number of the days in which ye spied out the land, even forty days, for every day a year* (Num. 14:34). R. Judah[5] says: Had Israel been meritorious for three days, they would have entered the land immediately, as it is said, *And the Ark of the Covenant of the Lord went before them three days' journey, to seek out a resting-place for them,* and "resting-place" always refers to the Land of Israel, as it is said, *For ye are not as yet come to the rest and the inheritance, which the Lord your God giveth thee* (12:9). R. Benaiah says: Had Israel been meritorious for one day, they would have entered the land immediately, as it is said, *This day ye go forth in the month Abib. And it shall be when the Lord shall bring thee into the land of the Canaanite,* etc. (Exod. 13:4–5)—immediately.[6] Abba Jose ben Ḥanan of Yanoaḥ says in the name of Abba Kohen ben Dalya: Had Israel been worthy when their feet had come up out of the Sea, they would have entered the land immediately, as it is said, *Go up, take possession*—immediately—*Go up, take possession, as the Lord, the God of thy fathers, hath spoken unto thee; fear not, neither be dismayed* (1:21).

And it came to pass in the fortieth year, in the eleventh month (1:3): Hence we learn that the year has twelve months.[7] But do we not know that the year has twelve months? Does not Scripture state elsewhere, *Even upon the thirteenth day of the twelfth month, which is the month Adar* (Esther 3:13), and similarly, *And Solomon had twelve officers over all Israel, (who provided victuals for the king and his household: each man had to make provision for a month in the year)* (1 Kings 4:7)? Scripture says further, *And one officer that was in the land* (1 Kings 4:19). What purpose did this one serve? He provided for the thirteenth intercalated month. R. Benaiah says: Before the time of Solomon would we not have known that the year has twelve months?[8] Does not Scripture say elsewhere, *And he said unto them, "I am a hundred and twenty years old this day?"* (31:2). Whenever Scripture uses the term "this day," it implies "my days have been brought to a conclusion on this day."

Another interpretation: *This day* implies that on that very day a specific period of time was completed, starting and ending on the same day. Elsewhere Scripture says, *And the people came up out of the Jordan on the tenth day of the first month* (Josh. 4:19). Now go and count back thirty-three days, and you will find that the year has twelve months.[9]

Another interpretation: *And it came to pass in the fortieth year*: Hence we learn that he rebuked them only when he was about to die. From whom did he learn this? From Jacob, who rebuked his sons only when he was about to die, as it is said, *And Jacob called unto his sons, and said, "Gather yourselves together, that I may tell you that which shall befall you in the end of days"* (Gen. 49:1). *Reuben, thou art my first-born* (Gen. 49:3)—do we not know that Reuben is the first-born? Rather this tells us that Jacob said to him, "Reuben, my son, let me tell you why I did not rebuke you all these years: so that you would not leave me and go off to cleave to my brother Esau." There are four reasons why A should not rebuke B until A is about to die: so that A would not be rebuking B over and over again; so that, whenever B sees A, he would not feel ashamed; so that B would not hold a grudge against A; and so that B would depart from A in peace,[10] for rebuke should bring about peace. You find the same thing concerning Abraham, as it is said, *And Abraham reproved Abimelech* (Gen. 21:25). And what does it say subsequently? *And they two made a covenant* (Gen. 21:27). So also concerning Isaac, as it is said, *And Isaac said unto them, "Wherefore are ye come unto me, seeing ye hate me, and have sent me away from you?"* (Gen. 26:27). And what does it say subsequently? *And Isaac sent them away, and they departed from him in peace* (Gen. 26:31). So also you find that Joshua rebuked Israel only when he was about to die, as it is said, *And if it seem evil unto you to serve the Lord, choose you this day whom ye will serve* (Josh. 24:15), followed by, *And the people said unto Joshua, "Nay; but we will serve the Lord." And Joshua said. . . . "Ye are witnesses,"* etc. (Josh. 24:21–22). So also you find that Samuel rebuked Israel only when he was about to die, as it is said, *"Here I am; witness against me before the Lord, and before His anointed."* . . . *And they said, "Thou hast not defrauded us,"* etc. . . . *And he said unto them, "The Lord is witness against you."* . . . *And they said, "He is witness"* (1 Sam. 12:3–5). And finally you find that David rebuked Solomon his son only when he was about to die, as it is said, *Now the days of David drew nigh that he should die; and he charged Solomon his son, saying, "I go the way of all the earth"* (1 Kings 2:1).[11]

Moses spoke unto the children of Israel (1:3): Did Moses prophesy only *these . . . words* (1:1)? Particularly, whence do we learn that (he also taught) all of the commandments of the Torah, arguments a fortiori, arguments from verbal analogy,[12] arguments from general categories and specific applications,[13] the major rules and the details? From the verse, *Moses spoke (unto the children of Israel) according unto all that the Lord had given him in commandment unto them* (1:3).[14]

Pisḳa 3

After he had smitten Sihon (1:4): A parable: A king went out into the wilderness with his troops. His troops said to him, "Give us fine warm white bread." He said to them, "I will give it to you." Again[1] they said to him, "Give us fine warm white bread." His lieutenant said to them, "(You trouble him) because he is so able.[2] Otherwise,[3] where would he have gotten grindstones and ovens out here in the wilderness?"[4] So also Moses said, "If I rebuke Israel first at this time, they will say of me, 'It is because he has no power to bring us into the land and to overthrow Sihon and Og before us that he is rebuking us!' " That is why he waited until he had brought them into the land and had overthrown Sihon and Og before them, and only then did he proceed to rebuke them. Hence Scripture says, *after he had smitten Sihon the king of the Amorites.*

Who dwelt in Heshbon (1:4): Had Sihon not been mighty but dwelt in Heshbon, it still would have been difficult (to conquer them), because the city itself was mighty. Had the city not been mighty but had Sihon dwelt in it, it would have been difficult (to conquer them) because of its mighty king. How much more difficult was it (to conquer) both a mighty king and a mighty city!

And Og the king of Bashan (1:4): Had Og not been mighty but dwelt in Ashtaroth, it still would have been difficult (to conquer them); and had the city not been so mighty but had Og dwelt in it, it would have been difficult (to conquer them) because the king was mighty. How much more difficult was it with both a mighty king and a mighty city!

In Ashtaroth—indicating that Ashtaroth was mighty[5]—*at Endrei* (1:4) which was the royal capital.

Pisḳa 4

Beyond the Jordan, in the land of Moab, took Moses upon him (hoʾil) to expound (1:5): R. Judah says: The verb *hoʾil* always means "to begin," as it is said, *Begin (hoʾel-naʾ) to tarry all night, and let thy heart be merry* (Judg. 19:6), and *Now begin (hoʾalta) to bless the house of thy servant, that it may continue forever before Thee* (1 Chron. 17:27). The Sages, however, say that the word *hoʾil* always means swearing an oath, as it is said, *Moses swore (way-yoʾel) to dwell with the man* (Exod. 2:21), and *Saul swore (way-yoʾel) to the people, saying, ("Cursed be the man")* (1 Sam. 14:24).[1]

To expound this law, saying (1:5): He said to them, "I am about to die. If there be anyone who had learned a verse but forgot it, let him come and go over it; if he forgot a whole lesson, let him come and go over it; if he forgot a chapter or a law, let him come and go over it. Hence *to expound this law, saying.*[2]

Pisḳa 5

The Lord our God spoke unto us at Horeb, saying (1:6): Moses said to them, "I am not speaking on my own—what I am saying to you comes from the mouth of the Holiness."[1]

Ye have dwelt long enough in this mountain (1:6): Your staying at this mountain is a reward for you—you have made for yourselves the Tabernacle, you have made for yourselves the Table (of Showbread), you have made for yourselves the Lampstand.

Another interpretation: Your staying at this mountain has been a benefit for you—you have accepted (the yoke of) the Torah upon yourselves, you have appointed seventy elders over yourselves, you have set up leaders of thousands, leaders of hundreds, leaders of fifties, and leaders of tens over yourselves. Thus staying at this mountain has been a great benefit to you.

Another interpretaion: Your staying at this mountain has been bad for you—*Turn you, and take your journey* (1:7), for idleness is bad.[2]

Pisḳa 6

Turn you, and take your journey, and go—by way of Arad and Hormah[1]—*to the hill-country of the Amorites and unto all the places nigh there unto*—Ammon, Moab, and Mount Seir[2]—*in the Arabah*—the plain of Zoar—*in the hill-country*—the mountain of the king—*and in the lowland*—the lowland of Lod and the lowland in the south—*and in the South, and by the sea-shore*—Gaza, Ashkelon, and Caesarea—*the land of the Canaanites* (1:7)—the border of the Canaanites, as it is said, *And the border of the Canaanites was from Zidon,* etc. (Gen. 10:19).

And Lebanon (1:7): Moses said to them, "When you enter the land, you will have to appoint for yourselves a king and build for yourselves the Chosen House."[3] Whence do we learn that *Lebanon* refers to a king? From the verses *(A great eagle) . . . came unto Lebanon, and took the top of the cedar*[4] (Ezek. 17:3), and *(And Jehoash the king of Israel sent to Amaziah king of Judah, saying), "The thistle that was in Lebanon (sent to the cedar that was in Lebanon")* (2 Kings 14:9). And whence do we learn that *Lebanon* refers to the Temple? From the verses *Thou art Gilead unto Me, the head of Lebanon; (yet surely will I make thee a wilderness)* (Jer. 22:6), and *And He shall cut down the thickets of the forest with iron, and Lebanon shall fall by a mighty one* (Isa. 10:34).[5]

Another interpretation: Why is the Temple called Lebanon? Because it whitens (*malbin*) the transgressions of Israel, as it is said, *Though your sins be as scarlet, they shall be as white as snow* (Isa. 1:18).

As far as the great river, the river Euphrates (1:7): Hence we learn that its main force is toward the Land of Israel.[6] As the common saying has it, "A king's servant is a king; cling to a warm person, and you will be warm."

Another interpretation: *The river Euphrates* (Pĕraṯ), so called because it branches off (*mafriḏ*)[7] and peters out, because it is ladled out (to irrigate the fields). Another interpretation: *The river Euphrates,* so called because it widens (*poreh*) and increases until it is passable by ships. All the rivers say to the Euphrates, "Why do you not let your voice be heard as our voices are heard from afar?" It replies, "My deeds speak for me. A man sows a seed in me, and it sprouts in three days; he plants a plant in me, and it sprouts in thirty days. Hence Scripture praises me, *As far as the great river, the river Euphrates.*"

Pisḳa 7

Behold I have set the land before you (1:8): Moses said to them, "I say this to you not on the basis of an estimate or a vague rumor[1] but from that which you can see with your own eyes."

Go in and possess the land (1:8): He said to them, "When you enter the land, you will need no weapons—just take a compass and divide it up."[2]

Pisḳa 8

Which the Lord swore unto your fathers (1:8): Why does the verse go on to say *to Abraham, to Isaac, and to Jacob?* If it is in reference to the oaths sworn to (each of) the fathers, Scripture says elsewhere, *The oaths proclaimed to the tribes* (Hab. 3:9).[1] Why then does Scripture say here, *to Abraham, to Isaac, and to Jacob?* To indicate that Abraham alone was worthy, Isaac alone was worthy, Jacob alone was worthy.

A parable:[2] A king gave his servant a certain field as a gift, gave it to him as it was. The servant went to work to improve it, saying, "What I have is only that which was given to me as it was," and planted a vineyard in it, saying again, "What I have is only that which was given to me as it was." So also when the Holy One, blessed be He, gave Abraham the land, He gave it to him only as it was, as it is said, *Arise, walk through the land in the length of it and in the breadth of it; for unto thee will I give it* (Gen. 13:17). Abraham then went to work to improve it, as it is said, *And Abraham planted a tamarisk tree in Beer-sheba* (Gen. 21:33). Isaac likewise went to work to improve it, as it is said, *And Isaac sowed in that land, and found in the same year a hundredfold* (Gen. 26:12). Jacob too went to work to improve it, as it is said, *And he bought the parcel of ground* (Gen. 33:19).[3]

To give unto them—to those who have entered the land—*and to their seed*—to their children—*after them* (1:8)—referring to those areas which were conquered by David and Jeroboam, as it is said, *He restored the border of Israel from the entrance of Hamath,* etc. (2 Kings 12:25).[4]

Rabbi (Judah the Prince) said: *To give unto them*—to those who returned from Babylon[5]—*and to their seed*—to their children—*after them*—referring to the time of the Messiah.

Pisḳa 9

And I spoke unto you at that time, saying (1:9): Moses said to Israel, "I am speaking not on my own—what I am saying to you comes from the mouth of the Holiness."[1]

I am not able to bear you myself alone (1:9): Is it possible that Moses could not sit in judgment over Israel, this man who had brought them out of Egypt, who had split the sea asunder for them, who had brought down the manna for them, who had fetched the quails for them, and had performed other signs and miracles for them? Such a man could not sit in judgment over them? Rather, he spoke to them thus: *The Lord your God hath multiplied you* (1:10) upon the backs of your judges.[2] Similarly Solomon says, *Give Thy servant therefore an understanding heart to judge Thy people* (1 Kings 3:9). Is it possible that Solomon could not sit in judgment over Israel, this man of whom it is said *And the Lord gave Solomon wisdom* (1 Kings 5:26), and *And Solomon's wisdom excelled the wisdom of all the children of the east, and all the wisdom of Egypt. For he was wiser than all men: than Ethan the Ezrahite, and Heman, and Calcol, and Darda, the sons of Mahal; and his fame was in all the nations round about* (1 Kings 5:10–11)? Such a man could not judge them? Rather he spoke to them thus: "I am not like all the other judges. A mortal king sits on his tribune and issues judgments for execution by the sword, by strangulation, by burning, or by stoning, and it means nothing (to him). And if by right he should take one selaʿ, he takes two, or if two, he takes three, or if a denar, he takes a mina.[3] I am not like this. If I (unjustly) find a person guilty in monetary matters, I am held to account for it as if it were a capital case."[4] Hence Scripture says, *Rob not the weak, because he is weak, neither crush the poor in the gate; for the Lord will plead their cause and despoil of life those that despoil them*[5] (Prov. 22:22).

Pisḳa 10

And behold, ye are this day as the stars of heaven for multitude (1:10): Behold, you are as eternal as the day.[1] Hence[2] the Sages have said: There are seven groups of the righteous in Paradise, one higher than the other: the first, *Surely the righteous shall give thanks unto Thy name; the upright shall dwell in Thy presence* (Ps. 140:14); the second, *Happy is the man whom Thou choosest, and bringest near* (Ps. 65:5); the third, *Happy are they that dwell in Thy House* (Ps. 84:5); the fourth, *Lord, who shall dwell in Thy Tabernacle?* (Ps. 15:1); the fifth, *Who shall dwell upon Thy holy mountain?* (Ps. 15:1); the sixth, *Who shall ascend into the mountain of the Lord?* (Ps. 24:3); the seventh, *and who shall stand in His holy place?* (Ps. 24:3)[3]

R. Simeon ben Yoḥai said: In the future the faces of the righteous will resemble seven joyous things:[4] the sun, the moon, the firmament, the stars, lightning, lilies, and the lampstand of the Temple. Whence the sun? From the verse, *But they that love Him be as the sun when he goeth forth in his might* (Judg. 5:31). Whence the moon? From the verse, *Fair as the moon* (Song 6:10). The firmament? *And they that are wise shall shine as the brightness of the firmament* (Dan. 12:3). The stars? *And they that turn the many to righteousness as the stars* (Dan. 12:3). Lightning? *They run to and fro like the lightnings* (Nah. 2:5). Lilies (*šošannim*)? *For the leader; upon šošannim* (Ps. 45:1). The lampstand of the Temple? *And two olive trees by it, one upon the right side of the bowl and the other upon the left side thereof* (Zech. 4:3).[5]

Pisḳa 11

The Lord, the God of your fathers, make you a thousand times so many more as ye are (1:11): They said to him, "Moses, our teacher, you cannot give us such a blessing, for God has already assured our father Abraham, *In blessing I will bless thee, and in multiplying I will multiply thy seed as the stars of the heavens and as the sand (which is upon the seashore)* (Gen. 22:17): and yet you limit our blessing!" A parable: A king who had many possessions and a young son found it necessary to journey to a place beyond the sea. He said, "If I leave all my possessions in the hands of my son, he will squander them. I will therefore appoint a guardian for him until he comes of age." When the son came of age, he said to the guardian, "Hand over to me the silver and the gold that my father had left with you for me." But the guardian, out of his own money, gave him only enough to maintain himself. The son then began to press him, saying, "You have all that silver and gold that my father had left for me!"[1] He replied, "Whatever I have given you was out of my own. What your father had left for you has been safely preserved." Thus also Moses said to Israel: *The Lord, the God of your fathers, make you a thousand times so many more as ye are*—that is my own blessing;[2] the blessing that is already yours is, *and bless you as He hath promised you* (1:11), that is to say, as many as the sand of the seashore, the plants of the earth, the fish of the sea, and the stars of the heavens.

Pisḳa 12

How can I myself alone bear your cumbrance (ṭarḥăḵem)? (1:12): This shows that they were troublemakers (*ṭarḥanim*).[1] If one of them saw the other besting him in a lawsuit, he would say, "I have (more) witnesses to bring. I have (more) evidence to present. Tomorrow I will add to the trial and demand additional judges." Hence *your cumbrance,*[2] showing that they were troublemakers.

And your burden (1:12): Hence we learn that they were *ʾapiḳorsim* (skeptics).[3] If Moses left his home early, they would say, "Why did the son of Amram see fit to leave (so early)? Perchance he is not happy at home." If he left late, they would say, "Why did the son of Amram fail to leave (earlier)? What do you think? Perchance he sits and concocts plots against you, and thinks hard and oppressive thoughts, even worse than the house of On," as it is said, *And On, the son of Peleth, sons of Reuben* (Num. 16:1).[4] Hence *and your burden,* showing that they were skeptics.

And your strife)1:12): Hence we learn that they were litigious:[5] they would spend a selaʿ to get two, two to get three.[6] Hence *and your strife,* showing that they were litigious.[7]

[Another interpretation: *Your cumbrance, and your burden, and your strife*: If Moses went out early, they would say, "Why did the son of Amram see fit to go out so hurriedly? So that his sons and members of his household might gather the largest pieces of manna." If he went out late, they would say, "He ate, drank, and had a nap (first)." If Moses walked in their midst, they would say, "He wants to make us stand up before him." If he walked on the side, they would say, "We have the commandment of standing up to honor an elder, and he seeks to uproot this commandment from our midst." Moses said to them, "If I walk in your midst, I do not satisfy you. If I walk on the side, I do not satisfy you."]

Pisḳa 13

Get you (1:13): Get (*haḇu*) always means "advise," as in *Give your counsel* (haḇu) *what we shall do* (2 Sam. 16:20), and *Come* (haḇu), *let us deal wisely with them* (Exod. 1:10).

Men (1:13): Would we ever think of appointing women? Why then does the verse say *men*? To indicate men that are as multifaceted as a mosaic,[1] that is to say, men who are trustworthy and suitable.

Wise (1:13): That is what Arios[2] asked R. Jose, saying, "Who is a wise man?" R. Jose replied, "One who establishes his teaching solidly." "Does it not mean simply an understanding man?" asked Arios. R. Jose replied, "Scripture goes on to say *understanding*."[3] What is the difference between a wise man and an understanding one? A wise man is like a rich money-changer: when people bring to him coins for examination, he examines them; when they do not, he takes out his own coins and examines them. An understanding man is like a poor money-changer: when people bring to him coins for examination, he examines them; when they do not, he is at a loss.

And known to your tribes (1:13): They should be known to you, for when such a man wraps himself up in his cloak[4] and comes to sit before me, I do not know what tribe he belongs to, but you know him, because you grew up with them. Hence *known to your tribes,* meaning they should be known to you. R. Simeon ben Gamaliel says: There is no session (of a court) without people complaining about it and saying, "What made So-and-so see fit to sit, and what made So-and-so see fit not to sit?" Hence *known to your tribes,* meaning that they should be known to you.[5]

And I will make them heads over you (1:13): One might think that Moses meant, "If you appoint them, their appointment is effective; if not, it is not effective."[6] Hence Scripture says, *I will make them heads over you*—if I appoint them, they are effectively appointed; if not, they are not. One might think that Moses meant, "If you raise them to high office, they are effectively raised; if not, they are not." Hence Scripture says, *I will make them heads over you*—if I raise them, they are effectively raised; if not, they are not.

Another interpretation: If you obey your leaders, your heads will be safe; if not, they will not be safe.[7]

Another interpretation: Read not *And I will make them (wa-ʾăśimem) heads over you* but "Their guilt (*wa-ʾăšamom*) is upon your heads."[8] Hence we learn that the guilts of Israel are visited upon the heads of their judges, as it is said, *So thou, son of man, I have set thee a watchman unto the house of Israel: therefore, when thou shalt hear the word of My mouth, warn them from Me. When I say unto the wicked: "O wicked man, (thou shalt surely die," and thou dost not speak to warn the wicked from his way, that wicked man shall die in his iniquity, but his blood will I require at thy hand). Nevertheless, if thou warn,* etc. (Ezek. 33:7–9).

Pisḳa 14

And ye answered me, and said, "The thing which thou hast spoken is good for us to do" (1:14): Moses said, "You should have said, 'Moses, our teacher, from whom is it best to learn Torah? From you, or from your students, or from your students' students? Is it not from you, who have suffered for it?' as it is said, *And he was there with the Lord forty days and forty nights; (he did neither eat bread, nor drink water)* (Exod. 34:28), and *Then I abode in the mount forty days and forty nights; I did neither eat bread nor drink water* (9:9). But I know that behind my back[1] you said, 'Now he will appoint over us some eighty thousand judges less a few, and it will be I, or else my son, or else my grandson, and then we can bring him a gift in order to induce him to favor our case.' Hence it is said, *ye answered me*; (that is to say,) when I was slow about it, you would say 'Do it right away.' "[2]

Pisḳa 15

So I took the heads of your tribes, wise men, etc., *and I charged your judges* (1:15–16): I attracted them with words, saying, "How fortunate you are! Over whom are you about to be appointed! Over the children of Abraham, Isaac, and Jacob, men who have been called brothers and friends, a pleasant vineyard and portion, sheep of His pasture, and all kinds of such endearing terms."

Wise men, and full of knowledge (1:15): This is one of the seven qualities which Jethro had mentioned to Moses, of which Moses found only three, *wise men and full of knowledge.*[1]

And made them heads over you (1:15): Meaning that they should be held in honor by you, leaders in buying and selling, in mutual negotiation, in coming in and in going out, such as come in first and go out last. Hence *And made them heads over you,* meaning that they should be held in honor by you.

Captains of thousands—if there were 1,999, only one captain of thousand was appointed—*captains of hundreds*—if there were 199, only one captain of hundred was appointed—*captains of fifties*—if there were 99, only one captain of fifty was appointed—*captains of tens*—if there were 19, only one captain of ten was appointed.[2]—*and officers* (1:15)—these were the Levites who administered the lashings, as it is said, *Also the officers of the Levites before you* (2 Chron. 19:11), and *So the Levites stilled all the people, saying: "Hold your peace"* (Neh. 8:11).

Pisḳa 16

And I charged your judges at that time saying, "Hear the causes between your brethren, and judge righteously" (1:16): I said to them, "Be deliberate in judgment. If a case comes before you two or three times, do not say, 'Such a case has already come before me repeatedly,' but be deliberate in judgment." The men of the Great Assembly likewise said, "Be deliberate in judgment, raise up many disciples, and make a fence for the Torah."[1]

At that time saying: In the past you were independent, but now you are the servants of the community. It happened once that R. Johanan ben Nuri and R. Eleazar Ḥisma were appointed by Rabban Gamaliel (to supervise) the academy,[2] but the disciples were not aware of them.[3] In the evening the two of them went to sit among the disciples. Now it was Rabban Gamaliel's custom that if when he entered, he said, "Ask (your questions)," this meant that no proctor was present. If he did not say "Ask" when he entered, this meant that a proctor was present.[4] When Rabban Gamaliel entered and found that R. Johanan ben Nuri and R. Eleazar Ḥisma were seated among the disciples, he said to them, "Johanan ben Nuri and Eleazar Ḥisma, you are doing a disservice[5] to the community, in that you do not seek to exercise control over it. In the past you were independent, but from now on you are the servants of the community."

Hear the causes between your brethren: It was R. Ishmael's custom that when two litigants, one an Israelite and the other a heathen, came before him for judgment, he would rule in favor of the Israelite, regardless of whether he ruled according to the laws of Israel or according to the laws of the nations; for he said, "What difference does it make to me? Does not the Torah say, *Hear the causes between your brethren?*"[6] Rabban Simeon ben Gamaliel, on the other hand, says: He should not have interpreted it in this sense; rather, if the litigants come to be judged by the laws of Israel, the judge should follow the laws of Israel, and if they come to be judged by the laws of the nations, he should follow the laws of the nations.[7]

And judge righteously: The righteous litigant brings a just claim and offers just evidence. For example: A is wrapped in his cloak, while B says, "It is my cloak"; A plows with his cow, while B says, "It is my cow"; A holds possession of his field, while B says, "It is my field"; A dwells in his house, while B says, "It is my house." Hence Scripture says, *and judge righteously.* The righteous litigant brings a just claim and offers just evidence.

Between a man (1:16): This excludes minors. Hence the Sages have said; Orphans may not be subject to lawsuits.[8]

Between a man and his brother (1:16): This seemingly applies only to contests between two men. Whence do we learn that it applies also to contests between a man and a woman, a woman and a man, a nation and a family, one family and another? From *between a man and his brother*—"brother" in the general sense (of another party).

And the stranger (gero) (1:16):[9] The one who piles up (*ʾāḡar*) charges: A says to B, "You plowed a furrow in my field," while B says, "I did not plow"; "Your ox killed my ox," while B says, "He did not kill"; "Your ox killed my servant," while B says, "He did not." Hence *and gero*—the one who piles up charges.

Another interpretation: *And the stranger*—his neighbor.

Another interpretation: His best man.

Another interpretation: The settler (on his property).

Piska 17

Ye shall not respect persons in judgment (1:17): This refers to him who appoints judges. You might say, "So-and-so is a fine man—I will appoint him judge"; "So-and-so is a mighty man—I will appoint him judge"; So-and-so is a kinsman[1] of mine—I will appoint him judge"; "So-and-so had lent me money [and is a hellenist[2]]—I will appoint him judge." The result might be that such a judge might free the guilty and convict the innocent, not because he is wicked but because he is simply not knowledgeable: yet he will be regarded as having respected persons in judgment.[3]

Ye shall hear the small and the great alike (1:17): You might say, "Since A is poor and B is rich, and it is our duty to sustain the poor, I will therefore rule in A's favor, so that he may be sustained honorably." Hence *Ye shall hear the small and the great alike.*[4]

Another interpretation: *Ye shall hear the small and the great alike*: You might say, "How can I dishonor this rich man A for a mere denar? I shall therefore rule in his favor, and then, when he goes outside, I will tell him, 'Give B (the denar), for you really owe it to him.' " Hence *Ye shall hear the small and the great alike.*

[*Ye shall not be afraid of the face of any man* (1:17):[5] If two litigants come before you, before you hear their arguments you may remain silent, but once you have heard them, you may not remain silent, for Scripture says, *The beginning of strife is as when one letteth out water; therefore leave off contention, before the quarrel break out* (Prov. 17:14). Before the case is revealed, you may remain silent, but once the case has been revealed, you may not remain silent. However, if you have heard the case but do not know who is innocent and who is guilty, you may still remain silent, as it is said, *These are the things that ye shall do: speak ye every man the truth with his neighbor, execute the judgment of truth and peace (in your gates)* (Zech. 8:16). What kind of *peace* includes *judgment of truth*? Arbitration. R. Simeon ben Gamaliel, however, says: "Arbitration raises the small to the place of the great and lowers the great to the place of the small." Hence the Sages say, "He who prescribes arbitration is a sinner,[6] as it is said, *The compromiser vaunteth himself,*[7] *though he contemn the Lord*" (Ps. 10:3)—the result is that one litigant praises the judge, while the other contemns his Creator.[8]]

Ye shall not be afraid of the face of any man (1:17): You might say, "I am afraid of So-and-so, lest he slay my children, or set fire to my stacks of grain, or uproot my planting." Hence *Ye shall not be afraid of the face of any man; for the judgment is God's.* So also Jehoshaphat said to the judges, "*Consider what ye do; for ye judge not for man, but for the Lord*" (2 Chron. 19:6).

And the cause that is too hard for you (ye shall bring unto me) (1:17): Said the Holy One, blessed is He, to Moses, "You think that you can decide difficult cases—by your life, I shall make you know that you cannot decide difficult cases. I shall bring you a case that your pupil's pupil will be able to judge, but you will not."[9] And what case was that? The case of the daughters of Zelophehad, of which Scripture says, *And Moses brought their cause before the Lord* (Num. 27:5). Similarly it says, *Then Saul drew near to Samuel in the gate, (and said, "Tell me, I pray thee, where the seer's house is"). And Samuel answered Saul and said, "I am the seer"* (1 Sam. 9:18–19). The Holy One, blessed be He, said to him, "You fancy yourself a seer—I shall make you know that you are not a seer." When did He make him know? When He said to him, *Fill thy horn with oil and go; I will send thee to Jesse the Beth-lehemite, for I have provided Me a king among his sons* (1 Sam. 16:1). What does Scripture go on to say? *And it came to pass, when they were come, that he beheld Eliab, and said, "Surely, the Lord's anointed is before Him"* (1 Sam. 16:6). The Holy One, blessed be He, said to him, "Did you not say that you were a seer? *Look not on his countenance, or on the height of his stature, because I have rejected him; (for it is not as man seeth; for man looketh on the outward appearance, but the Lord looketh on the heart)* (1 Sam. 16:7).

Pisḳa 18

And I commanded you at that time all the things which ye should do (1:18): This refers to the ten points of difference between civil cases and capital cases.[1]

And we journeyed from Horeb, and went through all that great and dreadful wilderness (1:19): To people who had seen serpents as large as beams and scorpions as large as bows stretched out and cast before them, to them he speaks of that *great and dreadful wilderness*? However, is this not a logical inference from the minor to the major: if I have overcome for you things that are not tame, how much more so will I be able to overcome things that are tame?[2] Hence *And we journeyed from Horeb,* etc.[3]

Pisḳa 19

And I said unto you (1:20): He said to them, "I am speaking to you not on my own—what I am saying to you comes from the mouth of the Holiness."

Ye are come unto the hill-country of the Amorites, which the Lord our God giveth unto us (1:20): A parable: A king handed his son over to a tutor who took him around and showed him many things, saying, "All these vines belong to you, all these olive trees belong to you." When he tired of showing him individual things, he said to him, "Everything you see belongs to you." So also during the forty years that Israel was in the wilderness Moses would say to them, *For the Lord thy God bringeth thee into a good land, a land of brooks of water, of fountains and depths, springing forth in valleys and hills* (8:7). Once they came to the land, he said to them: *Ye are come unto the hill-country of the Amorites, which the Lord our God giveth unto us.* Should you say that it is not yet time, it is time, for *Behold, the Lord thy God hath set the land before thee* (1:21). I say this to you on the basis not of an estimate or vague rumor but of that which you can see with your own eyes, *Go up, take possession*—immediately—*Go up, take possession, as the Lord, the God of thy fathers, hath spoken unto thee* (1:21).

Pisḳa 20

And ye came near unto me, every one of you, and said (1:22), (they came) in great confusion.[1] Later on Scripture says, *Ye came near unto me, even all the leaders of your tribes, and your elders* (5:20),[2] children honoring the elders, and the elders honoring the leaders; whereas here it says, *And ye came near unto me, every one of you, and said,* in great confusion, children pushing past the elders, elders pushing past the leaders.

And said, "Let us send men before us, that they may search out the land for us" (1:22): R. Simeon said: People who demand spies in this situation are really arrogant. Moses said to them, "When you were in a land of desolation and pits, you did not ask for spies; yet now that you are entering a good and spacious land, a land flowing with milk and honey, you demand spies!"[3]

And bring us back word—of what language they speak—*of the way by which we must go up*—every way has curves, every way has places for ambush, evey way has crossroads—*and the cities unto which we shall come* (1:22)—to let us know by which pathway we shall come upon them.[4]

Pisḳa 21

And the thing pleased me well (1:23): Moses said, "It pleased me, but it did not please God."[1] If it pleased Him, why did He record it together with words of rebuke?[2] A parable: A said to B, "Sell me your ass." B replied, "Very well." A said, "Will you let me have it for a trial?" B replied, "Very well. Let us both come along, and I will show you how much of a load it can carry on a mountain and how much in a valley." When A saw that B placed no obstacles in his way, he said, "Woe is me! It seems he is so obliging only in order to take my money." Hence *And the thing pleased me well.*[3]

And I took twelve men of you—from the best and finest among you—*one man for every tribe* (1:23): What need is there for the latter statement? Have we not already been told, *And I took twelve men of you?* Hence we learn that the tribe of Levi was not one of them.[4]

Pisḳa 22

And they turned and went up into the mountains (1:24): Hence we learn that spies usually go up into the mountains, and so also Rahab says to Joshua's spies, *Get you to the mountain, lest the pursuers light upon you, (and hide yourselves there three days, until the pursuers be returned)* (Josh. 2:16). We thus learn that the holy spirit rested upon her,[1] for had it not done so, how would she have known that they would return in three days? This proves that the holy spirit rested upon her.

And came unto the valley of Eshcol (1:24): Hence we learn that the valley was named after what was eventually to happen there. A similar instance is *And (Moses) came to the Mountain of God, unto Horeb* (Exod. 3:1), showing that the mountain was named after what was eventually to happen there.[2]

And spied it out (1:24): Hence we learn that they traveled through it in four ways, like the woof and warp (of a web).[3]

Pisḳa 23

And they took of the fruit of the land in their hands (1:25): R. Simeon said: How arrogant were the men who took it thus![1] They took it in their hands as does a man who buys an issar's worth of figs or grapes.

And brought it down unto us (1:25): This shows that the land of Canaan is higher than all the other lands, as is indicated also in the verses, *We should go up at once, and possess it; for we are well able to overcome it* (Num. 13:30), *So they went up, and spied out the land* (Num. 13:21), *And they went up into the South* (Num. 13:22), *And they went up out of Egypt* (Gen. 45:25).[2]

And brought us back word, and said, "Good is the land which the Lord our God giveth us" (1:25): Did they (really) speak favorably of the land? Did they not speak only in disfavor of it? Who (actually) spoke in favor of it? Only Joshua and Caleb.[3]

Nevertheless, *Ye would not go up, but rebelled against the commandment of the Lord your God* (1:26).

Pisḳa 24

And ye murmured in your tents, and said, "(Because the Lord) hated us" (1:27): Hence we learn that they sat in their tents and spoke in words of hypocritical sympathy, as it is said, *The words of a whisperer are as those of hypocritical sympathizers* (Prov. 26:22); but a knife descended from heaven and slit their bellies, as the verse goes on to say, *and they go down into the innermost parts of the body* (Prov. 26:22).[1]

Another interpretation: We learn therefrom that they sat in their tents and mourned as if for a deceased relative. They turned to their sons and said to them, "Woe unto you, O afflicted ones! Woe unto you, O suffering ones! Tomorrow some of you will be slain, some of you will be taken captive, some of you will be crucified upon crosses." Then they would turn to their daughters and say to them, "Woe unto you, O afflicted ones! Woe unto you, O suffering ones! Tomorrow some of you will be slain, some of you will be taken captive, some of you will be consigned to brothels."

Because the Lord hated us: Is it possible that God should hate Israel? Is it not said elsewhere, *I have loved you, saith the Lord* (Mal. 1:2)? Rather, it is they who hate God. As the popular proverb puts it, "Whatever you think of your friend, he thinks the same of you."

To deliver us into the hands of the Amorite, to destroy us (1:27): As it is said, *For when the Canaanites and all the inhabitants of the land hear of it, they will compass us round, and cut off our name from the earth; and what wilt Thou do for Thy great name?* (Josh. 7:9).

Pisḳa 25

Whither are we going up? Our brethren have made our heart to melt, (by) saying (1:28): They said to him, "Moses, our teacher, had we heard this from other persons, we would not have believed it; but we heard it from persons whose sons are our sons and whose daughters are our daughters."

The people is greater —hence we learn that they were tall in stature—*and many* (1:28)—hence we learn that they were numerous.

The cities are great and fortified up to heaven (1:28): R. Simeon ben Gamaliel says: Scripture uses hyperbole here, as it is said, *Hear, O Israel! Thou art to pass over the Jordan this day (to go in to dispossess nations greater and mightier than thyself, cities great and fortified up to heaven)* (9:1). But God's words to Abraham, *And I will multiply thy seed as the stars of the heaven* (Gen. 26:4), *and I will make thy seed as the dust of the earth* (Gen. 13:16), are not hyperbole.

And moreover we have seen the sons of the Anakim there (1:28): Hence we learn that they saw there giants (*ʿănaḳim*) standing on the shoulders of giants, as it is said, *Therefore pride is as a chain about their neck* (*ʿănaḳatmo*) (Ps. 73:6).

Then I said unto you (1:29): He said to them, "I say this to you not on my own, but from the mouth of the Holiness."

Dread not, neither be afraid of them (1:29): Why not? Because *The Lord your God who goeth before you, (He shall fight for you)* (1:30). Moses said to them, "He who has performed miracles for you in Egypt and all of these (latest) miracles, He will perform miracles for you when you enter the land." *According to all that He did for you in Egypt before your eyes* (1:30). If you will not believe in what is yet to be, believe at least in what has happened in the past.

Pisḳa 26

And I besought the Lord at that time, saying (3:23): This is explained by the verse, *The poor useth entreaties, but the rich answereth impudently*

(Prov. 18:23). {Israel[1] had two fine leaders, Moses and David, king of Israel. Moses said to the Holy One, blessed be He, "Master of the universe, let any transgression that I have committed be recorded against me, so that people will not say, 'Moses seems to have falsified the Torah,' or 'said something he had not been commanded to say.' " A parable: A certain king issued a decree to the effect that anyone who eats unripe figs grown in the Sabbatical year[2] shall be paraded (in disgrace) around the arena. Now a woman from a noble family proceeded to gather such figs and ate them, and as they were parading her around the arena, she said to the king, "I beg of you, my lord king, let my offense be publicly proclaimed, so that the citizens would not say, 'She seems to have been caught in an act of adultery or witchcraft.'[3] If they see figs draped around my neck, they will know that it is because of them that I am being paraded."[4] Thus also Moses said to God, "Let any transgression that I have committed be recorded against me." The Holy One, blessed be He, replied, "Behold, I am recording that it was only because of the transgression connected with the water, (that you were punished)," as it is said, *Because ye rebelled against My commandment (in the wilderness of Zin, in the strife of the congregation, to sanctify Me at the waters before their eyes)* (Num. 27:14).[5] R. Simeon says: A parable: A certain king was traveling with his son in his royal carriage. When they came to a narrow place, his carriage overturned upon his son, blinding his eye, amputating his hand, and breaking his leg. Thereafter, whenever the king passed that spot, he would say, "This is where my son was injured—this is where his eye was blinded, this is where his hand was cut off, this is where his leg was broken." Thus also God mentions three times *the waters of contention, the waters of contention, the waters of contention,* as much as to say, "This is where I doomed Miriam, this is where I doomed Aaron, this is where I doomed Moses."[6] Similarly, Scripture says, *Their judges are thrown down by the sides of the rock* (Ps. 141:6). David said to God, "Let not this transgression committed by me be recorded against me," but God said to him, "It is not fitting for you that people should say, 'God forgave him because He favors him.' " A parable: A man borrowed from the king a thousand *kor* of wheat per year. Everyone said, "Can it be possible for this man to manage a loan of one thousand *kor* of wheat in one year? It must be that the king has made him a gift of it and has written him a receipt!"[7] One time the man had nothing left over and could not repay anything to the king, so the king entered the man's house, seized his sons and daughters, and placed them on the auction block, whereupon everyone knew that the man had received no pardon from the king. So also all the punishments which came upon David were made multiple, as it is said, *And he shall restore the lamb fourfold* (2 Sam. 12:6). R. Ḥanina says: "*Fourfold* means sixteen times." Moreover, the prophet Nathan came by and rebuked David for that same misdeed. David said, *I have sinned against the Lord* (2 Sam. 12:13). How did Nathan reply? *The Lord also hath put away thy sin; thou shalt not die* (2 Sam. 12:13), and Scripture says, *Against Thee, Thee only, have I sinned, and done that which is evil in Thy sight* (Ps. 51:6).]

Israel had two fine leaders, Moses and David, king of Israel. Their meritorious deeds could have sustained the whole world, yet they begged the Holy One, blessed be He, only for a favor.[8] Is this not a matter of inference from the minor to the major? If those whose meritorious deeds could have sustained the whole world requested from the Holy One, blessed be He, only a favor, how much more so should a person who is not even one thousand-thousand-thousandth or ten-thousand–ten-thousandth part the disciples of their disciples beseech the Holy One, blessed be He, only for a favor.[9]

Another interpretation: *And I besought the Lord*: There are ten terms for prayer: cry (*zĕʿaḳah*), cry for help (*šawʿah*), moaning (*nĕʾaḳah*)—these three in the verses, *And it came to pass in the course of those many days that the king of Egypt died; and the children of Israel sighed by reason of the bondage, and they cried (way-yizʿaḳu), and their cry for help (šawʿatam), came up to God. And God heard their moaning (naʾăḳatam)* (Exod. 2:23–24); distress (*baṣ-ṣar*), calling out (*ḳĕriʾah*)—these two in the verse, *In my distress (baṣ-ṣar) I called out (ʾeḳraʾ) to the Lord* (2 Sam. 22:7); cry of prayer (*rinnah*), plea (*pĕgiʿah*)—these two in the verse, *Therefore pray not for this people, neither lift up cry (rinnah) nor prayer for them, neither plead (tifgaʿ) with Me* (Jer. 7:16); falling (*nafol*), as in the verse, *So I fell down before the Lord* (9:25); *pillul,* as in the verse, *And I prayed (ʾetpallel) unto the Lord* (9:26); entreating (*ʿăṯirah*), as in the verse, *And Isaac entreated (way-yeʿtar) the Lord for his wife* (Gen. 25:21); standing (*ʿămiḏah*), as in the verse, *Then stood (way-yaʿămoḏ) up Phinehas* (Ps. 106:30); imploring (*ḥilluy*), as in the verse, *And Moses implored (wayḥal) the Lord* (Exod. 32:11); and beseeching (*tĕḥinnah*), as in, *And I besought (wa-ʾetḥannen).*[10]

At that time, saying (3:23): A parable: The people of a certain city thought of asking the king to grant their city the status of a colony. When two of his enemies were defeated by him, the people of the city said, "This is a good time to ask the king to grant our city the status of a colony."[11] Thus also Moses thought of asking the Holy One, blessed be He, to permit him to enter the land. When he saw Sihon and Og defeated by Him, he said, "This is a good time for me to ask the Holy One, blessed be He, to let me enter the land"—hence *at that time.*

Saying: This is one of the things concerning which Moses said to God, "Let me know whether Thou wilt do it for me or not." The Holy One, blessed be He, replied, "Indeed I will do it." [*And*[12] *Moses cried unto the Lord, saying, "What shall I do unto this people?"* (Exod. 17:4)—Scripture does not use the term "saying" except for a special purpose, hence here it indicates that Moses said to God, "Let me know whether I will fall into their hands or not." Similarly Scripture says,] *And Moses spoke before the Lord, saying* (Exod. 6:12)—Scripture does not use the term "saying" except for a special purpose, hence here it indicates that Moses said to God, "Let me know whether Thou wilt redeem them or not." [Again Scripture says, *And Moses cried unto the Lord, saying, "Heal her now, O Lord, I beseech Thee"* (Num. 12:13)—Scripture does not use the term "saying" except for a special purpose, hence here it means "tell me whether Thou wilt heal her or not." Similarly Scripture says, *And Moses spoke unto the Lord, saying, "Let the Lord, the God of the spirits of all flesh, set"* (Num. 27:15–16)—Scripture does not use the term "saying" except for a special purpse, hence here it indicates that Moses said to God, "Let me know whether Thou wilt appoint leaders for them or not."] Here too, when Scripture says, *at that time, saying,* it does not use the term "saying" except for a special purpose; hence it indicates that Moses said to God, "Let me know whether I will enter the land or not."[13]

The Lord (3:24): Whenever Scripture says *the Lord* (*ʾĂḏonay*), it refers to His quality of mercy, as in the verse, *The Lord, the Lord, God, merciful and gracious* (Exod. 34:6). Wherever it says *God* (*ʾĔlohim*), it refers to His quality of justice, as in the verses, *The cause of both parties shall come before God* (*ʿĔlohim*) (Exod. 22:8), and *Thou shalt not revile God* (*ʾĔlohim*) *(nor curse a ruler)* (Exod. 22:27).[14]

Piska 27

Thou hast begun (3:24): thou hast released me from my vow.[1] When Thou saidst to me, *"Go, bring forth My people the children of Israel out of Egypt"* (Exod. 3:10), I said to Thee, "I cannot do so, for I have already sworn to Jethro that I would never leave him," as it is said, *And Moses was content (way-yo'el) to dwell with the man* (Exod. 2:21), and being content (*ho'alah*) always indicates an oath, as it is said, *But Saul adjured (way-yo'el) the people* (1 Sam. 14:24).

Another interpretation: *Thou hast begun*: "Thou hast given me an opening which allowed me to stand before Thee in prayer for Thy children after they had misdone in the matter of the (golden) calf," as it is said, *Let Me alone, that I may destroy them* (9:14). Did Moses actually seize hold of the Holy One? Rather, he spoke thus to Him, "Thou hast given me an opening which allowed me to stand before Thee in prayer for Thy children, and I stood and prayed for them; and Thou heardest my prayer and forgavest them their transgression.[2] I thought that I had them with me in this prayer, but they did not pray for me." For is it not a matter of inference from the minor to the major, that if the prayer of an individual for the whole group is accepted, certainly the prayer of the whole group for the individual would have been accepted?

To show Thy servant (3:24): There are those who called themselves servants, and the Holy One, blessed be He, also called them servants; there are those who called themselves servants, but the Holy One, blessed be He, did not call them servants; and there are those who did not call themselves servants, but the Holy One, blessed be He, did call them servants. Abraham called himself servant, as it is said, *Pass not away, I pray thee, from thy servant* (Gen. 18:3), and the Holy One, blessed be He, also called him servant, as it is said, *For My servant Abraham's sake* (Gen. 26:24). Jacob called himself servant, as it is said, *I am not worthy of all the mercies, and of all the truth, which Thou hast shown unto Thy servant* (Gen. 32:11), and God also called him servant, as it is said, *But thou, Israel, My servant* (Isa. 41:8). Moses called himself servant, as it is said, *To show Thy servant,* and the Holy One, blessed be He, also called him servant, as it is said, *My servant Moses is not so* (Num. 12:7). David called himself servant, as it is said, *I am Thy servant, the son of Thy handmaid* (Ps. 116:16), and the Holy One, blessed be He, also called him servant, as it is said, *For I will defend this city to save it, for Mine own sake, and for My servant David's sake* (2 Kings 19:34), *And David My servant shall be their prince for ever* (Ezek. 37:25). Isaiah called himself servant, as it is said, *And now saith the Lord that formed me from the womb to be His servant* (Isa. 49:5), and the Holy One, blessed be He, also called him servant, as it is said, *Like as My servant Isaiah hath walked naked and barefoot* (Isa. 20:3). Samuel called himself servant, as it is said, *Then Samuel said, "Speak, for Thy servant heareth"* (1 Sam. 3:10), but the Holy One, blessed be He, did not call him servant. Samson called himself servant, as it is said, *Thou hast given this great deliverance by the hand of Thy servant* (Judg. 15:18), but the Holy One, blessed be He, did not call him servant. Solomon called himself servant, as it is said, *Give Thy servant therefore an understanding heart* (1 Kings 3:9), but the Holy One, blessed be He, did not call him servant, but rather made him dependent upon his father David, as it is said, *For David My servant's sake* (1 Kings 11:13). Job did not call himself servant, but the Holy One, blessed be He, called him servant, as it is said, *Hast thou considered My servant Job?* (Job 2:3). Joshua did not call himself servant, but the Holy One, blessed be He, called him servant, as it is said, *Joshua the son of Nun, the servant of the Lord, died* (Josh. 24:29). Caleb did not call himself servant, but the Holy One, blessed be He, called him servant, as it is said, *But My servant Caleb* (Num. 14:24). Eliakim did not call himself servant, but the Holy One, blessed be He, called him servant, as it is said, *That I will call My servant Eliakim* (Isa. 22:20). Zerubbabel did not call himself servant, but the Holy One, blessed be He, called him servant, as it is said, *In that day, saith the Lord of hosts, will I take thee, O Zerubbabel, My servant, the son of Shealtiel, and will make thee as a signet; for I have chosen thee, saith the Lord of hosts* (Hag. 2:23). Daniel did not call himself servant, but the Holy One, blessed be He, called him servant, as it is said, *O Daniel, servant of the living God* (Dan. 6:21). Hananiah, Mishael, and Azariah did not call themselves servants, but the Holy One, blessed be He, called them servants, as it is said, *Shadrach, Meshach, and Abed-nego, ye servants of God Most High, come forth and come hither* (Dan. 3:26). The early prophets did not call themselves servants, but the Holy One, blessed be He, called them servants, as it is said, *For the Lord God will do nothing, but He revealeth His counsel unto His servants the prophets* (Amos 3:7).

Thy greatness (3:24): This is the basic statement which refers to every greatness mentioned in the Torah.[3]

And Thy strong hand (3:24): This refers to the ten plagues which the Holy One, blessed be He, brought upon the Egyptians in Egypt, as it is said of them, *Stretch forth thy hand* (Exod. 8:1).

For what god is there in heaven or on earth (3:24): The way of the Holy One, blessed be He, is not like that of creatures of flesh and blood. Among the latter, a prefect who rules over his province fears that his co-prefect may not agree to revoking the judgment. But Thou, who hast no co-prefect, why dost Thou not pardon me? A king of flesh and blood, who sits in his tribunal, fears that his viceroy may not agree to revoking the judgment. But Thou, who hast no viceroy, why wilt Thou not pardon me?

That can do according to Thy works—in Egypt—*and according to Thy mighty acts* (3:24)—at the sea. Another interpretation: *according to Thy works*—in Egypt—*and according to Thy might acts*—at the Jordan.

Piska 28

Let me go over, I pray Thee, and see (the good land) (3:25): Is it possible that Moses could have asked God to let him enter the land? Is it not stated elsewhere, *For thou shalt not go over this Jordan* (3:27)? A parable: A certain king who had two servants decreed that one of them should drink no wine for thirty days. The servant said, "He has decreed that I drink no wine for thirty days. I will taste none for a whole year or even for two years!" Why did he say this? In order to mitigate his master's words. The king then decreed that the other servant should likewise drink no wine for thirty days. This servant said, "How can I possibly be without wine for even a single hour?" Why did he say this? In order to show how precious to him were the words of his master. So also Moses demonstrated how precious to him were God's words by asking Him to let him enter the land. Hence, *Let me go over, I pray Thee, and see (the good land).*[1]

That goodly mountain, and Lebanon (3:25): Everyone called it mountain: Abraham called it mountain, as it is said, *In the mount where the Lord is seen* (Gen. 22:14); Moses called it mountain, as it is said, *That goodly mountain*; David called it mountain, as it is said, *Who shall ascend into the mountain of the Lord?* (Ps. 24:3); Isaiah called it mountain, as it is said, *And it shall come to pass in the end of days that the mountain of the Lord's House shall be established* (Isa. 2:2); the nations called it mountain, as it is said, *And many peoples shall go and say: "Come ye, and let us go up to the mountain of the Lord"* (Isa. 2:3).

And Lebanon: Whence do we know that Lebanon here means the Sanctuary? From the verses, *Thou art Gilead unto Me, the head of Lebanon* (Jer. 22:6), and *And He shall cut down the thickets of the forest with iron, and Lebanon shall fall by a mighty one* (Isa. 10:34). And why is the Sanctuary called Lebanon? Because it made white (*malbin*) the transgressions of Israel, as it is said, *Though your sins be as scarlet, they shall be as white as snow* (Isa. 1:18).[2]

Pisḳa 29

But the Lord was wroth (way-yiṯᶜabber) with me for your sakes, and hearkened not unto me (3:26): R. Eliezer says: He was filled with anger against me; R. Joshua says: Like a woman who is in no condition to converse because of (the pangs of) pregnancy.[1]

For your sakes—this was done to me because of you.

And hearkened not unto me—God did not accept my prayer.[2]

And the Lord said unto me, "Let it suffice (raḇ) thee" (3:26): God said to him, "Moses, when a man makes a vow, to whom does he go? Is it not to his master (*rabbo*) to release him from his vow? You too must obey the words of your Master (*rabbĕḵa*)."[3]

Another interpretation: *And the Lord said unto me, "Let it suffice thee (raḇ lĕḵa)"*: God said to Moses, "Moses, you are to serve as an example[4] for judges, who will say, 'If Moses, the wisest of the wise and the greatest of the great, was not forgiven for saying *Hear now, ye rebels* (Num. 20:10), for which it was decreed that he was not to enter the land, how much more so those who divert and distort justice.'" [If[5] Moses, who was told, *Let it suffice thee; speak no more,* did not desist from asking the Holy One, blessed be He, for mercy, how much more so anyone else! If Hezekiah, who was told, *Set thy house in order, for thou shalt die, and not live* (2 Kings 20:1), did not desist from asking for mercy—he reasoned that even when a sharp sword is poised over a man's neck, he should not despair of mercy, as it is said, *Then Hezekiah turned his face to the wall and prayed* (Isa. 38:2)—how much more so all other Israelites.]

Another interpretation: *And the Lord said unto me, "Let it suffice (raḇ) thee"*: God said to him, "Moses, I have much (*harbeh*) stored up for you for the world-to-come." It is like a man who says to his companion, "I have so much stored up for you; do not shame me."

Another interpretation: *And the Lord said unto me, "Let it suffice thee"*: It is like a man who says to his companion, "So-and-so has gone beyond the limit in his conduct toward So-and-so."[6]

Speak no more unto Me. . . . Get thee up into the top of Pisgah (3:26–

27): Hence R. Eliezer ben Jacob said:[7] One prayer is more efficacious than a hundred good deeds, for in respect to all of Moses' deeds he was never told "Get thee up," whereas in this matter he was told "Get thee up." This was the source of the saying,[8] "Those who are outside the land must face toward the Land of Israel when they pray, as it is said, *And pray unto Thee toward their land* (1 Kings 8:48). Those who are in the Land of Israel must face toward Jerusalem when they pray, as it is said, *And they pray unto Thee toward this city* (2 Chron. 6:34). Those who are in Jerusalem must face toward the Temple when they pray, as it is said, *And pray toward this house* (2 Chron. 6:32). Those who are within the Temple must direct their hearts toward the Holy of Holies when they pray, as it is said, *If they pray toward this place* (2 Chron. 6:26)." Thus those who are in the north must face the south, those in the south must face the north, those in the east must face the west, those in the west must face the east; thus all Israel will pray toward the same place.

And behold with thine eyes (3:27): A parable: A certain king forbade his son to enter his bedchamber. When the son entered the king's palace, the king drew him in and welcomed him. When the son went into the dining room entrance, the king drew him in and welcomed him once more. But when the son was about to enter the bedchamber, the king said to him, "Beyond this point you are forbidden to go." So also Moses said to the Holy One, blessed be He, "All I claim of the Land of Israel is just the width of this Jordan River, this area of fifty cubits." God replied, *And behold with thine eyes, for thou shalt not go over.*[9]

But charge Joshua (3:28): Charging always implies zeal,[10] as it is said, *And Moses called unto Joshua, and said unto him in the sight of all Israel, "Be strong and of good courage"* (31:7), *be strong* in Torah, *and of good courage* in good deeds.

For he shall go over before this people—if he[11] goes over before them, they will go over, and if he does not, they will not go over—*and he shall cause them to inherit* (3:28): If he causes them to inherit, they will inherit, and if he does not, they will not inherit. Similarly, you find that when they went to make war against Ai, about thirty-six righteous men fell in battle, as it is said, *And the men of Ai smote of them about thirty and six men, and they chased them. . . . and Joshua rent his clothes, and fell to the earth upon his face before the Ark of the Lord until the evening. . . . And Joshua said, "Alas, O Lord God, wherefore hast Thou at all brought this people over. . . . O Lord, what shall I say, after that Israel hath turned (their backs before their enemies?) . . ." And the Lord said unto Joshua, "Get thee up; wherefore now art thou fallen upon thy face?* (Josh. 7:5–8,10). Did I not tell your teacher Moses at the beginning that if you go over before them, they will go over, and if you do not, they will not go over, and that if you cause them to inherit, they will inherit, and if you do not, they will not inherit? Yet you sent them, and did not go with them."

Pisḳa 30

So we abode in the valley (3:29): Moses said to them, "What caused us to dwell in the valley? The evil deeds we had performed in Peor."[1] Another interpretation: He said to them, "See what a difference there is between you and me. For all of my prayers, requests, and pleas, it has been decreed that I am not to enter the land; whereas you have angered God for forty years in the wilderness, as it is said, *For forty years was I wearied with that generation* (Ps. 95:10); and not only that, but even the greatest of you worshiped Peor, yet His right hand is stretched out to receive the penitent."[2]

And now, O Israel, hearken unto the statutes (4:1): You are as if newly created—what had happened in the past has already been forgiven.

Pisḳa 31

Hear, O Israel, the Lord our God, the Lord is one (6:4): Why was this said?[1] Because Scripture says elsewhere, *Speak unto the children of Israel* (Exod. 25:2). It does not say, "Speak unto the children of Abraham," or "Speak unto the children of Isaac," but rather *Speak unto the children of Israel.* Our father Jacob merited such a declaration to be directed to his children, because all his days he was troubled by fear,[2] (for he said,) "Woe is me, perchance such unworthy ones will issue from me as they did issue from my forefathers."[3]

[From[4] Abraham issued Ishmael who worshipped idols, as it is said, *And Sarah saw the son of Hagar the Egyptian, whom she had borne unto Abraham, making sport* (Gen. 21:9). R. ʿAḳiba said that he was worshiping idols.[5]

R. Simeon ben Yoḥai says: There are four passages which R. ʿAḳiba interpreted (in his way) and I interpreted (in my way), and my own interpretations are preferable. He said that *Sarah saw the son of Hagar the Egyptian,* etc., means that he was worshiping idols, but I say that they[6] were quarreling[7] over fields and vineyards. When they came to divide them, Ishmael said, "I will take two portions, since I am the first-born." Sarah therefore said to Abraham, *Cast out this bondwoman and her son, for the son of this bondwoman shall not be heir with my son Isaac* (Gen. 21:10). I prefer my interpretation to his.

Another instance: Scripture says, *If flocks and herds be slain for them* (Num. 11:22). R. ʿAḳiba said that the meaning here is the same as that of *or if all the fish of the sea be gathered together for them* (Num. 11:22), that is to say, would it suffice for them?[8] But I say (that this means), even if Thou shouldst bring for them all the sheep and cattle in the world, they would still grumble against Thee. To which the holy spirit answered, *Now shalt thou see whether My word shall come to pass unto thee or not* (Num. 11:23).[9] I prefer my interpretation to his.

Another instance: Scripture says, *Son of man, they that inhabit those waste places in the Land of Israel speak, saying, Abraham was one, and he inherited the land, but we are many; the land is given us for inheritance* (Ezek. 33:24). (According to R. ʿAḳiba,) this is an instance of inference from the minor to the major: if Abraham, who worshiped only one God, inherited the land, is it not right that we, who worship many gods, should inherit the land? But I say that (they meant), if Abraham, who had been bound by only one commandment, inherited the land, is it not right that we, who have been bound by many commandments, should inherit the land? And how does the prophet reply to this? *Thus saith the Lord God: Ye eat with the blood, and lift up your eyes unto your idols, and shed blood—and shall ye possess the land? Ye stand upon your sword, ye work abomination, and ye defile everyone his neighbor's wife—and shall ye possess the land?* (Ezek. 33:25–26).[10] I prefer my interpretation to his.

Another instance: *Thus saith the Lord (of hosts): The fast of the fourth, and the fast of the fifth, and the fast of the seventh, and the fast of the tenth* (Zech. 8:19). (According to R. ʿAḳiba), *the fast of the fourth* refers to the seventeenth day of Tammuz, when the city (of Jerusalem) was breached. Why was it called *fast of the fourth?* Because it is in the fourth month. *The fast of the fifth* is the ninth of Ab, in which the Temple was destroyed, both the First and the Second. Why was it called *fast of the fifth?* Because it is in the fifth month. *The fast of the seventh* is the third of Tishri, when Gedaliah son of Ahikam was slain; and who slew him? Ishmael son of Nethaniah. Hence we learn that the assassination of righteous men is as grave a matter before the Holy One, blessed be He, as the destruction of the Temple.[11] Why was it called *the fast of the seventh?* Because it is in the seventh month. *The fast of the tenth* is the tenth of Tebet, when the king of Babylonia laid siege to Jerusalem, as it is said, *In the ninth year, in the tenth month, in the tenth day of the month, the word of the Lord came unto me, saying, Son of man, write thee the name of the day, even of this selfsame day: this selfsame day the king of Babylonia hath invested Jerusalem* (Ezek. 24:1–2). But I say that *the fast of the tenth* is in the fifth day of Tebet. In Judah the fast is observed on the date of the event itself, while in the Diaspora it is observed on the date of the report thereof, as it is said, *And it came to pass in the twelfth year of our captivity, in the tenth month, in the fifth day of the month, that one that had escaped out of Jerusalem came unto me, saying, The city is smitten* (Ezek. 33:21)—they heard of it and observed the same day in which they heard it as if it were the day of the conflagration itself. I prefer my interpretation to his.][12]

Ishmael issued from Abraham, and Esau from Isaac, but as for me, such unworthy ones shall not issue from me as they did from my forefathers, as it is said, *And Jacob vowed a vow, saying* (Gen. 28:20). Can one ever imagine that Jacob would have said, *If God . . . will give me bread to eat, and raiment to put on . . . then shall the Lord be my God?* (Gen. 28:20) (Could he have meant) that otherwise He shall not be my God? Hence Scripture goes on to say, *So that I come back to my father's house in peace, then shall the Lord be my God?* (Gen. 28:21), implying (that He will be Jacob's God) in any case.[13] What, then, does *then shall the Lord be my God* mean? (Jacob said:) "Let Him rest His name upon me, so that at no time whatever shall such unworthy ones issue from me."[14]

Similarly, Scripture says, *And it came to pass, while Israel stayed in that land, that Reuben went and lay with Bilhah, his father's concubine, and Israel heard of it* (Gen. 35:22). When Jacob heard about it, he was shaken and said, "Woe is me! Perchance an unworthy one has appeared among my children." Forthwith, however, the Holy One informed him that Reuben had repented, as it is said, *Now the sons of Jacob were twelve* (Gen. 35:22). Did we not know that they were twelve? Rather, this indicates that Jacob was told by the Holy One that Reuben had repented.[15] Hence we learn that Reuben fasted all his days, as it is said, *And they sat down to eat bread* (Gen. 37:25). Could one ever imagine that the brothers would sit down to eat bread without their eldest brother? (Yet he was in fact not with them on that occasion),[16] hence we learn that he fasted all his days, until Moses came along and accepted his repentance,[17] as it is said, *Let Reuben live, and not die* (33:6).

Thus also you find that when our father Jacob was about to depart from this world, he called his sons and reproved each one of them individually, as it is said, *And Jacob called unto his sons. . . . Reuben, thou art my first-born. . . . Simeon and Levi are brethren. . . . Judah, thee shall thy brethren praise* (Gen. 49:1–8). Having reproved each one individually, he again called them all together and said to them, "Do you have any doubts[18] concerning Him who spoke, and the world came into being?" They replied, "Hear, O Israel, our father! Just as you have no doubts about Him who spoke, and the world came into being, so do we have no doubts. Rather, *The Lord, our God, the Lord is one* (6:4). Hence it is said, *And Israel bowed down upon the bed's head* (Gen. 47:31). Did he actually bow upon the bed's head? Rather, he gave thanks and praise to God that unworthy ones had not issued from him.[19]

Some say[20] that *And Israel bowed down upon the bed's head* (means that he gave thanks) for Reuben's repentance.[21] Another interpretation: He said, "Blessed be the name of His glorious majesty for ever and ever."[22] The Holy One, blessed be He, said to him, "Jacob, surely this is what you desired all your days,[23] that your children should recite the Shemaʿ morning and evening."

Hear, O Israel (6:4): From this the Sages concluded that if one recites the Shemaʿ (so softly) that he cannot hear it, he has not fulfilled his obligation.[24]

The Lord, our God (6:4): Having already said *the Lord is One,* why does Scripture say also *our God?*[25] *Our God,* however, serves to teach us that His name rests in greater measure upon us.[26] A similar case is the verse, *Three times in the year shall all thy males appear before the Lord God, the God of Israel* (Exod. 34:23): having said *the Lord God,* why does Scripture go on to say *the God of Israel*? To indicate that His name rests in greater measure upon Israel. Another example is the verse, *Thus saith the Lord of hosts, the God of Israel* (Jer. 32:14): having said further on, *Behold, I am the Lord, the God of all flesh, is there anything too hard for Me?* (Jer. 32:27), Scripture nevertheless adds here *the God of Israel,* to indicate that His name rests in greater measure upon Israel. The same applies to *Hear, O My people, and I will speak, O Israel, and I will testify against thee. God, thy God, am I* (Ps. 50:7). Upon you rests My name in greater measure.

Another interpretation:[27] *The Lord, our God,* over us (the children of Israel); *the Lord is one,* over all the creatures of the world. *the Lord, our God,* in this world; *the Lord is one,* in the world to come, as it is said, *The Lord shall be king over all the earth. In that day shall the Lord be one and His name one* (Zech. 14:9).

Pisḳa 32

Thou shalt love the Lord thy God (6:5): Perform (God's commandments) out of love. Scripture makes a distinction between one who performs out of love and one who performs out of fear. He who performs out of love receives a doubled and redoubled reward,[1] as it is said,[2] *Thou shalt fear the Lord thy God, Him shalt thou serve* (10:20): A may (serve B) because he is afraid of him, but when B needs him,[3] A abandons him and goes his own way. You, however, must perform out of love. Only in regard to God do we find love combined with fear and fear combined with love.[4]

Another interpretation: *Thou shalt love the Lord thy God*: Make Him beloved to humanity, as did our father Abraham in the matter referred to in the verse, *And the souls that they had gotten in Haran* (Gen. 12:5). But is it not true that if all the creatures in the world were to convene in order to create just one gnat and endow it with a soul, they would not be able to do so? Hence we learn that Abraham converted people, thus bringing them under the wings of the Shekinah.[5]

With all thy heart (6:5): With both your Inclinations, the Inclination to good and the Inclination to evil.[6]

Another interpretation: *With all thy heart*: With all the heart that is within you;[7] your heart should not be divided in regard to God.[8]

And with all thy soul (6:5): Even if God takes away your soul, as it is said, *For Thy sake are we killed all the day; we are accounted as sheep for the slaughter* (Ps. 44:23). R. Simeon ben Menasya says: How can a man be slain all the day? Rather, the Holy One, blessed be He, credits the righteous as if they were slain daily.[9]

Simeon ben Azzai says: *With all thy soul*: love Him until the last drop of life is wrung out of you.

R. Eliezer says: Having said *with all thy soul,* why does Scripture go on to say *with all thy might?* And if it says *with all thy might,* why does it say *with all thy soul?* There are men whose bodies are more precious to them than their wealth, and *with all thy soul* is directed to them. There are other men whose wealth is more precious to them than their bodies, and *with all thy might* is directed to them.

R. ʿAḳiba says: Once Scripture says *with all thy soul, with all thy might* follows by inference from the major to the minor.[10] Why then *with all thy might?* Because *might* (*meʾoḏ*) implies whatever measure (*middah*) God metes out to you, whether of good or of punishment. Similarly David says, *(How can I repay unto the Lord all His bountiful dealings toward me?) I will lift up the cup of salvation, and call upon the name of the Lord* (Ps. 116:12–13), *I found trouble and sorrow, but I called upon the name of the Lord* (Ps. 116:3–4).[11] So also Job says, *The Lord gave, and the Lord hath taken away. Blessed be the name of the Lord* (Job 1:21), for the measure of good and for the measure of punishment.[12] What did his wife say to him? *Dost thou still hold fast thine integrity? Blaspheme God and die* (Job 2:9). What did he say in reply? *Thou speakest as one of the impious women speaketh. Shall we receive good at the hand of God, and shall we not receive evil?* (Job 2:10). The people of the generation of the flood were vile during good times, yet when punishment came upon them, they accepted it, whether they liked it or not. This is a matter of reasoning from the minor to the major: if one who is vile during good times is well behaved during punishment, should not we, who are well behaved during good times, be well behaved also during punishment?[13] That is what he meant when he said to her, "Speak like one of the impious women."

Furthermore, one should rejoice more in chastisement than in prosperity. For if one is prosperous all his life, no sin of his will be forgiven. What brings him forgiveness of sins? Suffering. R. Eliezer ben Jacob says: Scripture says, *For whom the Lord loveth He correcteth, even as a father the son in whom he delighteth.* (Prov. 3:12). What causes the son to be delighted in by his father? Suffering. R. Meir says: Scripture says, *And thou shalt consider in thy heart, that as a man chasteneth his son, so the Lord, thy God, chasteneth thee* (8:5). You and your heart know the deeds that you have committed, and that whatever sufferings I have brought upon you do not outweigh your deeds.

R. Jose ben R. Judah says: Precious are chastisements, for the name of the Omnipresent One rests upon him who suffers them, as it said, *So the Lord, thy God, chasteneth thee.* R. Nathan ben R. Joseph says: Just as a covenant is made concerning the land, so is a covenant made concerning chastisement, as it is said, *The Lord, thy God, chasteneth thee,* followed further on by *For the Lord, thy God, bringeth thee into a good land* (8:7).[14]

R. Simeon ben Yoḥai says: Precious are chastisements, for three goodly gifts coveted by all the nations of the world were given to Israel solely for the sake of sufferings, and they are: Torah, the Land of Israel, and the world-to-come. Whence Torah? From *To know wisdom and chastisement*[15] (Prov. 1:2), and *Happy is the man whom Thou chastisest, O Lord, and teachest out of Thy Torah* (Ps. 94:12). Whence the Land of Israel? From *The Lord, thy God, chasteneth thee. . . . For the Lord, thy God, bringeth thee into a good land* (8:5,7). Whence the world-to-come? From *The commandment is a lamp and the Torah is light, and reproofs of chastisement are the way of life* (Prov. 6:23). What is the road that leads a man to the world-to-come? Chastisements. R. Nehemiah says: Precious are chastisements, for just as sacrifices cause appeasement, so do chastisements. Concerning sacrifices Scripture says, *And it shall be accepted for him, to make atonement for him* (Lev. 1:4), while concerning chastisements it says, *And they shall be paid the punishment for their iniquity* (Lev. 26:43).[16] Indeed sufferings appease even more than sacrifices, for sacrifices involve one's money, while sufferings involve one's own body, as it is said, *Skin for skin, yea, all that a man hath will he give for his life* (Job 2:4).

Once R. Eliezer fell ill, and R. Tarfon, R. Joshua, E. Eleazar ben Azariah, and R. ʿAḳiba came to visit him. R. Tarfon said to him, "Master, you are more precious to Israel than the orb of the sun, for the orb of the sun sheds light on this world, while you have enlightened both this world and the world-to-come." R. Joshua said to him, "Master, you are more precious to Israel than the gift of rain, for rain grants life in this world, while you give it in this world and in the world-to-come." R. Eleazar ben Azariah said to him, "Master, you are more precious to Israel than one's father and mother, for father and mother bring one into this world, while you have brought us into this world and into the world-to-come." R. ʿAḳiba said to him. "Master, precious are chastisements."[17] R. Eliezer thereupon said to his disciples, "Prop me up." When R. Eliezer had sat up, he said to ʿAḳiba, "Go on, ʿAḳiba." R. ʿAḳiba went on: It is said, *Manasseh was twelve years old when he began to reign, and he reigned fifty and five years in Jerusalem* (2 Chron. 33.1), and *These also are proverbs of Solomon, which the men of Hezekiah king of Judah copied out*

(Prov. 25:1). Could one imagine that Hezekiah taught Torah to all Israel but not to Manasseh, his son? Rather, all his instruction and all his toil was of no avail to him. Only chastisements availed him, as it is said, *And the Lord spoke to Manasseh and to his people, but they gave no heed. Wherefore the Lord brought upon them the captains of the host of the king of Assyria, who took Manasseh with hooks, and bound him with fetters, and carried him to Babylon. And when he was in distress, he besought the Lord, his God, and humbled himself greatly before the God of his fathers, and he prayed unto Him, and He was entreated of him, and heard his supplication, and brought him back to Jerusalem, into his kingdom* (2 Chron. 33:10–13).[18] Hence, precious are chastisements.

R. Meir says: Scripture says, *Thou shalt love the Lord, thy God, with all thy heart.* Love Him with all your heart, as did your father Abraham, of whom it is said, *But thou, Israel, My servant, Jacob, whom I have chosen, the seed of Abraham My friend* (Isa. 41:8).[19] *And with all thy soul,* as did Isaac, who bound himself upon the altar, as it is said, *And Abraham stretched forth his hand, and took the knife to slay his son* (Gen. 22:10).[20] *And with all thy might* (*mĕ'oḏ*) thank him (*moḏeh*)[21] as did Jacob, as it is said, *I am not worthy of all the mercies and of all the truth, which Thou hast shown unto Thy servant, for with my staff I passed over this Jordan, and now I am become two camps* (Gen. 32:11).

Pisḳa 33

And these words which I command thee this day shall be upon thy heart (6:6): Rabbi (Judah the Prince) says: Why did Moses say this? Because Scripture says, *And thou shalt love the Lord, thy God, with all thy heart* (6:5). I do not know just how one is to love God. Hence Scripture goes on to say, *And these words which I command thee this day shall be upon thy heart,* meaning, take these words to heart, for thus will you recognize Him who spoke, and the world came into being, and you will cling to His ways.

Which I command thee this day: They should not be in your eyes like some antiquated edict to which no one pays any attention, but like a new edict which everyone runs to read.[1]

Upon thy heart: This was the source of R. Josiah's saying:[2] One must bind his Inclination by an oath, for you find everywhere that the righteous used to bind their Inclination by an oath. Concerning

Abraham, Scripture says, *I have lifted up my hand unto the Lord, God Most High, Maker of heaven and earth, that I will not take a thread nor a shoe-latchet nor aught that is thine* (Gen. 14:22–23). Concerning Boaz it says, *Then will I do the part of a kinsman to thee, as the Lord liveth; lie down until the morning* (Ruth 3:13). Concerning David it says, *And David said, "As the Lord liveth, nay, but the Lord shall smite him, or his day shall come to die, or he shall go down into battle and be swept away. (The Lord forbid it me, that I should put forth my hand against the Lord's anointed)"* (1 Sam. 26:10–11). Concerning Elisha it says, *As the Lord liveth, before whom I stand, I will receive none* (2 Kings 5:16). And just as the righteous used to bind their Inclination by an oath to prevent it from acting, so did the wicked bind their Inclination to make it act, as it is said, *As the Lord liveth, I will surely run after him, and take somewhat of him* (2 Kings 5:20).

Pisḳa 34

And thou shalt teach them diligently unto thy children (6:7): They should be so finely honed in your mouth that when someone asks you about them, you will not stutter, and will be able to reply immediately. Hence Scripture says, *Say unto wisdom, "Thou art my sister," and call understanding thy kinswoman* (Prov. 7:4), *Bind them upon thy fingers, write them upon the table of thy heart* (Prov. 7:3), *Thine arrows are sharp* (Ps. 45:6).[1] What is the reward for this? *The peoples fall under thee, (they sink) into the heart of the king's enemies* (Ps. 45:6), *As arrows in the hand of a mighty man, so are the children of one's youth* (Ps. 127:4). What does it say of such children? *Happy is the man that hath his quiver full of them; they shall not be put to shame when they speak with their enemies in the gate* (Ps. 127:5).

Another interpretation: *And thou shalt teach them diligently unto thy children*: These sections must be recited daily,[2] but *Sanctify unto Me all the first-born* (Exod. 13:2) and *It shall be when the Lord shall bring thee* (Exod. 13:11) need not be recited daily. Lest you should think that since *Speak* (Num. 15:38), which is not contained in the phylacteries,[3] is recited daily, certainly *Sanctify unto Me* and *It shall be,* which are contained in the phylacteries, should be recited, the verse here says explicitly *and thou shalt teach them,* meaning that these are to be recited, but *Sanctify unto Me* and *It shall be* are not to be recited.[4] Still I might say, if *Speak,* which is preceded by other commandments, is to be recited, should not the Ten Commandments,[5] which are preceded by no other commandments, also be recited? You might then say that this is a matter of inference from the minor to the major: if *Sanctify unto Me* and *It shall be,* which are contained in the phylacteries, are not to be recited, should the Ten Commandments, which are not contained in the phylacteries, also not be recited? The answer is that *Speak* proves the contrary, that even though the Ten Commandments are not contained in the phylacteries, they must be recited, hence Scripture says, *And thou shalt teach them diligently unto thy children,* meaning that these must be recited, but the Ten Commandments need not be recited.[6]

Unto thy children: This refers to your disciples, for you find that disciples are always referred to as children, as in the verse, *And the sons of the prophets that were at Beth-El came forth to Elisha* (2 Kings 2:3)—were they the children of the prophets? Were they not the disciples? Hence we learn that disciples are called children. So also in the verse *And the sons of the prophets that were at Jericho came near to Elisha* (2 Kings 2:5)—were they the children of the prophets? Were they not the disciples? Here too disciples are called children. Similarly, you find that Hezekiah, king of Judah, who taught the entire Torah to Israel, called them his sons, as it is said, *My sons, be not now negligent* (2 Chron. 29:11). Just as disciples are called sons, so the teacher is called father, as it is said, *And Elisha saw it, and he cried, "My father, my father, the chariots of Israel and the horsemen thereof," and he saw him no more* (2 Kings 2:12), and *Now Elisha was fallen sick of his sickness, whereof he was to die; and (Joash) the king of Israel came down unto him, and wept over him and said, "My father, my father, the chariots of Israel and the horsemen thereof"* (2 Kings 13:14).

And shalt talk of them (6:7): Make them matters of basic importance and not merely incidental, by having no discussion without them, and by not mixing other matters with them, as some[7] do. You might say, "I have learned the wisdom of Israel, so now I will go and learn the wisdom of the other nations"; hence Scripture says, *To walk therein* (Lev. 18:4) and not get free of them.[8] Similarly Scripture says, *Let them be only thine own, and not strangers with thee* (Prov. 5:17), *When thou walkest, it shall lead thee; when thou liest down, it shall watch over thee; and when thou awakest, it shall talk with thee* (Prov. 6:22). *When thou walkest, it shall lead thee,* in this world; *when thou liest down, it shall watch over thee,* in the hour of death; *and when thou awakest,* in the days of the Messiah, *it shall talk with thee,* in the world-to-come.[9]

And when thou liest down (6:7): You might think that this applies even if one lies down in the middle of the day, hence Scripture goes on to say, *And when thou risest up* (6:7); you might think that this applies even if one is awake in the middle of the night, hence Scripture says, *When thou sittest in thy house and when thou walkest by the way* (6:7)—the Torah is using common forms of speech.[10] Once R. Ishmael was reclining as he was expounding (his lesson), and R. Eleazar ben Azariah was standing. When the time came for the recitation of the Shemaᶜ, R. Ishmael got up and R. Eleazar ben Azariah lay down. R. Ishmael said to him, "What is this, Eleazar?" He replied, "Ishmael, my brother, once someone was asked, 'Why do you grow your beard long?' He replied, 'In protest against those who shave it off.'" Ishmael said to him, "You lay down in accord with the view of the School of Shammai, while I got up in accord with the School of Hillel." Another explanation: So that this matter should not become obligatory, since the School of Shammai taught that in the evening one must recline to recite the Shemaᶜ and in the morning one must stand up.[11]

Pisḳa 35[1]

And thou shalt bind them (6:8): These (verses) are contained in the phylacteries, while *Speak* (Num. 15:38) is not contained in them. Lest you should think that since *Sanctify unto Me* (Exod. 13:2) and *It shall be when the Lord shall bring thee* (Exod. 13:11), which are not recited daily, are contained in the phylacteries, *Speak,* which is recited daily, should certainly be contained in the phylacteries, the verse says (explicitly), *And thou shalt bind them,* meaning that these are to be contained in the phylacteries, while *Speak* is not to be contained in them. Still, I might say that if *Sanctify unto Me* and *It shall be when the Lord shall bring thee,* which are preceded by other commandments, are contained in the phylacteries, should not the Ten Commandments, which are preceded by no other commandments, be contained in the phylacteries? You might then say that this is a matter of inference from the minor to the major: if *Speak,* which is recited daily, is not contained in the phylacteries, should not the Ten Commandments, which are not recited daily, be likewise excluded from the phylacteries? The answer is that *Sanctify unto Me* and *It shall be when the Lord shall bring thee* would prove otherwise, for they are not recited and yet are contained in the phylacteries, which would prove that even though the Ten Commandments are not recited, they should be contained in the phylacteries. Hence Scripture says, *And thou shalt bind them*: these are to be "bound" in the phylacteries, but the Ten Commandments are not to be so "bound."

And thou shalt bind them for a sign upon thy hand (6:8): In one continuous scroll of all four sections. Lest you should think that since the Torah tells us to put phylacteries on the hand and on the head, it follows that just as the head phylactery contains four separate scrolls, so should the hand phylactery have four separate scrolls; therefore Scripture says (explicitly), *And thou shalt bind them for a sign*[2] *upon thy hand,* indicating one continuous scroll of all four sections. Or (one might ask), since the hand phylactery has one continuous scroll, should not the head phylactery also have one continuous scroll? Therefore Scripture goes on to say, *And they shall be for frontlets* (6:8). Now *frontlets* is spelled twice without the letter *waw* (of the plural suffix) and once with the letter *waw,* thus indicating four frontlets in all.[3] Or should there be four containers of four frontlets each? Therefore Scripture says, *And for a memorial*[4] *between thine eyes* (Exod. 13:9)—one container of four sections.

Upon thy hand: Upon the upper part of the arm. You might say, upon the upper part of the arm, but might it mean literally upon the hand itself? Logic answers that since the Torah tells us to put phylacteries both on the hand and on the head, just as the head phylactery is tied to the upper part of the head, so should the hand phylactery be tied to the upper part of the arm. R. Eliezer says: *Upon thy hand*—upon the upper part of the arm. You might say, upon the upper part of the arm, but might it mean literally upon the hand itself? Therefore Scripture says, *And it shall be for a sign unto thee upon thy hand* (Exod. 13:9)—it shall be a sign for you, not a sign for others.[5] R. Isaac says: Upon the upper part of the arm. You might say, upon the upper part of the arm, but might it mean literally upon the hand itself? Therefore Scripture says, *And these words . . . shall be upon thy heart* (6:6)—in a place opposite the heart. Where is that? On the upper part of the arm.

Upon thy hand: This is the left hand. You might say, this is the left hand, but might it be the right hand? There is a reference to this, though not proof of it, in the verses, *Yea, My hand hath laid the foundation of the earth, and My right hand hath spread out the heavens* (Isa. 48:13), and *Her hand she put to the tent-pin, and her right hand to the workmen's hammer; and with the hammer she smote Sisera, she smote through his head, yea, she pierced and struck through his temples* (Judg. 5:26). Hence whenever *hand* is used in Scripture, it means the left hand. R. Nathan says: *And thou shalt bind them . . . and thou shalt write them* (6:8–9)—just as writing is done with the right hand, so binding must be done by the right hand. R. Jose the net-maker, however, says: We find that the right hand also is sometimes called *hand,* as it is said, *And when Joseph saw that his father was laying his hand, the right one, upon the head of Ephraim, it displeased him, and he held up his father's hand, to remove it from Ephraim's head unto Manasseh's head* (Gen. 48:17). This being the case, why does Scripture say here, *Upon thy hand?* To include the man whose hand has been cut off, to the effect that he must put the phylactery upon his right arm.

And thou shalt bind them for a sign upon thy hand, and they shall be for frontlets between thine eyes (6:8): Once the hand phylactery is upon the hand, put the head phylactery upon the head. Hence the Sages said: When one puts on the phylacteries, he must put on the hand phylactery first, and then the head phylactery; when he removes them, he must remove the head phylactery first and then the hand phylactery.

Between thine eyes: Upon the upper part of the head. You might say, upon the upper part of the head, but does it rather mean literally between thine eyes? Logic suggests that since the Torah tells us to put phylacteries on both the hand and the head, it follows that just as the hand phylactery is tied to the upper part of the arm, so should the head phylactery be tied to the upper part of the head. R. Judah says: Since the Torah tells us to put phylacteries on both the hand and the head, it follows that just as the place on the hand is one that may become unclean through one of the marks of leprosy, so should the place on the head be one that may become unclean through one of the marks of leprosy.[6]

Pisḳa 36

And thou shalt write them (6:9): In perfect writing.[1] Hence the Sages said: If one writes *ʿayins* in place of *alefs,* or *alefs* in place of *ʿayins, kafs* in place of *bets, bets* in place of *kafs, ṣades* in place of *gimels, gimels* in place of *ṣades, rešs* in place of *dalets, dalets* in place of *rešs, ḥets* in place of *hes, hes* in place of *ḥets, yods* in place of *waws, waws* in place of *yods, nuns* in place of *zayins, zayins* in place of *nuns, pes* in place of *ṭets, ṭets* in place of *pes,*[2] straight letters in place of bent ones, bent ones in place of straight ones, *sameks* in place of *mems, mems* in place of *sameks,* open letters in place of closed ones, closed ones in place of open ones; if one writes a closed section open, or an open one closed; if one writes without ink, or writes the Song the same as the rest of the text,[3] or writes the Divine Names in gold[4]—in all these cases the scrolls must be hidden away.

And thou shalt write them: I might think that this means write them upon the stones,[5] because logic suggests that *write* is said here and *write* is said elsewhere (27:8);[6] just as *write* said there refers explicitly to writing upon stones, so must *write* said here mean writing upon stones. Or alternately you might argue thus: *write* is said here and *write* is said elsewhere (Num. 5:23); just as *write* there refers to writing with ink upon a scroll, so *write* said here means writing with ink upon a scroll. You can argue from the latter parallel, and I can argue from the former: *write* is said here and *write* is said elsewhere; just as *write* said there refers to writing upon stones, so *write* said here must mean writing upon stones.[7] If you say, let us then make a distinction and learn and judge one case from another similar case, (I reply,) let us learn something which is to be practiced through all generations from something else which is likewise to be practiced through all generations, rather than learn something which is to be practiced for all generations from something which was meant only for one specific occasion. Now *write* is said here and *write* is said elsewhere. Just as *write* there means writing with ink upon a scroll, so *write* here must mean writing with ink upon a scroll. Even though this is not proof, there is an indirect allusion to it in the verse, *Then Baruch answered them, "He pronounced all these words unto me with his mouth and I wrote them with ink in the book"* (Jer. 36:18).

Upon the door-posts (6:9): I might think that the plural presupposes (at least) two door-posts. Hence there is also a second verse which says *the door-posts* (11:20), and R. Ishmael taught that when one verse which adds to the number comes after another verse which adds to the number, it actually reduces the number. R. Isaac, however, says that this method of interpretation need not be applied here, for Scripture says elsewhere, *And they shall take of the blood, and put it on the two*[8] *side-posts and on the lintel* (Exod. 12:7), which provides the basic principle that only one door-post is meant, unless Scripture specifically says "two."

Of thy house (6:9): On the right side as one enters. You say, on the right side as one enters, but might it mean on the right side as one exits? Hence the verse says, *Upon the door-posts of thy house (beṯeḵa)*—read "upon thy entering" (*biʾaṯḵa*),[9] that is, on the right side as one enters.

And upon thy gates (6:9): I might think that this means (all) gates, to houses, chicken coops, cattle sheds, straw sheds, cow barns, storerooms, woodsheds, wine cellars, grain storage and oil storage rooms; hence the verse says, *Of thy house*—just as *thy house* refers to a dwelling structure, so *thy gates* refers to the gates of a dwelling structure. I might think that it includes also gates to basilicas,[10] demosias,[11] and bathhouses; hence the verse says, *thy house*—just as *thy house* refers to an honored place and a dwelling, so *thy gates* refers to an honored place and a dwelling. I might think that this includes even the gates of the Temple; hence the verse says, *thy house*—just as *thy house* refers to a place which is not sacred, so would it have to be a part of the Temple which is not sacred. Hence the Sages said: Chambers which open onto holy areas are holy, those which open onto nonsacred areas are not holy.[12]

Precious are Israel,[13] for Scripture has surrounded them with commandments: phylacteries on their heads, phylacteries on their arms, mezuzahs on their doors, ritual fringes on their garments.[14] Concerning them David said, *Seven times a day do I praise Thee because of Thy righteous ordinances* (Ps. 119:164). When he went into the bathhouse and saw himself naked, he said, "Woe is me, I am naked of commandments," but then he saw his mark of circumcision and began to praise it, saying, *For the Leader: on the eighth, a psalm of David* (Ps. 12:1). A parable: A king of flesh and blood said to his wife, "Deck yourself out with all your jewelry, so that you would look desirable to me." Thus also the Holy One, blessed be He, said to Israel, "My children, be marked by the commandments, so that you would look desirable to Me." Hence Scripture says, *Thou art beautiful, O my love, as Tirzah* (Song 6:4)—you are beautiful when you seem desirable[15] unto Me.

Pisḳa 37

And it shall come to pass because . . . (7:12), *For the land whither thou goest in to possess it (is not as the land of Egypt, from whence ye came out)*

11:10): This was said to pacify Israel at the time when they were leaving Egypt, for they kept saying, "Perchance we are going to a land not as fine as this one." Therefore God said to them, *For the land wither thou goest in to possess it is not as the land of Egypt,* indicating that the Land of Israel is superior to it. Does Scripture speak here in praise of the Land of Israel or in praise of the land of Egypt?[1] Another verse says, *Now Hebron was built seven years before Zoan in Egypt* (Num. 13:22). What kind of city was Zoan? It was the royal residence, as it is said, *For his princes are at Zoan* (Isa. 30:4). What kind of city was Hebron? The refuse of the Land of Israel, as it is said, *(And Sarah died in) Kiriath-Arba—the same is Hebron . . . (And Abraham rose up . . . saying, "Give me a possession of a burying-place with you")* (Gen. 23:2–4).[2] This is a matter of logical inference from the minor to the major: if Hebron, the refuse of the Land of Israel, is superior to the best place in Egypt—which is the best of all the other lands—it follows that the verse speaks in praise of the Land of Israel.[3] Should you say (that this[4] means nothing, since) they were not built by the same people,[5] another verse says, *And the sons of Ham: Cush, Mizraim, and Put, and Canaan* (Gen. 10:6). Since Ham who built one built also the other,[6] is it possible that he built the ugly one first and then built the beautiful one? Rather he built the beautiful one first and then the ugly one.[7] [A parable: When a man builds two great rooms, one beautiful and one ugly, he does not build the ugly one first and then the beautiful one, rather he builds first the beautiful one and then the ugly one, using the rejects from the beautiful one for the ugly one.] Thus, since Hebron was the more beautiful, it was built first.[8] This is also true concerning God's actions—whatever is more precious comes first: Torah, which is the most precious of all, was created before all else, as it is said, *The Lord made me as the beginning of His way, the first of His works of old* (Prov. 8:22), and *I was set up from everlasting, from the beginning, or ever the earth was* (Prov. 8:23). The Temple, since it is most precious of all, was created before all else, as it is said, *Thou throne of glory, on high from the beginning, thou place of our Sanctuary* (Jer. 17:12). The Land of Israel, which is the most precious of all, was created before all else, as it is said, *While as yet He had not made the earth nor the fields (nor the beginning of the dust of the world)* (Prov. 8:26)—(*earth* means all other lands, *fields* means wildernesses, *world* means the Land of Israel). R. Simeon ben Yoḥai says: *World* means the Land of Israel, as it is said, *Playing with the world, His land* (Prov. 8:31).

Why is it called "world" (*teḇel*)? Because it is enriched (*mĕṯubbeleṯ*)[9] by every thing. For every land has something lacking in other lands, whereas the Land of Israel lacks nothing, as it is said, *Thou shalt not lack anything in it* (8:9). Another interpretation: *Earth* means all the other lands, *fields* means wildernesses, *world* means the Land of Israel. Why is it called "world"? Because of the spice (*teḇel*) that is in it. And what spice does it contain? Torah, as it is said, *There is no Torah among the nations* (Lam. 2:9).[10] From this we learn that the Torah dwells in the Land of Israel. You find a similar instance in the case of Sennacherib, when he attempted to entice Israel: what did he say to them? *Until I come and take you away to a land like your own land* (2 Kings 18:32). He did not say, "a land finer than your land," but *a land like your own land.*[11] This is an inference from the minor to the major: if one who had come to speak the praises of his own land could not speak disparagingly of the Land of Israel, certainly (the afore-cited verses)[12] must be in praise of the Land of Israel. R. Simeon ben Yoḥai says: That one was a fool who did not know how to entice, (as witness) a parable: A man who wanted to betroth a woman said to her, "Your father is a king, and I am a king; your father is wealthy, and I am wealthy; your father feeds you meat and fish and gives you aged wine to drink, and I will feed you meat and fish and give you aged wine to drink"—that is not the proper way to entice. How then should he speak to her? He should say, "Your father is a commoner, but I am a king; your father is poor, but I am wealthy; your father feeds you vegetables and pulse, but I will feed you fish and meat; your father gives you new wine to drink, but I will give you aged wine; your father takes you to the bathhouse on foot, but I will take you there in a litter."[13] Is this then not an inference from the minor to the major? If one who had come to speak the praises of his own land could not speak disparagingly of the Land of Israel, certainly (the afore-cited verses) must be in praise of the Land of Israel.

Scripture says in one place, *Which Hermon the Sidonians call Sirion, and the Amorites call it Senir* (3:9), and in another, *Even unto Mount Sion—the same is Hermon* (4:48). Thus we find that it has four names. What use did people have (for all these names)? This indicates rather that four kingdoms had fought over it, each one saying, "It should be called after my name." Is this not a matter of inference from the minor to the major? If four kingdoms had fought over the most insignificant of the mountains of Israel, certainly (the afore-cited verses) must be in praise of the Land of Israel.[14] Similarly Scripture says, *And Dannah and Kiriat-sannah—the same is Debir* (Josh. 15:49), and in another place, *Now the name of Debir aforetime was Kiriath-Sepher* (Josh. 15:15). Thus we find that it had three names. What use do people have for (all these names)? They indicate rather that three kingdoms fought over it, each one saying, "It should be called after my name." Is this not a matter of inference from the minor to the major? If the most insignificant of the cities in Israel was fought over by four kingdoms, certainly (the afore-cited verses) must be in praise of the Land of Israel. In the same manner Scripture says, *Get thee up into this mountain of Abarim, unto Mount Nebo* (32:49), and in another place, *Get thee up into the top of Pisgah* (3:27). Thus we find that it had three names. What use did people have for all these names? They indicate rather that three kingdoms had fought over it, each one saying, "It should be called after my name." Is this not a matter of inference from the minor to the major? If three kingdoms had fought over the most insignificant of the hills of the Land of Israel, certainly (the afore-cited verses) speak in praise of the Land of Israel.

Behold, Scripture says, (*How would I*) . . . *give thee a pleasant land, the goodliest heritage of the nations* (Jer. 3:19). A land filled with magnificent fortifications[15] for kings and governors, for any king or governor who did not acquire (a place) in the Land of Israel would say, "I have accomplished nothing." (As) R. Judah says:[16] Were the thirty-one conquered kings really all in the Land of Israel? Rather, it is the same as what is now done in Rome—any king or governor who has not acquired (a place) in Rome says, "I have accomplished nothing." So also any king or governor who had not acquired palaces and fortresses in the Land of Israel would say, "I have accomplished nothing."

A pleasant land (*naḥălaṯ ṣĕḇi*):[17] As the deer is swifter of foot than any other domestic or wild animal, so the fruits of the Land of Israel are swifter to grow than those of any other land. Another interpretation: Just as the hide of the deer, once separated from the flesh, cannot contain it,[18] so also the Land of Israel cannot contain all its fruit so long as Israel is occupied with Torah. Just as deer (flesh) is the easiest to digest of that of all domestic and wild animals, so the fruits of the Land of Israel are easier to digest than those of any other land. You might think that since they are easy to digest they are not rich; hence Scripture says, *A land flowing with milk and honey*

(11:9)—rich as milk and sweet as honey. Similarly Scripture says, *Let me sing of my well-beloved, a song of my beloved touching his vineyard. My well-beloved had a vineyard in a very fruitful hill (bĕ-ḳeren ben šemen)*[19] (Isa. 5:1). Just as the horn is the highest part of the ox, so is the Land of Israel the highest of all lands. Or,[20] lest you should think that just as no part of the ox is less valuable than its horn, so is the Land of Israel the most insignificant of all the lands, the verse goes on to say, *the son of fat,* meaning that the Land of Israel is fat. Therefore the verse indicates that a place which is higher than other places is better than they. That the Land of Israel is indeed higher and therefore better than all other places (we learn from these verses): *We should go up at once, and possess it* (Num. 13:30), *so they went up, and spied out the land* (Num. 13:21), *And they went up into the south* (Num. 13:22), *And they went up out of Egypt* (Gen. 45:25). That the Temple was higher and therefore better than all other temples (we learn) from the verses, *Then shalt thou arise and get thee up unto the place* (17:18), *And many peoples shall go and say: "Come ye, and let us go up to the mountain of the house*[21] *of the Lord"* (Isa. 2:3), *For there shall be a day, that the watchmen shall call upon (the mount Ephraim: "Arise ye, and let us go up to Zion, unto the Lord our God")* (Jer. 31:6).

Pisḳa 38

It is not as the land of Egypt (11:10): The land of Egypt is watered[1] from below, while the Land of Israel is watered from above. The land of Egypt drinks the waters below but not those above, while the Land of Israel drinks both those below and those above. The land of Egypt drinks the waters below and then those which are above, while the Land of Israel drinks both those below and those above simultaneously.[2] In the land of Egypt what is exposed is watered but what is covered is not. In the Land of Israel both what is exposed and what is covered are watered. The land of Egypt is watered and then planted (only once). The Land of Israel is watered and then planted, planted again and then watered, and can be watered and planted (repeatedly) every day. The land of Egypt—only if you work over it with mattock and spade and give up sleep for it (will it yield produce);[3] if you do not, it will yield nothing. The Land of Israel is not like that—its inhabitants sleep in their beds while God sends down rain for them. A parable: A king who was walking along the way noticed a young man of noble family, and forthwith gave him a manservant to serve him. Later on the king saw another young man of noble family, well dressed and delicately reared, who was working as a hired laborer[4]—the king knew him and his parents—whereupon the king said, "I declare that I will personally see to his needs and feed him." Thus also all lands were given "servants" to tend them—Egypt is watered by the Nile, Babylon by its rivers—but the Land of Israel is not like that. Rather, there the inhabitants sleep in their beds while God causes the rains to fall for them. Hence we learn that God's ways are different from those of creatures of flesh and blood. A man acquires manservants to feed and sustain him, but He who spoke, and the world came into being, acquires manservants so that He Himself may feed and sustain them.

Once R. Eliezer, R. Joshua, and R. Zadok were reclining at a banquet for the son of Rabban Gamaliel. Rabban Gamaliel mixed a cup (of wine) for R. Eliezer, who declined it. R. Joshua took it, whereupon R. Eliezer said to him, "What's this, Joshua? Is it fitting for us to be reclining while R. Gamaliel son of Rabbi[5] stands and serves us?" R. Joshua replied, "Let him serve. After all Abraham, one of the great ones of the world, served the ministering angels when he thought that they were pagan Arabs, as it is said, *And he lifted up his eyes and looked, and lo, three men stood over against him* (Gen. 18:2)." Is this not an inference from the minor to the major? If Abraham, one of the great ones of the world, served angels when he thought that they were pagan Arabs, should not Gamaliel son of Rabbi serve us? R. Zadok thereupon said to them, "You have ignored God's honor in order to deal with the honor of flesh and blood. If He who spoke, and the world came into being, causes winds to blow, brings up clouds, brings down rains, and raises vegetation, thus setting a table for everyone, should not Gamaliel son of Rabbi serve us?"

You might ask, was this the intention of Scripture,[6] or did it contrast the Land of Israel with the land of Egypt because Egypt is the worst of all lands? Therefore Scripture says, *Like the garden of the Lord, like the land of Egypt* (Gen. 13:10):[7] *Like the garden of the Lord,* in its trees; *like the land of Egypt,* in its plants. Or is the contrast perhaps only with the unpleasant aspect of it?[8] Therefore Scripture says, *Wherein ye dwelt* (Lev. 18:3), and of the very same place wherein you dwelt it says, *In the best of the land* (Gen. 47:6). Or perhaps the contrast refers to the time of its degradation,[9] wherefore Scripture says, *From whence ye came out* (11:10):[10] When you were there, it was blessed because of you, but not so now, when it is not blessed as it was when you were there. Similarly you find that wherever the righteous go, blessing follows in their footsteps: when Isaac went down to Gerar, blessing followed in his footsteps, as it is said, *And Isaac sowed (in that land, and found in the same year a hundredfold)* (Gen. 26:12); when Jacob went down to be with Laban, blessing followed in his footsteps, as it is said, *I have observed the signs, and the Lord hath blessed me for thy sake* (Gen. 30:27); when Joseph went down to be with Potiphar, blessing followed in his footsteps, as it is said, *The Lord blessed the Egyptian's house for Joseph's sake* (Gen. 39:5); when Jacob went down to be with Pharaoh, blessing followed in his footsteps, as it is said, *And Jacob blessed Pharaoh* (Gen. 47:7). How did he bless him? By withholding from him the years of famine,[11] as it is said, *Now therefore fear ye not—I will sustain you* (Gen. 50:21). Just as the sustenance spoken of in Scripture elsewhere refers to a time of famine, so also here the sustenance spoken of in Scripture refers to a time of famine.[12]

R. Simeon ben Yoḥai says: It does not bring glory to God[13] if promises made by the righteous are kept while they are living, but are nullified once they die. R. Eleazar son of R. Simeon said: I prefer R. Jose's interpretation[14] to that of my father: indeed it does bring glory to God if when the righteous are in the world, there is blessing in the world, but when the righteous are removed from the world, blessing is removed from the world. Thus you find concerning the Ark of God that when it was taken to the house of Obed-edom the Gittite, the house was blessed because of it, as it is said, *And it was told King David, saying, "The Lord hath blessed the house of Obed-edom and all that pertaineth unto him, because of the Ark of God* (2 Sam. 6:12). Is this not an instance of inference from the minor to the major? If the Ark, which was made neither for profit nor for loss but for the broken pieces of the Tablets which were in it, brings blessings, how much more so should the righteous, for whose sakes the world was created, do the same. When our forefathers came to the Land of Israel, blessing followed in their footsteps, as it is said, *And houses full of all good things, which thou didst not fill, and cisterns hewn out, which thou didst not hew, (vineyards and olive trees, which thou didst not plant—and thou shalt eat and be satisfied)* (6:11). R. Simeon ben Yoḥai says: Is it not obvious that thou didst not fill them, since only now didst thou come into the land? *Cisterns hewn out, which thou didst not hew*—is it not obvious that thou didst not hew them, since only now didst thou come into the land? *Vineyards and olive trees, which thou didst not plant*—is it not obvious that thou didst not plant them, since only now didst thou come into the land? Why then does Scripture say, "didst fill," "didst hew," "didst plant"?[15] It was for the sake of your merit.[16] Thus you find that during the forty years when the children of Israel were in the wilderness the people of the (Holy) Land built houses, dug wells, ditches, and caves, planted fields, vineyards, and every fruit-bearing tree, so that when our forefathers came into the Land they would find it full of blessing.[17] Or, since this blessing had (now) come upon them, is it possible that it is they (the Canaanites) who shall eat and be satisfied?[18] Therefore Scripture says, *And thou shalt eat and be satisfied*—you shall eat and be satisfied, while they shall withhold it even from their wives, their sons, and their daughters, so that when our ancestors come to the land they shall find it full of blessing. The words *From whence ye came out* thus indicate that when you were there it was blessed for your sakes, but not now, when it is not blessed as it was when you were there.[19] You might say that such was the intention of Scripture.[20] Or did Scripture mean merely to draw an analogy[21] between the coming to the one (land) and the coming to the other, to the effect that just as you had been in Egypt for a specific number of years, including Sabbatical periods and Jubilee periods, so will you be in the land of Canaan? Therefore Scripture says, *To possess it* (11:11)—you are coming there to possess it,[22] not to sojourn there for only a specific number of years, including Sabbatical periods and Jubilee periods.[23] Indeed there is a distinction between their coming to the one and their coming to the other. Coming to Egypt was permissible, but coming to the Land of Israel was a duty. The land of Egypt—they will sojourn there whether or not they obey God's will. Not so with the Land of Israel—the land of Canaan is yours if you obey God's will; but if you do not, you will be exiled from it, as it is said, *That the land vomit not you out also, when ye defile it* (Lev. 18:28).

Pisḳa 39

But the land, whither ye go over to possess it, is a land of hills and valleys (11:11): Scripture speaks in praise of the Land of Israel. So you say. Or does Scripture perhaps speak disparagingly of the Land of Israel, since it mentions that there are hills there? Therefore it adds, *and valleys*—just as *valleys* indicates praise, so does *hills* indicate praise. Moreover, Scripture refers here to the difference in taste—the fruits of the hills have a light taste, while those of the valleys have a rich taste.[1] R. Simeon ben Yoḥai says: A valley has only one *bet̲ kor* of land,[2] but a hill has one *bet̲ kor* on the north side, another *bet̲ kor* on the south side, a third *bet̲ kor* on the east side, a fourth *bet̲ kor* on the west side, and a fifth *bet̲ kor* on the top, so that the sown ground is multiplied by five, as it is said, *Thus saith the Lord God: "This is Jerusalem! I have set her in the midst of the nations, and lands*[3] *are round about her"* (Ezek. 5:5). In another place it is called *land.* How can both of these be correct?[4] It is a land containing many different types of land—soil, sand, and dust. Another interpretation: *A land of hills and valleys*: This[5] indicates that the taste of the fruit of the hills is different from the taste of the fruit of the valleys, and vice versa. Whence do we learn that even the taste of the fruit of one hill is different from that of another hill, and the taste of the fruit of one valley is different from that of another valley? Scripture says, *A land of hills and valleys—hills* implies many hills, and *valleys,* many valleys. R. Simeon ben Yoḥai says further: Twelve lands were actually given, one to each of the twelve Tribes of Israel, and the flavor of the fruit of each Tribe was different from that of every other Tribe. And these are the proof-verses:[6]

For the land, whither thou goest in to possess it (11:10)
The land, whither ye go over to possess it (11:11)
A land of hills and valleys (11:11)
A land which the Lord thy God careth for (11:12)
For the Lord thy God bringeth thee into a good land (8:7)
A land of brooks of water (8:7)
A land of wheat and barley (8:8)
A land of olive trees and honey (8:8)
A land wherein thou shalt eat bread without scarceness (8:9)
A land where stones are iron (8:9)
For the good land which He hath given thee (8:10)
A land flowing with milk and honey (11:9).

Thus we have twelve lands given, one for each of the twelve Tribes of Israel. But the flavor of the fruits of one Tribe was not like that of any other Tribe, hence Scripture says, *A land of hills and valleys*: *hills*—many hills, *valleys*—many valleys. R. Jose ben ham-Meshullam says: Whence do you learn that just as different lands impart different flavors, so do different seas impart different flavors? From the verse, *And the gathering together of the waters called He seas* (Gen. 1:10). But was there not only one sea, as it is said, *Let the waters under the heaven be gathered unto one place* (Gen. 1:9)? What then is the meaning of *And the gathering together of the waters called He seas*? It indicates that the flavor of a fish from Acco is different from the flavor of a fish from Sidon, and the flavor of a fish from Sidon is different from the flavor of a fish from Paneas.[7]

Since the soil of a hill is light while that of a valley is rich, water might wash the (hill's) soil down into the valley, so that the valley would lack water;[8] therefore Scripture says, *A land of hills and valleys*—a hill which is a normal hill, and a valley which is a normal valley. Similarly Scripture says,[9] *Ask ye of the Lord rain in the time of the latter rain, (even of the Lord that maketh lightnings; and He will give them showers of rain, to every one grass in the field)* (Zech. 10:1). Or is it that since the Land of Israel is folded up into mountains, only exposed land would be watered, while land not exposed would not be watered? Therefore Scripture says, *And drinketh waters as the rain of heaven cometh down* (11:11), meaning that both land which is exposed and that which is not exposed are watered.[10] So also Scripture says, *Yea, He ladeth the thick cloud with moisture, He spreadeth abroad the cloud of His lightning . . . and they are turned round* (Job 37:11–12), so that clouds would surround the land and water it from every direction. Or is it that since it is watered by rain water it cannot be watered by irrigation conduits? Therefore Scripture says, *And drinketh waters as the rain of heaven cometh down*—when it says *waters,*[11] it means that the land is watered by irrigation conduits as well. Similarly Scripture says, *For the Lord thy God bringeth thee into a good land, a land of brooks of water* (8:7). Or is it that it is watered by irrigation conduits but not by water from (melted) snow? Therefore Scripture says, *And drinketh waters as the rain of heaven cometh down*—the word *waters* indicating that it is watered by water from (melted) snow as well. Again Scripture says, *For as the rain cometh down and the snow from heaven* (Isa. 55:10), and *For He saith to the snow, "Fall thou on the earth"* (Job 37:6). Or is it that the land is watered by water from (melted) snow but not by water from dew? Therefore Scripture says, *And drinketh waters as the rain of heaven cometh down*—*waters* indicating that it is watered by water from dew as well. Another interpretation:[12] Just as rain is a blessing, so is dew a blessing, for Scripture says, *So God give thee of the dew of heaven* (Gen. 27:28), *My doctrine shall drop as the rain, (my speech shall distill as the dew)* (32:2), *I will be as the dew unto Israel* (Hos. 14:6), *And the remnant of Jacob shall be . . . as dew from the Lord* (Mic. 5:6).

Piska 40

A land which the Lord thy God careth for (11:12): Is this the only land that He cares for? Does He not care for all lands, as it is said, *To cause it to rain on a land where no man is . . . to satisfy the desolate and waste ground* (Job 38:26–27)? What then does Scripture mean by *A land which the Lord thy God careth for*? It is as if it were possible to say[1] that He cares for it alone, but because of His care for it He cares for all the other lands along with it. Similarly you might ask, *Behold, He that keepeth Israel doth neither slumber nor sleep* (Ps. 121:4)—does He keep only Israel? Does He not keep all nations, as it is said, *In whose hand is the soul of every living thing and the breath of all mankind* (Job 12:10)? What then does *He that keepeth Israel* mean? It is as if it were possible to say that He keeps only Israel, but because He keeps them He keeps every other nation along with them. So also you might ask, *Mine eyes and My heart shall be there perpetually* (1 Kings 9:3),[2] yet elsewhere it is said, *The eyes of the Lord that run to and fro through the whole earth* (Zech. 4:10), *The eyes of the Lord are in every place, keeping watch upon the evil and the good* (Prov. 15:3)—what then does *Mine eyes and My heart shall be there perpetually* mean? It is as if it were possible to say that the Lord said, "My eyes and My heart shall be only there (especially)." The same applies to the verse *The voice of the Lord shaketh the wilderness; the Lord shaketh the wilderness of Kadesh* (Ps. 29:8): what does it (really) mean? That (the Lord shakes) this (wilderness of Kadesh) especially.

Careth for (doreš): The land is under the requirement (*dĕrišah*)[3] of separating the dough offering, the heave offering, and the tithes from it. Or are all other lands under the same requirement? (No,) for Scripture goes on to say *it*[4]—*it* is under this requirement, but the other lands are not.

Another interpretation: *Careth for* indicates that the land was given (to Israel) as a reward for the expounding (*dĕrišah*) of Torah,[5] as it is said, *And ye shall teach them your children, talking of them,* etc. . . . *that your days may be multiplied, and the days of your children* (11:19–

21), and also, *And He gave them the lands of the nations . . . that they might keep His statutes (and observe His laws)* (Ps. 105:44–45).

The eyes of the Lord thy God are always upon it (11:12): One verse says, *The eyes of the Lord thy God are always upon it,* while another verse says, *He looketh on the earth, and it trembleth, He toucheth the mountains, and they smoke* (Ps. 104:32)—how can both of these verses be true? When Israel does God's will,[6] *The eyes of the Lord thy God are always upon it,* and they suffer no injury; when Israel does not do God's will, *He looketh on the earth, and it trembleth.* Thus in regard to reward Scripture says, *The eyes of the Lord thy God are always upon it,* while in regard to punishment it says, *He looketh on the earth, and it trembleth.*[7] What was done in regard to reward? If they had been found guilty of evildoing on New Year's Day, and it was decreed that they should have but little rain, and if they forthwith repented, it was now impossible to add to the amount of rain, but still *The eyes of the Lord thy God are always upon it,* in that He would cause it to come down at the proper time and send a blessing with it, so that it would descend upon the land when it needed (water). What was done in regard to punishment? If they had been found righteous on New Year's Day, and it was decreed that they should have much rain, and if they thereupon fell into sin, it was now impossible to reduce it, but still *He looketh on the earth, and it trembleth*—He would cause it to come down at the wrong time and send a curse with it, causing it to descend on (parts of) the land that do not need it, on seas and on wildernesses, as it is said, *Drought and heat consume the snow waters, so doth the nether-world those that have sinned* (Job 24:19), meaning that what you had done against Me during the summer, when you did not separate heave offerings and tithes, has withheld the rain from you.[8]

From the beginning of the year even unto the end of the year (11:12): This shows that at the beginning of the year it is decreed how much rain and how much dew the land will have, how long sun will shine upon it, how long winds will blow over it.[9] Another interpretation: *From the beginning of the year*: I will bless you in commerce, building, planting, betrothal, marriage, and in whatever (else) you put your hands to, (in all this) I will bless you. A third interpretation: *From the beginning of the year even unto the end of the year*: Are there crops in the fields from the beginning of the year to its end? Rather, it is in My power to bless them in (your) home, just as it is in My power to bless them in the field, as it is said, *The Lord will command the blessing with thee in thy barns, and in all that thou puttest thy hand unto* (28:8), and *Is the seed yet in the barn? Yea, the vine, and the fig tree, and the pomegranate, and the olive tree hath not brought forth—from this day will I bless you* (Hag. 2:19). Whence do we learn that this applies to storehouses as well?[10] From the verse, *Blessed shalt thou be in the city, and blessed shalt thou be in the field* (28:3) And as to dough? From the verse, *Blessed shall be thy basket and thy kneading trough* (28:5). And as to entering and leaving? From the verse, *Blessed shalt thou be when thou comest in, and blessed shalt thou be when thou goest out* (28:6). As to eating to satiety? From the verse, *And thou shalt eat and be satisfied, and bless (the Lord)* (8:10). Does this apply even after the food has descended into your intestines? (Yes,) as Scripture says, *And I will take sickness away from the midst of thee* (Exod. 23:25). It is in My power to bless produce in the house just as it is in My power to bless it in the field. It will not be infested by vermin or rot, wine will not go sour, oil will not become rancid. Or is it that since the quality of goodness is greater (in Me) than the quality of punishment, it is not in My power to curse produce in the house as I can curse it in the field? Therefore Scripture says, *And when ye brought it home, I blew upon it* (Hag. 1:9), and *The Lord will send upon thee cursing, discomfiture, and rebuke* (28:20). Whence do we learn that this applies also to storehouses? From the verse, *Cursed shalt thou be in the city, and cursed shalt thou be in the field* (28:16). And as to dough? From the verse, *Cursed shall be thy basket and thy kneading trough* (28:17). And as to entering and leaving? From the verse, *Cursed shalt thou be when thou comest in, and cursed shalt thou be when thou goest out* (28:19). And as to eating to satiety? From the verse, *And ye shall eat, and not be satisfied* (Lev. 26:26). Does this apply even when the food has descended into your intestines? (Yes,) as Scripture says, *And thy sickness shall be in thy inward parts* (Mic. 6:14). It is indeed in My power to curse produce in the house just as it is in My power to curse it in the field: vermin and rot in produce, sourness in wine, and rancidity in oil.

R. Simeon ben Yoḥai says, by way of a parable:[11] A king of flesh and blood had many children and servants who were fed and sustained out of his hand. The keys to the storehouse were in his hands: when they did his will, he opened the storehouse, and they ate to satiety, but when they did not do his will, he locked the storehouse, and they died of starvation. Thus also is it with Israel: when they do God's will, *The Lord will open unto thee His good treasure, the heavens*

(28:12); but when they do not do His will, what does Scripture say?—*And the anger of the Lord be kindled against you, and He shut up the heaven, so that there shall be no rain* (11:17).

R. Simeon ben Yoḥai says: A loaf (of bread) and a cudgel tied together descended from heaven. God said to Israel, "If you observe the Torah, here is a loaf to eat; if not, here is a cudgel to be beaten with." Where is this set forth? In the verse, *If ye be willing and obedient, ye shall eat the good of the land: but if ye refuse and rebel, ye shall be devoured with the sword* (Isa. 1:19–20). R. Eleazar of Modiᶜin says: A scroll and a sword tied together descended from heaven. God said to them, "If you observe the Torah written in the one, you will be saved from the other; if not, you will be smitten by it." Where is this set forth? In the verse, *So He drove out the man, and He placed at the east of the Garden of Eden the cherubim, and the flaming sword which turned every way, to keep the way to the tree of life* (Gen. 3:24).[12]

Pisḳa 41

And it shall come to pass, if ye shall hearken diligently unto My commandments (11:13): Why was this said? Because it refers to the verse, *That ye may learn them, and observe to do them* (5:1). One might think that until they were obligated to perform them, they were not bound to learn them. Therefore Scripture says, *And it shall come to pass, if ye shall hearken diligently unto My commandments,* showing that they were bound to learn them immediately.[1] This might lead me to the conclusion that it applies only to commandments to be observed before Israel had entered the land (of Canaan), such as those governing the first born,[2] sacrifices,[3] and animal tithes.[4] Whence do we learn that this applies also to commandments that are to be observed only after Israel had entered the land, such as the sheaf of first fruits (*ᶜomer*),[5] the dough offering,[6] the two loaves,[7] and the showbread?[8] From the verse, *And it shall come to pass, if ye shall hearken diligently unto My commandments,* which is meant to include other commandments as well.[9] I might think that this refers only to commandments (performed) before they had conquered and settled (the land); what about those (performed) after they had conquered and settled (the land), such as gleanings, forgotten sheaves, corners of fields,[10] tithes,[11] heave offering,[12] and Sabbatical and Jubilee years?[13] Hence Scripture says, *And it shall come to pass, if ye shall hearken diligently unto My commandments (which I command you this day),*[14] thus including the other commandments as well.

That ye may learn them, and observe to do them (5:1)[15]: This indicates that deeds are dependent upon learning, but learning is not dependent upon deeds. Hence we find that one is punished more severely for failure in learning than for failure in deeds, as it is said, *Hear the word of the Lord, ye children of Israel! For the Lord hath a controversy with the inhabitants of the land, because there is no truth, nor mercy, nor knowledge of God in the land* (Hos. 4:1). *There is no truth*—words of truth are not spoken, as it is said, *Buy the truth, and sell it not, (also wisdom, and instruction, and understanding)* (Prov. 23:23). *Nor mercy*—words of mercy are not uttered, as it is said, *The earth, O Lord, is full of Thy mercy; (teach me Thy statutes)* (Ps. 119–64). *Nor knowledge*—words of knowledge are not spoken, as it is said, *My people are destroyed for lack of knowledge; (because thou hast rejected knowledge, I will also reject thee, that thou shalt be no priest to Me; seeing thou hast forgotten the law of thy God, I also will forget thy children)* (Hos. 4:6), and *Therefore, as stubble devoureth the tongue of fire, and as chaff consumeth the flame, (so their root shall be as rottenness)*[16] (Isa. 5:24). Can stubble devour fire? Rather, stubble refers to the wicked Esau; whenever Israel neglects the commandments, Esau gains mastery over them. Scripture says, *Who is the wise man, that he may understand this? And who is he to whom the mouth of the Lord hath spoken, that he may declare it? Wherefore is the land perished and laid waste like a wilderness, so that none passeth through? And the Lord saith: "Because they have forsaken My law which I set before them, and have not hearkened to My voice, neither walked therein"* (Jer. 9:11–12); and again, *Thus saith the Lord: "For three transgressions of Judah, yea, for four, I will not reverse it; because they have rejected the law of the Lord, and have not kept His statutes"* (Amos 2:4). Once R. Tarfon, R. ʿAḳiba, and R. Jose the Galilean were reclining at Bet ʿAris in Lod[17] when this question was presented to them, "What is more important, study or performance?" R. Tarfon said that performance is greater in importance, while R. ʿAḳiba said that study is greater. Everyone present agreed that study is greater because it leads to performance. R. Jose the Galilean said that study is greater because it preceded dough offering by forty years, tithes by fifty-four years, Sabbatical years by sixty-one years, Jubilees by one hundred and three years. Furthermore, just as God punished Israel more severely for not studying than for not performing, so too were they rewarded more for studying than for performance, since concerning study Scripture says, *And ye shall teach them your children, talking of them* (11:19). What does it say (subsequently)? *That your days may be multiplied, and the days of your children, (upon the land)* (11:21). Concerning performance, however, it says, *And He gave them the lands of the nations, and they took the labor of the peoples in possession; that they might keep His statutes and observe His laws* (Ps. 105:44–45).[18]

Which I command you this day (11:13): Whence do you learn that even if one learns an interpretation from the least learned of the Israelites, he should consider it as if he had learned it from a Sage? From the verse, *Which I command you.*[19] And moreover, not as if he had learned it from only one Sage but as if he had learned it from (many) Sages, as it is said, *The words of the sages are as goads* (Eccl. 12:11): just as a goad guides a cow along its furrows, thus producing livelihood for its owners, so do the words of Torah guide a man's thoughts toward knowledge of God. And furthermore, as if he had learned it not from (many ordinary) Sages but from the (most learned seventy members of the) Sanhedrin, as it is said, *Masters of assemblies* (*ʾăšufot̲*)[20] (Eccl. 12:11), *assemblies* meaning the Sanhedrin, as it is said, *Gather* (*ʾesfah*) *unto Me seventy men of the elders of Israel* (Num. 11:16). And still further, as if he had learned it not from the Sanhedrin but from Moses, as it is said, *They are given from one shepherd* (Eccl. 12:11), and *Then His people remembered the days of old, the days of Moses* (Isa. 63:11). And finally, as if he had learned it not from Moses but from the Almighty One, as it is said, *They are given from one Shepherd,* and *Give ear, O Shepherd of Israel, Thou that leadest Joseph like a flock* (Ps. 80:2), and *Hear, O Israel, the Lord our God, the Lord is one* (6:4).

Scripture says, *Thine eyes as the pools in Heshbon, by the gate of Bath-rabbim* (Song 7:5): *thine eyes*—these are the elders appointed over the community, as it is said, *For the Lord hath poured out upon you the spirit of deep sleep, and hath closed your eyes; (the prophets . . . hath He covered)* (Isa. 29:10); *pools*—just as one cannot know what is in a pool, so can he not fathom the words of the Sages; *in Heshbon*—in calculations (*ḥešbonot̲*) which result from consultation and thought; and where are these calculations made? In houses of study, *by the gate of Bath-rabbim.*[21] What is meant by *Thy nose is like the tower of Lebanon, which looketh toward Damascus* (Song 7:5)? If you perform the Torah, you may hope for (the coming of) Elijah,[22] to whom I had said, *Go, return on thy way to the wilderness of Damascus* (1 Kings 19:15), and I had also said, *Remember ye the Torah of Moses, My servant*, etc., *Behold, I will send you (Elijah the prophet before the coming of the great and terrible day of the Lord)* (Mal. 3:22–23).

To love the Lord your God (11:13): You might say, "I am going to study Torah in order to become rich," or "in order to be called Rabbi," or "in order to receive a reward in the world-to-come"; therefore Scripture says, *To love the Lord your God*—whatever you do should be done only out of love.[23]

And to serve Him (11:13):[24] This refers here to study. You might say, "This refers to study (according to you), but might it not refer to actual work?" (The answer is, No,) since Scripture says, *And the Lord God took the man, and put him into the Garden of Eden to work it and to guard it* (Gen. 2:15)—what kind of work or guarding was there at that time?[25] Thus you learn that *to work it* refers to study, and *to guard it* refers to the commandments. Just as serving at the altar is called "service," so is study called "service." Another interpretation of *and to serve Him*: This refers to prayer. You might say, "This refers to prayer (according to you), but might it not refer to (Temple) service?" (The answer is, No,) since Scripture says, *With all your heart and with all your soul* (11:13)—is there such a thing as (Temple) service in one's heart? Therefore what does the verse mean by *and to serve Him*? It refers to prayer. Similarly David says, *Let my prayer be set forth as incense before Thee, the lifting up of my hands as the evening sacrifice* (Ps. 141:2), and it is said, *And when Daniel knew that the writing was signed, he went into his house—now his windows were open in his upper chamber toward Jerusalem—and he kneeled upon his knees three times a day, and prayed* (Dan. 6:11), and *O Daniel, servant of the living God, is thy God, whom thou servest continually, able to deliver thee from the lions?* (Dan. 6:21). And is there (Temple) worship in Babylon? Therefore what does Scripture mean by *and to serve Him?* It means prayer, and just as the service of the altar is called "service," so is prayer called "service." R. Eliezer ben Jacob says: *And to serve Him with all your heart and with all your soul*—this is a warning to the priests not to be of two minds when serving (in the Temple).[26] Another interpretation: What does (the repetition of) *with all your heart and with all your soul* mean? Does not Scripture say elsewhere, *With all thy heart and with all thy soul* (6:5)? (The answer is,) the latter refers to the individual, while the former refers to the entire community;[27] the latter refers to study, while the former refers to performance.[28] Since, having heard, you performed what you were obligated to perform, I too will perform what I promised to perform—*I will give the rain of your land in its season* (11:14).

Piska 42

I will give—I Myself, not by the hands of an angel nor by the hands of a messenger[1]—*the rain of your land* (11:14)—not the rain of all the lands. Similarly Scripture says, *Who giveth rain upon the earth, and sendeth waters upon the fields* (Job 5:10).[2] R. Nathan says: *In its season* (11:14)—from Sabbath eve to Sabbath eve, as the rain used to fall in the days of Queen Shelomziyyon.[3] Why is this emphasized? Rabbi (Judah the Prince) says: So that people will not be able to say, "Where[4] is the reward for all the commandments?" Rather, *If ye walk in My statutes, and keep My commandments, and do them, then I will give you rains in their season* (Lev. 26:3–4), and *And it shall come to pass, if ye shall hearken diligently unto My commandments which I command you this day . . . that I will give the rain of your land in its season, the former rain and the latter rain* (11:13–14). Whence do we learn that one blessing[5] was given to Israel in which all blessings are encompassed? From the verses, *He that loveth silver shall not be satisfied with silver, nor he that loveth abundance with increase* (Eccl. 5:9), and *The profit of a land every way is a king that maketh himself servant to the field* (Eccl. 5:8)—a king rules over treasures of silver and gold, yet he is subject to that which comes out of the field. Thus you learn that the one blessing given to Israel emcompassed all blessings.

The former rain (*yoreh*)—so called[6] because it comes down and instructs (*moreh*) people to bring in their produce, to plaster their roofs, and to attend to all their (other) needs. Another interpretation: *The former rain*—it aims directly at the earth[7] and does not come down as a (wild) storm. Another interpretation: *The former rain*—it comes down and saturates (*marweh*)[8] the earth, watering it down to its nethermost depths, as in the verse, *Watering her ridges abundantly, settling down the furrows thereof* (Ps. 65:11). The former rain falls in Marheshvan, while the latter rain falls in Nisan. You say that the former rain falls in Marheshvan and the latter rain in Nisan, or is it that the former rain falls in Tishri and the latter rain in Iyyar? Therefore Scripture says, *in its season*—the former rain in Marheshvan and the latter rain in Nisan; similarly it says, *And I will cause the shower to come down in its season* (Ezek. 34:26).[9] Or does *former rain* indicate that it causes produce to fall down, washes away seeds, inundates granaries? Therefore, Scripture goes on to say *latter rain,* meaning that just as the latter rain is a blessing, so is the former rain a blessing. Or does *latter rain* indicate that it will cause houses to collapse, uproot trees, and bring on crickets? Therefore Scripture goes on to say, *former rain,* meaning that just as the former rain is a blessing, so is the latter rain a blessing. Similarly it says, *Be glad, ye children of Zion, and rejoice in the Lord your God, for He giveth you the former rain in just measure, and He causeth to come down for you the rain, the former rain and the latter rain* (Joel 2:23).

That thou mayest gather in thy corn, and thy wine, and thine oil (11:14): *Thy corn* in full, *thy wine* in full, *thine oil* in full. You may say, "Does it mean *thy corn* in full, *thy wine* in full, *thine oil* in full, or does it mean *that thou mayest gather in thy corn, and thy wine, and thine oil* because there is so little of this produce?" Therefore Scripture says elsewhere, *And your threshing shall reach unto the vintage* (Lev. 26:5). Threshing is compared to vintage: just as vintage cannot be halted once you begin it, so threshing, once you start it, you cannot interrupt it. Another interpretation: You will plow when harvesting, and harvest when plowing,[10] as Job says, *(My root shall be spread out to the waters,) and the dew shall lie all night upon my harvest*[11] (Job 29:19). Another interpretation: *That thou mayest gather in thy corn*—why is this said? Because elsewhere it is said, *This Book of the Law shall not depart out of thy mouth* (Josh. 1:8)—I might think that this is to be taken literally; therefore the other verse says, *That thou mayest gather in,* etc., for the Torah usually speaks of normal things in life.[12] This is the opinion of Rabbi Ishmael. Rabbi Simeon ben Yoḥai, however, says: There is no end to it. If one harvests at harvest time, ploughs at ploughing time, threshes in the hot season, and winnows in the windy season, when can one (find time to) study Torah? Rather, when Israel does God's will, their work is done for them by others, as it is said, *And strangers shall stand and feed your flocks, (and aliens shall be your plowmen and your vinedressers)* (Isa. 61:5). When Israel does not do God's will, they themselves will have to do their own work. Not only that, but they will have to do other people's work as well, as it is said, *Therefore shalt thou serve thine enemy,* etc. (28:48).

Another interpretation: *That thou mayest gather in thy corn, and thy wine, and thine oil*: The Land of Israel shall be full of corn, wine, and oil, and all the other lands shall send their overflow to fill it with silver and gold, as it is said, *And Joseph gathered up all the money (that was found in the land of Egypt)* (Gen. 47:14), and *And as thy days, so shall thy strength be* (33:25),[13] all the lands shall send their overflow of silver and gold to the Land of Israel.

Another interpretation: *Thy corn,* in the usual sense; thy wine,[14] here meaning (fermented) wine, as it is said, *Thus saith the Lord: As when wine is found in the cluster* (Isa. 65:8); *thine oil,*[15] (refined) oil, as it is said, *And the vats shall overflow with wine and oil* (Joel 2:24). Another interpretation: *Thy corn,* for you; *thy wine,* for you; *thine oil,* for you, in accordance not with the verse, *And so it was, when Israel had sown, that the Midianites came up, and the Amalekites, and the children of the east; they came up (against them . . . and destroyed the produce of the earth)* (Judg. 6:3–4), but rather with the verse, *The Lord hath sworn by His right hand, and by the arm of His strength, "Surely I will no more give thy corn to be food for thine enemies, and strangers shall not drink thy wine, for which thou hast labored. But they that have garnered it shall eat it, and praise the Lord; and they that have gathered it shall drink it in the courts of My Sanctuary"* (Isa. 62:8–9).

Pisḳa 43

And I will give grass in thy fields for thy cattle (11:15): So that you will not be troubled to go into the wildernesses.[1] You might say, "Is it as you explain it, so that you will not be troubled to go into the wildernesses, or does *And I will give grass in thy fields for thy cattle* mean literally just what it says?"[2] Therefore the verse goes on to say, *And thou shalt eat and be satisfied* (11:15).[3] How then am I to understand *And I will give grass in thy fields for thy cattle?* That you will not be troubled to go into the wildernesses. R. Judah ben Baba says: *And I will give grass in thy fields for thy cattle*—between the sections.[4] R. Simeon ben Yoḥai says: *And I will give grass in thy fields for thy cattle*—you will cut it and cast it before your cattle all through the rainy season; thereafter for thirty days before the harvest you will leave the field alone, and it will produce by itself, so that there will be no diminution of the grain.[5] Rabbi (Judah the Prince) says: *And I will give grass in thy fields for thy cattle*—this refers to flax, as in the verse, *Who causest the grass to spring up for the cattle, and herb for the service of man, to bring forth bread out of the earth*[6] (Ps. 104:14).

And thou shalt eat and be satisfied (11:15): It is a good omen for man when his beast eats and is satisfied, as it is said, *A righteous man regardeth the life of his beast, (but the tender mercies of the wicked are cruel)* (Prov. 12:10). Another interpretation: *And thou shalt eat and be satisfied*: When your beast eats and is satisfied, it can work the soil with strength, as it is said, *(Where no oxen are, the crib is clean), but much increase is by the strength of the ox* (Prov. 14:4).[7] Another interpretation: *And thou shalt eat and be satisfied,* from the young.[8] There is an indirect reference to this, though not direct proof, in the verse, *And they shall come and sing in the height of Zion, and shall flow unto the goodness of the Lord, to the corn, and to the wine, and to the oil, (and to the young of the flock and of the herd)* (Jer. 31:12).

And thou shalt eat and be satisfied. Take heed to yourselves lest your heart be deceived (11:15–16): He said to them, "Beware, lest you rebel against God, for one does not rebel against God except out of satiety," as it is said, *Lest when thou hast eaten and art satisfied, and hast built goodly houses, and dwelt therein; and when thy herds and thy flocks multiply, and thy silver and thy gold is multiplied, (and all that thou hast is multiplied)* (8:12–13); and then what does Scripture say?—*Then thy heart be lifted up and thou forget the Lord thy God* (8:14). Similarly Scripture says, *For when I shall have brought them into the land which I swore unto their fathers, flowing with milk and honey; (and they shall have eaten their fill)* (31:20); and then what does the verse say?—*And turned unto other gods (and served them).* So also Scripture says, *And the people sat down to eat and to drink* (Exod. 32:6); and then what does it say?—*They have made them a molten calf* (Exod. 32:8). Likewise you find that the generation of the flood rebelled against God only out of satiety, for what does Scripture say about them?—*Their houses are safe, without fear . . . their bull gendereth . . . they send forth their little ones like a flock . . . they spend their days in prosperity,* etc. (Job 21:9–13)—it is precisely this that caused them to say to God, *"Depart from us, for we desire not the knowledge of Thy ways. What is the Almighty that we should serve Him?"* etc. (Job 21:14–15). They said, "Not even for one drop of rain do we need Him, seeing that *There goes up a mist from the earth*" (Gen. 2:6).[9] Therefore God said to them, "You use the favor that I have bestowed upon you to exalt yourselves therewith before Me. Therefore will I use it to punish you—*And the rain was upon the earth forty days and forty nights* (Gen. 7:12).

R. Jose son of the Damascene woman says: Just as they did cast their eyes both up and down in order to satisfy their lust, so did God open upon them both the upper and lower fountainheads in order to destroy them,[10] as it is said, *All the fountains of the great deep (were) broken up, and the windows of heaven were opened* (Gen. 7:11). Likewise you find that the men of the tower (of Babel) rebelled against God only out of satiety, for what does Scripture say about them?—*And the whole earth was of one language and one speech. And it came to pass, as they journeyed east, that they found a plain in the land of Shinar, and they dwelt there* (Gen. 11:1–3). Now "dwelling" here means nothing but eating and drinking, as it is said, *And the people sat down*[11] *to eat and to drink, and rose up to make merry* (Exod. 32:6). It is precisely this that caused them (to rebel), as it is said of them, *And they said, "Come, let us build us a city,"* etc. (Gen. 11:4).[12] What does Scripture say further about them?—*So the Lord scattered them abroad from thence upon the face of all the earth* (Gen. 11:8). You find the same about the people of Sodom, who rebelled against God only out of satiety, for what does Scripture say about them?—*As for the earth, out of it cometh bread. . . . The stones thereof are the place of sapphires. . . . That path no bird of prey knoweth . . . the proud beasts have not trodden it,* etc. (Job 28:5–8). The people of Sodom said, "We have food. We have silver and gold. Let us therefore rise up and eradicate (the custom of) hospitality from our land." But God said to them, "You use the favor that I have bestowed upon you to eradicate hospitality from amongst you. I will therefore eradicate you from the world." What does Scripture then say about them? *He breaketh open a shaft away from where men sojourn (they are forgotten of the foot*[13] *that passeth by)* (Job 28:4), and *A contemptible brand (in the thought of him that is at ease, a thing ready for them whose foot slippeth). The tents of robbers prosper, and they that provoke God are secure* (Job 12:5–6). What caused them to rebel was *whatsoever God bringeth into their hand* (Job 12:6). Hence Scripture says (of Sodom), *As I live, saith the Lord God, Sodom thy sister hath not done . . . as thou hast done. . . . Behold, this was the iniquity of thy sister Sodom,* etc., which was so great that *neither did she strengthen the hand of the poor and needy. And they were haughty* (Ezek. 16:48–50). The same applies (to Lot's daughters), as it is said, *(And Lot lifted up his eyes, and behold, all the plain of the Jordan,) that it was well watered everywhere* (Gen. 13:10). What does it say further on?—*And they made their father drink wine* (Gen. 19:33).[14] Where did they get wine in the cave (in which they dwelt)? They came upon it in that very hour, for Scripture says elsewhere, *And it shall come to pass on that day that the mountains shall drop down sweet wine* (Joel 4:18). If this is what God provides for those who anger Him, how much more so will He do for those who fulfill His will.[15]

[R. Meir says: Scripture says, *Hangings of white, fine cotton, and blue* (Esth. 1:6)—is Scripture concerned with telling us only about Ahasuerus' wealth? Rather, it indicates that if this is what God has given to those who had angered Him, how much more so will He give to those who fulfill His will.]

Once, as Rabban Gamaliel, R. Joshua, R. Eleazar ben Azariah, and R. ᶜAḳiba were journeying to Rome, they heard the murmuring sound of the (great) city from as far as Puteoli, a distance of one hundred and twenty miles, whereupon they burst into tears, except for R. ᶜAḳiba, who laughed. They asked him, "ᶜAḳiba, why are you laughing while we are weeping?" He replied, "Why are you weeping?" They said, "Should we not weep when these pagans, who sacrifice to idols and bow down to images dwell in security, peace, and serenity, while the House which is our God's footstool has been reduced to a charred ruin and a lair for beasts of the field?" To which R. ᶜAḳiba retorted, "But this is exactly why I laughed—if this is what God has given to those who have angered Him, how much more so will He give to those who fulfill his will."[16] [They said to him, "ᶜAḳiba, you have comforted us."] Another time they were going up to Jerusalem. When they reached Mount Scopus, they rent their garments, and when they came to the Temple Mount and saw a fox running out of the (ruined) building of the Holy of Holies, they began to weep, while R. ᶜAḳiba laughed. They said to him, "ᶜAḳiba, you never cease to astonish us—we are weeping, yet you laugh!" He replied, "Why are you weeping?" They said to him, "Should we not weep when a fox emerges from the place of which it is written, *And the common man that draweth nigh shall be put to death* (Num. 1:51)? This is indeed how the verse, *For this our heart is faint, for these things our eyes are dim—for the mountain of Zion which is desolate, the foxes walk upon it* (Lam. 5:17–18), has been fulfilled for us." He said to them, "This is exactly why I laughed, for it is said, *And I will take unto me faithful witnesses to record, Uriah the priest and Zechariah the son of Jeberechiah* (Isa. 8:2). Now what is the connection between Uriah and Zechariah? Uriah said, *Zion shall be plowed as a field, and Jerusalem shall become heaps, and the Mountain of (the Lord's)*

House as the high places of a forest (Jer. 26:18).[17] What did Zechariah say? *Thus saith the Lord of hosts: There shall yet old men and old women sit in the broad places of Jerusalem,* etc. (Zech. 8:4). Said God, 'These are My two witnesses'—if the words of Uriah are fulfilled, so will the words of Zechariah; if the words of Uriah are not fulfilled, neither will the words of Zechariah. I rejoice therefore that in the end the words of Uriah have been fulfilled, because this means that so will the words of Zechariah." They said to him again in the same words, "ʿAḳiba, you have comforted us."

Another interpretation: *And thou shalt eat and be satisfied. Take heed to yourselves, (lest your heart be deceived, and ye turn aside, and serve other gods, and worship them)*: God said to them, "Take care, lest the Inclination to evil should lead you astray, and you separate yourselves from the Torah, for when a person separates himself from the Torah, he goes and clings to idolatry, as it is said, *They have turned aside quickly out of the way which I commanded them; they have made them a molten calf* (Exod. 32:8), and *If it be the Lord that hath stirred thee up against me, let Him accept an offering, but if it be the children of men, cursed be they before the Lord, for they have driven me out this day that I should not cleave to the inheritance of the Lord, saying, "Go serve other Gods"* (1 Sam. 26:19). Could it possibly occur to you that King David would worship idols? Rather, having ceased studying Torah, he as much as went and cleaved to idolatry.[18]

And ye turn aside—from the way of life to the way of death.

And serve other gods—are they "gods"? Does not Scripture say elsewhere, *And have cast their gods into the fire; for they were no gods, but the work of men's hands, wood and stone, therefore they have destroyed them* (Isa. 37:19)? Why then are they called other (*ʾăḥerim*) gods? Because they delay (*meʾăḥerim*)[19] the coming of goodness into the world. Another interpretation: *Other gods*—that turn their worshipers into heretics (*ʾăḥerim*).[20] Another interpretation: *Other gods*—others consider them true deities. Another interpretation: *Other gods*—they are estranged (*ʾăḥerim*) from their worshipers, as it is said, *Yea, though one cry unto him, he cannot answer, nor save him out of his trouble* (Isa. 46:7). R. Jose says: Why are they called *other gods?* In order not to give people an excuse to say, "If they were called by God's name, they too would have been effective." For even though they are indeed called by His name, yet they are useless. When were they called by His name? In the days of Enosh son of Seth, as it is said, *Then began men to call (idols) by the name of the Lord*[21] (Gen. 4:26).

At that time the ocean rose up and flooded one-third of the world, and the Holy One, blessed be He, said to mankind, "You did a new thing by your own decision in calling (idols by My name). I too shall do a new thing by My own decision and call forth (the ocean)," as it is said, *That calleth for the waters of the sea, and poureth them out upon the face of the earth; the Lord is His name* (Amos 5:8).[22] R. Isaac says: If all the idols were called by their individual names, no amount of punishments[23] would suffice. R. Eliezer says: Why are they called *other gods*? Because every day men create new deities—if (the original idol) was made of gold, and one is in need of it, he will make a copy of it of silver, or if of silver, he will make it of copper, or if of copper, he will make it of iron, or if of iron, he will make it of tin, or if of tin, he will make it of lead, or if of lead, he will make it of wood. R. Ḥanina ben Antigonus says: Come and note the terms used by the Torah, (for example,) "Molech"—whatever you make king (*melek*) over you for even one hour. Rabbi (Judah the Prince) says: Why are they called *other gods*? Because they are of later creation (*ʾăḥerim*)[24] than (man), the latest of the creatures, for they were called deities by those who were created last.

And worship them—you worship them, you do not worship Me, as it is said, *And have worshiped it, and have sacrificed unto it, and said, "These are thy gods,*[25] *O Israel"* (Exod. 32:8). Others say: Had Israel not associated God's name with the idols, they would have been destroyed.[26] Rabban Simeon ben Gamaliel[27] says: Is not anyone who associates God's name with an idol liable to extirpation, as it is said, *He that sacrificeth unto the gods, save unto the Lord only, shall be utterly destroyed*[28] (Exod. 22:19)? What then does the verse mean by *thy gods?*[29] It means that they made many (golden) calves.

Similarly[30] Scripture says, *Also they have shut up the doors of the porch, and put out the lamps, and have not burned incense nor offered burnt offerings in the holy place to the God of Israel* (2 Chron. 29:7)—they did in fact offer incense to other gods; *nor offered burnt offerings,* but did offer burnt offerings to other gods; *in the holy place* they did not offer offerings, but in profane places they did offer; *to the God of Israel* they did not offer them, but to other gods they did.

If you do such (wicked things), *And the anger of the Lord be kindled against you* (11:17): A parable: A king who was about to send his son to a banquet house sat down and gave him instructions, saying, "My son, do not eat more than you need, do not drink more than you need, so that you might return to your home in a decent condition." The son paid no attention, and ate more than he needed and drank more than he needed, and as a result vomited, soiling all the other participants in the banquet, whereupon they seized him by his arms and legs and threw him out behind the palace. So also the Holy One, blessed be He, said to Israel, "I brought you into a good and broad land, a land flowing with milk and honey, so that you might eat of its produce and be satisfied with its goodness, and bless My name for it. You (chose to) disregard prosperity—suffer then the affliction of *the anger of the Lord be kindled against you.*

The anger of the Lord be kindled against you: [I might think that this means that they will be depleted from the world; therefore the verse goes on to say, *and He shut up the heaven* (11:17)—(all) kinds of afflictions will be spent (upon them),[31] as it is said, *I will spend Mine arrows upon them* (32:23), My arrows will be spent, but they will not be depleted, for Scripture says elsewhere, *The Lord hath accomplished His fury, He hath poured out His fierce anger* (Lam. 4:11)]. *Fierce anger* is spoken of here, and *fierce anger* is spoken of elsewhere (Exod. 22:23)—just as *fierce anger* there refers to the sword, so *fierce anger* here refers to the sword; just as *fierce anger* there refers to pestilence and evil beasts (cf. Lev. 26:16), so *fierce anger* here refers to pestilence and evil beasts; just as *fierce anger* here means withholding of rain and exile, so the *fierce anger* elsewhere means withholding of rain and exile. Thus we learn that wherever "fierce anger" is mentioned, five types of punishment are implied: sword, pestilence, evil beasts, withholding of rain, and exile.

Another interpretation: *And the anger of the Lord be kindled against you*: Not against the nations of the world, for the nations of the world will enjoy prosperity while Israel will suffer punishment, the nations of the world will not be burying their sons and daughters while Israel will be burying their sons and daughters.

And He shut up the heaven (11:17): Clouds will be laden (with moisture) but will remain so, without releasing even a drop of rain. Whence do we learn that even dew and winds (will be withheld)?—from the verse, *And I will make your heaven as iron* (Lev. 26:19); or that even irrigated fields will bring forth no produce?—from the verse, *And your earth as brass* (Lev. 26:1).

And the ground shall not yield her fruit (11:17)—not even spontaneous growth. *And the ground shall not yield her fruit*—not even what you have brought[32] to it. Shall trees bring forth fruit? (No,) since Scripture says, *Neither shall the trees of the land yield their fruit*

(Lev. 26:20). Shall they at least produce firewood for ovens and stoves? (No,) since Scripture says, *Neither shall the trees of the land yield their fruit,* (meaning any kind of yield). Or will an Israelite go outside the Land (of Israel) and live there in prosperity? (No,) since Scripture says, *And thy heaven that is over thy head shall be brass, and the earth that is under thee shall be iron* (28:23)—everywhere.

Another interpretation: *And the anger of the Lord be kindled*: After all these sufferings that I shall bring upon you, I will exile you. So severe is exile that it is weighed against all (other punishments), as it is said, *And the Lord rooted them out of their land in anger, and in wrath, and in great indignation, and cast them into another land, as it is this day* (29:27); *And it shall come to pass when they say unto thee, "Whither shall we go forth?" then thou shalt tell them, "Thus saith the Lord: Such as are for death, to death; and such as are for the sword, to the sword; and such as are for the famine, to the famine; and such as are for captivity, to captivity"* (Jer. 15:2); *Thus says the Lord: Thy wife shall be a harlot in the city, and thy sons and thy daughters shall fall by the sword, and thy land shall be divided by line; and thou thyself shalt die in an unclean land, and Israel shall surely be led away captive out of his land* (Amos 7:17); and *Weep ye not for the dead, neither bemoan him; but weep sore for him that goeth away, for he shall return no more, nor see his native country* (Jer. 22:10). *Weep ye not for the dead* refers to Jehoiakim, king of Judah, for what does Scripture say about him?—*He shall be buried with the burial of an ass* (Jer. 22:19). *Weep sore for him that goeth away* refers to Jehoiachin, king of Judah, for what does Scripture say about him?—*And he changed his prison garments, and did eat bread before him continually all the days of his life,* etc. (Jer. 52:33). From this we learn that the corpse of Jehoiakim, king of Judah, which was exposed to the heat of the day and to the chill of the night, was more fortunate than the life of Jehoiachin, king of Judah, whose throne was placed above that of other kings and who ate and drank in the royal banquet hall.[33]

And ye perish quickly (11:17): I will exile you immediately, and I will grant you no extension. Should you say, "The people of the flood, God granted them an extension of one hundred and twenty years," (I will reply,) "The people of the flood had no one to learn from, whereas you have those from whom you can learn."

Another interpretation: *And ye perish quickly*: Through one exile after another. Thus also you find one exile after another in the case of the Ten Tribes, and the same in the case of the Tribes of Judah and Benjamin: they were exiled in the seventh year of Nebuchadnezzar, in the eighteenth year, and in the twenty-third year. R. Joshua ben Ḳorḥah says by way of a parable: A robber entered a householder's field and cut down his heap (of harvested grain), but the owner raised no objection; the robber then cut down his (standing) ears, but the owner still raised no objection; the robber finally went on until he had his own heap full and departed. The same is meant by the verse, *For is there no gloom to her that was steadfast? Now the former hath lightly afflicted the land of Zebulun and the land of Naftali, but the latter hath dealt a more grievous blow (by the way of the sea, beyond the Jordan, in the district of the nations)* (Isa. 8:23). R. Simeon ben Yoḥai says: If those of whom it was said *quickly* were not exiled until sometime afterward, how much more so is this the case of those of whom *quickly* was not said.[34]

Another interpretation: *And ye perish quickly . . . therefore shall ye lay up these My words* (11:17–18): Even though I am about to exile you from the Land (of Israel) to a foreign land, you must continue to be marked there by the commandments, so that when you return they will not be new to you.[35] A parable: A king of flesh and blood grew angry with his wife and sent her back to her father's house, saying to her, "Be sure to continue wearing your jewelry, so that whenever you return, it will not be new to you." Thus also the Holy One, blessed be He, said to Israel, "My children, you must continue to be marked by the commandments, so that when you return, they will not be new to you." Hence Jeremiah says, *Set thee up waymarks*—that is to say, commandments by which Israel is marked—*make thee guideposts* (Jer. 31:21)—that is to say, (do not forget) the destruction of the Temple, for Scripture says, *If I forget thee, O Jerusalem, let my right hand forget her cunning, let my tongue cleave to the roof of my mouth if I remember thee not,* etc. (Ps. 137:5–6). *Set thy heart toward the highway, even the way by which thou wentest* (Jer. 31:21)—the Holy One, blessed be He, said to Israel, "Consider the ways which you had followed, and repent, whereupon you will forthwith return to your cities," as it is said, *Return, O virgin of Israel, return to these thy cities* (Jer. 31:21).

Another interpretation: *And ye perish quickly from off the good land* (11:17): You will be exiled from the good land to a land that is not like it in goodness. R. Judah says: *Good* refers to Torah, as it is said, *For I give you good doctrine*—[in the Land of Israel][36]—*forsake ye not My Torah* (Prov. 4:2)—outside the Land.

Pisḳa 44

Therefore shall ye lay up these My words in your heart—this refers to study of Torah—*and ye shall bind them for a sign upon your hand* (11:18)—these are the phylacteries. Thus I have here only phylacteries and study of Torah. Whence do we learn that the same applies also to the other commandments of the Torah?[1] From analogy[2] between these two passages. Phylacteries are not by nature like study of Torah, nor is study of Torah by nature like phylacteries. The sole similarity between them is that they are both commandments incumbent upon the person and not dependent upon the Land (of Israel), and must be performed both in the Land (of Israel) and outside of it. Hence all commandments incumbent upon the person and not dependent upon the Land (of Israel) must be performed both in the Land (of Israel) and outside of it. Those dependent upon the Land (of Israel) must be performed only there, except for *ʿorlah*[3] and mixed seeds (*kilʾayim*).[4] R. Eliezer says: New produce (*ḥadaš*)[5] is also included (among the exceptions).[6]

Pisḳa 45

Therefore shall ye lay up these My words in your heart (11:18): This tells us that words of Torah are comparable to the elixir of life.[1] A parable: A king grew angry with his son and struck him a violent blow, but then put a bandage on the wound and said to him, "My son, so long as this bandage is on your wound, you may eat whatever you please, drink whatever you please, and bathe in hot or cold water (as you please), and you will suffer no injury; but if you remove it, the wound will forthwith become ulcerated." Thus also the Holy One, blessed be He, said to Israel, "My children, I created an Inclination to evil in you than which there is none more evil. *If thou doest well, shall it not be lifted up?* (Gen. 4:7)—busy yourselves with words of Torah, and the Inclination to evil will not rule over you; but if you abandon the words of Torah, it will gain mastery over you, as it is said, *Sin coucheth at the door, and unto thee is its desire* (Gen. 4:7). It has no business but with you, but if you wish, you can gain mastery over it, as it is said, *But thou mayest rule over it* (Gen. 4:7), and *If thine enemy be hungry, give him bread to eat, and if he be thirsty, give him water to drink, for thou wilt heap coals of fire upon his head* (Prov. 25:21–

22)."[2] Evil indeed is the Inclination to evil, for even He who created it testifies to its evil nature, as it is said, *For the imagination of man's heart is evil* (Gen. 8:21).

Pisḳa 46

And ye shall teach them your children (*bĕneḳem*) (11:19): Your sons,[1] not your daughters, so taught R. Jose ben ʿAḳiba. Hence the Sages have said:[2] Once an infant begins to talk, his father should converse with him in the holy tongue and should teach him Torah, for if he fails to do so it is the same as if he had buried him (alive), as it is said, *And ye shall teach them your children, talking of them* (11:19). If you teach them to your children, *Your days may be multiplied, and the days of your children* (11:21); if not, your days may be shortened.[3] For thus are words of Torah to be expounded: the positive implies the negative, and the negative implies the positive.

Pisḳa 47

That your days may be multiplied—in this world—*and the days of your children . . .*—in the days of the Messiah—*as the days of the heavens above the earth*—in the world to come—*(upon the land) which the Lord swore unto your fathers to give them* (11:21)—Scripture does not say here "to give you" but rather *to give them*; hence we find that we can deduce (the doctrine of) the resurrection of the dead from the Torah.[1]

As the days of the heavens above the earth: The faces of the righteous will (shine as bright) as the day, as it is said, *But they that love Him (shall) be as the sun when he goeth forth in his might* (Judg. 5:31). R. Simeon ben Yoḥai says:[2] In the future, when the righteous greet the Sheḵinah, their faces will resemble seven joyous things, to wit, *But they that love Him (shall) be as the sun when he goeth forth in his might* (Judg. 5:31), *Fair as the moon (shall they be), clear as the sun* (Song. 6:10), *And they that are wise shall shine as the brightness of the firmament, and they that turn the many to righteousness as the stars for ever and ever* (Dan. 12:3), *They (shall) run to and fro like lightnings* (Nah. 2:5), *(They shall be as) the leader, upon lilies* (Ps. 45:1), and *His beauty shall be as the olive tree* (Hos. 14:7). Scripture says also, *A song of ascents* (Ps. 121:1)—(intended) for the one who in the future shall make ascents for his servants, the righteous.[3] R. ʿAḳiba says:[4] Scripture does not say "a song of an ascent," but *a song of ascents*—there are thirty ascents,[5] one above the other; Rabbi (Judah the Prince) says that there are sixty ascents, one above the other. Since there are several ascents, one above the other, am I to think that enmity, hatred, jealousy, or rivalry prevail among them? (No,) for Scripture says, *And they that turn the many to righteousness (shall shine) as the stars for ever and ever* (Dan. 12:3).—just as there is no enmity, hatred, jealousy, or rivalry among the stars, so is there none among the righteous; just as the brightness of one star is not like that of another, so is this true of the righteous. Another interpretation: *They that turn the many to righteousness*—this refers to alms collectors.[6] R. Simeon ben Menasya says: This refers to the elders, as it is said, *But they that love Him (shall) be as the sun when he goeth forth in his might* (Judg. 5:31). Who is greater, those who love or those who cause others to love? Certainly those who cause others to love. Hence, if it is said of those who love *But they that love Him (shall) be as the sun when he goeth forth in his might,* how much more is this true of those who cause others to love. *And they that turn the many to righteousness (shall shine) as the stars for ever*: Just as the stars are exalted and placed above all the creatures of the world, so are the righteous; just as the stars rule and govern from one end of the world to the other, so do the righteous; just as the stars are sometimes hidden and sometimes visible, just as the stars are grouped in so many clusters that they cannot be counted, so are the righteous. Or does this mean,[7] regardless of whether they do God's will or not? (No,) for Scripture says, *And thy seed shall be as the dust of the earth* (Gen. 28:14)—if they do God's will, they will be like the stars; if not, they will be like the dust of the earth, for Scripture says, *For the king of Aram destroyed them and made them like the dust in threshing* (2 Kings 13:7).

Another interpretation: *As the days of the heavens above the earth*: They will live and endure for all eternity, as it is said, *For as the new heavens and the new earth, (which I will make, shall remain before Me, saith the Lord, so shall your seed and your name remain)* (Isa. 66:22). And is this not a matter of reasoning from the minor to the major? If the heavens and the earth, which were created only for the glory of Israel, shall live and endure for all eternity, how much more so will this be true with the righteous, for whose sake the whole world was created. R. Simeon ben Yoḥai says: Scripture says, *For as the days of a tree shall be the days of My people* (Isa. 65:22)—*tree* means Torah, as it is said, *She (wisdom) is a tree of life to them that lay hold upon her* (Prov. 3:18). Is this not a matter of reasoning from the minor to the major? If the Torah, which was created only for the glory of Israel, shall endure for all eternity, how much more so shall the righteous, for whose sake the whole world was created. R. Joshua ben Ḳorḥah says: Scripture says, *One generation passeth away, and another generation cometh, and the earth abideth for ever* (Eccl. 1:4)—it should have said here, "the earth passeth away, and the earth cometh, and the generation abideth for ever," but since Israel changed their deeds, God changed the order of the world.[8]

One Scriptural verse begins by saying, *Yet the number of the children of Israel shall be,* and then goes on to say, *as the sand of the sea, which cannot be measured nor numbered* (Hos. 2:1)—when Israel does God's will, they are *as the sand of the sea, which cannot be measured nor numbered*; when they do not, *yet the number of the children of Israel shall be.*[9] Similarly, one verse says, *(One thousand shall flee at the rebuke of one, at the rebuke of five shall ye flee,) till ye be left as a beacon upon the top of a mountain* (Isa. 30:17), while another verse says, *For thus saith the Lord God: The city that went forth a thousand shall have a hundred left* (Amos 5:3). Another interpretation: *Yet the number of the children of Israel shall be*—as numbered by heaven—*as the sand of the sea*—as numbered by man.[10]

Piska 48

For if ye shall diligently keep all this commandment (11:22): Why was this said? Because of *If ye shall hearken*[1] *diligently unto My commandments* (11:13). I might assume that even if one has heard[2] the words of Torah, he may remain idle and not study them again. Therefore Scripture says here, *ye shall diligently keep,* indicating that just as one must be careful not to lose his money,[3] so must he be careful not to lose his learning. Similarly Scripture says, *If thou seek her* (wisdom) *as silver* (Prov. 2:4)—just as silver is difficult to acquire, so words of Torah are difficult to acquire. Or could it mean that just as silver is difficult to destroy,[4] so words of Torah are difficult to destroy? Therefore another verse says, *Gold and glass cannot equal it* (wisdom)—words of Torah are as difficult to acquire as gold, and as easy to destroy as glass vessels—*neither shall the exchange thereof be vessels of fine gold* (Job 28:17). R. Ishmael used to say: *Only take heed to thyself, and keep thy soul diligently* (4:9)—a parable: A king of flesh and blood snared a bird and handed it to his servant, saying, "Be careful with this bird, which is for my son. If you lose it, do not think of it as if you had lost a bird worth an *isar,*[5] but rather as if you had forfeited your life." Hence Scripture says, *For it is no vain thing for you, because it*—what you say is vain—*is your very life* (32:47). R. Simeon ben Yoḥai says by way of a parable: Two brothers inherit money from their father. One converts it into a denar and spends it, while the other converts it into a denar and puts it aside. He who has converted his denar and spent it now has nothing, whereas he who has converted his denar and has put it aside eventually grows wealthy. Even so is it with the disciples of the wise: one who studies two or three things a day, two or three chapters in a week, two or three Scriptural lessons in a month, eventually becomes rich (in Torah),[6] and of him it is said, *He that gathereth little by little shall increase* (Prov. 13:11). He who says, "Today I will study (only what I need now), tomorrow I will study (what I shall need then); today I will review (only what I need now), tomorrow I will review (what I shall need then),"[7] will have nothing, and of him it is said, *A wise son gathereth in summer, but a son that doeth shamefully sleepeth in harvest* (Prov. 10:5), *The sluggard will not plow when winter setteth in; therefore he shall beg in harvest and have nothing* (Prov. 20:4), *He that observeth the wind shall not sow* (Eccl. 11:4), and *I went by the field of the slothful man, (and by the vineyard of the man void of understanding); and lo, it was all grown over with thistles, (the face thereof was covered with nettles, and the stone wall thereof was broken down)* (Prov. 24:30–31). *I went by the field of the slothful man,* who had already purchased a field, *and by the vineyard of the man void of understanding,* who had already purchased a vineyard—since he had already purchased the field or the vineyard and is called *man,* why is he called *slothful* and *void of understanding*? Because he had purchased a field or a vineyard, but did not toil in them. What indicates that such a disciple will overlook two or three things in the Scriptural lesson (that he has studied)? The statement, *and lo, it was all grown over with thistles.* And what indicates that he will seek the true interpretation of the lesson but will not find it? The statement, *the face thereof was covered with nettles.* Hence it is said of him, *and the stone wall thereof was broken down*—although he sees that nothing remains in his hand, he sits (in judgment) nevertheless and pronounces the clean unclean and the unclean clean, and thus breaks down the fences erected by the Sages. What is his punishment? Solomon proceeded to specify it in the Writings: *and whoso breaketh through a fence, a serpent shall bite him* (Eccl. 10:8)—thus whosoever breaks down the fences erected by the Sages will be punished in the end.[8]

R. Simeon ben Menasya says: Scripture says, *The full soul loatheth a honeycomb, (but to the hungry soul every bitter thing is sweet)* (Prov. 27:7)—this refers to a disciple who at the outset contains nothing but that which he has learned.[9] Another interpretation: *The full soul loatheth a honeycomb* (*nofet*)—just as a sieve (*nafah*) sets apart flour, bran, and coarse meal, so does a student sit and sift words of Torah and weigh them: this Sage forbids, while that Sage permits, this Sage declares an object unclean, while that Sage declares it clean. R. Judah says: An able student is like a sponge that absorbs everything; one who is not, is like a rag that absorbs only up to its limit. Such a student says, "What my teacher has taught me is sufficient for me."[10] R. Simeon ben Yoḥai says: Scripture says, *Drink waters out of thine own cistern, (and running waters out of thine own well. Let thy springs be dispersed abroad, and courses of water in the streets)* (Prov. 5:15–16)—learn from whosoever is with you in the city, and afterwards spread it out in other places, as it is said, *She is like the merchant ships, she bringeth her food from afar* (Prov. 31:14). R. Simeon ben Menasya says: Scripture says, *Drink waters out of thine own cistern*—drink of the waters of Him that created you; do not drink of muddy waters, lest you be attracted to the words of heretics. R. ʿAḳiba says: Scripture says, *Drink waters out of thine own cistern*—at the outset a cistern cannot bring forth a drop of water of its own, except only that which is already in it; so also a disciple at the outset contains nothing but that which he has learned—*and running waters out of thine own well*—he is like a well; just as a well distills living water from all sides, so do disciples come and learn from their teacher, as it is said, *Let thy springs be dispersed abroad,* etc. Words of Torah are likened to water: just as water endures forever, so do words of Torah live forever, as it is said, *For they are life unto those that find them* (Prov. 4:22). Just as water cleanses the unclean of their uncleannesses, so do words of Torah cleanse the unclean of their uncleannesses, as it is said, *Thy word is tried to the utmost, and Thy servant loveth it* (Ps. 119:140). Just as water restores a man's soul, as it is said, *As cold waters to a faint soul* (Prov. 25:25), so do words of Torah restore a man's soul, as it is said, *The law of the Lord is perfect, restoring the soul* (Ps. 19:8). Just as water is forever free to everyone, so are words of Torah forever free to everyone, as it is said, *Ho, every one that thirsteth, come ye for water, (and he that hath no money, come ye, buy and eat . . . without money)* (Isa. 55:1). Just as water is priceless, so are words of Torah priceless, as it is said, *She* (wisdom) *is more precious than rubies* (Prov. 3:15). Or might one think that just as water does not make the heart to rejoice, so words of Torah do not make the heart to rejoice? (No,) for Scripture says *For thy love is better than wine* (Song 1:2)—just as wine makes the heart to rejoice, so do words of Torah make the heart to rejoice, as it is said, *The precepts of the Lord are right, rejoicing the heart* (Ps. 19:9). Just as you cannot relish the taste of wine when it is still new, and the longer it ages in the vessel, the better it tastes, so too words of Torah, the longer they age within a person, the more they improve, as it is said, *Wisdom is with aged men* (Job 12:12). Just as wine cannot keep well in silver or gold vessels, but only in the lowliest of vessels—earthen ones—so words of Torah do not keep well in one who considers himself to be the same as silver or gold vessels, but only in one who considers himself the same as the lowliest of vessels—earthen ones. Or is it possible that just as wine is sometimes bad for the head and bad for the body, so too are words of Torah? (No,) for Scripture says, *Thine ointments have a goodly fragrance* (Song 1:3)—just as ointment is beneficial for the head and beneficial for the body, so are words of Torah beneficial for the head and beneficial for the body, as it is said, *For they shall be a chaplet of grace unto thy head, and chains about thy neck,* etc. (Prov. 1:9), and *She will give to thy head a chaplet of grace* (Prov. 4:9). Words of Torah are compared (not only) to oil (but) also to honey, as it is said, *Sweeter also than honey and the honeycomb* (Ps. 19:11).

Another interpretation: *For if ye shall diligently keep all this commandment*: Whence do we learn that if one learns several interpretations of Torah one by one and retains them in his mind, just as the first ones (to be learned) will be retained, so will the later ones be retained? From this same verse, *For if ye shall diligently keep.* And whence do we learn that if one learns several interpretations of Torah one by one but then forgets them, just as the first ones are not retained in his mind, so will the later ones not be retained? From the verse, *And it shall be, if thou shalt forget* (8:19); no sooner do you lose sight of it than it vanishes, as it is said, *Wilt thou set thine eyes upon it?—it is gone* (Prov. 23:5). And it is written in the Scroll of Pottery,[11] "If you abandon me for one day, I will abandon you for two."

Another interpretation: *For if ye shall diligently keep all this commandment*: You might say, "Let the sons of the elders study, let the sons of the great study, let the disciples of the prophets study." Therefore the verse says, *For if ye*[12] *shall diligently keep,* showing that all are equal in regard to Torah. Similarly Scripture says, *Moses commanded us a law, an inheritance of the congregation of Jacob* (33:4)—it does not say "priests, Levites, and Israelites," but *the congregation of Jacob.*[13] Similarly it says, *Ye are standing this day, all of you, before the Lord your God: your heads, your elders, and your officers, even all the men of Israel* (29:9). But for those who arose and established the Torah, would it not have been forgotten from among Israel? Had not Shaphan in his time, Ezra in his time, and R. ʿAḳiba in his time stood up, would it not have been forgotten? Hence Scripture says, *A word in good season, how good is it!* (Prov. 15:23)—the word of each one (of them) was as valuable as that of all others.[14]

Scripture says, *They shall run to and fro to seek the word of the Lord, and shall not find it* (Amos 8:12)—they go from city to city and from province to province (to inquire about the rule) governing an insect that has touched a loaf of bread, in order to determine whether it is a case of primary or secondary (degree of uncleanness).[15] R. Simeon ben Yoḥai[16] says: Should one conclude then that the Torah will be forgotten in Israel? Does not Scripture say, *For it shall not be forgotten out of the mouths of their seed* (31:21)? Rather (the verse in Amos means that) one authority will forbid while another will permit, one will declare unclean while another will declare clean, and no clear teaching will be found.

Another interpretation: *For if ye shall diligently keep all this commandment*: Lest you say, "I will study a difficult Scriptural lesson and ignore the easy one," Scripture says, *For it is no vain thing for you, because it is your life* (32:47)—something which you say is worthless is your very life. You must not say, "I have learned a sufficiency of rules," for the verse says not "a commandment" nor "the commandment" but *all this commandment*; hence you must study Midrash, halaḵah, and haggaḏah.[17] Similarly Scripture says, *That man doth not live by bread alone*—referring to Midrash—*but by everything that proceedeth out of the mouth of the Lord* (8:3), referring to halaḵah and haggaḏah. It also says elsewhere,[18] *My son, be wise, and make My heart glad, (that I may answer him that taunteth Me)* (Prov. 27:11), and *My son, if thy heart be wise, My heart will be glad, even Mine* (Prov. 23:15). R. Simeon ben Menasya says: I am bound to think that *my heart* refers to one's earthly father; whence do I learn that it refers to one's Father in heaven? From the following *even Mine*—thus applying it also to one's Father in heaven.[19]

Which I command you, to do it (11:22): Why did Scripture say this, seeing that it has already said *For if ye shall diligently keep?* I might think that once one has kept the words of Torah,[20] he may stop with that and need not perform them; therefore Scripture goes on to say, *to do it*—the purpose is *to do it*. If one merely learns Torah, he has fulfilled one commandment; if he learns and keeps what he has learned, he has fulfilled two commandments; if he learns, keeps, and performs, there is no one more meritorious.

To love (11:22): You might say, "I am studying Torah in order to be called a sage, in order to sit in the academy, in order to prolong my days in the world-to-come;" therefore Scripture says, *to love*—study it for its own sake, and honor will come eventually,[21] for Scripture says, *She* (wisdom) *is a tree of life to them that lay hold upon her* (Prov. 3:18), *For they are life unto those that find them* (Prov. 4:22), *She* (wisdom) *will give to thy head a chaplet of grace*—in this world—*a crown of glory will she bestow on thee* (Prov. 4:9)—in the world-to-come, and *Length of days is in her right hand*—in the world-to-come—*in her left hand are riches and honor* (Prov. 3:16)—in this world.

R. Eliezer ben R. Zadok says: Perform deeds for the sake of doing them, and speak of them for their own sake. He used to say: If Belshazzar, who used Temple vessels after they had been profaned, was uprooted from this world and the world-to-come, how much more so will one who uses (improperly) the vessel with which the world was created[22] be uprooted from this world and the world-to-come.

Pisḳa 49

To walk in all His ways (11:22): These are the ways of *The Lord, God, merciful and gracious* (Exod. 34:6). Scripture says, *And it shall come to pass, that whosoever shall call by*[1] *the name of the Lord shall be delivered* (Joel 3:5)—how is it possible for man to be called by the name of the Lord? Rather, as God is called *merciful*, so should you be merciful;[2] as the Holy One, blessed be He, is called *gracious,* so too should you be gracious, as it is said, *The Lord is gracious and full of compassion* (Ps. 145:8), and grants free gifts.[3] As God is called righteous, *For the Lord is righteous, He loveth righteousness* (Ps. 11:7), so you too should be righteous. As God is called merciful, as it is said *For I am merciful (ḥasiḏ), saith the Lord* (Jer. 3:12), so too should you be merciful.[4] Therefore Scripture says, *And it shall come to pass, that whosoever shall call by the name of the Lord shall be delivered* (Joel 3:5), *Every one that is called by My name* (Isa. 43:7), and *The Lord hath made every thing for His own purpose* (Prov. 16:4).

And cleave unto Him (11:22): Is it possible for man to ascend to (fiery) heaven and cleave to fire, seeing that Scripture has said, *For the Lord thy God is a devouring fire* (4:24), and *His Throne was fiery flames* (Dan 7:9)? Rather, (the meaning is,) cling to the Sages and to their disciples, and I will account it to you as if you had ascended to heaven and had received it (the Torah) there, and not only that but also as if you had ascended and had received it not in peace but only after waging war in order to receive it, as it is said, *Thou hast ascended on high, thou hast led captivity captive* (Ps. 68:19). Expounders of haggaḏic texts (*haggaḏoṯ*)[5] say: If you wish to come to know Him who spoke, and the world came into being, study haggaḏah, for thereby you will come to know Him and to cling to His ways.

If you do what is your duty to do, I will do what I made it My duty to do, *Then will the Lord drive out all those nations from before you* (11:23).

Pisḳa 50

Then will the Lord drive out—the Lord will drive out, human beings will not drive out—*all (these) nations* (11:23): I might take this literally, therefore Scripture inserts *these* after *all,* whence I learn that it refers only to these seven (nations). Whence do we learn that this applies also to their helpers? From the full phrase, *all these nations from before you* (11:23)—you will constantly grow more numerous, while they will constantly grow less numerous. Similarly Scripture says, *By little and little I will drive them out from before thee* (Exod. 23:30), and *I will not drive them out from before thee in one year, lest the land become desolate, and the beasts of the field multiply against thee* (Exod. 23:29)—so taught R. Jacob.[1] R. Eleazar ben Azariah said to him: Or (should we we ask that) if (the people of) Israel are righteous, why would they be afraid of wild beasts? Is it not true that if they are righteous, they need not fear wild beasts, as it is said, *For thou shalt be in league with the stones of the field, (and the beasts of the field shall be at peace with thee)* (Job 5:23)? Should you ask, why then did Joshua go to all that trouble?[2] The answer is, because Israel had sinned, and that is why it was decreed for them that *By little and little I will drive them out from before thee.*

And ye shall dispossess nations greater and mightier—*greater* in height *and mightier* in strength[3]—*than yourselves* (11:23). You also are great and mighty, but they are greater and mightier than you. R. Eliezer ben Jacob says: It is like a person who says, "A is a mighty man, and so is B, but A is mightier than B."

Another interpretation: *Than yourselves*—why was this said, seeing that Scripture says elsewhere, *Seven nations greater and mightier than thou* (7:1)? Why then *than yourselves*? To show that each one of the seven nations was greater and mightier than all of Israel,[4] as it is said, *Yet destroyed I the Amorite before them, whose height was like the height of the cedars, and he was strong as the oaks* (Amos 2:9).[5]

Pisḳa 51

Every place whereon the sole of your foot shall tread shall be yours; (from the wilderness, and Lebanon, from the river, the river Euphrates, even unto the hinder sea shall be your border) (11:24): If the purpose here was to define the territorial boundaries of the Land of Israel, having said, *from the wilderness, and Lebanon,* etc., why does Scripture say first, *Every place whereon the sole of your foot shall tread?* Because Moses said to them, "Every place you shall conquer, excepting these places, shall be yours."[1] Or was it to permit them to conquer places outside of the Land of Israel before conquering the Land itself? (No,) for Scripture says first, *Ye shall dispossess nations greater and mightier than yourselves* (11:23), and afterwards, *Every place whereon the sole of your foot shall tread,* thus indicating that the Land of Israel must not remain contaminated by idols while you turn back and conquer other lands; rather, only after you have conquered the Land of Israel will you be permitted to conquer places outside of it. Once they have conquered these foreign places, whence do we learn that the commandments are to be observed there also?[2] Judge for yourself: here

Scripture says *shall* and there also it says *shall.*[3] Just as in the former place referred to by *shall*[4] the commandments are to be observed, so in the latter places referred to by *shall* they are likewise to be observed.[5] Should you ask, "Why do not the commandments apply to Aram-Naharaim and Aram-Zobah which were conquered by David?," the answer is, David disobeyed the Torah, for the Torah said, "After you have conquered the Land of Israel, you may conquer places outside the Land," but he did not do so; rather, he turned back and conquered Aram-Naharaim and Aram-Zobah without first dispossessing the Jebusites who were adjacent to Jerusalem. God said to him, "You have neglected to dispossess the Jebusites who are hard by your own palace; how then can you turn back to conquer Aram-Naharaim and Aram-Zobah?" Granting that they may conquer (adjacent) lands outside the Land of Israel, whence do we learn that anything opposite (the Land) across the sea likewise belongs to them?[6] From the verse, *From the wilderness, and Lebanon—from the wilderness* is your border, though the wilderness itself is not your border,[7] but if you conquer it, it shall be your border, *the wilderness . . . shall be your border;*[8] *from the river, the river Euphrates—from the river* is your border, though the river itself is not your border, but if you conquer it, it shall be your border; *even unto the hinder sea shall be your border*—though the sea itself is not your border, but if you conquer it,[9] it shall be your border. Similarly Scripture says, *and for the Western border ye shall have the Great Sea for a border*[10] (Num. 34:6)—*the . . . border* will be your border, (but if you conquer it), the Sea itself will be your border. Thus one concludes (from all this): in all places in the Land of Israel up to Achzib, seized by those who had come up from Babylonia, produce may not be eaten nor land worked; in all places occupied earlier by those who had come up from Egypt, produce may be eaten, but land may not be worked. Anywhere else produce may be eaten and land worked.[11]

These are the boundaries of the Land of Israel as seized by those who came up from Babylonia:[12] the Ashkelon junction, the walls of Strato's Tower, Dor, and the walls of Acco, the headwaters of Gaton and Gaton itself, Kabraṯa and Beṯ Zeniṯa, the fort (*castrum*) of Galila, Kabya of ʿAita, Masya of ʿAbṯa, Kamuṯa of Biryin, Paḥurta of Yattir, the brook of ʾAbṣel, Beṯ ʿEr, Marʿashta, greater Lulʾa, Karḵa of Bar Sangara, Mesaf Sefanta, the channel of ʿIyyun, upper Tarnegola of Caesarea Philippi, Beṯ Sukkoṯ, Yoneḳeṯ and Reḳem of Ḥagra, Trachonitis of Zimra at the limits of Biṣra, Saḳḳa and Heshbon, and the brook of Wered, Sakuṯa, Nimrin, the fort of Zariza, Reḳem of Gaia, the Garden of Ashkelon, and the great road leading to the wilderness.

Pisḳa 52

There shall no man be able to stand against you (11:25): This refers to a single man; what about a nation, a family, or even a woman plying her witchcraft? Hence the verse says, *There shall no man be able to stand*—in any combination. If so, why does Scripture say *man*? To include even (a man) like Og king of Bashan, of whom it is said, *For only Og king of Bashan remained of the remnant of the Rephaim* (3:11).

The fear of you and the dread of you (11:25): If they fear, do they not also dread? Rather, *fear* felt by those who are nearby, and *dread* felt by those who are far off.[1] Similarly Scripture says, *And it came to pass, when all the kings of the Amorites, that were beyond the Jordan westward, and all the kings of the Canaanites, that were by the sea, heard how that the Lord had dried up the waters of the Jordan from before the children of Israel, until they were passed over, that their heart melted, neither was there any spirit in them any more, because of the children of Israel* (Josh. 5:1). So also Rahab the harlot says to Joshua's messengers, *For we have heard how the Lord dried up the water of the Red Sea before you, when ye came out of Egypt, and what ye did unto the two kings of the Amorites that were beyond the Jordan. And as soon as we heard it, our hearts did melt* (Josh. 2:10–11). Should you say that the people of Jericho were not large and tough, does not Scripture say elsewhere, *And Joshua the son of Nun sent out of Shittim two spies secretly, saying, "Go view the land, and Jericho"* (Josh. 2:1)? Now Jericho was part of the land as a whole, why then was it specified? To imply that it was as strong as all the others put together. The same applies to *And Moses sent them, a thousand of every tribe, to the war, them and Phinehas* (Num. 31:6). Now Phinehas was part of the whole expedition, why then was he specified? To indicate that he was equal in worth to all the others put together. The same is true in the case of *Then sang Moses and the children of Israel this song* (Exod. 15:1). Now Moses was part of the whole nation, why then was he specified? To show that he was equal in worth to all of them put together.[2] Again Scripture says, *And David spoke unto the Lord the words of this song (in the day that the Lord delivered him out of the hand of all his enemies, and out of the hand of Saul)* (2 Sam. 22:1) Now Saul was part of the whole group (of enemies), why then was he specified? To indicate that he was as mighty as all the others put together. Similarly Scripture says, *There lacked of David's servants nineteen men, and Asael* (2 Sam. 2:30). Now Asael was part of the whole group (of servants), why then was he specified? To imply that he was as mighty as all of them put together. Likewise Scripture says, *Now King Solomon loved many foreign women, besides the daughter of Pharaoh* (1 Kings 11:1). Now the daughter of Pharaoh was one of them, why then was she specified? To show that he loved her more than all the others, yet she caused him to sin more than all the rest of them.[3]

The Lord your God shall lay (the fear of you and the dread of you upon all the land) (11:25): Why was this said? Because Scripture says, *Three times in a year (shall all thy males appear before the Lord thy God in the place which He shall choose)* (16:16). Israel might ask, "If we go up to worship, who will guard our land?" To which God replied, "Go up—I will guard what is yours," as it is said, *Neither shall any man covet thy land when thou goest up to appear (before the Lord thy God three times in the year)* (Exod. 34:24). If he will not first covet it with his eyes, how will he come to take your goods and cattle? Similarly you find that when Israel fulfilled God's will, what did Naaman say to Elisha? *If not, yet I pray thee, let there be given to thy servant two mules' burden of earth* (2 Kings 5:17). Is it not a case of inference from the minor to the major? If he is afraid to take earth from the Land of Israel without permission, how much more so would he (fear to) take goods or cattle?

As He hath spoken unto you (11:25): Where did he speak? In the verse, *I will send My terror before thee, and I will discomfit all the people to whom thou shalt come* (Exod. 23:27).[4]

Pisḳa 53

Behold, I set before thee this day a blessing and a curse (11:26): Why is this stated?[1] Because Scripture says, *I have set before thee life and death, the blessing and the curse* (30:19). Israel might say, "Since God has placed before us two paths, the path of life and the path of death, we will follow whichever one we want"; therefore the verse says, *choose life* (30:19). A parable: A person was sitting at a crossroads, with two paths before him, one which started out smoothly but ended amidst thorns, and one which started out amidst thorns but ended smoothly. He therefore informed passers-by, saying to them, "Do you see this path which starts out smoothly? For two or three steps you will walk easily, but it ends up with thorns. And do you see that other path that is full of thorns at the beginning? For two or three steps you will walk through thorns, but it ends smoothly."

So also Moses said to Israel: Do you see the wicked who prosper in this world? For two or three days they will prosper, but in the end they will be full of regret, as it is said, *For there shall be no reward*[2] *for the evil man* (Prov. 24:20), *The tears of such as were oppressed,*[3] *(and they had no comforter)* (Eccl. 4:1), *the fool foldeth his hands together, (and eateth his own flesh)* (Eccl. 4:5), and *The way of the wicked is as darkness, (they know not at what they stumble)* (Prov. 4:19). On the other hand, you may see the righteous suffer in this world. For two or three days they suffer, but eventually they are bound to rejoice, as it is said, *That He might prove thee, to do thee good at thy latter end* (8:16), *Better is the end of a thing than the beginning thereof* (Eccl. 7:8), *For I know the thoughts that I think toward you, (saith the Lord, thoughts of peace and not of evil, to give you a future and a hope)* (Jer. 29:11), and *But the path of the righteous is as the light of dawn, (that shineth more and more unto the perfect day)* (Prov. 4:18).

R. Joshua ben Ḳorḥah says: A parable: A king arranged a banquet and invited several guests, amongst them his friend. The king would discreetly motion to him as he reclined (at the table) to take a choice portion, but he did not understand, as it is said, *I will instruct thee and teach thee in the way which thou shalt go; I will give counsel, Mine eye being upon you* (Ps. 32:8). When the king saw that he did not understand, he grasped his hand and placed it over a choice portion, just as it is said, *O Lord, the portion of mine inheritance and of my cup, Thou maintainest*[4] *my lot* (Ps. 16:5). There are people who receive their portion but are not content with it, but Israel acknowledge that they are completely satisfied and that there is no portion as choice as theirs, no inheritance like theirs, and no fate like theirs, and for this they are thankful and give praise. Hence Scripture says, *The lines are fallen unto me in pleasant places, (yea, I have a goodly heritage); I will bless the Lord, who hath given me counsel* (Ps. 16:6–7).[5]

Piska 54

A blessing and a curse (11:26): The blessing if you obey and the curse if you do not obey. Similarly you say, *If thou doest well, shall it not be lifted up?* (Gen. 4:7)—if you do right, you will receive a blessing, and if you do not do right, you will earn a curse.[1] R. Eliezer the son of R. Jose the Galilean says: Who has whispered this to you?[2] The Torah says, *The blessing, (if) ye shall hearken . . . and the curse, if ye shall not hearken.*[3] Similarly you say, *Death and life are in the power of the tongues, and they that indulge it shall eat the fruit thereof* (Prov. 18:21). He who loves goodness will eat its fruits, and he who loves evil will eat its fruits.[4] R. Eliezer the son of R. Jose the Galilean says further: Who has whispered this to you? The Torah states, *Keep thy tongue from evil* (Ps. 34:14). Similarly you say, *Behold, the righteous shall be requited in the earth; how much more the wicked and the sinner* (Prov. 11:31). R. Eliezer the son of R. Jose the Galilean says finally: Who has whispered this to you? The Torah says, *The Lord hath made every thing for His own purpose, yea, even the wicked for the day of evil*[5] (Prov. 16:4).

And the curse, if ye shall not hearken: We learn that our father Jacob did not command his sons until his days were completed, when he was close to death and had already seen all the miracles wrought for him. So also Moses our teacher did not rebuke Israel until his days were completed, when he was close to death and had seen all the miracles that were wrought for him; hence Scripture says, *After he had smitten Sihon*[6] (1:14).

But turn aside out of the way—from the path of life to the path of death[7]—*which I command you this day, to go after other gods* (11:28): Hence the Sages have said that anyone who acknowledges idolatry denies the entire Torah, and anyone who denies idolatry acknowledges the entire Torah.[8]

Pisḳa 55

And it shall come to pass, when the Lord thy God shall bring thee (11:29): *it shall come to pass* always implies "immediately," while *shall bring thee* means accept upon yourself the commandment uttered in this connection, for as a reward therefor you will enter *into the land*[1] *whither thou goest to possess it* (11:29)—meaning as a reward for entering you will possess it.

That thou shalt set the blessing upon Mount Gerizim (11:29): Is it the intent of this verse to teach us that the blessing is on Mount Gerizim and the curse on Mount Ebal? Does not Scripture say elsewhere,

These shall stand upon Mount Gerizim to bless the people . . . and these shall stand upon Mount Ebal for the curse (27:12–13)? Why then does Scripture say, *Thou shalt set the blessing upon Mount Gerizim?* Because one might think that all the blessings precede the curses. Hence Scripture says, *Thou shalt set the blessing*[2] *upon Mount Gerizim*—one blessing may precede a curse, but several blessings may not precede the curses. Another reason is to indicate the analogy between curses and blessings: just as the curses were pronounced by the Levites, so were the blessings pronounced by the Levites; just as the curses were pronounced aloud, so were the blessings pronounced aloud; just as the curses were spoken in the holy tongue, so were the blessings spoken in the holy tongue; just as the curses were general or particular,[3] so were the blessings general or particular; just as both groups[4] answered Amen to the curses, so did they answer Amen to the blessings, turning toward Mount Gerizim for the blessings and toward Mount Ebal for the curses.

Piska 56

Are they not beyond the Jordan[1]—from the other side of the Jordan and beyond, according to R. Judah—*beyond the way of the going down of the sun*—where the sun rises[2]—. . . *beside the terebinths of Moreh?* (11:30): Elsewhere Scripture says, *And Abram passed through the land unto the place of Shechem, unto the terebinth of Moreh* (Gen. 12:6). Just as *the terebinth of Moreh* referred to there is Shechem, so is *the terebinth of Moreh* referred to here Shechem. R. Eleazar son of R. Jose said: I said to the scribes of the Cutheans (Samaritans), "You have falsified the Torah but have not benefited from it in the least. You have written, 'by the terebinths of Moreh, which is Shechem,'[3] but we conclude that this refers to Mount Gerizim and Mount Ebal," which are likewise situated where the Samaritans live, as it is said, *Are they not beyond the Jordan*, etc., *beside the terebinths of Moreh,* while elsewhere it is said, *And Abram passed through the land (unto the place of Shechem, unto the terebinth of Moreh).* Just as *the terebinth of Moreh* referred to there is Shechem, so is *the terebinth of Moreh* referred to here Shechem. R. Eliezer says:[4] This does not refer to the Mount Gerizim and Mount Ebal that are situated among the Samaritans, since Scripture says, *Are they not beyond the Jordan*—next to the other side of the Jordan—*beyond the way of the going down of the sun*—the place where the sun sets—*in the land of the Canaanites*—the land of the Hivites[5]—*that dwell in the Arabah*—whereas these dwell among the hills—*over against Gilgal* (11:30)—whereas these are not even within sight of Gilgal. R. Eliezer ben Jacob says:[6] The intent of Scripture was only to show them the rest of the way as it had shown them the way in the beginning: *the way*—take the road, do not go through the fields—*that dwell*—through inhabited country, not through the wilderness—*in the Arabah*—through the plain, not through the mountains.

Pisḳa 57

For ye are to pass over the Jordan, to go in to possess the land—from the fact that you are to cross the Jordan you will know that you will occupy the land—*which the Lord your God giveth you*—because of your merit—*and ye shall possess it, and dwell therein* (11:31)—as a reward for possessing, you will dwell therein.

Pisḳa 58

And ye shall observe—this refers to study[1]—*to do*—this refers to performance—*all the statutes*—these are the interpretations[2]—*and the ordinances*—these are the regulations—*which I set before you this day* (11:32)—let them be as precious to you as if you had received them from Mount Sinai today, let them be part of your discourse as frequently as if you had heard them today.

Pisḳa 59

These are the statutes—these are the interpretations[1]—*and the ordinances*—these are the regulations—*which ye shall observe*—this refers to study—*to do*—this refers to performance—*in the land* (12:1): One might think that all the commandments are to be observed also outside of the Land of Israel; hence Scripture specifies *to do in the land.* Again, one might think that all the commandments are to be observed only in the Land of Israel; hence Scripture goes on to say, *All the days that ye live upon the earth* (12:1). After extending, Scripture limits.[2] We learn this from that which is said further in this matter. What is said further in the matter? *Ye shall surely destroy all the places* (12:2): Just as the prohibition of idolatry, a commandment incumbent upon the person and not dependent on the land, is observed both in the Holy Land and outside of it, so also all other commandments incumbent upon the person and not dependent on the Holy Land, are to be observed both in the Holy Land and outside of it. On the other hand, those dependent on the Holy Land are to be observed only in that land, except for *ʿorlah* and diverse kinds. R. Eliezer adds new crops.[3]

Pisḳa 60

Ye shall surely destroy all the places (12:2): Whence do we learn that if one cuts down an asherah and it grows back even ten times, one must cut it down each time? From the emphatic verb *shall surely destroy.*[1]

All the places wherein (the nations) . . . served (their gods) (12:2): This tells us that the Canaanites were steeped in idolatry more than all the other nations of the world.

(The nations) that ye are to dispossess (served) their gods[2]: Why must you dispossess their gods? So that you should not follow their[3] ways, whereupon others would come and dispossess you. R. Jose the Galilean says: One might think that if they worship mountains and hills you are commanded to destroy them, too. Hence the verse goes on to say, *Upon the high mountains, and upon the hills, and under every leafy tree* (12:2). Their gods are under the leafy trees, but the leafy trees themselves are not their gods; their gods are on the hills, but the hills themselves are not their gods; their gods are on high mountains, but the high mountains themselves are not their gods. Why then is the asherah forbidden?[4] Because it is man's handiwork, and anything that is man's handiwork is forbidden.

R. ʿAḳiba said: I will make it clear to you. Wherever you find a high mountain, a lofty hill, or a leafy tree, you know that there is an idol there, for Scripture says, *Upon the high mountains, and upon the hills, and under every leafy tree.*[5]

Pisḳa 61

And ye shall break down their altars—[this refers to a stone that was hewn specifically for idol worship—*and dash in pieces their pillars*—this refers to a pillar that had been hewn first and later used for worship—*and burn their asherahs with fire*—this refers to an asherah made specifically for idol worship—*and ye shall hew down the graven images of their gods* (12:3)—this refers to an asherah which had been planted first and later used for worship. Another interpretation: *And ye shall break down their altars:*] Hence the Sages have said:[1] There are three kinds of asherahs—if a tree was planted originally for idol worship, it is forbidden, as it is said, *And burn their asherahs with fire*; if the branches had been trimmed and then grew back, they must be removed,[2] as it is said, *And ye shall hew down the graven images of their gods*; if one did not trim the branches in order to cause them to grow back, but erected an idol under the tree and then removed it,[3] it is permitted, as it is said, *And ye shall destroy their name out of that place. Ye shall not do so unto the Lord your God* (12:3–4).

There are three types of houses:[4] if a house was originally built for idol worship, it is forbidden, as it is said, *Ye shall surely destroy all the places* (12:2); if it was renovated, that which was renovated must be removed, as it is said, *Ye shall destroy their name*; if it was not renovated, but one has placed an idol in it and then removed it, it is permitted, as it is said, *Break down their altars, and dash in pieces their pillars*—once you have torn down the altar, you may leave it, and once you have smashed the pillar, you may leave it. You might think that you are commanded to pursue their destruction even outside of the Land of Israel; hence the verse goes on to say, *And ye shall destroy their name out of that place*—in the Land of Israel you are commanded to pursue their destruction, outside of the Land of Israel you are not commanded to do so.

R. Eliezer says: Whence do we learn that when you cut down a sacred pole, you must also uproot it? From the verse, *And ye shall destroy their name.* R. ʿAḳiba said to him: Why do I need this (verse)? Does not Scripture say previously, *Ye shall surely destroy* (12:2)? What then is the purpose of *Ye shall destroy their name*? (It implies that we must) also change their name. But does this mean even if this serves to praise them? (No,) for Scripture says elsewhere, *Thou shalt utterly detest it, and thou shalt utterly abhor it*[5] (7:26). Whence do we learn that if one chips out one stone from the Hall of the Temple, from its altar, or from its courtyards,[6] he violates a negative commandment? From the verse, *Break down their altars and dash in pieces their pillars. . . . Ye shall not do so unto the Lord your God.*[7]

R. Ishmael says: Whence do we learn that if one erases even one letter from the the (Holy) Name, he violates a negative commandment? From the verse, *Ye shall destroy their name. . . . Ye shall not do so unto the Lord your God.*

Rabban Gamaliel says: Could you possibly imagine that Israelites would tear down their own altars? Heaven forbid! Rather, the verse means: do not do as the heathen do, for your evil deeds would then cause the Temple of your fathers to be destroyed.

Pisḳa 62

But unto the place which the Lord your God shall choose out of all your Tribes (12:5): Inquire of a prophet.[1] You might think that you must wait until a prophet tells you; hence the verse goes on to say, *Even unto His habitation shall ye seek and thither thou shalt come* (12:5)—search for and find the place, then the prophet will tell you.[2] You find the same in the case of David, as it is said, *Lord, remember unto David all his afflictions; how he swore unto the Lord, and vowed unto the Mighty One of Jacob: Surely I will not come into the tent of my house, nor go up into the bed that is spread for me; I will not give sleep to mine eyes, nor slumber to mine eyelids, until I find out a place for the Lord, a dwelling-place for the Mighty One of Jacob* (Ps. 132:1–5).

Whence do we learn that he did nothing without a prophet's guidance? From the verse, *And Gad came that day to David and said unto him, "Go up, rear an altar unto the Lord in the threshing-floor of Araunah the Jebusite"* (2 Sam. 24:18), and again, *Then Solomon began to build the House of the Lord at Jerusalem in Mount Moriah, where the Lord appeared to David his father, for which provision had been made in the place of David, in the threshing-floor of Araunah the Jebusite* (2 Chron. 3:1).

One verse says, *In one of thy Tribes* (12:14), while another says, *Out of all your Tribes*—how can both verses be maintained? They knew that in the time to come the Temple will be built in the territory of Judah and Benjamin, and therefore they set aside the pasture of Jericho.[3] Who benefited from it all those years?[4] The descendants of the Kenite, Moses' father-in-law, benefited from it, as it is said, *And the children of the Kenite, Moses' father-in-law, went up out of the city of palm trees* (Judg. 1:16); but after the Temple was built, they journeyed away from there—so taught R. Simeon.[5] R. Judah says: They went to Jabez to learn Torah, as it is said, *And the families of scribes that dwelt at Jabez, the Tirathites, the Shimeathites, the Sucathites. These are the Kenites* (1 Chr. 2:55).

Another interpretation: One verse says, *In one of thy Tribes,* while another says, *Out of all your Tribes*—the money will come from all of your Tribes, but (the land for) the Temple will come from only one Tribe. Another interpretation: *In one of thy Tribes*—this refers to Shiloh; *Out of all your Tribes*—this refers to Jerusalem.[6]

Scripture says, *So David bought the threshing-floor and the oxen for fifty shekels of silver* (2 Sam. 24:24), while elsewhere it says, *So David gave to Ornan for the place six hundred shekels of gold by weight* (1 Chron. 21:25)—how can both these verses be maintained? Since there were twelve Tribes, David took fifty shekels from each one, for a total of six hundred shekels from all the Tribes.

To put His name there (12:5): Here Scripture says, *His name,* while elsewhere it says, *My name* (Num. 6:27)—just as *His name* here refers to the Chosen House (the Temple), so does *My name* there refer to the Chosen House; just as *My name* there refers to the priestly blessing, so does *His name* here refer to the priestly blessing. This informs me only about (the priestly blessing) in the Temple. Whence do we learn (that it is to be practiced) also outside of Jerusalem?[7] From the verse, *In every place where I cause My name to be mentioned* (Exod. 20:21). If so, why does Scripture say, *To put His name there?*[8] (To show) that in the Temple the (Holy) Name was pronounced as written, while in the rest of the country the substitute was used.

Piska 63

And thither thou shalt come; and thither ye shall bring (12:5–6): Why is this said? Because Scripture says, *These are the appointed seasons of the Lord, which ye shall proclaim to be holy convocations, to bring an offering made by fire unto the Lord . . . each on its own day* (Lev. 23:37). One might think that on the festivals only the festival offering is to be brought. Whence do we learn that communal sacrifices consecrated prior to the festival as well as individual sacrifices consecrated prior to, or on, the festival should likewise be offered on the festival? From the verse, *And beside your gifts, and beside all your vows, and beside all your freewill-offerings, which ye give unto the Lord* (Lev. 23:38), thus including fowl and meal offerings, and permitting all of them to be brought on the festival. One might think that this is merely permissive;[1] hence Scripture says elsewhere, *These ye shall offer unto the Lord in your appointed seasons* (Num. 29:39). Since permission has already been given,[2] why does Scripture say, *These ye shall offer unto the Lord in your appointed seasons?* In order to appoint that all of them must be brought on the festival day.[3] One might think that they may be brought on whatever festival one chooses; hence Scripture says, *And thither thou shalt come, and thither ye shall bring.* Again, if as far as permission is concerned, it has already been granted, and as far as appointment is concerned, it has already been declared,[4] why does Scripture say, *And thither thou shalt come, and thither ye shall bring?* In order to appoint as a duty that they must be brought on the nearest festival that comes along. One might think that if one festival has passed by and one has failed to bring them, he must forgo them entirely, on the principle of "thou shalt not delay";[5] hence Scripture says, *These ye shall offer unto the Lord in your appointed seasons,*[6] implying that one may not forgo them on the principle of "thou shalt not delay," unless the entire year's cycle of festivals has passed.[7]

Your burnt offerings—both individual and communal—*and your sacrifices*—the peace offerings of individuals and the communal peace offerings—*and your tithes*—R. ʿAḳiba says: Scripture refers here to two tithes, that of grain and that of animals[8]—*and the offering of your hand*—these are the first fruit offerings, as it is said, *And the priest shall take the basket out of thy hand* (26:4)—*and the firstlings*—this is the first-born—*of your herd and of your flock* (12:6)—these are the sin offerings and the guilt offerings.

Piska 64

And there ye shall eat before the Lord your God—within the compartment[1]—*and ye shall rejoice*—"rejoicing" is used both here and later on (27:7), and just as the rejoicing spoken of later on refers to peace offerings, so does the rejoicing spoken of here refer to peace offerings—*in all that ye put your hand unto*—in whatever you put your hand unto I will send a blessing for it—*ye and your households*—

meaning one's wife[2]—*wherein the Lord thy God hath blessed thee* (12:7)—one must bring (his offering) in accordance with this blessing.

Pisḳa 65

[*Ye shall not do after all that we do here this day* (12:8): (Bringing obligatory offerings) at the Permanent House (the Temple) and voluntary ones on the altars. Another interpretation: *Ye shall not do*—go out and do—hence the Sages have said:[1] Before the Tabernacle was erected, the altars were permitted, and the sacrifices were offered by the first-born. Once the Tabernacle was erected, the altars were forbidden, and the sacrifices were offered by the priests. When they came to Gilgal, the altars were permitted, but when they came to Shiloh, they were again forbidden. When they came to Nob and Gibeon, the altars were again permitted. From the time they came to Jerusalem and thereafter the altars were once more forbidden and were never again permitted.]

Ye shall not do after all that we do here this day: Today we move the Tabernacle (from place to place), and are forbidden to sacrifice at altars. Once we come into the (Holy) Land, we shall not be forbidden to sacrifice at altars. R. Judah says: One might think that the community may bring sacrifices at the altar; hence Scripture says, *Every man* (12:8)—an individual may bring a sacrifice at the altar, but the community may not.[2]

Every man whatsoever is right in his own eyes (12:8): Anyone who makes a vow or pledges a freewill offering may offer at his own altar,[3] and anyone who does not vow or pledge does not offer at the altar of the individual. R. Simeon says: Today we may bring sin offerings and guilt offerings, but once we come to the (Holy) Land, we may not bring them.[4]

Pisḳa 66

For how long? *For ye are not as yet come* (12:9): The altar was permitted from the time of resting (within the Holy Land) until the time of possessing it. "Possessing" refers to Shiloh, while "resting" refers to Jerusalem, as it is said, *This is My resting place for ever* (Ps. 132:14)—so said R. Simeon. R. Judah says: The other way around.[2]

Pisḳa 67

But when ye go over the Jordan, and dwell in the land (12:10): R. Judah says: Three commandments were given to Israel to be performed when they entered the (Holy) Land: to appoint a king for themselves, to build the Chosen House (the Temple) for themselves, and to cut off the seed of Amalek. I might not know which took precedence, appointing a king for themselves, building the Chosen House for themselves, or cutting off the seed of Amalek; hence Scripture says, *The hand upon the throne of the Lord: the Lord will have war with Amalek from generation to generation* (Exod. 17:16)—once a king is enthroned upon the Lord's throne, you shall cut off the seed of Amalek. And whence do we learn that *the throne of the Lord* refers to the king? From the verse, *Then Solomon sat on the throne of the Lord as king* (1 Chron. 29:23). But I still might not know which commandment takes precedence, building the Chosen House for themselves or cutting off the seed of Amalek; hence Scripture goes on to say, *which the Lord your God causeth you to inherit (and He giveth you rest from all your enemies round about)*[1] . . . *then it shall come to pass that the place which the Lord your God shall choose to cause His name to dwell there, thither shall ye bring all that I command you* (12:10–11), and also, *And it came to pass, when the king sat in his house, and the Lord had given him rest from all his enemies round about, that the king said unto Nathan the prophet, "See now, I dwell in a house of cedar, but the Ark of God dwells within curtains"* (2 Sam. 7:1–2).

Then it shall come to pass that the place which the Lord your God shall choose to cause His name to dwell there, thither shall ye bring all that I command you: *there, thither*[2]—there were two areas there, one for the holiest sacrifices and one for the lesser sacrifices.[3]

Pisḳa 68

Your burnt offerings—individual and communal—*and your sacrifices*—the peace offerings, individual and communal—*and your tithes*—

R. ʿAḳiba says: Scripture speaks of two tithes, one of grain and the other of animals—*and the offering of your hand*—these are the first-born—*and all your choice vows which ye vow unto the Lord* (12:11)—this adds the stipulation that vows and freewill offerings must be brought only from the choicest items. Now I might think that this stipulation applies only to vows and freewill offerings; whence do we learn that it applies to the first-born and to tithes, sin offerings, and guilt offerings as well? From the fact that Scripture says (not merely) *your choice vows* (but) *and all your choice vows*. Rabbi (Judah the Prince) says: Scripture has already mentioned vows earlier;[1] why then are they mentioned here again? The former command refers to Shiloh, the latter to Jerusalem.[2]

Pisḳa 69

And ye shall rejoice—rejoice is said here, and *rejoice* is said elsewhere (27:7); just as the *rejoice* said there refers to peace offerings, so does *rejoice* said here refer to peace offerings—*before the Lord your God*—within the compartment[1]—*ye, and your sons, and your daughters, and your menservants and your maidservants*—the more precious take precedence—*and the Levite that is within your gates* (12:12)—wherever you find the term *the Levite*,[2] it indicates: give him out of his portion; if he does not have (enough out of his) portion, give him the tithe of the poor; if he does not have (enough out of) the tithe of the poor, give him (of) the peace offerings.

Pisḳa 70

Take heed—this refers to a negative command[1]—*lest*—this again refers to a negative command—*thou offer thy burnt offerings* (12:13): Not the burnt offerings of the Gentiles; so taught R. Simeon[2]. R. Judah says: Not the burnt offerings of the Gentiles, which were consecrated outside of the (Holy) Land.[3]

In every place that thou seest (12:13): But only in any place that a prophet will tell you to offer them, as in the case of Elijah who brought offerings on Mount Carmel.[4]

But in the place which the Lord shall choose in one of thy Tribes (12:14): One verse says *In one of thy tribes*, while another verse says *Out of all your Tribes* (12:5); this is why R. Judah says that the money came *Out of all your Tribes,* but the site for the Chosen House came from only one Tribe.[5]

There shalt thou offer thy burnt offerings (12:14): This, I see, refers only to the burnt offering; whence do we learn that this refers also to the other sacrifices? From the conclusion of the verse, *and there thou shalt do all that I command thee* (12:14). I might still contend that the burnt offering is subject to both a positive and a negative commandment,[6] whereas the other sacred offerings are subject only to a positive commandment; hence the verse says, *There shalt thou offer thy burnt offerings*—the burnt offering comes under the general rule and is singled out to indicate that just as the burnt offering, which is subject to both a positive and a negative commandment, is singled out, so also is everything else, that is subject only to a positive commandment, thereby subjected to a negative commandment as well.

Pisḳa 71

Notwithstanding thou mayest kill and eat flesh (within all thy gates), after all the desire of thy soul (12:15): To what does this verse refer? If to meat slaughtered for personal pleasure, it has already been mentioned elsewhere; if to the eating of sacrifices, this too has already been mentioned elsewhere. Therefore this must refer solely to animals dedicated but found unfit, which must be redeemed.[1] One might think that they must be redeemed also when the imperfection is only temporary; hence the verse says, *notwithstanding.*[2]

Thou mayest kill and eat—but not make use of its fleece—*flesh*—but not milk.[3] One might think that all this is also forbidden after slaughtering; hence the verse goes on to say, *According to the blessing of the Lord thy God which He hath given thee* (12:15).[4] One might think that if the permanent flaw occurred before the beasts were dedicated, and they were then redeemed, they are likewise forbidden; hence again the verse says, *notwithstanding.*

How do we learn that the beasts may be slaughtered only if there is a permanent imperfection? By your reasoning from the minor to the major. If the firstling,[5] which does not include all newborn animals and which becomes fit for profane use[6] without being redeemed, may be slaughtered only when there is a permanent imperfection, should not consecrated animals, which include all the newborn and which must be redeemed before they become fit for profane use, also be slaughtered only when there is a permanent imperfection? (One might argue that) this is not so, because if you say that this applies to the firstling, which is consecrated from the womb and whose consecration remains in force even with a permanent imperfection, how can you infer the same about consecrated animals, which are not consecrated from the womb and whose consecration lapses once they are afflicted with a permanent imperfection? Hence the verse says, *Which He hath given thee* (and) *within all thy gates*. The phrase *thy gates* (here) and *thy gates* (in 15:22) indicates an analogy:[7] just as (the animals referred to by) *thy gates* there (in 15:22) are not to be slaughtered unless there is a permanent imperfection, so *thy gates* here indicates that they are not to be slaughtered unless there is a permanent imperfection.[8]

The unclean . . . may eat (12:15): This implies to me only the unclean; what about the clean? The verse says *as one* (12:22),[9] which proves that both of them may eat from the same dish.[10] You might think that heave offering may also be eaten from the same dish; hence the verse goes on to say, *as one* (12:22)—these may be eaten from the same dish, but heave offering may not. You might think that these are included in the requirement of priestly gifts; hence the verse goes on to say, *as the gazelle* (12:22). (You might say,) I will exclude it from the requirement of priestly gifts, but not from the gift of breast and thigh (Lev. 7:31–32); hence the verse says, *And as of the hart* (12:15).[11] Or (you might say that) just as the gazelle is permitted in its entirety, so all of this; hence the verse says, *notwithstanding*.[12] R. Simeon says: You might think that just as the Torah differentiates between sacrifices of greater sanctity and those of lesser sanctity when they are perfect, so does Torah differentiate between them when they have imperfections; hence the verse says, *As of the gazelle and as of the hart*—Scripture thus indicates that just as the Torah does not differentiate between the gazelle and the hart, so does it not differentiate between the sacrifices of greater sanctity and those of lesser sanctity when they have imperfections.

Only ye shall not eat the blood (12:16): R. Judah says: You might think Israelites are liable for violating two prohibitions concerning these animals' blood, as in the case of the blood of consecrated offerings;[13] hence the verse says, *Only ye shall not eat the blood*—there is only one prohibition concerning blood, and not two.

Thou shalt pour it out upon the earth—not into seas, rivers, or vessels—*as water* (12:16)—not into the water itself. *As water*—just as one is permitted to derive benefit from water, so is one permitted to derive benefit from blood.[14] Just as water makes seeds fit, so does blood.[15] Just as water need not be covered, so this blood need not be covered.

Pisḳa 72

Thou mayest not eat within thy gates (12:17): R. Joshua ben Ḳorḥah says: I am able to do so but am not permitted.[1] The same applies to *And as for the Jebusites, the inhabitants of Jerusalem, the children of Judah could not drive them out*[2] (Josh. 15:63). They were able to do so, but were not permitted.

The tithe (12:17): I might think that this refers only to clean tithe; whence unclean tithe?[3] From the following *of thy corn*. Whence that this applies to what is purchased with second tithe money? The following *of thy wine*. This refers only to what is clean; whence that which is unclean? From the following *of thine oil*.[4] R. Simeon says: From the verse, *I have not eaten thereof in my mourning, neither have I put away thereof being unclean* (26:14), I would not know where there is a warning; hence Scripture says here, *Thou mayest not eat within thy gates the tithe*. I might think that he who gives it as a gift is also liable; hence Scripture says, *Thou mayest not eat within thy gates the tithe*—he who eats of it is liable, but he who gives it as a gift is not. R. Jose the Galilean says:[5] I might think that one is liable only for produce from which the priestly and Levitic dues have not yet been separated (*ṭebel*), or from which the heave offering has been separated but not first tithe, or first tithe but not second tithe, or even not the poor man's tithe; hence Scripture says, *Thou mayest not eat within thy gates*.[6] R. Simeon says: The purpose of the verse is only to distinguish among various (types) of holy objects.[7] *Nor the offering of thy hand* (12:17): This refers to first fruits. And what do we learn from this verse? If it is about the eating of first fruits outside the wall (of Jerusalem), this may be inferred from tithes by arguing from the minor to the major: if in the case of tithes, which are permitted to laymen, one who eats of them outside the wall has violated a negative commandment, then in the case of first fruits, which are forbidden to laymen, would not one who eats of them outside the wall be even more so in violation of a negative commandment? Hence what we learn from this verse can be nothing else but that if one eats of first fruits without making the prescribed declaration,[8] he has violated a negative commandment.[9]

Nor thy freewill offerings (12:17): This refers to the thanksgiving offerings and the peace offerings. What do we learn from this verse? If it is about the eating of thanksgiving offerings and the peace offerings outside of the wall, this could be deduced from tithes by arguing from the minor to the major: if in the case of tithes, where one is not liable[10] for *piggul,*[11] he who eats outside the wall of what is left over, and is therefore unclean, has transgressed a negative commandment, then in the case of thanksgiving offerings and peace offerings, where one is liable for *piggul,* should not he who eats outside the wall of what is left over, and is therefore unclean, be even more guilty of transgressing a negative commandment? Hence what we learn from this verse can be nothing else but that if one eats of thanksgiving offerings and peace offerings before sprinkling the blood, he has violated a negative commandment.

Or the firstlings (12:17): This refers to the first-born young. What do we learn from this verse? If it is about eating its flesh outside of the wall, this could be deduced from tithes by arguing from the minor to the major. If it is about eating of it before sprinkling the blood, this may be deduced from thanksgiving and peace offerings by arguing from the minor to the major: if in the case of thanksgiving and peace offerings, which are permitted to laymen, one who eats of them before sprinkling the blood violates a negative commandment, should not he who eats of the first-born, which is forbidden to laymen, before sprinkling the blood, be even more in violation of a negative commandment? Hence what we learn from this verse can be nothing else but that if a layman eats of the flesh of the first-born either before or after sprinkling the blood, he has violated a negative commandment.

Pisḳa 73

Of thy herd or of thy flock (12:17): This refers to sin offerings and guilt offerings. What do we learn from this verse? If it is about eating of sin or guilt offerings outside the wall (of Jerusalem), this could be deduced from tithes by arguing from the minor to the major. If it is about eating before sprinkling the blood, this too could be deduced from thanksgiving and peace offerings by arguing from the minor to the major. If it is about (eating) after sprinkling the blood, this also could be deduced from the first-born by arguing from the minor to the major: if in the case of the (sacrifice of the) first-born, which is of lesser sanctity, (a layman)[1] who eats of it after sprinkling the blood transgresses a negative commandment, then in the case of sin and guilt offerings, which are of greater sanctity, should not (a layman) who eats of it after sprinkling the blood be violating a negative commandment? Therefore the verse must refer to none else but the one who eats of sin or guilt offerings outside of the hangings,[2] since he violates a negative commandment.

Pisḳa 74

Any of thy vows (12:17): This refers to the burnt offerings. What do we learn from this verse? If it refers to eating of the burnt offering outside of the wall (of Jerusalem), this could be deduced from tithes by arguing from the minor to the major; if it refers to (eating of it) before sprinkling the blood, it could be deduced in the same way from thanksgiving and peace offerings; if to (eating of it) after sprinkling the blood, this could be deduced in the same way from the first-born. If it refers to (eating of it) outside of the hangings,[1] this could be deduced in the same way from sin and guilt offerings: if in the case of sin and guilt offerings, which are permitted to be eaten, one who eats of them outside of the hangings has violated a negative commandment, should he not, in the case of a burnt offering, which is forbidden to be eaten, be guilty of violating a negative commandment if he eats of it outside the hangings? Therefore the verse must refer to none else but one who eats of a burnt offering, whether before or after sprinkling the blood, whether within or without the hangings, to the effect that he violates a negative commandment.

Before the Lord thy God—this refers to Shiloh—*in the place which the Lord thy God shall choose*—this refers to Jerusalem[2]—*thou, and thy son, and thy daughter, and thy manservant, and thy maidservant*—the more precious takes precedence—*and the Levite that is within thy gates* (12:18)—wherever you find the term *the Levite,*[3] it indicates, give him out of his portion; if he does not have (enough out of) his portion, give him out of the poor man's tithe; if he does not have (enough out of) the poor man's tithe, give him out of the peace offerings.

Take heed—this a negative commandment—*lest*—referring again to a negative commandment—*thou forsake the Levite as long as thou livest*—even during the Sabbatical and Jubilee years—*upon thy land* (12:19)—but not in the Diaspora.[4]

Piska 75

When the Lord thy God shall enlarge thy border—fulfill the commandment set forth here, so that as a reward *the Lord thy God shall enlarge thy border, as He hath promised thee* (12:20): What did He say to you? *(Unto thy seed have I given) this land, (from the river of Egypt unto the great river, the river Euphrates); the Kenite, and the Kenizzite, and the Kadmonite* (Gen. 15:18–19). Rabbi (Judah the Prince) says: These have been mentioned elsewhere.[1] What then does *As He hath promised thee* refer to?[2] To *And they shall have their sides east and west: Dan one portion . . . Asher one portion . . . Judah one portion* (Ezek. 48:1–7).

And thou shalt say, "I will eat flesh," because thy soul desireth it (12:20): R. Ishmael says: From this we learn that meat for profane consumption was forbidden to Israel in the wilderness, but when they came to the (Holy) Land, Scripture permitted it to them. R. ʿAḳiba, however, says: The purpose of the verse is to do nothing but teach you the commandments set forth in it.[3] R. Eleazar ben Azariah says: The purpose of the verse is merely to teach you proper conduct—one should not eat meat unless he has a desire for it.[4] You might think he might buy it at the market place and eat it (immediately); hence Scripture goes on to say, *Then thou shalt kill of thy herd and of thy flock* (12:21)—one should not eat meat until he has cattle and flocks.[5] You might think that he must slaughter all of his flock and all of his herd; hence the verse says *of thy herd,* not all of thy herd, and *of thy flock,* not all of thy flock.

As I have commanded thee (12:21): Just as consecrated animals must be slaughtered in the ritual manner, so also profane animals must be slaughtered in the ritual manner. (One might think that) just as consecrated animals must be slaughtered in *the place,* so also profane animals must be slaughtered in *the place*; hence the verse says, *If the place which the Lord thy God shall choose to put His name there be too far from thee, then thou shalt kill,* etc. (12:21)—when *the place* is far away from you, you may kill[6] them, but not when *the place* is near, with the sole exception of profane meat slaughtered in the Temple court. This can refer only to unblemished animals; whence do we learn that this applies also to blemished animals? From the verse, *And kill it at the door of the Tent of Meeting* (Lev. 3:2). You might think that wild beasts and fowl may also be slaughtered at the door of the Tent of Meeting; hence Scripture goes on to say again, *And kill it* (Lev. 3:8)—*it* (the sacrificial animal) is slaughtered at the entrance to the Tent of Meeting, not wild beasts and fowl. Again, you might think that just as consecrated animals must be slaughtered at the specified time, so too profane animals (must be slaughtered) at the specified time; hence Scripture goes on to say, *And thou shalt eat within thy gates, after all the desire of thy soul* (12:21). You might think that just as consecrated animals must be slaughtered within the Temple partition, so also profane animals must be slaughtered within it; hence the verse says, *Thou shalt eat within thy gates.* You might think that just as consecrated animals must be slaughtered during the day, so also profane animals must be slaughtered during the day; hence the verse says, *Thou shalt eat within thy gates, after all the desire of thy soul.* You might think that just as consecrated animals must be slaughtered in a state of cleanness, so also profane animals must be slaughtered in a state of cleanness; hence Scripture goes on to say, *The unclean . . . may eat thereof* (12:22). This refers only to the unclean person; whence do we learn that this applies also to the clean? From the full statement here, *The unclean and the clean may eat thereof as one* (12:22), indicating that both may eat from the same dish.[7] One might think that heave offering also may be eaten from the same dish; hence the verse says, *May eat thereof as one*—this (profane meat) may be eaten from the same dish, but not heave offering. One might think that they are obligated to offer the breast and the thigh;[8] hence the verse says, *As the gazelle* (12:22). Lest one should suppose that such profane meat is excluded from the rule of breast and thigh but not from the rule of the two kidneys and the lobe above the liver,[9] the verse goes on to say, *As the hart* (12:22). Lest one should suppose that just as all of the gazelle is permitted, so is all of this (meat) permitted, the verse begins with *Howbeit* (12:22).

Howbeit as the gazelle and as the hart is eaten (12:22): R. Eleazar ha-Ḳappar be-Rabbi says: Is this verse meant to inform us about the difference between the gazelle and the hart? (No.) Rather it is like a person who has come to act as the teacher but finds that he is the pupil: just as domestic animals must be slaughtered ritually, so must wild beasts be slaughtered ritually; but the ritual slaughtering of fowls is only a Rabbinic ordinance.[10] Rabbi (Judah the Prince) says: *As I have commanded thee* (12:21) indicates that Moses was commanded concerning the windpipe and the gullet, that (in slaughtering) the greater part of one of these (must be cut) in fowls, and the greater part of both in cattle.[11]

Pisḳa 76

Only be steadfast in not eating the blood (12:23): R. Judah says: This indicates that Israel was bathed in blood before the giving of Torah. One might think that this situation continued even after they had joyfully received it from Mount Sinai; hence the verse begins with *Only.*[1] R. Simeon ben Azzai says: Are there not three hundred other positive commandments like this in the Torah?[2] (The emphasis on) it indicates that if in the case of the interdict of blood, which is the least[3] of all the commandments, Scripture emphatically warns you, how much more so does this apply to other, (more grave,) commandments. R. Simeon says: Every commandment which Israel accepted with joy at Mount Sinai, they perform with joy, and every commandment which they accepted without joy at Mount Sinai, they perform without joy. Rabban Simeon ben Gamaliel says: Every commandment for which Israelites had sacrificed their lives in times of persecution is performed in public, while any commandment for which Israelites had not sacrificed their lives in times of persectuion is still vacillatingly observed.[4] *For the blood is the life* (12:23): This indicates the reason (for the commandment).

And thou shalt not eat the life with the flesh (12:23): This refers to a limb cut off from a living animal. But is it not obvious that if flesh seethed in milk, which was permitted to all descendants of Noah, was (later) forbidden to Israel, the limbs of a living animal, which was forbidden to all descendants of Noah, should certainly be forbidden also to Israel? (Not necessarily so,) as evidenced by the case of the (captive) *woman of goodly form* (21:11), who was forbidden to all descendants of Noah but was (later) permitted to Israel, and by other similar cases. You should not therefore be surprised if the limb of a living animal, too, were (later) permitted to Israel although previously prohibited to all descendants of Noah.[5] Hence, *Thou shalt not eat the life with the flesh,* referring to the limb of a living animal. R. Ḥanina ben Gamaliel, however, says: This refers to the blood of a living animal.

Thou shalt not eat it (12:24): This includes flesh seethed in milk. But is it not obvious that if in the case of *nĕḇelah,*[6] for which one is not liable if he only cooks it, he is liable if he eats of it, then in the case of flesh seethed in milk, for which one is liable even if he only cooks it, he should certainly be liable for eating of it? (Not necessarily so,) as evidenced by mixed seeds, where one is liable for sowing them but not for eating of them. You should not therefore be surprised if in the case of flesh seethed in milk, one were not liable for eating of it even though he is liable for seething it. Hence *Thou shalt not eat it,* so as to include (eating) flesh seethed in milk.

R. Eliezer says: If in the case of the Paschal lamb, where one is not liable for seething it,[7] one is liable for eating of it, is it not obvious that in the case of flesh seethed in milk, where one is liable for seething it, he is liable also for eating of it? (Not necessarily so,) as evidenced by the compounding of frankincense, where one is liable for mixing it (improperly) but not for inhaling the fragrance of it. Therefore you should not be surprised if in the case of flesh seethed in milk, even though one is liable for seething it, one were not liable for eating of it. Hence, *Thou shalt not eat it,* so as to include (eating) flesh seethed in milk.[8]

Rabban Gamaliel be-Rabbi says: Scripture says, *Only be steadfast in not eating the blood*—if in the case of blood, which is the least of all the commandments, Scripture warns you of it, how much more so must one beware in the case of all the other commandments!

Pisḳa 77

Only thy holy things which thou hast, and thy vows, thou shalt take, and go unto the place (which the Lord shall choose) (12:26): To what does the verse refer? If to the consecrated offerings of the (Holy) Land, they have already been spoken of elsewhere;[1] hence the verse must refer to the consecrated offerings from outside the (Holy) Land. *Thou shalt take, and go* indicates that one is responsible for taking care of them on the way until they are brought into the Chosen House itself.

R. Judah, however, says: One is responsible for them only up to the Cistern of the Diaspora;[2] from that Cistern and onward he is not responsible for them. One might think that this applies to the first-born and the tithes as well;[3] hence the verse says, *thy vows,* indicating consecrated offerings resulting from vows or freewill pledges, thus excluding the first-born and the tithes, which are not the result of vows or freewill pledges. I might at this point exclude also sin and guilt offerings; hence the verse says, *thy holy things.* Who then tells you to include sin and guilt offerings but exclude the first-born and the tithes? (The fact that) after the verse includes, it proceeds to exclude: I include the sin and guilt offerings, which have no remedy except in their own place, and I exclude the first-born and the tithes, which have a remedy anywhere.[4]

R. ʿAḳiba says: The verse speaks about substitution of consecrated objects. *Thou shalt take, and go unto the place*—one might think that this applies also to the first-born and the tithes; hence the verse says, *and thy vows.* One might think that the tithe of cattle applies also to partnerships; hence the verse says, *which thou hast.*[5] I might exclude brothers who had acquired it from the estate and have afterwards divided it; hence the verse says, *which thou hast.* Ben Azzai says: One might think that the tithe of cattle applies also to an orphan; hence the verse says, *only.*[6]

Pisḳa 78

And thou shalt offer thy burnt offerings, the flesh and the blood (12:27): R. Joshua says: If there is no blood, there is no flesh, and if there is no flesh, there is no blood.[1] R. Eliezer says: *And the blood of thy sacrifices shall be poured out* (12:27)—even when there is no flesh. In that case, how can I draw an analogy between this part of the verse and the part which says, *Thou shalt offer thy burnt offerings, the flesh and the blood*? The connection is that just as blood requires casting, so does flesh require casting.[2] One might think that he may stand far off and cast it; hence Scripture says, *And the priest shall lay them* (Lev. 1:12), showing that he must stand close and arrange the sacrifices on the pile of wood (upon the altar).

Since Scripture says, *And the priest shall make the whole smoke on the altar* (Lev. 1:9), this must include the bones, the sinews, the horns, and the hoofs.[3] One might therefore think that this is so even if they are separated; hence the verse here says, *Thou shalt offer thy burnt offerings, the flesh and the blood.* One might think further that *Thou shalt offer thy burnt offerings, the flesh and the blood* means that one must first remove the sinews and the bones and then offer up the flesh alone upon the altar; hence Scripture says, *(The priest shall offer) the whole* (Lev. 1:13). How so? If they are still connected, offer them up; if they have been separated, even if they are on top of the altar, take them down. Whence do we learn that in the case of all consecrated offerings blood must be applied at the base of the altar and poured once upon the altar? From the verse, *Thou shalt offer thy burnt offerings, the flesh and the blood (upon the altar of the Lord thy God, and the blood of thy sacrifices shall be poured out against the altar)* (12:27). Whence do we learn that in the case of the tithe and the Paschal lamb, if the blood is applied all at once, they are effective? From the verse, *Thou shalt offer thy burnt offerings.* Whence do we learn that the tithe and the Paschal lamb should have only one application of the blood? From the verse, *And the blood*[4] *of thy sacrifices shall be poured out.*

R. Ishmael says: Scripture here refers to the substitution of consecrated animals. *Thou shalt take, and go unto the place* (12:26)—when it arrives at the place, what is to be done with it? The answer is, *Thou shalt offer thy burnt offerings, the flesh and the blood.* Just as the burnt offering must be flayed, cut up, and completely burned, so must the substitute for it. Just as the burnt offering must have one application of blood at the base of the altar and one pouring out on the altar, so must the substitute. Just as with the burnt offering, if some of its limbs split off the altar they must be replaced over the pile of wood, so must the limbs of the substitute. Just as none of the flesh of the consecrated offerings is permitted until the blood has been sprinkled, so is the flesh of the substitute.[5]

Pisḳa 79

[*Observe and hear* (12:28): If you listen (to your teacher) a little, you will eventually listen a great deal. If you observe (what he teaches you) a little, you will eventually observe a great deal. If you observe what you have listened to, you will eventually observe what you have not yet listened to. Observe what you can, and you will learn (to observe more) in the future. Another interpretation: If one has acquired the merit of learning Torah, not only will the merit be his but it will also extend to his descendants until the end of all generations.]

Observe and hear—whatever is not included in the generality of teaching is not included in the generality of performance—*all these words which I command thee*—indicating that a light commandment should be as precious to you as a grave one—. . . *when thou doest that which is good and right* (12:28): That which is good in the sight of heaven and right in the sight of man; so taught R. ʿAḳiba. And similarly Scripture says, *So shalt thou find grace and good favor in the sight of God and man* (Prov. 3:4). R. Ishmael, however, says: *And right*—likewise in the sight of heaven.[1]

Pisḳa 80

When the Lord thy God shall cut off the nations—perform the commandment prescribed in this matter, and as a reward *the Lord thy God shall cut off the nations . . . whither thou goest in to dispossess them*—as a reward for going in, you will dispossess—*and thou dispossessest them, and dwellest in their land* (12:29):[1] From the verse *And thou dost succeed them, and dwell in their cities, and in their houses* (19:1) one might think that you are not permitted to build anything more than what already exists; hence Scripture says here, *And thou dispossessest them, and dwellest in their land*—wherever you wish to build, go ahead and build.[2]

[*And thou dispossessest them, and dwellest*: It once happened that R. Judah ben Betherah, R. Mattiah ben Ḥeresh, R. Hananiah ben Aḥi, R. Joshua, and R. Jonathan were going abroad. When they reached Platana and remembered the Land of Israel, they raised their eyes (heavenward) and wept, rent their garments, and recited the verse, *And ye shall possess it and dwell therein, and ye shall observe to do all the statutes and the ordinances* (11:31–32). They said: (The duty of) dwelling in the Land of Israel is equivalent to all the other commandments of the Torah put together.[3] At another time R. Eleazar ben Shammuʿa and R. Johanan the Sandal-maker were going to Nisibis to study Torah under R. Judah ben Betherah. When they got to Sidon, they remembered the Land of Israel, raised their eyes (heavenward) letting their tears flow, rent their garments, and recited this same verse, *And ye shall possess it and dwell therein, and ye shall observe to do all the statutes and the ordinances.* They said: (The duty of) dwelling in the Land of Israel is equivalent to all the other commandments of the Torah put together. Thereupon they returned to the Land of Israel.[4]]

Pisḳa 81

Take heed (to thyself)—this indicates a negative commandment—*lest*—this too indicates a negative commandment—*that thou be not ensnared to follow them*—perhaps you will be drawn after them or become like them, by doing what they do, so that they will become a snare for you—*after that they are destroyed from before thee*—why am I destroying them from before you? So that you might not do as they do, causing others to come and destroy you (also)—*and that thou inquire not after their gods, saying*—you should not say, "Since they go out clad in a toga, so will I go out clad in a toga; since they go out wearing purple, so will I go out wearing purple; since they go out wearing a *tulas,*[1] so will I go out wearing a *tulas*"—*even so will I do likewise* (12:30).

Thou shalt not do so unto the Lord thy God (12:31): The word *so* may apply either to the worship or to the object of worship. Hence the Sages have taught:[2] If one offers to an idol something which is also offered on the altar (of God), he is liable; if he offers on the altar something which is also offered to an idol, he is exempt. If he offers to an idol that which is not offered on the altar, the rule is as follows: if similar things are offered (on the altar), he is liable; if not, he is exempt. You might then think that sin offerings were not to be offered; hence the verse says next, *For every abomination to the Lord, which He hateth, (have they done unto their gods)* (12:31)—(do not offer) that which is hateful and abominable to God. Another interpretation: They (really) intended to offer nothing but what God hates.

For even their sons and (even) their daughters (do they burn) (12:31): This informs me only concerning their sons and daughters; whence do I learn that this applies also to the Canaanites' fathers and mothers? From the expression *even their sons,* not just "their sons", *even their daughters,* not just "their daughters". R. ʿAḳiba said: I myself saw a heathen who tied up his father and left him before his dog, whereupon the animal devoured him.

Pisḳa 82

All this word which I command you—(indicating) that a light commandment should be as precious to you as a weighty one—*that shall ye observe to do*—R. Eliezer ben Jacob says: This adds a negative commandment to every positive commandment uttered in this lesson[1]—*thou shalt not add thereto, nor diminish from it* (13:1): Hence the Sages have said:[2] If (blood) which was to be sprinkled once is mixed with other blood which was also to be sprinkled once, it is to be sprinkled once. Another interpretation: *Thou shalt not add thereto*: Whence do we learn that one may not add anything to the lulaḇ[3] or to the ritual fringe? From the verse, *Thou shalt not add thereto.* Whence do we learn that one may not diminish anything from them? From the verse, *Nor diminish from it.* Whence do we learn that if one has already commenced to recite the priestly blessing he should not say, "Since I have already commenced the blessing, I will go on to say, *The Lord, the God of your fathers, make you a thousand times (so many more as ye are, and bless you)* (1:11)"? From the expression, *this word*—do not add even one word to (anything commanded).

Pisḳa 83

If there arise in the midst of thee a prophet (13:2): Just as Moses used the formula *Thus saith (the Lord)* (Exod. 5:1, etc.), so did the (false) prophets use the same formula. Just as Moses spoke only part and fulfilled only part, so did these (false) prophets speak only part and fulfill only part. Just as Moses used the principle of deducing the general from the particular, and vice versa, so did these (false) prophets use the same principle. Does it then follow that just as Moses was an elder, eighty years of age, and Amram's son, so must all those (false) prophets have been? (No,) for the verse says, *a prophet,* of any kind, (even a false one).[1]

Or a dreamer of dreams (13:2): Since concerning Moses it is said, *With him do I speak mouth to mouth* (Num. 12:8), one might think that this would be the case also with all prophets; hence the verse adds, *Or a dreamer of dreams.*[2]

In the midst of thee—including women—*and he give thee a sign*—in the heavens, as in the verse, *(Let there be lights in the firmament of the heaven . . .) and let them be for signs* (Gen. 1:14)—*or a wonder*

(13:2)—on earth, as in the verse, *If there be dew on the fleece only, and it be dry upon all the ground* (Judg. 6:37), which is followed by, *And God did so* (Judg. 6:40).

Pisḳa 84

And the sign or the wonder come to pass . . .—R. Jose the Galilean said: See how far Scripture goes in that it permits heathens to have power even over sun and moon, stars and planets![1]—*thou shalt not hearken*—to them; why not?—*for the Lord your God putteth you to proof, to know whether ye do love the Lord your God* (13:3–4): Said R. ʿAḳiba: Heaven forbid that God should give the heathens dominion over sun, moon, stars, and planets. Scripture speaks here only of those who were at first true prophets but then lapsed and became false prophets,[2] such as Hananiah ben Azzur.[3]

Thou shalt not hearken unto the words of that prophet—except the one who has repented[4]—*or unto that dreamer of dreams*—except the one suspected retroactively[5]—*for the Lord your God putteth you to proof, to know whether ye do love the Lord* (13:4).

Pisḳa 85

After the Lord your God shall ye walk—this refers to (following the pillar of) cloud—*and Him shall ye fear*—meaning that the awe (of the Lord) shall be upon you—*and His commandments*—referring to positive commandments—*shall ye keep*—including (the implied) negative commandments—*and unto His voice shall ye hearken*—meaning the voice of His prophets[1]—*and Him ye shall serve*—serve Him according to His Torah and in His Sanctuary—*and unto Him shall ye cleave* (13:6)—separate yourselves from idolatry and cleave unto the Lord.

Pisḳa 86

And that prophet—but not one who is acting under compulsion—*or that dreamer of dreams*—but not one who is innocently mistaken—*shall be put to death, because he hath spoken perversion against the Lord your God* (13:6): Is this not a matter of inference from the minor to the major? If one who falsifies the words of his companion is liable to death, so certainly is he who falsifies the words of God.

Who brought you out of the land of Egypt—even if He had no other claim upon you than that He had taken you out of the land of Egypt, that would have been sufficient—*and redeemed thee out of the house of bondage*—even if He had no other claim upon you other than that He had redeemed you from the house of bondage, that would have been sufficient—*to draw thee aside out of the way* (13:6): "Drawing aside" is mentioned both here and elsewhere (13:11); just as the "drawing aside" there is punishable by stoning, so is "drawing aside" here punishable by stoning. R. Simeon, however, says that his execution in this case is by strangulation.[1]

Another interpretation: *To draw thee aside out of the way*—this refers to positive commandments—*which the Lord thy God commanded thee*—this refers to negative commandments—*to walk in*—but not who says (to abandon) part of them and to observe the other part[2]—*so shalt thou put away the evil from the midst of thee* (13:6)—remove the evildoer from Israel.

Piska 87

If thy brother, the son of thy mother . . . entice thee (13:7): Enticement always implies acting in error, as it is said, *Whom Jezebel his wife enticed* (1 Kings 21:25). Others, however, say that enticement always indicates deliberate action, as it is said, *Now therefore, I pray thee, let my lord the king hear the words of his servant. If it be the Lord that hath stirred thee up against me, let Him accept an offering* (1 Sam. 26:19).

From the verse *The fathers shall not be put to death for the children* (24:16) we learn that they may not testify against one another.[1] You might think that just as they cannot testify against one another, so can they not entice one another; hence the verse says, *If thy brother, the son of thy mother (or thy son) . . . entice thee.*

Thy brother—son of your father—*the son of thy mother*—your mother's son[2]—*or thy son*—any son (by whatever woman)—*or thy daughter*—any daughter—*or thy wife*—one betrothed to you—*of thy bosom*—one wedded to you—*or thy friend*—this refers to the proselyte—*that is as thine own soul*—this refers to your father—*(entice thee) secretly*—showing that they speak their words (of enticement) only in secret, as it is said, *In the twilight, in the evening of the day, in the blackness of night and the darkness* (Prov. 7:9), whereas words of Torah are always spoken publicly, as it is said, *Wisdom crieth aloud in the street . . . she calleth at the head of the noisy streets* (Prov. 1:20–21)—*(saying, "Let us go and serve other gods") which thou hast not known, thou, nor thy fathers* (13:7): R. Jose the Galilean says: This is meant as a reproach to Israel—the nations of the world do not abandon the tradition handed over to them by their fathers, but Israel do abandon the tradition handed over to them by their fathers in order to go and worship idols.

Pisḳa 88

Of the gods of the people that are round about you, nigh unto thee, (or far off from thee)—from the ones that are near, you can judge what the ones far away are like[1]—*from the one end of the earth even unto the other end of the earth* (13:8)—this refers to the sun and the moon which revolve from one end of the world to the other.

Pisḳa 89

Thou shalt not consent unto him (13:9): Because of what is said elsewhere, *But thou shalt love thy neighbor as thyself* (Lev. 19:18), you might think you must love this one too; hence the verse says, *Thou shalt not consent unto him, nor hearken unto him.* Because of what is said elsewhere, *Thou shalt surely release it with him* (Exod. 23:5), you might think that you may help him release his beast;[1] hence the verse says, *nor hearken unto him.*

Neither shall thine eye pity him (13:9): Because of what is said elsewhere, *Neither shalt thou stand idly by the blood of thy neighbor* (Lev. 19:16), you might think that you are not permitted to stand idly by while his blood is being shed; hence the verse here says, *neither shall thine eye pity him.*

Neither shalt thou spare—do not seek to justify him—*neither shalt thou conceal him* (13:9): If you know that he is guilty, you are not permitted to keep silent. Whence do we learn that if he is found guilty by the court, he may not be subsequently considered justified? From the (following) verse, *But thou shalt surely kill him* (13:10). If he is cleared (by the court), whence do we learn that he may be subsequently found guilty? From the expression, *surely kill him.*[2]

Thy hand shall be upon him (13:10): The one enticed by him is commanded[3] to kill him. Whence do we learn that if he is not killed by the hand of the enticed, he may be put to death by anyone else? From the following, *And afterwards the hand of all the people* (13:10).

Pisḳa 90

And thou shalt stone him with stones (13:11): You might think that it is to be done with many stones, but elsewhere Scripture says, *With a stone* (Lev. 20:27),[1] from which you might conclude that this means one stone only; hence the verse here says, *with stones,* showing that if he does not die by the first stone, he may be killed by a second one.

Because he has sought to draw thee aside (13:11): Drawing aside is mentioned both here and elsewhere (13:6); just as the drawing aside mentioned here is punishable by stoning, so is the drawing aside elsewhere punishable by stoning.[2]

From the Lord thy God, who brought thee out (of the land of Egypt) (13:11): Even if He had no claim on you other than that He had brought you out of the land of Egypt, from the house of slavery, that would have been sufficient.

Pisḳa 91

And all Israel shall hear, and fear (13:12): [He is to be kept in custody until the festival, and then put to death on the festival day, as it is said, *And all the people shall hear, and fear* (17:13); so taught R. ʿAḳiba. R. Judah, however, says: There must be no delay in execution[1]].

This applies only to this specific instance. Whence do we learn that (this applies) also to the one who (without mentioning other gods) says, "I will worship," "I will go and worship," "Let us go and worship," "I will sacrifice," "I will go and sacrifice," "Let us go and sacrifice," "I will burn incense," "I will go and burn incense," "Let us go and burn incense," "I will offer a libation," "I will go and offer a libation," "Let us go and offer a libation," "I will prostrate myself," "I will go and prostrate myself," "Let us go and prostrate outselves"? From what the verse goes on to say, *And shall do no more any such evil deed as this* (13:12), neither anything like that *deed,* nor as *evil,* nor like *this.* One might think that this includes one who embraces (an idol), kisses it, sprinkles it, bathes it, anoints it, dresses it, shoes it, or wraps it; hence the verse says *this*—for *this* one is to be stoned, but not for the other actions.[2]

Piska 92

If thou shalt hear tell (13:13): [But one need not go searching for it.[1] One might then think that such (information) might be ignored; hence Scripture goes on to say, *Then shalt thou inquire, and make search, and ask diligently* (13:15)—*thou shalt inquire* into what the Torah (prescribes), *and make search* by (examining) the witnesses, *and ask diligently* of the disciples (of the wise)].

Concerning one of thy cities (13:13): One city may be declared condemned, but three cities may not be so declared.[2] One might think that (even) two cities may not (be declared condemned); hence the verse says, *One of thy cities.*[3]

Which the Lord thy God giveth thee—wherever it may be—*to dwell there* (13:13)—excluding Jerusalem, which was not given as a dwelling place.[4]

Piska 93

Certain men are gone out—not women, nor minors,[1] and not fewer than two—*base fellows* (*běne běliyaʿal*)—without the yoke,[2] that is to say, people who have cast off God's yoke—*from the midst of thee*—and not from border areas[3]—*and have drawn away the inhabitants of their city*—and not the inhabitants of another city—*saying*—(indicating that) a warning (is required)[4]—*Let us go and serve other gods which ye have not known* (13:14).

Then shalt thou inquire, and make search, and ask diligently (13:15): As it is said, *And it be told thee, and thou hear it, then shalt thou inquire diligently* (17:4). The word *diligently* used in both verses indicates an analogy,[5] showing that we must examine the witness with seven examinations. Whence do we learn that we must also cross-examine him?[6] From the following, *And behold, if it be truth, and the thing certain* (13:15). If in any case we are going to cross-examine eventually, why does the verse say *inquire*? In the case of inquiries, if even one (witness) says, "I do not know," the testimony of all witnesses is nullified. In the case of cross-examinations, if one witness—or even two—says, "I do not know," their testimony stands. In both inquiry and cross-examination, if the witnesses flatly contradict each other, their testimony is nullified.

That such abomination is wrought (in the midst of thee) (13:15): To include proselytes and manumitted slaves.[7]

Pisḳa 94

Thou shalt surely smite (13:16): Whence do we learn that if you cannot slay the offender in the manner prescribed here, you may slay him in some other statutory manner, whether prescribed for lesser or greater offenses? From the verse, *Thou shalt surely smite.*[1] Whence do we learn that even if he has escaped my hand he shall not escape yours? From the expression, *Thou shalt surely smite.*[2]

The inhabitants of that city (13:16): [Hence the Sages have said: Even children may not be spared.[3] Abba Ḥanan, however, says: *The fathers shall not be put to death for the children, neither shall the children be put to death for the fathers* (24:16)—this verse refers to the condemned city].

Thou shalt surely smite the inhabitants of that city—not the inhabitants of any other city; hence the Sages have said: A passing caravan of asses or camels saves (the condemned city)[4]—*with the edge of the sword*—with the blade of the sword, so as not to disfigure them[5]—*destroying it utterly*—with the exception of such possessions of the righteous as are outside the city—*and all that is therein*—including such possessions of the righteous as are within the city; hence the Sages have said: Such possessions of the righteous as are within the city are to be destroyed, whereas such as are outside of it are to be spared;[6] (all possessions) of wicked persons, however, are to be destroyed, whether they are within the city or outside of it—*and the cattle thereof* (13:16)—except consecrated cattle.

Pisḳa 95

[*And thou shalt gather*] *all the spoil of it*—this includes also the possessions of the wicked that are outside of it—*into the midst of the broad place thereof* (13:17): If it does not have such a broad place, one is to be made for it.[1] If the broad place is outside of the city, whence do we learn that it may be included within the city? From the following, *Into the midst of the broad place thereof.*

And shalt burn with fire the city, and all the spoil thereof (13:17): But not the spoil of heaven.[2] [Hence the Sages have said: Trees rooted (in the soil) are permitted, but uprooted ones are forbidden; wells, ditches, caves, and Holy Scriptures are permitted, since Scripture says, *The spoil thereof,* thus excluding the spoil of heaven.[3] Another interpretation: *The spoil thereof*: Thus excluding the spoil of heaven.] Hence the Sages have said: Sanctified objects within it are to be redeemed; heave offerings are to be left to rot; second tithe and Holy Scriptures are to be hidden away.[4]

Every whit unto the Lord thy God; and it shall be a heap for ever (13:17): Similarly Scripture says, *And Joshua charged the people with an oath at that time, saying: Cursed be the man before the Lord that riseth up and buildeth this city, even Jericho*—do we not know already that its name was Jericho? Rather, this indicates that they may not rebuild it and call it by another name, nor may they build another city and call it Jericho—*with the loss of his first-born shall he lay the foundation thereof, and with the loss of his youngest son shall he set up the gate of it* (Josh. 6:26). You might think that this applies also to one who does it unwittingly; hence Scripture says elsewhere, *According to the word of the Lord, which He spoke by the hand of Joshua the son of Nun* (1 Kings 16:34), indicating that from that time on anyone who does so does it deliberately.[5]

Pisḳa 96

[*It shall not be built again* (13:17): Do not even turn it into fruit or pleasure gardens, not even cotes for Herodian doves; so said R. ʿAḳiba.][1]

And there shall cleave naught of the devoted thing to thy hand (13:18): Hence the Sages have said: If one takes a stick, a fork, a whorl (turning stick), or a staff, no benefit may be derived from them. If these are mixed with other things, no benefit may be derived from all of them. What then should be done with them? Their value (in coins) should be cast into the Dead Sea.[2] The general rule is that one who benefits from objects of idolatry must cast their value (in coins) into the Dead Sea.

That the Lord may turn from the fierceness of His anger—as long as idolatry exists in the world, fierce anger exists in the world; once idolatry is removed from the world, fierce anger will be removed from the world—*and show thee mercy, and have compassion upon thee*—mercy for you but not for others;[3] hence Rabban Gamaliel be-Rabbi used to say: Whenever you show mercy to others, mercy is shown to you from heaven; when you show no mercy to others, no mercy will be shown to you from heaven[4]—*and multiply thee*—as it is said, *And I will multiply thy seed as the stars of heaven* (Gen. 26:4)—*as He hath sworn unto thy fathers* (13:18)—all for the sake of the merit of your fathers.[5]

When thou shalt hearken to the voice of the Lord thy God—hence the Sages have said: If a person begins by listening to a little, in the end he will hear a great deal[6]—*to keep all His commandments which I command thee this day*—so that a minor commandment should be as precious to you as a major one—*to do that which is right in the eyes of the Lord thy God* (13:19)—this is what R. Ishmael meant when he said: (Do) what is right in the eyes of heaven.[7]

Ye are the children of the Lord your God (14:1): R. Judah says: If you conduct yourselves like (dutiful) children, you are His children; if not, you are not His children. R. Meir, however, says: In either case, *Ye are the children of the Lord your God.*[8] Similarly Scripture says, *Yet the number of the children of Israel (shall be as the sand of the sea, which cannot be measured nor numbered; and it shall come to pass, that instead of that which was said unto them: "Ye are not My people," it shall be said unto them, "Ye are the children of the living God")*[9] (Hos. 2:1).

Ye shall not cut yourselves (*tiṯgoḏĕḏu*) (14:1): Do not split yourselves up into several factions (*ʾăḡuddoṯ*) but rather be one faction, as it is said, *It is He that buildeth His upper chambers in the heaven, and hath founded His (single) vault* (*ʾăḡuddaṯo*) *upon the earth* (Amos 9:6).[10]

Another interpretation: *Ye shall not cut yourselves*—you shall not cut yourselves in the same manner as others cut themselves, as it is said, *And they (the prophets of Baal) cut themselves after their manner*[11] (1 Kings 18:28)—*nor make any baldness (between your eyes for the dead)* (14:1): You might think that one is liable only for cutting between his eyes. Whence do we learn that any part of the head is included (in this prohibition)? From the verse, *(They shall not make baldness) upon their head* (Lev. 21:5), meaning upon any part of the head. You might think that since Scripture has imposed upon the priests many additional commandments, they alone are liable for every sort of baldness on any part of the head as well as between the eyes, and that Israelites, upon whom Scripture did not impose any additional commandments, are liable only once[12] and only for the baldness between the eyes; hence Scripture states: *baldness* (here) and *baldness* (there) (Lev. 21:5), indicating an analogy[13]—just as priests are liable for every act of making baldness anywhere on the head as well as between the eyes, so are Israelites liable for every act of making baldness anywhere on the head as well as between the eyes; and just as Israelites are liable only for (making) baldness (as a mark of mourning) for the dead, so are priests liable for (making) baldness only for the dead.

Piṣka 97

For thou art a holy people unto the Lord thy God (14:2): That is to say, you must make yourself holy. [*For thou art a holy people unto the Lord thy God:* The (divine) holiness that rests upon you has made you holy.[1] Another interpretation: Do not cause any other people to become as holy as you are. *And the Lord hath chosen thee* (14:2): (As it is said,) *For the Lord hath chosen Jacob unto Himself*—to be His treasured people—*and Israel for His own treasure* (Ps. 135:4).]

And the Lord hath chosen thee to be His own treasure, out of all peoples that are on the face of the earth (14:2): Hence we learn that each individual (Israelite) is more precious to the Holy One, blessed be He, than all the nations of the world.[2] You might think that this means more precious than the early patriarchs;[3] hence the verse says, *Out of all peoples that are on the face of the earth*—say, then, more precious than those who were before them and those who were after them, but not the early patriarchs themselves.

Piṣka 98

[*And every beast that parteth the hoof, and hath the hoof wholly cloven in two, and cheweth the cud* (14:6): Unless it has these three marks, it may not be eaten. Abba Ḥanan says in the name of R. Eliezer: *Šĕsuʿah* (*cheweth the cud*) is the name of an animal.[1]

R. Josiah said: Wherever Scripture says *bird* (*ṣippor*), it implies a clean bird. R. Isaac, however, says, A clean fowl is called either *fowl* (*ʿof*) or *bird*; unclean fowl is termed only *fowl*.[2]

And the glede (*raʾah*) (14:13): This is the same as the *dayyah* ("kite")[3] (14:13). All of them are varieties of the kite. Isi ben Judah says: There are a hundred species of fowl in the east, and all of them are varieties of the kite.

The kite, the glede, the *dayyah* and the *daʾah*—why are they specified in Deuteronomy? The beasts are specified because of the *šĕsuʿah,* and the fowls because of the *dayyah.*][4]

Pisḳa 99

Thou shalt not eat any abominable thing (14:3): R. Eliezer says: Whence do we learn that he who slits the ear of a first-born animal and eats of it, is violating a negative commandment? From the verse, *Thou shalt not eat any abominable thing.*[1] Others say that this applies only to consecrated animals which have become unfit, since Scripture says here *abominable thing,* and says again elsewhere, *Thou shalt not sacrifice unto the Lord thy God an ox, or a sheep, (wherein is a blemish) . . . for that is an abomination unto the Lord thy God* (17:1)—just as the abominable thing spoken of in the latter verse refers to consecrated animals that have become unfit, so does the abominable thing spoken of in the former verse refer to consecrated animals that have become unfit.

Pisḳa 100

These are the animals which ye may eat: the ox, the sheep, and the goat, the hart, and the gazelle, and the roebuck (14:4–5): Hence we learn that wild beasts are included with domestic animals. Whence do we learn that (by the same token) domestic animals are included with wild beasts? From the verse, *These are the beasts (which ye may eat among all the animals that are on the earth)* (Lev. 11:2), which shows that a beast is called an animal and an animal is called a beast, and that there are more unclean animals than clean ones, since in every instance Scripture itemizes the fewer kind, since it says in this instance, *These are the beasts which ye may eat . . . the hart, and the gazelle, and the roebuck, (and the wild goat,* etc.) (14:4–5).[1]

And the antelope (*te᾽o*) (14:5): R. Jose says: This is rather the wild ox.

Pisḳa 101

And every animal that parteth the hoof (14:6): Since we find that the law of unclean animals has been applied to laymen and not confined to sacred use alone,[1] let me also declare as forbidden for food those that are forbidden to men for other purposes. And which are they? The ox and the ass that are used for plowing together. But the verse states, *The ox, the sheep, and the goat . . . ye may eat* (14:4,6). Even if I add these,[2] I still do not know whether or not to include (as permitted) the animal used in active or passive bestiality, one set aside or actually used for idolatrous worship, a harlot's hire, the price of a dog, a hybrid, one torn in the field, or one born by way of Caesarean section;[3] therefore the verse states, *The ox, the sheep, and the goat,* etc.[4] Again, Even if I add these, I still do not know whether or not to permit an animal used in commission of some transgression and attested by only one witness or by its owner alone; therefore the verse states, *The ox, the sheep, and the goat,* etc. If I permit these, I still do not know whether or not to include an animal used in commission of some crime and attested by two witnesses, but whose trial has not been completed; therefore the verse says, *The ox, the sheep, and the goat . . . you may eat.* Even if I permit these that had grown up in cleanness, I still do not know whether or not to include a clean animal that was suckled by an unclean animal; therefore the verse states, *Among the animals* (14:6). Even if I add the permitted animal that was suckled by an unclean animal, I still do not know whether or not to include the unclean animal that was suckled by a clean animal together with an unclean animal; therefore the verse says, *Among the animals,* (indicating) any (fit) animal.[5]

Among the animals, that ye may eat (14:6): This includes the placenta. You might think that this applies even if only part of it has emerged; hence the verse goes on to say, *That*[6] *ye may eat* (14:6). Moreover, *that* may be eaten, but not an unclean animal. But this is no more than a positive commandment. Whence do I learn that an unclean animal is forbidden also by a negative commandment?[7]

From the verse, *The camel, and the hare, and the rock-badger . . . and the swine . . . of their flesh ye shall not eat* (14:7–8). This informs me only about (the prohibition of) these particular animals; whence do I learn that (this applies also to) all other unclean animals? It is a matter of logical conclusion: if the aforementioned particular animals are prohibited by a negative commandment even though they have some of the marks of clean animals, should not other unclean animals which do not have such marks of cleanness be likewise prohibited by the same negative commandment as regards the consumption of them? Hence the camel, the hare, the rock-badger, and the swine are expressly prohibited by Scripture, while other unclean animals (are prohibited) by an inference from the minor to the major. Thus the positive commandment governing these animals is found in Scripture, while the pertinent negative commandment is derived by logical inference.

Pisḳa 102

Nevertheless these ye shall not eat of them that only chew the cud, etc. (14:7): R. ʿAḳiba said: Was Moses a hunter or an archer? This is the answer to those who assert that the Torah is not from heaven.[1]

Pisḳa 103

Of all clean birds ye may eat (14:11): Since Scripture says, *Then shall the priest command to take for him that is to be cleansed two living clean birds* (Lev. 14:4), one might think that just as the slaughtered bird is forbidden,[1] so is the released mother-bird forbidden;[2] hence the verse says, *Of all clean birds ye may eat.*[3] Or (should one think that) just as the released mother-bird is permitted (for consumption later on), so should the slaughtered bird[4] be permitted (for consumption)? (Not so, for) Scripture goes on to say, *These are they of which ye shall not eat*[5]: *the great vulture, and the bearded vulture, and the osprey* (14:12).

R. ʿAḳiba says: Here we read *the great vulture* and elsewhere we read *the great vulture* (Lev. 11:13)—just as *the great vulture* in the latter verse includes all other birds mentioned with it in the prohibition of letting both others eat of it and oneself eat of it, so does *the great vulture* in the former verse also include all the other birds mentioned with it in the same prohibition. R. Simeon says: Here we read *ʾayyah* (*falcon*) (14:3) and elsewhere we read *ʾayyah* (Lev. 11:14)—just as the *ʾayyah* spoken of here includes the *raʾah* (*glede*) (14:13), so does the *ʾayyah* spoken of there also include the *raʾah*.[6]

Raven—this is the giant raven—*And every raven*—this includes the raven of the valleys and the raven that flies ahead of the doves—*after its kinds*—including the starling—[(*and*) *the hawk*—this is the (common) hawk—] *after its kinds* (14:14–15)—including the *ben horayah*.[7]

And the ostrich, etc., *the little owl,* etc., *and the pelican, and the carrion vulture, and the cormorant* (14:15–17): Hence we learn that clean birds are more numerous than unclean ones, for in each instance Scripture itemizes the fewer kind.[8] The distinguishing marks of domestic and wild animals are stated in the Torah, whereas the distinguishing marks of birds are not stated there. Hence the Sages have said: All birds of prey are unclean, as it is said, *the great vulture* (14:12)—just as the great vulture clearly has neither crop nor extra toe, has a craw that cannot be peeled, is a bird of prey, eats unclean things, (and is therefore forbidden), so is any other bird that shares these marks forbidden, while those that do not share them are permitted.[9]

Of all clean winged things ye may eat (14:20)—this is a positive commandment—*and all winged swarming things are unclean to you* (14:19)—this is a negative commandment. R. Simeon says: *Of all clean winged things ye may eat*—this refers to clean locusts; *and all winged swarming things are unclean to you; they shall not be eaten*—this refers to unclean locusts.

Piska 104

Ye shall not eat of any thing that dieth of itself (14:21): This informs me only about that which has died of itself. Whence do we learn that this applies also to that which has been torn (by beasts of prey)? From the expression *Any thing that dieth of itself*—any animal that has died of itself.[1]

(Thou mayest give it) unto the stranger that is within thy gates (14:21): Hence we learn that it may be given as a gift to a resident alien. Whence do we learn that it may be given also to a (nonresident)

foreigner? From the following *(Or thou mayest sell it) unto a foreigner* (14:21). Whence do we learn that it may be sold to a resident alien as well? From the expression *Or thou mayest sell it.*[2] Whence do we learn that the preceding *(Thou mayest give it)* applies also to the foreigner? From the expression *Or unto a foreigner*—whichever one you find, you may sell it or give it as a gift to him, foreigner or resident alien.[3] R. Judah, however, says: The rule is (to be understood) as written.[4]

For thou art a holy people unto the Lord thy God (14:21): (Therefore) make yourself holy. [Permitted things that are customarily used by others are forbidden (to you), and you may not act as if they were permitted.

Thou shalt not seethe a kid in its mother's milk (14:21): Why was this said?[5] In order to refer to the three convenants that the Holy One, blessed be He, had made with Israel, on three occasions: once at Horeb, another time in the Plain of Moab, and a third time on Mount Gerizim and Mount Ebal.] R. ʿAḳiba says: (The prohibition of mixing milk and meat in the case of) beasts and fowls is not from the Torah, which says only, *Thou shalt not seethe a kid in its mother's milk*—this is stated three times to exclude beasts, fowls, and unclean animals.[6] R. Jose the Galilean says:[7] Scripture says, *Ye shall not eat of any thing that dieth of itself* and *Thou shalt not seethe a kid in its mother's milk*—[what is forbidden when it dies of itself is forbidden to be seethed in milk. Is it to be inferred that fowl which is forbidden when it dies of itself is likewise forbidden to be seethed in milk? (No,) since the verse specifies *in its mother's milk,*][8] thus excluding fowl, which has no mother's milk.

Pisḳa 105

Thou shalt surely tithe all the increase of thy seed, that which is brought forth in the field year by year (14:22): Hence we learn that one may not tithe from one year for (the crops of) another year.[1] This (seemingly) applies only to second tithe,[2] which is the one spoken of in this passage. Whence do we learn that this applies also to the other tithes? From the expression *Thou shalt surely tithe.*[3] Whence do we learn that in the case of animals also one may not tithe from one year for another? From the verse, *Thou shalt surely tithe all the increase of thy seed,*[4] *that which is brought forth in the field year by year.* R. Simeon ben Judah says in the name of R. Simeon: Whence do we learn that one is commanded to give actively[5] a tithe of his animals? From the expression, *Thou shalt surely tithe.* One might think that even such things growing out of the soil[6] as woad[7] or thorns are also subject to tithing; therefore Scripture says, *Thou shalt surely tithe . . . and thou shalt eat* (14:23).[8] Since one might think that this applies to honey and milk[9] as well, the verse specifies, *That which is brought forth in the field year by year,* showing that this covers only products of the field itself.

From the verse, *And thou shalt eat before the Lord thy God, in the place which He shall choose to cause His name to dwell there, the tithe of thy corn, of thy wine, and of thine oil* (14:23), one might conclude that only corn, wine, and oil are subject to tithing. Whence do we learn that all other produce is to be included? From the expression, *The increase of thy seed.* One might say that if this is so, I would say that since such produce is distinct in that it can be stored and is customarily consumed in its natural state, I will include nothing (as liable to tithing) but that which shares these characteristics. What would I therefore include? Rice, millet, poppy seed, and sesame. Whence do we learn that this includes also other legumes? From the expression *Thou shalt surely tithe.* Having included legumes which are customarily consumed in their natural state, I still have not included lupine and mustard, which are not customarily consumed in their natural state. Therefore (I deduce their inclusion from) the expression *Thou shalt surely tithe.* One might further think that this applies even if they have not yet taken root;[10] therefore the verse states, *And thou shalt eat.* Whence do we learn that herbs are also liable to tithing? From the verse, *And all the tithe of the land* (Lev. 27:30), followed by *(whether) of the seed of the land,* which includes garlic, garden cress, and garden rock.[11] I might include also turnips, radishes, and such garden seeds as are not eaten; therefore the verse states *Of the seed of the land* (Lev. 27:30), and not "all the seed of the land." *(Or) of the fruit of the tree* (Lev. 27:30) includes the (edible) fruit of trees. I might think that this includes the pod of the sycamore, the pod of the Zalmonah tree, and the pod of the Gederah tree[12] that are not edible; therefore the verse states *(Or) of the fruit of the tree,* and not "all the fruit of the tree." Whence do we learn that one must tithe everything edible? From the expression *Thou shalt surely tithe.* One might think that this applies also to produce that has not yet completed its growth in the field; therefore Scripture says, *As though it were the corn of the threshing floor*—which is already (fully grown) in the field—*and as the fullness of the winepress* (Num. 18:27)—not until it is already in the winepress. One might think that he may eat of such incidentally in the field (without tithing); therefore the verse states, *Thou shalt surely tithe.*[13] Whence do we learn that if the produce is meant to be used as seed it must also be tithed? From the following, *That which is brought forth in the field.* Whence do we learn that this applies also to stored produce? From the expression *The increase of thy seed.* The Sages said: The (produce) stores of the children of Hanan were destroyed three years before the rest of the Land of Israel because they failed to set aside tithes from their produce, for they interpreted *Thou shalt surely tithe . . . and thou shalt eat* as excluding the seller, and *The increase of thy seed* as excluding the buyer.[14]

Piska 106

And thou shalt eat before the Lord thy God, in the place which He shall choose (14:23): R. Jose transmitted three interpretations[1] in the names of three elders: R. ʿAḳiba says: One might think that he may import firstlings from outside the Land (of Israel) to the Land; therefore the verse states, *And thou shalt eat before the Lord thy God, in the place which He shall choose (to cause His name to dwell there, the tithe of thy corn, of thy wine, and of thine oil, and the firstlings of thy herd and of thy flock)* (14:23)—from the place whence you may bring the tithe of corn, you may also bring firstlings; from outside the Land, whence you may not bring the tithe of corn, you may not bring firstlings.[2]

Simeon ben Zoma[3] says: One might think that just as the Torah has made a distinction between consecrated offerings of greater sanctity and those of lesser sanctity,[4] so has the Torah made a distinction between firstlings and second tithe. Hence, if you argue that since a firstling must be brought to the holy place and the second tithe must be brought to the holy place, therefore, just as a firstling may be consumed only within (Jerusalem's) wall, so may second tithe be consumed only within that wall, (one can counter that) the place of consuming the firstlings has been limited because the time for consuming it has been limited, whereas in the case of second tithe the time for consuming it has been expanded; therefore, since the time for consuming second tithe has been expanded, the place for consuming it should also be expanded. (To answer this reasoning) the verse states, *And thou shalt eat before the Lord thy God, in the place which He shall choose*—just as the firstling may be consumed only within (Jerusalem's) wall, so second tithe may be consumed only within that wall.[5]

R. Ishmael says: One might think that at this time[6] also he may bring second tithe to Jerusalem and consume it there. Hence the rule should be that firstlings must be brought to the (holy) place and so should second tithe be brought to the (holy) place; therefore, just as a firstling may be consumed only while the Temple is standing, so may second tithe be consumed only while the Temple is standing. Should you counter that a firstling's blood and portions of fat must be placed on the altar, whereas second tithe has no blood or portions of fat to be placed on the altar;[7] the case of first fruits proves the contrary,[8] for they too have no blood or portions of fat to be placed on the altar, and yet they may be consumed only while the Temple is standing. Should you counter further that while first fruits must indeed be brought before the altar, how can the same rules apply to second tithe, seeing that it does not have to be brought before the altar? (To answer this) the verse states, *And thou shalt eat before the Lord thy God in the place which He shall choose,*[9] thus drawing an analogy between the consumption of the firstling and that of second tithe: just as the firstling may be consumed only while the Temple is standing, so second tithe may be consumed only while the Temple is standing.

Others say: One might think that a firstling whose time has passed from one year to the next should be disqualified[10] in the same way as disqualified consecrated offerings;[11] therefore the verse states, *And thou shalt eat before the Lord thy God.*[12] If (the intent of this phrase is) to imply that the firstling must be consumed within the (Temple) wall, it is superfluous, since Scripture elsewhere states, *Thou shalt eat it before the Lord thy God (year by year in the place which the Lord shall choose)* (15:20)—why then say here again, *And thou shalt eat before the Lord thy God?* If (the intent of this phrase is) to imply that second tithe must be eaten within the (Temple) wall,[13] it is again superfluous, since it is stated elsewhere, *Thou mayest not eat within thy gates (the tithe of thy corn)* (12:17)—why then say here *And thou shalt eat before the Lord thy God*? (The answer is,) to draw an analogy between the firstling and second tithe—just as second tithe of one year may be consumed in the next year, so may the firstling of one year be consumed in the next year.

That thou mayest learn to fear the Lord thy God—hence we learn that tithing leads one to study of Torah[14]—*always* (14:23)—whether one is in the Land (of Israel) or outside of it.[15]

Pisḳa 107

And if the way be too long for thee (14:24): One might think that Scripture is referring to the duration (of travel); therefore the verse goes on to explain, *Because the place is too far from thee*—thus making clear that it speaks of distance being too far and not of duration being too long. Now this obviously refers only to long duration; but what about short duration (of travel)? The answer is supplied by the phrase in the same verse, *So that thou art not able to carry it.*[1] Now this obviously refers only to a poor man;[2] whence do we learn the rule for a rich man? From another phrase in the same verse, *When the Lord thy God shall bless thee.*[3]

Then shalt thou turn it into money (14:25): Hence we learn that tithe may be redeemed only with silver money.[4] Whence do we learn that other coins may be used as well as silver ones? One might argue that since both property dedicated to the Temple and second tithe may be redeemed, and since in the case of dedicated property other coins may be used as well as silver ones, so also in the case of second tithe other coins may be used as well as silver ones.[5] (One could counter) that in the case of dedicated property not only other coins may be used as well as silver ones, but also movable property, whereas this is not so in the case of second tithe, where movable property may not be used in lieu of silver. Therefore the same verse goes on to say, *And bind up* (*wĕ-ṣarta*) *the money (in thy hand)* (14:25): (Meaning) the kind of money that is usually bound up;[6] so taught R. Ishmael.[7] R. ʿAḳiba, however, says: *Wĕ-ṣarta* means something which has a figure on it,[8] excluding the *asimon,*[9] which has no figure on it.

In thy hand—excluding that which has gone out of your possession[10]—*and shalt go unto the place which the Lord thy God shall choose* (14:25)—referring to Shiloh and to the Temple.[11]

And thou shalt bestow the money for whatsoever thy soul desireth (14:26): R. Judah says: One might think that if that which was purchased with this tithe money has become defiled, it too may be redeemed,[12] and the rule should be that since second tithe itself may be redeemed if it becomes defiled,[13] that which has been purchased with tithe money, if it too becomes defiled, might surely be redeemed. Therefore the verse says expressly *money,*[14] meaning only the first money and not also the second money. This obviously refers only to clean money. Whence do we learn that the same applies also to defiled money? From the same term *money,* meaning the first money and not the second money. [Three kinds of money are discussed here: money realized from clean tithe, money realized from defiled tithe, and goods purchased with tithe money.]

For whatsoever thy soul desireth (14:26): One might think (that this money may be used to purchase) male or female slaves, or land; hence the verse goes on to say, *For oxen or for sheep,*[15] which refers only to what is eaten. Whence do we learn that this applies also to what is drunk? From the following *Or for wine, or for strong drink.* All this covers only food and drink; what about things that improve (the flavor of) food and drink, such as costus root, amomum, heads of spices, crowfoot root, asafetida, peppers, and saffron lozenges? The same verse goes on to state, *Or for whatsoever thy soul asketh of thee.* One might think that this includes even water and salt; therefore the verse specifies, *For oxen, or for sheep, or for wine, or for strong drink*—just as these are distinct as being the product of produce and as nourished out of the soil, so only those things which are the product of produce and are nourished out of the soil are permitted. Ben Bag-Bag says: *For oxen*—you may purchase a cow together with her hide—*or for sheep*—a ewe together with her wool—*or for wine*—the jar of wine together with its decanter—*or for strong drink*—together with the fermented pressed grapes.[16] One might think that he may purchase an animal also for his son's feast, but we can reason otherwise, since rejoicing is mentioned here (14:26) and rejoicing is mentioned elsewhere (27:6–7). Just as the rejoicing mentioned there refers to peace offerings, so the rejoicing mentioned here must refer to peace offerings.[17] Perhaps just as the rejoicing mentioned there refers to burnt offerings[18] as well as peace offerings, so the rejoicing mentioned here must refer to both burnt offerings and peace offerings? Therefore the same verse states, *And thou shalt eat . . . and thou shalt rejoice,* meaning rejoicing combined with eating, thus excluding burnt offerings which do not involve eating.

Pisḳa 108

And the Levite that is within thy gates—wherever you find mention of the Levite, the intent is to instruct you to give him his portion; if he has no portion (due to him), give him of the poor man's tithe; if he has no (part of the) poor man's tithe, give him of the peace offerings; if he has no (part of the) peace offerings, give him sustenance out of charity funds—*for he hath no portion nor inheritance with thee* (14:27)—this explains the cause (of this law).[1]

Piska 109

At the end of every three years (14:28): One might think that this refers to the festival (of Tabernacles); therefore Scripture says elsewhere, *When thou hast made an end of tithing* (26:12).[1] But might *When thou hast made an end of tithing* refer to Hanukkah?[2] (No,) for this verse (14:28) says *end* and a later verse (31:10) also says *end* (meaning that), just as *end* there (31:10) refers to a pilgrim festival, so does *end* here (14:28) refer to a pilgrim festival. Or does this mean that just as *end* there (15:1) refers to the festival of Tabernacles, so does *end* here (14:28) refer to the festival of Tabernacles? (No,) for the verse there states, *When thou hast made an end of tithing,* meaning the festival when the tithes are concluded, which is Passover. Hence the Sages have said:[3] On the eve of the last day of the Passover festival, in the fourth and seventh years, removal (of the past tithes) took place: in the fourth year, because of the poor man's tithe of the third year, and in the seventh year, because of the second tithe of the sixth year. One might think that (the produce of) the seventh year should also be liable to tithing; therefore the verse goes on to say, *Which is the year of tithing* (26:12), meaning the year which is liable to tithing,[4] thus excluding the seventh year which is not liable to tithing. One might think that two tithes must be set aside in the third year; hence the verse (26:12) states, *The year of tithing*—only one tithe must be set aside in that year, not two.[5] This obviously refers to none but the poor man's tithe,[6] which is the subject of this verse. Whence do we learn that the other tithes are also to be included? From the verse, *(All) the tithe of thine increase* (14:28), which includes (the tithing of the entire increase).

Even in the same year, thou shalt bring forth all the tithe of thine increase (14:28): Hence we learn that it may be brought out of an unclean place[7] into a clean place.[8] One might think that tithe of the other years may also be brought out of an unclean place into a clean place; therefore the verse states, *Even in the same year*—you may bring out the tithe of that year, but not that of other years, out of an unclean place into a clean place. You may remove (the tithe) of that same year but not the (tithe) out of herbs that came out between New Year's Day and Passover.[9]

And shalt lay it up within thy gates (14:28): If there is no poor man on hand there, store it in a granary. This leaves me in doubt as to which tithe is to be postponed, the first or the second; therefore the next verse states, *And the Levite, because he hath no portion or inheritance (with thee . . . shall come)* (14:29): Let the Levite come and take his portion in any case; so taught R. Judah.[10] R. Eliezer ben Jacob, however, says: Not necessarily, for Scripture says elsewhere, *And unto the children of Levi, behold, I have given all the tithe in Israel for an inheritance* (Num. 18:21)—just as an inheritance cannot move, so cannot first tithe move.[11] One might think that gleanings, forgotten sheaves, and corner crop are also liable to tithe; therefore the verse states, *And the Levite, because he hath no portion or inheritance with thee, and the stranger, and the fatherless . . . (shall come)*—those things in which he has no portion or inheritance with you, you must give him, thus excluding those things in which he does have a portion and an inheritance with you.

Pisḳa 110

And the stranger, and the fatherless, and the widow, that are within thy gates (14:29): One might think that this means whether or not they are in need.[1] Do not be astonished,[2] for Scripture states elsewhere, *(Thou shalt not pervert the justice due to the stranger, or to the fatherless): nor take the widow's raiment to pledge* (24:17)—(seemingly) meaning whether she be rich or poor. Therefore another Scriptural verse states (expressly), *(Thou shalt leave them) for the poor* (Lev. 19:10)[3]—just as *the poor* here means the needy, so all of these persons must be needy (in order to be eligible). One might think that it applies equally to those who are members of the covenant and to those who are not;[4] therefore the verse includes *the Levite* (14:29)—just as the Levite is a member of the covenant, so all of them must be members of the covenant.

And shall eat and be satisfied (14:29): Give them enough to satisfy them. Hence the Sages have said:[5] One may not give the poor less than half a *ḳab̲* of wheat or one *ḳab̲* of barley from the threshing floor.

That are within thy gates (14:29): Hence we learn that the poor man may not be taken outside of the (Holy) Land.[6] It is said that when the family of the house of Nebalṭa was living in Jerusalem, they were given six hundred talents of gold in order to induce them not to leave Jerusalem.[7]

Pisḳa 111

At the end of every seven years (15:1): You might think that this could be counting either from the beginning of the year or from the conclusion of it;[1] but since *end* is stated here and *end* is stated (in the same context) elsewhere (31:10), you must conclude that just as *end* there refers to the end (of the year)[2] and not to the beginning, so *end* here refers to the end (of the year) and not to the beginning.

Thou shalt make a release. . . . shall release (15:1–2): As long as release (of land) is in force so is release of (money).[3]

Seven years: You might ask whether the count of seven years may differ in the case of each person, and you might reply that since in the case of both land and loan one is required to perform release after seven years, then just as the seven years mentioned in connection with land refer to uniform counting for everyone, so the seven years mentioned in connection with a loan must refer to one uniform counting for everyone. Or one might say that since in both the case of a Hebrew slave and the case of a loan one is required to perform release after seven years,[4] and since the count of seven years mentioned in connection with the Hebrew slave is different in the case of each slave, so the count of seven years mentioned in connection with a loan should be different for each person. Let us see which case[5] resembles that of a loan: If we are to draw conclusions concerning something which is not dependent upon the law of Jubilee[6] from something else which is likewise not dependent upon that law, then the law affecting the Hebrew slave proves nothing, since his release is dependent upon the Jubilee. Or if we are to draw conclusions concerning something practiced both in the (Holy) Land and outside of it[7] from something which is likewise practiced both in the (Holy) Land and outside of it, then the release of land proves nothing, since it is obligatory only in the (Holy) Land. That is why Scripture mentions seven years twice,[8] indicating an analogy: just as the count of seven years mentioned in connection with release must be uniform for everyone, so the count of seven years mentioned in connection with a loan must be uniform for everyone. R. Jose the Galilean says: Scripture says, *The seventh year, the year of release is at hand* (15:9)—if the count of seven years may be different for each person, how can it be at hand? Hence you must admit that it must mean the same count of seven years for everyone. One might think that the release of loans was practiced already in the wilderness;[9] hence the verse states, *Thou shalt make a release. . . . shall release.*[10] Or does Scripture mean by *Thou shalt make a release. . . . shall release* that in the Land of Israel, where you must release land, you must also release loans, whereas outside of the Land, where you need not release land, you need not release loans? (No,) for the next verse states, *Because the Lord's release hath been proclaimed* (15:2)—both in the (Holy) Land and outside of it.[11]

Piska 112

And this is the manner of the release (15:2): Hence the Sages have said:[1] If the debtor attempts to repay the debt in the seventh year, the creditor should say to him, "I release you." If the debtor retorts, "Nevertheless, (I insist on repaying it,)" the creditor may accept the repayment from him, as it is said, *And this is the manner of the release.*[2]

[*And this is the manner of the release*:] The Sabbatical year releases loans, but the Jubilee year does not. One might have reasoned that since the Sabbatical year, which does not release slaves, releases loans, should not the Jubilee year, which does release slaves, certainly release loans? Therefore the verse states, *And this is the manner of the release*—the Sabbatical year does release loans, but the Jubilee year does not. Again, one might reason from the minor to the major about the Sabbatical year releasing slaves: if the Jubilee year, which does not release loans, does free slaves, should not the Sabbatical year, which does release loans, surely free slaves? Therefore Scripture says elsewhere, *In this year of Jubilee* (Lev. 25:13)—the Sabbatical year releases loans, while the Jubilee year frees slaves.[3]

Every creditor shall release (15:2): One might think that this applies also to stolen or deposited property; therefore the verse goes on to say, *That which he hath lent*. Or *that which he hath lent* might (be thought to) include the wages of a hired laborer or store debts; therefore the verse goes on to say, *Lent to his neighbor* (15:2). But since we were eventually to include all of them in any case,[4] why does the verse state *that which he hath lent?* Just as a loan represents an obligation, so do wages and store debts represent obligations.

He shall not exact it—imposing upon the creditor a negative commandment—*of his neighbor*—excluding others[5]—*and his brother*—excluding the resident alien—*because the land's release hath been proclaimed* (15:2)—whether in the (Holy) Land or outside of it.[6]

Pisḳa 113

Of a foreigner thou mayest exact it—this is a positive commandment—*but whatever of thine is with thy brother*—and not whatever of your brother's is in your hand; hence you conclude that a loan secured by a pledge need not be released[1]—*with thy brother, thy hand shall release* (15:3)—but not a loan the bonds of which have been handed over to a court. Hence the Sages have said:[2] Hillel instituted the *prosbul*[3] [to uphold the social order. When he saw that people had become reluctant to extend credit to each other, thus transgressing that which is written in the Torah, he arose and instituted the prosbul. And this is the form of the prosbul: "I declare unto you, So-and-so and So-and-so, judges in such-and-such place, that whatsoever debt is owed to me, I am to be free to collect it at any time I wish"; and the judges or the witnesses must sign below].

Pisḳa 114

Howbeit there shall be no needy among you (15:4): Yet elsewhere Scripture says, *For the poor shall never cease out of the land* (15:11). So long as you do God's will, the needy will be found only among others; when you fail to do God's will, the needy will be among you.[1] *For the Lord will surely bless thee in the land*—this indicates that blessing is dependent upon the land alone—*which the Lord thy God giveth thee (for an inheritance) to possess it* (15:4)—you will conquer it because you are to inherit it.

Pisḳa 115

If only thou diligently hearken unto the voice of the Lord thy God—hence the Sages have said:[1] If a person listens to a little, he is enabled to listen to a great deal; if he listens to the teachings of Torah, he is enabled to listen to the teachings of the Scribes—*to observe to do all this commandment* (15:5)—meaning that a lesser commandment should be as precious to you as a weighty commandment.

Pisḳa 116

For the Lord thy God will bless thee, as He promised thee (15:6): What did He promise you? *Blessed shalt thou be in the city,* etc. (28:3).[1]

And thou shalt lend unto many nations (15:6): You might think that this means that you will lend one *selaᶜ* (= two shekels) and borrow one shekel, as others do; therefore the verse goes on to say, *But thou shalt not borrow, and thou shalt rule over many nations* (15:6). You might think that this means that (at times) you will rule over others and (at other times) others will rule over you, as is stated in the case (of Adoni-bezek), *And Adoni-bezek said, "Threescore and ten kings (having their thumbs and their great toes cut off, gathered food under my table; as I have done, so God hath requited me)*[2] (Judg. 1:7); therefore the verse goes on to say, *But they shall not rule over thee* (15:6).

If there be among you—not among others—*a needy man*—the one most needy takes precedence—*one of thy brethren*—your brother on your father's side,[3] indicating that your brother on your father's side takes precedence over your brother on your mother's side—*within any of thy gates*—the inhabitants of your own city take precedence over the inhabitants of any other city—*in thy land*—the inhabitants of the (Holy) Land take precedence over those who dwell outside the Land; when Scripture says *within any*[4] *of thy gates,* it means that if he resides in the one place, you are commanded to support him, but if he goes around (begging) from place to place, you are under no obligation to support him[5]—*which the Lord thy God giveth thee* (15:7)—wherever that may be.

Thou shalt not harden thy heart—there are persons who agonize over whether they should give or not—*nor shut thy hand*—there are some who first extend their hand but then withdraw it and shut it—*from thy needy brother* (15:7): If you fail to give to him, you will end up by having to beg from him. Whence do we learn that having opened (your hand) to him once, you must continue to do so even a hundred times? From the verse, *But thou shalt surely open*[6] *thy hand unto him, and shalt surely lend him* (15:8). [*Thou shalt surely open*—open first with words, for if he is ashamed, you should say to him, "Do you need a loan?" Hence the Sages have said: Charity should be extended the same way as a loan.] *And shalt surely lend him*—you should first give him (what he needs), and then suggest that he deposit a pledge (with you); so taught R. Judah. The Sages say: You may say to him, "Bring a pledge," in order to encourage him.[7]

Sufficient for his need—you are not commanded to make him rich—*in that which he wanteth*[8] (15:8)—be it even a horse or a slave. It happened once that Hillel the Elder gave a certain poor man from a noble family a horse to exercise on and a slave to wait on him. On another occasion in Upper Galilee a guest was served a pound of meat every day.[9] *To him* includes his wife, as it is said, *I will make him a help meet to him* (Gen. 2:18).

Piska 117

Beware (15:9): [Be careful not to withhold mercy, for whosoever withholds mercy is analogous to transgressors and throws off the yoke of heaven, as is indicated by the following *base thought* (*bĕliyaʿal*), meaning "without the yoke (*bĕli ʿol*)."][1] Another interpretation: *Beware* signifies a negative commandment, and the following *lest* also signifies a negative commandment, (thus emphasizing the gravity of the command).

Lest there be a base thought in thy heart, saying (15:9): Such thought is termed idolatry, since *base* is used here and also in *Certain base fellows are gone out* (13:14); just as *base* there refers to idolatry, so *base* here refers to idolatry.[2]

The seventh year, the year of release, is at hand (15:9): This is what R. Jose the Galilean was referring to when he said: If the seventh year were a separate reckoning for each person, how could it be at hand? Hence you must conclude that the reckoning of seven years is the same for everyone.[3]

And thine eye be evil against thy needy brother, and thou give him naught; and he cry unto the Lord against thee (15:9): One might think that one is here commanded not to cry out; therefore the verse states,

And he cry.[4] Or contrariwise, one might think that he is commanded to cry out; therefore Scripture says elsewhere, *Lest he cry*[5] *against thee* (24:15). Again, one might think that if he cries out against you, a sin is charged against you, but if he does not cry out against you, no sin is charged against you; therefore the verse goes on to say, *And it be sin in thee* (15:9)—in any event.[6] If so, why does the verse end with *And he cry unto the Lord against thee?*[7] Because I, (the Lord,) will exact punishment more quickly in response to the one who cries out than to the one who does not cry out. Whence do we learn that even if you had already given once, you must continue to give even a hundred times? From the following verse, *Thou shalt surely give*[8] *him* (15:10)—it is (an obligation) between you and him. Hence the Sages have said: That is why there was a Chamber of Secrets in Jerusalem.[9]

Because that for this thing (the Lord thy God will bless thee in all thy work, and in all that thou puttest thy hand unto) (15:10): If a person had said that he would give and then gave, he would receive one reward for the saying and another reward for the act of giving. If he had said that he would give but was then unable to do so, he would receive a reward for the saying equivalent to the reward for the act of giving. If he did not say that he would give but told others to give, he would receive a reward for that, as it is said, *Because that for this thing.*[10] If he neither said that he would give nor told others to give, but comforted the donee with kind words, whence do we learn that he would receive a reward even for that? From the statement, *Because that for this thing the Lord thy God will bless thee in all thy work.*[11]

Pisḳa 118

For the poor shall never cease out of the land (15:11): Earlier, Scripture has said, *Howbeit there shall be no needy among you* (15:4). How can both these promises be fulfilled? So long as you perform God's will, there will be poor only among others, but when you do not perform God's will, the poor will be also among you.[1]

Therefore I command thee, saying—therefore means for this reason; *I command thee, saying* means I am giving you good advice for your own benefit[2]—*Thou shalt surely open thy hand unto thy poor and needy brother* (15:11): Why are all of these specified? To indicate that one should give bread to the one who requires bread, dough to the who requires dough, a *meʿah* coin to the one who requires a *meʿah* coin, and even actually feed by mouth one who requires such feeding.[3]

If (thy brother, a Hebrew man, or a Hebrew woman), be sold unto thee (15:12): Whence do we learn that when you purchase a slave, you should purchase only a Hebrew one? From the verse, *If thou buy a Hebrew servant* (Exod. 21:2). Whence do we learn that when he is sold, he should be sold only to (an Israelite like) you? From the verse, *Be sold unto thee.* Whence do we learn that if a court decrees that he be sold, he should be sold only to (an Israelite like) you? From the same verse, *Be sold unto thee.*[4] *Thy brother, a Hebrew man, or a Hebrew woman*: The law differentiates between a Hebrew man and a Hebrew woman.[5] A Hebrew man goes free after (he has served the statutory six) years, or in the Jubilee year, or by paying the balance of his indebtedness, which is not so in the case of a Hebrew woman; while a Hebrew woman attains freedom upon reaching maturity, cannot be resold,[6] and must be redeemed even against her will, this is not so in the case of a Hebrew man. Since different laws thus apply to the Hebrew man and to the Hebrew woman, it was necessary to specify *a Hebrew man* and *a Hebrew woman.*

He shall serve thee six years (15:12): This includes the purchaser's son. One might think that this includes also the purchaser's heir; therefore Scripture says elsewhere, *Six years he shall serve* (Exod. 21:2).[7] Who has whispered to you to include the son but to exclude the heir?[8] I include the son because he takes his father's place in designating (the Hebrew bondswoman as his wife)[9] and in (redeeming) the ancestral field,[10] and I exclude the heir because he cannot take the father's place in these two matters. Whence do we learn that a runaway Hebrew slave who returns (to his master) must complete his (six) years of servitude? From the verse, *Six years he shall serve.*[11] One might think that if the Hebrew slave had become ill and then recovered, he must make up for the period of his disability; therefore the same verse goes on to say, *He shall go out free for nothing* (Exod. 21:2).[12]

Pisḳa 119

And when thou lettest him go free from thee, etc., *thou shalt furnish him liberally* (15:13–14): One might think that this applies only to a

Hebrew slave who is freed after serving six years.[1] Whence do we learn that this applies also to one who is freed in the Jubilee year or upon the death of his master, or to a Hebrew bondswoman (who is freed) upon reaching maturity? From the verses, "let him go free," *When thou shalt let him go free* (15:12), and *And when thou lettest him go free* (15:13).[2] One might think that you must furnish also one who redeems himself with money; therefore the verse states, *And when thou lettest him go free from thee,* etc.—you must furnish only the one whom you yourself set free, not one who sets himself free by his own action.

Whence do we learn that if you furnish him once, you must furnish him even a hundred times? From the verse, *Thou shalt furnish him liberally*[3]—*him* alone, not his heirs—*out of thy flock, and out of thy threshing floor, and out of thy winepress* (15:14). One might think that one must furnish him only out of the flock, the threshing floor, and the winepress that are here specified. Whence do we learn that everything else is also included? From the same verse, *Thou shalt furnish him liberally*—out of everything. But if so, why does Scripture specify *out of thy flock, and out of thy threshing floor, and out of thy winepress?* The special quality of the flock, the threshing floor, and the winepress is that they all are fit to be blessed,[4] thus excluding money, which is not fit to be blessed; so taught R. Simeon. R. Eliezer ben Jacob says: Excluding also mules, since they cannot give birth to young.

Of that wherewith the Lord thy God hath blessed thee (thou shalt give unto him) (15:14): One might think that if the household has been blessed for his sake, one must furnish him, but if the household has not been blessed for his sake, one need not furnish him; therefore the verse states, *Thou shalt furnish him liberally*—in either case.[5] But if so, why does Scripture say, *Of that wherewith the Lord thy God hath blessed thee thou shalt give unto him?* To indicate that you must furnish him according to the blessing (that you have received).[6]

Piska 120

And thou shalt remember that thou wast a bondman in the land of Egypt (15:15): Just as I repeatedly furnished you in Egypt, so must you furnish the Hebrew slave repeatedly. Just as I furnished you with a generous hand in Egypt, so must you furnish him with a generous hand. Similarly Scripture says, *The wings of the dove are covered with silver*—referring to the spoil of Egypt—*and her pinions with the shimmer of gold* (Ps. 68:14)—referring to the spoil of the (Red) Sea; and again, *We will make thee circlets of gold*—referring to the spoil of the (Red) Sea—*with studs of silver* (Song 1:11)—referring to the spoil of Egypt.[1]

Therefore I command thee this thing today (15:15): One may pierce (the ear of a Hebrew slave who refuses to be set free) in daytime, but not at night.[2]

Pisḳa 121

And it shall be, if he say unto thee: "I will not go out from thee" (15:16): One might think that the Hebrew slave's saying this once is sufficient; therefore Scripture says elsewhere, *But if the servant shall plainly say* (Exod. 21:5),[1] indicating that he must say so once and then repeat it.[2] If he says so within the six years but not at the end of them, his ear may not be pierced, since Scripture goes on to say, *I will not go out free* (Exod. 21:5), indicating not until he says so at the time of his going free. If he says so at the end of the six years but not within the six years, his ear may not be pierced, as it is said, *but if the servant shall plainly say,* indicating that he must say so while he is still a servant.[3]

Because he loveth thee (and thy house) (15:16): Since Scripture says elsewhere, *I love my master* (Exod. 21:5), {would I not know that he loves his master?}.[4] Hence we learn that if he loves his master but his master does not love him, or if he is loved by his master but does not love him, his ear may not be pierced, as it is said, *Because he loveth thee.* If he has a wife and children but his master does not, his ear may not be pierced, as it is said, *Because he loveth thee and thy house.*

Because he fareth well with thee (15:16): Hence if he has fallen ill, or his master has fallen ill, his ear may not be pierced.

Pisḳa 122

Then thou shalt take an awl (15:17): Whence do we learn that this includes also a thorn, (a sharp sliver of) glass, or a splinter of reed?[1]

From the expression, *Thou shalt take;*[2] so taught R. Jose son of R. Judah. Rabbi (Judah the Prince) says: *An awl*—since an awl is made of metal, I must conclude that only metal instruments (may be used).[3] [This was the source of R. Ishmael's saying:[4] In three places the halakah circumvents Scripture: the Torah says, *He shall pour out the blood thereof, and cover it with dust* (Lev. 17:13), while the halakah says, with anything that grows plants;[5] the Torah says, *He writeth her a book of divorcement* (24:1), while the halakah says, (he may write) on anything that was separated from the ground;[6] the Torah says, *With an awl* (Exod. 21:6), while the halakah says, with anything. Rabbi (Judah the Prince) says: *To the door or to the doorpost* (Exod. 21:6)—(while the door is) in an upright position.][7] *An awl*—this refers to a large awl.[8]

[*Then thou shalt take an awl*: This might indicate that it may be done privately; hence Scripture says elsewhere, *Then his master shall bring him unto God, (and shall bring him to the door, or unto the doorpost)* (Exod. 21:6), that is, to the judges, so that he may convey this to the sellers.[9] *With an awl* (Exod. 21:6)—with anything that effects a puncture.] R. Eleazar said: Has not Yudan bĕ-Rabbi taught that the piercing may be done only through the ear-lobe, while the Sages say that a priest may not have his ear pierced lest he be blemished?[10] Yet if he is pierced through the ear-lobe, how can he be blemished? Hence we learn that the piercing must be done through the upper part of the ear.[11] [R. Meir says: Also through the cartilage (of the ear)—seeing that R. Meir held the view that a priest may not have his ear pierced.][12]

(And thrust it through) his ear (15:17): *His ear* is stated here, and *his ear*[13] is stated elsewhere (Lev. 14:14). Just as *his ear* there refers to the right ear, so *his ear* here refers to the right ear, through the upper part of the ear.

Through[14] *his ear* (15:17): One might think that this means through the side of his ear; therefore the verse specifies further, *Through his ear and into the door,* that is, put the awl through the ear until it reaches the door.[15]

And he shall be thy bondman for ever (15:17): As long as the "ever"[16] of his master exists, even if the slave was sold thirty or forty years before the Jubilee year. Hence you must conclude that a Hebrew slave must serve his master's son,[17] but not his master's daughter. If his ear has been pierced, he need serve neither the son nor the daughter.[18] Whence do we learn that that which applies here[19] applies also there,[20] and vice versa? From the fact that both verses use the term *for ever,* indicating an analogy.

And also unto thy bondwoman thou shalt do likewise (15:17): This refers to furnishing liberally.[21] One might think that it refers also to piercing the ear; therefore Scripture says elsewhere, *But if the servant*[22] *shall plainly say* (Exod. 21:5), showing that a bondsman is meant, not a bondwoman.

Pisḳa 123

It shall not seem hard unto thee, when thou lettest him go free from thee; (for to the double of the hire of a hireling hath he served thee six years)— hence you conclude that a hireling labors only during the day, whereas the slave labors both by day and by night[1]— *and the Lord thy God will bless thee* (15:18): One might think that this will be so even if you are idle; therefore the verse goes on to say, *in all that thou doest.*

[*And the Lord thy God will bless thee*—wherever Scripture deals with matters involving a possible monetary loss, it mentions a blessing.][2]

Pisḳa 124

All the firstling males that are born of thy herd and of thy flock (thou shalt sanctify unto the Lord thy God. . . . Thou shalt eat it before the Lord year by year) (15:19–20): This shows that the firstling may be consumed all through its first year. I might think that this refers only to the unblemished firstling; whence do we learn that this applies to the blemished one as well? From the expression, *All the firstling males.*[1]

From the verse, *Thou shalt do no work with the firstling of thine ox, nor shear the firstling of thy flock* (15:19), we learn that one may not shear the firstling or work him. I might think that this applies only to the unblemished firstling; whence do we learn that this applies to the blemished one as well? From the expression, *All the firstling males.*

That are born (15:19): Thus excluding the one born by Caesarean section.[2]

(All the firstling males) . . . of thy herd and of thy flock thou shalt sanctify unto the Lord thy God (15:19): This shows that the firstling

may be consumed at any time within its first year. I might think that this applies only to the firstling; whence do we learn that this includes all consecrated offerings? From the expression, *All the firstling males.*[3]

From the verse, *Thou shalt do no work with the firstling of thine ox, nor shear the firstling of thy flock* (15:19), we learn that one may not shear the firstling or work him. I might think that this applies only to the firstling; whence do we learn that it applies also to all the other consecrated offerings? Should not the law be that if the firstling, which is subject to rules that do not govern all offspring in general and which becomes permitted for profane use without first being redeemed, may not be sheared or worked, then sanctified offerings, the laws of which do apply to all offspring and which become permitted for profane use only after redemption, must surely be forbidden to be sheared or worked? One might argue to the contrary that while this applies to the firstling, whose sanctity begins once he leaves the womb, and to whom sanctity applies even if he is permanently impaired, how can you say the same about consecrated offerings, whose sanctity does not begin at the womb and does not apply in case of permanent impairment? Therefore the verse states, *(All the firstling males . . . of) thy herd and (of) thy flock thou shalt sanctify . . . thou shalt do no work . . . nor shear.*[4]

Thou shalt sanctify unto the Lord thy God: R. Ishmael says: One verse states, *Thou shalt sanctify,* while another verse states, *He shall not sanctify* (Lev. 27:26).[5] [If[6] you say (in one verse), *he shall not sanctify,* you cannot possibly say (in another verse), *thou shalt sanctify,* and vice versa. Hence you must conclude that you may consecrate it by consecrating its value,[7] but you may not consecrate it] as a sacrifice on the altar. One might think that this applies also to an animal consecrated for the repair of the Temple,[8] which is not the same as consecrating it for the altar; therefore the verse states, *firstling* (Lev. 27:26)—just as the firstling is characterized by being consecrated for the altar, [so is anything else consecrated for the altar].[9] Or (one might say) that something found to be applicable in one way may be assumed to be applicable in all other possible ways. Hence, since a firstling is characterized by the fact that it is of lesser sanctity, may be consumed when over two days old, and includes both cattle and sheep, I may apply the same rule only to those other cases which have the same characteristics. Whence do we learn that sacrifices of both greater sanctity and lesser sanctity, offered both by the individual and by the community, should also be included? From the verse, *Of thy herd and of thy flock . . . thou shalt sanctify . . . thou shalt do no work . . . nor shear.*[10] The firstling is specified only in order to teach you that since it is characterized by being consecrated for the altar, this excludes the animal consecrated for the repair of the Temple, which is not consecrated for the altar.

R. Judah says: *Thou shalt do no work with the firstling of thine ox*—but you may do work with an ox that belongs to others—[11] nor shear the firstling of thy flock—but you may shear one that belongs to others. R. Simeon says:[12] *(Thou shalt do no) work with the firstling of thine ox*—but you may have a human firstling work for you—*nor shear the firstling of thy flock*—but you may shear the firstling of an ass. Now this refers only to the firstling of an ox in regard to work, and to the firstling of the flock in regard to shearing. Whence the rule forbidding shearing the firstling of the ox and working the firstling of the flock? You may argue that if a blemished head of cattle, which is not equal to an unblemished head of cattle in regard to being offered on the altar, is nevertheless equal to it in regard to doing work, then should not an unblemished head of sheep, which is equal to an unblemished head of cattle in regard to being offered on the altar, be likewise equal to it in regard to doing work? The same would apply to shearing. And conversely, if a blemished head of sheep, which is not equal to an unblemished head of sheep in regard to being offered upon the altar, is nevertheless equal to it in regard to shearing, should not an unblemished head of cattle, which is equal to an unblemished head of sheep in regard to being offered upon the altar, be equal to it in regard to shearing? As yet we have learned only the rule governing unblemished animals. Whence do we learn that it applies also to blemished animals? If an unblemished head of cattle, which is not equal to a blemished head of cattle in regard to being offered upon the altar, is nevertheless equal to it in regard to work, should not a blemished head of sheep, which is equal to an unblemished head of cattle in regard to being offered upon the altar, be equal to it in regard to work? The same should also apply to shearing. Again, if an unblemished head of sheep, which is not equal to a blemished head of sheep in regard to the consumption of it outside of the Temple, is nevertheless equal to it in regard to shearing, should not a blemished head of cattle, which is equal to a blemished head of sheep in regard to the consumption of it outside of the Temple, be equal to it in regard to shearing? Therefore the verse states, *Thou shalt do no work with the firstling of thine ox, nor shear the firstling of thy flock.*

Pisḳa 125

Thou shalt eat it before the Lord thy God year by year (15:20): This shows that the firstling must be eaten over a period of two days, the concluding day of this year (of its life) and the first day of the next year.[1]

Pisḳa 126

And if there be any blemish therein (15:21): I conclude that this refers only to an animal which was born perfect and later became blemished. Whence do we learn that this applies also to one born blemished? From the following *any ill blemish* (15:21).[1] Whence do we learn that this applies also to one afflicted with scurf, warts, or lichen, or old, or sick, or emitting an offensive odor?[2] From the same verse, *Any blemish . . . any ill blemish whatsoever, thou shalt not sacrifice it unto the Lord thy God* (15:21). One might think that all these[3] may not be slaughtered because of those (defects) within the Temple, but may be slaughtered outside of the Temple;[4] therefore the verse states, *Lameness or blindness* (15:21). Now the lame and the blind are the general rule; why did the Sages single them out? To serve as a basis for analogical deduction. They reasoned that since the lame and the blind[5] are characterized by a blemish which is visible and incurable, the same (rule) must apply only to such other blemishes as are likewise visible and incurable.

[*Only thou shalt not eat the blood thereof* (15:23): Drinking is included in (the prohibition of) eating. The adverb *only* refers to the warning of witnesses.[6] *Only* fixes the minimum amount as the size of an olive, according to the law of the Torah.[7]

(Thou shalt pour it out) Upon the ground (15:23): And not over a pit or a hole, nor over water or flowing streams.[8] But one may enter into his house and slaughter the animal there beside a hole, so that the blood would slowly flow into the hole without dirtying the entire house. But he may not do this in the street, in order not to imitate the heretics.[9]

Thou shalt pour it out: Pouring means out of (an incision in) the neck.[10] R. Eliezer says: *Thou shalt pour it out upon the ground as water*: Just as water renders seeds fit (to acquire uncleanness),[11] so does the blood of slaughtering render them fit (to acquire uncleanness). Perhaps also blood flowing from a stab wound, a torn wound, a severed blood vessel,[12] or a blood-letting incision, from the spleen or the embryo, the final draining of blood,[13] from the liver, the heart, or an animal which died naturally? Hence the verse states, *Thou shalt pour it as water*—only blood that is poured as water renders (food susceptible to uncleanness), thus excluding types of blood which do not render (food susceptible to uncleanness).}[14]

Piska 127

Observe the month of Abib (16:1): Observe the month nearest to spring (*ʾaḇiḇ*), so that spring will come in its proper season.[1] One might think that if a year lacks fourteen or fifteen days, you might add these fourteen or fifteen days to it; therefore the verse states, *month*—neither more nor less. One might think that if a year lacks forty or fifty days, you might add these forty or fifty days to it; therefore the verse states, *month*—neither more nor less.

{(*Observe the month of Abib*: Scripture discusses the festivals in three places: in Leviticus, in regard to their chronological order;[2] in Numbers, in regard to the prescribed sacrifices;[3] and in Deuteronomy, in regard to the intercalation of the year. This shows you that Moses heard the section on the Festivals (at Sinai), proclaimed it to Israel, and then repeated it to them at the particular times when the festivals were due to be observed.[4] Another interpretation: Moses told Israel the laws of Passover at Passover, the laws of Pentecost at Pentecost, and the laws of Tabernacles at Tabernacles. This is the source of the Sages' statement: Moses cautioned Israel to study the matter and expound it.}[5]

Piska 128

And perform[1] *the Passover* (16:1): This indicates that it must be performed specifically as the Passover sacrifice, for if it is slaughtered for some other purpose, it is invalid. This refers only to its slaughtering; whence do we learn that it applies also to receiving the blood and sprinkling it? From the term, *perform*. It might be thought that I may include also the roasting of it and the washing of its entrails; therefore Scripture goes on to say, *And thou shalt sacrifice* (16:2). Since sacrificing is merely part of the entire matter, why was it singled out? To serve as a basis for analogical deduction: since sacrifice is characterized by being intended solely for divine worship, such other acts as are not intended for divine worship are excluded.[2]

Unto the Lord thy God (16:1): Unto the one and only (Holy) Name.

For in the month of Abib (16:1): In the month which is most suitable, neither hot nor cold, as it is said, *God maketh the solitary to dwell in a house: He bringeeth out the prisoners into prosperity*[3] (Ps. 68:7).

The Lord thy God brought thee forth out of Egypt by night (16:1): Did they actually go out by night? Did they not go out in the daytime, as it is said, *On the morrow after the Passover* (Num. 33:3)? (Indeed so,) but we must conclude from this same verse that they were redeemed on the preceding night.[4]

Pisḳa 129

And thou shalt sacrifice the Passover offering (16:2): This indicates that it must be slaughtered specifically as the Passover sacrifice, for if it is slaughtered for some other purpose, it is invalid. This refers only to its slaughtering; whence do we learn that this applies also to receiving the blood and sprinkling it? From the preceding term *perform* (16:1). It might be thought that I might include also the offering up of its fat; therefore the verse states, *And thou shalt sacrifice.* Since sacrificing is merely part of the entire matter, why was it singled out? To serve as a basis for analogical deduction: since sacrificing is characterized by being indispensable for expiation, anything else indispensable for expiation is also included; hence burning (of the fat), which is not indispensable for expiation, is excluded.

Unto the Lord thy God (16:2): Unto the one and only (Holy) Name.

Of the flock and the herd (16:2): But is it not a fact that the Passover sacrifice is brought only of sheep or goats? If so, why does Scripture say, *of the flock and the herd?* Because *flock* refers to the Passover sacrifice[1] and *herd* to the festival sacrifice. [Another interpretation:] In order to draw an analogy between all that is brought of the flock and of the herd and the Passover sacrifice: just as the Passover sacrifice, which is obligatory, must be brought only of that which is not consecrated, so everything which is obligatory must be brought only of that which is not consecrated.[2]

In the place which the Lord shall choose to cause His name to dwell there (16:2): This refers to Shiloh and to the Eternal House (the Temple in Jerusalem).

Pisḳa 130

Thou shalt eat no leavened bread with it (16:3): R. Judah says: Whence do we learn that if one eats leaven after the sixth hour (on Passover eve) he violates a negative commandment? From the verse, *Thou shalt eat no leavened bread with it.*[1] R. Simeon says: Is this really the case? The verse states, *Thou shalt eat no leavened bread with it; seven days shalt thou eat unleavened bread therewith* (16:3). The time indicated in the command to eat unleavened bread is the same as the time indicated in the prohibition of eating leaven, and that which is not included in the command to eat unleavened bread is not included in the prohibition of eating leaven.[2]

The bread of affliction (16:3): This excludes dumplings[3] and pancakes.[4] One might think that a person could not fulfill his obligation with coarse bread;[5] therefore the verse states, *unleavened bread*—even (King) Solomon's (fine) unleavened bread.[6] If so, why does Scripture say, *the bread of affliction*? To exclude dumplings and pancakes.[7] R. Simeon says: Why is it called *the bread of affliction*? Only because of the affliction with which the Israelites were afflicted in Egypt.[8]

For in haste didst thou come forth out of the land of Egypt (16:3): One might think that the haste[9] applies both to Israel and Egypt; therefore Scripture says elsewhere, *But against any of the children of Israel shall not a dog whet his tongue* (Exod. 11:7). Hence you must conclude that there was haste only for the Egyptians, not for Israel.

That thou mayest remember the day when thou camest forth out of the land of Egypt (all the days of thy life) (16:3): It was in reference to this that R. Eleazar ben Azariah said:[10] I am now about seventy years old, but I was never privileged to (learn) that the exodus from Egypt should be recited at night, until Ben Zoma interpreted the verse, *That thou mayest remember the day when thou camest forth out of the land of Egypt all the days of thy life,* in this way: *the days of thy life* means the days; *all the days of thy life* means including the nights. And the Sages say: *the days of thy life* means in this world; *all the days of thy life* includes the time of the Messiah.

Pisḳa 131

And there shall be no leaven seen with thee (16:4): You may see that of others.[1] *And there shall be no leaven seen with thee*—you may see that of the One on high;[2] *and there shall be no leaven seen with thee*—you may see it in the street;[3] *and there shall be no leaven seen with thee*—nullify it in your heart. Hence the Sages have said: In the case of a person who is about to slaughter the Passover lamb or circumcise his son, and who remembers that he still has some leaven in his house, the rule is as follows: if he can go back and clear it out, and then fulfill his obligation, he may go back; if not, he must nullify the leaven in his heart.[4]

And there shall no leavened bread be seen with thee, neither shall there be leaven seen with thee (Exod. 13:7): This is a matter of controversy between the School of Shammai and the School of Hillel. The School of Shammai says: The legal minimum of leaven is the size of an olive, and of leavened bread the size of a *koṯeḇeṯ* date.[5] The School of Hillel says: In both cases the minimum is the size of an olive.[6]

Neither shall any of the flesh, which thou sacrificest the first day at even, remain (all night until the morning) (16:4): What sacrifice is slaughtered in order to be eaten in the evening? You must conclude that it is the Passover.

The first day . . . until the morning: Does this mean the morning of the third day, or might it be the morning of the second day? Scripture says elsewhere, *A vow*—if a vow, it includes a free-will offering—*or a free-will offering* (Lev. 7:16)—thus including the festive offering that must accompany the Passover sacrifice, which may be consumed during two days. How then am I to interpret the words *until the morning*? Until the morning of the third day.[7]

Pisḳa 132

Thou mayest not sacrifice the Passover offering within one of thy gates (16:5): R. Judah says: Whence do we learn that if one slaughters the Passover in behalf of a single individual, he violates a negative commandment? From the verse, *Thou mayest not sacrifice the Passover offering within one of thy gates.*[1] R. Jose says: There are times when one may slaughter it for a single individual, and there are times when one may not slaughter it even for ten individuals. How so? If a single individual can consume it all, one may slaughter it for him; if ten persons cannot consume it, one may not slaughter it for them, lest one should render the Passover offering unfit.[2] R. Eleazar ben Mattithiah says: Since we find that the community may perform the Passover in a state of uncleanness when the majority of them is unclean, one might think that a single (unclean) individual could determine the matter;[3] therefore the verse states, *Thou mayest not sacrifice the Passover offering within one.*[4] R. Simeon says: If one slaughters the Passover offering on behalf of a single individual at a private altar and at a time when altars are forbidden, he violates a negative commandment.[5] Hence one might think that this is also true at a time when altars are permitted; therefore the verse states, *Within one of thy gates,* that is to say, when Israel is gathered in one place for this purpose, meaning when private altars are forbidden, not when they are permitted.[6]

Pisḳa 133

But at the place which the Lord thy God shall choose . . . (there thou shalt sacrifice the Passover offering at even, at the going down of the sun, at the season that thou camest forth out of Egypt) (16:6): R. Eliezer says: *At even* you must slaughter it, *at the going down of the sun* you must eat of it, and *at the season that thou camest forth out of Egypt* you must burn (the remainder of) it.[1] R. ʿAḳiba says: *At even* you must slaughter it, and *at the going down of the sun* you must eat of it. Until when? Until *the season that thou camest forth out of Egypt.*[2] [Another interpretation: *At the season that thou camest forth out of Egypt,* for the slaughtering of it; *at the going down of the sun,* for roasting it; *at even,* for eating of it.][3]

Pisḳa 134

And thou shalt roast and eat it in the place which the Lord thy God shall choose (16:7): Hence we learn that one may return the cut pieces and the limbs;[1] so taught R. Judah. R. Jose says: On the Sabbath, in both cases, it is forbidden; on the holy day, in both cases, it is permitted.

And thou shalt turn in the morning, and go unto thy tents (16:7):

Hence we learn that this requires an overnight stay (in Jerusalem).[2] Now this applies only to animal sacrifices; whence do we learn that it applies also to fowls, meal-offerings, wine, incense, and wood? From the expression, *And thou shalt turn*—any time you turn (from the Temple), it must be from the morning onward.[3] R. Judah says: One might think that the minor Passover[4] also requires an overnight stay (in Jerusalem); therefore the verse states, *And thou shalt turn in the morning, and go unto thy tents* followed by, *Six days thou shalt eat unleavened bread* (16:8)—that which requires six days also requires staying overnight, thus excluding the minor Passover, which is observed for only one day. And the Sages say: This is comparable to wood and incense which do require staying overnight.

Six days thou shalt eat unleavened bread: R. Simeon says: One verse says *Six days thou shalt eat unleavened bread,* while another verse says, *Seven days shall ye eat unleavened bread* (Exod. 12:15)—unleavened bread must be eaten all seven days, six from the new crop and the seventh from the old one.[5]

Pisḳa 135

And on the seventh day shall be a solemn assembly to the Lord thy God (16:8): Rabbi (Judah the Prince) says: One might think that he must be closeted[1] in the house of study the entire day; therefore Scripture says elsewhere, *Unto you (a solemn assembly)* (Num. 29:35).[2] One might think that he must eat and drink all day long; therefore the verse states, *A solemn assembly to the Lord thy God.* How so? One must devote a part of the day to the house of study and a part to eating and drinking.

R. Ishmael says: Since we have not learned (from Scripture) that on festival days it is forbidden to perform work,[3] whence else do we learn it? From the verse, *Six days thou shalt eat unleavened bread, and on the seventh day shall be a solemn assembly to the Lord*—just as the seventh day involves restraint[4] (in regard to work), so do the six days involve restraint (in regard to work). Perhaps one could conclude that just as the seventh day involves restraint from all work, so do the six days involve restraint from all work? Therefore the verse states, *Six days thou shalt eat unleavened bread, and on the seventh day shall be a solemn assembly to the Lord,* meaning that the seventh day involves restraint from all work, but the six days do not.[5] Thus it is evident that Scripture had left it to the Sages alone to decide on which days work is forbidden and on which days it is permitted, which kind of work is permitted and which is forbidden.[6]

Piska 136

Seven weeks shalt thou number unto thee (16:9): (The counting to be done) by the court.[1] Whence do we learn that each person must also count? From the verse, *And ye shall count unto you from the morrow after the day of rest* (Lev. 23:15)—each person (must count) individually.[2]

From the time the sickle is first put to the standing corn (16:9): From the time when you first apply the sickle to the standing corn, meaning that everything must be standing corn,[3] that everything to be harvested must have begun to sprout,[4] and that the harvesting is to be done only by sickle.

One might think that he may first harvest and bring in (the sheaf), and then count whenever he wishes; therefore the verse states, *From the time the sickle is first put to the standing corn shalt thou begin to number.* Or he might think that he may first harvest and count, and then bring in (the sheaf) whenever he wishes; hence Scripture says elsewhere, *From the day that ye brought (the sheaf) . . . shall ye number* (Lev. 23:15–16). One might think further that he must harvest only in daytime, count only in daytime, and bring in (the sheaf) only in daytime; hence Scripture says, *Seven weeks shall there be complete* (Lev. 23:15)—when are they complete? When you begin in the evening.[5] One might again think that he may harvest only in nighttime, count only in nighttime, and bring in (the sheaf) only in nighttime; therefore the same verse states, *From the day that ye brought (the sheaf)* (Lev. 23:15)—the bringing must be done in daytime. What then is the procedure? Harvesting and counting in nighttime, bringing in (the sheaf) in daytime.[6]

Piska 137

And thou shalt keep the Feast of Weeks unto the Lord thy God (16:10): Since Scripture says elsewhere, *And the feast of harvest, the first fruits of thy labors* (Exod. 23:16), one might think that if you have a harvest, you must keep the festival, and if you have no harvest, you need not keep the festival; therefore the verse states, *And thou shalt keep the Feast of Weeks unto the Lord thy God*—whether you have a harvest or not, you must keep the festival.[1]

After the measure of the free-will offering of thy hand, which thou shalt give (16:10): Hence we learn that one must bring his obligatory offering out of unconsecrated money.[2] Whence do we learn that if he wishes to bring it out of tithe-money, he may do so? From the verse, *According as the Lord thy God blesseth thee* (16:10).[3]

Piska 138

And thou shalt rejoice (16:11): Rejoicing is spoken of here, and rejoicing is spoken of elsewhere (27:7). Just as the rejoicing mentioned there refers to peace offerings,[1] so the rejoicing stated here refers to peace offerings.

Thou, and thy son, and thy daughter, and thy manservant, and thy maidservant, and the Levite that is within thy gates, and the stranger (16:11): The most precious come first.

R. Jose the Galilean says:[2] There are three commandments that must be performed on festivals, to wit: the festival offering, the pilgrimage offering, and the rejoicing offering.[3] The pilgrimage offering has a feature lacking in the other two, the festival offering has a feature lacking in the other two, and the rejoicing offering has a feature lacking in the other two. The pilgrimage offering belongs entirely to the Most High, which is not the case with the other two; the festival offering was brought both before and after the revelation (at Sinai),[4] which is not the case with the other two; the rejoicing offering may be brought by both men and women,[5] which is not the case with the other two. Since each of them has something that the other two lack, Scripture had to list all of them.

Piska 139

And thou shalt remember that thou wast a bondman in Egypt, and thou shalt observe and do (these statutes) (16:12): This (seems) to imply that whatever is observed on the Festival of Weeks is to be observed on Passover and on Tabernacles, or even that whatever is observed on

Passover and Tabernacles is to be observed on the Festival of Weeks; therefore the verse states, *These statutes—these* are to be observed on the Festival of Weeks, but booth, lulab̠, seven days' duration, and unleavened bread are not to be observed on this festival.[1]

Pisḳa 140

Thou shalt keep the Feast of Tabernacles seven days (16:13): This applies to the commoner; whence do we learn that it applies also to the Most High?[1] From the verse, *The Feast of Tabernacles for seven days unto the Lord* (Lev. 23:34). If so, why does Scripture say, *Thou shalt keep*? When you erect a booth I shall account it to you as if you had made it for the Most High.

Thou shalt make:[2] Thus excluding an old booth;[3] hence you conclude that if one first trains a vine, a pumpkin, or an ivy (over the booth), and then places a proper covering over them, the booth is invalid.[4]

R. Eliezer says: Just as one cannot fulfill his obligation on the first day of the festival with a lulab̠ belonging to his fellow, so can he not fulfill his obligation on the first day of the festival with a booth belonging to his fellow, as it is said, *Thou shalt make.* The Sages, however, say: He cannot fulfill his obligation with a lulab̠ belonging to his fellow, as it is said, *And ye shall take you (on the first day the fruit of goodly trees)* (Lev. 23:40), (the plural) *you* meaning each one of you; but he does fulfill his obligation with a booth belonging to his fellow, as it is said, *All that are homeborn in Israel shall dwell in booths* (Lev. 23:42)—all Israel may sit in the same booth.[5]

R. Simeon[6] says: Passover and Tabernacles, which are not work seasons,[7] are seven and eight days (respectively), while the Festival of Weeks, which is a work season, is only one day, showing that Scripture is considerate of Israel's welfare.

After that thou hast gathered in from thy threshing floor and from thy winepress (16:13): Since the products of the threshing floor and of the winepress are characterized by having been nourished by the water of the past year, this excludes vegetables, which are not nourished by the water of the past year; so taught R. Jose the Galilean. R. ʿAḳiba, however, says: Since the products of the threshing floor and of the winepress are characterized by the fact that they are not nourished by all types of water, and are therefore tithed as produce of the past year, this excludes vegetables, which are nourished by all types of water, and are therefore tithed as produce of the next year.[8]

Pisḳa 141

And thou shalt rejoice (16:14): In all ways of rejoicing.[1] One might think that this includes fowls and meal offerings as well; therefore the verse goes on to say, *In thy feast* (16:14)—in whatever may be brought as a festival offering, thus excluding fowls and meal offerings, which cannot be brought as festival offerings.

Thou, and thy son, and thy daughter, and thy manservant, and thy maidservant, and the Levite . . . that are within thy gates (16:14)—the most precious come first.

Pisḳa 142

Seven days shalt thou keep a feast unto the Lord thy God in the place which the Lord shall choose (16:15): But did not Scripture already state elsewhere, *The Feast of Tabernacles for seven days unto the Lord* (Lev. 23:34)? Why then say here again, *seven days*? Hence we learn that one may make up (the sacrifice) of the first day during the entire festival.[1] [One might think that he must bring a festival offering on each of the seven days; therefore Scripture says elsewhere, *(And ye shall keep) it (a feast unto the Lord)* (Lev. 23:41).] Why then say here again, *seven days*? To indicate that one may make up the offering during the entire seven days.

Because the Lord thy God shall bless thee (16:15): One might think that this means only in the same kind;[2] therefore the verse goes on to say, *in all thine increase, and in all the work of thy hands* (16:15).

And thou shalt be altogether joyful (16:15): This includes the first night of the festival as the time for the offering of rejoicing. I might think that I should include also the last night as well for the offering of rejoicing; therefore the verse says, *altogether.*[3] Hence the Sages have said: An Israelite may fulfill his obligation with vow-offerings and freewill offerings. One might think that he may bring fowl and meal-offerings as well; therefore the verse says, *altogether.*[4]

Pisḳa 143

Three times (16:16): *times* means seasons;[1] [another interpretation: *times* means festivals,] as in the verse, *The foot shall tread it down, even the feet of the poor, and the steps of the needy* (Isa. 26:6).[2]

(Shall all thy males) appear (16:16): As one comes to see, so does he come to be seen.[3] *Thy males,* thus excluding women. *All thy males,* thus including minors. Hence the Sages have said: Who is a minor? He who is too small to ride on his father's shoulder while going up from Jerusalem to the Temple Mount; so taught the School of Shammai,[4] on the basis of *thy males.* The School of Hillel, however, says: He who is too small to hold his father's hand while going up from Jerusalem to the Temple Mount, on the basis of *three festivals*[5] (Exod. 23:14).

Before[6] *the Lord thy God* (16:16): If you do all that was said in this matter, I will turn away from all My other business and will busy Myself only with you.

On the Feast of Unleavened Bread, and on the Feast of Weeks, and on the Feast of Tabernacles (16:16): R. Simeon says: Why does not the verse mention first the Feast of Tabernacles, which is the subject of this section? Why does it mention it last?[7] To indicate that one does not become liable for transgressing the commandment of *Thou shalt not be slack*[8] (23:22) until all of the festivals of the year have passed.

And they shall not appear before the Lord empty (16:16)—of charity.[9] The Sages have set a fixed amount (for the offering). The School of Shammai says: The pilgrimage offering is two silver *mĕʿah,*[10] the offering of rejoicing[11] one silver mĕʿah. The School of Hillel says: The pilgrimage offering is one silver mĕʿah and the offering of rejoicing two silver mĕʿah.

Every man shall give as he is able (16:17): Hence the Sages have said: If one has many mouths to feed but few possessions, he may offer many peace offerings but few burnt offerings; if he has few mouths to feed but many possessions, he must offer many burnt offerings and few peace offerings; if he has few of both, he may offer, respectively, one and two silver *mĕʿah*; if he has many of both, of him Scripture says, *Every man shall give as he is able, according to the blessing of the Lord thy God which He hath given thee* (16:17).[12]

Piska 144

Judges and officers (shalt thou make thee) (16:18): Whence do we learn that both judges and officers should be appointed for all Israel? From the verse, *Judges and officers shalt thou make thee.*[1] R. Judah says: Whence do we learn that one of them should be appointed over all of them? From the verse, *Shalt thou make thee.*[2] And Scripture says also, *The officers of the Levites before you* (2 Chron. 19:11).[3] Whence do we learn that courts should be appointed for every city? From the verse, *Judges . . . in all thy gates* (16:18). Whence do we learn that officers also should be appointed for every city? From the same verse, *And officers . . . in all thy gates.* Whence do we learn that courts should be appointed for every Tribe? From the verse, *Judges . . . Tribe by Tribe* (16:18). And whence do we learn that officers also should be appointed for every Tribe? From the same verse, *And officers . . . Tribe by Tribe.* R. Simeon ben Gamaliel says: *Tribe by Tribe, and they shall judge* (16:18): This indicates that it is the duty of each Tribe to judge its own members.[4] [*In all thy gates*: This is stated in order to compare the great Sanhedrin with the lesser Sanhedrin. Just as the great Sanhedrin is authorized to try cases involving the death penalty, so is the lesser Sanhedrin.[5]]

And they shall judge the people—even against their will[6]—*with righteous judgment* (16:18): Does not Scripture say further on, *Thou shalt not wrest judgment* (16:19)? Why then does it say here, *righteous judgment*? Here it refers to the appointment of judges.

Thou shalt not wrest judgment—do not say, "So-and-so is a fine man, So-and-so is a leader in prayer"[7]—*thou shalt not respect persons*—do not say, "So-and-so is poor, So-and-so is rich"—*neither shalt thou take a gift*—while it goes without saying that this applies to acquitting the guilty and condemning the innocent, it applies also even to acquitting the innocent and condemning the guilty—*for a gift doth blind the eyes of the wise*—it goes without saying that it blinds also the eyes of the foolish—*and pervert the words of the righteous* (16:19)—it goes without saying that it perverts also the words of the wicked. Another interpretation: *For a gift doth blind the eyes of the wise*—it causes them to declare the clean unclean, and vice versa—*and pervert the words of the righteous*—it causes them to declare the forbidden permitted, and vice versa. Another interpretation: *For a gift doth blind the eyes of the wise*—he will not leave this world as long as he teaches justice—*and pervert the words of the righteous*—he will not leave this world so long as he understands what he is saying.[8]

[Another interpretation: *Thou shalt not wrest judgment*—in matters of money—*thou shalt not respect persons*—in matters of justice.[9] Another interpretation: *Thou shalt not respect persons*—in matters of honor: do not seat one who should sit below, above, nor one who should sit above, below.[10]]

(Justice), justice shalt thou follow (16:20): Whence do we learn that if one has been acquitted by the court, he may not be cited again (on the same charge)? From the repetition, *justice, justice.* If he has been convicted, however, whence do we learn that he may be cited again (if new evidence speaks) for acquittal? From the same repetition, *justice, justice.*[11]

Another interpretation: *Justice, justice shalt thou follow*: Seek out a court whose judgments are proper, (like) the court of R. Johanan ben Zakkai or the court of R. Eliezer.[12]

That thou mayest live, and inherit the land (16:20): Hence we learn that the appointment of (just) judges is to be effective in restoring Israel and resettling them on their Land, and in preventing them from being felled by the sword.

Pisḳa 145

Thou shalt not plant thee an Asherah of any kind of tree (beside the altar of the Lord thy God which thou shalt make thee) (16:21): Hence we learn that one who plants an Asherah transgresses a negative commandment. Whence do we learn that if one plants a tree on the Temple Mount, he likewise transgresses a negative commandment? From the same verse, *Any kind of tree beside the altar of the Lord thy God.* R. Eliezer ben Jacob says: Whence do we learn that it is forbidden to build an exedra[1] in the Temple court? From the same verse, *Any kind of tree beside the altar of the Lord thy God. Which thou shalt make thee* implies (the prohibition of planting trees) near an altar.[2]

[*Thou shalt not plant thee an Asherah*: The Torah says elsewhere, *And burn their Asherim with fire* (12:3), from which it follows by reasoning from the minor to the major that one certainly should not plant them. Whence do we learn that (if already planted) they should not be allowed to stand? From the verse, *Thou shalt not plant thee*—in any manner.[3] Another interpretation: even a house[4] or a booth.[5]]

Pisḳa 146

Neither shalt thou set thee up a pillar (16:22): This refers only to a pillar. Whence do we learn that this applies also to an idol?[1] It is a matter of logic: if pillars, which were favored by the Patriarchs, are to be an abomination to the children, idols, which were an abomination to the Patriarchs, should certainly be an abomination to the children.

Pisḳa 147

Thou shalt not sacrifice unto the Lord thy God an ox, or a sheep, (wherein is a blemish) (17:1): R. Judah says: One might think that if one merely slaughters a sin offering in the south (part of the Temple court), he transgresses a negative commandment; therefore the verse says, *Thou shalt not sacrifice unto the Lord thy God an ox, or a sheep, wherein is a blemish*—he trangresses a negative commandment if he offers a blemished animal, but not if he merely slaughters the animal in the south.[1] The Sages, however, say that if one merely slaughters it in the south, he transgresses a negative commandment. One might think that if one offers consecrated offerings out of the correct order, the burnt offering before the sin offering, the Passover sacrifice before the daily burnt offering, or the additional offerings before the daily burnt offerings, he likewise transgresses a negative commandment;[2] therefore Scripture says elsewhere, *Thou mayest not eat within thy gates the tithe of thy corn, or of thy wine, or of thine oil* (12:17), and *Thou mayest not sacrifice the Passover offering within any of thy gates* (16:5), as well as *Thou shalt not sacrifice unto the Lord thy God an ox, or a sheep, wherein is a blemish*—in these cases one transgresses a negative commandment, but not when offering the sacred offerings out of the correct order.

Wherein is a blemish (17:1): This refers only to one born without a blemish which later became blemished; whence do we learn that this applies also to an animal congenitally blemished from its mother's womb? From what follows, *even any evil thing* (17:1). Whence do we learn that this applies also to an animal with itch, warts, or scabs? From the same verse, *A blemish, even any evil thing*. What about one which is old, ill, or emits an offensive odor? From the same verse, *An ox or a sheep . . . even any evil thing*. Whence do we learn that in the case of consecrated offerings slaughtered at the improper time or in an improper place, one likewise violates a negative commandment? From the words *(any) . . . thing*—when any (improper) thing is involved. What about an animal used in bestiality by woman or man, or set aside for idolatrous sacrifice or worship?[3] The same verse goes on to say, *For that is an abomination unto the Lord thy God* (17:1).[4] What about (an animal bought with) harlot's hire, or the price (of a dog), or an animal of mixed breed,[5] unfit for slaughtering (*ṭĕrefah*), or born by Caesarean section? The verse says, *For that is an abomination.* R. Judah says: The (mother) animal itself is an abomination, but not its offspring. R. Simeon says: One might think that since we find that animals used in bestiality are disqualified, the same would apply to human beings as well;[6] therefore the verse says, *that*—I was speaking of the sacrifice and not of the sacrificer.

Piska 148

If there be found (17:2): Before witnesses. Scripture says later on, *At the mouth of two witnesses, or three witnesses* (17:6)—this is the general principle: wherever Scripture says *if there be found,* the finding must be attested by two or three witnesses.[1]

In the midst of thee, within any of thy gates (17:2): What does the plural *gates* indicate? Since Scripture says further on, *Then shalt thou bring forth that man or that woman, who have done this evil thing, unto thy gates* (17:5), I would have thought that this refers to the gate in which they are found and to the gate in which they are judged. But the use of the term *thy gates* in both verses indicates an analogy: just as *thy gates* there means the gates in which they are found and not the gates in which they are judged, so *thy gates* here must refer to the gates in which they are found, and not the gates in which they are judged.[2]

Since we find that the inhabitants of a city that has been led astray into idolatry are to be executed by the sword,[3] one might think that the same applies to those who have led them astray as well; therefore the verse here goes on to say, *That man or that woman . . . and thou shalt stone them with stones, that they die* (17:5).[4]

Since we find that the inhabitants are not to be declared as having strayed into idolatry on the testimony of only one male witness or of a woman, one might think that in such a case the trangressor here is to be exempt (from punishment); therefore the verse says, *That man or that woman*[5] (is to be punished).

That doeth that which is evil in the sight of the Lord thy God, in transgressing His covenant (17:2): He is called by five names: banned, abominable, hated, detested, and perverse.[6] God also calls him by five names: evildoer, breaker of the covenant, blasphemer, angerer, rebel. He causes five things: pollution of the Land, desecration of the Holy Name, departure of the Shekinah, downfall of Israel by the sword, and their exile from their Land.[7] This covers only such a one;[8] whence do we learn that this applies also to one who worships idols? The verse says, *And hath gone and served other gods* (17:3). What about one who merely bows down? The verse goes on to say, *And bows down to them, or the sun, or the moon, or any of the host of heaven which I have commanded not* (17:3), (and Scripture adds elsewhere), *To serve them* (28:14),[9] thus including one who joins (God's name to idolatrous worship).[10]

R. Jose the Galilean says: From the verse, *Which the Lord thy God hath allotted unto all the peoples under the whole heaven* (4:19), one might conclude that He had allotted them to the nations (for worship);[11] therefore Scripture says elsewhere, *Gods that they knew not, and that He had not allotted unto them* (29:25).[12] R. Jose says: My son Eliezer offers these interpretations: *Which I commanded not*—in the Torah—*nor spoke it*—in the Ten Commandments[13]—*neither came it into My mind* (Jer. 19:5)—that a man should actually offer up his son upon the altar.[14] Others say that *which I commanded not* refers to Jephthah, *nor spoke it* refers to Mesha, king of Moab,[15] *neither came it into My mind* that Abraham should actually offer up his son upon the altar.

Pisḳa 149

And it be told thee, and thou hear it, then shalt thou inquire diligently (17:4): Elsewhere Scripture says, *Then shalt thou inquire, and make search, and ask diligently* (13:15). The word *diligently* in both verses indicates an analogy: one must conduct seven inquiries. This refers only to inquiries; whence do we learn that we must also conduct examinations? From the following, *And behold, if it be truth, and the thing certain* (17:4). But if in any case we are eventually going to conduct examinations, why also inquiries? In the case of inquiries, if even one witness says, "I do not know," the entire testimony is null and void. In the case of examinations, if one witness says, "I do not know," or even if two say, "We do not know," their testimony stands. In both inquiry and examination, however, if the witnesses contradict one another, their testimony is null and void.[1]

In Israel (17:4): This refers only to male Israelites. What about proselytes, women, and slaves? Scripture goes on to say, *Then shalt thou bring forth that man or that woman* (17:5)—(this applies to everyone).

Unto thy gates (17:5): I might conclude that this refers to the gate in which they are found and the gate in which they are judged. Since the term *thy gates* is used in both verses (17:2 and 17:5), this indicates an analogy: just as *thy gates* there means the gates in which they are found, and not the gates in which they are judged, so *thy gates* here refers to the gates in which they are found, and not the gates in which they are judged.[2]

That (man) (17:5): Not one who was coerced, nor one who did it inadvertently, nor one who is (innocently) misled.[3]

And thou shalt stone them with stones (17:5): One might think that this means many stones; but another verse says, *With a stone* (Lev. 20:27), from which one might conclude that this means only one stone, yet the verse here says *with stones*. From this we learn that if the culprit did not die from the first stone, let him die from the second stone.[4]

Pisḳa 150

At the mouth of two witnesses, or three witnesses, shall he that is to die be put to death (17:6): I might think that this applies only to this kind of culprit. Whence do we learn that this applies to all those who are condemned to death? From this verse, *At the mouth of two witnesses, or three witnesses, shall he that is to die be put to death*—(any condemned culprit).

Whence do we learn that conviction may not be based on the testimony of only one witness? From the following, *At the mouth of one witness he shall not be put to death* (17:6). [Whence do we learn that a disciple (of the wise) may not testify for conviction? From this same verse, *At the mouth of one witness he shall not be put to death*.[1]]

Pisḳa 151

The hand of the witnesses shall be first upon him to put him to death (17:7): It is a positive commandment that the witnesses must put him to death.[1] Whence do we learn that if he did not die at the hand of the witnesses, he may be executed by anyone else? From the following, *And afterward the hand of all the people. So thou shalt put away the evil from the midst of thee* (17:7)—put away the evildoers from Israel.

Pisḳa 152

If there arise a matter too hard—this shows that Scripture speaks here of an expert judge[1]—*for thee*—referring to advice[2]—*a matter*—in halaḵah[3]—*in judgment*—in judicial judgment[4]—*between blood and blood*—whether menstrual blood, blood of birth, or blood of flux[5]—*between plea and plea*—whether in civil law, capital law, or bodily injury law—*between plague and plague*—between plagues which affect persons and those affecting clothing or houses—*even matters*—of evaluation,[6] devotion, or consecration—*of controversy*—this refers to the (bitter) water to be drunk by the wayward woman,[7] the breaking of the heifer's neck,[8] and the cleansing of a leper[9]—*within thy gates* (17:8)—this refers to gleanings,[10] forgotten sheaf,[11] and corner crop.[12]

Then shalt thou arise (17:8): You must arise immediately, and in court. Hence the Sages have said: There were three courts there, one at the entrance to the Temple Mount, one at the entrance to the Temple court, and one in the Chamber of Hewn Stone. They[13] would come to the court at the gate of the Temple Mount, and one would say, "Thus have I expounded, and thus have my colleagues expounded. Thus have I taught, and thus have my colleagues taught." If they had a tradition on this matter, they would relate it, but if not, they would go to the court at the entrance to the Temple court and say, "Thus have I expounded, and thus have my colleagues expounded. Thus have I taught, and thus have my colleagues taught." If they had a tradition on this matter, they would relate it, but if not, they would all go to the great court in the Chamber of Hewn Stone, from which Torah used to be dispensed to all Israel, as it is said, *(And get thee up) unto the place which the Lord thy God shall choose* (17:8).

Then shalt thou arise, and get thee up (17:8): This shows that the Land of Israel is higher than all other lands, and that the Temple is higher than all of the Land of Israel.

Pisḳa 153

And thou shalt come—including the court at Jabneh[1]—*unto the priests the Levites* (17:9): It is a positive commandment to have priests and Levites in the court; but lest one should think that, since this is a commandment, if a court does not have them, it is disqualified, the verse goes on to say, *And unto the judge* (17:9)—even if the court has no priests and Levites, it is legal.[2]

That shall be in those days (17:9): R. Jose the Galilean said: Would it occur to you to go before a judge who is not living in your own days? (Of course not.) Rather this means a judge who is qualified and approved in those days. If he had been a relative (of one of the parties) and subsequently ceased being so, he is qualified.[3] Similarly Scripture says, *Say not thou: "How was it that the former days were better than these?", for it is not out of wisdom that thou inquirest concerning this* (Eccl. 7:10).[4]

And they shall declare unto thee the sentence of judgment (17:9): (By telling you), "These are the details of the judgment."

Pisḳa 154

And thou shalt do according to the tenor of the sentence (17:10): The death penalty may be imposed by the great court which is in Jerusalem, but not by the court at Jabneh.[1]

According to the law which they shall teach thee—one may be sentenced to death for transgressing the ordinances of the Torah, but not for transgressing ordinances of the Scribes[2]—*and according to the judgment which they shall tell thee, thou shalt do*—a positive commandment—*thou shalt not turn aside from the sentence which they shall declare unto thee*—a negative commandment—*to the right hand, nor to the left* (17:11)—even if they point out to you that right is left and left is right, obey them.[3]

Pisḳa 155

And the man that doeth presumptuously (17:12): Who does not obey the instructions of the court, but teaches (his own interpretation); *that doeth*—he is liable only for deed, not for teaching;[1] *presumptuously*—he is liable for doing it deliberately, not for doing it in error.

In not hearkening—but not in the case of hearing it from someone else who had heard it[2]—*unto the priest that standeth to minister*—this tells us that lawful ministering must be performed while standing; hence if he is seated while performing his service, it is invalid[3]—*or unto the judge*—as indicated previously, even if there are no priests or Levites, (the court) is legal[4]—*even that man shall die*—execution indicated by the Torah without further specification refers to strangulation[5]—*that (man)*—not one who was coerced, or acted inadvertently, or was (innocently) mistaken—*and thou shalt exterminate the evil from Israel* (17:12)—exterminate the evildoers from Israel.

Pisḳa 156

When thou art come unto the land—perform the commandment which is prescribed in this matter, and as a reward for it you will enter the land[1]—*which the Lord thy God giveth thee*—because of your merit—*and shalt possess it, and shalt dwell therein* (17:14)—as a reward for possessing it, you shall dwell in it.

And shalt say: I will set a king over me (17:4): R. Nehorai says: This is in disparagement of Israel, as it is said, *For they have not rejected thee, but they have rejected Me, that I should not be king over them* (1 Sam. 8:7). R. Judah said: But is it not a positive commandment in the Torah itself that they should demand a king for themselves, as it is said, *Thou shalt in any wise set him king over thee* (17:15)? Why then were they punished for doing so in the days of Samuel? Because they initiated it prematurely on their own.[2]

Like all the nations that are round about me (17:14): R. Nehorai says: They demanded a king only so that he might lead them into idolatry, as it is said, *That we also may be like all the nations; and that our king may judge us, and go out before us, and fight our battles* (1 Sam. 8:20).

Pisḳa 157

Thou shalt in any wise set—if he dies, appoint another in his place[1]—*a king*—but not a queen—*whom the Lord thy God shall choose*—through the word of a prophet—*one from among*—and not from outside the (Holy) Land—*thy brethren*—and not from among Gentiles—*shalt thou set a king over thee* (17:15): Having already said, *Thou shalt in any wise set a king over thee,* why does the verse say again *shalt thou set a king over thee?* In order that fear of him should be upon you. Hence the Sages have said:[2] As for a king, one may not ride his horse, nor sit upon his throne, nor use his scepter, nor view him when he is naked, is being barbered, or is in the bathhouse.

Another interpretation: *Thou shalt in any wise set a king over thee*—this is a positive commandment—*thou mayest not put a foreigner over thee* (17:5)—this is a negative commandment. *A foreigner*[3]—hence the Sages have said: A man may be appointed leader of the community, but not a woman.

Who is not thy brother (17:15): Whenever Agrippa[4] came to this verse, he wept, and all the people of Israel said to him, "Fear not, Agrippa, you are our brother, you are our brother."[5]

Pisḳa 158

Only he shall not multiply horses to himself (17:16): One might think that he also may not multiply horses for his chariots and for his horsemen;[1] therefore the verse says, *To himself*—to himself he may not multiply them, but he may multiply them for his chariots and his horsemen. If this is so, why does it go on to say, *(Nor cause the people to return to Egypt,) to the end that he should not multiply horses* (17:16)? *Horses* means those that are idle. Whence do we learn that even one idle horse is enough to cause the people to return to Egypt? From the same verse, *Only he shall not multiply horses to himself, nor cause the people to return (to Egypt.).*[2] Is this not a matter of inference from the minor to the major?—if a transgression can cause the people to return to Egypt, which is specifically prohibited in the covenant, how much more so can sin cause them to be brought to other lands, which are not thus prohibited.[3]

Pisḳa 159

Neither shall he multiply wives to himself (17:17): In excess of eighteen.[1] R. Judah says: He may multiply them to himself so long as they do not cause his heart to go astray.[2] R. Simeon says: He should not wed even one wife if she will lead him astray. If so, why does Scripture say, *Neither shall he multiply wives to himself?* Even (if they are all) like Abigail.[3] [*Neither shall he multiply wives to himself*: Even if she is like Abigail and her companions, who were virtuous, he may not wed her, nor if she is like Jezebel and her companions, who were evil; she will turn his heart astray.]

Neither shall he greatly multiply to himself silver and gold (17:17): One might think that he may not multiply them even for the purpose of maintaining an army; therefore the verse says, *to himself*—for himself he may not multiply them, but he may multiply them to maintain the army. [Another interpretation: (But may he multiply them) to maintain the army? The verse goes on to say, *multiply to himself*—for himself he may not multiply them, but he may multiply them to maintain the army. That is what David had done, as it is said, *Now behold, in my straits I have prepared for the House of the Lord (a hundred thousand talents of gold and a hundred thousand talents of silver)* (I Chron. 22:14); but Solomon changed that, as it is said, *And the king made silver to be in Jerusalem as stones* (1 Kings 10:27).[4]]

Pisḳa 160

And it shall be, when he sitteth upon the throne of his kingdom—if he does all that has been said here in this matter, he is worthy of sitting upon the throne of his kingdom—*that he shall write him*—for himself, and not pride himself on that of his ancestors[1]—*a copy*[2] *(of this law)* (17:18): This can refer only to Deuteronomy; whence do we learn that this includes also the rest of the words of the Torah? From the following *To keep all the words of this law and these statutes, to do them* (17:19). If so, why does Scripture say, *a copy of this law*? Because in the future it will be changed.[3] Others say: When reading before the assemblage,[4] only the Book of Deuteronomy should be read.

In a book—and not on a tablet, nor on paper, but on a scroll,[5] as it is said, *In a book; out of that which is before the priests the Levites* (17:18)—it must have been corrected by the priests and Levites.[6]

[*In a book*—on the skin of a clean animal, and corrected against the Scroll in the Temple Court by a court of seventy-one—*out of that which is before the priests and the Levites*—hence R. Eleazar ben ʿArak taught that in the future the Torah will be forgotten.[7]]

Pisḳa 161

And it shall be with him, and he shall read therein all the days of his life (17:19): Hence the Sages have said:[1] When the king goes out to war, it should be with him; when he returns, it should be with him; when he sits in judgment, it should be by his side; when he reclines, it should face him, as it is said, *And it shall be with him, and he shall read therein all the days of his life*—*the days of his life* refers to the days, *all the days of his life* refers to the nights.

That he may learn to fear the Lord his God (17:19): Hence we learn that fear[2] leads to Scripture, Scripture leads to Targum, Targum leads to Mishnah, Mishnah leads to Talmud, Talmud leads to performance, performance leads to reverence.

Since we have found that a commoner is equal to a king in matters of Torah, should he also be equal to him in other matters? Therefore the verse goes on to say, *To keep all the words of this law (and these statutes)* (17:19)—in matters of Torah they are equal, but not in other matters. Hence the Sages have said:[3] A king may break down fences to make a road for himself, and should not be prevented from doing so; he may widen streets, and should not be prevented from doing so; for there is no limit to the width of the king's highway.[4] When the people take booty, they must place it before him and let him take his share first. [Another interpretation: *And these statutes*—this refers to the statutes of kingship.]

Pisḳa 162

That his heart be not lifted up above his brethren—nor above the Holy One[1]—*and that he turn not aside from the commandment, to the right hand, or to the left*—he should not deviate right or left from the commandment—*to the end that he may prolong his days in his kingdom*—if he does that which is written in this matter, he is worthy of having his days prolonged in his kingdom—*he and his children (in the midst of Israel)* (17:20)—if he dies, his son will reign in his place. This applies only to kings; whence do we learn that this applies also to all leaders[2] in Israel, in that their children will fill their places? From the verse, *He and his children, in the midst of Israel*—anyone who is in the midst of Israel, his son will fill his place. R. Hananiah ben Gamaliel says: Scripture says, *And I have also given thee that which thou hast not asked, both riches and honor* (1 Kings 3:13)—those things which I did not stipulate as contingent upon the observance of the Torah, I have given you, but those things that I have stipulated as contingent upon the observance of the Torah, I will not give you unless you observe it. Hence Scripture goes on to say, *And if thou wilt walk in My ways (to keep My statutes and My commandments)* (1 Kings, 3:14).

Pisḳa 163

The priests the Levites, even all the Tribe of Levi, shall have no (portion nor inheritence with Israel) (18:1): From the following verse, *Then he shall minister in the name of the Lord his God* (18:7), I conclude that this refers only to able-bodied individuals; whence do we learn that this applies also to blemished ones?[1] From the phrase, *even all the Tribe of Levi. Portion* refers to booty, while *inheritance* refers to the inherited portion in the (Holy) Land.

(They shall eat) the offerings of the Lord made by fire (18:1): This refers to the consecrated offerings brought in the Temple. Whence do we learn that this includes also the consecrated offerings brought outside of the Temple?[2] From the following, *they shall eat . . . His inheritance* (18:1).

Pisḳa 164

(And they shall have) no inheritance—this refers to the portion of the three (Tribes)[1]—*among their brethren*—this refers to the portion of the five[2]—*the Lord is their inheritance, as He hath spoken unto them* (18:2)—this explains the reason for this rule.

Pisḳa 165

And this shall be the priests' due (18:3): Hence we learn that these dues may be claimed through the judges.[1] One might argue that consecrated animals are also liable to these dues: if unconsecrated animals, which are not liable to the chest and thigh offering, are liable to these dues, surely consecrated animals, which are liable to the chest and thigh offering, are also liable to these dues. Therefore the verse says, *And this shall be the priests' due.*[2]

From the people—but not from others, nor from priests—*from them that offer a sacrifice* (18:3): Except *ṭĕrefah* meat[3]; and he has a right to it only once it is sacrificed. Hence the Sages have said: If a proselyte has a cow and slaughters it before he is converted, it is exempt; if he slaughters it after he is converted, it is liable. If there is a doubt, it is exempt, on the ground that a person who claims something from another person bears the burden of proof.[4]

Whether it be ox or sheep (18:3): This includes a hybrid as well, and whether in the Land (of Israel) or outside of it.[5] One might argue that he is liable both in this case and in the case of the first fleece: just as the first fleece is due both in the (Holy) Land and outside of it, so these dues should be given both in the Land and outside of it. Or one might argue in the same way that he is liable both in this case and in the case of the first fruits:[6] just as he is liable to the first fruits only in the Land, so should these dues be given only in the Land. Let us see to what this matter may be best compared: one should judge something which is not dependent upon the Land and is not sacred by something else which is likewise not dependent upon the Land and is not sacred,[7] and not by the first fruits which are dependent upon the Land and are sacred. In the same way, one may argue that one should judge something which is either small or great in quantity by something else which is likewise small or great in quantity, and not by the first fleece which is due only when its quantity is large.[8] Therefore the verse says, *Whether it be ox or sheep*—whether in the Land or outside of it.[9]

That they shall give unto the priest—to the priest himself— *the shoulder*—the right shoulder—*and the two cheeks*—the lower cheeks[10]—*and the maw* (18:3)—just as it says. R. Judah says: Those who interpret the law metaphorically[11] say that the priest was given the shoulder as a reward for the hand, as it is said (of Phinehas), *He rose up from the midst of the congregation and took a spear in his hand* (Num. 25:7); the cheeks as a reward for the prayer, as it is said, *Then stood up Phinehas, and prayed*[12] (Ps. 106:30); and the maw as a reward for the belly,[13] as it is said, *And the woman through her belly* (Num. 25:8).

Pisḳa 166

The first fruits of thy corn, of thy wine, and of thine oil (18:4): Hence we learn that the priests' portion must be given only from the choicest part of the produce.[1] Just as we have found that if there are two different kinds of fruits of trees, one may not give one kind for the other, so also when there are two different kinds of grain or vegetable, one may not give one kind for the other.

And the first of the fleece of thy sheep (18:4): Not the *šeṭef*,[2] nor the fleece of *ṭĕrefah* animals, whether in the (Holy) Land or outside of it.[3]

Of thy sheep: But not of one belonging to others. Hence the Sages have said: If one purchases sheep's fleece from a Gentile, he is exempt from the law of the first fleece.[4] If he purchases sheep's fleece from another Israelite, the rule is as follows: If the seller retains part of the fleece, he is liable (for the priests' portion); if not, the purchaser is liable for it.[5]

Shalt thou give him (18:4): Enough to make a (substantial) gift.[6] Hence the Sages have said: How much shall he give the priest? The weight of five *selaᶜ*[7] in Judea, equal to ten selaᶜ in Galilee, of bleached, not dirty, wool, sufficient to make a small garment out of it, as it is said, *Shalt thou give him,* enough to make a (substantial) gift.[8]

How many sheep must one own to be liable to the first fleece? The School of Shammai says two ewes, as it is said, *And it shall come to pass in that day, that a man shall rear a young cow, and two sheep* (Isa. 7:21). The School of Hillel says five, as it is said, *And five sheep ready dressed* (1 Sam. 25:18). R. ᶜAḳiba says: *And the first of the fleece*—(meaning at least of) two (sheep)[9]—*of thy sheep*—(making) four[10]—*shalt thou give him*—making a total of five.[11]

Pisḳa 167

For the Lord thy God hath chosen him out of all thy Tribes, (to stand)—hence we learn that he must stand when ministering properly; therefore, if the priest is seated while ministering, his service is invalid—*him and his*[1] *sons for ever* (18:5)—in the (Holy) Land or outside of it.[2]

Pisḳa 168

And if a Levite come (18:6): One might think that this refers to anyone who is of Levite descent; therefore the verse goes on to say, *from any of thy gates* (18:6), meaning those who did not take their gates elsewhere, thus excluding Levites who have taken their gates elsewhere.[1] (The next verse,) *Then he shall minister* (18:7), refers to those who are fit for ministering, thus excluding Levites who are not fit for ministering.[2]

Out of all Israel, where he sojourneth—out of all the places where you reside—*and come with all the desire of his soul* (18:6): Whence do you conclude[3] that this includes a priest who comes and offers the blessing in a priestly watch to which he does not[4] belong? From the verse, *And come with all the desire of his soul.* Whence do you conclude that all of the watches may share equally in offering the festival sacrifices? From the same verse, *And come with all the desire of his soul.* One might think that they can do this at all times; therefore the verse says, *from one*[5] *of thy gates*[6]—only at the time when all Israel enter through the same gate, namely on the three festivals.

Pisḳa 169

Then he shall minister in the name of the Lord his God, (as all his brethren the Levites do, who stand) (18:7): On the floor. Hence you conclude that a priest who is uncircumcised, or unclean, or seated, or standing on some utensils, or on an animal's back, or on another priest's feet is unfit.[1] Whence do you learn that all the watches share equally in the festival sacrifices and in the division of the shewbread? From the next verse, *They shall have like portions to eat* (18:8)—a portion to eat, a portion to serve; the portion in eating like the portion in serving.[2] One might think that all the watches are equal also in regard to the festival sacrifices that were not connected with the festival itself; therefore the verse goes on to say, *Beside that which is sold*[3] *according to the fathers' houses* (18:8). What did the fathers sell to one another? (One said to the other:) "You take your week and I will take my week."[4]

Pisḳa 170

When thou art come into the land—perform the commandment stated in this matter, and as a reward for it you will enter the land—*which the Lord thy God giveth thee*—because of your merit—*thou shalt not learn to do after the abominations of those nations* (18:9): You might think that you are not permitted to learn and to instruct about them, or to understand them; therefore the verse says, *to do*—you may not learn (their ways) in order to do them, but you may learn them in order to instruct and to understand.[1]

Pisḳa 171

There shall not be found among you—this is a warning to the court (not to permit it)[1]—*any one that maketh his son or his daughter to pass through the fire* (18:10): This instructs me only about one's son and one's daughter; whence do we learn that this applies also to one's grandson or granddaughter? From the verse, *And thou shalt not give any of thy seed to pass unto Molech* (Lev. 18:21).[2] However, here Scripture says *the fire* and there it says *unto Molech*; whence do we learn that what is stated here applies there, and what is stated there applies here? The term "passing" is used in both places to indicate an analogy: just as the passing stated here is through fire, so is the passing stated there through fire, and just as the passing stated there means (sacrificing to) Molech, so does the passing stated here mean (sacrificing to) Molech. Thus you conclude that (one is not guilty) unless he has violated both of these verses, delivering (his son) and making him pass through the fire unto Molech.[3] If not, we do not hold him guilty.

One that useth divination (18:10): It is the same whether he performs many divinations or only a few—he is liable for each act of divination. Who is a diviner? One who seizes his staff and says,

"Shall I go or not go?", as it is said, *My people ask counsel at their stock, and their staff declareth unto them* (Hos. 4:12).[4] [Another interpretation: (A diviner is) one who has a fox (pass) at his right or at his left.

Another interpretation: *One that maketh his son or his daughter to pass through the fire*: This refers to one who cohabits with an Aramean woman and by her produces a son who is an enemy of God.[5] We learn here[6] of the punishment, but where is the warning? (In the verse,) *There shall not be found among you one that maketh his son or his daughter to pass through the fire*. R. Judah says: This refers to one who makes his son or daughter pass to an idol and makes a covenant with it, as it is said, *When they cut the calf in twain and passed through the parts thereof* (Jer. 34:18)].[7]

A soothsayer (18:10): R. Ishmael says: This is one who passes (something) over his eye.[8] R. ʿAḳiba says: They are those who calculate seasons,[9] like those who say, "I learn that (we can expect) wheat ripening before the beginning of the Sabbatical year to be good, and beans pulled up to be bad."[10] But the Sages say: They are those who produce illusions.[11]

Or an enchanter (18:10): Who is an enchanter? For example, one who says, "My morsel of bread has dropped out of my mouth," "My staff has dropped out of my hand," "A serpent passed me on my right, a fox on my left, and a deer blocked the way in front of me," "Do not begin with me," "It is early morning," "It is the new moon," "It is the night following the Sabbath."[12]

Or a sorcerer (18:10): One who actually performs magic tricks and not merely creates illusions. R. ʿAḳiba says in the name of R. Joshua: If two persons gather cucumbers (by magic), one may gather and be exempt, while the other may gather and be liable—the one who performs the magic trick is liable, while the one who merely creates an illusion is exempt.[13]

Piska 172

Or a charmer—whether he charms many things or only a few, whether he charms a serpent or a scorpion—*or one that consulteth a ghost*—a necromancer[1] who makes (the dead) speak out of his armpit—*or a familiar spirit*—one who speaks out of his own mouth;[2] they themselves are to be punished by stoning, and those who inquire of them are to be warned—*or a necromancer* (18:11)—both one who conjures the dead by divination and one who inquires of a skull.[3] What is the difference between one who conjures by divination and one who conjures by a skull? The spirit conjured by divination does not ascend naturally and may not be questioned on the Sabbath, while the spirit conjured by the skull does ascend naturally and may be questioned on the Sabbath.

Piska 173

For whosoever doeth these things is an abomination (18:12): One might think that a person is not liable until he has transgressed in all of these matters;[1] therefore the verse says, *whosoever doeth these things*—even one of them.[2]

And because of these abominations the Lord thy God is driving them out from before thee (18:12): R. Simeon said:[3] This proves that the Canaanites had been warned about all of these practices, for a person may not be punished unless he has been first warned. When R. Eliezer would come to this verse he would say: How unfortunate we are! Since he who clings to anything unclean, the spirit of uncleanness rests upon him, he who clings to the Shekinah, the holy spirit should surely rest upon him. What causes this (not to happen)? *But your iniquities have separated between you and your God* (Isa. 59:2).

Thou shalt be whole-hearted with the Lord thy God (18:13): When you are whole-hearted, your portion is with the Lord your God. Similarly David said, *But as for me, I will walk in my whole-heartedness; redeem me and be gracious unto me* (Ps. 26:11), *And as for me, Thou upholdest me because of my whole-heartedness, and settest me before Thy face for ever* (Ps. 41:13). *Thou shalt be whole-hearted with the Lord thy God*: If you do everything which is stated in this matter, you will be[4] whole-hearted with the Lord your God.

Piska 174

For these nations, that thou art to dispossess—perform the commandment stated in this matter, for as a reward you will dispossess these nations—*hearken unto soothsayers, and unto diviners* (18:14): Lest you should say, "They have ways of inquiring, and I do not," the verse goes on to say, *But as for thee, the Lord thy God hath not suffered thee so to do.*[1] *(A prophet will the Lord thy God raise up unto thee)* (18:14–15). [*Suffered thee*—it has been given to you, but you forsake the words of Torah and busy yourselves with making it void.[2]]

Pisḳa 175

A prophet from the midst of thee—and not from outside the (Holy) Land—*of thy brethren*—and not from foreigners—*will the Lord thy God raise up unto thee* (18:15)—and not unto the nations. How then am I to obey the command, *I have appointed thee a prophet unto the nations* (Jer. 1:5)? (A prophet) unto those who behave like the nations.[1]

Unto him ye shall hearken (18:15): Even if he tells you to disobey one of the commandments of the Torah in order to meet the needs of the hour, as did Elijah at Mount Carmel, hearken unto him.[2]

Pisḳa 176

According to all that thou didst desire of the Lord thy God in Horeb—because of this, they merited having prophets raised up for them— . . . *(saying,) Let me not hear again the voice of the Lord my God*[1] (18:16).

And the Lord said unto me: They have well said—they deferred to My desire[2]—*I will raise them up a prophet*—thus you learn that as a reward for their fear (of God), they merited having prophets raised up for them—. . . *and I will put My words into his mouth* (18:17–18)—[I will put My words into his mouth, but I will not speak to him face to face]. Another interpretation: *And I will put My words into his mouth*—henceforth you will know how the holy spirit is put into the mouths of the prophets—*and he shall speak unto them*—without employing an aide[3]—*all that I shall command him* (18:8)—saying first things first and last things last.

Pisḳa 177

And it shall come to pass, that whosoever will not hearken unto My words (18:19): There are three kinds of persons whose deaths are in the hands of heaven: one who suppresses his prophecy, like Jonah the son of Amitai;[1] one who ignores the words of a prophet, like the companion of Micah;[2] and the prophet who violates his own words, like Iddo.[3] And there are three kinds of persons who may be put to death by the court: one who prophesies something he has not heard (from God), like Zedekiah son of Chenaanah;[4] one who says something which was not said to him, like Hananiah the son of Azzur,[5] who heard prophecies from the mouth of Jeremiah as he prophesied in the upper market, and then himself prophesied (the same) in the lower market; and one who prophesies in the name of an idol and says, "This is what the idol said to me," even if he intends to conform to the law by declaring the unclean unclean and the clean clean.[6]

Piska 178

But the prophet that shall speak a word presumptuously in My name . . . (that same prophet) shall die (18:20): Unspecified death mentioned in the Torah signifies strangulation.[1]

And if thou say—as you will say in the future—. . . *"How shall we know the word?"* (18:21): Jeremiah said, "The vessels of the Lord's House shall be brought to Babylon,"[2] while Hananiah says, *Behold the vessels of the Lord's House shall now shortly be brought back from Babylon* (Jer. 27:16)—and I do not know to whom to listen. Therefore the following verse says, *When a prophet speaketh in the name of the Lord, if the thing follow not, nor come to pass, that is the thing which the Lord hath not spoken* (18:22). What is the thing which the Lord has spoken? That which (the prophet) had spoken, and it came to pass.

The prophet hath spoken it presumptuously—he is liable for his presumptuousness, but not for acting in error—*thou shalt not be afraid of him* (18:22)—do not shrink from arguing for his condemnation.

Piska 179

When the Lord thy God shall cut off the nations—because of your merit—. . . *and thou dost succeed them, and dwell in their cities and in their houses* (19:1): One might think that *and dwell in their cities and in their houses* means that you are not permitted to add anything to what has already been built; therefore Scripture says elsewhere, *And dwellest in their land* (12:29)—wherever you wish to build, do so.[1]

Pisḳa 180

Three cities—cities and not castles, cities and not metropolises, cities and not villages—*shalt thou separate for thee*—and not for foreigners—*in the midst of thy land*—and not on the border—*which the Lord thy God giveth thee to possess it* (19:2)—what you possess you shall have conquered.[1]

Thou shalt prepare thee the way—prepare highways that lead directly into (such a city of refuge)—*and divide the borders of thy land into three parts*—they must not be scattered, rather the division must be straight like that between two rows of vines in a vineyard—*which the Lord thy God causeth thee to inherit*—including the other side of the Jordan—*that every manslayer may flee thither* (19:3)—so that he need not wander from one city to another.[2]

Pisḳa 181

And this is the case[1] *of the manslayer* (19:4): Hence you conclude that if a manslayer is exiled from his city to a city of refuge, (and the people of that city wish to honor him, he must tell them, "I am a manslayer." If they say to him, "Nevertheless, (we insist on honoring you)," he may accept the honor).[2]

Since Scripture goes on to say, *Lest the avenger of blood pursue the manslayer* (19:6), I conclude that this refers only to the pursuer who is also the blood avenger. What about cases where the pursuer is not the blood avenger, or the blood avenger is not the pursuer, or (the person) is neither the blood avenger nor the pursuer? The word *manslayer* is repeated (in these two verses) in order to include these other possibilities as well.

Since Scripture says, *While his heart is hot* (19:6), I conclude that this refers only to a person hot of heart.[3] What about the case of a father pursuing his son or a son pursuing his father?[4] Again, the word *manslayer* is repeated (in these two verses) in order to include these other possibilities as well.

Why is the word *there* repeated three times?[5] There he shall dwell,[6] there he shall die, and there he shall be buried.

Why is the word *his neighbor* repeated three times?[7] *His neighbor,* excluding foreigners; *his neighbor,* excluding the resident alien; *his neighbor*—the Torah has already designated him as *his neighbor* in saying, *Whoso killeth his neighbor unawares, and hated him not* (19:4);[8] hence if he did hate him, he is not to be sent into exile.

Yesterday or the day before (19:4): R. Judah says, *Yesterday* means two days, *the day before* means three days.

Pisḳa 182

As when a man goeth into the forest with his neighbor (19:5): Just as both the one who was injured and the one who has inflicted the injury had the right to enter the forest, so does this apply to any other place where both of them had the right to enter, thus excluding the injurer's private courtyard, which he had the right to enter while the injuree had not.[1]

To hew wood (19:5): Abba Saul says: Just as hewing wood is a voluntary action, so does this apply to any other voluntary action, excluding a father who strikes his son, a teacher who lashes his pupil, or an officer of the court.[2]

Pisḳa 183

And his hand fetcheth a stroke with the axe to cut down the tree (19:5): Hence you conclude that if one meant to cut down the tree, and the head of the axe fell on a man and killed him, he must go into exile.[1]

And the head slippeth from the wood (19:5): The head split off of the helve. Rabbi (Judah the Prince) says: (From the tree) which is being split.[2]

And findeth (his neighbor) (19:5): His neighbor was already to be found in that spot. Hence R. Eliezer ben Jacob said: If the victim stuck his head out after the stone had already left the slayer's hand, and it struck him, the slayer is exempt.[3]

He shall flee unto one of these cities and live (19:5): He need not wander from one city to another.[4]

Lest the avenger of blood pursue the manslayer—it is the blood avenger's duty to pursue (him)[5]—*while his heart is hot . . . inasmuch as he hated him not*—hence if he did hate him, he is not to be sent into exile—*yesterday or the day before* (19:6)—this is what R. Judah says: *Yesterday* means two days, *the day before* means three days.

Wherefore I command thee, saying (19:7): This is a warning to the court about this matter.[6]

Piska 184

And if the Lord thy God enlarge thy border—perform the commandment which is stated in this matter, and as a reward *the Lord thy God will enlarge thy border*[1]—*as He hath sworn unto thy fathers*—everything is due to the merit of your fathers—*and give thee all the land (which He promised to give unto thy fathers)* (19:8)—everything is due to the merit of your fathers.[2]

Piska 185

If thou shalt keep all this commandment to do it . . . then shalt thou add three cities more for thee, besides these three (19:9): Hence you conclude that Moses set aside three cities on the other side of the Jordan, and after the Israelites came to the (Holy) Land, they set aside three more; in the future they will set aside an additional three. Three and three makes six, and *three . . . more* makes nine. R. Nehorai says: Three plus three and *more* makes nine, plus *besides . . . three* makes twelve. R. Saul says: Three plus three plus *more* makes nine, plus *besides . . . three* makes twelve, plus *these* makes fifteen.[1]

Piska 186/87

That innocent blood be not shed . . . and so blood be upon thee (19:10): This is a warning to the court in this matter.[1]

But if any man hate his neighbor, and lie in wait for him, and rise up against him (19:11): Hence the Sages have said: If a person transgresses a minor[2] commandment, he will eventually transgress a major commandment. If he transgresses *Thou shalt love thy neighbor as thyself* (Lev. 19:18), he will eventually transgress *Thou shalt not take ven-*

geance, nor bear any grudge (Lev. 19:18), *Thou shalt not hate thy brother* (Lev. 19:17), and *That thy brother may live with thee* (Lev. 25:36), until he ends up shedding blood.[3] Therefore Scripture says, *But if any man hate his neighbor, and lie in wait for him, and rise up against him, (and smite him mortally that he die; and he flee into one of these cities)* (19:11).[4] Hence R. Jose ben R. Judah said: Those who slay a human being, whether by error or by design, proceed first to the cities of refuge. The court then sends messengers to bring them thence, and he who is found guilty is condemned to death and is executed, as it is said, *Then the elders of his city shall send and fetch him thence, (and deliver him into the hand of the avenger of blood, that he may die)* (19:12). He who is found not guilty is acquitted, as it is said, *And the congregation shall deliver the manslayer (out of the hand of the avenger of blood)* (Num. 35:25). If he is found to be liable to exile, he is returned to the place where he was found, as it is said, *And the congregation shall restore him (to his city of refuge)* (Num. 35:25). Rabbi (Judah the Prince) says: If a deliberate manslayer flees to a city of refuge thinking that it will offer him refuge as it does to one who has slain unwittingly, the elders of his city must send messengers to bring him thence, as it is said, *Then the elders of his city shall send.*

Into the hand of the avenger of blood, that he may die (19:12): Whence do we learn that if he does not die by the hand of the blood-avenger, he may be put to death by any other man? From the verse, *Into the hand of the avenger of blood, that he may die;*[5] *thine eye shall not pity him, but thou shalt put away the blood of the innocent* (19:12–13). You might say, "Since the victim has already been slain, why should we become responsible for the blood of the slayer?" Therefore the verse says, *Thine eye shall not pity him, but thou shalt put away the blood of the innocent*—put those who do evil out of Israel.

Piska 188

Thou shalt not remove thy neighbor's landmark (19:14): Did not Scripture already say elsewhere, *Thou shalt not . . . rob* (Lev. 19:13)? Why then does it say here, *Thou shalt not remove?* To show that if one uproots his neighbor's landmark, he transgresses two negative commandments. One might further think that this applies also outside of the (Holy) Land; therefore the verse here goes on to say, *In thine inheritance which thou shalt inherit* (19:14)—in the Land of Israel he transgresses two negative commandments; outside of the Land he transgresses only one negative commandment. Whence do we learn that if one uproots the several landmarks of an entire Tribe, he transgresses a negative commandment? From the same verse, *Thou shalt not remove thy neighbor's landmark.* Whence do we learn that if one substitutes R. Joshua's view for that of R. Eliezer, or vice versa, or says that the unclean is clean or that the clean is unclean, he transgresses a negative commandment? From the same verse, *Thou shalt not remove thy neighbor's landmark.* Whence do we learn that if one sells his ancestral burial plot, he violates a negative commandment? From the selfsame verse, *Thou shalt not remove thy neighbor's landmark.* One might think that this applies even if no one has ever been buried therein; therefore the verse says, *In thine inheritance which thou shalt inherit.* Thus, if permission was given to bury there even a fetus, one does not violate a negative commandment.[1]

One witness shall not rise up against a man (19:15): I conclude that this applies only to capital cases; whence do we learn that it applies to monetary matters as well? From the following, *for any iniquity* (19:15). What about matters concerning sacrifices? The verse goes on to say, *or for any sin* (19:15). What about cases of battery? The verse goes on to say, *in any sin that he sinneth* (19:15). What about elevating a person to act as priest or demoting him therefrom? The verse says, *for any iniquity, or for any sin* (19:15).[2] I conclude further that this applies only to testimony against a man; whence do we learn that this applies to testimony against women as well? From the verse, *For any iniquity, or for any sin, in any sin that he sinneth.* But if we end up by including women, why does the verse say, *against a man*? To indicate that one witness may not arise in matters of iniquity, but he may arise in order to permit a woman to be married;[3] so taught R. Judah. R. Jose says: One witness may not arise in matters of iniquity, but he may arise in matters of oaths.[4] R. Jose said: if in instances where the accused cannot join his own testimony with that of the lone witness, namely in capital cases, he may take an oath all by himself, then in cases where he can join his testimony with that of the lone witness, namely in monetary cases, should not the law be that he may take an oath all by himself? Not necessarily, for where he takes an oath all by himself he also pays all by himself, but where his testimony can join with the testimony of the lone witness, he does not pay on the testimony of the lone witness; therefore the verse says, *for any iniquity*—one witness may not arise in matters of iniquity, but he may testify concerning an oath.[5]

At the mouth of two witnesses, or at the mouth of three witnesses, shall a matter be established (19:15): Not through their writing nor through an interpreter.[6] *(At the mouth of two)*—hence the Sages have said: In the case of a man who suspects his wife of infidelity, R. Eliezer says: He must warn her[7] in the presence of two witnesses, and may compel her to drink (the bitter waters) on the testimony of only one witness.[8] Logic would seem to require that if the first testimony,[9] which does not render her forever forbidden to her husband, cannot be established with less than two witnesses, surely the latter testimony, which does render her forever forbidden to him, should not be established with less than two witnesses. Therefore Scripture says, *And there be no witness against her* (Num. 5:13), indicating that if there is a witness against her, she would not need to drink (the bitter waters).

Pisḳa 189

If an unrighteous witness rise up against any man to bear perverted witness against him (19:16): The word *unrighteous* (*ḥamas*) can mean only intending robbery. *To bear perverted witness against him*: The word *perverted* (*sarah*) can only imply a transgression,[1] as it is said, *Because he hath spoken perversion* (*sarah*) *(against the Lord)* (13:6), and, *This year thou shalt die, because thou hast spoken perversion* (*sarah*) *against the Lord* (Jer. 28:16). (*Witness against him*:) This indicates that the witness is not liable until he incriminates himself.[2] Hence the Sages have said:[3] Witnesses are not to be held false until they incriminate themselves. How so? (If some witnesses say,) "I testify that So-and-so has committed the murder," (and the other witnesses say to him, "How can you testify to that when the person who was slain—or the one who you say has slain him—was with us on that day in a certain place," they are not to be regarded as false witnesses. But if the others say to them, "How can you testify to that when you yourselves were with us on that day in a certain place," they are false witnesses).[4]

Pisḳa 190

[*Then the two men . . . shall stand* (19:17): The judges shall sit and the litigants shall stand. Another interpretation: This is a warning to the litigant not to state his case to the judge before his fellow-litigant has appeared.]

Shall stand: It is a commandment that the parties to the suit must stand. *The two men*: This can only mean two men. Whence do we learn that this applies also to cases involving a man versus a woman, or a woman versus a man, or two women contending with one another? From the verse, *Between whom the controversy is* (19:17)—whatever the sex of the contending parties. One might think therefore that a woman is qualified to act as a witness; however, Scripture says *two* here and *two* elsewhere (19:15):[1] just as *two* there refers to men and not to women, so *two* here refers to men and not to women.

Between whom the controversy is—let the owner of the ox come and stand by his ox[2]—*(shall stand) before the Lord*—they think that they are standing before creatures of flesh and blood, but they are really standing before God Himself—*before the priests and the judges that shall be in those days* (19:17): It is in this connection that R. Jose the Galilean said: Would it occur to us to go before a judge who is not living in your own days? Rather it means a judge who is qualified and approved in those days. If he had been a relative (of one of the parties) and subsequently ceased being one, he is still qualified,[3] as it is said, *Say not thou, "How was it (that the former days were better than these?" for it is not out of wisdom that thou inquirest concerning this)* (Eccl. 7:10).

And the judges shall inquire diligently (19:18): Elsewhere Scripture says, *And it be told thee, and thou hear it, then thou shalt inquire diligently* (17:4). Both verses use the term *diligently,* thus indicating an analogy; hence here, too, we must test the witness with seven inquiries. This refers only to inquiries; whence do we learn that this applies also to examinations? From the verse, *And behold, if it be truth, and the thing certain* (13:15).[4] Whence do we learn that a witness may confess that he had testified falsely? From the verse, *And behold, if the witness be a false witness* (19:18). Whence do we learn that he may declare that the other witness had spoken falsely? From the same verse, *And behold, if the witness be a false witness.* One might think that this applies also even after inquiry had been made by the court into their testimony; therefore the verse goes on to say, *And hath testified falsely against his brother* (19:18). Hence you conclude that this may be done only as long as the court requires their presence, but not after the court had completed the inquiry into their testimony.[5] From this verse[6] we conclude also that witnesses may be declared false, even if there are a hundred of them.[7]

Then shall ye do unto him as he had purposed to do unto his brother (19:19): If he had intended to deprive him of money, he is to be sentenced to a fine of money; if to have him flogged, he is to be flogged; if to have him executed, he is to be executed. So much for punishment. Whence do we derive the prohibition itself? From the verse, *(Thou shalt not bear false witness against thy neighbor)* (Exod. 20:13).[8]

Then shall ye do unto him (as he had purposed): Hence we learn that false witnesses may not be executed until after the sentence has been passed;[9] (this is meant) to refute the Sadducees who say, until after the accused has been executed, as it is said, *Life for life* (19:21).[10] R. Jose the Galilean says: What is the meaning of the verse, *Then shall ye do unto him as he had purposed to do unto his brother?* We find that regarding all the capital punishments prescribed in the Torah, the manner of execution is identical for both men and women, and this is true also of the punishment prescribed for the false witnesses involved in these cases. But in the case of the priest's daughter and her lover, their manner of execution is not identical, since the man is executed by strangulation and the woman by burning; and we are not told how the false witnesses (involved in this case) are to be executed. Therefore the verse here states, *Then shall ye do unto him as he had purposed to do unto his brother*—his manner of execution is to be the same as that of *his brother* and not as that of "his sister."

Whence do we learn that one who inflicts an indignity upon another must pay a monetary compensation? *Thine eye shall not pity* is stated here (19:21), and *Thine eye shall not pity* is stated there (25:12)[11]—just as *Thine eye shall not pity* in one place[12] means a monetary compensation, so *Thine eye shall not pity* in the other means a monetary compensation. R. Judah says: *Hand* and *foot* are listed here (19:21), and *hand* and *foot* are listed elsewhere (Exod. 21:24)—just as *hand* and *foot* there mean a monetary compensation, so do *hand* and *foot* here mean a monetary compensation.[13]

R. Jose the Galilean says: Whence do we learn that a man should not go forth to war unless he has arms, legs, eyes, and teeth? From the verse, *And thine eye shall not pity: life for life, (eye for eye, tooth for tooth, hand for hand, foot for foot,) when thou goest forth to battle* (19:21–20:1).[14] [R. Judah said: To what kind of war does this apply? To a war prescribed by a commandment; in a defensive war, everyone must go forth, even the groom from his bridal chamber and the bride from her bridal canopy.[15]

(Horse and chariot) (20;1): When Israel does God's will, all the nations become as one horse before them, as it is said, *The horse and his rider hath he thrown into the sea* (Exod. 15:1)—was there only one horse there?, etc.[16]]

When thou goest forth to battle against thine enemies (20:1): This refers to a nonobligatory war.[17] *Against thine enemies*—you are fighting against your own enemies.[18]

And seest horse and chariot (and many people) (20:1): Just as these go out against you with horse and chariot, so shall you go out against them with horse and chariot; just as they go out against you with many people, so shall you go out against them with many people.

Thou shalt not be afraid of them; for the Lord thy God is with thee, who brought thee out of the land of Egypt (20:1): He who had brought you out of the land of Egypt is with you in time of trouble.[19]

Pisḳa 191

And it shall be, when ye draw nigh unto the battle (20:2): One might think that this refers to the day in which they actually approach the battle. However, the next words, *And (the priest) shall say unto them: Hear, O Israel, ye draw nigh this day unto battle* (20:3), make it obvious that the words *this day* refer to the day in which they actually approach the battle. What then is the meaning of the preceding *And it shall be, when ye draw nigh unto the battle?* It is that when they reach the actual battle, a priest must explain to them all of the pertinent conditions and say to them, *Hear, O Israel.*[1]

Pisḳa 192

[*What man is there that is fearful and faint-hearted* (20:8): *And the officers shall speak further* (20:8): Why were all these matters spoken of? So that the cities of Israel should not become desolate; so taught R. Johanan ben Zakkai.[1] Come and see how considerate God is for the honor of His creatures, even such as are fearful and faint-hearted, so that when such a person returns, the others would say, "Perhaps he left to build a house, or to plant a vineyard, or to wed a wife."[2] Other absentees had to present valid proof, but not the fearful and faint-heared, in whose case the proof is self-evident: he heard the crashing of shields and was terrified, he heard the neighing of horses and trembled, he heard the piercing sound of trumpets and was frightened, he saw the unsheathing of swords and water[3] ran down between his knees. Another interpretation:] *And shall say unto them: Hear, O Israel, ye draw nigh this day unto battle against your enemies* (20:3): Not against your brothers—not Judah against Simeon nor Simeon against Judah—for if you fall into their hands, they will have mercy on you, as witness (the case of Benjamin), of whom it is said, *And they said: "O Lord, the God of Israel, why is this come to pass in Israel, (that there should be today one Tribe lacking in Israel?* (Judg. 21:3), whereupon they restored the Tribe (of Benjamin) to its former place, and not as in the matter of which it is said, *And the children of Israel carried away captive of their brethren two hundred thousand women, sons, and daughters, and took also away much spoil from them, and brought the spoil to Samaria. But a prophet of the Lord was there, whose name was Oded; and he went out to meet the host that came to Samaria, and said unto them: "Behold, because the Lord, the God of your fathers, was wroth with Judah, He hath delivered them into your hand, and ye have slain them in a rage which hath reached up unto heaven. And now ye purpose to bring the children of Judah and Jerusalem (into subjection for bondmen and bondwomen unto you; but are there not even with you acts of guilt of your own against the Lord your God?) Now hear me therefore, and send back the captives that ye have taken captive of your brethren"* (2 Chron. 28:8–11). And it is said further, *And the men that have been mentioned by name rose up, and took the captives, and with the spoil clothed all that were naked among them, and arrayed them, and shod them, and gave them to eat and to drink, and anointed them, and carried all the feeble of them upon asses, and brought them to Jericho, the city of palm trees, unto their brethren; then they returned to Samaria* (2 Chron. 28:15). You are now going against your enemies, who, should you fall into their hands, will have no mercy on you.

Let not your heart faint; fear not, nor be alarmed, neither be ye affrighted at them (20:3): *Let not your heart faint* at the neighing of their horses, *fear not* the crashing of their shields and the tramp of their nail-studded shoes, *nor be alarmed* at the sound of the trumpets, *neither be ye affrighted* at the sound of their shouting. This refers to the four methods used by the nations of the world (to frighten their enemies): crashing (shields), trumpeting, shouting (battle cries), and stamping (their heavy shoes).[4]

For the Lord your God is He that goeth with you (20:4): The enemies come (trusting) in the triumph of flesh and blood, but you come (trusting) in the triumph of the Omnipresent One.[5]

Pisḳa 193

For the Lord your God is He that goeth with you (20:4): He who was with you in the wilderness will be with you in time of trouble. Similarly Scripture says, *The Lord will fight for you, and ye shall hold your peace* (Exod. 14:14).

[*To fight for you against your enemies, to save you*—from venomous serpents, scorpions, and evil spirits—*(and the officers shall speak . . .)*—thus far the priest anointed to serve the army has spoken; from this point on the officers shall speak—*(What man is there that hath betrothed a wife . . .)*—even if she is a widow, or is awaiting release by her levir,[1] even if he has just heard that his brother had died in battle, he must return—*(let him go and return unto his house)* (20:4–7)—all such who hear the words of the priest assigned to the army of battle must return and take care of the supply of water and food for their brothers and of the repair of roads.]

And the officers shall speak (20:5): One might think that they speak other words,[2] but since Scripture says later on, *And the officers shall speak further unto the people* (20:8), this shows that they speak the very same words. What then is the meaning of *And the officers shall speak?* Once the officer begins to speak, the priest proclaims these conditions to them.[3]

Pisḳa 194

What man is there that hath built (a new house) (20:5): This obviously refers only to one who has built it. Whence do we learn that this applies also to one who has inherited a house, or purchased it, or was given it as a gift? From the expression, *What*[1] *man is there that hath built.*

A house: This obviously means only a dwelling house. Whence do we learn that this includes also a hut for straw, a barn for cattle, a shed for wood, or a storehouse? From the phrase *that hath built*. One might think that this includes also one who has built a gatehouse, an exedra, or a balcony; therefore the verse uses the term *house*—"house" is generally understood as a dwelling place, hence places that are not suitable for dwelling are excluded.

And hath not dedicated it—thus excluding one who has acquired it by robbery[2]—*let him go and return to his house*—let him go and listen to the priest of the armies of battle, and then return home—*lest he die in the battle*—if he does not obey the words of the priest, he will in the end die in battle[3]—*and another man dedicate it* (20:5)—one might think that this refers to his uncle or his cousin; but Scripture says here *another* and says elsewhere *another* (28:30):[4] just as *another* there refers to a stranger, so does *another* here refer to a stranger.

Pisḳa 195

And what man is there that hath planted (a vineyard) (20:6): This refers only to the one who has planted it; whence do we learn that it applies also to one who has inherited it, or has purchased it, or had it given to him as a gift? From the verse, *And what man is there that hath planted*.[1]

A vineyard: This refers only to a vineyard; whence do we learn that this applies also to one who has planted the five kinds of fruit trees or even five different species (of plants)?[2] From the phrase, *that hath planted*. One might think that this would include one who has planted four fruit trees or five trees which do not bear fruit; therefore the verse says, *a vineyard*, which means, according to R. Eliezer ben Jacob, nothing other than a vineyard.[3]

And hath not used the fruit thereof (20:6): Thus excluding training a vine into the ground[4] or grafting.

Let him go and return unto his house—let him go and listen to the priest of the armies of battle and return home—*lest he die in the battle*—if he does not obey the words of the priest, he will in the end die in battle—*and another man use the fruit thereof* (20:6)—one might think that this refers to his uncle or his cousin; but Scripture says here *another* and says elsewhere *another* (28:30): just as *another* there refers to a stranger, so does *another* here refer to a stranger.[5]

Pisḳa 196

And what man is there that hath betrothed a wife—whether he betroths a virgin or a widow, or one awaiting release by her levir, once he hears that his brother has died in battle,[1] he must return—*and hath not taken her*—this refers to a wife who is fit for him, thus excluding a man who remarries his divorced wife, a widow married to a high priest, a divorcée or a widow released by her levir and married to a common priest, a female bastard or Nathin[2] married to an Israelite, or an Israelite woman married to a Nathin or a bastard—*let him go and return unto his house* (20:7)—let him go and listen to the priest of the armies of battle and then return home.

Pisḳa 197

And the officers shall speak further unto the people, and they shall say—we learn from this that they must say the very same words[1]—*What man is there that is fearful and faint-hearted?*—because of some sin which he has committed in secret[2]—*let him go and return unto his house* (20:8): R. ʿAḳiba says that *fearful and faint-hearted* means just what it says, whereas R. Jose the Galilean says that *fearful and faint-hearted* means that he has a deformity.[3]

Lest his brethren's heart melt as his heart (20:8): Showing that if one of them is afraid because of his sins, all would return home.[4]

Pisḳa 198

And it shall be, when the officers have made an end (20:9): The officers should post guards in front of them and behind them with iron axes in their hands, and if anyone tries to return, they are permitted to smite them sorely on the thigh, for flight is the beginning of defeat, as it is said, *Israel is fled before the Philistines, and there hath been also a great slaughter among the people* (1 Sam. 4:17). When does this apply? In the case of a nonobligatory war. In the case of an obligatory war, everyone must go forth (to battle), even the bridegroom from his chamber and the bride from her bridal canopy.[1]

Piska 199

When thou drawest nigh unto a city—Scripture speaks here of a nonobligatory war—*unto a city*—not to a metropolis, nor to a village—*to fight against it*—not to reduce it through lack of food or water nor to slay its inhabitants through disease[1]—*then proclaim peace unto it* (20:10)—great is peace, for even the dead require peace. Great is peace, for even in their war Israel requires peace. Great is peace, for even those who dwell on high require peace, as it is said, *He maketh peace in His high places* (Job 25:2). Great is peace, for the priestly blessing concludes with it.[2] And even Moses was a lover of peace, as it is said, *And I sent messengers out of the wilderness of Kedemoth unto Sihon king of Heshbon with words of peace* (2:26).[3]

Piska 200

And it shall be, if it make thee answer of peace (20:11): One might think that this applies even when only some of the inhabitants (make answer of peace); therefore the verse goes on to say, *and open unto thee*—meaning the entire city does so, and not only some of its inhabitants.

(Then it shall be) that all the people that are found therein—including the Canaanites that are within[1]—*shall become tributary unto thee, and shall serve thee* (20:11): If they say, "We are willing to pay tribute to you but not to serve you," or "We will serve you but not pay tribute to you," they are not to be heeded. They must accept both conditions.

And if it will make no peace with thee, but will make war against thee—Scripture informs you that if it will not make peace with you, it will eventually make war against you—*then thou shalt besiege it* (20:12)—even by reducing it through lack of food or water or by slaying its inhabitants through disease.

And when the Lord thy God delivereth it into thy hand—if you do everything that is prescribed in this matter, the result will be that the Lord your God will deliver it into your hand—*thou shalt smite every male thereof with the edge of the sword* (20:13): I might conclude therefrom that this includes the male minors who are within it; therefore Scripture goes on to say, *But the women, and the little ones, and the cattle . . . (shalt thou take for a prey unto thyself)* (20:14). Or does this refer only to female children? You could reason that if in the case of Midian[2] the adult females were slain but the female children were spared, certainly here, where the adult females are spared, should not the female children be spared also? Therefore, when Scripture states here *little ones* it must mean male children.[3] Whence do we learn that (this does not apply to) a minor who wages war against you? From the phrase, *But the women, and the little ones, and the cattle.*[4]

And all that is in the city, even all the spoil thereof, shalt thou take for a spoil unto thyself (20:14): One might think that their spoil should be forbidden[5] to you; therefore the verse goes on to say, *Shalt thou take for a spoil unto thyself; and thou shalt eat the spoil of thine enemies* (20:14).

Pisḳa 201

Thus shalt thou do unto all the cities which are very far off—those cities which are far off are included in this rule, but those that are near are not—*which are not of the cities of these nations* (20:15)—the cities of these nations are not included in this rule.

Howbeit of the cities of these peoples . . . thou shalt save alive nothing that breatheth (20:16): Put them to the sword.[1]

But thou shalt utterly destroy them—one might think that their spoil would be forbidden to you; therefore Scripture states elsewhere, *(To give thee) . . . houses full of good things* (6:10–11)[2]—*the Hittite, and the Amorite, the Canaanite, and the Perizzite, the Hivite, and the Jebusite* (20:17)—the following *as the Lord thy God hath commanded thee* (20:17) implies that the Girgashites are included as well.[3]

Pisḳa 202

That they teach you not to do (after all their abominations)—showing that if they repent, they are not to be slain[1]—*and so ye sin against the Lord your God* (20:18)—if you do not do everything which is stated in this matter, you too will be called sinners against the Lord your God.

Pisḳa 203

When thou shalt besiege a city (20:19): Scripture refers here to a voluntary war. *A city*—not a metropolis, nor a village.

Many days (20:19): The plural *days* implies at least two, *many* implies at least three; hence the Sages have said: A siege against a Gentile city may not be laid less than three days before the Sabbath.[1]

In making war against it to take it—not merely to take its inhabitants captive—*thou shalt not destroy the trees thereof by wielding an axe against them* (20:19): I conclude that this applies only to using an axe; whence do we learn that one may not even divert a water conduit from them? From the verse, *Thou shalt not destroy the trees thereof*—by any means whatsoever. [Another interpretation: *When thou shalt besiege a city*: This informs us that we must sue for peace for two or three days before waging war against it, as it is said, *And David had abode two days in Ziklag* (2 Sam. 1:1). One may not begin the siege against a city on the Sabbath, but only three days before the Sabbath. But once the city has been surrounded, and the Sabbath arrives, the Sabbath need not suspend the war. This is one of three rules that Shammai the Elder had taught,[2] one of which is the rule that one may not sail a ship to the Great (Mediterranean) Sea less than three days before the Sabbath. When does this apply? For a long distance journey, but for a short journey one may do so.]

For thou mayest eat of them—this is a positive commandment—*but thou shalt not cut them down* (20:19)—this is a negative commandment.

For is the tree of the field man (20:19): This shows that man's living comes from the tree,[3] and R. Ishmael says: Hence we learn that God has pity on the fruits of the tree; we learn this by reasoning from the minor to the major: if Scripture cautions you concerning the tree which merely grows fruit, how much more so must this apply to the fruit itself.

That it should be besieged of thee? (20:19): Hence you learn that if the tree prevents you from laying siege, you may cut it down.

Pisḳa 204

Only the trees of which thou knowest—this refers to fruitful trees[1]—*that they are not trees for food* (20:20)—this refers to an unfruitful tree. But if eventually we are going to include fruit trees, why does the verse state, *(that they are not) trees for food*? To show that an unfruitful tree takes precedence over a fruitful tree.[2] One might think that this is so even when the unfruitful tree is worth more (for other things than for its fruit), but, as R. Eleazar ben R. Simeon says, the verse goes on to say, *Them thou mayest destroy and cut down*[3]—from them you may construct arks and boats[4]—*that thou mayest build bulwarks against the city*—you may make all kinds of *tormenta* and bring up all kinds of *ballistae*[5]—*until it fall* (20:20)—even on the Sabbath.[6]

Pisḳa 205

If one be found (21;1): But not when frequently found.[1] Hence the Sages have said: Since the time when murderers multiplied, the breaking of the heifer's neck was discontinued.[2] This was when Eliezer ben Dinai and Teḥina ben Perishah appeared; originally called son of Perishah, he was then renamed "son of the murderer."[3]

Slain—not strangled, nor writhing in agony—*in the land*—not hidden under a heap of stones—*lying*—not hanging from a tree—*in the field* (21:1)—and not floating on the surface of the water.[4]

Which the Lord thy God giveth thee (21:1): This includes the other side of the Jordan. R. Eleazar says: In all of such cases, (if the victim was slain by the sword,)[5] the heifer's neck was broken. R. Jose ben R. Judah said to him: But is it not true that if the victim was strangled and thrown into the field, the heifer's neck need not be broken?[6] (So it is,) but in all such cases, if he was slain (by the sword), the heifer's neck was broken.[7]

And it be not known who hath smitten him (21:1): Hence if it is known who smote him, even if only one witness saw him, the heifer's neck need not be broken. R. ʿAḳiba says: Whence do we learn that if the court saw someone smite him, but did not recognize him, the heifer's neck was not broken? From the verse, *And they shall speak and say: Our hands have not shed this blood, (neither have our eyes seen it)* (21:7).

Then thy elders (and thy judges) shall come forth (21:2): *Thy elders* means two, *and thy judges* means two; since a court may not consist of an even number of judges, one more must be added, so that there are five. So taught R. Judah. R. Simeon says: *Thy elders and thy judges* means two; since a court may not consist of an even number of judges, one more must be added, so that there are three.[8]

And they shall measure unto the cities (21:2): (They must measure) from the slain man to the cities, not from the cities to the slain man. Hence the Sages have said: If his head is found in one place and his body in another, the head should be placed next to the body; so taught R. Eliezer. R. ʿAḳiba says: The body (should be placed) next to the head.[9] If he was found near the border, or near a city in which there are Gentiles, or near a city which has no court, they did not measure. Measuring may be done only to a city which has a court.[10]

Pisḳa 206

And it shall be, that the city which is nearest (unto the slain man) (21:3): Whichever is closest. Hence the Sages have said:[1] If the corpse was found equidistant between the two cities, both of them must bring a heifer whose neck is to be broken; so taught R. Eliezer. The Sages say: Only one city must bring it; both cities need not bring two heifers, and Jerusalem need not at all bring a heifer whose neck is to be broken.

Even the elders of that city shall take—but not the elders of Jerusalem[2]—*a heifer of the herd* (21:3): R. Eliezer says: A heifer is not yet one year old, a cow is no more than two years old. The Sages say: A heifer is two years old, a cow is three or four years old.[3] [Another interpretation: *A heifer of the herd*: It must have two marks.[4] How so? It must be two years old; it must be a heifer of the herd. Another interpretation: Washing is done by the elders and the atonement by the priests.[5]]

Which hath not been wrought with (21:3): In any sort of work. Whence do we learn (that it has not yet borne) a yoke? From the following, *and which hath not drawn in the yoke* (21:3).[6]

Pisḳa 207

And the elders of that city shall bring down—it is a commandment incumbent upon the elders of that city—*the heifer unto a rough valley*

(21:4)—this is to be understood literally: rough, but even if it is not rough, it is fit (for this rite).

Its neck is to be broken with a butcher's hatchet from behind, and the site may be neither sown nor tilled. One might think that the site is forbidden also for carding flax therein or for chiseling stones; therefore the verse goes on to say, *which may neither be cultivated nor sown* (21:4). Sowing is part of cultivation; why then was it singled out? In order to indicate an analogy: since sowing is an integral part of cultivating the ground, anything which is not part of cultivating the ground is not included (in the prohibition).[1]

And shall break the heifer's neck there (21:4): Breaking the neck is mentioned here, and breaking the neck is mentioned elsewhere.[2] Just as the breaking of the neck mentioned here is done by a butcher's hatchet from behind, and the carcass must be buried and is forbidden for benefit, so the breaking of the neck mentioned there is to be done with a butcher's hatchet from behind, and the carcass requires burial and is forbidden for benefit.

In the valley (21:4): Even if it is not rough.[3]

Pisḳa 208

And the priests the sons of Levi shall come near (21:5): Since Scripture has said earlier, *Then he shall minister in the name of the Lord his God* (18:7), I conclude that here also it meant only those who are unblemished. Whence do we learn that here those who are blemished are also included? From the phrase, *the sons of Levi.*[1]

For them the Lord thy God hath chosen (to minister unto Him, and to bless in the name of the Lord) (21:5): This indicates that the priestly blessing is improper if pronounced by those who are blemished.[2]

To minister unto Him, and to bless in the name of the Lord: An analogy is drawn between blessing and serving: just as serving is performed while standing, so is blessing pronounced while standing.

And according to their word shall every controversy and every plague-spot be (21:5): An analogy is drawn between controversies and plague-spots: just as plague-spots may be examined only during the day, so controversies are to be tried only during the day; just as controversies may not be tried by relatives, so leprosy may not be examined by relatives. Or (are we to conclude also that) just as controversies are to be tried by three (priests), so should plague-spots be examined by three (priests)? By rights, if three (priests) are required to sit in judgment over a person's money, should not three (priests) be required to examine his body for plague-spots? Hence Scripture says elsewhere, *Or unto one of his sons the priests* (Lev. 13:2), showing that only one priest need examine plague-spots.[3]

Pisḳa 209

And all the elders of that city (21:6): Even if there are a hundred of them. Since previously we have specified only three or five,[1] should the same number be understood here also? (No,) for the verse states, *And all the elders of that city,* even if there are a hundred of them.

Shall wash their hands over the heifer whose neck was broken in the valley (21:6): Over the spot where the heifer's neck was broken. One might think that they might ascend from the valley and then make the declaration; therefore the verse states, *in the valley,* meaning that they must speak and make the declaration in the valley.

Pisḳa 210

And they shall speak and say—in the holy tongue—*Our hands have not shed (this blood)* (21:7): Did it ever occur to us that the elders of the court are shedders of blood? Rather it means: The deceased did not come to us, and we did not send him away {without food}, nor did we see him and allow him to go on his way {without an escort}.[1]

The priests say, *Forgive, O Lord, Thy people Israel, (whom Thou hast redeemed)* (21:8): When Scripture says, *whom Thou hast redeemed,* it indicates that this atonement applies also to those who had left the land of Egypt.[2] {*Forgive Thy people*—those who are now alive—*whom Thou hast redeemed*—those who are dead. This indicates that the dead too require atonement; hence we learn that he who sheds blood is a sinner even as far back as those who had left Egypt. *Whom Thou hast redeemed*—Thou hast redeemed us on condition that there should be no shedders of blood among us. Another interpretation: Thou hast redeemed us on condition that should we sin, Thou wilt atone for us. And the holy spirit says: As long as you do so, the blood will be atoned for you.[3]}

So shalt thou put away (the innocent blood) (21:9): Put away those who do evil out of Israel.

Pisḳa 211

When thou goest forth to battle—Scripture speaks of non-obligatory wars[1]—*upon thine enemies*—against[2] your enemies—*and the Lord thy God delivereth them into thy hands*—if you do all that is indicated in this matter, the result will be that the Lord your God will deliver them into your hands—*and thou carriest them away captive* (21:10)—including any Canaanites that are there.[3]

And seest among the captives—at the time of her capture[4]—*a woman*—even if she is a married woman[5]—*of goodly form*—I conclude that this refers only to an attractive woman; whence do we learn that this includes also an unattractive one? From the following, *and thou hast a desire unto her*—even though she is not attractive—*and wouldst take her to thee to wife* (21:11)—so that you may not say, "This one is for my father," or "This one is for my brother."

Pisḳa 212

Then thou shalt bring her home to thy house—and not to any other house—*and she shall shave her head, and do her nails* (21:12): R. Eliezer says, cut them; R. ʿAḳiba says, grow them. Rejoined R. Eliezer: Doing is stated in regard to her head,[1] and doing is stated in regard to her nails; just as the doing in regard to her head means trimming (of hair), so must the doing in regard to her nails mean trimming (of them). R. ʿAḳiba objected: Doing is stated in regard to her head, and doing is stated in regard to her nails; just as the doing in regard to her head means disfigurement, so the doing in regard to her nails must mean disfigurement. Support for R. Eliezer's interpretation may be found in the verse, *And Mephibosheth the son of Saul came down to meet the king; and he had neither dressed his feet, nor trimmed his beard* (2 Sam. 19:25).[2]

Pisḳa 213

And she shall put the raiment of her captivity from off her—this indicates that the captor must divest her of her attractive raiment and clothe her in widow's weeds, for these accursed nations make their daughters adorn themselves in time of war in order to cause their foes to go awhoring after them[1]—*and shall remain in thy house*—in a house that the captor habitually uses, so that he will chance upon her when he goes in and when he goes out; if she looks like a pumpkin-shell, he will see her in all her unattractiveness—*and bewail her father and her mother a full month* (21:13): Her actual father and mother; so taught R. Eliezer. R. ᶜAḳiba says: *Her father and her mother* refers to none other than her idols, as it is said, *Who say to a stock: "Thou art my father," (and to a stone: "Thou hast brought us forth")* (Jer. 2:27). *A full month*—thirty days.[2] [Another interpretation: *A month*—one month; *full*—two months, totaling three months, in order that her beautiful and precious garments (might wear out), and in order that it may be established whether the child that she may subsequently be delivered of is the seed of her previous (heathen) husband or the seed of her second (Israelite) husband; so taught R. ᶜAḳiba. R. Eliezer says: *A full month*—literally. And what is the reason for all this (procedure)? So that an Israelite woman would rejoice while the captive one is in tears; the Israelite woman would wear her adornments while this one is stripped of them.

And after that thou mayest go in unto her, and be her husband, (and she shall be thy wife) (21:13): This indicates that if he does not do for her all the aforementioned things, and goes in unto her, it is an act of illicit intercourse.][3]

And after that thou mayest go in unto her, and be her husband—the only (remaining) commandment incumbent upon you is to go in unto her[4]—*and she shall be thy wife*—she shall be entitled to *Her food, her raiment, and her conjugal rights, shall he not diminish* (Exod. 21:10).

Pisḳa 214

And it shall be, if thou have no delight in her—Scripture is informing you that you will come to hate her—*then thou shalt let her go whither she will,* but not to a place of idolatry[1]—[*thou shalt let her go* with a bill of divorcement, as R. Jonathan taught; if she is ill, he shall wait until she recovers; all the more is this the case concerning Israelite women who are holy and pure]—*but thou shalt not sell her at all for money* (21:14): I conclude from this only that he may not sell her for money; whence do we learn that he may not give her away as a gift or as a favor? From the following, *but thou shalt not sell her at all for money; thou shalt not deal with her as a slave* (21:14)—meaning that you may not make use of her. [Another interpretation: *Thou shalt not deal with her as a slave;* as R. Jonathan taught.[2] Another interpretation: This is a warning for the court.][3]

Because thou hast humbled her (21:14)—even if only one act of intercourse has been performed.

Pisḳa 215

[*If a man have two wives, (the one beloved, and the other hated)* (21:15): Whose (marital) status is legal, thus excluding a female slave and a Gentile woman, whose status is not legal. It would follow that since we exclude these, we should also exclude the widowed sister-in-law subject to levirate marriage and the bethrothed woman, since they too do not yet have legal marital status; (therefore the verse states, *two wives*).[1]

R. Ishmael says: Scripture speaks here of the normal course of events, and tells us that in the end he will come to hate her and love another woman.

And they have borne him children, (both the beloved and the hated) (21:15): Thus excluding a child of doubtful parentage, namely a nine-months child of the former husband or a seven-months child by the current husband. I conclude that this refers only to a normal birth; whence do we learn that this refers also to a Caesarean birth? From the phrase, *borne him*—in any manner whatsoever.[2]

Another interpretation: *If a man have two wives* (21:15): I conclude that this refers only to two wives; whence do we learn that it refers also to more than two? From the (plural) *wives.* I still conclude that this refers only to several wives, some of whom are beloved and some of whom are hated; whence do we learn that this applies even when all of them are beloved or all of them are hated? From the repetition of *beloved* and *the beloved, hated* and *the hated,*[3] thus extending the meaning. I again conclude that this applies only to several wives, all beloved or all hated; whence do we learn that it applies even when there are only two? From the words, *two wives.* Once more I conclude that this refers only to the case of two wives, one beloved and the other hated; whence do we learn that this applies even if there is only one wife, either beloved or hated? From the repetition, *beloved* and *beloved, hated* and *hated,* thus extending the meaning. What is meant by *beloved*? Is it possible that *beloved* means beloved before God and *hated* means hated before God?[4] Perhaps I should conclude that this refers only to a woman who was raped or seduced, since his relationship to them is not like that to other women; whence do we learn that this applies also to such (undesirable) marriages as that of a widow to a high priest, or a divorcée, or a widowed sister-in-law rejected by her levir, to a common priest? From the repetition *hated* and *hated,* thus including marriages banned by a negative commandment. I still might not include those forbidden marriages for which one is liable to excision at the hand of heaven; therefore the verse repeats *hated* and *hated,* thus including forbidden marriages punishable by excision at the hand of heaven. Again I might not include those forbidden marriages for which one is liable to death at the hand of the court; therefore the verse repeats *hated* and *hated,* thus including the latter. One might think that this includes a female slave and a Gentile woman; therefore the verse states, *If a man have* (*tihyena*), meaning a woman with whom he is involved in lawful marriage (*hawayah*), thus excluding those who do not have legal (marital) status.[5]

And they have borne him children (21:15): *Children* means that they are his, thus excluding those that are not his. Another interpretation: *And they have borne him children*: Male children are implied here, not female children.[6] Since we find that female children may receive their hereditary portions through their brothers, dividing them equally, one might think that the law of the first-born would apply to them as well; therefore the verse states, *And they have borne him children,* showing that the sons are included here, but not the daughters.

And if the first-born son—not a *ṭumṭum,*[7] a hermaphrodite, or one whose primogeniture is in doubt—*be hers that was hated* (21:15)—Scripture announces to you that the first-born will be the child of the hated wife.

Piska 216

Then it shall be, in the day that he causeth his sons to inherit—inheritances must be distributed in daytime, not at night[1]—*that which he hath*—showing that the son is to receive that which will accrue in the future as well as that which is now in his father's possession—*that he may not make (the son of the beloved) the first-born* (21:16): showing that he may not make the other child the first-born. One might think that while he is not permitted to make the other child the first-born, once he has done so, the child becomes the first-born; therefore the verse states, *that he may not make . . . the first-born.* Hence even if he has declared him first-born, he is not first-born. *The son of the beloved*—once the head and most of the body (of the first-born) has emerged alive, the child born after him is released from the obligations of the first-born.[2]

Before the son of the hated (21:16): Even though the first-born is the son of the hated wife.

Pisḳa 217

But he shall acknowledge the first-born, the son of the hated (21:17): He shall acknowledge him to others; hence we learn that a man is to be believed when he declares, "This is my first-born son." R. Judah says: Just as a man is to be believed when he declares, "This is my first-born son," so is he to be believed when he declares, "This is the son of a divorced woman," or "This is the son of a widowed sister-in-law rejected by her levir." The Sages, however, say: He is not to be believed.[1]

By giving him a double portion (21:17): Twice as much as any one else receives, or two-thirds of the entire estate? You may reason as follows: since he may be the coinheritor with as few as one or with as many as five, just as he receives twice the amount of his coinheritor when there is only one, so should he receive twice the amount of any one of the five.[2] Or you may reason otherwise: since he may be the coinheritor with as few as one or with as many as five, just as he receives two-thirds of the entire estate when there is only one, so should he receive two-thirds of the entire estate when there are five.[3] Therefore the preceding verse states, *Then it shall be, on the day that he causeth his sons to inherit* (21:16). Thus Scripture expressly adds mention of the portion of the other brothers, in the light of which fact you cannot but conclude that the first alternative was correct,[4] namely that since he may be coinheritor with as few as one or with as many as five, just as he receives twice the amount of his coinheritor when there is only one, so should he receive twice the amount of any one of the five. Similarly Scripture says, *I have given to thee one portion above thy brethren* (Gen. 48:22), *And the sons of Reuben the first-born of Israel—for he was the first-born. . . . For Judah prevailed above his brethren, and of him came he that is the prince; but the birthright was Joseph's* (1 Chron. 5:1–2). Since we find that primogeniture is mentioned in connection with Joseph and in connection with future generations,[5] just as the primogeniture mentioned in connection with Joseph involves twice the amount of any one else, so the birthright mentioned in connection with future generations must involve twice the amount of any one else.

Of all that he hath—showing that the first-born may not receive a double portion of that which will accrue in the future, as he does of that which is now in his father's possession—*for he is the first fruits of his strength*—but not the first fruits of the mother's strength—*the right of the first-born is his* (21:17)—showing that the right of primogeniture may be enforced by the judges.[6]

Pisḳa 218

If a man have a (stubborn and rebellious) son (21:18): But not if a woman have such a son. *A son,* but not a daughter, nor an adult son. A minor is exempt, since he has not yet come under the rule of the commandments.[1] *Stubborn*—twice[2]—*and rebellious*—a fool.[3] Another interpretation: *Stubborn*—an apostate who teaches himself a different way.[4] [Another interpretation: Just because he has squandered his father's money, do you say that a stubborn and rebellious son should die?[5] Rather he is judged according to what he is bound to come to in the end: it is better that he should die innocent than die guilty. His father must have fallen in love with a comely captive woman and thus introduced a disturber into his house, so that the son became stubborn and rebellious, and will in the end cause his father to die an unnatural death. *And if a man have committed a sin worthy of death and he be put to death* (21:22)—but not on the Sabbath or on festivals.[6]

Another interpretation: *Stubborn*—against the words of his father—*and rebellious*—against the words of his mother; *stubborn*—against the teachings of the Torah—*and rebellious*—against the teachings of the prophets; *stubborn*—against the testimony of witnesses—*and rebellious*—against the rulings of the judges.[7]

R. Josiah said: Zeʿera told me three rulings on the authority of the scholars of Jerusalem: If a husband wishes to forgive his wife whom he has suspected of adultery, he may do so; if a father and mother wish to forgive a stubborn and rebellious son, they may do so; if the members of a court wish to forgive an elder who has rebelled against their verdict, they may do so. When I came and recited these rulings before R. Judah ben Beterah, he agreed with two of them but disagreed with one; he agreed with the rulings about the wayward wife and the stubborn and rebellious son, and he disagreed with the ruling concerning the elder who rebels against the verdict of the court, since he would cause controversy in Israel.[8]]

That will not hearken to the voice of his father, or the voice of his mother (21:8): Even if his father and mother tell him to kindle a light and he does not do so? (No,) and that is why Scripture repeats *that will not hearken* twice,[9] in order to draw an analogy: just as *that will not hearken* there applies only to one who is a *glutton and a drunkard* (21:20), so *that will not hearken* here refers to one who is *a glutton and a drunkard.* Just as *that will not hearken* there does not apply until he steals from his father and mother, so *that will not hearken* here does not apply until he steals from his father and mother.

And though they chasten him, will not hearken unto them (21:18): Showing that he is to be flogged in the presence of three (judges).[10]

Pisḳa 219

Then shall his father and his mother lay hold on him (21:19): This shows that he is not liable unless he has a father and a mother; so taught R. Meir. R. Judah says: If his mother was not fit for his father, he cannot be declared a stubborn and rebellious son.[1]

And bring him out unto the elders of his city, and unto the gate of his place (21:19): This is a positive commandment specifying the elders of his city and the gate of his place.

And they shall say unto the elders of his city: This our son (is stubborn and rebellious) (21:20): This is the one who was (previously) flogged in your presence. Hence we learn that if one of the judges has since died, the son may not be stoned. If one (of the parents) is an amputee, lame, mute, blind, or deaf, the son may not be declared stubborn and rebellious, since Scripture says, *Lay hold on him*—therefore they may not be amputees—*and bring him out* (21:19)—therefore they may not be lame—*and they shall say*—therefore they may not be mute—*this our son*—therefore they may not be blind—*doth not hearken to our voice* (21:20)—therefore they may not be deaf.[2] He should then be admonished in the presence of three (judges) and flogged. If he misbehaves again, he must be judged before a court of twenty-three (judges), but may not be stoned unless the original three judges are present, since it is said, *This our son*—this is the one who was flogged in your presence.

He is a glutton, and a drunkard (21:20): A glutton in eating meat and a drunkard in drinking wine. There is a reference to this (rule), though not a proof (for it), in the verse, *Be not among winebibbers, among gluttonous eaters of flesh, for the drunkard and the glutton shall come to poverty, and drowsiness shall clothe a man with rags* (Prov. 23:20–21).

Pisḳa 220

And all the men of his city shall stone him (with stones) (21:21): Are literally all the men of his city to stone him? Rather, the meaning is (that it shall be done) in the presence of all the men of his city.[1] *With stones*: One might think that this means with many stones; therefore Scripture says elsewhere, *With a stone* (Lev. 20:27).[2] One might therefore think that this means with only one stone; yet the verse here states *with stones* (in the plural). From this we conclude that if he does not die from the first stone, he is to die from the second. R. Jose said: Should he be stoned to death just because he has eaten a *tarṭemar*[3] of meat and had drunk half a *loḡ* of wine? Rather, the Torah foresaw what he will eventually come to do, and decreed that it is better for him to die while yet innocent than to die when guilty, for the death of the wicked is beneficial for them and beneficial for the world, whereas the death of the righteous is bad for them and bad for the world. Wine and (drunken) stupor for the wicked are beneficial for them and beneficial for the world, but for the righteous they are bad for them and bad for the world. Quietude for the wicked is bad for them and bad for the world, but for the righteous it is beneficial for them and beneficial for the world.[4]

So shalt thou put away the evil (21:21): Remove the evildoers from the midst of Israel.

Pisḳa 221

And if a man have committed a sin worthy of death, and he be put to death, (and thou hang him on a tree) (21:22): A man may be hanged, but a woman may not. R. Eliezer said to the Sages: Did not Simeon ben Sheṭaḥ[1] hang women in Ashkelon? They replied: He hanged eighty women (in one day);[2] although no two persons may be sentenced to death on the same day, his was an emergency measure intended as a lesson to others.[3]

And thou hang him: One might conclude that all those who are stoned to death should then be hanged; therefore Scripture goes on to say, *For he that is hanged is a reproach unto God* (21:23)—after extending the rule, Scripture limits it. We learn this from the case of the blasphemer: just as the blasphemer is characterized as one who extends his hand to threaten the fundamental principle (of faith) and is therefore liable to hanging, so also all who threaten the fundamental principle (of faith) are liable to hanging. R. Eliezer says: Just as the blasphemer is characterized by being liable to stoning, and then to hanging, so also all who are liable to stoning should then be hanged.[4] One might think that he is to be hanged alive, as is the practice of the (Roman) government; therefore the verse states, *And he be put to death, and thou hang him on a tree.*

Him, but not his garments; *him,* but not those who (falsely) testified against him; *him,* but not his rebuttal witnesses;[5] *him,* but not two persons on the same day.

On a tree: One might think that this may be either a tree which has been cut off or one still attached to the ground; therefore the verse states, *But thou shalt surely bury him* (21:23),[6] indicating a tree that is to be buried wih him. From this we deduce that it is a tree which has been cut off, and not one still attached to the ground.

Whence do we learn that he who permits a body to hang overnight transgresses a negative commandment? From the verse, *His body shall not remain all night upon the tree* (21:23). One might think that even if he lets the body remain hanging in order to honor the dead, so that he may fetch a coffin and shrouds, he is still transgressing this command; therefore the verse states, *upon the tree*—just as the tree is characterized as inflicting disgrace upon the body, so is anything else that inflicts disgrace upon the body, which excludes letting it remain in order to honor the dead and not to inflict disgrace.

His body shall not remain all night upon the tree—this is a negative commandment—*but thou shalt surely bury him* (21:23)—this is a positive commandment. What is actually to be done with the culprit? We execute him before dark, then hang him, after which we release the body. If it remains overnight, we transgress a negative commandment, as it is said, *His body shall not remain all night upon the tree.*[7]

For he that is hanged is a curse unto God (21:23): That is to say, why was he hanged? Because he cursed God, thus profaning the Name of heaven.

[A man must be stoned naked, but not a woman. R. Judah says: Both men and women are (to be stoned naked), but thereafter the man is to be hanged with his face towards the people and his back towards the tree, while the woman is to be hanged with her face towards the tree and her back towards the people. The man is to be covered with a strip of cloth in front, and the woman with two strips, one in front and one in back, since all of her nakedness is illicit.][8]

That thou defile not thy land which the Lord thy God giveth thee for an inheritance (21:23): This is a warning to the court in this matter.

Pisḳa 222

[*If thou see* (Exod. 23:5):[1] One might think that this applies even if one is a full mile away from him; therefore the preceding verse states, *If thou meet* (Exod. 23:4). Lest *If thou meet* should be taken literally,[2] the former verse states, *If thou see.*[3] What then is the distance? The Sages fixed it as one-seventh-and-a-half of a mile, which is a *ris.*[4] *Thou shalt forbear to pass by him; thou shalt surely release it with him* (Exod. 23:5): Thus we learn that he (who fails to do so) transgresses both a positive commandment and a negative commandment. *Thou shalt surely release it with him* refers to unloading; *Thou shalt surely help him to lift them up again* (22:4) refers to loading; so taught R. Judah ben Betherah.]

Thou shalt not see thy brother's ox (22:1): This is a negative commandment; elsewhere Scripture says, *If thou meet* (Exod. 23:4), which is a positive commandment. *Thy brother's ox*—this tells me only concerning *thy brother's ox*; whence do we learn that it applies to your enemy's ox as well? From the verse, *thine enemy's (ox)* (Exod. 23:4), indicating that this applies in all cases. If so, why does Scripture say here *thy brother's*? Because the Torah speaks in opposition to the Inclination to evil.[5]

Or his sheep driven away (22:1): In any way they may be driven away.[6] Hence you are led to say:[7] When is (an animal considered) lost? If one finds an ass or a cow grazing on the roadway, it is not considered lost; but if an ass is found with its harness in disarray, or a cow is found running through vineyards, it is considered lost.

And hide thyself from them (22:1): There are times when you may hide yourself from them, and times when you may not. How so? If one is a priest and the beast is in a cemetery,[8] or if one is an elder and it is beneath his dignity (to take care of animals), or if his own loss would be greater than that of his fellow,[9] he is exempt. Therefore it is said, *And hide thyself*—there are times when you may hide yourself from them, and times when you may not.[10]

Thou shalt surely bring them back (unto thy brother) (22:1): If one returns the beast, and it runs away again, and when he once more returns it, it runs away a second time, even if this goes on five times, he must return it each time, as it is said, *Thou shalt surely bring them back.* If he brings it back to a place where others can see it, and they do not take care of it,[11] and it is stolen or lost, the responsibility is still his. The responsibility remains his until he restores it to the possession of its owner, as it is said, *Thou shalt surely bring them back unto thy brother.*

Pisḳa 223

And if thy brother be not nigh (unto thee) (22:2): I conclude that this refers only to one who is (not) near; whence do we learn that this applies also to one who is (not) far? From the following, *and thou know him not.*

Then thou shalt bring it home to thy house—and not to someone else's house—*and it shall be with thee until thy brother require it* (22:2): Would you possibly think that you are to surrender it to him without his describing its distinguishing marks? Why then is it said, *until thy brother require it?* Until you first examine him as to whether or not he is deceiving you.[1]

And thou shalt restore it to him (22:2): You must also restore him (to his home) if he himself is lost.[2]

Pisḳa 224

And so shalt thou do with his ass (22:3): If it is an ass, one may work it and then feed it; if it is a garment, one must shake it out every thirty days and spread it out in order to keep it in good condition, but not in order to use it for his own adornment; if it is utensils of silver or copper, he may make normal use of them, but not to the extent of wearing them out; if it is wooden utensils, he may use them so that they would not rot.[1]

(And so shalt thou do with his garment) (22:3):[2] The garment is included in the general rule;[3] why then was it specified? In order to draw an analogy: just as the garment is characterized by having identification marks and by being likely to be claimed, so does anything else which has identifiable marks and is likely to be claimed, (and thus comes under the same rule). So much for these particular things; whence do we learn that this applies also to all other lost articles? From the following, *(And so shalt thou do) with every lost thing of thy brother's which he hath lost*—excluding anything worth less than a *pĕruṭah*.[4] R. Judah, however, says: *And thou hast found* means including anything worth even less than a *pĕruṭah*.[5]

Thou mayest not hide thyself (22:3): This shows that there is here a negative commandment as well.

Pisḳa 225

Thou shalt not see—this is a negative commandment, while elsewhere, *If thou see* (Exod. 23:5), it is a positive commandment—*thy brother's ass* (22:4): I conclude that this refers only to your brother's ass; what about your enemy's ass? The verse elsewhere states, *The ass of him that hateth thee* (Exod. 23:5), showing that the rule applies to both. If so, why does Scripture say here, *thy brother's ass?* To indicate that the Torah speaks solely in opposition to the (finder's) Inclination to evil.[1]

Or his ox fallen down—not standing—*by the way* (22:4)—not in the barn. Hence the Sages have said: If the beast is found in the barn, one is not obligated (to do anything), but if it is found in the public domain, he is obligated (to help).[2]

And hide thyself (22:4): There are times when you may hide yourself, and times when you may not. How so? If one is a priest and the beasts are in a cemetery, or if he is an elder and it is beneath his dignity (to take care of animals), or if his own loss would be greater than that of his fellow, he is exempt, as it is said, *and hide thyself*—there are times when you may hide yourself, and times when you may not.[3]

Thou shalt surely help him to lift them up again (22:4): If one lifts it up, and it falls down again, he must lift it up again, and if it falls down once more, he must once more lift it up; even if this goes on five times, he is obligated to lift it up, as it is said, *Thou shalt surely help him to lift them up again.* If the owner of the beast[4] is merely sitting down and tells him, "Since you are commanded to do this, if you wish to lift the beast up, do so," he is exempt, as it is said, *Thou shalt surely help him to lift them up.*[5] One might think that this is so even when the owner is old or sick, or afflicted with boils; therefore the verse states, *Thou shalt surely help him to lift them up again.*[6]

Piska 226

A woman shall not wear that which pertaineth unto a man (22:5): What does Scripture mean to tell you? That a woman may not wear white garments, and that a man may not cover himself with colored clothes? (No,) for the verse goes on to say, *(for whosoever doeth these things is) an abomination* (22:5)—something which results in abomination. This is the general principle in this matter: a woman may not dress like a man and go among men, and a man may not adorn himself with women's finery and go among women.[1] R. Eliezer ben Jacob says: Whence do we learn that a woman may not arm herself with weapons and go out to battle? From the verse, *A woman shall not wear that which pertaineth unto a man.* And (whence do we learn) that a man may not adorn himself with women's finery? From what follows, *neither shall a man put on a woman's garment* (22:5).

For whosoever doeth these things is an abomination unto the Lord thy God (22:5): He is called by five names: banned, abominated, hated, loathsome, and perverted.

Piska 227

If a bird's nest chance (to be before thee) (22:6): This excludes one that is ready at hand.[1] The minimum number implied by (the plural) *young ones* (22:6) is two; the minimum number implied by *eggs* (22:6) is also two. Whence do we learn that if there is only one young one or only one egg, one is still required to release the mother-bird? The verse states, *nest*—any nest whatsoever. Since the verse goes on to say, *In the way . . . and the dam sitting upon the young, or upon the eggs* (22:6), one might think that I am to exclude ducks and chickens that nest in an orchard; therefore the verse states, *before thee.* This refers only to birds nesting on private property. What about those that nest on public property? The verse states, *in the way.* What about those that nest in trees? The verse states, *in any tree* (22:6). What about those that nest on the ground? The verse states, *or on the ground* (22:6).[2] *And the dam sitting upon the young, or upon the eggs*—just as the young must be capable of survival, so must the eggs be capable of survival, thus excluding eggs that are addled. Just as eggs require their mother-bird, so the young birds must be such as require their mother-bird, thus excluding those which can fly and do not require their mother-bird.[3] *And the dam sitting*—meaning that this applies only when she is actually sitting on them, excluding one that is hovering over them. One might think that this does not apply even when her wings are touching the nest; therefore the verse states, *And the dam sitting upon the young*—even though she is not bodily upon them. One might think that if an unclean bird sits upon the eggs of a clean bird, or vice versa, one is required to release her; therefore the verse states, *And the dam sitting*—only when all of them are of the same species.

Thou shalt not take the dam with the young (22:6): Since Scripture says, *(Then shall the priest command) to take for him that is to be cleansed two living clean birds* (Lev. 14:4), one might think that it is permitted to take these (found) birds in order to cleanse a leper; therefore the verse states, *Thou shalt not take the dam with the young*—even in order to purify a leper.[4]

Thou shalt not take the dam (22:6): This is a negative commandment.

Pisḳa 228

Thou shalt in any wise let the dam go (22:7): This is a positive commandment. If he releases her and she returns, he must release her again, and if she returns again, he must once more release her; even if this goes on five times, he must release her, as it is said, *Thou shalt in any wise let the dam go.* [Ducks and chickens that have escaped[1] and have nested in an orchard must be released; but if they are inside the house, one is not required to release them. *Young ones or eggs* (22:6): Just as "young ones" refers to those that are useful, thus excluding dead ones that are not useful, so "eggs" refers to those that are useful, thus excluding addled eggs that are not useful. *Young ones* indicates a minimum of two and *eggs* indicates a minimum of two, but even if there is only one egg or only one young, one is required to release the dam. Another interpretation: *If a bird's nest chance to be before thee*—in any place—*in the way, in any tree, or on the ground* (22:6): Since *way* refers to something permitted for use by everyone, birds which are tied up are excluded, inasmuch as they are in someone else's possession.[2] Another interpretation: *Thou shalt in any wise let the dam go*: Is Scripture referring to birds that are clean, or does it include the unclean as well? Scripture says elsewhere: *Of all clean birds ye may eat* (14:11). This is the basic principle: wherever "bird" is mentioned (in Scripture) it refers to a clean bird; so taught R. Josiah. Hence if one has released the dam (and taken the young ones), but then returned them (to the nest, and the dam came back to them), he is exempt from releasing her again.[3] *Thou shalt in any wise let the dam go*: Scripture refers to females and not to males.[4]] In regard to the male partridge, R. Eliezer requires that he be released, as it is said, *Thou shalt in any wise let the dam go,* but the Sages exempt it, as it is said *the dam,*[5] hence excluding the male partridge. If one nevertheless takes the mother-bird with the young, R. Judah says: He is liable to a flogging, but need not release her; the Sages, however, say: He must release her but is not to be flogged. [This is the general rule: in the case of any negative commandment which can be remedied by the performance of an act, one is not to be flogged for transgressing it. One may not take the mother-bird with the young even in order to cleanse the leper. If in the case of such an easy commandment, involving no more than the value of an *isar,*[6] the Torah says, *That it may be well with thee, and that thou mayest prolong thy days* (22:7), how much more must this be so in the case of weighty commandments in the Torah.[7]]

Pisḳa 229

When thou buildest a new house (22:8): I conclude that this refers only to him who builds it; whence do we learn that it applies also to him who acquires it by purchase, inheritance, or gift? From the term *a house*—acquired in any manner.

(Then thou shalt make a parapet for thy roof), that thou bring not blood upon thy house (22:8): I conclude that this refers only to a dwelling house; whence do we learn that this includes also one who builds a storehouse for straw, a cow-shed, a woodshed, or a produce storehouse? From the verse, *That thou bring not blood upon thy house.*[1] One might think that this applies also to one who builds a gatehouse, an exedra,[2] or a gallery; therefore the verse states, *a house*—a house is characterized as a structure housing something, thus excluding structures that do not house anything.

Then thou shalt make a parapet for thy roof: I conclude that this refers only to (house) roofs; whence do we learn that it refers also to wells, ditches, caves, trenches, and wedge-shaped grooves? From the verse, *That thou bring not blood upon thy house.* If so, why does it specifically mention *roof*? Because *roof* excludes a ramp, whereas *house* includes the Temple Hall.[3] *Roof* excludes also the Temple Porch.[4] *New*: Rabbi (Judah the Prince) says: Make a parapet from the time that the house is new. What is the measurement of a parapet? Three handbreadths at the higher point, ten at the lower.[5]

Then thou shalt make a parapet for thy roof—this is a positive commandment—*that thou bring not blood upon thy house*—this is a negative commandment.

If he who falls should fall from thence (22:8): It may be fitting that he should fall, nevertheless merit is brought about by the meritorious and guilt by the guilty.[6] *From thence*—but not unto it, for if the public domain is ten handbreadths higher, as it is said *from thence,* not "unto it."[7] [Another interpretation: *When thou buildest*: R. Ishmael says: Scripture intends to teach you (that one cannot know) how he will be judged, as it is said, *For man also knoweth not his time, as the fishes that are taken in an evil net* (Eccl. 9:12). (*House*:) Hence the Sages have said: A house which is not four by four cubits[8] is not required to have a parapet, a mezuzah, or an *ᶜeruḇ,*[9] nor can it be used to connect cities[10] or to make untithed produce liable for tithes,[11] nor does its entrance acquire four cubits of room.[12] One who vows not to benefit from such a house may continue to dwell in it. It does not acquire uncleanness through leprosy, does not become irredeemable in the Jubilee year, nor does it entitle its owner to leave the battle line in order to return to it.][13]

Piska 230

Thou shalt not sow thy vineyard with two kinds of seed (22:9): Why is this necessary? Has it not already been said elsewhere, *Thou shalt not sow thy field with two kinds of seed* (Lev. 19:19)? The repetition, however, implies that if one sows two kinds of seeds in a vineyard, he violates two negative commandments. I conclude that this applies only to a complete vineyard; whence do we learn that it applies even to a single vine which produces fruit? From the term *vineyard*—of any size. Whence do we learn that one is forbidden even to derive benefit from the mixed seeds of a vineyard? From the fact that holiness is spoken of here,[1] and holiness is spoken of elsewhere;[2] just as it is forbidden to derive benefit from the holiness mentioned elsewhere, so is it forbidden to derive benefit from the holiness stated here.[3]

Lest the fulness of the seed (which thou hast sown) be forfeited (22:9): When does the fulness of the seed become forbidden because of mixed seeds? From the time when the plants become rooted.[4] Vines are forbidden from the time that the grapes grow to the size of white beans.[5] *The seed*: This excludes seed that has come (into the soil) with manure or with irrigation water, or was blown in by the wind as one was sowing. I might not exclude[6] the case of the seed blown in by the wind as the sower was sowing; therefore the verse states, *Which thou has sown.*[7] If one lets thorns grow in a vineyard, he renders vines forbidden, as it is said, *which thou hast sown*; so said R. Eliezer. The Sages, however, say that the term *seed* excludes the one who lets thorns grow in a vineyard.[8]

The increase of the vineyard (22:9): When does the increase become forbidden? From the time that the plants become rooted. And the vines are forbidden from the time that the grapes grow to the size of white beans. I conclude that this refers only to a vineyard that produces fruit; whence do we learn that it applies also to a vineyard which does not produce fruit? From the term *vineyard*—of any kind. Again I conclude that this refers only to your own vineyard;[9] whence do we learn that this applies also to a vineyard owned by others? From the verse, *Thou shalt not sow thy vineyard with two kinds of seed*—any vineyard.[10]

[If one stretches a grapevine over other plants, even in an area of a hundred cubits, the vine and its fruit are forbidden. *Thou shalt not plow with an ox and an ass* (22:10): One might think that this means that one may not plow with one of them alone or with the other alone; therefore the verse adds, *together,* showing that plowing with one of them alone is permitted. Another interpretation: *Two kinds of seed*: This indicates that liability applies to both vineyards and fields.[11] Another interpretation: *Lest the fulness . . . be forfeited*: Lest the fulness be forbidden; so taught R. Josiah. *Which thou hast sown*: I conclude that this applies only to seed sown by one's self; whence do we learn that this applies also to seed sown by someone else which one wishes to retain? From the phrase, *thou hast sown*—even if indirectly.][12]

Pisḳa 231

Thou shalt not plow with an ox and an ass together (22:10): One might think that this means (that oxen and asses may) never (be used for plowing); but since Scripture says elsewhere, *That thine ox and thine ass may have rest* (Exod. 23:12), it is obvious that oxen and asses may be used for work. Why then is it said, *Thou shalt not plow with an ox and an ass?* To indicate, with the two of them together. *An ox and an ass*: I conclude that this applies only to oxen and asses; whence do we learn that this applies also to other domestic animals, wild beasts, and fowl? From the phrase, *Thou shalt not plow*—with mixed breeds of any kind. If so, why does Scripture say, *with an ox and an ass*? To indicate that you may not plow with an ox and an ass together, but you may plow with a man and an ass together.

Thou shalt not plow: I conclude that this refers only to plowing; whence do we learn that this applies also to threshing, sitting (in a wagon pulled by the animals), and driving (such a wagon)? From the term, *together*—in all these cases.[1] R. Meir, however, considers one who sits (in a wagon) to be exempt. *Together*—excluding a mule.[2] *Together*—excluding one who ties a horse to the side of a wagon or behind a wagon, and (one who works) a Libyan ass[3] with a camel.

Pisḳa 232

Thou shalt not wear a mingled stuff, (wool and linen together) (22:11): One might think that it is forbidden to wear woolen fleece with linen fibers; therefore Scripture uses the term *šaʿaṭnez* ("mingled stuff"), a composite of *šuʿa* ("carded"), *ṭawuy* ("spun"), and *nuz* ("woven").[1] R. Simeon ben Eleazar says: He (who violates this rule) is perverse (*naloz*) and causes his Father in heaven to remove Himself (*meliz*) from him.[2]

Thou shalt not wear: I conclude that this refers only to wearing; whence do we learn that this applies also to covering one's self? From the verse, *Neither shall there come upon thee (a garment of two kinds of stuff mingled together)* (Lev. 19:19). One might think that he may not bundle up such a garment [and put it] into a basket behind him;[3] therefore the verse states, *Thou shalt not wear*—don it in any manner whatsoever. Why then was wearing singled out? In order to draw an analogy and inform you that just as wearing is characterized as giving comfort to the body, so any other use (of the garment) which gives comfort to the body is equally forbidden. *Together*: One might think that he may not wear a woolen shirt over a linen shirt, or a linen shirt over a woolen shirt; therefore the verse states, *together.* R. Hananiah ben Gamaliel says: Whence do we learn that one may not tie a woolen strip to a linen strip in order to gird his loins, even if a leather strap is tied between them?[4] From the term, *together*—in any manner whatsoever. Thus one may say that a sack and a basket combine the two kinds to create mixed kinds.[5]

[*Wool and linen together*: But each one separately is permitted. Felted stuffs, however, even though not woven, are forbidden as mixed seeds, because they are carded.[6]]

Pisḳa 233

[*Thou shalt not wear a mingled stuff. . . . Thou shalt make thee twisted cords* (22:11–12): These two were said together in one utterance.[1] *Remember* and *observe*[2] (Exod. 20:8, Deut. 5:12) were said together in one utterance. *Every one that profaneth it shall surely be put to death* (Exod. 31:14) and *And on the Sabbath day two he-lambs of the first year* (Num. 28:9) were said in one utterance. *Thou shalt not uncover the nakedness of thy brother's wife* (Lev. 18:16) and *And perform the duty of a husband's brother unto her* (25:5) were said in one utterance. *And every daughter that possesseth an inheritance . . . (shall be wife unto one of the family of the Tribe of her father)* (Num. 36:8) and *So shall no inheritance remove from one Tribe to another Tribe* (Num. 36:9) were said in one utterance. A human being cannot utter two utterances at the same time, (but God can,) as it is said, *God hath spoken once, twice have I heard this* (Ps. 62:12).]

Pisḳa 234

[*Thou shalt make thee twisted cords* (22:12): Why was this said, seeing that Scripture has already said elsewhere, *That they make them . . . fringes* (Num. 15:38)? I might think that I should make them of only one thread; therefore the verse states, *twisted cords*. How are twisted cords made? According to the School of Hillel, of not less than three threads, while according to the School of Shammai, of (not less than) four threads of blue and four threads of white, each of four finger-lengths, and the law is according to the School of Shammai.[1] To what part of the fringe does this apply? To the beginning of it, but as for remainders and stubs of it, any length is valid.[2] *Upon the four (corners of thy covering)* (22:12)—thus excluding garments with three, five, six, seven, or eight corners. Another interpretation:] *Thou shalt make thee twisted cords*: This refers to the white threads; whence do we learn that this applies also to the blue threads? From the verse, *That they put with the fringe of each corner a thread of blue* (Num. 15:38). *Make*: Do not use that which is already made, indicating that one may not pull threads out of the prayer shawl and make (the fringes) out of them.

Upon the four (corners)—and not on eight (corners)—*of thy covering* (22:12): Excluding the following (types of clothing): toga, *tuḇla,*[3] *tiḇalṭir,*[4] *taḳraḳ,*[5] *buras,*[6] and *burdas,*[7] since they are not four-cornered. R. Eliezer ben Jacob says: Whence do we learn that the cords may not be attached to the middle of the garment but only to the border? From the verse, *Upon the four corners*.

Of thy covering—excluding a *sadin*[8]—*wherewith thou coverest (thyself)* (22:12)—excluding *sagus*.[9] *Wherewith*—excluding a duster,[10] which does not cover (most of) one's head and body.

Pisḳa 235

If any man take a wife, and go in unto her, and hate her (22:13): R. Judah says: If he goes in unto her, he is liable to a flogging; if he does not go in unto her, he is not liable.[1] *(And hate her)*:[2] Hence you learn[3] that if one transgresses a minor commandment, he will eventually come to transgress a major commandment. If he transgresses *Thou shalt love thy neighbor as thyself* (Lev. 19:18), he will eventually transgress *Thou shalt not take vengeance, nor bear any grudge* (Lev. 19:18), *Thou shalt not hate thy brother in thy heart* (Lev. 19:17),[4] and *That thy brother may live with thee* (Lev. 25:36), until he ends by shedding blood. Therefore Scripture says, *If a man take a wife . . . (and hate her)*.

And lay wanton charges against her (22:14): One might think that this applies even if he tells her, "You have spoiled my dinner," when in fact she had not; therefore the verse states, *wanton charges*, (that is to say, false charges). *Wanton charges*: This is meant to draw an analogy: just as *wanton charges* mentioned further on (22:17) refer to charges of lack of virginity,[5] so *wanton charges* stated here refer to charges of lack of virginity. Or (one might argue that) if *wanton charges* mentioned further on refer to lack of virginity, and that therefore wanton charges stated here must also refer to lack of virginity, whence do we learn that this applies also to intercourse which does not result in loss of virginity? From the following words, *And bring up an evil name upon her* (22:14).

And say: I took this woman—this shows that he must say these words in her presence[6]—*and when I came nigh to her, I found not in her the tokens of virginity* (22:14)—hence there are witnesses that she had become unchaste in her father's house.[7]

{*If a man take a wife*: Why is this said? Because Scripture says elsewhere, *And the man that committeth adultery with another man's wife* (Lev. 20:10). Whether the witnesses who testify that she had become unchaste in her father's house come from her husband's house or from her father's house, she must be judged at the city gate. But does not Scripture make an exception of the case when the witnesses to her unchastity in her father's house come from her husband's house, so that she is to be judged at the door of her father's house?[8] That is precisely why Scripture says, *If a man take a wife . . . (and hate her)*. R. Ishmael says: Come and see what terrible things hate may lead to, down to defamation of character.[9]}

Then shall the father of the damsel and her mother (22:15): I conclude that this refers only to a damsel whose father and mother are living. What about one who has a father but not a mother, a mother but not a father, or neither father nor mother? The verse states, *damsel*—

irrespective of her parents. If that is so, why does Scripture go on to say, *the father of the damsel and her mother?* So that those who had raised evil progeny shall come and be disgraced together with their progeny.[10]

(Take) and bring forth the tokens of the damsel's virginity . . .—literally[11]—*and the damsel's father shall say unto the elders*—hence we learn that a woman may not speak in the man's stead[12]—*I gave my daughter unto this man* (22:15–16): Hence we learn that a father is authorized to betroth his minor daughter.[13]

Pisḳa 236

(I gave my daughter unto this man) to wife, and he hateth her; and lo, he hath laid wanton charges, saying: "I found not in thy daughter the tokens of virginity"; and yet these are the tokens of my daughter's virginity (22:16–17): Here are witnesses to rebut his witnesses.

[R. Judah says: He may never be held liable unless he had had intercourse with her. *(And the damsel's father shall say)*: Hence we learn that he who initiates a claim must speak first.][1]

(If a man be found lying with a woman) married to a husband (22:22): R. Ishmael says: Scripture means to indicate to you that in the case of a widow subject to levirate marriage, one who has intercourse with her is not liable until she has had intercourse (with her husband).[2]

Pisḳa 237

[*And they shall spread the garment (before the elders)* (22:17): They must make their words as clear as if the garment itself were exhibited. This is one of the instances in which R. Ishmael interpreted the Torah symbolically.[1] Another instance is: *If the sun be risen upon him, there shall be bloodguiltiness for him* (Exod. 22:2). Does the sun rise only upon him? What then does the verse mean by, *If the sun be risen upon him, there shall be bloodguiltiness for him?* Just as the sun has peaceful intentions towards the entire world, so too, if the householder knew that the thief had peaceful intentions toward him, yet slew him nevertheless, he is liable. Another instance is: *If he rise again, and walk abroad upon his staff* (Exod. 21:19), meaning, if he is restored to health. Accordingly, *And they shall spread the garment* means that they must make their words as clear as if the garment itself were exhibited. R. ʿAḳiba says: *And they shall spread the garment before the elders of the city* indicates that the husband's witnesses are thus shown to be false.] *And they shall spread the garment*: The witnesses for each side must come forward and give their testimony before the elders of the city. R. Eliezer ben Jacob, however, says: The matter is to be taken literally.[2]

Pisḳa 238

And the elders of that city shall take the man—but not if he is a minor—*and chastise him* (22:18)—by flogging.

And they shall punish him[1]—monetarily—*a hundred shekels of silver*—Tyrian silver[2]—*and give them unto the father of the damsel*—to be his property—*and give them unto the father of the damsel*—but not if she is an adult woman—*and give them unto the father of the damsel*—except in the case of a proselyte damsel who was conceived in paganism but was born in holiness, since she does not come under the law of one hundred shekels of silver[3]—*because he hath brought up an evil name* (22:19)—not only upon this damsel but upon all virgins in Israel.

And she shall be his wife (22:19): Hence we learn that he must drink out of his refuse-vessel[4]—even if she is lame or blind, even if she is afflicted with boils. But if unchastity is discovered about her, or if she is (otherwise) unworthy of entering into Israel, may he retain her? (No, for) the verse states, *And she shall be his wife*—only if she is a suitable wife for him.

He may not put her away all his days (22:20): Even at a later time. [*All his days*:] He may, however, send her away in order to release her from a (subsequent) levirate marriage.[5]

Pisḳa 239

But if this thing be true (22:20): I conclude that this refers only to intercourse performed in the normal fashion. Whence do we learn that this applies also to abnormal intercourse? From the expression, *be (true)*.[1] One might think that I should include also intercourse by way of other organs of the body; therefore the verse states, *this (thing)*.[2]

That the tokens of virginity were not found in the damsel (22:20): There are no witnesses to prove that his witnesses are false.

Then they shall bring out the damsel to the door of her father's house (22:21): I conclude that this refers only to a damsel who has a father and whose father's house has a door. What about one whose father's house has a door but who has no father?[3] The verse states, *Then they shall bring out the damsel*—whatever her circumstances may be. If that is so, why does Scripture say, *to the door of her father's house?* To indicate that this is the preferable way.[4]

Pisḳa 240

And all[1] *the men of her city shall stone her (with stones)* (22:21): Are all the men of her city to stone her? Rather, it must be done in the presence of all the men of her city. *With stones*: One might think that this is to be done with many stones; therefore Scripture says (elsewhere), *With a stone* (Lev. 20:27). But since it says there, *with a stone,* one might think that only one stone may be used; therefore the verse here states, *with stones,* from which you conclude that if she does not die from the first (stone), she is to die from the second.

Because she hath wrought a wanton deed in Israel—she has disgraced not only herself but also all the virgins in Israel—*to play the harlot in her father's house* (22:21): *Her father* is stated here, and *her father* is stated elsewhere (Lev. 21:9).[2] Just as *her father* stated here[3] refers to unchastity in spite of marital ties, so *her father* stated there must refer to unchastity in spite of marital ties.

So shalt thou put away the evil from the midst of thee (22:21): Remove evildoers from Israel.

Pisḳa 241

If a man be found—by witnesses—*lying with a woman*—any manner of lying—*married to a husband*—including one who had intercourse while in her father's house[1] and is still in the state of betrothal—*(then they shall, even both of them), die* (22:22)—in the manner indicated whenever the Torah prescribes death without further specification, namely by strangulation. *Both of them*—excluding one who practices Herod's deed.[2] By adding the word *even,* the verse includes also those others who may have intercourse with her subsequently.[3]

The man that lay with the woman—even if she is a minor—*and the woman*—even if she had intercourse with a minor—*so shalt thou put away the evil* (22:22)—remove evildoers form Israel.

Pisḳa 242

If there be a damsel that is a virgin betrothed unto a man—showing that the rapist is not liable unless the damsel is a virgin and is betrothed to a man[1]—*and a man find her in the city*—had she not gone out about the city, he would not have come upon her—*in the city and lie with her*—showing that a breach invites a thief—*and lie with her*—in any manner of lying—*then ye shall bring them both out unto the gate of that city*—meaning, as has been said before,[2] the gate within which they were found, and not the gate where they are judged—*and ye shall stone them with stones* (22:23–24): One might think that this is to be done with many stones; therefore Scripture states elsewhere, *With a stone* (Lev. 20:27). Since it states there *with a stone,* one might think that only one stone may be used; therefore the verse here states, *with stones,* from which you conclude that if they do not die from the first (stone), they will die from the second.

The damsel, because she cried not—the word *because*[3] indicates that a prior warning is required, thus including one who deliberately fails to cry out even after being warned in the presence of witnesses—*and the man, because he hath humbled his neighbor's wife* (22:24)—the word *because* indicating that a prior warning is required.

Lest I should conclude that this refers only to (rape occurring within the limits of) a city, Scripture goes on to say, *but if the man (find the damsel) . . . in the field . . . and lie with her*—excluding the case when one man holds her and another man lies with her; so taught R. Judah—*then the man only that lay with her shall die* (22:25)—the rapist by stoning, the other man by strangulation.[4]

Pisḳa 243

But unto the damsel thou shalt do nothing; (there is in the damsel no sin worthy of death) (22:26): Hence we learn that she is exempt from execution. Whence do we learn that she is exempt also from bringing a sacrifice? From the words, *(no) sin.* Whence do we learn that she is exempt also from flogging? From the words, *(no) sin worthy of death.*

For as when a man riseth against his neighbor, and slayeth him (22:26): Hence we learn that a person who acts unlawfully under threat of violence is exempt and may be saved even at the cost of the assailant's life.[1] I might think that this refers only to actual assault; whence do we learn that this applies also to one who merely pursues another person in order to slay him, or pursues a male (in order to rape him)? From what follows, *even so in this matter* (22:26). One might think that this applies also to one who pursues an animal (for sexual purposes), or violates the Sabbath, or commits idolatry; therefore the verse states, *this—this* is a matter which is punishable by stoning, whereas the others are not punished by stoning.[2]

For he found her in the field (22:27): One might think that she is liable if the rape takes place in the city, but exempt if it takes place in the field; therefore the verse goes on to say, *the betrothed damsel cried, and there was none to save her* (22:27)—indicating that if there was someone who could have saved her, whether in the city or in the field, she is liable; if there were none who could have saved her, whether in the city or in the field, she is exempt. *Cried*—except when she said, "Leave him be"; so taught R. Judah.[3]

Pisḳa 244

If a man find a damsel that is a virgin (22:28): *Virgin* is stated here, and *virgin* is stated in the case of seduction (Exod. 22:15). If in the case of rape, which is a greater trespass, the man is not liable unless the woman is a virgin, then in the case of seduction, which is a lesser trespass, should not he be liable only if she is a virgin?[1] Or, (if the term *virgin* had not been used in Exod. 22:15,)[2] one might reason the other way around: If in the case of seduction, which is a lesser trespass, the man is liable both when the woman is a virgin and when she is not a virgin, then in the case of rape, which is a greater trespass, should not he be liable both when she is a virgin and when she is not a virgin? In that case, the fact that *virgin* is stated in the case of rape might be understood to indicate that her father is not entitled to payment for damage (if she is not a virgin), but she is so entitled. Therefore the verse states *virgin,*[3] in order to exclude one who had already lost her virginity. From this I conclude that this refers only to a woman who had been deflowered by way of sexual intercourse. Whence do we learn that this applies also to one who has lost her virginity by accident?[4] From the term *virgin,* thus excluding the latter.[5]

That is not betrothed (22:28) is stated here, and *that is not bethrothed* (Exod. 22:15) is stated in the case of seduction. If in the case of rape, which is a greater trespass, the man is not liable if the woman had been betrothed and then divorced, should not he be free of liability in the case of seduction, which is a lesser trespass, if she had been betrothed and then divorced? Or, (if the term *not bethrothed* had not been used for seduction,) one might reason the other way around: If in the case of seduction, which is a lesser trespass, the man is liable when she had been betrothed and divorced, then in the case of rape, which is a greater trespass, should not he be liable when she had been betrothed and divorced? In that case, the fact that *that is not betrothed* is stated in the case of rape might be understood to indicate that her father is not entitled to payment for damage, but she is. Therefore Scripture states *that is not betrothed* here and *that is not betrothed* there, to indicate that in such a case neither she nor her father is entitled to such payment.

However, *damsel* is stated here, but not in the case of seduction. If in the case of rape, which is a greater trespass, the man is not liable unless the woman is a *damsel,* certainly in the case of seduction, which is a lesser trespass, should not he be liable only if she is a damsel?[6] Or, (if the term *damsel* had been used in Exod. 22:15,) one might reason the other way around: If in the case of seduction, which is a lesser trespass, he is liable both when she is a damsel and when she is older, then in the case of rape, which is a greater trespass, should not he be liable both when she is a damsel and when she is older? Therefore Scripture goes on to say, *Then the man shall give unto the damsel's father (fifty shekels)* (22:29)—but not to the father of the adult woman.[7] Is this not a matter of inference form the minor to the major? If in the case of rape, which is a greater trespass, the man is not liable when she is an adult woman, certainly in the case of seduction, which is of lesser severity, is it not logical that he should not be liable when she is an adult woman? You cannot change the reasoning[8] since *damsel* is stated twice.

And lie with her—in any manner of lying—*and they be found* (22:28)—by witnesses.

Pisḳa 245

Then the man—but not a minor—*that lay with her*—in any manner of lying—*shall give unto the damsel's father*—to be his—*unto the damsel's father*—not unto the father of an adult woman—*fifty shekels of silver*—Tyrian silver—*and she shall be his wife* (22:29): Hence we learn that he must drink from his refuse-vessel, even if she is lame, or blind, or afflicted with boils. But if unseemly things are found about her, or if she is not worthy of entering into Israel, may he retain her? The verse states, *And she shall be his wife*—only when she is a wife suitable for him.[1]

Because he hath humbled her (22:29): Including the case of an orphan girl. Hence the Sages have said:[2] In the case of an orphan girl who has been widowed or divorced, R. Eliezer says: He who rapes her is liable, but he who seduces her is not liable.

He may not put her away all his days (22:29): But he may divorce her in order to free her from the obligation of levirate marriage.

Pisḳa 246

A man shall not take his father's wife (23:1): Hence the Sages have said:[1] One may marry the near relatives of a woman whom he had raped or seduced, but if he rapes or seduces a near relative of his wife, he is liable. One may also marry a woman raped or seduced by his father, or raped or seduced by his son. R. Judah forbids marriage with a woman raped or seduced by one's father, on the ground of *A man shall not take his father's wife.*

Pisḳa 247

He that is crushed (or maimed in his privy parts) shall not enter (into the assembly of the Lord) (23:2): What is meant by *he that is crushed?* One whose testicles are crushed, even if only one of them. I conclude that this refers only to total crushing; whence do we learn that this applies also when the damage is only partial? From the term [*dakka*[1]]. *Or maimed in his privy parts*: Meaning one whose member has been severed. R. Ishmael son of R. Johanan ben Barokah said: I heard (it said) in a vineyard in Jabneh that one who has only one testicle is regarded as a congenital[2] eunuch. [What is the difference between *crushed* and *maimed in his privy parts? He that is crushed* may be restored,[3] while *he that is maimed in his privy parts* cannot be restored. This is the rule of the healers.[4]]. *Into the assembly of the Lord*: R. Judah says: There are four assemblies: the assembly of the priests, the assembly of the Levites, the assembly of Israel, and the assembly of the proselytes. The Sages say: There are only three.[5]

Pisḳa 248

A bastard shall not enter into the assembly of the Lord (23:3): Whether it be a man or a woman. *A bastard shall not enter*—anyone who is a bastard. What is the definition of a bastard? The issue of any union forbidden because of consanguineous relationship;[1] so taught R. ᶜAḳiba, as it is said, *A man shall not take his father's wife* (23:1). . . . *A bastard shall not enter into the assembly of the Lord*: just as the father's wife is characterized as a consanguineous relative, so that she is forbidden for cohabitation, and the offspring is considered a bastard, so too is any consanguineous relative forbidden for cohabitation, and the offspring is considered a bastard. Simeon the Yemenite says: The offspring of any union forbidden under penalty of excision[2] at the hands of heaven is considered a bastard, as it is said, *A man shall not take his father's wife. . . . A bastard shall not enter into the assembly of the Lord*: just as in the case of the father's wife, who is characterized as forbidden under threat of excision at the hands of heaven, the offspring is considered a bastard, so too in the case of any other union that is forbidden under penalty of excision at the hands of heaven, the offspring is considered a bastard.[3] R. Joshua says: The offspring of any union forbidden under penalty of death at the hands of the court is considered a bastard, as it is said, *A man shall not take his father's wife. . . . A bastard shall not enter into the assembly of the Lord*: just as the father's wife is characterized as forbidden under penalty of death at the hands of the court, and the offspring is considered a bastard, so too in any union forbidden under penalty of death at the hands of the court, the offspring is considered a bastard.

Even to the tenth generation(23:3): *The tenth generation* is mentioned here, and *the tenth generation* is mentioned in the next verse (23:4); just as *the tenth generation* there is explained by the following *for ever* (23:4), so *the tenth generation* here must also mean "for ever."

Pisḳa 249

An Ammonite or a Moabite shall not enter into the assembly of the Lord (23:4): [Scripture is speaking here of males and not of females]—a male Ammonite but not a female one, a male Moabite but not a female one; so taught R. Judah.[1] The Sages[2] say: *Because they met you not with bread and with water* (23:5): Who is it that goes out to meet guests? Men, not women. One might reason[3] that since in the case of the bastard, where "for ever" is not used, both women and men are included, certainly in the case of Ammonites and Moabites, where *for ever* is used, both women and men should be included. Or one might reason the other way around: If in the case of Ammonites and Moabites, where *for ever* is used, women are not included along with men, should not the same apply in the case of the bastard, where "for ever" is not used, so that women should not be included along with men? Therefore the verse states, *A bastard shall not enter* (23:3)—whether male or female; thus after the Scripture has added, it now excludes.[4] Thus one is forced to reason as first suggested, namely that if in the case of the bastard, where "for ever" is not used, both women and men are included, should not the same apply to the case of Ammonites and Moabites, where *for ever* is used, so that both women and men should be included? Hence that is why Scripture uses the masculine gender *Ammonite,* not "Ammonitess"; so taught R. Judah.

If Scripture states *the tenth generation,* why add *for ever* (23:4)?[5] In order to suggest an analogy:[6] *Tenth generation* is stated here, and *tenth generation* is stated earlier;[7] just as *tenth generation* here is *for ever, so tenth generation* stated earlier also means "for ever."

Pisḳa 250

Because they met you not with bread and with water (23:5): *Because*[1] refers to their (devious) advice, as it is said, *O my people, remember now what Balak king of Moab devised* (Mic. 6:5).

In the way—at the time of your trouble—*when ye came forth out of Egypt*—at the time of your redemption—*and because they hired against thee Balaam the son of Beor (. . . to curse thee)*—this is a compliment[2] to Balaam—*nevertheless the Lord thy God would not hearken unto Ba-*

laam—showing that he who curses is himself accursed—showing that the one who curses (Israel) in fact curses himself;[3] and why?—*because the Lord thy God loved thee* (23:5–6).

Pisḳa 251

Thou shalt not seek their peace nor their prosperity (23:7): Since Scripture says, *When thou drawest nigh unto a city to fight against it, then proclaim peace unto it* (20:10), one might think that this would apply here as well. Therefore the verse states, *Thou shalt not seek their peace nor their prosperity.* Since Scripture says, *In his prosperity, thou shalt not wrong him* (23:17),[1] one might think that this would apply here as well; therefore the verse states, *nor their prosperity.*

All thy days for ever (23:7): And for ever and ever.

Pisḳa 252

Thou shalt not abhor an Edomite—for what reason?—*for he is thy brother*—and great is brotherhood—*thou shalt not abhor an Egyptian*—for what reason?—*because thou wast a stranger in his land* (23:8): R. Eleazar ben Azariah said: The Egyptians accepted the Israelites only in order to exploit them for their own benefit; nevertheless God granted them a reward. Is this not a matter of inference from the minor to the major? If he who without intending to perform a meritorious deed performs it is spoken of by Scripture as having earned merit for it, how much more so should he who performs the deed intentionally earn merit for it? R. Simeon says: The Egyptians drowned the Israelite infants in water, and the Edomites confronted the Israelites with the sword, yet Scripture prohibited (their entry into the assembly of the Lord) for only three generations. Since the Ammonites and the Moabites plotted to make Israel sin, Scripture prohibited them forever, thus showing you that causing a person to sin is a greater offense than slaying him, for he who slays him removes him from this world, whereas he who causes him to sin removes him from both this world and the world to come.

Pisḳa 253

The children (23:9): Male children, but not female children;[1] so taught R. Simeon. The Sages, however, say: *That are born unto them* (23:9) adds the female children.[2] R. Simeon says: This is a matter of inference from the minor to the major: If in a case where the males are prohibited forever, the females are permitted immediately,[3] in a case where the males are prohibited for only three generations, should not the females be permitted immediately? The Sages said to him: If you are reporting a rule, we will accept it; but if it is a matter of logical reasoning, we have an answer.[4] He said to them: It is definitely a rule that I am reporting, and Scripture supports me, for it says, *The children,* (implying only male,) not female, children.

Of the third generation (23:9): Is it possible that the first and second generation would be permitted and only the third prohibited?[5] Therefore the verse states, *The third generation . . . may enter into the assembly of the Lord* (23:9): This indicates that the first and second generations are prohibited but the third is permitted. R. Judah said: Benjamin, an Egyptian proselyte who was my colleague among the disciples of R. ʿAḳiba, said, "I am an Egyptian proselyte married to an Egyptian female proselyte. I intend to have my son marry the daughter of an Egyptian female proselyte, so that my grandson may be fit to enter the congregation, thus fulfilling that which is stated in Scripture, *The third generation may enter into the assembly of the Lord.*"[6]

Pisḳa 254

When thou goest forth in camp against thine enemies—when you go forth, go forth in a camp[1]—*against thine enemies*—when you are about to wage war against your enemies—*then thou shalt keep thee from every evil thing* (23:10): I might take this as indicating that Scripture is speaking here of cleanness, uncleanness, and tithes; however, Scripture further on uses the term *unseemly thing* (*ʿerwah*) (23:15).[2] I conclude that this refers only to sexual matters. Whence do we learn that this includes also idolatry, bloodshed, and blasphemy? From what the verse goes on to say, *Then thou shalt keep thee from every evil thing.* Or one might think that *then thou shalt keep thee* refers only to cleanness, uncleanness, and tithes; therefore the verse further on uses the term *unseemly thing*: just as *unseemly thing* is characterized as any action for which the Canaanites were exiled and which causes the Shekinah to depart (from this world),[3] so is any other action for which the Canaanites were exiled and which causes the Shekinah to depart. When Scripture says *thing (dabar)*,[4] it refers also to (verbal) slander.

[Another interpretation: *Then thou shalt keep thee*: Take care not to think about lecherous matters which will cause you a seminal discharge at night.]

Piska 255

If there be among you—and not among others—*a man*—thus excluding a minor—*that is not clean by reason of that which chanceth him by night* (23:11): I conclude that this refers only to a seminal discharge at night. What about such a discharge during the day? The verse states, *that is not clean*—at any time. But if so, why does Scripture state, *that which chanceth him by night*? To indicate that Scripture speaks here of that which happens ordinarily.

Then shall he go abroad out of the camp—this is a positive commandment—*he shall not come within the camp* (23:11)—this is a negative commandment. R. Simeon says: *Then shall he go abroad out of the camp* refers to the Levitical camp; *he shall not come within the camp* refers to the camp of the Shekinah.[1]

Piska 256

But it shall be, when evening cometh on, he shall bathe himself in water—showing that a seminal discharge exempts one from becoming unclean by reason of a flux for a twenty-four hour period[1]—*and when the sun is down, (he may come within the camp)* (23:12): The setting of the sun prevents his re-entering the camp, but a flux discharge does not prevent him from re-entering it.[2]

Piska 257

Thou shalt have a hand[1] *also without the camp*—*hand* means a place, as it is said, *Behold, he is setting himself up a hand*[2] (1 Sam. 15:12), and *Every man in his hand,*[2] *by their standards* (Num. 2:17)—*whither thou shalt go forth abroad* (23:13)—not in standing position.[3]

And thou shalt have a paddle among thy weapons—thy weapons (ʾăzeneḵa) means the place where your weapons (*zeyneḵa*) are kept—*and it shall be, when thou sittest down abroad*—and not when sitting[4]—*thou shalt dig therewith, and shalt turn back and cover that which cometh from thee* (23:14): I might think that one must have one tool for digging and another tool for covering; therefore the verse states, *Thou shalt dig therewith.*

R. Simeon says: Whence do we learn that one may not turn his loins toward the south?[5] From the verse, *Thou shalt dig therewith, and shalt turn back and cover that which cometh from thee. (For the Lord thy God walketh in the midst of thy camp. . . . that He see no unseemly thing in thee, and turn away from thee)* (23:14–15).

Pisḳa 258

For the Lord thy God walketh in the midst of thy camp (23:15): Hence the Sages have said:[1] One should not recite the Shemaʿ next to the launderers' soaking tub,[2] nor should one enter a bathhouse or a tannery holding in his hand scrolls or phylacteries.[3]

To deliver thee, and to give up thine enemies before thee—if you do all that was said in this matter, in the end He will deliver you and give up your enemies before you—*therefore shall thy camp be holy* (23:15): Make it holy. Hence the Sages have said: One should not enter the Temple Mount carrying his staff, sandals, purse, or even the dust upon his feet.[4]

That He see no unseemly thing in thee, and turn away from thee (23:15): This indicates that unchastity drives away the Shekinah.[5]

Pisḳa 259

Thou shalt not deliver unto his master a bondman—hence the Sages have said: If one sells his slave to a heathen or to someone outside the Land (of Israel), he goes free[1]—*that is escaped from his master unto thee* (23:16)—including a resident alien.[2]

He shall dwell with thee—and not in the city by himself[3]—*in the midst of thee*—and not in the border area—*in the place which he shall choose*—in the place where he earns his livelihood—*within one of thy gates*—within your gates, but not in Jerusalem;[4] Scripture states *within one of thy gates* in order to indicate that he should not have to wander from city to city—*where it liketh him best*—away from an evil dwelling place to a good dwelling place—*thou shalt not wrong him* (23:17)—this refers to wronging him with words.[5] [Another interpretation: *Thou shalt not deliver unto his master a bondman*: Scripture is speaking here of a Gentile who has been rescued from idolatry.]

Piska 260

There shall be no harlot of the daughters of Israel—you are not warned concerning (a harlot) of the other nations—*neither shall there be a sodomite of the sons of Israel* (23:18)—you are not warned concerning (a sodomite) of the other nations. One might reason that if in the case of an Israelite harlot, whose trespass is of lesser severity, you are warned against her, should you not be warned also against an Israelite sodomite, whose trespass is of greater severity? Or one might reason the other way around: If in the case of the sodomite, whose trespass is of greater severity, one is not warned against a Gentile sodomite, what need was there in the case of the harlot, whose trespass is of lesser severity, to warn against a Gentile harlot?[1] Why then does the verse add *a sodomite*? It was necessary to add this, for had the verse mentioned the harlot alone, and not the sodomite, I might have reasoned that if in the case of the harlot, whose trespass is of lesser severity, you are warned only against an Israelite harlot, should you not in the case of the sodomite, whose trespass is of greater severity, be warned also against a Gentile sodomite? Therefore the verse states, *There shall be no harlot of the daughters of Israel*—you are not warned against a Gentile harlot—*neither shall there be a sodomite of the sons of Israel*—you are not warned against a Gentile sodomite. [Another interpretation: *There shall be no harlot*: This is a warning open for interpretation, as it is said, *there hath been no harlot here* (Gen. 38:21).[2]]

Piska 261

Thou shalt not bring the hire of a harlot (23:19): I conclude that this refers only to the hire of a harlot; whence do we learn that this refers also to the hire of any other sexual transgression? From the term, *the hire*—any kind of such hire. What is meant by *the hire of a harlot?* If one says to a harlot, "Take this lamb for your hire," even if there are a hundred lambs, they are all forbidden.[1] If one says to his fellow, "Take this lamb, and have your maidservant sleep with my manservant," Rabbi (Judah the Prince) says that this is not hire, but the Sages say that it is hire.[2]

Or the price of a dog (23:19): What is meant by *the price of a dog?* When one says to his fellow, "Take this lamb (in exchange) for your dog."[3] One might think that he is guilty even if he merely walks it[4] through the Temple Court; but Scripture here terms it *an abomination* (23:19), as it does elsewhere (17:1)—just as the abomination stated there refers to an animal intended as a sacrifice, so the abomination stated here refers to an animal intended as a sacrifice.

(For any) vow (23:19): Excluding that which has already been vowed. When Scripture says *for any vow,* it includes the temporary altar.[5]

Into the house of the Lord thy God (23:19): This excludes the heifer of the sin offering[6] that does not come into the Temple; so taught R. Eliezer. The Sages say: This includes the plates of beaten gold.[7]

For any vow (23:19): This includes birds.[8] For one might have reasoned that if in the case of dedicated animals, which are unfit if they have a blemish, the law of the harlot's hire and of the dog's price does not apply, should not the law be inapplicable also in the case of birds, which are not disqualified by a blemish? Therefore the verse states, *for any vow*—including birds. One might think that payment for the time that the heifer has been taken away from her work would also be forbidden; therefore the verse states, *For even both these are an abomination* (23:19)—*both,* but not four;[9] *these,* but not their issue or their substitutes.

Pisḳa 262

Thou shalt not lend upon interest to thy brother (23:20): This refers to the borrower.[1] Whence do we learn that it refers also to the lender? From the verse, *Take thou no interest of him or increase* (Lev. 25:36).[2] Since the following verse says, *thy money* (Lev. 25:37), it follows, not the money of others; *thy victuals* (Lev. 25:37), not the victuals of others. Or one could argue that *thy money* implies not tithe money, and *thy victuals,* not animal victuals. But Scripture goes on to say here, *interest of money* (23:20), thus including tithe money, *interest of victuals* (23:20), thus including animal victuals. I conclude that this applies only to interest of money and interest of victuals. What about interest of all other things? The verse goes on to say, *Interest of anything that is lent upon interest* (23:20). R. Simeon says: Whence do we learn that the lender may not say to the borrower, "Go and see how So-and-so is," or "Let me know if So-and-so from such-and-such place has arrived"?[3] From the verse, *Interest of anything that is lent upon interest.*

Pisḳa 263

Unto a foreigner thou mayest lend upon interest; but unto thy brother thou shalt not lend upon interest (23:21): *Unto a foreigner thou mayest lend upon interest*—that is a positive commandment—*but unto thy brother thou shalt not lend upon interest*—that is a negative commandment. Rabban Gamaliel says: Why does Scripture say again, *But unto thy brother thou shalt not lend upon interest,* having already said, *Thou shalt not lend upon interest to thy brother* (23:20)? Because there is advanced interest and delayed interest. How so? When B, intending to borrow from A, sends him (some money), saying (to himself), "This is so that he will lend me (more money)," that is advanced interest. If B, having borrowed from A, repays the loan, and then sends him (more money), saying (to himself), "This is (to reimburse him for not having) the use of his money while it was in my possession," that is delayed interest.

That the Lord thy God may bless thee in all that thou puttest thy hand unto—Scripture has appointed a blessing for him in his endeavors—*in the land whither thou goest in to possess it* (23:21): As a reward for going in, you will possess it.

Pisḳa 264

When thou shalt vow a vow unto the Lord (thy God) (23:22): *Vow* is stated here, and *vow* is stated elsewhere (Lev. 7:16). Just as *vow* stated there includes both vow and freewill offering, so *vow* stated here includes both vow and freewill offering; and just as concerning the vow stated here, *Thou shalt not be slack to pay it* (23:22), so concerning the vow stated there, *Thou shalt not be slack to pay it. Unto the Lord thy God*—this refers to (offerings of) valuation and dedication to the priesthood or to the Temple.

Thou shalt not be slack to pay it—it, not a substitute for it—*for the Lord thy God will surely require it—it* refers to sin offerings and guilt offerings,[1] while *the Lord thy God* refers to that which is dedicated to the repair of the Temple—*of thee*—this refers to gleanings, forgotten sheaves, and corner crop[2]—*and it will be sin in thee* (23:22)—it will be a sin in you but not in your sacrifice.[3]

Piska 265

But if thou shalt forbear to vow (23:23): R. Meir says:[1] *Better is it that thou shouldest not vow, than that thou shouldest vow and not pay* (Eccl. 5:4)—even better than either[2] is not vowing at all. R. Judah, however, says: *Better is it that thou shouldest not vow*—even better than either[3] is vowing and paying.

That which is gone out of thy lips—this is a positive commandment—*thou shalt observe*[4]—this is a negative commandment—*and do*—this is a warning to the court to make you fulfill (your vow)—*according as thou hast vowed freely*—this refers to the (ordinary) vow—*unto the Lord thy God*—this refers to valuations and vows to the priesthood and to the Temple—*a donation*—this refers to freewill offerings—*even that which thou hast spoken*—this refers to gifts dedicated to the repair of the Temple—*with thy mouth* (23:24)—this refers to alms.

Piska 266

When thou comest unto thy neighbor's vineyard, (then thou mayest eat grapes) (23:25): One might think that this means at any time;[1] therefore the verse goes on to say, *but thou shalt not put any in thy vessel* (23:25)—meaning at the same time that you put grapes into the vessel of the owner. *Thy neighbor's*—excluding others; *thy neighbor's*—excluding the Most High. *Then thou mayest eat*—but not press—*grapes*—but not figs. Hence you conclude that if one is gathering figs, he may not eat of the grapes; or if he is gathering grapes, he may not eat of the figs. Rather, he must restrain himself until he comes to the place where the best fruit is and then eat of it.[2] R. Eliezer Ḥismah says: Whence do we learn that a laborer may not eat more than the value of his wages? From the following, *(Until thou have enough) at thine own pleasure*[3] (23:25). The Sages, however, say: *Until thou have enough*—this shows that a laborer may eat more than the value of his wages.

But thou shalt not put any in thy vessel (23:25): During the time when you are putting them into the owner's vessels.[4]

Pisḳa 267

When thou comest into thy neighbor's standing corn (23:26): One might think that this means at any time; therefore the verse goes on to say, *But thou shalt not move a sickle* (23:26)—only at the time when you move a sickle unto the owner's standing corn. *Thy neighbor's*—excluding others; *thy neighbor's*—excluding the Most High.

Then thou mayest pluck ears with thy hand—but not harvest with a scythe—*but thou shalt not move a sickle* (23:26)—at the time when you move a sickle upon the owner's standing corn.[1]

Pisḳa 268

When a man taketh a wife, and marrieth her (24:1): This shows that a woman may be acquired in marriage with money.[1] For one might reason that if a Hebrew maidservant, who may not be acquired in marriage by way of intercourse, may be acquired with money, should not a (free) woman, who may be acquired in marriage by way of intercourse, be acquired also with money? The case of a childless widow might indicate the opposite, for she may be acquired by way of intercourse but not with money; therefore do not be amazed that a woman, even though acquired by way of intercourse, may not be acquired with money. Hence Scripture states here, *When a man taketh a wife, and marrieth her,* showing that a woman may be acquired in marriage with money.[2]

And marrieth her: This shows that a woman may be acquired in marriage by way of intercourse. For one might reason that if a childless widow, who may not be acquired with money, may be acquired by way of intercourse, should not a woman who may be acquired with money, be acquired also by way of intercourse? The case of a Hebrew maidservant might indicate the opposite, for she may be acquired with money but not by way of intercourse; therefore do not be amazed that a woman, even though acquired with money, may not be acquired by way of intercourse. Hence Scripture states here *and marrieth her,* showing that a woman may be acquired in marriage by way of intercourse.

Whence do we learn that a woman (may also be acquired) by way of a document? One might reason that if (payment of) money, which cannot effect a divorce, can acquire her, should not a document, which does effect a divorce, effect also acquisition? Not so, for while you can say this about money, which may purchase consecrated property and second tithe, you cannot say it about a document, which cannot purchase consecrated property and second tithe. Hence Scripture goes on to say, *That he writeth her a bill of divorcement, and giveth it in her hand, and sendeth her out of his house, and she departeth out of his house, and goeth and becometh another man's wife* (24:1–2), thus drawing an analogy between her wedlock with her second husband and her divorce from her first husband: just as her divorce from the latter is effected by a document, so her wedlock with the former is effected by a document.

Pisḳa 269

Then it cometh to pass, if she find no favor in his eyes (24:1): Hence the School of Shammai taught:[1] A man may not divorce his wife unless he has found her guilty of sexual misconduct, as it is said, *Because he hath found some unseemly thing in her* (24:1). The School of Hillel, however, says: (He may dismiss her) even if she has merely spoiled his meal, as it is said, *thing.*[2] The School of Hillel retorted to the School of Shammai: If Scripture says *thing,* why does it say *unseemly?* And if it says *unseemly,* why does it say *thing?* For had it said *thing* without saying *unseemly,* I would have said that a woman divorced for a *thing* may remarry, whereas one divorced because of unseemliness may not. And do not be amazed, for if she is forbidden to the man who is permitted to her,[3] should she not be forbidden to the man who is forbidden to her?[4] Therefore Scripture says, *Unseemly (thing).* . . . *And she departeth out of his house, and goeth and becometh another man's wife* (24:1–2). And had it said *unseemly* without saying *thing,* I would have said that she may be divorced only for something *unseemly* but not for a *thing.* Therefore Scripture says, *Thing. . . . And she departeth out of his house.*[5] R. ʿAḳiba says: (He may divorce her) even if he finds another woman more comely than she is, as it is said, *Then it cometh to pass, if she find no favor in his eyes.*

That he writeth her (a bill of divorcement) (24:1): Specifically in her name. Hence the Sages have said: Any bill of divorcement not written specifically in the name of the woman is not valid. How so? If the husband was passing through the market place, etc.[6]

That he writeth: I conclude that this refers only to writing with plain ink; what about pigment (*sam*),[7] red paint (*siḳra*), gum ink (*ḳumos*), or vitriol ink (*ḳanḳantum*)? The verse states, *that he writeth*—with any kind of fluid.

A bill[8]: I conclude that this refers only to a scroll (*sefer*); what about (a bill written on) the leaves of reed, of nut tree, of olive tree, of carob tree? The verse goes on to say, *and giveth (it)* (24:1)—whatever it is written on. If so, why does it say, *a bill*? Just as a bill is characterized as something which endures, so anything else which endures is permitted, thus excluding anything which does not endure.[9] R. Judah ben Betherah says: Since a bill is characterized as something which is separated from the ground, anything which is still attached to the ground is excluded.

Divorcement[10]: Meaning that the couple are cut off from each other.[11] Hence you conclude that if a man says to his wife, "Behold, this is your bill of divorcement, on condition that you never again go to your father's house," or "on condition that you never again drink wine," this does not constitute a cutting off. (If he says,) "on condition that you do not go to your father's house for the next thirty days," or "on condition that you do not drink wine for the next thirty days," this constitutes a cutting off. If one divorces his wife by saying to her, "Behold, you are permitted to any man except So-and-so,"[12] R. Eliezer permits it[13] but the Sages forbid it.[14] After R. Eliezer's death, four elders gathered together to reply to his ruling: R. Tarfon, R. Jose the Galilean, R. Eleazar ben Azariah, and R. ʿAḳiba.[15] R. Tarfon said: If she went and married So-and-so's brother, who then died without issue, how could she fulfill the obligation of levirate marriage?[16] Would this not be an instance of attaching a condition to an ordinance written in the Torah? Yet the rule is that such a condition is null and void; hence you learn that such a conditioned divorce is not considered a valid cutting off. R. Jose the Galilean said: Where do we find in the Torah that a woman is permitted to one man but forbidden to another man? Rather, if she is permitted to one man, she is permitted to any other man, and if she is forbidden to one man, she is forbidden to any other man. Thus you learn that such a divorce is not a valid cutting off. R. Eleazar ben Azariah said: *Divorcement* means something that makes a cutting between him and her.[17] R. Jose the Galilean said: I concur with the view of R. Eleazar ben Azariah. R. ʿAḳiba said: In which case is the Torah stricter, that of the divorcée or that of the widow? The law of the divorcée is more strict than the law of the widow. If the widow, whose case is more lenient, is forbidden to marry a man who is otherwise permitted to her, should not a divorcée, whose case is more strict, be forbidden to marry a man who is otherwise also forbidden to her? Thus we learn that this is not a valid cutting off.[18] Another case is that of a woman who marries a man and has children by him; after his death she marries this (second) husband (who was forbidden to her by her first husband). Would not the children of her first husband be bastards?[19] Thus you learn that this is not a valid cutting off.

In her hand (24:1): I conclude that this refers only to (depositing the bill in) her hand; what about (depositing it) in her garden, her courtyard, or the ruins (of her house)? The verse states, *and giveth it*—anywhere.[20] If this is so, why does Scripture say, *in her hand?* Just as her hand is characterized by belonging to her, so does anything else that belongs to her.

And giveth it in her hand, and sendeth her out of his house (24:1): Having given the bill into her hand, he is to send her out of his house. Hence the Sages have said: If one throws the bill of divorcement to his wife while she is in her house or her courtyard, she is divorced, etc. If he says to her, "Take in this bill of debt," or if she finds it behind him, etc.[21]

Pisḳa 270

And she departeth out of his house—hence you learn that the woman must leave the man—*and goeth and becometh another man's wife* (24:2): She may not marry him in the same neighborhood. *Another*—the Torah already designates him as different.[1]

And the latter husband hateth her—Scripture informs you that you too will eventually come to hate her—*or if the latter husband die* (24:3)—Scripture informs you that she will eventually bury him. I conclude that this refers only to a divorcée;[2] what about a widow? The verse states, *Or if the latter husband die.* If we are eventually going to include the widow in any case, why does Scripture speak only of a divorcée?[3] Because a levir may marry his brother's widow, but not his divorcée.[4] One might also think that if a woman was unfaithful to her husband after she had been divorced, she would also be forbidden to return to him;[5] therefore the preceding verses state, *And writeth her a bill of divorcement. . . . And she departeth (. . . and becometh another man's wife).* A woman who received a writ of divorce (from her second husband) is forbidden to return to her first husband, whereas one who has been unfaithful to him after she had been divorced[6] is not forbidden to return to him.

Whence do we learn that if a levir gives a writ of divorce to his widowed sister-in-law, he is forbidden to return to her? From the verse, *Her former husband, (who sent her away,) may not (take her again to be his wife)* (24:4). But what about a woman whose husband had gone to a place beyond the sea, and who was informed that he had died, whereupon she married again, and then her first husband returned? Must she leave both of them, and does she require a writ of divorce from both of them? The verse states, *Her former husband, who sent her away, may not take her again to be his wife*—he cannot take again the wife he had sent away.[7]

Who sent her away: I conclude that this means only from matrimony to matrimony;[8] what about espousal to espousal,[9] espousal to matrimony, or matrimony to espousal? The verse states, *Her former husband, (who sent her away,) may not (take her again)*—the first husband may not take back the woman he has sent away. R. Jose ben Kippar says in the name of R. Eleazar ben Azariah: After espousal she may be taken back, after matrimony she may not, as it is said, *After that she is defiled*[10] (24:4). The Sages, however, say: She is forbidden in either case. If so, why does Scripture say, *After that she is defiled*? In order to include the case of a wayward wife who had secluded herself with another man.[11] Similarly Scripture says, *If a man put away his wife, and she go from him, (and become another man's, may he return unto her again?)*[12] (Jer. 3:1).

For she[13] *is abomination (before the Lord)*—R. Judah says: She is an abomination, but her child is not an abomination—*and thou shalt not cause the land to sin* (24:4)—this is a warning to the court about this matter.

Piska 271

When a man taketh a new wife (. . . he shall be free for his house one year) (24:5): I conclude that this refers only to a virgin; what about a widow or a woman awaiting levirate marriage? The verse goes on to say, *and shall cheer his wife* (24:5)—whichever one she may be. If so, why does Scripture say, *new*? One who is new to him, thus excluding the case of a man who takes back his divorced wife, of a widow married to a High Priest, of a divorcée or a woman released from levirate marriage who is married to a common priest, of a female bastard or a woman of Gibeonite descent married to an Israelite, or of an Israelite woman married to a bastard or to a man of Gibeonite descent.[1]

He shall not go out in the host (24:5): One might think that he may not go out in the host, but may supply them with weapons, water, and food;[2] therefore the verse goes on to say, *Neither shall he be charged with any business* (24:5)—if he is not to be charged with any business, perhaps this applies even if he had built a house but had not dedicated it, planted a vineyard but not yet used the fruit thereof, betrothed a wife but had not yet wed her?[3] Therefore the verse states *neither shall he be charged*—he may not be charged with (military) business, but all others may be so charged.[4]

He shall be free for his house—this refers to his house, while *shall be* refers to his vineyard—*and shall cheer his wife*—this refers to his wife—*whom he hath taken* (24:5)—this includes his widowed sister-in-law.

Piska 272

No man shall take the mill or the upper millstone to pledge (24:6): I conclude that this refers expressly to the mill or the upper millstone; what about all other such objects? The verse goes on to say, *for he taketh a man's life to pledge* (24:6). If so, why does Scripture say, *the mill or the upper millstone?* Just as the mill and the upper millstone are characterized as two tools which are used to perform one task, yet the pledgee is liable for each one of them separately, so in the case of any other two tools which are used to perform one task, the pledgee is liable for each one of them separately.[1] *For he taketh a man's life to pledge* (24:6)—this explains the reason (for the rule).

Pisḳa 273

If a man be found—before witnesses[1]—*man*—excluding a minor—*stealing any of his brethren*—and not of others—*of the children of Israel* (24:7): Thus including him who steals his own son and sells him, who is equally liable. So taught R. Johanan ben Baroḳah, while the Sages say: He who steals his own son and sells him is not liable.

And he deal with him as a slave, (and sell him) (24:7): This shows that he is not liable until he takes him into his possession. R. Judah, however, says: Until he takes him into his possession and uses him, as it is said, *And he deal with him as a slave,*[2] *and sell him.*

Then that thief shall die—by the method of execution intended whenever unspecified death penalty is mentioned in the Torah, namely strangulation[3]—*that (thief)*—but not one who steals someone who is a slave or is half-slave and half-free—*and thou shalt put away the evil from the midst of thee* (24:7)—remove the evildoers from Israel.

Pisḳa 274

Take heed—this is a negative commandment—*in the plague*—this means a white hair—*of leprosy* (24:8)—this means a scab. I conclude that this refers only to the time before the patient has been proclaimed unclean. What about the time after he has been proclaimed unclean and after he has been exempted?[1] The verse states, *That thou observe diligently, and do* (24:8). I conclude that this applies only to plagues which afflict human beings; what about plagues afflicting clothing and houses? The verse goes on to say, *According to all that the priests the Levites shall teach you* (24:8). I conclude that this refers only to the time when a decision has been reached; what about the time of temporary confinement? The verse states, *as I commanded them* (24:8). I conclude that *them* refers to all (the white hairs); what about part of them? The verse states, *That thou observe diligently, and do*—you may go about doing (what you normally do), without fearing that this may cause the leprous scab to fall off.[2]

Piska 275

Remember what the Lord thy God did unto Miriam (24:9): What does this have to do with the matter under discussion? The connection here is intended to show you that plagues come only as a result of evil talk.[1] Is this not a matter of reasoning from the minor to the major? If Miriam, who spoke only when Moses was not present, and for Moses' own benefit and in praise of God and the upbuilding of the world,[2] was punished in this way, how much more so should punishment come upon him who speaks disparagingly of his fellow in public.[3]

By the way—at the time of your confusion—*as ye came forth out of Egypt* (24:9)—at the time of your redemption. This verse was connected with Miriam in order to show you that the banners did not journey forth until Miriam went before them, as it is said, *And I sent before thee Moses, Aaron, and Miriam* (Mic. 6:40).[4]

Piska 276

When thou dost lend thy neighbor (24:10): I conclude that this refers only to a loan;[1] what about the wages of a hired man or store debts? The verse goes on to say, *Any manner of loan,*[2] *thou shalt not go into his house.* One might think that the creditor may not seize the pledge from within but may seize it from without; therefore the verse goes on to say, *to fetch his pledge without* (24:10).[3] One might think that he may not seize his pledge from without, but may seize it from within; therefore the Scripture goes on to say, *Thou shalt stand without* (24:11). When Scripture says, *And the man . . . (shall bring forth the pledge)* (24:11), it includes the messenger of the court.

Piska 277

And if he be a poor man (24:12): I conclude that this applies only to a poor man; what about a rich man? The verse states, *And if he be a man.*[1] If so, why does it say *poor*? Because I requite the cause of a poor man more quickly than that of a rich man.[2]

Thou shalt not sleep with his pledge (24:12): Would you possibly think of actually sleeping (wrapped) in[3] his pledge? The meaning is rather that you should not sleep overnight with his pledge in your possession.

Thou shalt surely restore to him the pledge (24:13): This shows that one must restore a daytime garment to him in the daytime and a nighttime garment in the nighttime,[4] a blanket[5] at night and a plow during the day, but not the blanket during the day and the plow at night.

That he may sleep in his garment, and bless thee (24:13): Hence we learn that the pledger is commanded to bless you. Lest one should think that if he blesses you, you are blessed, but if he fails to bless you, you are not blessed, the verse goes on to say, *and it shall be righteousness unto thee* (24:13)—you create your righteousness by your action. *And it shall be righteousness unto thee*—hence you learn that righteousness ascends before the throne of glory, as it is said, *Righteousness shall go before Him, and shall make His footsteps a way* (Ps. 85:14).

Pisḳa 278

Thou shalt not oppress a hired servant that is poor and needy (24:14): Does not Scripture say elsewhere, *Nor rob him* (Lev. 19:13)? Why then does it say here, *Thou shalt not oppress?*[1] Because you learn therefrom that if one withholds the wages of a hired servant, he transgresses four[2] negative commandments, to wit: *Thou shalt not oppress* (Lev. 19:13), *Nor rob* (Lev. 19:13), *The wages . . . shall not abide with thee all night* (Lev. 19:13), and *In the same day thou shalt give him his hire, neither shall the sun go down upon it* (24:15). *(For he is poor), and setteth his heart upon it* (24:15): I conclude therefrom that this applies only to work which he sets his heart upon; what about work which he does not set his heart upon, such as carding and combing (flax)? The verse states, *Thou shalt not oppress* (24:14)—in any kind of work. *(That is poor and needy)*:[3] I conclude that this applies only to a workman who is poor and needy; what about any other workman? The verse states, *Thou shalt not oppress*—any workman, (whether needy or not). If so, why does Scripture say, *poor and needy*? Because I requite the cause of a poor and needy workman more quickly than that of any other person.[4]

Of thy brethren—but not of others—*or of thy strangers* (24:14): This refers to the righteous proselyte, showing that in his case one transgresses two negative commandments.[5] R. Jose ben R. Judah says: (He transgresses) only the commandment not to oppress.[6]

{*Within thy gates* (24:14): This is the resident alien. I conclude therefrom that this applies only to the wages of a hired man; what about the wages of a hired animal or of hired tools? The verse states, *That are in thy land* (24:14)—anything (hired) in your land.[7]}

Pisḳa 279

In the same day thou shalt give him his hire (24:15): This shows that the laborer may collect his wages for the preceding night during all of the next day. Whence do we learn that he may collect his wages for the day during all of the next night? From the verse, *The wages of a hired servant shall not abide with thee all night until the morning* (Lev. 19:13).[1]

Neither shall the sun go down upon it; for he is poor—excluding the time when it is not with him[2]—*and setteth his heart upon it* (24:15): After all, why did he go up on the scaffold and risk his life for you?[3] Was it not so that you would pay him his wages that same day? But if so,[4] why does the verse state, *And setteth his heart upon it?* To indicate that he who withholds the laborer's wages is considered by Scripture as if he had taken his life.

Lest he cry[5] *against thee unto the Lord* (24:15): One might think that this implies a negative commandment not to cry out; therefore Scripture says elsewhere, *And he cry unto the Lord against thee* (15:9). One might think that it is a (positive) commandment to cry out; therefore the verse here states, *Lest he cry against thee unto the Lord.* One might think that if he cries out against you, you will be considered as having sinned, but if he does not cry out against you, you will not be considered as having sinned; therefore the verse here states, *And it be a sin in thee* (24:15)—in any case. But if so, why does Scripture say elsewhere, *And he cry unto the Lord against thee* (15:9)? Because I will requite the cause of him who cries out more quickly than that of him who does not cry out.

Piska 280

The fathers shall not be put to death for the children (24:16): What is it that Scripture wishes to teach us here? That fathers are not to be executed because of (the deeds of) their children? Does it not say elsewhere,[1] *Every man shall be put to death for his own sin* (24:16)? Scripture means rather to tell us that fathers shall not be executed on the testimony of their own children, nor children on the testimony of their own fathers. When it goes on to say, *neither (shall) the children (be put to death for the fathers)* (24:16), it means to include relatives, to wit, one's brother, father's brother, mother's brother, sister's husband, father's sister's husband, mother's sister's husband, mother's husband, father-in-law, and brother-in-law.

Every man shall be put to death for his own sin (24:16): Fathers shall die for their own sin and children for their own sin.

Piska 281

Thou shalt not pervert the justice due to the proselyte[1] (24:17): What do I need this (reminder) for? Is it not stated elsewhere, *Thou shalt not wrest judgment; thou shalt not respect persons* (16:19)? Rather, we learn therefrom that he who perverts the judgment of a proselyte violates two negative commandments, and if the proselyte is also an orphan, he violates three such commandments.

Nor take the widow's raiment to pledge (24:17): Whether she is poor or rich, even if she is (as rich) as Martha daughter of Boethus.[2] R. Simeon says: When you take a pledge from a man, you may not return it to a woman,[3] lest you should go back and forth to her home and thus tarnish her reputation.

Piska 282

When thou reapest thy harvest (24:19): This excludes crops harvested by robbers, nibbled by ants, or broken by wind or by animals.[1] *Thy harvest*—this excludes fields harvested by heathens. Hence the Sages have said: A Gentile who has harvested his field and subsequently became a proselyte is not liable for gleanings, forgotten sheaves, and corner crop. R. Judah, however, requires liability for forgotten sheaves, since such sheaves occur only at the time when the sheaves[2] are formed.

Thy harvest—excluding that of others; *thy harvest*—excluding crops dedicated to the Sanctuary. Thus you may say that if one harvests a dedicated crop, and another Israelite takes it, it is exempt. If a Gentile harvests it, and an Israelite takes it, it is likewise exempt. R. Jose the Galilean says: Since Scripture says, *When thou reapest thy harvest in thy field, and hast forgot a sheaf in the field* (24:19), it follows that whenever one has his own harvest, he has his own sheaves, and is therefore liable for forgotten sheaves; whenever the harvest is not his, he has no sheaves, and is therefore not liable for forgotten sheaves. Thus you may say that if one harvests a dedicated crop, and an Israelite takes it, it is exempt. If a heathen harvests it, and an Israelite takes it, it is likewise exempt.

In thy field (24:19): This excludes one who binds sheaves in his neighbor's field; so taught R. Meir, but the Sages hold him liable. Hence you learn that a sheaf forgotten by the laborers but not by the owner, or vice versa, or a sheaf before which the poor had stationed themselves (to hide it), or which they hid (by covering it) with straw, is not considered a forgotten sheaf.[3]

Pisḳa 283

And hast forgot a sheaf (in the field) (24:19): But not a stack of sheaves. Since one might think that this excludes also two sheaves, the verse goes on to say, *it shall be for the stranger, for the fatherless, and for the widow*[1] (24:19). Hence the Sages have said: Two sheaves may be considered forgotten, but three may not; two bundles of olives or carobs may be considered forgotten, but three may not. Two berries may be considered droppings, but three may not.[2]

In the field—excluding sheaves that have been stored away; so taught R. Judah. The Sages, however, say: *In the field* includes those that have been stored away.[3]

In the field—including the standing corn; for one might have reasoned that if in the case of the sheaf, where the right of the poor is weakened, the rule of forgotten sheaves applies, should it not apply in the case of standing corn, where the right of the poor is strengthened?[4] (The answer is:) No. If you say this of the (forgotten) sheaf, which does not save either the sheaf or the standing corn, can you say it of the standing corn, which does save both the sheaf and the standing corn?[5] Therefore the verse states, *in the field,* in order to include the standing corn.[6]

Thou shalt not go back to fetch it (24:19): Thus excluding the beginnings of rows (of plants). Hence the Sages have said: The sheaves lying opposite the beginnings of rows serve as an indication. If the owner takes up a sheaf with the intention of conveying it to the city, but then forgets it, all agree that it is not a forgotten sheaf.[7]

Thou shalt not go back to fetch it: All of it in one piece.[8] How much should it amount to? The Sages estimated it as enough to yield two sĕᶜah (of produce). Hence the Sages have said: If a sheaf yields two sĕᶜah and is forgotten, it is not considered a forgotten sheaf. If two sheaves yield two sĕᶜah, Rabban Gamaliel says that it belongs to the owner, while the Sages say that it belongs to the poor, etc.[9]

Thou shalt not go back to fetch it: Hence R. Ishmael said: If an ear of corn is left over after the harvest, and its head touches the standing corn, the rule is as follows: if it can be cut together with the standing corn, it belongs to the owner; if not, it belongs to the poor.[10] If the owner wishes to take it from the poor, he must show cause, for he who wishes to take something from another person must show cause.[11] Whence do we learn that doubtful gleanings are gleanings, doubtful forgotten sheaf is forgotten sheaf, and doubtful corner crop is corner crop? From the verse, *It shall be for the stranger, for the fatherless, and for the widow* (24:19).[12]

Said R. Eleazar ben Azariah: Whence do we learn that if one loses a selaᶜ (coin), and a poor man finds it and maintains himself with it, Scripture accounts it to the loser as if he had performed a meritorious deed? From the verse, *It shall be for the stranger, for the fatherless, and for the widow: (that the Lord thy God may bless thee in all the work of thy hands)* (24:19).[13] Is this not a matter of inference from the minor to the major? If one who unintentionally performs a meritorious deed is spoken of by Scripture as having earned merit, how much more so one who performs it intentionally.[14]

Pisḳa 284

When thou beatest thine olive tree, (thou shalt not go over the boughs again) (24:20): In earlier times[1] people, while beating their olive trees, would do it in a generous manner.[2] Hence the Sages have said:[3] If an olive tree stands between three rows (of corn), at a distance of two garden plots from one another, and is forgotten, it is not considered forgotten sheaf. (. . . As long as fruit belonging to the owner is at the foot of the tree, that at the top also belongs to him. R. Meir says: The law[4] applies only after those who wielded the beating rod have departed.)

Thine olive tree—excluding one belonging to others; *thine olive tree*—excluding one dedicated to the Sanctuary.

Thou shalt not go over the boughs (again) (24:20): Do not lord it over the poor.[5] Hence the Sages have said:[6] He who does not permit the poor to gather (their share), or permits it to one but not to another, or helps one of them, is robbing the poor. Of such as he it is said, *Remove not the ancient landmark* (Prov. 22:28).

Again—showing that the law of forgotten sheaves applies to him, and so does the law of corner crop.[7]

It shall be for the stranger, for the fatherless, and for the widow (24:20): *Stranger* and *fatherless* is stated here, and *stranger* and *fatherless* is stated elsewhere (24:19): just as *stranger* and *fatherless* stated there applies only when there is enough to yield two sĕᶜah (of produce), so *stranger* and *fatherless* stated here applies only when it yields two sĕᶜah.[8]

Pisḳa 285

When thou gatherest the grapes of thy vineyard (24:21): Hence R. Eliezer used to say: If a vineyard consists solely of bunches,[1] it belongs to the owner. R. ᶜAḳiba, however, says: It belongs to the poor.

Thou shalt not glean it (after thee) (24:21): What is considered a bunch? That which has neither a shoulder nor pendent grapes. If it has a shoulder but not a pendent, or a pendent but not a shoulder, it belongs to the owner. If not, it belongs to the poor.[2]

After thee[3]—showing that the law of forgotten sheaf applies here; *after thee*—showing that the law of corner crop applies here. Hence the Sages have said:[4] What is considered forgotten sheaf in the case of a grape arbor? Anything which one cannot reach and grasp by extending his hand. And in the case of runners? Anything remaining after the gleaners have passed by.

(It shall be) for the stranger, for the fatherless (24:21): *Stranger* and *fatherless* is stated here, and *stranger* and *fatherless* is stated elsewhere

(24:19); just as *stranger* and *fatherless* stated there applies only when there is enough to yield two sĕʿah, so *stranger* and *fatherless* stated here applies only when it yields two sĕʿah.[5]

Piska 286

If there be a controversy between men (25:1): Peace never results from strife, as it is said, *And there was a strife between the herdmen of Abram's cattle and the herdmen of Lot's cattle* (Gen. 13:7). What caused Lot to separate himself from that righteous man?[1] You must conclude that it was strife. The same is meant by *If there be a controversy between men.* What causes the (wicked) man referred to here to be beaten? You must conclude that it is strife.

Between men: I conclude that this refers only to (strife between) men; what about strife between a man and a woman, a woman and a man, or two women? The verse goes on to say, *And they come unto judgment*—whosoever the parties may be—*and the judges judge them* (25:1)—even if against their will.

By justifying (the righteous, and condemning the wicked) (25:1): One might think that everyone who is convicted is to be beaten; therefore the verse goes on to say, *then it shall be, if the wicked man deserve to be beaten* (25:2)—there are times when he is to be beaten, and times when he is not to be beaten. But I still do not know who is to be beaten; therefore Scripture states further on, *Thou shalt not muzzle the ox when he treadeth out the corn* (25:4)[2]—just as muzzling the ox is forbidden by a negative commandment, and the transgressor is liable to be beaten, so he is to be beaten for the violation of any other negative commandment. Or is he to be beaten also for violation of a negative commandment which can be rectified by a positive action? (No,) for the aforecited verse states, *Thou shalt not muzzle the ox*—just as muzzling the ox is characterized as subject to a negative commandment which cannot be rectified by a positive action, and the guilty party is to be beaten for it, so is he to be beaten for violating any other negative commandment which cannot be rectified by a positive action.[3] R. Simeon says: *By justifying the righteous*: You must justify him so that he will not be beaten.

Then it shall be, if the wicked man deserve to be beaten—there are times when he is to be beaten, and times when he is not to be beaten—*that the judge shall cause him to lie down*—one may not be beaten while standing—*and to be beaten*—one-third of the lashes in front and two-thirds in the back[4]—*before his face* (25:2): Meaning that when he is beaten, the judge's eyes must be upon him, so that it may not be done in such a way that while he is beaten, the judge's eyes are on something else.[5] One might think that he may be first beaten and then executed; therefore the verse goes on to say, *according to the measure of his wickedness* (25:2)—he is not to be both beaten and executed. One might think that he may be both beaten and fined; therefore the verse states, *according to the measure of his wickedness*—he is not to be both beaten and fined.[6]

Forty (stripes) (25:3): One might think that this means the full forty; *forty,* however, must be joined to the preceding *by number* (25:2)[7] (to read *by number forty*), meaning a number that comes up next to forty.[8] R. Judah, however, says: The full forty. Where is he to be beaten with this odd lash? Between the shoulders.[9]

He may give him (25:3): He may not strike the ground, nor his garment, nor may two culprits be beaten together.[10]

He shall not exceed (25:3): If he exceeds, he transgresses a negative commandment. I conclude that this applies only to addition to the statutory number[11] of lashes; what about any other number that may be estimated by the court?[12] The verse goes on to say, *above these* (25:3), meaning whatever the number may be.

With many stripes (25:3): I conclude that this refers to lashes over thirty-nine; what about lashes under thirty-nine? The verse states, *above*[13] *these* (25:3), (meaning any number). But if so, why does Scripture state, *with many stripes*? To indicate that the first lash is not considered *many stripes*.

Then thy brother should be dishonored before thine eyes (25:3): Hence the Sages have said:[14] If he befouls himself with feces or urine, he is exempt.[15] R. Judah says: In the case of a man, if he befouls himself with feces; in the case of a woman, even if only with urine. Another interpretation: *Then thy brother should be dishonored before thine eyes*: Once he has been beaten, he is (again) your brother. Hence the Sages have said:[16] As soon as those who are liable to the penalty of excision are beaten, they are immediately released from this liability. R. Hananiah ben Gamaliel says: All along Scripture calls him "wicked," as it is said, *Then it shall be, if the wicked man deserve to be beaten* (25:2), but once he has been beaten, it calls him "your brother," as it says, *Then thy brother should be dishonored.*[17] R. Simeon says: This can be determined from its own Scriptural passage, as it is said, *For whosoever shall do any of these abominations, even the souls that do them, shall be cut off from among their people* (Lev. 18:29), and, *Which, if a man do, he shall live by them* (Lev. 18:5). Is this not a matter of inference from the minor to the major? If in the case of a lesser measure of punishment,[18] he who associates himself with transgressors is regarded as if he himself were a transgressor, how much more is this so in the case of him who associated himself with those who perform the commandments.[19] R. Simeon bĕ-Rebbi[20] says: Behold, Scripture says, *Only be steadfast in not eating the blood* (12:23). If in the case of blood, which is repulsive to a man's soul, one who refrains from it receives a goodly reward, how much more will he be rewarded who refrains from theft and unchastity, which a man's soul lusts after and covets—he and his descendants, until the end of all generations. Rabbi (Judah the Prince) says: Behold, Scripture says, *Lord, who shall sojourn in Thy tabernacle? . . . He that walketh uprightly, and worketh righteousness . . . that hath no slander upon his tongue . . . in whose eyes a vile person is despised . . . he that putteth not out his money on interest* (Ps. 15:1–5), and elsewhere it says, *But if a man be just,* etc. (Ezek. 18:5), followed in conclusion by, *he is just, he shall surely live* (Ezek. 18:9). Yet what has this one really done? Thus (we see that) he who merely sits and does not transgress is rewarded in the same way as is he who performs a commandment.[21]

Pisḳa 287

Thou shalt not muzzle the ox (25:4): I conclude that this refers only to the ox; what about other domestic animals, wild beasts, and fowls? The verse states, *Thou shalt not muzzle*—whatsoever animal it may be. But if so, why does Scripture say, *the ox?* You may not muzzle an ox, but you may muzzle a man.[1]

When he treadeth out the corn (25:4): I conclude that this refers only to treading; what about other types of work? The verse states, *Thou shalt not muzzle*—whatever the work involved. But if so, why does Scripture say, *when he treadeth out the corn?* Since treading involves something which grows out of the soil and is plucked from the soil, and (the animal) eats of it as it performs the final stage of the work, the same rule applies to anything else which grows out of the soil and is plucked from the soil—(the animal) may eat of it as it performs the final stage of the work. R. Jose ben R. Judah says: Since treading is something done with one's hands, feet, and the whole body, anything done with one's hands but not with one's feet, or with one's feet but not with one's whole body is excluded.[2]

Pisḳa 288

If brethren dwell (together) (25:5): This excludes the wife of a deceased brother who was not alive at the same time as the surviving brother.[1] Hence the Sages have said:[2] If there are two brothers, and one of them dies, and thereafter another brother is born to their parents, and if later on the second brother takes the widow to wife,[3] etc. *Together*: Excluding his brother by the same mother. Since we find in the Torah that some brothers by the same mother are considered the same as brothers by the same father,[4] one might think that this is so here as well; therefore the verse here states, *together,* thus excluding his brother by the same mother only.

And one of them die (25:5): I conclude therefrom that this refers only to two brothers, one of whom dies; whence do we learn that this applies even when there are many brothers? From the verse, *And one of them die.* What if all[5] of them die? The verse states, *And one of them die.*[6] But if so, why does it say, *one of them?* To imply that he must take the widow of only one of them in levirate marriage, but not the widows of two of them. Hence the Sages have said:[7] If three brothers are married to three unrelated women, and if one of the brothers dies, and one of the surviving brothers declares his willingness to marry the widow but then dies (before doing so), the two widows must perform the ceremony of *ḥăliṣah,*[8] and may not marry the surviving brother.

And have no son[9] (25:5): I conclude therefrom that this refers only to a son; what about a son's son, a son's daughter, a daughter's son, or a daughter's daughter? The verse states, *and have no son*—any sort of progeny.[10] But if so, why does it say, *and have no son?* To exclude his children by a maidservant or a heathen wife.[11]

The wife of the dead shall not be married abroad unto one not of his kin (25:5): Why do I need this (rule)? Since we have already said that he must take the wife of one of the dead brothers in levirate marriage, but not the wives of two of them, one might think that this applies here too;[12] therefore the verse states, *The wife of the dead shall not be married abroad unto one not of his kin.* What then must she do? Either perform *ḥăliṣah* or enter into levirate marriage. If the surviving brother gives a bill of divorcement to his wife by levirate marriage, she is forbidden both to him and to the other brothers. One might think that she should be free (to marry anyone) through a bill of divorcement, and might reason that if *ḥăliṣah,* which does not free a married woman, does free a widow, should not a bill of divorcement, which frees a married woman, certainly free a widow? Therefore the verse states, *The wife of the dead shall not be married abroad unto one not of his kin,* except through *ḥăliṣah.*[13] The brother who declares his willingness to marry the widow acquires her for himself and renders her forbidden to the other brothers. One might think that with this declaration he concludes the matter; therefore the verse states, *Her husband's brother shall go in unto her* (25:5)—intercourse concludes the matter, while the declaration alone does not conclude it.

Her husband's brother shall go in unto her: Whether unintentionally or intentionally, unwillingly or willingly, even if unintentionally on his part and intentionally on hers, or intentionally on his part and unintentionally on hers.[14]

And he shall take—*And take her (to him to wife)*—in levirate marriage—*and perform the duty of a husband's brother unto her* (25:5)—excluding co-wives forbidden because of some incestuous relationship.[15] Hence the Sages have said:[16] Fifteen women exempt their co-wives and co-wives of co-wives from *ḥăliṣah* and from levirate marriage.

Pisḳa 289

And it shall be that the first-born that she beareth (shall succeed in the name of his brother that is dead) (25:6): One might think that if the deceased brother's name had been Jose, the child's name should also be Jose, or if his name had been Johanan, the child's name should also be Johanan; therefore the verse states, *shall succeed in the name of his brother*—whatever the child's name may be. But if so, why does it say, *And it shall be that the first-born that she beareth?* To indicate that it is the duty of the eldest surviving brother to perform levirate marriage.[1]

That she beareth—thus excluding a sterile woman who cannot bear children—*shall succeed in the name of his brother*—(that is to say, of his actual father,) and not in the name of his father's brother[2]—*that is dead*: Since we have said elsewhere that the widow of one of the brothers may be taken in levirate marriage, not that the widow of two of them may be so taken, whence do we learn that if the first brother dies, the second brother must take her in levirate marriage, and if then the second brother too dies, the third brother must take her? From the phrase, *that is dead,* which must imply something additional.[3]

That his name be not blotted out of Israel (25:6): Thus excluding a eunuch, whose name has already been blotted out.

And if the man like not (to take his brother's wife) (25:7): Not that God likes her not;[4] hence I exclude those incestuous relationships for which one is liable to death by the court. But I have not yet excluded those incestuous relationships for which one is liable to excision at the hands of heaven. Therefore the verse goes on to say, *My husband's brother refuseth* (25:7)—not that God refuses her; hence I exclude those incestuous relationships for which one is liable to excision at the hands of heaven. But I have not yet excluded those incestuous relationships which are forbidden by a negative commandment. Therefore the verse goes on to say, *he does not wish* (25:7),[5] and not that God does not wish.

To take his brother's wife (25:7): Why do I need these words, seeing that Scripture has already said, *And it shall be that the first-born that she beareth* (25:6)? I might have excluded a woman who is barren,[6] elderly, or a minor, who is incapable of giving birth; therefore the verse states, *his brother's wife,* the phrase "his brother's wife" indicating something additional.[7]

Then his brother's wife shall go up to the gate (unto the elders) (25:7): It is a positive commandment that the court be located at the highest place in the city and that it consist of elders.

My husband's brother refuseth—not that God refuses her—*to raise up unto his brother (a name in Israel)* (25:7)—excluding a eunuch, who could not raise up a name even if he wished to do so.

A name: R. Judah says: *Name* is stated here and *name* is stated elsewhere (25:6); just as *name* stated there refers to inheritance, so does *name* stated here refer to inheritance, and just as *name* stated here refers to progeny, so does *name* stated there refer to progeny.

In Israel—and not among proselytes. Hence you learn[8] that two proselyte brothers conceived not in holiness but born in holiness are exempt from both *ḥălîṣah* and levirate marriage, as it is said, *in Israel,* not among proselytes.[9]

He does not wish—not that God does not wish.

Pisḳa 290

Then the elders of his city shall call him—it is a commandment that it be done by the elders of his city—*and speak unto him* (25:8): Provided that she is suitable for him. If he is a child and she an elderly woman, or vice versa, they should say to him, "Go to someone who is of your own age; why should you bring dissension into your house?"

And if he stand and say—showing that he must say it while standing[1]—*I like not to take her* (25:8)—not that God likes her not.

Pisḳa 291

Then shall his brother's wife draw nigh unto him in the presence of the elders, [*(and loose his shoe from off his foot,) and spit in his face* (25:9): With spittle that is visible to the elders]. This shows that she must be face to face with him in the presence of the elders.[1]

And loose his shoe: I conclude that this refers only to his own shoe; what about someone else's shoe? The next verse states, *Him that had a shoe loosed* (25:10)—regardless of who owned it.[2] But if so, why does it say here, *and loose his shoe?* To exclude a shoe so large that one cannot walk in it, or one so small that it does not cover most of his foot, or a slipper which has no heel, for in these cases the *ḥălîṣah* is invalid.

From off his foot: *His foot* is stated here, and *his . . . foot* is stated elsewhere (Lev. 14:14). Just as *his . . . foot* there refers to his right foot, so *his foot* here refers to his right foot. *From off his foot*: Hence you learn that from the knee downward *ḥălîṣah* is valid, but from the knee upward it is invalid.[3]

And spit in his face: One might think that this means directly in his face; therefore the verse states, *in the presence of the elders* (25:9)—her spittle must be visible to the elders.[4] Hence the Sages have said:[5] If she removes the shoe and spits, but does not recite the declaration, her *ḥălîṣah* is valid; if she recites the declaration and spits, but does not remove the shoe, her *ḥăliṣah* is invalid; if she removes the shoe and recites the declaration, but does not spit, R. Eliezer says that her *ḥăliṣah* is invalid, while R. ʿAḳiba says that it is valid.

And she shall answer and say (25:9): Answering is mentioned here and answering is mentioned elsewhere (27:15);[6] just as the answering there must be in the holy tongue, so the answering here must be in the holy tongue.

So shall it be done unto the man that doth not build up his brother's house (25:9): R. Eliezer says: He that did not build it up and that will not build it up in the future.

[*So shall it be done*:] R. Eliezer said: *So shall it be done* means that lack of the act (of spitting) invalidates (the ceremony).[7] But R. ʿAḳiba said to him: You cite this as proof? (The verse says,) *So shall it be done unto the man,* meaning what is done to the man.[8] R. Simeon says: Lack of either the removal of the shoe or the spitting invalidates (the ceremony).

[*And his name shall be called in Israel* (25:10): R. Ishmael says: Removal of the shoe should be done lying down, and spitting is analogous to intercourse.][9]

And his name shall be called in Israel: *In Israel* is stated here, and *in Israel* is stated elsewhere (25:7); just as *in Israel* elsewhere excludes a court consisting of proselytes, so *in Israel* here excludes a court consisting of proselytes.[10]

The house of him that had his shoe loosed (25:10): This is a commandment for the judges and not for the disciples.[11] R. Judah says: It is a commandment for all who are standing there to say, *him that had his shoe loosed, him that had his shoe loosed.* R. Judah said: Once we were sitting in the presence of R. Tarfon, and he said to us, "All of you must respond and say, *him that had his shoe loosed, him that had his shoe loosed.*"

Pisḳa 292

When men strive (together) (25:11): Peace never results from strife,[1] as it is said, *And there was a strife between the herdmen of Abram's cattle and the herdmen of Lot's cattle* (Gen. 13:7). What caused Lot to separate himself from that righteous man? One must conclude that it was strife, as it is said, *If there be a controversy between men* (25:1)—

what causes the man referred to here to be beaten? You must conclude that it is strife.

Men: I conclude that this refers only to men; what about strife between a man and a woman, or a woman and a man? The verse states, *together*—regardless of the participants' sex.

One with his brother[2]—excluding slaves, who are not subject to the relationship of brotherhood[3]—*and the wife of the one draweth near*—and not the wife of the messenger of the court[4]—*to deliver her husband* (25:11): Rabbi (Judah the Prince) says: Since we find that there are cases in the Torah of unintentional damages which are treated as if they were intentional, one might think that such is the case here also; therefore the verse goes on to say, *and taketh (him) by his secrets*[5] (25:11), showing that one is liable for causing disgrace only when he does it deliberately. *By the secrets*: I conclude that this applies only to seizing the genital organs; what about any other part of the body where there is danger of injury? The verse states, *and taketh*—by any part of his body. But if so, why does Scripture state, *by the secrets?* Just as the genitals are characterized by being subject to injury involving danger to life and therefore require the penalty of *Thou shalt cut off her hand* (25:12), so does any other part which may cause danger to life if injured, come under the same law of *Thou shalt cut off her hand.*

Pisḳa 293

Then thou shalt cut off her hand (25:12): Hence you learn that you are required to "save" her by cutting off her hand.[1] Whence do we learn that if you cannot "save" her by cutting off her hand, you must "save" her by taking her life? The verse goes on to say, *Thine eye shall have no pity* (25:12). R. Judah says: *Thine eye shall have no pity* is stated here, and *Thine eye shall have no pity* is stated elsewhere (19:21);[2] just as *Thine eye shall have no pity* stated there refers to money, so *Thine eye shall have no pity* stated here refers to money.[3]

Pisḳa 294

Thou shalt not have in thy bag diverse weights, (a great and a small) (25:13): One might think that this means that one may not make (a set of three) weights, a liṭra and a half, a liṭra and a quarter, and one liṭra; therefore the verse states, *a great and a small*—a great one which falsifies the small one, so that one would not use the great weight for receiving, and the small one for dispensing. R. ʿAḳiba says: Whence do we learn that one may not have a selaʿ which is smaller than a shekel or a dinar which is smaller than a quinarius?[1] From the phrase, *Thou shalt not have.* R. Jose ben Judah says: If you keep the worn-out weight, that too is a violation of *Thou shalt not have.*[2]

Thou shalt not have in thy house diverse measures, (a great and a small) (25:14): One might think that this means that one may not make (a set of three) measures, a *tarḳab̲*[3] and a half, a *tarḳab̲* and a quarter, and one *tarḳab̲*; therefore the verse states, *a great and a small*—a great one which falsifies the small one, so that one would not use the great weight for receiving, and the small one for dispensing. R. Eliezer says: Whence do we learn that one may not make a measure the size of four *ḳab̲*[4] even in measuring for himself in his own house?[5] The verse states, *Thou shalt not have.* Whence do we learn that one may not give exact weight in a place where the custom is to give overweight, or overweight in a place where the custom is to give exact weight?[6] From the next verse, *A perfect (and just) weight (shalt thou have)* (25:15). One might think that this does not apply if he says (to the purchaser), in a place where the custom is to give overweight, "I am going to give you the exact weight, but am going to reduce the price accordingly"; or in a place where the custom is to give exact weight, "I am going to give you overweight, but am going to add to the price accordingly."[7] Therefore the verse states, *Justice*[8] *shalt thou have.* Whence do we learn that one may not give a heaping measure in a place where the custom is to level off, nor level off in a place where the custom is to give a heaping measure? The verse states, *A perfect . . . weight.* One might think that he may say (to the purchaser), "I am going to level off" in a place where the custom is to give a heaping measure, and reduce the price, or "I am going to give a heaping measure" in a place where the custom is to level off, and increase the price; no heed should be paid to him, for the verse states, *Justice shalt thou have.*

Shalt thou have (25:15): Appoint a market commissioner[9] for this purpose. Hence the Sages have said:[10] The wholesaler must clean off his measures every thirty days, and the householder every twelve months, etc. Eleazar ben Hananiah ben Hezekiah ben Garon says:

Scripture says, *An ephah for a bullock, and an ephah for a ram, and* [an ephah][11] *for the lambs* (Ezek. 46:11). But is the amount designated for bullocks, rams, and lambs the same? Does it not say elsewhere, *Three tenth parts for the bullock, two tenth parts for the ram, and one tenth part for every lamb* (Num. 29:3–4)? Rather, this shows that both the large ephah and the small ephah are called ephah.

Pisḳa 295

That thy days may be long (25:15): This is one of the commandments in the Torah which are closely accompanied by a statement of the reward for their observance. And is this not a matter of inference from the minor to the major? If the Torah grants length of days for (the expenditure of) a dried fig, which weighs not more than one one-hundredth of an issar, how much more is this so in the case of other commandments which involve a substantial monetary loss.

For all that do such things, (even all that do unrighteously), are an abomination unto the Lord thy God (25:16): One might think that one is not liable until he transgresses all of the aforementioned things; therefore the verse states, *all that do such things*—even only one of them.

[*All that do unrighteously*:] Hence the Sages have said:[1] One may not mix produce with other produce, not even the new with the old. He may not mix a sĕʿah of (inferior) produce worth one denar per sĕʿah, with superior produce worth one denar and a tressis per sĕʿah, and sell the mixture at one denar per sĕʿah.[2]

All that do unrighteously: Such a one is called five names: banned, abominable, detested, hated, and perverse.[3]

Pisḳa 296

Remember (25:17)—with (the utterance of) your mouth—*Thou shalt not forget* (25:19)—in your heart,[1] as it is said, *The peoples have heard, they tremble* (Exod. 15:14).[2]

By the way—at the time of your trouble—*as ye came forth out of Egypt* (25:17)—at the time of your redemption.

How he met thee—"meeting" here can mean only meeting

providentially[3]—*and smote the hindmost of thee, all that were enfeebled in thy rear*—showing that he slew only those among them who were drawn to stray from God's ways and were therefore so enfeebled as to drop out of the protection of the cloud—*when thou wast faint and weary; and he feared not God* (25:18): By the measure with which you measured out, was it measured out to you; just as you were faint and weary because you feared not God, so will he be faint and weary because he feared not God.[4]

Therefore it shall be, when the Lord thy God hath given thee rest from all thine enemies round about—meaning that they will not form an alliance against you—*in the land which the Lord thy God giveth thee for an inheritance to possess it*—that which you are to possess you will conquer—*that thou shalt blot out the remembrance of Amalek* (25:19): Elsewhere Scripture states, *For I will utterly blot out the remembrance of Amalek . . . the hand upon the throne of the Lord: the Lord will have war with Amalek from generation to generation* (Exod. 17:14–15).[5]

Piska 297

And it shall be, when thou art come in unto the land—"and it shall be" always means "immediately"—*when thou art come in unto the land*—perform the commandment stated in this matter, for as a reward you will enter the land—*which the Lord thy God giveth thee for an inheritance, and dost possess it, and dwell therein*—that which you are to possess you shall conquer—*and dost possess it, and dwell therein* (26:1)—once you possess it, you will dwell in it.[1]

That thou shalt take of the first of all the fruit of the ground, (which thou shalt bring in from thy land) (26:2): One might think that all produce is liable for first fruits; therefore the verse says, *of the first,* not "all the first." But I still do not know which are liable and which are not liable. I might reason: "bringing" is used for both the community's first fruits and the individual's first fruits; just as the community's first fruits spoken of elsewhere (Lev. 23:17) consist of seven species, so the individual's first fruits spoken of here must consist of seven species, and just as there wheat and barley are meant, so here wheat and barely are meant.[2] Whence do we learn that this includes the rest of the seven species? From the verse, *The choicest first fruits of thy land* (Exod. 23:19). An inclusion following an inclusion in Scripture indicates an exclusion, hence one must follow the original rule, to wit, that "bringing" is used for both the community's first fruits and the individual's first fruits; just as the community's first fruits must consist of the seven species spoken of in praise of the land, so the individual's first fruits must consist of the seven species spoken of in praise of the land, namely, *A land of wheat and barley, and vines and fig trees and pomegranates, a land of olive trees and honey* (8:8).[3] The olive is the storage olive;[4] the honey is date-honey.

Of the first—even if only one cluster, or even only one grain (or berry).

The fruit—you must bring the (original) fruit, not the wine or oil made therefrom.

Of the ground—this excludes tenants, lessees, holders of confiscated land, and robbers,[5] who need not bring them for the same reason, as it is said, *The choicest first fruits of thy land (thou shalt bring)* (Exod. 23:19).[6] You might think that you may bring them whenever you make the pertinent declaration; therefore the verse states, *Which thou shalt bring in from thy land* (26:2)—when they are found upon your land. You might think that you may make the declaration whenever you bring them; therefore Scripture goes on to say, *And thou shalt say unto him . . . and thou shalt rejoice* (26:3, 11)—the declaration must be made only at the time of rejoicing,[7] which means that from Pentecost to Tabernacles one may bring the first fruits and make the declaration, whereas from Tabernacles to Hanukkah one may bring the first fruits but may not make the declaration. R. Judah ben Betherah, however, says: One may both bring the first fruits and make the declaration (all year through).

That the Lord thy God giveth thee (26:2): Excluding one who plants in his own soil but sinks a shoot into soil belonging to another individual or into the soil of the public domain, or one who sinks in his soil a shoot from something growing in the soil of the public domain or in the soil of another individual, or one who plants in his soil and sinks a shoot in his own soil, with a public path or a path owned by another individual in between the two soils—he need not bring first fruits. R. Judah, however, says: In this case he must bring first fruits. What is the reason for his not bringing them? Because Scripture says, *The choicest first fruits of thy land* (Exod. 23:19)—only when the entire growth is from your own land.[8]

Pisḳa 298

And thou shalt put it in a basket—showing that a vessel is required—*and shalt go unto the place which the Lord thy God shall choose* (26:2)—this refers to Shiloh and to the Eternal House (in Jerusalem).

And thou shalt come unto the priest that shall be in those days (26:3): This is what R. Jose the Galilean referred to when he said: Would it ever occur to you to go to a priest who does not live in your own days? Rather, the meaning is a priest who is qualified and acknowledged in those days. If he had been a relative but subsequently ceased being one, he is still qualified, as it is said, *Say not thou: how was it that the former days were better than these?* (Eccl. 7:10).[1]

Pisḳa 299

And say unto him—be not an ingrate—*I profess this day unto the Lord thy God, that I am come* (26:3)—you must make this declaration once a year, not twice a year.[1]

That I am come unto the land which the Lord swore unto our fathers—thus excluding proselytes[2]—*to give us* (26:3)—thus excluding slaves. R. Simeon says: Excluding also the other side of the Jordan, which you took on your own.[3]

Pisḳa 300

And the priest shall take the basket out of thy hand (26:4): Hence the Sages have said:[1] The wealthy must bring their first fruits in vase-shaped baskets of silver or gold, while the poor may bring theirs in wicker baskets of peeled willow. Both the baskets and the first fruits are given to the priests as a gift, in order to multiply gifts to the priests.

Out of thy hand—hence you learn that they require waving;[2] as taught by R. Eliezer ben Jacob—*and set it down before the altar of the Lord thy God* (26:4): So long as there is an altar, you are obligated to bring first fruits; when there is no altar, you are not so obligated.[3] *And set it down*: Hence the Sages have said:[4] If they were stolen or lost, one is required to bring replacements; if they are rendered unclean while in the Temple Court, one must scatter them and need not make the declaration.

Pisḳa 301

And thou shalt respond[1] *and say* (26:5): "Responding" is stated here, and "responding" is stated elsewhere (27:14);[2] just as "responding" there means in the holy tongue, so "responding" here means in the holy tongue. Hence the Sages have said:[3] Originally all those who knew how to make the declaration did so, while those who did not know how to do it had it recited to them.[4] When people consequently refrained from bringing (first fruits), it was decided that both those who knew how and those who did not would have the declaration recited to them. For this they relied upon the verse, *And thou shalt respond,* since responding implies prompting to respond by someone else.[5]

And thou shalt respond and say before the Lord thy God: A wandering Aramean was my father (26:5): This shows that our father Jacob went to Aram assuming that he would perish,[6] and that Laban is considered as if he had destroyed him.[7]

And he went down into Egypt (26:5): [This shows that he went there not to settle but only to sojourn.] Should you say that he went there in order to assume the crown of kingship for himself, the verse goes on to say, *and sojourned there*; should you say that he went there with a great multitude of people, the verse continues, *few in number* (26:5)—as it is said of this same event, *Thy fathers went down into Egypt with threescore and ten persons* (10:22).

And he became there a nation, great (26:5): This shows that Israel was distinguishable there.

And (the Lord) saw our affliction—as it is said, *Ye shall look upon the birthstool* (Exod. 1:16)—*and our toil* (26:7)—as it is said, *Every son that is born ye shall cast into the river,* etc. (Exod. 1:22). R. Judah supplied a mnemonic abbreviation for the ten plagues of Egypt: *DṢḴ ʿDŠ BʾḤB.*[8]

And He hath brought us into this place (26:9): This refers to the (site of the) Temple. Might it mean the Land of Israel? (No,) for the verse goes on to say, *and hath given us this land* (26:9). Hence the Land of Israel is referred to here.[9] Why then say, *And he hath brought us into this place?*[10] As a reward for our coming to this place, He has given us this land.

A land flowing with milk and honey (26:9): *A land flowing with milk and honey* is stated here, and *A land flowing with milk and honey* is stated elsewhere (Exod. 13:5). Just as *A land flowing with milk and honey* there refers to the territory of the five nations, so *A land flowing with milk and honey* here refers to the territory of the five nations. R. Jose the Galilean says: First fruits may not be brought from the other side of the Jordan, since it is not a land flowing with milk and honey.[11]

And now — immediately — *behold* — with rejoicing[12] — *I have brought*—of my own[13]—*the first of the fruit of the land* (26:10): Hence the Sages have said:[14] When one goes into his field and sees a ripened fig, a ripened cluster, a ripened pomegranate, he should tie it with a reed string and say, "These shall be first fruits."

Which thou, O Lord, hast given me (25:10): Hence the Sages have said:[15] A guardian, a slave, an agent, a woman, a person of doubtful sex, or a hermaphrodite may bring first fruits but may not make the declaration, since they cannot rightfully say, *Which thou, O Lord, hast given me.*

And thou shall set it down before the Lord thy God, and worship before the Lord thy God (26:10): This shows that the fruits must be set down twice, once at the time of the declaration and once at the time of the worship.

And thou shalt rejoice—with all manner of rejoicing—*in all the good*—this refers to the song[16]—*which the Lord thy God hath given unto thee, and unto thy house*—showing that one may bring first fruits from the property of his wife and make the declaration over it[17]—*thou, and the Levite, and the stranger that is in the midst of thee* (26:11): Hence the Sages have said:[18] Israelites and bastards may make the declaration, but not proselytes and freed slaves, since they have no portion in the (Holy) Land.

Pisḳa 302

When thou hast made an end of tithing (26:12): Perhaps this refers to Hanukkah? You might reason: *end* is stated here, and *end* is stated elsewhere (31:10); just as *end* there refers to a pilgrim festival,[1] so *end* here refers to a pilgrim festival; or, just as *end* there refers to the

Feast of Tabernacles, so *end* here refers to the Feast of Tabernacles; therefore the verse states, *When thou hast made an end of tithing*—the festival when the tithes are concluded, which is Passover. Hence the Sages have said:[2] On the eve of the last day of the Passover holiday in the fourth and seventh years, there must be removal (of the tithe).[3]

In the third year (26:12): One might think that the seventh year should also require tithing; therefore the verse states, *In the third year, which is the year of the tithe* (26:12)—the year which requires tithing, thus excluding the seventh year, which does not require tithing. Perhaps there should be two tithes in that year? (No,) for the verse states, *the year of the tithe*—one tithe is to be observed in it, not two tithes.[4] I conclude that Scripture refers here only to the poor man's tithe;[5] whence do we learn that this applies also to the other tithes? From the verse, *the tithe of thine increase* (26:12)—implying all the other tithes as well.

Pisḳa 303

And hast given it unto the Levite, to the stranger, to the fatherless, and to the widow—give each one the proper share due him—*that they may eat within thy gates, and be satisfied* (26:12)—give them enough to satisfy them. Hence the Sages have said:[1] One may not give the poor man at the threshing floor less than half a *ḳab̲* of wheat or one ḳab̲ of barley; so said R. Judah. Rabbi (Judah the Prince), however, says, Half a ḳab̲.

Within thy gates: This shows that he may not be taken outside of the Land (of Israel). It is said that when the family of the house of Nebalṭa was in Jerusalem, the Sages offered them six hundred talents of gold, because they did not want them to leave Jerusalem.[2]

Then thou shalt say—in any language—*before the Lord thy God*—this is the confession of the tithe—*I have put away the hallowed things out of my house*—this refers to the second tithe and the fourth year's planting[3]—*and also have given them unto the Levite*—this refers to the tithe of the Levite—*and also have given them*—*them* includes heave offering, and also heave offering of the tithe—*and unto the stranger, to the fatherless, and to the widow* (26:13)—this refers to poor man's tithe, gleanings, forgotten sheaf, and corner crop, even though lack of them does not invalidate the confession.

Out of my house: This refers to dough offering.[4] Another interpretation: *Out of my house*: Since you have separated it from your house, you are not in need of it for any other purpose.

According to all Thy commandment—if one separates the second tithe before the first, it is of no consequence—*which Thou hast commanded me*—I have not given it to anyone who is not entitled to it—*I have not transgressed any of Thy commandments*—I have not separated a gift from one species of produce for another species, nor taken it from plucked produce for produce still attached to the soil, or vice versa, nor from new produce for old, or vice versa[5]—*neither have I forgotten them* (26:13)—I did not forget to bless Thee and mention Thy name over it.[6]

I have not eaten thereof in my mourning—hence if one eats of it while in mourning, he may not make the confession—*neither have I put away thereof, being unclean*—when I was unclean while the produce was clean, or vice versa—*nor given thereof to the dead* (26:14): I did not use funds realized from it to purchase a coffin or a shroud for the dead;[7] so taught E. Eliezer. R. ʿAḳiba said to him: It is forbidden to do so not only for the dead but also for the living. What then does the verse mean by *for the dead*? That such a gift may not even be exchanged for clean produce.

I have hearkened to the voice of the Lord my God—and have brought it to the Chosen House—*I have done according to all that Thou hast commanded me* (26:14)—I have rejoiced, and caused others to rejoice, therein.[8]

Look forth from Thy holy habitation—we have done that which Thou hast decreed for us; do Thou, therefore, unto us what Thou hast promised us—*look forth from Thy holy habitation, from heaven, and bless Thy people,* etc. (26:15).[9]

Pisḳa 304

And the Lord said unto Moses: Behold, thy days approach that thou must die (31:14): R. Simeon ben Yoḥai says: Blessed be the Truthful Judge,[1] Master of all that happens, before whom there is no corruption or favoritism, as it is said, *Trust not in a friend, put ye not confidence in a chief* (Mic. 7:5).[2]

Moses responded to the Holy One, blessed be He, "Master of the world, since it is in great agony that I depart from this world, show me a trustworthy man who can take charge of Israel, so that I might relieve myself of their charge," as it is said, *Who may go out before them and who may come in before them* (Num. 27:17).[3] (This anticipates) Scripture's statement, *We have a little sister, and she hath no breasts* (Song 8:8), meaning that four kingdoms will rule over Israel when Israel will have no wise or understanding man (to lead them). (Such was the case) in the days of Ahab, king of Israel, and Jehoshaphat, king of Judah, when *All Israel (was) scattered upon the mountains as sheep that have no shepherd* (1 Kings 22:17). *That the congregation of the Lord be not as sheep which have no shepherd* (Num. 27:17).

Pisḳa 305

And the Lord said unto Moses: Take thee Joshua the son of Nun (Num. 27:18)[1]: *Take thee*[2]—a man as heroic[3] as yourself. [*Take thee*:[4] One can do this only by seizing,[5] for one cannot acquire a friend except by great effort, as the Sages have said: One should acquire a friend for himself, to study Torah with him, to study Mishnah with him, to eat with him, to drink with him, and to reveal his secrets to him, as it is said, *Two are better than one* (Eccl. 4:9) and *A threefold cord is not quickly broken* (Eccl. 4:12).]

The Holy One, blessed be He, replied to Moses,[6] saying, "Give Joshua a spokesman,[7] and let him question, respond, and give instruction while you are still living, so that when you depart from this world, Israel might not say to him, 'During your master's lifetime you did not speak out, and now you do!'" Some say that Moses lifted Joshua up from the ground, and placed him between his knees,[8] so that Moses and Israel had to raise their heads in order to hear Joshua's words. What did Joshua say? "Blessed be the Lord who has given the Torah to Israel at the hands of our master Moses"—those were Joshua's words.

R. Nathan says: Moses was saddened by the fact that one of his sons had not been appointed leader. So the Holy One, blessed be He, said to him: "Why are you saddened because one of your sons had not been appointed? Are not your brother Aaron's sons like your own sons? The man whom I am appointing over Israel will still have to go and stand humbly at Eleazar's[9] doorway." To what may this be likened? To a king of flesh-and-blood who had a son unworthy of kingship, so he took the kingship away from him and gave it to his favorite's son, saying to him, "Even though I have conferred upon you royal majesty, go and stand humbly at my son's doorway." So also did the Holy One, blessed be He, say to Joshua, "Even though I have made you leader, go and stand humbly at Eleazar's doorway," as it is said, *And he shall stand before Eleazar the priest* (Num. 27:21).

At that moment Moses was filled with strength with which he fortified Joshua in the sight of all Israel, as it is said, *And Moses called unto Joshua, and said unto him in the sight of all Israel, "Be strong and of good courage"* (31:7). He said to him, "This people that I am giving into your care are still as young kids, still mere infants. Do not be too strict with them about all that they do, for even their (Divine) Master has not been strict with them about all their deeds," as it is said, *When Israel was a child, then I loved him* (Hos. 11:1).[10] R. Nehemiah says: (Moses said to Joshua:) "I do not have permission, but if I had permission, I would bring them in to dwell beside the tents of the shepherds."[11]

It once happened that while Rabban Johanan ben Zakkai was riding an ass and his disciples were following him, he saw a young woman gathering barley grains from under the feet of Arab cattle. When she saw Rabban Johanan ben Zakkai, she covered her face with her hair, stood up before him, and said to him, "Master, grant me sustenance." He asked her, "Whose daughter are you?" She replied, "I am the daughter of Naḳdimon ben Gorion." "Master," she continued, "you no doubt remember when you signed my marriage contract." Rabban Johanan ben Zakkai then said to his disciples, "I did indeed sign this woman's marriage contract, and I noticed in it a stipulation of one million gold denar payable to her by her father-in-law's family and her own family. Whenever they went to worship at the Temple Mount, fine woollen carpets were spread out for them to walk on, and they would enter, prostrate themselves, and return joyfully to their homes.[12] All my life I wondered about the meaning of the verse, *If thou know not, O thou fairest among women, go thy way forth by the footsteps of the flock, and feed thy kids beside the shepherds' tents* (Song 1:8), but now I found it—read not *gĕḏiyoṯayiḵ* ("your kids") but *gĕwiyoṯayiḵ* ("your bodies"). As long as Israel do the will of God, no nation or kingdom can rule over them, but when Israel do not do God's will, He delivers them into the hand of the lowliest of nations, and not only into the hands of the lowliest of nations but also under the feet of the cattle of the lowliest of nations."

Three righteous persons died in the same year: Moses, Aaron, and Miriam, and after Moses died, Israel felt no more satisfaction, as it is said, *And I cut off the three shepherds in one month*[13] (Zech. 11:8). But did they all die in the same month? Did they not die in the same year? Rather, as Scripture says, *The well which the princes digged, which the nobles of the people delved* (Num. 21:18).[14] This means that when Miriam died, the well disappeared, but then returned because of the merit of Moses and Aaron. When Aaron died, the pillar of cloud disappeared, but both well and pillar returned because of the merit of Moses. When Moses died, all three disappeared and returned no more. At that time Israel was scattered and devoid of all gifts.[15]

(When Aaron died,)[16] all Israel gathered before Moses and said to him, "Where is your brother Aaron?" He replied, "God has secreted him for the life in the world to come." They did not believe him and said to him, "We know that you are cruel. It may be that he had said something improper before you, and you condemned him to death." What did the Holy One, blessed be He, do? He brought back Aaron's bier and suspended it in the upper heavens, and the Holy One, blessed be He, stood over him eulogizing him, while the ministering angels responded after Him. What did they say? *The Torah of truth was in his mouth, and unrighteousness was not found in his lips; he walked with Me in peace and uprightness, and did turn many away from iniquity* (Mal. 2:6).

At that same time[17] the Holy One, blessed be He, said to the angel of death, "Go and fetch Me the soul of Moses." The angel went and stood before Moses, and said to him, "Moses, give me your soul." Moses replied, "You do not even have the right to be in the place where I dwell, and yet you dare say to me, Give me your soul?" Moses thus rebuked him, and the angel left crestfallen. The angel of death then went back and reported to God, whereupon the Holy One, blessed be He, told him once more, "Go and fetch Me his soul." The angel went looking for him at his home but could not find him. He went to the sea and asked it, "Moses, have you seen him?" The sea replied, "Since the day that he made Israel pass through me, I did not see him." He then went to the mountains and the hills and asked them, "Moses, have you seen him?" They replied, "Since the day that Israel received the Torah on Mount Sinai, we have not seen him." He thereupon went to Gehenna and asked it, "Moses, have you seen him?" She replied, "I have heard his name, but I have not seen him." He then went to the ministering angels and asked them, "Moses, have you seen him?" They replied, "Go and ask human beings." He finally went to Israel and asked them, "Moses, have you seen him?" They said to him, "God has fathomed his way, and has secreted him for the life of the world to come, and no creature knows his whereabouts," as it is said, *And he was buried in the valley* (34:6).[18]

Upon the death of Moses, Joshua wept, wailed, and mourned bitterly,[19] saying, "My father, my father, my master, my master, my father who has raised me, my master who has taught me Torah!" He kept mourning over him for many days, until the Holy One, blessed be He, said to him, "Joshua, how long will you continue mourning? Does his death affect you alone? Does not his death truly affect Me? For from the day he died there has been great mourning before Me, as it is said, *And in that day did the Lord, the God of hosts, call to weeping, and to lamentation,* etc. (Isa. 22:12); but he is assured of the world to come,"[20] as it is said, *And the Lord said unto Moses, Behold, thou art about to sleep with thy fathers and . . . wilt arise* (31:16).[21]

Piṣḳa 306

Give ear, ye heavens, and I will speak (32:1): R. Meir says: When Israel[1] was meritorious, they gave witness against themselves, as it is said, *And Joshua said unto the people, Ye are witnesses against yourselves* (Josh. 24:22). When they corrupted themselves, as it is said, *Ephraim compasseth Me about with lies, and the house of Israel with deceit* (Hos. 12:1), the Tribes of Judah and Benjamin witnessed against them, as it is said, *And now, O inhabitants of Jerusalem and men of Judah, judge, I pray you, betwixt me and my vineyard. What could have been done more to my vineyard?* (Isa. 5:3–4). When the Tribes of Judah and Benjamin too were corrupted, as it is said, *Judah hath dealt treacherously* (Mal. 2:11), God called the prophets to witness against them, as it is said, *Yet the Lord forewarned Israel, and Judah, by the hand of every prophet* (2 Kings 17:13). When they rebuffed[2] the prophets, as it is said, *But they mocked the messengers of God* (2 Chron. 36:16), God called the heavens to witness against them, as it is said, *I call heaven and earth to witness against you this day* (Deut. 4:26). After they had corrupted the heavens,[3] as it is said, *Seest thou not what they do (in the cities of Judah)? The children gather wood, and the fathers kindle the fire, and the women knead the dough, to make cakes to the queen of heaven* (Jer. 7:17–18), God called the earth[4] to witness against them, as it is said, *Hear, O earth, behold, I will bring evil (upon this people)* (Jer. 6:19). After they had corrupted the earth, as it is said, *Yea, their altars shall be as heaps in the furrows of the field* (Hos. 12:12), God called the highways to witness against them, as it is said, *Thus saith the Lord: Stand ye in the ways and see* (Jer. 6:16). After they had corrupted the highways, as it is said, *Thou hast built thy lofty place at every head of the way* (Ezek. 16:25), God called the nations to witness against them, as it is said, *Therefore hear, ye nations, and know, O congregation, what is against them* (Jer. 6:18). After they had been corrupted by the nations, as it is said, *But (our fathers) mingled themselves with the nations and learned their works* (Ps. 106:35), God called the mountains to witness against them, as it is said, *Hear, O ye mountains, the Lord's controversy* (Mic. 6:2). After they had corrupted the mountains, as it is said, *They sacrifice upon the tops of the mountains* (Hos. 4:13), God called cattle to witness against them, as it is said, *The ox knoweth his owner (and the ass his master's crib; but Israel doth not know)* (Isa. 1:3). After they had corrupted the cattle, as it is said, *Thus they exchanged their glory for the likeness of an ox that eateth grass* (Ps. 106:20), God called the fowls to witness against them, as it is said, *Yea, the stork in the heaven knoweth her appointed times . . . (but My people knoweth not the ordinance of the Lord)* (Jer. 8:7). After they had corrupted the cattle, the beasts, and the fowls, as it is said, *So I went in and saw; and behold, every detestable form of creeping things and beasts* (Ezek. 8:10), God called the fishes to witness against them, as it is said, *Or speak to the earth, and it shall teach thee; and the fishes of the sea shall declare unto thee* (Job 12:8). After they had corrupted the fishes, as it is said, *And makest man as the fishes of the sea* (Hab. 1:14), God called the ant to witness against them, as it is said, *Go to the ant, thou sluggard . . . which . . . provideth her bread in the summer* (Prov. 6:6–8). R. Simeon ben Eleazar says: What a humiliation for this fellow to have to learn from the ant! Had he learned from her and acted accordingly, it would have been humiliating enough; but here he should have learned from her ways, but did not even learn![5]

In the future the congregation of Israel will say before the Holy One, blessed be He: "Master of the universe, my witnesses[6] still exist," as it is said, *I call heaven and earth to witness against you this day* (30:19). God replies[7] to her: "Behold, I shall cause them to pass away," as it is said, *For behold, I create new heavens and a new earth* (Isa. 65:17). She says to Him: "Master of the universe, I now see the places which I corrupted, and I am ashamed," as it is said, *See thy way in the valley, (know what thou hast done)* (Jer. 2:23). God replies: "I shall cause them to pass away," as it is said, *Every valley shall be lifted up* (Isa. 40:4). She says to Him: "Master of the universe, my (old) name exists."[8] God replies: "I shall cause it to pass away," as it is said, *And thou shalt be called by a new name* (Isa. 62:2). She says to Him: "Master of the universe, my name[9] is tied with that of the Baalim." God replies: "I shall cause it to pass away," as it is said, *For I will take away the names of the Baalim (out of her mouth)* (Hos. 2:19). She says to Him: "Master of the universe, nevertheless members of my house[10] will remind (me) of it." God replies: "*And they shall no more be mentioned by their name* (Hos. 2:19)."

Once again, on the morrow, she will say before Him: "Master of the universe, Thou hast already written down, *saying: If a man put away his wife, and she go from him, and become another man's wife, may he return unto her again?* (Jer. 3:1)." God replies: "Did I not specifically write *a man*? And has it not already been said, *For I am God, and not man* (Hos. 11:9)?" Another version (of God's reply): "Have you been divorced from Me, O house of Israel? Has it not already been said, *Thus saith the Lord: Where is the bill of your mother's divorcement, wherewith I have put her away? Or which of My creditors is it to whom I have sold you?* (Isa. 50:1)."

Another interpretation: *Give ear, ye heavens*: A parable: A king turned over his son to a tutor to stay with him and guard him.[11] The son said to himself, "Does father really think that handing me over to the tutor will benefit him? Now I will watch the tutor as he eats, drinks, and falls asleep, and then I will go out and do whatsoever I wish to do." Whereupon his father said to him, "I have handed you over to the tutor for the sole purpose that he not let you out of his sight." So also Moses said to Israel: Do you possibly think that you can escape from under the wings of the Shekinah, or leave the earth?[12] Furthermore, the heavens themselves record (everything), as it is said, *The heavens shall reveal his iniquity* (Job 20:27). Whence do we learn that the earth also is aware of everything? From the verse, *And the earth shall rise up against him* (Job 20:27).

In the future the congregation of Israel will stand in judgment before God, saying to Him: Master of the universe,[13] I do not know at first who rebuffed whom, and who changed his attitude toward whom—did Israel rebuff God, or did God change His attitude toward Israel? But when Scripture says, *And the heavens declare His righteousness* (Ps. 50:6), it becomes obvious that Israel has rebuffed God, whereas God did not change His attitude toward Israel, as it is said, *For I the Lord change not* (Mal. 3:6).

Another interpretation: *Give ear, ye heavens*: R. Judah says: A parable: A king had two deputies in the city, to whom he entrusted his possessions and into whose care he gave his son, saying to them, "As long as my son conducts himself according to my will, indulge him in every luxury and give him (fine) food and drink. Whenever my son does not conduct himself according to my will, he is not to taste anything of mine." So also, whenever Israel fulfill God's will, what does Scripture say concerning them? *The Lord will open unto thee His good treasure, the heaven (to give the rain of thy land in its season)* (28:12). Whenever they do not fulfill God's will, what does Scripture say of them? *And the anger of the Lord be kindled against you, and He shut up the heaven, so that there shall be no rain, and the ground shall not yield her fruit* (11:17).

Another interpretation: *Give ear, ye heavens*: R. Nehemiah says: A parable: A king had a son who fell into depraved ways. The king began to complain about him to his brothers, to his friends, to his neighbors, and to his relatives. This father did not cease complaining until he said, "O heaven and earth, to whom am I to complain about you[14] except to these?"[15] Therefore Scripture says, *Give ear, ye heavens, and I will speak, and let the earth hear the words of my mouth* (32:1).

Another interpretation: *Give ear, ye heavens*: R. Judah says: These are insufficient for the righteous. Rather, the world is enlarged[16] when they are in it. When Israel perform God's will, what does Scripture say about them? *The Lord will open unto thee His good treasure, (the heaven)* (28:12). And opening means enlarging, as it is said, *And He opened her womb* (Gen. 29:31). Nor are these sufficient for the wicked.[17] Rather, the world is straitened when they are in it, for when Israel do not perform God's will, what does it say of them? *And the anger of the Lord be kindled against you, and He shut up the heaven* (11:17). And shutting up means making strait, as it is said, *For the Lord had fast shut up (the wombs)* (Gen. 20:18).

Another interpretation: *Give ear, ye heavens, and I will speak*: The Holy One, blessed be He, said to Moses: Say to Israel: Look at the heavens which I have created to serve you. Have they changed their character? Has the sphere of the sun said, "I am not going to rise in the east and illuminate the whole world"? On the contrary, it is said, *The sun also ariseth, and the sun goeth down* (Eccl. 1:5). And furthermore, it rejoices to perform My will, as it is said, *(The sun), which is as a bridegroom coming out of his chamber, and rejoiceth as a strong man to run his course* (Ps. 19:5–6). *And let the earth hear the words of my mouth* (32:1): Look at the earth which I have created to serve you. Has it changed its character? Have you sown seed in it, and it did not cause the seed to sprout? Have you sown wheat, and it brought forth barley? Or has this cow (of yours) said, "I am not going to thresh or plough today"? Or has this ass (of yours) said, "I am not going to carry or walk today"? And as for the sea, Scripture says, *Fear ye not Me? saith the Lord: will ye not tremble at My presence? Who have placed the sand for the bound of the sea* (Jer. 5:22). From the time that I had decreed its (bounds), has it changed its character? Has it said, "I will arise and flood the world"? On the contrary, it is said, *And prescribe for it My decree, and set bars and doors, and said: Thus far shalt thou come, but no further; and here shall thy proud waves be stayed* (Job 38:10–11). Furthermore, the sea is troubled and knows not what to do, as it is said, *And though the waves thereof toss themselves, yet can they not prevail* (Jer. 5:22). Is this not a matter of inference from the minor to the major? If those who were created for neither reward nor loss, who when worthy receive no reward, and when guilty of sin receive no punishment, and who need have no concern for their sons and daughters, yet do not change their character, how much less should you, who when worthy receive a reward, and when guilty of sin receive punishment, and who are concerned about your sons and daughters, change your character?

Another interpretation: *Give ear, ye heavens*: R. Benaiah says: When a man has been found guilty, the witnesses should be the first to lay a hand on him, as it is said, *The hand of the witnesses shall be first upon him to put him to death* (17:7). And afterwards other individuals may join in, as it is said, *and afterward the hand of all the people* (17:7). So also, when Israel does not perform God's will, what does Scripture say about them? *And the anger of the Lord be kindled against you, and He shut up the heaven, (so that there shall be no rain, and the ground shall not yield her fruit)* (11:17);[18] and afterwards other punishments follow, as it is said, *and ye perish quickly from off the good land which the Lord giveth you* (11:17). When Israel performs God's will, what is said of them? *And it shall come to pass in that day, I will respond, saith the Lord, I will respond to the heavens (and they shall respond to the earth) . . . and I will sow her unto Me in the land* (Hos. 2:23–25).

Another interpretation: *Give ear, ye heavens, and I will speak*: R. Judah ben Hananiah used to say: When Moses said, *Give ear, ye heavens, and I will speak,* the heavens and the heavens of heavens stood still, and when he said, *and let the earth hear the words of my mouth,* the earth and everything upon it stood still. And if you are astounded at this, consider what is said concerning Joshua, *And he said in the sight of Israel: Sun, stand thou still upon Gibeon; and thou, Moon, in the valley of Aijalon. . . . And there was no day like that before it* (Josh. 10:12–14). Thus we learn that the righteous have dominion over the entire world.[19]

Another interpretation: *Give ear, ye heavens*: Since Moses was (at that moment) close to heaven, he said, *Give ear, ye heavens,* and since he was far from the earth he said, *and let the earth hear the words of my mouth.* Isaiah came and added, *Hear, O heavens* (Isa. 1:2), since he was far from heaven, *and give ear, O earth* (Isa. 1:2), since he was close to the earth.[20] Another interpretation: Since the heavens are multiple, Moses used the plural for them, and since the earth is only one, he used the singular for it, *and let the earth hear the words of my mouth.* Isaiah came and added, *Hear, O heavens, and give ear, O earth,* giving the plural to the multiple and the singular to the one.[21] The Sages, however, say that this is not so. Rather, when witnesses come forth to testify, if their words are identical, their testimony stands; if not, their testimony does not stand. So also, had Moses said[22] only, *Give ear, ye heavens,* and nothing more, the heavens would have said, "We have heard only by giving ear, (and not also by hearing.)" And had he said, *and let the earth hear the words of my mouth,* the earth would have said, "I have heard only by hearing, (and not also by giving ear.)"[23] Isaiah came and added, *Hear, O heavens, and give ear, O earth,* in order to ascribe giving ear and hearing to both heavens and earth.

Another interpretation: *Give ear, ye heavens, and I will speak*—this refers to the fact that the Torah was given from the heavens, as it is said, *Ye yourselves have seen that I have talked with you from heaven* (Exod. 20:19)—*and let the earth hear the words of my mouth*—since Israel stood upon the earth and said, *All that the Lord hath spoken will we do and obey* (Exod. 24:7).

Another interpretation: *Give ear, ye heavens*—that Israel had not fulfilled the commandments given to them concerning[24] the heavens, namely, the intercalation of the year and the determination of the new months, as it is said, *And let them be for signs and for seasons, and for days and years* (Gen. 1:14)—*and let the earth hear*—that they had not fulfilled the commandments given to them concerning the earth, namely, those concerning gleanings, forgotten sheaves, corner crop, heave offering, tithes, Sabbatical years, and Jubilee years.

Another interpretation: *Give ear, ye heavens*—that Israel had not fulfilled all the commandments given to them from heaven—*and let the earth hear the words of my mouth*—that they had not fulfilled all the commandments given them on earth.[25] Moses called two witnesses against Israel that will exist for all eternity, as it is said, *I call heaven and earth to witness against you this day* (30:19). And the Holy One, blessed be He, called the song[26] to testify against them, as it is said, *Now therefore write ye this song for you* (31:19). We do not know whose testimony stands,[27] that of the Holy One, blessed be He, or that of Moses. When Scripture says, *This song shall testify before them as a witness* (31:21), it indicates that the testimony of the Holy One, blessed be He, confirms the testimony of Moses, not that the testimony of Moses confirms the testimony of the Holy One, blessed be He. Why then did Moses call two witnesses against Israel which will exist for all eternity? Because he said, "I am but flesh-and-blood—tomorrow I will die. What if Israel decide to say, 'We did not receive the Torah'? Who will controvert them?" Therefore he called two witnesses to testify against them which will exist for all eternity. The Holy One, blessed be He, called the song to testify against them, saying, "The song will testify against them from below, and I (will testify) from above." Whence do we learn that God is called a witness? From the verses, *And I will come near to you to judgment, and I will be a swift witness* (Mal. 3:5), *But I am He that knoweth, and am witness, saith the Lord* (Jer. 29:23), and, *And let the Lord God be witness against you, the Lord from His holy Temple* (Mic. 1:2).

My doctrine shall drop as the rain (32:2): *My doctrine* means words of Torah, as it is said, *For I give you good doctrine, foresake ye not My Torah* (Prov. 4:2), *Receive My instruction, and not silver* (Prov. 8:10)—*instruction* means words of Torah, as it is said, *Hear, my son, the instruction of thy father, and foresake not the Torah of thy mother* (Prov. 1:8)—*Hear instruction, and be wise, and refuse it not* (Prov. 8:33), *Take fast hold of instruction, let her not go* (Prov. 4:13), and, *Take with you words, and return unto the Lord* (Hos. 14:3)—*words* means words of Torah, as it is said, *These words the Lord spoke unto all your assembly* (5:19).

As the rain: Just as rain lives forever, so words of Torah live forever. Or could it be that just as in the case of rain, where part of the world rejoices in it and part is distressed by it—if one's tank is full of wine and his threshing floor is (full of grain) before him, he will be distressed by it—so also in the case of the words of Torah? Therefore the verse goes on to say, *My speech shall distill as the dew* (32:2)—just as the whole world rejoices in dew, so does it rejoice in words of Torah.

As the small rain upon the tender grass (32:2): Just as this small rain comes down upon the grass and makes it go up and grow, so do words of Torah make you go up and grow, as it is said, *Extol her, and she will exalt you* (Prov. 4:8).

And as the showers upon the herb (32:2): Just as these showers come down upon the herbs, refreshing them and filling them out, so words of Torah will refresh you and fill you out, as it is said, *For they shall be a chaplet of grace unto they head* (Prov. 1:9), and, *She will give to thy head a chaplet of grace* (Prov. 4:9).

Another interpretation: *My doctrine shall drop as the rain, (my speech shall distill as the dew)*: R. Nehemiah used to say: You should always assemble the words of Torah into general rules. You might think that just as you assemble them into general rules, so should you dispense them as general rules. Therefore the verse states, *My doctrine shall drop as the rain*—"drop" (*yaᶜărof*) is a Canaanite term;[28] one does not say to another, "*pĕroṭ* (break) this selaᶜ for me," but "*ᶜărof* this selaᶜ for me." Thus, assemble the words of Torah into general rules, but then break them up and dispense them like drops of dew—not like drops of rain which are large, but like drops of dew that are small.[29]

As the small rain upon the tender grass: Just as the small raindrops come down upon the tender grasses and permeate them thoroughly, so that they do not become wormy, so should you thoroughly permeate[30] the words of Torah in order that you do not forget them. Thus R. Jacob be-R. Hanilai once said to Rabbi (Judah the Prince): Come, let us permeate some rules, so that they will not become moldy (in our minds).

And as the showers upon the herb: Just as these showers come down upon the herbs, cleanse them, and perfume them, so should you perfume words of Torah and go over them time and time again.

Another interpretation: *My doctrine shall drop as the rain*: R. Eliezer ben R. Jose the Galilean says: *Drop* (*yaᶜărof*) means "kill," as it is said, *And shall break (wĕ-ᶜorfu) the heifer's neck there in the valley* (21:4). What does the heifer atone for? For the shedding of blood. So, too, do words of Torah atone for all transgressions.

As the small rain (śĕᶜirim) upon the tender grass: What do goats (*śĕᶜirim*)[31] (when sacrificed) atone for? Sins. So, too, do words of Torah atone for sins.

And as the showers upon the herb: Just as the showers are pure and cover[32] (everything), so do words of Torah atone for all sins and transgressions.

Another interpretation: *My doctrine shall drop as the rain*: The Sages say that Moses said to Israel: Perhaps you do not know how much I suffered for the sake of the Torah, how much I toiled in it, how much I labored in it, as it is said, *And he was there with the Lord forty days and forty nights; he did neither eat bread, nor drink water* (Exod. 34:28), and, *Then I abode in the mount forty days and forty nights, I did neither eat bread nor drink water* (9:9). I went among the angels, among the (heavenly) beasts, among the seraphim, each one of which is capable of burning the entire world over its inhabitants, as it is said, *Above Him stood the seraphim* (Isa. 6:2).[33] I gave my soul for the Torah, I gave my blood for it. Just as I learned it in suffering, so shall you learn it in suffering. Or does it mean that just as you learn it in suffering, so shall you teach it in suffering? Therefore the verse states, *My speech shall drop*[34] *as the dew*—think of it as to be sold at a low price, as when three or four sĕʾah (of wheat) sell for one selaᶜ.[35]

As the small rain (śĕᶜirim) upon the tender grass: When one begins to learn Torah, it pounces on him like a *śĕᶜir*, meaning a satyr, as it is said, *And the satyr (śĕᶜir) shall dance there* (Isa. 13:21).

Another interpretation: *My doctrine shall drop as the rain*: R. Benaiah used to say: If you fulfill the words of Torah for their own sake, they will bring you life, as it is said, *For they are life unto those that find them* (Prov. 4:22); if you do not fulfill them for their own sake, they will bring you death, as it is said, *My doctrine shall drop (yaᶜărof) as the rain, yaᶜărof* meaning "shall kill," as it is said, *And shall break (wĕ-ᶜorfu) the heifer's neck there in the valley* (21:4), and it is said also, *For she hath cast down many wounded; yea, a mighty host are all her slain* (Prov. 7:26).

Another interpretation: *My doctrine shall drop as the rain*: R. Dostai ben Judah says: If you gather the words of Torah together as one gathers water into a (watertight) cistern, the result will be that you yourself will merit attaining your learning,[36] as it is said, *Drink waters out of thine own cistern* (Prov. 5:15). If, however, you gather the words of Torah as one gathers rain (water) into ditches, pits, and caves, the result will be that you will irrigate and water others (as well), as it is said, *And running waters out of thine own well* (Prov. 5:15)[37] and, *Let thy springs be dispersed abroad* (Prov. 5:16).

Another interpretation: *My doctrine shall drop as the rain*: R. Meir used to say: You should always gather the words of Torah together into general rules, for if you assemble them as individual details, they will weary you.[38] How then can you know what to do? A parable: A man who went to Caesarea needed one hundred or two hundred zuz for expenses. If he took this sum in small change, it would weary him. (At first) he did not know what to do, but finally he converted the money into selaᶜ-coins, which he then changed (into smaller coins) and spent wherever it suited him. So, too, one who goes to the market at Bet Ilias[39] needs one hundred minas or two myriads[40] for expenses. If he took this sum in selaᶜ-coins, it would weary him. (At first) he does not know what to do, but finally he converts the money into gold denar, which he changes and spends wherever it suits him.

As the small rain (śĕᶜirim) upon the tender grass: When one goes to learn Torah, at first he does not know what to do, but after he learns two books or two sections, the rest follows after him like *showers (rĕbibim)*[41] *upon the herb*.

Another interpretation: *My doctrine shall drop as the rain*: Just as rain falls on trees and infuses them with the particular flavor (of their fruit)—the grapevine according to its flavor, the olive tree according to its flavor, the fig tree according to its flavor—so also words of Torah are all the same, yet they comprise Scripture, Mishnah, Talmud, Halakah, and Haggadah.[42]

As the small rain upon the tender grass: Just as the small rain falls upon the (tender) grasses and causes them to grow, some red, some green, some black, and some white, so also words of Torah—some men (who study Torah) are wise, some are worthy, some are righteous, and some are pious.[43]

Another interpretation: Just as rain cannot be anticipated in advance, until it actually arrives, as it is said, *And it came to pass in a little while, that the heaven grew black with clouds (and wind, and there was a great rain)* (1 Kings 18:45),[44] so also a disciple of the wise—you do not know what his character is until he teaches the interpretation of Halakah and Haggadah, or until he is appointed administrator[45] over the community.

Another interpretation: *Shall drop as the rain*: Not like the rain that comes from the south and causes only blast and mildew, and is nothing but a curse, but like the rain that comes from the west, which is entirely a blessing. R. Simai[46] used to say: Whence do we learn that just as Moses invoked the heavens and the earth as witnesses against Israel, so did he invoke the four winds of heaven? From the verse, *My doctrine shall drop (yaʿărof) as the rain*—referring to the west wind, which comes from the back (*ʿoref*) of the world and is entirely a blessing—*my speech shall distill as the dew*—referring to the north wind, which makes the sky as clear as (refined) gold—*as the small rain (śĕʿirim) upon the tender grass*—referring to the east wind, which makes the sky as black as demons—*and as the showers upon the herb*—referring to the south wind, which plows up the sky like a *rabib*.[47]

Another interpretation: *My doctrine shall drop as the rain*: R. Simai used to say: These four winds refer to the four winds of heaven: the north wind is pleasant in the summer but harsh in the rainy season; the south wind is harsh in the summer but pleasant in the rainy season; the east wind is always harsh; the west wind is always pleasant.[48] The north wind is favorable for wheat when the first third (of the crop) is being harvested, but bad for olive trees when their fruit is being formed. The south wind is bad for olive trees when the first third (of the crop) is being harvested, but good for wheat when it is being formed. R. Simai used to say further: Both the soul and the body of creatures created from heaven are from heaven; both the soul and the body of those creatures created from the earth are from earth, except for that one creature, man, whose soul is from heaven and whose body is from the earth. Therefore, if man lives by the Torah and performs the will of his Father in heaven, he is like the heavenly creatures, as it is said, *I said, Ye are godlike beings, and all of you sons of the Most High* (Ps. 82:6). But if he does not live by the Torah and does not perform the will of his Father in heaven, he is like the creatures of the earth, as it is said, *Nevertheless ye shall die like Adam*[49] (Ps. 82:7).

R. Simai used to say: There is no Scriptural lesson lacking a reference to the resurrection of the dead, but we do not know how to interpret it properly. (For example,) it is said, *He calleth to the heavens above, and to the earth, that He may judge His people* (Ps. 50:4):

He calleth to the heavens above—this refers to the soul; *and to the earth*—this refers to the body; *that he may judge His people* (*ᶜammo*)—who judges with Him (*ᶜimmo*)?[50] And whence do we learn that this[51] refers to the resurrection of the dead? From the verse, *(Thus saith the Lord God): Come from the four winds, O breath, and breathe upon these slain, that they may live* (Ezek. 37:9).

For I will proclaim the name of the Lord (32:3): We find that Moses did not mention the name of the Holy One, blessed be He, until after he had spoken twenty-one words.[52] From whom did he learn this? From the ministering angels, for the ministering angels mention the name (of God) only after the threefold Sanctification, as it is said, *And one called unto another,* and said: *Holy, holy, holy, is the Lord of hosts* (Isa. 6:3). Said Moses, "It is enough for me to be seven times as modest as the ministering angels."[53] The matter lends itself to inference from the minor to the major: if Moses, the wisest of the wise, the greatest of the great, and the father of the prophets, mentioned God's name only after twenty-one words, how much more must one be cautious not to mention God's name in vain. R. Simeon ben Yoḥai says: Whence do we learn that one should not say, "unto the Lord, a burnt offering," "unto the Lord, a meal offering," "unto the Lord, a peace offering," but rather, "a burnt offering unto the Lord," "a meal offering unto the Lord," "a peace offering unto the Lord"? From the verse, *An offering unto the Lord* (Lev. 1:2). This is a matter of inference from the minor to the major: If in connection with that which is consecrated to heaven, the Holy One, blessed be He, has said, "Do not invoke My name upon them until they have been sanctified,"[54] how much more must one be cautious about mentioning the name of the Holy One, blessed be He, in vain or in a place of shame.

For I will proclaim the name of the Lord: R. Jose says: Whence do we learn that when those who lead in the synagogue call out, "Bless ye the Lord, who is to be blessed,"[55] the congregation must respond, "Blessed is the Lord, who is to be blessed, for ever and ever"? From the other half of the verse, *For I will proclaim the name of the Lord; ascribe ye greatness unto our God* (32:3).[56] R. Nehorai said to R. Jose: By heaven, that is the way things go on this earth—the rank and file soldiers begin the battle, but it is the heroes who triumph.[57] Whence do we learn that one may not recite Grace after meals unless there are at least three persons present? From the same verse, *For I will proclaim the name of the Lord; ascribe ye greatness unto our God.*[58]

And whence do we learn that one must respond with Amen to a blessing? From the verse, *Ascribe ye greatness unto our God.* Whence do we learn that we must go on to say, "Blessed be His glorious majesty forever and ever"?[59] From the verse, *For I will proclaim the name of the Lord.* Whence do we learn that when one says, "May His great name be blessed," the others must respond, "For ever and for all eternity"?[60] From the verse, *Ascribe ye greatness unto our God.* Whence do you learn that our ancestors went into Egypt only so that the Holy One, blessed be He, might perform miracles and mighty acts for them in order to sanctify His great name in the world? From the verses, *And it came to pass in the course of those many days that the king of Egypt died, (and the children of Israel sighed by reason of the bondage, and they cried)*[61] . . . *and God heard their groaning, and God remembered His covenant* (Exod. 2:23–24), and, *For I will proclaim the name of the Lord; ascribe ye greatness unto our God.*[62]

And whence do we learn that God brought punishment and the ten plagues upon Pharaoh and upon Egypt only in order to sanctify His great name in the world? From the fact that at the beginning of the matter Pharaoh says, *Who is the Lord, that I should hearken unto His voice?* (Exod. 5:2), but at the conclusion of it he says, *The Lord is righteous, and I and my people are wicked* (Exod. 9:27).

And whence do we learn that God worked miracles and mighty deeds at the (Red) Sea, and at the Jordan, and at the valleys of Arnon[63] only in order to sanctify His name in the world? From the verse, *And it came to pass, when all the kings of the Amorites that were beyond the Jordan westward, and all the kings (of the Canaanites, that were by the sea, heard how that the Lord had dried up the waters of the Jordan from before the children of Israel, until they were passed over, that their heart melted, neither was their spirit in them any more)* (Josh. 5:1). Similarly Rahab says to Joshua's messengers, *For we have heard how the Lord dried up the water of the Red Sea before you (when ye came out of Egypt; and what ye did unto the two kings of the Amorites that were beyond the Jordan, unto Sihon and to Og, whom ye utterly destroyed)* (Josh. 2:10). Therefore the verse here states, *For I will proclaim the name of the Lord.*[64] And whence do we learn that Daniel went down into the lions' den only so that the Holy One, blessed be He, might work miracles and mighty deeds for him and in order to sanctify His great name in the world? From the verses, *For I will proclaim the name of the Lord,* and *I make a decree, that in all the dominions of my kingdom men tremble and fear before the God of Daniel. . . . (He worketh signs and wonders in heaven and in earth)* (Dan. 6:27–28). And whence do we learn that Hananiah, Mishael, and Azariah went down into the fiery furnace only so that the Holy One, blessed be He, might work miracles and mighty deeds in order to sanctify His great name in the world?[65] From the verse, *It hath seemed good unto me to declare the signs and wonders that God Most High hath wrought toward me. . . . How great are His signs! And how mighty are His wonders! His kingdom is an everlasting kingdom* (Dan. 3:32–33).

And whence do we learn that the ministering angels do not mention the name of the Holy One, blessed be He, on high until Israel mention it below? From the verses, *Hear, O Israel, the Lord our God, the Lord is One* (6:4), and, *When the morning stars sang together, and all the sons of God shouted for joy* (Job 38:7)—*the morning stars* are Israel, who are symbolized by the stars, as it is said, *I will multiply thy seed as the stars of the heaven* (Gen. 22:17); *and all the sons of God shouted for joy* refers to the ministering angels, as it is said, *The sons of God came to present themselves before the Lord* (Job 1:6).

Pisḳa 307

The Rock (haṣ-Ṣur)—the Artist (*ṣayyar*), for He first designed (*ṣar*) the world and then formed man in it, as it is said, *Then the Lord God formed (way-yiṣer) man* (Gen. 2:7)—*His work is perfect* (32:4): His workmanship in regard to all creatures of the world is perfect; there can be no complaint whatsoever[1] about His work. None of them can look at himself and say, "If only I had three eyes, if only I had three arms, if only I had three legs, if only I walked on my head, if only my face were turned the other way, how nicely it would become me!" Hence the verse goes on to say, *For all His ways are justice*—He sits in judgment on everyone and dispenses to each that which is appropriate for him—*a God of faithfulness*—who believed in the world and created it[2]—*and without iniquity*—for men were created not in order to be wicked but in order to be righteous, as it is said, *Behold, this only have I found, that God made man upright; but they have sought out many inventions* (Eccl. 7:29)—*just and right is He* (32:4)—He conducts Himself uprightly with all the creatures of the world.

Another interpretation: *The Rock*—the Powerful One—*His work is perfect*: His actions in regard to all creatures of the world are perfect; there can be no complaint whatsoever about His work. None of them can look at himself and say, "Why should the generation of the flood have been swept away by water? Why should the people of the tower (of Babel) have been scattered from one end of the earth to the other? Why should the people of Sodom have been swept away by fire and brimstone? Why should Aaron have assumed the priesthood? Why should David have assumed the kingship? Why should Korah and his followers have been swallowed up by the earth?" Therefore the verse goes on to say, *For all His way are justice*—He sits in judgment on everyone and dispenses to each what is appropriate[3] for him—*a God of faithfulness*—who keeps His trust[4]—*and without iniquity*—He collects that which is His only at the end. For the way of the Holy One, blessed be He, is not like the way of creatures of flesh and blood: if A deposits with B a purse of two hundred (shekels) while owing B a *manah*,[5] when A comes to retrieve it, B says to him, "I will subtract the *manah* you owe me, and here is the balance, (one hundred shekels)"; similarly if a workman working for B owes him a *denar*, when he comes to collect his wages, B says to him, "I will subtract the denar you owe me, and here is the balance (of your wages)." but He-who-spoke-and-the-world-came-into-being is not like that; rather, *He is a God of faithfulness*—who keeps His trust—*and without iniquity*—collecting that which is His only at the end[6]—*just and right is He,* as it is said, *For the Lord is righteous, He loveth righteousness* (Ps. 11:7).

Another interpretation: *The Rock*—the Powerful One—*His work is perfect*: The work of all creatures of the world is complete before Him, both the dispensing of reward to the righteous and the infliction of punishment to the wicked. Neither takes anything due to them in this world. Whence do we learn that the righteous take nothing due to them in this world? From the verse, *Oh how abundant is Thy goodness, which Thou hast laid up for them that fear Thee!* (Ps. 31:20). And whence do we learn that the wicked take nothing due to them in this world? From the verse, *Is not this laid up in store with Me, sealed up in My treasuries?* (32:34).[7] When do both of them take (that which is due them)? *For all His ways are justice*—in the future, when He will sit upon the throne of justice, He will sit in judgment on each one and give him what is appropriate for him.

A God of faithfulness: Just as He grants the perfectly righteous a reward in the world-to-come for his performance of the commandments in this world, so does He grant the perfectly wicked a reward in this world for any minor commandment performed in this world;

and just as He requites the perfectly wicked in the world-to-come for any transgression performed in this world, so does He requite the perfectlay righteous in this world for any minor transgression committed in this world.[8]

And without iniquity:[9] When one departs from this world, all his deeds will come before him one by one and say to him, "Thus did you do on such-and-such a day, and thus did you do on such-and-such other day—do you acknowledge these matters?" And he will reply, "Yes." He will be told, "Sign!," as it is said, *The hand of every man shall seal (it), so that all men may know his deeds*[10] (Job 37:7).

Just and right is He: The man thereupon will justify the verdict and say, "Well was I judged," as it is said, *That Thou mayest justify (the judgment) when Thou speakest*[11] (Ps. 51:6).

Another interpretation: *The Rock, His work is perfect*: When they apprehended R. Ḥaninah ben Teradion,[12] he was condemned to be burned together with his Torah Scroll.[13] When he was told of it, he recited this verse, *The Rock, His work is perfect.* When his wife was told, "Your husband has been condemned to be burned, and you to be executed," she recited the verse, *A God of faithfulness and without iniquity.* And when his daughter was told, "Your father has been condemned to be burned, your mother to be executed, and you yourself to be assigned to (disgraceful) work,"[14] she recited the verse, *Great in counsel, and mighty in work, whose eyes are open (upon all the ways of the sons of men, to give every one according to his ways)* (Jer. 32:19). Rabbi (Judah the Prince) said: How great were these righteous persons, in that at the time of their trouble they invoked[15] three verses justifying (God's) judgment, which are unequaled in the Scripture. The three directed their hearts (toward God) and accepted the justice of God's judgment. A philosopher protested to the prefect, saying, "My master, do not boast that you have burned the Torah, for it has now returned to the place whence it had come—its Father's house." The prefect replied, "Tomorrow your fate will be the same as theirs," whereupon the philosopher said to him, "You have conveyed good tidings to me, that tomorrow my portion will be with them in the world to come."[16]

Another interpretation: *The Rock, His work is perfect*: When Moses descended from Mount Sinai, all Israel gathered together around him and said to him, "Our master Moses, tell us, what is the measure of justice on high?"[17] He replied, "I do not tell you merely that He does not justify the guilty or punish the innocent,[18] but that He does not even exchange (one for the other).[19] He is *A God of faithfulness, and without iniquity.*"

Pisḳa 308

Is corruption His? No; His children's is the blemish (32:5): Even though they are full of blemishes, they are called "children," as it is said, *His children's is the blemish*; so taught R. Meir. R. Judah, however, says: They have no blemishes, as it is said, *His children have no blemish.*[1] Similarly,[2] Scripture calls them *A seed of evil-doers, children that deal corruptly* (Isa. 1:4). If they are called "children" when they deal corruptly, how much more would they be called so if they did not deal corruptly. In a similar vein (Scripture says), *They are wise to do evil* (Jer. 4:22). Is this not a matter of inference from the minor to the major: if they are called "wise" when they do evil, how much more would they be so called if they did good. The same verse says also, *They are sottish children* (Jer. 4:22): if they are called "children" when they are sottish, how much more would they be called so if they were understanding. Another verse says likewise, *And cometh unto thee as the people cometh, and sit before thee as My people, and hear thy words* (Ezek. 33:31)—lest you think that they both hear and do them, the verse goes on to say, *but do them not* (Ezek. 33:31)—if they are called "My people" when they hear but do not do, how much more would they be so called if they both heard and did.

The Sages taught in the name of Abba Hedores:[3] Israel has corrupted itself by violating all the prohibitions in the Torah.[4] Why is this stated?[5] In order not to give the wicked an excuse to say that whenever we sin, we trouble Him.[6] To what may this be likened? To one who is about to be crucified. His father weeps for him, and his mother prostrates herself before him (in her grief). The father cries, "Woe is me!" The mother cries, "Woe is me!" But the one really affected is only he who is about to be crucified. Thus Scripture says, *Woe unto their soul! For they have wrought evil unto themselves* (Isa. 3:9).[7]

A generation crooked and perverse (32:5): Moses said to Israel, "You are twisted. You are devious. You are headed for the fire." To what may this be likened? To one who has in his hand a twisted staff and gives it to an artisan to be straightened. The artisan first tries to fix it (by heating it) with fire.[8] If that does not succeed, he tries to straighten it in a wood-press, and if that too does not succeed, he chips it up with an adze and casts it into the fire,[9] as it is said, *And I will deliver thee into the hand of brutish men, skillful to destroy. (Thou shalt be for fuel to the fire)* (Ezek. 21:36–37).

Another interpretation: Moses said to Israel, "I have measured out to you with the same measure with which you have measured out, as it is said, *With the pure Thou dost show Thyself pure, with the crooked Thou dost show Thyself perverse* (2 Sam. 22:27)—(and you are) *a generation crooked and perverse.*"[10]

Pisḳa 309

Do ye thus requite the Lord? (32:6): A parable: To what may this be likened? To one who stood up in the forum and insulted a senator.[1] The bystanders said to him, "You stupid fool! You stand up and insult a senator. Why, if he decided to strike you, or to rip your garment, or to imprison you, could you restrain him? If he were a centurion, who is even more important, how much more harm could he do to you. If he were a consul,[2] who is more important than both of them, how much more and more harm could he do to you."

Another interpretation: *Do you thus requite the Lord?* A parable: To what may it be likened? To one who stood up in the forum and insulted his own father. The bystanders said to him, "You stupid fool! Whom are you insulting? It is your own father! How he labored for your sake, how much weariness he suffered for your sake! If you did not honor him in the past, surely you should honor him now, lest he should will all his possessions to others." So also did Moses say to Israel, "If you do not remember the miracles and mighty deeds that the Holy One, blessed be He, performed for you in Egypt, at least consider how many good things He plans to grant you in the world to come."

O foolish people and unwise (32:6): *Foolish* in the past and *unwise* in the future. Similarly (Scripture says), *But Israel doth not know*—in the past—*My people doth not consider* (Isa. 1:3)—in the future.[3] What caused Israel to be so disgraceful and so stupid? Their failure to gain wisdom through the words of Torah, as it is said, *Is not their tent-*

cord plucked up within them? They die, and that without wisdom[4] (Job 4:21).

Is not He thy father that hath gotten thee? (32:6):[5] Simeon ben Ḥalafta says: If (in a battle) a weakling is on top and a valiant man underneath, who would win? Could you be sure to defeat the valiant man? How much less so if the valiant man is on top and the weakling underneath. Similarly Scripture says, *Be not rash with thy mouth, and let not thy heart be hasty to utter a word before God, for God is in heaven, and thou upon earth* (Eccl. 5:1).

Is not He thy father that hath gotten thee?: Moses said to Israel, "You are precious to Him. You are His own possession and not His inheritance."[6] A parable: A certain person who had inherited ten fields from his father purchased a field of his own, which he therefore loved more than all the fields that he had inherited from his father. Similarly, a person who had inherited ten palaces from his father purchased one palace of his own, which he loved more than all the palaces that he had inherited from his father. So also did Moses say to Israel, "You are precious to Him. You are His own acquisition and not His inheritance."

That hath gotten thee: This is one of three[7] called God's acquisition. Torah is called God's acquisition, as it is said, *The Lord acquired me at the beginning of His way* (Prov. 8:22). Israel is called God's acquisition, as it is said, *Is not He thy father that hath gotten thee?* The Temple (in Jerusalem) is called God's acquisition, as it is said, *This mountain, which His right hand had acquired* (Ps. 78:54).[8]

Hath He not made thee, and established thee? (32:6): R. Meir used to say: It is a city containing every sort of men: priests are within it, prophets are within it, wise men are within it, scribes are within it,[9] as it is said, *Out of them shall come forth the cornerstone, out of them the stake, (out of them the battle bow, out of them every master together)* (Zech. 10:4). R. Judah says: *(Established thee)* means "make thee full of cavities."[10] R. Simeon ben Judah says: He settled you upon your base, fed you the spoil of seven nations, gave you what He had pledged unto you, and let you possess what He had promised you. R. Dostai ben Judah says: *(Established thee)* means "made thee full of inner chambers":[11] if any one of them were to be misplaced, you would not be able to exist.[12]

Pisḳa 310

Remember the days of old (32:7): Moses said to Israel, "Bethink yourselves of what I have done to the earlier generations—what I have done to the people of the generation of the flood, what I have done to the people of the generation of the dispersion, and what I have done to the people of Sodom."

Consider the years of each generation (32:7): There is no generation but that it includes people like those of the generation of the flood and like those of Sodom, but each individual is judged according to his deeds.

Ask thy father, and he will declare unto thee—this refers to the prophets, the same as in the verse, *And Elisha saw it, and he cried, "My father, my father"*[1] (2 Kings 2:12)—*thine elders, and they will tell thee* (32:7)—this refers to the elders (of Israel), the same as in the verse, *Gather unto Me seventy men of the elders of Israel* (Num. 11:16).[2]

Another interpretation: *Remember the days of old*: Moses said to them, "Whenever the Holy One, blessed be He, brings sufferings upon you, remind yourselves of all the good things and consolations that He will give you in the world-to-come."[3]

Consider the years of each generation: This refers to the generation of the Messiah, which will endure for three generations, as it is said, *They shall fear Thee while the sun endureth, and so long as the moon, throughout all generations*[4] (Ps. 72:5).

Ask thy Father, and He will declare unto thee—in the future Israel will see and hear as if from the mouth of the Holy One, blessed be He, Himself, as it is said, *And thine ears shall hear a word behind thee, saying . . .* (Isa. 30:21), and, *Yet shall not thy Teacher hide Himself anymore, but thine eyes shall see thy Teacher* (Isa. 30:20)—*thine elders, and they will tell thee*—what I have revealed to the elders on the Mountain (of Sinai), as it is said, *And unto Moses He said, Come up unto the Lord, thou, (and Aaron, Nadab, and Abihu, and seventy of the elders of Israel)* (Exod. 24:1).

Pisḳa 311

When the Most High gave to the nations their inheritance (32:8): Before the appearance of our father Abraham, the Holy One, blessed be He, judged the world with the measure of harshness,[1] if one may say such a thing. When the people of the flood sinned, He quenched them like sparks in water; when the people of the tower (of Babel) sinned, He scattered them from one end of the world to the other; when the people of Sodom sinned, He inundated them with fire and brimstone. But when our father Abraham came into the world, he was privileged to endure sufferings which began to appear gradually, as it is said, *And there was a famine in the land, and Abram went down into Egypt* (Gen. 12:10). Should you ask, why do sufferings come? (the answer is,) because of the preciousness of Israel—*He set the borders of the people according to the number of the children of Israel* (32:8).

Another interpretation: *When the Most High gave to the nations their inheritance*: When the Holy One, blessed be He, gave the peoples their inheritance, He specified the area of each nation,[2] so that they would not be mixed. He assigned the children of Gomer to Gomer, the children of Magog to Magog, the children of Media to Media, the children of Javan to Greece, the children of Tubal to Tubal. He specified the areas of the nations, so that they would not enter the Land of Israel—*He set the borders of the peoples* (32:8).

Another interpretation: *When the Most High gave to the nations their inheritance*: When the Holy One, blessed be He, gave the Torah to Israel, He stood up,[3] looked out, and scrutinized, as it is said, *He standeth, and shaketh the earth, He beholdeth, and maketh the nations to tremble* (Hab. 3:6), and there was no nation among the nations worthy to receive the Torah other than Israel—*He set the borders of the peoples*.[4]

Another interpretation: *When the Most High gave to the nations their inheritance*: When the Holy One, blessed be He, gave the peoples their inheritance, He made Gehenna their portion, as it is said, *Asshur is there and all her company* (Ezek. 32:33), *There are the princes of the north, all of them, and all the Zidonians* (Ezek. 32:30), *There is Edom, her kings* (Ezek. 32:29).[5] Should you ask, who will possess their wealth and honor? the answer is, Israel—*He set the borders of the peoples (according to the number of the children of Israel)* (32:8).

Another interpretation: *When the Most High gave to the nations their inheritance*: When the Holy One, blessed be He, gave inheritance to the sin-fearing and worthy ones from among the peoples.[6]

When He separated the children of men (32:8): This refers to the generation of the dispersion, as it is said, *And from thence did the Lord scatter them abroad* (Gen. 11:9).

He set the borders of the peoples: R. Eliezer the son of R. Jose the

Galilean says: But Scripture says, *There are threescore queens, and fourscore concubines* (Song 6:8)—sixty and eighty make one hundred and forty. Yet of our forefathers only seventy souls went down to Egypt, as it is said, *Thy fathers went down into Egypt with threescore and ten persons* (10:22).[7] So also Scripture says here, *the borders of the peoples*[8]—it does not say "the border"[9] of the peoples," but *the borders of the peoples*; the nations were privileged to take twice the portion given to the children of Israel.

Pisḳa 312

For the portion of the Lord is His people (32:9): A parable: A king had a field which he leased to tenants. When the tenants began to steal from it, He took it away from them and leased it to their children. When the children began to act worse than their fathers, he took it away from them and gave it to (the original tenants') grandchildren. When these too became worse than their predecessors, a son was born to him. He then said to the grandchildren, "Leave my property. You may not remain therein. Give me back my portion, so that I may repossess it." Thus also, when our father Abraham came into the world, unworthy (descendants) issued from him, Ishmael and all of Keturah's children. When Isaac came into the world, unworthy (descendants) issued from him, Esau and all the princes of Edom, and they became worse than their predecessors. When Jacob came into the world, he did not produce unworthy (descendants), rather all his children were worthy,[1] as it is said, *And Jacob was a perfect man, dwelling in tents* (Gen. 25:27). When did God repossess His portion? Beginning with Jacob,[2] as it is said, *For the portion of the Lord is His people, Jacob the lot of His inheritance* (32:9), and, *For the Lord hath chosen Jacob unto Himself* (Ps. 135:4). Yet the matter remains unclear,[3] since we do not know whether the Holy One, blessed be He, chose Jacob or whether Jacob chose the Holy One, blessed be He; therefore Scripture states, *And Israel for his own treasure* (Ps. 135:4). Yet the matter still remains unclear, since we do not know whether the Holy One, blessed be He, chose Israel to be His own treasure, or whether Israel chose the Holy One, blessed be He, (to be their own treasure); therefore Scripture states, *And the Lord hath chosen thee to be His own treasure* (14:2). And whence do we learn that Jacob also chose God? From the verse, *Not like these is the portion of Jacob* (Jer. 10:16).[4]

Jacob the lot of His inheritance: *Ḥebel* ("lot") always involves the casting of lots (*goral*), as it is said, *The lines* (*ḥăbalim*) *are fallen unto me in pleasant places* (Ps. 16:6), *And there fell ten parts* (*ḥable*) *to Manasseh* (Josh. 17:5), and, *Out of the allotment* (*me-ḥebel*) *of the children of Judah was the inheritance of the children of Simeon* (Josh. 19:9).

Another interpretation: Just as this portion is triple,[5] so also was Jacob the third of the fathers and received the reward of all (three) of them. When Abraham was born, what does Scripture say? *And a brother is born for adversity* (Prov. 17:17). When Isaac was born, what does Scripture say? *Two are better than one* (Eccl. 4:9). When Jacob was born, what does Scripture say? *And a threefold cord is not quickly broken* (Eccl. 4:12).

Pisḳa 313

He found him in a desert land (32:10): This refers to Abraham. A parable: A king[1] went out to the wilderness together with his army. His troops deserted him in a place where there were marauders, wandering soldiers, and robbers, and went their own way. One valiant man remained loyal to him and said to him, "My lord the king, be not despondent, nor fearful of anything. By your life, I will not leave you until you enter your own palace and sleep in your own bed." Just so it is said, *And He said unto him, "I am the Lord that brought thee out of Ur of the Chaldees* (Gen. 15:7).

He compassed him about—this refers back to *Now the Lord said unto Abram, "Get thee out of thy country"* (Gen. 12:1)—*He cared for him* (32:10): Until Abraham came into this world, the Holy One, blessed be He, reigned, if one dare say such a thing, only over the heavens, as it is said, *The Lord, the God of heaven, who took me* (Gen. 24:7); but when Abraham came into the world, he made Him king over both the heaven and the earth, as it is said, *And I will make thee swear by the Lord, the God of heaven and the God of the earth* (Gen. 24:3).

He kept him as the apple of His eye (32:10): Had the Holy One, blessed be He, asked Abraham for his eyeball, he would have given it to Him; and not only his eyeball but his very soul, the thing most precious to him of all, as it is said, *Take now thy son, thine only one . . . even Isaac* (Gen. 22:2). But is it not well known that Isaac was his only son? Rather, this refers to Abraham's soul, which is called "only one," as it is said, *Deliver my soul from the sword; mine only one from the power of the dog* (Ps. 22:21).

Another interpretation: *He found him in a desert land*—this refers to Israel, as it is said, *I found Israel like grapes in a desert land* (Hos. 9:10)—*and in the waste, a howling wilderness* (32:10)—in a place of marauders, a place of wandering soldiers, a place of robbers—*He compassed him about*—before Mount Sinai, as it is said, *And thou shalt set bounds unto the people round about* (Exod. 19:12)—*He cared for him*—through the Ten Commandments. This shows that when the pronouncement came forth from the mouth of the Holy One, blessed be He, Israel perceived it, acquired wisdom[2] through it, and knew what interpretations were contained in it, what rules were contained in it, what inferences from the minor to the major were contained in it, what analogies were in it.

He kept him as the apple of His eye: They went backwards twelve miles and forward again twelve miles at each of the pronouncements, yet they were afraid neither of the thunders nor of the lightnings.[3]

Another interpretation: *He found him in a desert land*—everything was prepared[4] and supplied to them in the wilderness: a well arose for them, manna descended for them, quails were made available to them, the cloud of glory encompassed them—*and in the waste, a howling wilderness*—in a place of marauders, a place of wandering soldiers, a place of robbers—*He compassed him about*—with banners, three from the north, three from the south, three from the east, three from the west.[5]

He cared for him—in regard to two gifts: when anyone from among the nations stretched out his hand to take a handful of manna, he came away with nothing, and when he tried to take water from the well, he again came away with nothing—*He kept him as the apple of His eye*—as it is said, *Rise up, O Lord, and let thine enemies be scattered, and let them that hate Thee flee (before Thee)* (Num. 10:35).

Another interpretation: *He found him in a desert land*—this is a reference to the future, as it is said, *Therefore, behold, I will allure her, and bring her into the wilderness, and speak tenderly unto her* (Hos. 2:16)—*and in the waste, a howling wilderness*—this refers to the four kingdoms,[6] of which it is said, *Who led thee*[7] *through the great and dreadful wilderness* (8:15)—*He compassed him about*—with elders—*He cared for him*—with prophets—*He kept him as the apple of His eye*—

He protected them, so that evil spirits should not injure them, as it is said, *Surely he that toucheth you toucheth the apple of his eye* (Zech. 2:12).

Pisḳa 314

As an eagle that stirreth up her nest (32:11): Just as the mother-eagle does not enter her nest without first shaking her chicks with her wings, as she flies between one tree and another, between one bush and another, in order to rouse them, so that they would be strong enough to receive her, so also when the Holy One, blessed be He, revealed Himself in order to give the Torah to Israel, He revealed Himself to them not from only one direction but from all four directions, as it is said, *And he said: The Lord came from Sinai, and rose from Seir unto them, (He shined forth from Mount Paran)* (33:2). What about the fourth direction? *God cometh from Teman* (Hab. 3:3).

Spreadeth abroad her wings, taketh them—as it is said, *And in the wilderness, where thou hast seen how that the Lord thy God bore thee* (1:31)—*beareth them on her pinions* (32:11)—as it is said, *How I bore you on eagles' wings* (Exod. 19:4).

Another interpretation: *As an eagle that stirreth up her nest*—this refers to the future, as it is said, *Hark, my beloved! Behold, he cometh* (Song 2:8)—*spreadeth abroad her wings*—as it is said, *I will say to the north: "Give up," and to the south: "Keep not back"* (Isa. 43:6)—*beareth them on her pinions*—as it is said, *And they shall bring thy sons in their bosom* (Isa. 49:22).

Pisḳa 315

The Lord alone shall lead him[1] (32:12): Said the Holy One, blessed be He, to them: "Just as you dwelt alone in this world, receiving no benefit from the nations, so will I set you apart in the future, and the nations will not benefit from you in the least."

And there was no strange god with Him (32:12): None of the princes[2] that rule the nations will have the right to rule over you, as it is said, *And when I go forth, lo, the prince of Greece shall come* (Dan. 10:20), *But the prince of the kingdom of Persia withstood me*

(Dan. 10:13), *Howbeit I will declare unto thee that which is inscribed in the writing of truth; (and there is none that holdeth with me against these, except Michael your prince)* (Dan. 10:21).[3]

Another interpretation: *The Lord alone shall lead him*: In the future[4] I will give you portions of inheritance from one end of the world to another, as it is said, *From the east side unto the west side: Asher, one portion . . . from the east side even unto the west side; Reuben, one portion, from the east side unto the west side: Judah, one portion* (Ezek. 48:2,6,7). What does Scripture mean by saying, *Asher, one portion . . . Reuben, one portion . . . Judah, one portion?* That in the future Israel will encompass an area stretching (all the way) from east to west in length, and twenty-five thousand rods, or seventy-five miles, in width.

And there shall be[5] *no strange god with Him* (32:12): There will be no idolators among you, as it is said, *Therefore by this shall the iniquity of Jacob be expiated . . . (so that the Asherim and the sun images shall rise no more)* (Isa. 27:9).

Another interpretation: *The Lord alone shall lead him*—in the future I will set you amidst pleasure[6] in the world—*and there shall be no strange god with Him*—there will be none among you engaged in fruitless endeavors, as it is said, *May he be as a rich cornfield (pissaṯ bar) in the land* (Ps. 72:16), meaning that the wheat will yield handfulls (*pissah*) of cakes, *May his fruit rustle like Lebanon* (Ps. 72:16), (meaning) that the stalks of wheat will rustle one against another, so that fine flour will be sifted down upon the ground, and you will come and take handfulls of it, sufficient to sustain yourself.[7]

Pisḳa 316

He made him ride on the high places of the earth (32:13): This refers to the Land of Israel, which is higher than all the other lands, as it is said, *We should go up at once and possess it* (Num. 13:30), *So they went up, and spied out the land* (Num. 13:21), *And they went up into the South, and came unto Hebron* (Num. 13:22), and, *And they went up out of Egypt* (Gen. 45:25).[1]

And he did eat the fruitage of the field—this refers to the fruits of the Land of Israel, which are more digestible than the fruits of all the other lands—*and He made him to suck honey out of the crag* (32:13)—as in Siknin and its environs. It happened once that

R. Judah said to his son, "Go out and bring me figs from the jar." The son said to him, "Father, the jar is filled with honey." Replied R. Judah, "Dip your hand in the jar, and you will pull out figs from deep down in it."[2]

And oil out of the flinty rock (32:13): This refers to the olives of Gush Halab. It happened once that R. Jose said to his son in Sepphoris, "Go and bring us olives from the upper room." The son went up and found the upper room awash with oil.[3]

Pisḳa 317

Curd of kine, and milk of sheep—this was the situation at the time of Solomon, as it is said, *Ten fat oxen, and twenty oxen out of the pastures, and a hundred sheep* (1 Kings 5:3)—*with fat of lambs and rams*—this was the situation at the time of the Ten Tribes, as it is said, *And eat the lambs out of the flock, and the calves out of the midst of the stall* (Amos 6:4)—*with the kidney-fat of wheat*—this was the situation at the time of Solomon, as it is said, *And Solomon's provision for one day was thirty measures of fine flour* (1 Kings 5:2)—*and of the blood of the grape thou drankest foaming wine* (32:14)—this was the situation at the time of the Ten Tribes, as it is said, *That drink wine in bowls* (Amos 6:6).

Another interpretation: *He made him ride on the high places of the earth*: This refers to the Temple, which was situated higher than the entire world, as it is said, *Then shalt thou arise, and get thee up unto the place (which the Lord thy God shall choose)* (17:8), and, *And many peoples shall go and say: Come ye, and let us go up to the mountain of the Lord* (Isa. 2:3).

And he did eat the fruitage of the field—this refers to the baskets of first fruits[1]—*and He made him to suck honey out of the crag and oil out of the flinty rock*—this refers to the libations of oil—*curd of kine, and milk of sheep*—this refers to sin offering, burnt offerring, peace offerings, thank offering, guilt offering, and offerings of lesser sanctity—*with the kidney-fat of wheat*—this refers to the offerings of fine flour—*and of the blood of the grape thou drankest foaming wine*—this refers to the libations of wine.

Another interpretation: *He made him ride on the high places of the earth*—this refers to the Torah, as it is said, *The Lord made me*[2] *as the beginning of His way . . . (I was set up from everlasting . . . or ever the earth was*) (Prov. 8:22–23)—*and he did eat the fruitage of the field*—this refers to Scripture—*and He made him to suck honey out of the crag*—this refers to Mishnah—*and oil out of the flinty rock*—this refers to Talmud—*curd of kine and milk of sheep with fat of lambs*—this refers to the inferences from the minor to the major, analogies, rules, and answers (to arguments)—*with the kidney-fat of wheat*—this refers to laws that are the essence of Torah—*and of the blood of the grape thou drankest foaming wine*—this refers to homiletic lessons that attract man's heart like wine.

Another interpretation: *He made him ride on the high places of the earth*—this refers to the world, as it is said, *The boar out of the wood doth ravage it, (that which moveth in the field feedeth on it)* (Ps. 80:14)[3]—*and he did eat the fruitage of the field*—this refers to the four kingdoms—*and He made him*[4] *to suck honey out of the crag, and oil out of the flinty rock*—this refers to the oppressors who have taken possession of the Land of Israel, and from which it is as difficult to extract a *pĕruṭah*[5] as from rock; but in the near future Israel will inherit all of their possessions and will derive pleasure from them as from oil and honey.

Curd of kine—this refers to their consuls[6] and their generals[7]—*and milk of sheep*—this refers to their colonels[8]—*and rams*—this refers to their centurions—*of the breed of Bashan*—this refers to the privileged soldiers,[9] who extract (food) from between the teeth[10]—*and he-goats*—this refers to their senators[11]—*with the kidney-fat of wheat*—this refers to their noble ladies—*and of the blood of the grape thou drankest*[12] *foaming wine*—in the near future Israel will inherit their possessions and will derive pleasure from them as from oil and honey.

Another interpretation: *With the kidney-fat of wheat*: In the future each grain of wheat will be as large as the two kidneys of a large bull and will weigh four *liṭra* of Sepphoris. And if this surprises you, look at turnip heads. It once happened that they weighed a turnip head (and found it) to weigh thirty *liṭra* of Sepphoris. On another occasion a fox (was found to have) made his nest in a turnip head. It once happened in Shiḥin that a mustard stalk had three twigs. They split off one of them and used it to cover a potter's hut. When they knocked it open, they found that it contained nine *ḳab̲* of mustard seed. R. Simeon ben Ḥalafta said: There was a stalk of cabbage in my house, and I used to climb up and down it as one climbs up and down a ladder.[13]

Another interpretation: *And of the blood of the grape thou drankest foaming wine*: You will not have to weary yourselves with treading and cutting grapes. Rather, you will bring in (the vine) in a wagon, set it up in a corner, and then repeatedly drink (wine) from it as one drinks it out of a large jar.[14]

Pisḳa 318

But Jeshurun waxed fat, and kicked (32:15)[1]: Satiety leads to rebellion. Thus you find that the people of the generation of the flood rebelled against the Holy One, blessed be He, only out of (abundance of) food and drink and out of ease of life. For what is said of them? *Their houses are safe, without fear,* etc. (Job 21:9) (this comment is found earlier in this commentary on Deuteronomy).[2] Similarly we find that the people of the tower (of Babel) rebelled against the Holy One, blessed be He, only out of ease of life, as it is said, *And the whole earth was of one language* (Gen. 11:1). Again we find that the people of Sodom rebelled only out of (abundance of) food, as it is said, *As for the earth, out of it cometh bread* (Job 28:5) (and so forth, as in the earlier comment),[3] and, *As I live, saith the Lord God, Sodom thy sister hath not done (as thou hast done. . . . This was the iniquity of thy sister Sodom: pride, fulness of bread, and careless ease)* (Ezek. 16:48–49). Once R. Gamaliel, R. Joshua, R. Eleazar ben Azariah, and R. ʿAḳiba were approaching Rome, etc. (this comment is found earlier in this commentary on Deuteronomy).[4] Similarly you find that the people of the wilderness rebelled only out of (abundance of) food and drink, as it is said, *And the people sat down to eat and to drink, and rose up to make merry* (Exod. 32:6). What is said concerning them? *They have turned aside quickly out of the way (which I commanded them)* (Exod. 32:8). Said the Holy One, blessed be He, to Moses, "Say to the Israelites, when you enter the (Holy) Land only (abundance of) food and drink and ease of life will lead you to rebel," as it is said, *For when I shall have brought them into the land which I swore unto their fathers, flowing with milk and honey, and they shall have eaten their fill, and waxen fat; and turned unto other gods (and served them, and despised Me, and broken My covenant)* (31:20). Therefore Moses said to Israel, "When you enter the (Holy) Land only (abundance of) food and drink and ease of life will lead you to rebel, as it is said, *Lest when thou hast eaten and art satisfied . . . and when thy herds and thy flocks multiply . . . then thy heart be lifted up, and thou forget the*

Lord thy God (8:12–14)." So also you find that suffering came upon the sons and daughters of Job only because of (abundance of) food and drink, as it is said, *While he was yet speaking, there came also another, and said: "Thy sons and thy daughters were eating and drinking wine in their eldest brother's house, and behold, there came a great wind"* (Job 1:18–19). Again you find that the Ten Tribes were exiled only because of (abundance of) food, drink, and ease, as it is said, *That lie upon beds of ivory . . . that drink wine in bowls. . . . Therefore now shall they go captive at the head of them that go captive* (Amos 6:4,6,7). Similarly you find that in the days of the Messiah Israel will rebel only because of (abundance of) food and drink, as it is said, *But Jeshurun waxed fat, and kicked . . . and he forsook God who made him* (32:15). A parable: Once a man who had a calf groomed and curried it, and fed it bitter vetch,[5] so that he might use it for plowing. When the calf matured, the man placed a yoke upon it, but it bucked, breaking the yoke and snapping off the carved tips of the yoke. Hence Scripture says, *Thou hast broken the bars of wood; but thou shalt make in their stead bars of iron* (Jer. 28:13).

Thou didst wax fat—in the days of Jeroboam—*thou didst grow thick*—in the days of Ahab—*thou didst become gross* (32:15)—all in the days of Jehu. Another interpretation: *Thou didst wax fat*—in the days of Ahaz—*thou didst grow thick*—in the days of Manasseh—*thou didst become gross*—all in the days of Zedekiah. Another interpretation: *Thou didst wax fat, thou didst grow thick, thou didst become gross*: When a person is fat inside, it makes his loins protrude, as it is said, *Because he hath covered his face with his fatness, and made collops of fat on his loins* (Job 15:27).

Another interpretation: *Thou didst wax fat, thou didst grow thick, thou didst become gross*: This refers to the three generations preceding the days of the Messiah, as it is said, *Their land also is full of silver and gold, neither is there any end of their treasures. . . . Their land also is full of idols; every one worshipeth the work of his own hands, that which his own fingers have made* (Isa. 2:7–8).

And he forsook God who made him: As it is said, *For My people have committed two evils: (they have forsaken Me)* (Jer. 2:13). The Holy One, blessed be He, said to them, "By the measure with which you have measured to Me, I have measured to you"—*I have forsaken My house, I have cast off My heritage* (Jer. 12:7), *And He forsook the Tabernacle of Shiloh* (Ps. 78:60), and, *For Thou hast forsaken Thy people, the house of Jacob* (Isa. 2:6).[6]

Another interpretation: *And he forsook God who made him:* As it is said, *And He brought me into the inner court of the Lord's House, and behold, at the door of the Temple of the Lord, between the porch and the altar, were about five and twenty men, with their backs toward the Temple of the Lord* (Ezek. 8:16). R. Dostai ben Judah says: Read not *And he forsook God who made him, and was contemned (by the Rock of his salvation),* but "and contemned the Rock of his salvation,"[7] as it is said, *Do not contemn us, for Thy name's sake, do not dishonor the throne of Thy glory* (Jer. 14:21).

They roused Him to jealousy with strange gods (32:16): Meaning that they went and made strange things, as it is said, *And also Maacah his mother he removed from being queen, because she had made an abominable image for an Asherah* (1 Kings 15:13).

With abominations did they provoke Him (32:16): This refers to sodomy, as it is said, *Thou shalt not lie with mankind, as with womankind; it is an abomination* (Lev. 18:22), and, *And there were also sodomites in the land; (they did according to all the abominations of the nations)* (1 Kings 14:24).

They sacrificed unto demons, no-gods, (gods that they knew not) (32:17): Had they worshiped the sun, the moon, the stars, the planets, or other things that are necessary for the world and are beneficial to it, His jealousy would not have been redoubled; but they worshiped things that could neither benefit them nor harm them. *Unto demons*: What does a demon do? He enters into a person and compels him (to sin). *Gods that they knew not*: That (even) the nations of the world would not recognize.

New gods that came up of late (32:17): So that whenever someone from another nation saw it, he would say, "This is an idol of the Jews," as it is said, *As my hand hath reached the kingdoms of the idols, whose graven images did exceed them of Jerusalem and of Samaria* (Isa. 10:10)—this shows that Jerusalem and Samaria supplied molds (for idols) to all mankind.

Which your fathers dreaded not (32:17): Your ancestors' hair did not stand on end (in fear of) them.[8] Another interpretation: *Which your fathers dreaded not*: Your ancestors did not evaluate[9] them to see if they were of any use or not. Another interpretation: *Which your fathers dreaded not*: Read not *which your fathers dreaded (śĕᶜarum) not* but "which your fathers respected (*šaᶜum*) not," for even though they offered sacrifices and incense to them, they feared them not, as it is said, *But unto Cain and his offering He had not respect (šaᶜah)* (Gen. 4:5).

Piska 319

Of the Rock that begot thee thou wast unmindful (32:18): The Holy One, blessed be He, said to them, "You caused Me to feel like a male trying to give birth." If a woman about to give birth is sitting on the birth-stool, is she not anxious, as it is said, *For the children are come to the birth, and there is not strength to bring forth* (2 Kings 19:3)?[1] If she is in travail and giving birth for the first time, would she not be anxious, as it is said, *For I have heard a voice as of a woman in travail, the anguish as of her that bringeth forth her first child* (Jer. 4:31)? If there are twins in her womb, would she not be anxious, as it is said, *And the children struggled together within her; (and she said: "If it be so, wherefore do I live?")* (Gen. 25:22)? If it is a male, who does not ordinarily give birth but is trying to give birth, would not the pain be doubled and redoubled, as it is said, *Ask ye now, and see whether a man doth travail with child* (Jer. 30:6).

Of the Rock that begot thee thou wast unmindful: You forgot Me through the merit of the fathers,[2] as it is said, *Look unto the rock whence ye were hewn, and to the hole of the pit whence ye were digged, (look unto Abraham your father, and unto Sarah that bore you)* (Isa. 51:1–2).

Another interpretation: *Of the Rock that begot thee thou wast unmindful*: Whenever I want to do good things for you, you weaken[3] the power of heaven. When you stood at the (Red) Sea and said, *This is my God, and I will glorify Him* (Exod. 15:2), I wanted to do good things for you, but you relapsed and said, *Let us make a captain, and let us return into Egypt* (Num. 14:4). When you stood before Mount Sinai and said, *All that the Lord hath spoken will we do, and obey* (Exod. 24:7), I wanted to do good things for you, but you relapsed and said to the (golden) calf, *This is thy god, O Israel* (Exod. 32:4). Thus whenever I want to do good things for you, you weaken the power of heaven.

And didst forget God that bore thee (mĕḥolĕleḵa) 32:18): R. Meir interpreted this as "God that travailed (*ḥeḥil*) and suffered for you," as it is said, *Pangs,*[4] *as of a woman in travail* (Ps. 48:7). R. Judah interprets it as: "God that made you full of cavities (*mĕḥillim*)."[5] Another interpretation: *And didst forget God that bore thee*: The God who made His name rest (*ḥeḥil*) upon you,[6] and not upon any other nation or kingdom, as it is said, *I am the Lord your God, who brought you out of the land of Egypt, to be your God* (Num. 15:41).[7] R. Nehemiah interprets it as "God that made you vulnerable[8] to any (nation) in the world when you do not fulfill the Torah," as it is said, *The voice of the Lord is upon the waters,* and so forth, to *the voice of the Lord maketh the hinds to calve (yĕḥolel)*[9] (Ps. 29:3–9). Another interpretation: *And didst forget God that bore thee*: God that pardons (*moḥel*) you for all your sins.

Piska 320

And the Lord saw, and spurned (32:19): R. Judah says: They spurned Him with the very things that He gave them for their own benefit.[1] R. Meir says: *Because of the provoking of His sons and His daughters* (32:19)—is this not a matter of inference from the minor to the major: if they are called "children" when they provoke Him, how much more would this be so when they do not provoke Him?[2]

And He said: "I will hide My face from them"—said the Holy One, blessed be He: I shall now remove My presence from among them—*"I will see what their end shall be"* (32:20)—and I will know what will become of them. Another interpretation: I shall now deliver them into the hands of the four kingdoms,[3] which will enslave them.

I will see what their end shall be—I will inform them of their fate[4]—*for they are a very forward generation*—neither "a generation which is inverted" nor "a generation which shall be overturned" is written here, but *a very forward generation,*[5] (meaning that) they are fickle, they are perfidious—*children in whom is no faithfulness* (32:20): You are children who are not trustworthy. You stood at Mount Sinai and said, *All that the Lord hath spoken will we do, and obey* (Exod. 24:7), (whereupon) *I said: Ye are godlike beings* (Ps. 82:6); but when you said to the (golden) calf, *This is thy god, O Israel* (Exod. 32:4), I said to you, *Nevertheless, ye shall die like men* (Ps. 82:7).[6] When I brought you into the land of your fathers, and you built for yourselves the Chosen House, I said that you will never be exiled from it; but when you said, *We have no portion in David* (2 Sam. 20:1), I said, *And Israel shall surely be led away captive out of his land* (Amos 7:17).

R. Dostai ben Judah says: Read not *in whom is no faithfulness* (*ʾemun*) but "who say not Amen,"[7] for they did not want to respond with Amen to the prophets when they blessed them, as (it happened when Jeremiah prophesied) *That I may establish the oath which I swore unto your fathers, to give them a land flowing with milk and honey, as at this day* (Jer. 11:5), to which not one of them opened his mouth to respond with Amen, until Jeremiah himself responded with Amen, as it is said, *Then answered I, and said: Amen, O Lord* (Jer. 11:5).

They have roused Me to jealousy with a no-god; they have provoked Me with their vapors[8] (32:21): There are those who worship an idol, something which can be seen, but they worship a mere shadow,[9] and not even a shadow but the vapor that rises from a (boiling) kettle, as it is said, *They have provoked Me with their vapors.*

And I will rouse them to jealousy with a no-people (bĕ-loʾ ʿam) (32:21): Read not *bĕ-loʾ ʿam (a no-people)* but *bi-lĕway ʿam,* "with associates of a people,"[10] those who come from among the nations and kingdoms and expel them from their homes. Another interpretation: This refers to those who come from Barbaria[11] and Martania,[12] who go about naked in the market place, for there is none more despised and contemptible than one who goes about naked in the market place.[13]

I will provoke them with a vile nation (32:21): This refers to the heretics, as it is said, *The fool*[14] *hath said in his heart: "There is no God"* (Ps. 14:1).

For a fire is kindled in My nostril (32:22): When punishment issues forth from before Me, it always issues from the nostril;[15] and whence do we learn that this is so even in Gehenna? From the following words, *and burneth upon the depths of the netherworld, and devoureth the land with her produce*—this refers to the Land of Israel—*and setteth ablaze the foundations of the mountains* (32:22)—this refers to Jerusalem, as it is said, *As the mountains are round about Jerusalem* (Ps. 125:2). Another interpretation: *And devoureth the land with her produce*—this refers to the world and all its fullness—*and setteth ablaze the foundations of the mountains*—this refers to the four kingdoms, as it is said, *And behold there came four chariots (out from between the two mountains; and the mountains were mountains of brass)* (Zech. 6:1).

Pisḳa 321

I will heap evils upon them (32:23): I will now gather and bring upon them all the punishments, all of them at once. Another interpretation: I will now gather together in a trap and bring upon them all the punishments, all of them at once. Another interpretation: Scripture says here not "I will gather[1] evils upon them" but rather "I will stop,"[2] meaning that all sufferings will cease but they (Israel) will not cease. The same applies to what follows, *I will spend Mine arrows upon them* (32:23)—Scripture says not "Mine arrows will destroy[3] them" but rather *I will spend[4] Mine arrows upon them,* (meaning) Mine arrows will be spent, but they will not be spent. Another interpretation, *I will spend Mine arrows upon them*—this refers to the arrows of famine, as it is said, *When I shall send upon them the evil arrows of famine, that are for destruction* (Ezek. 5:16).

The wasting of hunger, and the devouring of the fiery bolt (32:24): Indicating that they will be staggering[5] with hunger and be cast out into the streets, as it is said, *And the people to whom they prophesy shall be cast out in the streets of Jerusalem* (Jer. 14:16).

And bitter destruction (ḳeṭeḇ) (32:24): From this you can learn that whosoever is possessed by a demon[6] salivates.[7]

And the teeth of beasts will I send upon them (32:24): Read not *of beasts (bĕhemoṯ)* but rather "of beastliness" (*bahamuṯ*)," meaning that they will be lustful and will seek out all sins.[8] Another interpretation: (Each) one of them will be lustful and will extend (his foreskin),[9] causing an ulcerous growth that will kill him. Another interpretation: *And the teeth of beasts will I send upon them,* meaning that his animal will bite him, causing an ulcerous growth that will kill him. The Sages have said that it happened once that ewes bit people, killing them.[10]

With the venom of crawling things of the dust (32:24): They will be made to crawl in the dust. Rabbi (Judah the Prince), however, says that this refers to snakes, who rule only over dust.

Without shall the sword bereave (32:25): Hence the Sages have said: When there is warfare, retreat indoors; when there is famine, go elsewhere,[11] as it is said, *If I go forth into the field, then behold the slain with the sword; and if I enter into the city, then behold them that are sick with famine* (Jer. 14:18), and, *The sword is without, and the pestilence and the famine within* (Ezek. 7:15).

And in the chambers terror (32:25): Even if one saw the sword coming into the street and managed to flee and escape from it, the chambers of his heart would be beating so hard that he would be overcome and die.

Another interpretation: *Without (mi-ḥuṣ) shall the sword bereave:* Because of what they had done in the streets (*ḥuṣoṯ*) of Jerusalem, as it is said, *For according to the number of thy cities are thy gods, O Judah; and according to the number of the streets (ḥuṣoṯ) of Jerusalem have ye set up altars to the shameful thing (Baal)* (Jer. 11:13).

And in the chambers terror: Because of what they had done in inner chambers, as it is said, *Son of man, hast thou seen what the elders of the house of Israel do in the dark, every man in his chambers of imagery? For they say: The Lord seeth us not, the Lord hath forsaken the land* (Ezek. 8:12).

(Slaying) both young man and virgin—these I might have been able to overlook,[12] but not—*the suckling with the man of gray hairs* (32:25): As it is said, *(Pour it out upon the babes in the street, and upon the assembly of young men together); for even the husband with the wife shall be taken, the aged with him that is full of days* (Jer. 6:11).

Another interpretation: *Both young man (baḥur)*—you caused Me to lay a hand upon My chosen ones (*bĕḥiray),* as it is said, *And Joshua the son of Nun, the minister of Moses, one of his chosen (mib-bĕḥuraw)*[13] *answered* (Num. 11:28)—*and virgin*—showing that they were as free from sin as is a virgin who has never tasted sin—*the suckling*—showing that they sucked words of Torah just as a suckling sucks milk from its mother's breast—*with the man of gray hairs*: Read not[14] "man of *śeḇah* ("gray hairs") but rather "man of *yĕšiḇah* ("sitting"), showing that all of them were worthy of sitting in the house of study, as it is said, *(And all the men of might) . . . all of them strong and apt for war* (2 Kings 24:16). What might can be demonstrated by men going into exile, and what war can be waged by men bound with fetters and chains?[15]—rather, these mighty men were mighty in Torah, as it is said, *Bless the Lord, ye angels of His, ye mighty in strength, that fulfill His word* (Ps. 103:20). *Apt for war,* meaning that they engaged in the warfare of Torah,[16] as it is said, *Wherefore it is said in the book of the Wars of the Lord* (Num. 21:14), and, *And the craftsmen and the smiths a thousand* (2 Kings 24:16)—*craftsmen,*[17] (meaning) one who speaks while all others keep still; *smiths (misger)*: everyone sits before him and learns from him, and he opens and closes (*soḡer*) (the discussion), to fulfill that which is written, *And he shall open, and none shall shut; and he shall shut, and none shall open* (Isa. 22:22).[18]

Pisḳa 322

I thought I would make an end of them—I thought in My anger, "Where are they?"[1]—*I would make their memory cease from among men* (32:26): I thought they should not be in the world, but what shall I do to them? *If it had not been (lule) the Lord who was for us, when men rose up against us* (Ps. 124:2).[2]

Another interpretation: I thought in My anger, "Where are they?", *I would make their memory cease from among men,* so that they will not be in the world, but what shall I do? *Except*[3] *the Lord of hosts had left unto us a very small remnant* (Isa. 1:9). Another interpretation: *I thought I would make an end of them*: Were it not that it is said, *Therefore He said that He would destroy them, had not (lule) Moses His chosen stood before Him in the breach* (Ps. 106:23).

Were it not that I dreaded (ʾagur) the enemy's provocation (32:27): What caused them to be punished?[4] The anger of the nations which was heaped up within their innards. *ʾAgur* means here "heaped up,"[5] as it is said, *The words of the Gatherer (ʾAgur) the son of Jakeh* (Prov. 30:1), and it is said, *May He incite death against them, let them go down alive into the netherworld; for evil is in their gathering,*[6] *and within them* (Ps. 55:16).

Lest their adversaries should misdeem (yĕnakru) (32:27): When Israel is in trouble,[7] the nations of the world estrange (*mĕnakkĕrim*) themselves from them and pretend that they never knew them. Thus we find that when Israel sought to flee to the north, the nations would not take them in, but delivered them up, as it is said, *Thus saith the Lord: For three transgressions of Tyre, yea, for four, I will not reverse it: because they delivered up a whole captivity to Edom* (Amos 1:9). When Israel sought to flee to the south, the nations again delivered them up, as it is said, *Thus saith the Lord: For three transgressions of Gaza, (yea, for four, I will not reverse it;) because they carried away captive a whole captivity to deliver them up to Edom* (Amos 1:6). When they sought to flee to the east, the nations once more delivered them up, as it is said, *Thus saith the Lord: For three transgressions of Damascus . . . (because they have threshed Gilead with sledges of iron)* (Amos 1:3). When Israel sought to flee to the west, the nations again delivered them up, as it is said, *The burden upon the west.*[8] *In the thickets in the west shall ye lodge, O ye caravans of Dedanites* (Isa. 21:13). When Israel prospers, the nations of the world flatter them and act as if they were brothers. Thus Esau said to Jacob, *I have enough; my brother, let that which thou hast be thine* (Gen. 33:9), and Hiram said to Solomon, *What cities are these which thou hast given me, my brother?* (1 Kings 9:13).

Lest they should say: Our hand is exalted, and not the Lord hath wrought all this (32:27): Such as what those fools[9] had said, *Have we not taken to us horns by our own strength?* (Amos 6:13).

For they are a nation void of counsel (32:28): R. Judah applied this to Israel, while R. Nehemiah applied it to the nations of the world.

R. Judah applied it to Israel thus: Israel voided the good counsel given to them, and "counsel" always means Torah, as it is said, *Counsel is mine and sound wisdom* (Prov. 8:14). *And there is no understanding in them* (32:28): There is not one among them who would upon reflection say, "Just the other day one of us could pursue a thousand men of the nations, and two could make ten thousand of them flee, but now one man of the nations pursues a thousand of us, and two of them make ten thousand of us flee.[10] (This could not happen,) *Except their Rock had given them over* (32:30)."

R. Nehemiah applied it to the nations thus: The nations voided the seven (Noachian) commandments[11] that I had given them. *And there is no understanding in them*: There is not one among them who would upon reflection say, "Now one of us pursues a thousand Israelites, and two of us make ten thousand flee. In the days of the Messiah one Israelite will pursue a thousand of us, and two will make ten thousand flee. (This could not have happened), *Except their Rock had given them over.*" It once happened during the revolt[12] in Judea that a mounted decurion[13] pursued an Israelite in order to kill him. For a while he could not overtake him, but just as he was about to reach him, a serpent emerged and stung the Israelite on his heel. Said the Israelite to the decurion, "Do not think that because you are mighty[14] we have been delivered into your hands, *Except their Rock had given them over.*"

Pisḳa 323

If they were wise, they would understand this, (they would discern their latter end) (32:29): If Israel would but look[1] closely at the words of Torah which I have given them, no nation or kingdom could dominate them. (The word) *this* always means Torah, as it is said, *And this is the Torah which Moses set (before the children of Israel)* (4:44). Another interpretation: *If they were wise, they would understand this*: If Israel would but look closely at what their father Jacob[2] had said to them, no nation or kingdom could dominate them. What did he say to them? Accept upon yourselves the kingdom of heaven, vie with each other in fear of heaven, and act toward each other with loving-kindness.

How should one chase a thousand? (32:30): If you do not observe My Torah, how can I keep the promise which you requested (of Me) that one of you should pursue a thousand men of the nations, and two cause ten thousand to flee? Rather, now one man of the nations pursues a thousand of you, and two of them cause ten thousand to flee.

Except their Rock had given them over, and the Lord had delivered them up (32:30): I will deliver you up not by Myself but through others.[3] It once happened in Judea that flies delivered them up. R. Ḥanina of Ṭibᶜin says: A parable: A man may say to his fellow, "I will sell you a slave, to be delivered some time in the future."[4] But I, (the Lord,) do not act like that—I both sell (Israel) and deliver (them) immediately.[5] [Another interpretation: *And the Lord had delivered them up*: Do I deliver][6] you as the unclean ones into the hands of the clean ones, or as the clean ones into the hands of the unclean ones? We learn that only the unclean are delivered up, as it is said, *Then the priest shall deliver up him*[7] *that hath the plague (for) seven days* (Lev. 13:4).

For their rock is not as our Rock (32:31): The power[8] that You give them is not the same as that which You give us. When You give us power, we treat them according to the measure of mercy, but when You give them power, they treat us according to the measure of cruelty. They kill us, burn us, and crucify us.

Even our enemies themselves being judges (32:31): You wrote in the Torah that an enemy may not judge nor give testimony, (as it is said,) *And he was not his enemy*—only in such a case may he testify—*neither sought his harm* (Num. 35:23)—only then may he judge him.[9] And yet You have appointed enemies as witnesses and judges over us.

For their vine is of the vine of Sodom (32:32): R. Judah applied this to Israel, while R. Nehemiah applied it to the nations of the world.

R. Judah says: Are you of the vine of Sodom or of the planting of Gomorrah? Are you not rather of a holy planting, as it is said, *Yet I had planted thee a noble vine, wholly a right seed* (Jer. 2:21)?[10]

Their grapes are grapes of gall—you are the descendants of primeval[11] Adam, for whom I decreed death, both for him and for his descendants who follow him, until the end of all generations—*their clusters are bitter* (32:32); The gall of the great ones among you is spread out in them like a cluster. "Cluster" always means (a) large (bunch of grapes), as it is said, *There is no cluster to eat; nor first-ripe fig which my soul desireth* (Mic. 7:1).

Their wine is the venom of serpents—you envenomed[12] the pious ones and God-fearing ones amongst you like serpents—*and the cruel poison (roʾš) of asps* (32:33)—meaning that your leaders (*roʾšim*) will be like the asp that is cruel. Another interpretation: *Their wine is the venom of serpents*—you envenomed the patient and sin-fearing among you like serpents—*and the cruel poison of asps*—your leaders are like the asp that is cruel.

R. Nehemiah applied it to the nations of the world: you are certainly of the vine of Sodom and of the planting of Gomorrah. You are the disciples of the primeval serpent[13] that caused Adam and Eve to go astray. *Their clusters are bitter*—the gall of the great ones among them is spread out in them like a serpent. *Their clusters are bitter*—"cluster" always means (a) large (bunch of grapes), as it is said, *There is no cluster to eat* (Mic. 7:1).

Pisḳa 324

Is not this laid up in store with Me? (32:34): R. Eliezer the son of R. Jose the Galilean says: A cup which is filled up,[1] and yet empty? (No.) One might think that it is weak wine; therefore Scripture says *foaming wine* (Ps. 75:9).[2] One might think that it is only half-full; therefore Scripture goes on to say, *full of mixture* (Ps. 75:9). One might think that (it is so full that) it lacks not one drop;[3] therefore Scripture goes on to say, *and He poureth out of the same* (Ps. 75:9). From that one drop have drunk the generation of the flood, the generation of confusion of tongues, the people of Sodom, Pharaoh and all his host, Sisera and all his multitudes, Sennacherib and all his hosts, Nebuchadnezzar and all his army, and from that same one drop are destined to drink all the inhabitants of the world until the end of all generations. Similarly Scripture states, *And in this mountain will the Lord of hosts make unto all peoples a feast of fat things, a feast of wines on the lees* (Isa. 25:6). One might think that this means fat things which are nourishing and wines which are not nutritious; therefore Scripture goes on to say, *of fat things full of marrow, of wines on the lees well refined* (Isa. 25:6), fat things which contain nothing but foul matter. Similarly Scripture states, *Babylonia hath been a golden cup in the Lord's hand, that made all the earth drunken* (Jer. 51:7):

Just as broken (vessels of) gold can be restored, so after the punishment of the nations ceases, it will be brought upon them once more. But concerning Israel's punishment what does Scripture say? *Thou shalt even drink it and drain it, and thou shalt crunch the sherds thereof* (Ezek. 23:34): Just as broken vessels of clay cannot be restored, so after the punishment of Israel ceases, it will never be reimposed.

Sealed up in my treasuries (32:34): Just as this treasury is sealed up and brings forth no further crops, so the deeds of the wicked shall bring forth no gains, for should you say that they do, they would destroy the world. Hence Scripture says, *Woe unto the wicked! it shall be ill with him; for the work of his hands shall be done to him* (Isa. 3:11). But the deeds of the righteous shall bring forth gains and gains upon gains,[4] as it is said, *Say ye of the righteous, that it shall be well with him; for they shall eat the fruit of their doing* (Isa. 3:10). Another interpretation: Just as this treasury is sealed and therefore nothing is missing from it, so do the righteous take nothing (of the reward that) they deserve from this world. Whence do we learn that the righteous take nothing they deserve from this world? From the verse, *Oh how abundant is Thy goodness, which Thou hast laid up for them that fear Thee* (Ps. 31:20). And whence do we learn that the wicked take nothing (of the punishment that) they deserve from this world? From the verse, *Is not this laid up in store with Me?* (32:34). And when will all of these receive (their just due)? On the morrow, when redemption will come for Israel, as it is said, *Vengeance is Mine, and recompense* (32:35).

Piska 325

Vengeance is Mine, and recompense (32:35): I will requite it of them, I Myself, not through an angel nor through a messenger, as it is said,[1] *Come now, therefore, and I will send thee unto Pharaoh* (Exod. 3:10), and, *And it came to pass that night that the angel of the Lord went forth, and smote in the camp of the Assyrians* (2 Kings 19:35).

Another interpretation: "Vengeance is Mine, and I will recompense" is not written here, but rather *Vengeance is Mine, and recompense.* I recompense (Israel) for the deeds which their forefathers performed before Me in this world, as it is said, *I will not keep silence, except I have requited* (Isa. 65:6), and, *And first I will recompense their iniquity and their sin double* (Jer. 16:18).

Against the time when their foot shall slip (32:35): As it is said, *The foot shall tread it down, even the feet of the poor, and the steps of the needy* (Isa. 26:6).

For the day of their calamity is at hand (32:35): R. Jose said: If calamities are coming so slowly for those of whom it is said, *For the day of their*[2] *calamity is at hand,* how much more is this true of those of whom it is said, *And after many days shall they be punished* (Isa. 24:22).

And the things that are to come upon them shall make haste (32:35): When the Holy One, blessed be He, brings calamity upon the nations, He will shake the very earth, as it is said, *(And their horsemen spread themselves; yea, their horsemen come from far). They fly as a vulture that hasteth to devour* (Hab. 1:8), and, *That say: Let Him make speed, let Him hasten His work, that we may see it: and let the counsel of the Holy One of Israel draw nigh and come, that we may know it* (Isa. 5:19).[3] But when the Holy One, blessed be He, brings suffering upon Israel, He does not inflict it immediately, but waits. How so? He delivers them to the four kingdoms to be subjected to them, as it is said, *For I am with thee, saith the Lord, to save thee; (for I will make a full end of all the nations whither I have scattered thee, but I will not make a full end of thee; for I will correct thee in measure, and will not utterly destroy thee)* (Jer. 30:11).[4]

Pisḳa 326

For the Lord will judge His people—when the Holy One, blessed be He, judges the nations,[1] He rejoices in it, but when He judges Israel, He, as it were, regrets it, as it is said, *and repent Himself for His servants* (32:36)—"repent" always means regret, as it is said, *For it repenteth Me that I have made them* (Gen. 6:7), and, *It repenteth Me that I have set up Saul to be king* (1 Sam. 15:11).

When He seeth that their stay is gone (32:36): When He sees their destruction as they all go into captivity. Another interpretation: When He sees that they have despaired of redemption. Another interpretation: *That their stay is gone and there is none remaining, shut up or left at large* (32:36): When He sees that there is not one *peruṭah* in their pockets, as it is said, *And when they have made an end of breaking in pieces the power*[2] *of the holy people, all these things shall be finished* (Dan. 12:7). Another interpretation: *When He seeth that their stay is gone*: When He sees that there are no men among them who would plead for mercy for them, as did Moses, as it is said, *Therefore He said that He would destroy them, had not Moses His chosen (stood before Him in the breach, to turn back His wrath, lest He should destroy them)* (Ps. 106:23). Another interpretation: *When He seeth that their stay is gone*: When He sees that there are no men among them who would plead for mercy for them, as did Aaron, as it is said, *And he stood between the dead and the living; and the plague was stayed* (Num. 17:13). Another interpretation: *When He seeth*: When He sees that there are no men among them who would plead for mercy for them, as did Phinehas, as it is said, *Then stood up Phinehas, and wrought judgment, (and so the plague was stayed)* (Ps. 106:30). Another interpretation: *When he seeth that their stay is gone and there is none remaining, shut up or left at large*: None shut up, none at large, none to help Israel.

Pisḳa 327

And it is said: Where are their gods? (32:37): R. Judah applied this to Israel, while R. Nehemiah applied it to the nations of the world. R. Judah says: In the future, Israel will say to the nations of the world, "Where are your consuls and generals?"[1]

Pisḳa 328

Who did eat the fat of their sacrifices—to whom we used to give *opsonia, donativa,* and *salaria*[1]—*let them*[2] *rise up and help you* (32:38): It is written not "let them rise up and let them help you" but "let them rise up and let him help you."[3] R. Nehemiah says: This[4] refers to the wicked Titus, son of Vespasian's wife, who entered the Holy of Holies, cut down the two curtains with his sword, and said, "If He is God, let Him come and stop me!"[5] *Who did eat the fat of their sacrifices . . .*—Titus said, "Moses misled these people and told them, 'Build for yourselves an altar, and upon it offer up burnt offerings and pour out libations,'" as it is said, *The one lamb shalt thou offer in the morning, and the other lamb shalt thou offer at dusk* (Num. 28:4)[6]—*let Him rise up and help you, let Him be your protection* (32:38): The Holy One, blessed be He, will forgive anything, but desecration of His name He will requite immediately.[7]

Pisḳa 329

See now that I, even I, am He (32:39): This is an answer to those who say, "There is no authority in heaven." As for him who says, "There are two authorities in heaven,"[1] one should respond by saying, "Is it not also written, *And there is no god with Me?* (32:39)." Or if one contends that He has no power to kill or give life, to harm or to benefit, the verse states, *See now that I, even I, am He . . . I kill, and I make alive* (32:39), and it is also written, *Thus saith the Lord, the King of Israel and his Redeemer, the Lord of hosts: I am the first, and I am the last, and beside Me there is no God* (Isa. 44:6).

Another interpretation: *I kill, and I make alive*: This is one of the four assurances given to Israel which hint at the resurrection of the dead: *I kill and I make alive, Let me die the death of the righteous (and let mine end be like his)* (Num. 23:10), *Let Reuben live, and not die* (33:6), and, *After two days He will revive us* (Hos. 6:2). I might think that death here refers to one person, and life to another; therefore the verse goes on to say, *I have wounded, and I heal* (32:39)—just as wounding and healing there refer to the same person, so death and life here refer to the same person.[2]

And there is none that can deliver out of My hand (32:39): Fathers cannot save their children; Abraham cannot save Ishmael, nor can Isaac save Esau. This shows only that fathers cannot save sons; whence do we learn that brothers cannot save brothers? From the verse, *No man can by any means redeem his brother* (Ps. 49:8); Isaac cannot save Ishmael, nor can Jacob save Esau. Even if one were to offer all the money in the world, he cannot be granted atonement, as it is said, *No man can by any means redeem his brother, (nor give to God a ransom for him,) for too costly is the redemption of their soul* (Ps. 49:8–9)—the soul is precious, and when one sins against it, there is no payment (that would redeem it).[3]

Pisḳa 330

For I lift up My hand to heaven (32:40): When the Holy One, blessed be He, created the world, He did so by a spoken word alone and not with an oath.[1] Who caused Him to swear an oath? Those who lacked faith were the ones who caused Him to swear an oath, as it is said, *Therefore He swore concerning them, that He would overthrow them in the wilderness* (Ps. 106:26),[2] and, *I have lifted up My hand: Surely the nations that are round about you, (they shall bear their shame)* (Ezek. 36:7).[3]

And say: As I live for ever (32:40): For the way of the Holy One, blessed be He, is not like the way of creatures of flesh and blood. The way of the latter, when a governor goes into his province, if he can collect (the revenue) from his province, he does so, and if not, he cannot collect it. But He who spoke, and the world came into being, is not like that: if He does not collect from the living, He collects from the dead, and if He does not collect in this world, He collects in the world to come.[4]

Pisḳa 331

If I whet My glittering sword—when calamity issues from before Me, it is as swift as lightning;[1] nevertheless—*and My hand take hold on judgment,* [*I will render vengeance to Mine adversaries*—this is one (punishment)—*and will recompense them that hate Me* (32:41)—this is a second (punishment). Another interpretation:] *I will render vengeance to Mine adversaries*—this refers to the Cutheans,[2] as it is said, *Now when the adversaries of Judah and Benjamin heard* (Ezra 4:1)—*and will recompense them that hate Me*—this refers to the heretics, as it is said, *Do not I hate them, O Lord, that hate Thee? And do not I strive with those that rise up against Thee?* (Ps. 139:21).

Pisḳa 332

I will make Mine arrows drunk with blood (32:42): Is it possible for arrows to become drunk with blood? Rather, I will make the others drunk with what My arrows will do.

And My sword shall devour flesh (32:42): Is it possible for a sword to eat flesh? Rather, I will make the others eat of what My sword will do, as it is said, *And thou, son of man, (thus saith the Lord God:) Speak unto the birds of every sort* (Ezek. 39:17), *And ye shall eat fat till ye be full, and drink blood (till ye be drunken)* (Ezek. 39:19), *The flesh of the mighty shall ye eat* (Ezek. 39:18), *And ye shall be filled at My table with horses and horsemen* (Ezek. 39:20), and, *The sword of the Lord is filled with blood, it is made fat with fatness* (Isa. 34:6). Why so? *For the Lord hath a sacrifice in Bozrah, and a great slaughter in the land of Edom* (Isa. 34:6).

With the blood of the slain and the captives (32:42): From what they did with the slain of My people, as it is said, *Oh that my head were waters, and mine eyes a fountain of tears, that I might weep day and night for the slain of the daughter of my people!* (Jer. 8:23). *And the captives*—as it is said, *And they shall take them captive, whose captives they were; and they shall rule over their oppressors* (Isa. 14:2).

From the long-haired heads of the enemy (32:42): When the Holy One, blessed be He, brings calamity[1] upon the nations, He will inflict upon them not only the punishment earned by them but also that earned by their ancestors from Nimrod down. When He bestows benefits upon Israel, He will bestow upon them both those earned by them and those earned by their ancestors from Abraham down.

Another interpretation: *From the long-haired heads of the enemy*: Why was it proper to place all calamities upon the head of Pharaoh?[2] Because he was the first to enslave Israel.

Pisḳa 333

Sing aloud, O ye nations, of His people (32:43): Tomorrow, when the Holy One, blessed be He, brings redemption to Israel, the nations of the world will rage before Him,[1] nor will this be the first time for them, for they had raged before, as it is said, *The peoples have heard, they raged* (Exod. 15:14).

Another interpretation: *Sing aloud, O ye nations, of His people*: In the future[2] the nations of the world will sing praise before Israel, as it is said, *Sing aloud, O ye nations, of His people.*

Even heaven and earth (will sing praise), as it is said, *Sing, O ye heavens, for the Lord hath done it; shout, ye lowest parts of the earth* (Isa. 44:23). Whence do we learn that mountains and hills also will sing praise? From the verse, *The mountains and the hills shall break forth before you into singing* (Isa. 55:12). Whence do we learn that the trees also will sing praise? From the verse, *And all the trees of the field shall clap their hands* (Isa. 55:12). Whence do we learn that patriarchs and matriarchs also will sing praise? From the verse, *Let the inhabitants of Sela exult, let them shout from the top of the mountains* (Isa. 42:11).[3]

For He doth avenge the blood of His servants, and doth render vengeance to His adversaries (32:43): There will be two acts of vengeance, one for the blood and one for the violence. Whence do we learn that all the violence perpetrated by the nations of the world against Israel will be accounted as if they had shed innocent blood? From the verses, *I will gather all nations, and will bring them down into the valley of Jehoshaphat, and I will enter into judgment with them there for My people (and for My heritage) Israel* (Joel 4:2), and, *Egypt shall be a desolation, and Edom shall be a desolate wilderness, for the violence against the children of Judah, because they have shed innocent blood in their land* (Joel 4:19). But at that same time, *Judah shall be inhabited for ever, and Jerusalem from generation to generation. And I will hold as innocent their blood that I have not held as innocent; and the Lord dwelleth in Zion* (Joel 4:20–21).

And doth make expiation for the land of His people (32:43): Whence do we learn that when Israelites are slain by the nations of the world, it serves them as expiation in the world to come? From the verses, *A Psalm of Asaph: O God, the heathen are come into Thine inheritance. . . . They have given the dead bodies of Thy servants (to be food unto the fowls of the heaven, the flesh of Thy saints unto the beasts of the earth). They have shed their blood like water* (Ps. 79:1–3).[4] Another interpretation: *And doth make expiation for the land of His people*: Whence do we learn that the descent of the wicked into Gehenna brings them[5] expiation? From the verses, *I have given Egypt as thy expiation,*[6] *Ethiopia and Seba for thee, since thou are precious in My sight, and honorable, and I have loved thee* (Isa. 43:3–4).

R. Meir used to say: The Land of Israel makes expiation for anyone who dwells in it, as it is said, *The people that dwell therein shall be forgiven their iniquity* (Isa. 33:24). Nevertheless, this matter is still in doubt, for we do not know whether they must suffer their iniquities upon it, or whether their iniquities are atoned for upon it.[7] But when Scripture states *And doth make expiation for the land of His people,* we learn that their iniquities are atoned for upon it. Similarly R. Meir used to say: He who lives in the Land of Israel, recites the Shemaᶜ morning and evening, and speaks the holy tongue, he is assured of the world to come.

(To sum up,) you may well say: How great is this song, for it contains references to the present, to the past, and to the future to come, as well as to this world and the world to come!

Pisḳa 334

And Moses came (32:44): Here Scripture says *And Moses came,* while previously it says *And Moses went* (31:1). It is impossible to say

"Moses came" when previously it was said "Moses went," and it is impossible to say "Moses went" when later on it is said "Moses came." Hence you conclude that Moses' successor[1] (Joshua) had come and that authority was given into the hands of another.

And spoke all the words of this song in the ears of the people (32:44): This shows that he made them sink into their ears.

He, and Hoshea the son of Nun (32:44): What purpose does this (statement) serve? Has it not been stated already, *And Moses called Hoshea the son of Nun Joshua* (Num. 13:16)? Why then does the verse here state *He, and Hoshea the son of Nun?* To inform you of Joshua's righteousness. I might think that he became haughty once he was appointed to lead (Israel); therefore the verse states, *He, and Hoshea the son of Nun*—Joshua remained as righteous as Hoshea (had always been); even though he had been appointed leader of Israel, he remained as righteous as Hoshea (had always been). Similarly Scripture says, *And Joseph was in Egypt already* (Exod. 1:5). Do we not know that Joseph was in Egypt? Rather, this is intended to indicate the righteousness of Joseph. He had once been a shepherd of his father's flock, and even though he was now appointed viceroy of Egypt, he remained as righteous as Joseph (had always been). The same applies to the verse, *And David was the youngest* (1 Sam. 17:14). Do we not know that David was the youngest? Rather, this is meant to inform you of David's righteousness; he had once been a shepherd of his father's flock, and even though he was now appointed king of Israel, he remained as "young"[2] as David had always been.

Pisḳa 335

He said unto them: Set your heart unto all the words wherewith I testify against you this day (32:46): One should direct his heart, his eyes, and his ears toward the words of Torah, as it is said, *Son of man, set thy heart, and behold with thine eyes, and hear with thine ears all that I say unto thee . . . and set thy heart to the entering in of the House* (Ezek. 44:5). There is an inference from the minor to the major here: if one must direct his heart, his eyes, and his ears toward the Temple, which can be seen by the eye and can be measured by the hand, how much more is this true of the words of the Torah, which are as mountains suspended by a hair.[1]

That ye may charge your children therewith to observe (32:46): Moses said to them: I must be grateful to you for observing the Torah (as I have taught it) after me, and you must be grateful to your children who will observe the Torah (as you teach it) after you. It once happened that Rabbi (Judah the Prince) came up from Laodicea, and R. Jose son of R. Judah and R. Eleazar son of R. Judah came in and sat before him. He said to them: Draw near—I shall be grateful to you for observing the Torah (as I have taught it) after me, and you shall be grateful to your children who will observe the Torah (as you teach it) after you. For there was none greater than Moses, yet had others not accepted the Torah through him, it would have been worthless. How much more is this true of us. Therefore it is said, *That ye may charge your children.*

Pisḳa 336

For it is no vain thing for you (32:47): There is nothing vain in the Torah, nothing that, when interpreted, will not earn you a reward in this world, with the principal remaining intact for the world to come. You know that this is so, for the Sages have said: Why is it said, *And Lotan's sister was Timna* (Gen. 36:22) and *And Timna was concubine (to Eliphaz, Esau's son)* (Gen. 36:12)? Because she said, "I am not worthy to be his wife; I will therefore be his concubine."[1] Why so? To indicate to you how much Abraham was beloved, so much so that Gentiles forsook royal power and sought to attach themselves to him. Is not this a matter of inference from the minor to the major? If kings and rulers sought to attach themselves to Esau, who observed only one commandment, that of honoring his father, how much more did they seek to attach themselves to Jacob the righteous, who observed the entire Torah, as it is said, *And Jacob was a quiet man, dwelling in tents*[2] (Gen. 25:27).

And through this thing ye shall prolong your days (32:47): This is one of the things for the performance of which one enjoys their fruit in this world and prolongs his days in the world to come. Study of Torah is explicitly referred to here; but whence do we learn that this applies also to honoring one's father and mother? From the verse, *Honor thy father and thy mother, that thy days may be long* (Exod. 20:12). And the same applies also to releasing the mother-bird, as it is said, *Thou shalt in any wise let the dam go, but the young thou mayest take unto thyself, that it may be well with thee, and that thou mayest prolong thy days* (22:7). The same applies also to establishing peace, as it is said, *And all thy children shall be taught of the Lord, and great shall be the peace of thy children* (Isa. 54:13).[3]

Pisḳa 337

And the Lord spoke unto Moses that selfsame day (32:48): The phrase "that selfsame day" is used in three places.[1] *That selfsame day* (Gen. 7:13) refers to Noah, showing that the generation of Noah said, "By our oath, if we see him (going into the ark), we will not let him go; rather, we will take picks and axes and wreck his ark over him." Said the Holy One, blessed be He: "Behold, I will bring him into (the ark) at midday, and if anyone wishes to stop him, let him come and try." Concerning (the exodus from) Egypt, what was Scripture's purpose in saying, *That selfsame day it came to pass, that all the hosts of the Lord went out from the land of Egypt* (Exod. 12:41)? The reason was that the Egyptians said, "By our oath, if we see them (preparing to leave), we will not let them go; furthermore, we will take hold of our swords and cutlasses and slay them." Said the Holy One, blessed be He: "Behold, I will bring them out (of Egypt) at midday, and if anyone wishes to stop them, let him come and try." And what was Scripture's purpose in saying *that selfsame day* here? The reason was that Israel said, "By our oath, if we see Moses (leaving us), we will not let the man who had brought us out of Egypt, had split the (Red) Sea for us, had brought down manna for us, had supplied us with the quail, had performed miracles and wonders for us—we will not let him go." Said the Holy One, blessed be He: "Behold, I will bring him into the cave at midday, and if anyone wishes to stop (Me), let him come and try." Hence Scripture says, *And the Lord spoke unto Moses that selfsame day,* etc.[2]

Pisḳa 338

Get thee up into this mountain of Abarim, (unto Mount Nebo) (32:49): This is an elevation for you and not a degradation.

This mountain of Abarim, which is known by four names: Mount Abarim, Mount Nebo, Mount Hor, and Top of Pisgah. Why is it called Mount Nebo? Because three prophets (*nĕḇiʾim*) who died not because of sin were buried there, namely Moses, Aaron, and Miriam.[1]

Which is in the land of Moab—hence we learn that God showed Moses the dynasty of kings who would spring from Ruth the Moabitess—*that is over against Jericho*—this shows that He showed him the succession of prophets who were to issue from Rahab the harlot[2]—*and behold the land of Canaan* (32:49): R. Eliezer says: The finger of the Holy One, blessed be He, became Moses' guide, pointing out to him all the borders of the Land of Israel: this far is Ephraim's section, this far is the section of Manasseh. R. Joshua says: Moses saw it all by himself. How so? God gave power to Moses' eyes, which enabled him to see from one end of the world to the other.

Piska 339

And die in the mount whither thou goest up (32:50): Moses said to God, "Master of the universe, why must I die? Would it not be better for people to say 'Moses is good' out of personal knowledge rather than as mere rumor? Would it not be better for people to say, 'This here is Moses, who had brought us out of Egypt, had split the (Red) Sea for us, had brought down the manna for us, and had performed miracles and wonders for us,' rather than to say, 'Moses was like that, and did such-and-such?'" God replied, "Enough, Moses. Such is My decree, which applies equally to all men," as it is said, *This is the law: when a man dieth in a tent* (Num. 19:14),[1] and, *This is the law of a man, O Lord God* (2 Sam. 7:19). The ministering angels said to the Holy One, blessed be He, "Master of the universe, why did primeval Adam die?" He replied, "Because he did not obey My commands." They said to Him, "But Moses does obey Thy commands!" He replied, "It is My decree, and it applies equally to all men, as it is said, *This is the law: when a man dieth in a tent.*"[2]

And be gathered unto thy people (32:50): Unto Abraham, Isaac, and Jacob, unto Amram and Kohath, unto Miriam and Aaron, your brother.

As Aaron thy brother died (32:50): The same manner of death that you desired. And whence do we know that Moses desired (for himself) Aaron's manner of death? When the Holy One, blessed be He, said to Moses, *Take Aaron and Eleazar his son . . . and strip Aaron of his garments* (Num. 20:25–26), Moses put these priestly garments, one by one, upon Eleazar. Moses then said to Aaron, "Go into the cave," and Aaron went into it; "lie down upon the couch," and Aaron did so; "stretch out your arms," and Aaron did so; "stretch out your legs," and Aaron did so; "close your mouth," and Aaron did so; "close your eyes," and Aaron did so. At that time Moses exclaimed, "Happy is he who dies in this manner of death!" Therefore Scripture says, *As Aaron thy brother died*—the same manner of death that you desired.

Pisḳa 340

Because ye trespassed against Me—you caused (Israel) to trespass against Me—. . . *because ye sanctified Me not* (32:51)—you caused (them) not to sanctify Me.

Because ye rebelled against My commandment (Num. 27:14): You caused (Israel) to rebel against My commandment. Said the Holy One, blessed be He, to Moses, "Did I not say to you, *What is that in thy hand? . . . Cast it on the ground* (Exod. 4:2–3). And you did cast it. In the case of such miracles, you did not hold back. But in this light matter[1] you had to hold back!" Whence do we learn that Moses did not depart from this world until the Holy One, blessed be He, enveloped his soul in His wings? From the verse, *Therefore ye shall not bring this assembly (into the land)* (Num. 20:12).[2]

Pisḳa 341

For thou shalt see the land afar off: but thou shalt not go thither (32:52): Here Scripture says, *But thou shalt not go thither,* and elsewhere it says, *But thou shalt not go over thither* (34:4). It is impossible to say *But thou shalt not go over thither* when it is already said *But thou shalt not go thither,* and it would be impossible to say *But thou shalt not go thither* if it were already said *but thou shalt not go over thither.* Said Moses before the Holy One, blessed be He, "If I do not enter it as a king, let me enter it as a commoner. If I do not enter it alive, let me enter it dead." Replied the Holy One, blessed be He, "*Thou shalt not go thither* and *Thou shalt not go over thither*; not as a king, nor as a commoner, neither alive, nor dead."[1]

Pisḳa 342

And this is the blessing, wherewith Moses . . . blessed (the children of Israel) (33:1): Since Moses had spoken harsh words to Israel previously—*The wasting of hunger . . . without shall the sword bereave* (32:24–25), *Also in Horeb ye made the Lord wroth* (9:8), *Ye have been rebellious against the Lord* (9:7)—he now spoke words of comfort to them: *And this is the blessing, wherewith Moses . . . blessed.* It was from Moses that all the prophets learned to speak first harsh words to Israel and then words of comfort. You cannot find anyone among the prophets whose words were more harsh than those of Hosea. He began by saying to them, *Give them, O Lord, whatsoever Thou wilt give. Give them a miscarrying womb* (Hos. 9:14), but later he spoke words of comfort to them, *His branches shall spread, and his beauty shall be as the olive tree, and his fragrance as Lebanon. They that dwell under his shadow shall again make corn to grow, and shall blossom as the vine* (Hos. 14:7–8), and, *I will heal their backsliding, I will love them freely . . . I will be as the dew unto Israel: He shall blossom as the lily* (Hos. 14:5–6). Similarly Joel said to them first, *Hear this, ye old men, and give ear, all ye inhabitants of the land. Hath this been in your days, or in the days of your fathers? Tell ye your children of it. . . . That which the palmer-worm hath left hath the locust eaten* (Joel 1:2–4), but later he spoke words of comfort to them, *And I will restore to you the years that the locust hath eaten, the canker-worm, and the caterpillar, and the palmer-worm* (Joel 2:25). Similarly Amos said to them first, *Hear this word, ye kine of Bashan, that are in the mountain of Samaria, that oppress the poor, that crush the needy, that say unto their lords, "Bring, that we may feast"* (Amos 4:1), but later he spoke words of comfort to them, *Behold, the days come . . . that the plowman shall overtake the reaper* (Amos 9:13). Similarly Micah said to them first, *Who hate the good, and love the evil, who rob. . . . Who also eat the flesh of my people, and flay their skin from off them* (Mic. 3:2–3), but later he spoke words of comfort to them, *Who is a God like unto Thee, that pardoneth the iniquity, and passeth by the transgression of the remnant of His heritage? He retaineth not His anger for ever, because He delighteth in mercy. He will again have compassion upon us, He will subdue our iniquities, and Thou wilt cast all their sins into the depths of the sea. Thou wilt show faithfulness to Jacob, mercy to Abraham, as Thou hast sworn unto our fathers from the days of old* (Mic. 7:18–20). Similarly Jeremiah said to them first, *Then will I cause to cease from the cities of Judah, and from the streets of*

Jerusalem, the voice of mirth and the voice of gladness (Jer. 7:34), but later he spoke to them words of comfort, *Then shall the virgin rejoice in the dance* (Jer. 31:13). One might think that having spoken words of comfort to Israel the prophets would then speak more words of rebuke; therefore the prophecy of Jeremiah ends with *And thou shalt say: Thus shall Babylon sink, and shall not rise again because of the evil that I will bring upon her; (and they shall be weary). Thus far are the words of Jeremiah* (Jer. 51:64). This indicates that once they have spoken words of comfort to them, they will not speak words of rebuke to them.

And this is the blessing (wherewith Moses . . . blessed) (33:1): This is additional to the first blessing with which their father Jacob had blessed them, as it is said, *And this is it that their father spoke unto them, and blessed them* (Gen. 49:28). From this we learn[1] that Moses commenced to bless them at the place where our father Jacob had stopped, as it is said, *And this is the blessing wherewith (Moses) . . . blessed. And this is the blessing*—this is additional to the first blessing. But which one? *A prayer of Moses, the man of God* (Ps. 90:1). Yet the matter is still in doubt, for we do not know whether prayer precedes blessing or blessing precedes prayer. Since Scripture says, *And this is the blessing,* we deduce that prayer precedes blessing and that blessing does not precede prayer.[2]

Wherewith Moses . . . blessed: Had others blessed Israel, their blessing would have been deserved. But Moses himself blessed them, hence we learn that Moses was deserving[3] of blessing Israel, and Israel was deserving of being blessed by Moses.

(Moses), the man of God (33:1): Moses is one of ten men called "man of God." Moses is called "man of God": *A prayer of Moses, the man of God* (Ps. 90:1). Elkanah is called "man of God": *And there came a man of God unto Eli* (1 Sam. 2:27).[4] Samuel is called "man of God," as it is said, *Behold now, there is in this city a man of God* (1 Sam. 9:6). David is called "man of God," as it is said, *According to the commandment of David the man of God* (Neh. 12:24). Shemaiah is called "man of God," as it is said, *But the word of God came unto Shemaiah the man of God, saying* (1 Kings 12:22). Iddo is called "man of God," as it is said, *And behold there came a man of God out of Judah by the word of the Lord*[5] (1 Kings 13:1). Elijah is called "man of God," as it is said, *O man of God, I pray thee, let my life . . . be precious* (2 Kings 1:13). Elisha is called "man of God," as it is said, *Behold now, I perceive that this is a holy man of God* (2 Kings 4:9). Micah is

called "man of God," as it is said, *And a man of God came near and spoke unto the King of Israel* (1 Kings 20:28). Amoz is called "man of God," as it is said, *But there came a man of God unto him, saying, "O king, let not the army of Israel go with thee"* (2 Chron. 25:7).[6]

Before his death (33:1): Did it ever come to your mind that Moses blessed Israel after his death? What then is meant by *Before his death?* Close to his death. Similarly Scripture says, *Behold, I will send you Elijah the prophet before the coming of the great and terrible day of the Lord* (Mal. 3:23). Did it ever come to your mind that Elijah was to prophesy to them after the coming of that day? What then is meant by *before the coming of the . . . day*? Close to the coming of that day.

Pisḳa 343

And he said: The Lord came from Sinai, and rose from Seir unto them (33:2): Scripture shows that Moses opened (the blessing) not with the needs of Israel but with the praise of God. This may be compared to an advocate (rhetor) hired by a certain individual to plead his cause. The advocate, standing on the podium, opens not with the needs of his client but with the praise of the king. Happy is the world because he is its king. Happy is the world because he is its judge. The sun shines upon us (for his sake). The moon shines upon us (for his sake). The audience joins him in praising (the king). Only then does he turn to the needs of his client, and finally concludes with (repeated) praise of the king.[1] So too our teacher Moses opened not with the needs of Israel but with the praise of God, as it is said, *And he said: The Lord came from Sinai.* Only thereafter did he begin to speak of the needs of Israel, (as it is said,) *And there was a king in Jeshurun* (33:5). Finally he concluded with the praise of God, (as it is said,) *There is none like unto God, O Jeshurun* (33:26). King David also spoke first in praise of God, as it is said, *Hallelujah. Sing unto the Lord a new song* (Ps. 149:1), and only afterwards spoke in praise of Israel,[2] (as it is said,) *For the Lord taketh pleasure in His people* (Ps. 149:4); finally he concluded with the praise of God, (as it is said,) *Praise God in His Sanctuary* (Ps. 150:1). His son Solomon likewise spoke first in praise of God, (as it is said,) *There is no God like Thee, in the heaven, or in the earth, who keepeth the covenant and mercy* (2 Chron. 6:14); then he spoke of the needs of Israel, (as it is said,) *If there be in the land famine* (2 Chron. 6:28), and he concluded with the praise of God, (as it is said,) *Now therefore arise, O Lord God, into Thy resting place* (2 Chron. 6:41). So too the Eighteen Benedictions, which the early prophets ordained that Israel should recite daily, commence not with the needs of Israel but with the praise of God: "The great, mighty, and awesome God, Thou art holy, and Thy name is awesome," followed by "Who releases the captives," and concluding with, "Who heals the sick," and "We give thanks unto Thee."[3]

And he said: The Lord came from Sinai: When God revealed Himself in order to give the Torah to Israel, He did so not from just one direction but from all four directions, as it is said, *And he said: The Lord came from Sinai, and rose from Seir unto them: He shined forth from Mount Paran* (33:2). And what is the fourth direction? *God cometh from Teman* (Hab. 3:3).

Another interpretation: When God revealed Himself to give the Torah to Israel, He spoke to them not in one language but in four languages, as it is said, *And He said: The Lord came from Sinai*—this refers to the Hebrew language—*and rose from Seir unto them*—this refers to the Roman language[4]—*He shined forth from Mount Paran*—this refers to the Arabic language—*and He came from the Myriads of Ḳodesh*[5]—this refers to the Aramaic language.

Another interpretation: *And he said: The Lord came from Sinai*: When God revealed Himself to give the Torah to Israel, He revealed Himself not only to Israel but to all the nations.[6] He went first to the children of Esau and asked them, "Will you accept the Torah?" They replied, "What is written in it?" He said to them, *Thou shalt not murder* (Exod. 20:13). They replied that this is the very essence of these people, and that their forefather was a murderer, as it is said, *But the hands are the hands of Esau* (Gen. 27:22),[7] and, *By thy sword shalt thou live* (Gen. 27:40). He then went to the Ammonites and the Moabites and asked them, "Will you accept the Torah?" They replied, "What is written in it?" He said, *Thou shalt not commit adultery* (Exod. 20:13). They replied that adultery is their very essence, as it is said, *Thus were both the daughters of Lot with child by their father* (Gen. 19:36).[8] He went next to the Ishmaelites and asked them, "Will you accept the Torah?" They replied, "What is written in it?" He said, *Thou shalt not steal* (Exod. 20:13). They replied that theft is their very essence and that their forefather was a thief, as it is said, *And he shall be a wild ass of a man* (Gen. 16:12). And thus it was with every other nation—He asked them all, "Will you accept the Torah?," as it is said, *All the kings of the earth shall give Thee thanks, O Lord, for they have heard the words of Thy mouth* (Ps. 138:4). One might think (from this verse) that they heard and accepted (His offer); therefore Scripture states elsewhere, *And I will execute vengeance in anger and fury upon the nations, because they hearkened not* (Mic. 5:14). It was not enough for them that they did not hearken—they were not even able to observe the seven commandments that the children of Noah had accepted upon themselves, and they cast them off. When the Holy One, blessed be He, saw that, He surrendered them to Israel.[9] A parable: A man took his ass and his dog to the threshing floor and loaded the ass with a *leṯeḵ* (of grain) and the dog with three *seʾah*.[10] The ass went along (easily), but the dog began to pant, so the man took off[11] a *seʾah* and put it on the ass, and so too with the second and the third *seʾah*. So also Israel accepted the Torah, with all of its explanations and details, as well as the seven commandments which the children of Noah had not been able to observe and had cast off. Therefore it is said, *And he said: The Lord came from Sinai, and rose from Seir unto them.*[12]

Another interpretation: *And rose from Seir unto them*: In the future, when the Holy One, blessed be He, will punish Seir, He will shake the entire world, together with its inhabitants, as He did at the giving of the Torah, as it is said, *Lord, when Thou didst go forth out of Seir, when Thou didst march out of the field of Edom, the earth trembled, the heavens also dropped water, yea, the clouds dropped water* (Judg. 5:4), and, *And after that came forth his brother, and his hand had hold on Esau's heel; and his name was called Jacob* (Gen. 25:26). The Holy One, blessed be He, said to Israel, "No nation or tongue will be able to come between you."[13] A parable:[14] A king wanted to present a gift to one of his sons, but was afraid of the son's brothers, of his favorites, and of his relatives. What did that son do? He adorned himself[15] and arranged his hair, whereupon the king said to him, "To you I am presenting this gift." So also, when our father Abraham came into the world, he had unworthy children, Ishmael and the children of Keturah, who were more evil than the previous generations (of men). When Isaac came along, he had an unworthy child, Esau, and all the princes of Edom became more evil than the previous generations. But when Jacob came along, he had no unworthy children, for all the children born to him were worthy,[16] as it is said, *And Jacob was a worthy man, dwelling in tents* (Gen. 25:27). Whereupon the Holy One, blessed be He, said to him, "To you shall I give the Torah." Hence Scripture says, *The Lord came from Sinai, and rose from Seir unto them.*

Another interpretation: *Came from Sinai*: When the Holy One, blessed be He, revealed Himself to give the Torah, He shook the entire world, together with its inhabitants, as it is said, *The voice of the Lord is upon the waters. . . . The voice of the Lord is powerful* (Ps. 29:3–4). At that time all the nations gathered together and came to Balaam, saying to him, "It seems to us that the Holy One, blessed be He, is about to destroy the world with water." He replied by citing, *The waters shall no more become a flood* (Gen. 9:15). They said to him, "What then is this (mighty) sound?" He replied, *"The Lord will give strength unto His people"* (Ps. 29:11)—"strength" always refers to the Torah, as it is said, *With Him is strength and sound wisdom* (Job 12:16). They said to him, "If that is so, *The Lord will bless His people with peace* (Ps. 29:11)."[17]

He shined forth from Mount Paran: There are four occasions when God shines forth. The first was in Egypt, as it is said, *Give ear, O Shepherd of Israel, Thou that leadest Joseph like a flock; Thou that art enthroned upon the cherubim, shine forth* (Ps. 80:2). The second, at the time of the giving of the Torah, as it is said, *He shined forth from Mount Paran.* The third will occur at the time of Gog and Magog, as it is said, *O Lord, Thou God to whom vengeance belongeth, Thou God to whom vengeance belongeth, shine forth* (Ps. 94:1). The fourth will occur in the days of the Messiah, as it is said, *Out of Zion, the perfection of beauty, God hath shined forth* (Ps. 50:2).

And He came from the myriads holy (33:2): The way of the Holy One, blessed be He, is not like that of flesh and blood. When a man arranges a banquet for his son in celebration of the son's wedding, he displays his treasures and all his possessions. But He who spoke, and the world came into being, is not like this—rather, *And He came from the myriads holy,* and not "all the myriads holy."[18]

Another interpretation: *And He came from the myriads holy*: When a king of flesh and blood holds court in his palace, there are present men more handsome than he, more praiseworthy than he, more mighty than he. Not so in the case of Him who spoke, and the world came into being—*And He is a mark among the myriads holy,* He stands out[19] from among the myriads holy. When He revealed Himself at the (Red) Sea, they immediately recognized Him, as it is said, *This is my God, and I will glorify Him, my father's God, and I will exalt him* (Exod. 15:2). Thus it was that the nations of the world asked Israel, "*What is thy beloved more than another beloved* (Song 5:9), that you are prepared to die for His sake, as it is said, *Therefore do they love thee unto death*[20] (Song 1:3), and, *Nay, but for Thy sake are we killed all the day* (Ps. 44:23)? You are all pleasant, you are all mighty. Come therefore and let us mingle together." And Israel replied, "You have been told only a fraction of His praise, yet you think that you know Him! *My beloved is white and ruddy . . . His head is as the most fine gold . . . His eyes are like doves beside the water-brooks . . . His cheeks are as a bed of spices . . . His hands are as rods of gold . . . His legs are as pillars of marble . . . His mouth is most sweet, yea, he is altogether sweet* (Song 5:10–16)."[21] When the nations of the world heard of the beauty and the praise of the Holy One, blessed be He, they said to Israel, "Let us come with you, as it is said, *Whither is thy beloved gone, O thou fairest among women? Whither hath thy beloved turned him, that we may seek him with thee?* (Song 6:1)." What does Israel reply? They have no part in Him—"*I am my beloved's, and my beloved is mine, that feedeth among the lilies* (Song 6:3)."

At His right hand was a fiery law unto them (33:2): When the word went forth from the mouth of the Holy One, blessed be He, it would go forth from the right side of the Holy One, blessed be He, to the left side of Israel, encircle the camp of Israel twelve miles by twelve miles, and return through the right side of Israel to the left side of the Holy One, blessed be He. The Holy One, blessed be He, would receive it in His right hand and engrave it upon the tablet. His voice would reach from one end of the world to the other, as it is said, *The voice of the Lord heweth out flames of fire* (Ps. 29:7).

At his right hand was a fiery law unto them: This shows that the words of Torah are likened to fire. Just as fire was given from heaven, so were the words of Torah given from heaven, as it is said, *Ye yourselves have seen that I have talked with you from heaven* (Exod. 20:19). Just as fire lives forever, so do the words of Torah live forever. Just as fire scorches him who draws near it, while he who is far away from it is chilled, so is it with words of Torah: if one occupies himself with them, they give him life, but if he departs from them, they cause his death. Just as fire is used both in this world and in the world to come, so the words of Torah are used both in this world and in the world to come. Just as fire leaves a mark upon the body of one who uses it, so the words of Torah leave a mark upon the body of him who uses them. Just as those who work with fire are recognizable among other people, so disciples of the wise are recognized by their manner of walking, by their speech, and by their outdoor dress.[22]

A fiery law unto them: Were it not for the laws given with it, no man could withstand it.[23]

Pisḳa 344

Yea, He loveth the peoples (33:3): This shows that God loved Israel in a way different from the way He loved any other nation or kingdom.

All His holy ones, they are in Thy hand (33:3): This refers to the leaders of Israel, who give their lives for Israel. Thus it is written that Moses said, *Yet now, if Thou wilt forgive their sin; and if not, blot me, I pray Thee, out of Thy book, which Thou hast written* (Exod. 32:32). And it is written that David said, *Is it not I that commanded the people to be numbered? . . . (Let Thy hand, I pray Thee, O Lord my God, be against me, and against my father's house, but not against Thy people, that they should be plagued)* (1 Chron. 21:17).

And they sit down at Thy feet—even though they are persecuted, even though they are smitten, even though they are despoiled—*receiving of Thy words* (33:3)—they accept them upon themselves and say, *All that the Lord hath spoken will we do, and obey* (Exod. 24:7).[1]

Another interpretation: *Yea, He loveth the peoples*: This shows that the Holy One, blessed be He, did not dispense love to the nations of the world as He did to Israel. You learn that this is so from the Sages' saying, "That which was stolen from a non-Jew is permitted, while that which was stolen from a Jew is forbidden."[2] The government (of Rome) once sent out two officials, ordering them, "Go and disguise yourselves as Jews, and find out what is the nature of their Torah." They went to Rabban Gamaliel at Usha,[3] where they studied Scripture, Mishnah, Midrash, halakah and aggadah.[4] As the officers were taking their leave, they said to the Sages, "All of the Torah is fine and praiseworthy, except for one thing, and that is your saying 'That which is stolen from a non-Jew is permitted, while that which was stolen from a Jew is forbidden,' but we will not report this exception to the government."[5]

All His holy ones, they are in Thy hand: This refers to the great ones in Israel who are seized as hostages for Israel,[6] as it is said of Ezekiel, *Moreover lie thou upon thy left side, and lay the iniquity of the house of Israel upon it; according to the number of the days that thou shalt lie upon it, thou shalt bear their iniquity. For I have appointed the years of their iniquity to be unto thee a number of days . . . and again, when Thou hast accomplished these, thou shalt lie on thy right side, and shalt bear the iniquity of the house of Judah* (Ezek. 4:4–6).

And they sit down at Thy feet—even though they anger Thee, even though they are sinners—*receiving of Thy words*—they accept the yoke of Thy Torah upon themselves, (as it is said,) *All that the Lord hath spoken will we do, and obey* (Exod. 24:7).

Another interpretation: *Yea, He loveth the peoples*: This shows that the Holy One, blessed be He, loved Israel in a way different from the way He loved any other nation or kingdom.

All His holy ones, they are in Thy hand: This refers to the souls of the righteous, which are kept in His treasury, as it is said, *Yet the soul of my lord shall be bound in the bundle of life with the Lord thy God* (1 Sam. 25:29).

And they sit down at Thy feet—even if they are shoved back twelve miles and then forward twelve miles[7]—*receiving of Thy words*—accepting upon themselves, *All that the Lord hath spoken will we do, and obey.*

Pisḳa 345

Moses commanded us a law (33:4): This command is meant only for us, only for our sakes, as it is said, *And have built the house for the name of the Lord, the God of Israel* (1 Kings 8:20). What is the purpose of this house? To house the Ark (of the Covenant), as it is said, *And there have I set a place for the Ark* (1 Kings 8:21).[1] Thus we see that this command is meant only for us, only for our sakes.

Another interpretation: *Moses commanded us a law*: Is it from our teacher Moses that we took possession of the Torah? Is it not that our forefathers had attained it through their merit, as it is said, *An inheritance of the congregation of Jacob* (33:4)? From this I conclude that it is an inheritance for the children of kings. Whence do we learn that it is an inheritance for the children of commoners as well? From the verse, *Ye are standing this day, all of you, (before the Lord your God)* (29:9).[2] Another interpretation: [*An inheritance of the congregation of Jacob*]: Read not *an inheritance* (*morašah*) but "a betrothed" (*mě᾿orašah*), showing that the Torah is betrothed to Israel and has therefore the status of a married woman in relation to the nations of the world,[3] as it is said, *Can a man take fire in his bosom, and his clothes not be burned? Can one walk upon hot coals, and his feet not be scorched? So he that goeth in to his neighbor's wife; whosoever toucheth her shall not go unpunished* (Prov. 6:27–29).

Another interpretation: Read not "a betrothed" (*mĕʾoraśah*) but *an inheritance* (*moraśah*).[4] This shows that the Torah is the inheritance of Israel. To what may this be likened? To a king's son who when small was taken away into captivity to a country across the sea. Should he desire to return, even after a hundred years, he will not be embarrassed to do so, because he can say, "I am returning to my inheritance." So also a disciple of the wise who has turned away from the words of Torah in order to attend to other matters, will not be embarrassed to return to them, should he so desire, even after a hundred years, because he can say, "I am returning to my inheritance." Therefore Scripture says, *An inheritance of the congregation of Jacob.*

Piska 346

And there was a king in Jeshurun (33:5): When all of Israel is united in their counsel below, His great name is praised above, as it is said, *And there was a king in Jeshurun.* When (does this occur)? *When the heads of the people were gathered* (33:5)—"gathering" always implies the chiefs of the people, as it is said, *And the Lord said unto Moses, "Take all the chiefs of the people"* (Num. 25:4).

Another interpretation: When the prince seats the elders in the academy below,[1] His great name is praised above, as it is said, *And there was a king in Jeshurun.* When? *When the heads of the people were gathered*—"gathering" implies the elders, as it is said, *Gather unto Me seventy men of the elders of Israel* (Num. 11:16).

All the Tribes of Israel together (33:5): (This will apply)[2] when they form one (unified) group (*ʾăguddah*) and not when they are formed into several groups, as it is said, *It is He that buildeth His upper chambers in the heaven, and hath founded His vault* (*ʾăguddaṯo*) *upon the earth* (Amos 9:6). R. Simeon ben Yoḥai says: A parable: A man brought two ships, tied them to anchors and iron weights, stationed them in the middle of the sea, and built a palace upon them. As long as the two ships are tied to each other, the palace stands firm. Once the ships are separated, the palace cannot stand. Thus is it also with Israel: when they do the will of God, He builds His upper chambers in the heaven; when they do not do His will, He founds His vault upon the earth,[3] if one may say so. Similarly Scripture says: *This is my God, and I will glorify Him* (Exod. 15:2)—when I acknowledge Him, He is glorious, but when I do not acknowledge Him, He is (not) glorious,[4] if one may say such a thing—*For I will proclaim the name of the Lord; ascribe ye greatness unto our God* (32:3)—when I proclaim His Name, He is great, but when I do not, (He is not great,) if one may say such a thing—*Therefore ye are My witnesses, saith the Lord, and I am God* (Isa. 43:12)—when you are My witnesses, I am God, but when you are not My witnesses, I am not God, if one may say such a thing—*Unto thee I lift up mine eyes, O Thou that art enthroned in the heavens* (Ps. 123:1)—were it not for me, Thou wouldst not be enthroned in the heavens, if one may say such a thing. So too in this case *(And there was a king in Jeshurun), all the Tribes of Israel together*—(He is King) when they form one (unified) group; (He is) not (King) when they form several groups.

Pisḳa 347

All the Tribes of Israel together. Let Reuben live, and not die (33:5–6): What is the connection between these two sentences? A parable: A king used to come from time to time to visit his children. When he left them, his sons and relatives would escort him. He said to them, "My children, is there anything you need? Is there any matter you wish to raise? If so, tell me." They replied, "Father, there is nothing we need, and no matter to raise, except that we wish you would be reconciled with our elder brother." So also here, were it not for the (other) Tribes, God would not have been reconciled with Reuben. Therefore Scripture says, *All of the Tribes of Israel together. Let Reuben live, and not die.*

Let Reuben live, and not die: But was he not already dead? What then does Scripture mean by *and not die?* In the world to come.

Another interpretation: *Let Reuben live*—because of his action in the matter of Joseph—*and not die*—because of his action in the matter of Bilhah.[1] R. Hananiah ben Gamaliel says: Merit is never replaced by guilt, nor guilt by merit, except in the cases of Reuben and David, as it is said, *And Shimei went along on the side* (2 Sam. 16:13), but nevertheless *of the hill over against him* (2 Sam. 16:13),[2] (as it is said, *Solomon built Millo* (1 Kings 11:27), but nevertheless, *and repaired the breach of the city of David his father* (1 Kings 11:27). The Sages, however, say: Merit is never replaced by guilt, nor guilt by merit, but one receives a reward for (performance of) religious duties and punishment for transgressions. What then is the meaning of *Let Reuben live, and not die?* It indicates that Reuben repented.[3] Rabban Simeon ben Gamaliel says: Reuben was saved from that (grievous) sin and did not commit that deed. Is it possible that he who was to stand at the head of the Tribes on Mount Ebal and say, *Cursed be he that lieth with his father's wife* (27:20), would commit such a deed? What then does Scripture mean by *Because thou wentest up to thy father's bed* (Gen. 49:4)? He avenged his mother's shame.[4]

In that his men become few (33:6): In this world, in which his days are few in number, but in the future, *Let Reuben live, and not die.*[5]

Another interpretation: *In that his men become few* (*Men* refers to those who are) mighty in strength and mighty in Torah. Mighty in strength, as it is said, *Thy men shall fall by the sword, and thy mighty in the war* (Isa. 3:25); mighty in Torah, as it is said, *Ye mighty in strength, that fulfill His word* (Ps. 103:20). And Scripture says also, *Beerah, his son, whom Tillegath-pilneser king of Assyria carried away captive, he was prince of the Reubenites* (1 Chron. 5:6).

Pisḳa 348

Let Reuben live, and not die. . . . And this for Judah (33:6–7): What is the connection between these two verses: When Judah committed that (evil) deed and then stood up and admitted, *She is more righteous than I* (Gen. 38:26), Reuben witnessed this admission and then himself confessed what he had done (in the matter of Bilhah).[1] One might say therefore, that Judah caused Reuben to repent. Concerning them Scripture says, *Which wise men have told from their fathers and have not hid it. Unto whom alone the land was given, and no stranger passed among them* (Job 15:18–19).

Hear, Lord, the voice of Judah (33:7): This shows that Moses prayed for the Tribe of Judah, saying, "Master of the universe, whenever the Tribe of Judah finds itself in trouble and prays unto Thee, deliver them from it."

And bring him unto his people (33:7): Meaning that he would be buried with the patriarchs in the Land (of Israel). R. Judah says: Were the bones of Joseph the only ones that Israel brought out of Egypt? Did not each Tribe bring the bones of its own forefather[2] out of Egypt, as it is said, *And ye shall carry up my bones away hence with you* (Exod. 13:19)? Now the words *with you* seem at first superfluous. What then does *with you* indicate? That each Tribe brought the bones of its own forefather out of Egypt. Therefore what does *And bring him unto his people* mean?[3] That he would be buried with the patriarchs in their burial place. R. Meir says: Scripture says, *In my grave which I have digged for me in the land of Canaan* (Gen. 50:5), I (Jacob) shall be buried in it,[4] meaning that no one else will be buried in it. What then does *And bring him unto his people* mean? That he would be buried with the (other) patriarchs in the Land of Israel.

His hands shall contend for him—when he killed Esau[5]—*and Thou shalt be a help against his adversaries* (33:7)—when he stood before Joseph.

And this for Judah 33:7): This shows that Moses prayed for the Tribe of Simeon,[6] saying, "Master of the universe, whenever the Tribe of Simeon finds itself in trouble and prays unto Thee, deliver them from it."

And bring him unto his people (*ᶜammo*) (33:7): Meaning that Judah brought Simeon with him (*ᶜimmo*) for the blessing,[7] as it is said, *And Judah said unto Simeon his brother, "Come up with me unto my lot"* (Judg. 1:3).

His hands shall contend for him—when *Two of the sons of Jacob, Simeon and Levi . . . (took each man his sword)* (Gen. 34:25)—*and Thou shalt be a help against his adversaries*—in the matter of which it is said, *And they journeyed; and a terror of God was upon the cities that were round about them, and they did not pursue after the sons of Jacob* (Gen. 35:5).

And this for Judah: This shows that Moses prayed for David, king of Israel, saying, "Master of the universe, whenever David, the king of Israel, finds himself in trouble and prays to Thee, deliver him from it."

And bring him unto his people—return him in peace to his brethren—*his hands shall contend for him*—when he killed Goliath—*and Thou shalt be a help against his adversaries*—when he says, *I will lift up mine eyes unto the mountains: from whence shall my help come?* (Ps. 121:1).

And this for Judah: This shows that Moses prayed for the kings of the house of David, saying, "Master of the universe, whenever the kings of the house of David find themselves in trouble and pray to Thee, deliver them from it."

And bring him unto his people—this refers to Josiah, as it is said, *Therefore, behold, I will gather thee to thy fathers* (2 Kings 22:20)—*his hands shall contend for him*—this refers to Manasseh, as it is said, *Moreover, Manasseh shed innocent blood very much* (2 Kings 21:16); what is said of him later? *And he prayed unto Him; and He . . . (heard his supplication, and brought him back to Jerusalem into his kingdom)* (2 Chron. 33:13).

And Thou shalt be a help against his adversaries: This refers to Jehoshaphat, as it is said, *But Jehoshaphat cried out, and the Lord helped him* (2 Chron. 18:31).

Pisḳa 349

And of Levi he said (33:8): Why is this said?[1] Because Simeon and Levi drank from the same cup, as it is said, *Cursed be their anger, for it was fierce, and their wrath, for it was cruel: I will divide them in Jacob, and scatter them in Israel* (Gen. 49:7). A parable: Two men borrowed money from the king. One repaid the king and even lent him some money, while the other not only did not repay the debt but even borrowed more money. So also both Simeon and Levi "borrowed"[2] in the matter of Shechem, as it is said, *Two of the sons of Jacob, Simeon and Levi, Dinah's brethren, took each man his sword, and came upon the city unawares, and slew all the males* (Gen. 34:25). In the wilderness Levi repaid his debt, as it is said, *Then Moses stood in the gate of the camp, and said, ("Whoso is on the Lord's side, let him come unto me." And all the sons of Levi gathered themselves together unto him). And he said unto them, "Thus saith the Lord, the God of Israel: Put ye every man his sword upon his thigh . . ." And the sons of Levi did according to the word of Moses*[3] (Exod. 32:26–28). Then Levi even "lent" something to God at Shittim, as it is said, *Phinehas, the son of Eleazar, the son of Aaron the priest, hath turned My wrath away from the children of Israel, in that he was very jealous for My sake among them, so that I consumed not the children of Israel in My jealousy* (Num. 25:11). But Simeon not only did not repay his "debt" but even "borrowed" more, as it is said, *Now the name of the man of Israel that was slain, who was slain with the Midianitish woman, was Zimri, the son of Salu, a prince of a father's house among the Simeonites* (Num. 25:14). Therefore Scripture says, *And of Levi he said.*[4]

Thy Thummim and Thy Urim be with Thy holy one—he who is destined to wear the Urim and Thummim in the future; (or,) *with Thy holy one,* with him who is dealt with graciously by your children[5]—*whom Thou didst prove at Massah*—Thou hast proven him with many trials, and he proved steadfast in all of them—*with whom Thou didst strive at the waters of Meribah* (33:8)—Thou hast accused him falsely, for while Moses said, *Hear now, ye rebels, (are we to bring you forth water out of this rock?)* (Num. 20:10), what did Aaron and Miriam do?[6]

Piska 350

Who said of his father, and of his mother, "I have not seen him" (33:9): Could one possibly imagine that (the Tribe of) Levi was guilty of idolatry?[1] Was it not stated elsewhere, *Then Moses stood in the gate (of the camp . . . and all the sons of Levi gathered themselves together unto him)* (Exod. 32:26–27)? Rather, this refers to his mother's father who was an Israelite.

Neither did he acknowledge his brethren—this refers to his mother's brother who was an Israelite—*nor knew he his own children*—this refers to his daughter's son who was an Israelite—*for they have observed Thy word*—in Egypt—*and keep Thy covenant* (33:9)—in the wilderness.[2] Another interpretation: *For they have observed Thy word*—in Egypt—*and keep Thy covenant*—in the matter of the spies.[3]

Piska 351

They shall teach Jacob Thine ordinances (33:10): This shows that all instructions must issue from their mouths alone, as it is said, *And according to their word shall every controversy and every stroke be* (21:5). *Controversy* refers to any controversies concerning the (red) heifer,[1] the heifer (of the herd),[2] and the woman suspected of adultery.[3] *Stroke*[4] refers to plagues affecting both men and houses.

And Israel Thy Torah (33:10): This shows that two Torahs[5] were given to Israel, one Oral and one Written. Agnitus,[6] the (Roman) general, asked Rabban Gamaliel, "How many Torahs were given to

Israel?," to which R. Gamaliel replied, "Two, one Oral and one Written."[7]

They shall put incense before Thee—this refers to the incense[8] which is within—*and whole burnt offering upon Thine altar* (33:10)—this refers to the meal offering of the priest, as it is said, *And every meal offering of the priest shall be wholly made to smoke* (Lev. 6:16). Another interpretation: *They shall put incense before Thee*—this refers to the incense which is within—*and whole burnt offering upon Thine altar*—this refers to the parts of the burnt offering.

Piṣḳa 352

Bless, Lord, his substance (33:11): (Bless him with) possessions. Hence the Sages have said: Most priests are wealthy. The Sages said in the name of Abbah Hedores[1]: Scripture says, *I have been young, and now am old; yet have I not seen the righteous forsaken nor his seed begging bread* (Ps. 37–25)—this refers to the seed of Aaron.

And accept the work of his hands—the Levites make Israel acceptable to their Father in heaven—*smite through the loins of them that rise up against him* (33:11)—anyone who disputes the legitimacy of their priesthood immediately falls.

Another interpretation: *Smite through the loins of them that rise up against him*—this refers to Korah[2]—*and of them that hate him, that they rise not again* (33:11)—this refers to Uzziah.[3]

Of Benjamin he said: The beloved of the Lord (33:12): Favored is Benjamin, for he is called the beloved of God. A king has many favorites, but the most favored of all is the one whom the king loves. Six are called "beloved"; the Holy One, blessed be He, is called "beloved," as it is said, *Let me sing of my Beloved* (Isa. 5:1). Abraham is called "beloved," as it is said, *What hath my beloved to do in My house?* (Jer. 11:15). Benjamin is called "beloved," as it is said, *Of Benjamin he said: The beloved of the Lord.* Solomon is called "beloved," as it is said, *And He sent by the hand of Nathan the prophet, and he called his name Jedidiah ("beloved of the Lord")* (2 Sam. 12:25). (The people of) Israel are called "beloved," as it is said, *I have given the beloved one of My soul* (Jer. 12:7). The Temple (in Jerusalem) is called "beloved," as it is said, *How beloved are Thy tabernacles* (Ps. 84:2). Let the beloved son of the beloved one come and build the beloved house for the Beloved (God). Let Israel, who are called "beloved," the children of Abraham, who is called "beloved," come and build the Temple, which is called "beloved," in the portion of Benjamin, who is called "beloved," for the Holy One, blessed be He, who is called "Beloved."[4]

Shall dwell in safety by Him (33:12): *Safety* means security, as it is said, *And they shall dwell in safety in the wilderness, and sleep in the woods* (Ezek. 34:25).

He covereth him all the day—this refers to the First Temple—*all the day*—this refers to the Second Temple—*and He dwelleth between his shoulders* (33:12)—built and beautified in the future.[5] Another interpretation: *He covereth him*—in this world—*all the day*—in the days of the Messiah—*and He dwelleth between his shoulders*—built and beautified in the future. Similarly you find that Abraham saw it built, saw it destroyed, and saw it rebuilt,[6] as it is said, *And Abraham called the name of that place Adonai-Jireh*—indicating that it was built—*as it is said to this day, "In the mount*—indicating that it was destroyed—*where the Lord is seen"* (Gen. 22:14)—indicating that (he saw it) built and beautified in the future.[7] Similarly you find that Isaac also saw it built, saw it destroyed, and saw it rebuilt, as it is said, *See, the smell of my son*—indicating that it was built—*is as the smell of a field*—indicating that it was destroyed—*which the Lord hath blessed* (Gen. 27:27)—indicating that (he saw it) built and beautified in the future, as it is said, *For there the Lord commanded the blessing, even life for ever* (Ps. 133:3).[8] So also you find that Jacob saw it built, saw it destroyed, and saw it rebuilt, as it is said, *And he was afraid, and said, "How full of awe is this place*—indicating that it was built—*this is none*—indicating that it was destroyed—*other than the house of God, and this is the gate of heaven"* (Gen. 28:17)—indicating that (he saw it) built and beautified in the future.[9]

And He dwelleth between his shoulders (33:12): Whether the Temple is destroyed or not, as it is said, *All the Kingdoms of the earth hath the Lord, the God of heaven, given me, (and He hath charged me to build Him a house in Jerusalem, which is in Judah)* (2 Chron. 36:23). Another interpretation: *And He dwelleth between his shoulders*: Just as the shoulders are the highest part of the ox, so the Temple is the highest part of the world, as it is said, *Then shalt thou arise and get thee up unto the place (which the Lord . . . shall choose)* (17:8), and, *And many peoples shall go and say, "Come ye, and let us go up to the mountain of the Lord"* (Isa. 2:3). Scripture does not say "Gad from the east, and Dan from the west," but *many peoples*. Rabbi (Judah the Prince) says: In (the descriptions) of all the borders Scripture says, *And the border shall go down,* or *And the border was drawn,*[10] while here it says, *And the border went up by the valley of the son of Hinnom unto the side of the Jebusite southward—the same is Jerusalem* (Josh. 15:8). This shows that the Chosen House was built in the portion of Benjamin. R. Meir says: The Chosen House was built in the portion of Benjamin, and a triangular section[11] extended from that portion to that of Judah, as it is said, *And He*[12] *dwelleth between his shoulders.* How then am I to understand the passage, *The scepter shall not depart from Judah* (Gen. 49:10)? That it refers to the Hall of Hewn Stones[13] which was situated in the portion of Judah, as it is said, *Moreover He abhorred the tent of Joseph, and chose not the Tribe of Ephraim, but chose the Tribe of Judah* (Ps. 78:67–68). However, the main building was built in the portion of Joseph in Shiloh. [R. Judah says: The Temple was in the portion of Judah,] as it is said, *But thou, Beth-lehem Ephrathah, which art little to be among the thousands of Judah, (out of thee shall one come forth unto Me that is to be ruler in Israel)* (Mic. 5:1), and *Ephrathah* always refers to Beth-lehem, as it is said, *And Rachel died, and was buried in the way to Ephrath—the same is Beth-lehem* (Gen. 35:19). R. Meir says: She died in the portion of her son Benjamin, as it is said, *And as for me, when I came from Paddan, Rachel died unto me in the land of Canaan in the way, when there was still some way to come unto Ephrath* (Gen. 48:7), and *Ephrathah* always refers to Beth-lehem, as it is said, *But thou, Beth-lehem Ephrathah* (Mic. 5:1). I might conclude therefrom that Ephrath was situated in the portion of Joseph, Rachel's son; therefore Scripture says (elsewhere), *Lo, we heard of it as being in Ephrath; we found it in the field of the wood* (Ps. 132:6), in the (portion) of him who is likened to a beast of the forest. And who is that? Benjamin, as it is said, *Benjamin is a wolf that raveneth* (Gen. 49:27). Benjamin was thus found worthy of having the Shekinah dwell in his portion. You find therefore that when Joshua apportioned the Land of Israel among the Tribes, he set aside the lush pasture of Jericho, five hundred cubits by five hundred cubits, and gave the major portion of it to the children of Jonadab the son of Rechab,[14] and they benefited from it for four hundred and forty years, as it is said, *And it came to pass in the four hundred and eightieth year . . . (that he began to build the house of the Lord)* (1 Kings 6:1). Exclude from that the forty years when Israel was in the wilderness, and you find that the Rechabites benefited from it for four hundred and forty years, but that when the Shekinah came to dwell in the portion of

Benjamin, they left it in the Benjamites' favor,[15] as it is said, *And the children of the Kenite, Moses' father-in-law, went up out of the city of palm trees with the children of Judah* (Judg. 1:16).

[*And Moses said unto Hobab, the son of Reuel the Midianite, Moses' father-in-law* (Num. 10:29): Would it ever occur to anyone that Moses said to Jethro, "Come, and we will give you a portion in the land"? Is it not said also, *Come thee with us, and we will do thee good* (Num. 10:29)? What does the verse mean by saying further, *For the Lord hath spoken good concerning Israel* (Num. 10:29)? This refers to the lush pasture of Jericho, from which the descendants of Jethro benefited until the Chosen House was built for the Tribes. *And he said unto him, "I will not go"* (Num. 10:30): Jethro said to Moses, "When you apportion the Land of Israel among the Tribes tomorrow, what Tribe from amongst you will be willing to give me one vineyard out of his portion or one furrow out of his portion? Rather, will I go to my own land, and eat the fruit of my own land, and drink the wine of my own vineyard." Thus also you find that some Israelites left a place (in Israel) of fruit, food, and drink, and went instead to hoe (the soil) in the wilderness and to study Torah with Jabez; such a one was Otniel son of Kenaz.[16]

Scripture states in one place, *So David bought the threshing floor and the oxen for fifty shekels of silver* (2 Sam. 24:24), while in another place it states, *So David gave to Ornan for the place six hundred shekels of gold by weight* (1 Chron. 21:25). How can it say *shekels of gold* when elsewhere it says *shekels of silver*? Or how can it say *shekels of silver* when elsewhere it says *shekels of gold*? It is impossible. One must therefore conclude that David purchased the place for silver, but weighed it out in gold.[17] But how can Scripture say *fifty* when elsewhere it says *six hundred*? Or how can it say *six hundred* when elsewhere it says *fifty*? It is impossible. One must therefore conclude that when David saw that the place was suitable for building the Chosen House, he collected fifty shekels from each Tribe, totaling six hundred shekels from all the Tribes together.][18]

Why was Benjamin deemed worthy[19] of having the Shekinah dwell in his portion? A parable: A king used to come for periodic visits to his sons, and each one of them would say, "He will stay with me." The youngest of them all, however, said, "Is it possible that my father would leave my elder brothers to stay with me?" He then arose, his face downcast and his soul sad. Said (the king), "Did you notice how my youngest son arose, his face downcast and his soul sad? Now therefore you shall supply me with food and drink, but I shall stay with him." Thus also the Holy One, blessed be He, said, "The Chosen House shall be in the portion of Benjamin, but the sacrifices shall come from all the Tribes." Another interpretation: Why was Benjamin deemed worthy of having the Shekinah dwell in his portion? Because all the other (fathers of the) Tribes were born outside of the Land of Israel while Benjamin was born in the Land. Another interpretation: All the other Tribes were involved in the selling of Joseph while Benjamin was not. Said the Holy One, blessed be He, "If I tell them to build the Chosen House for Me, and they then pray before Me, I will not be moved to be merciful towards them, since they were not merciful towards their brother." Another interpretation: Why was Benjamin deemed worthy of having the Shekinah dwell in his portion? A parable: A king had many sons. When they grew up, each one of them went forth and seized a place for himself. But the youngest son, who was his father's favorite, would eat and drink with him, and the king would lean on him when he went out and when he came back. Thus also Benjamin the righteous was the youngest of all the (fathers of the) Tribes, and his father Jacob would eat and drink with him and would lean upon him when he went out and when he came back. Said the Holy One, blessed be He, "I shall cause My Shekinah to dwell in the place where that righteous man[20] placed his hands," as it is said, *And He dwelleth between his shoulders.*

Pisḳa 353

And of Joseph he said: Blessed of the Lord be his land—this shows that the land of Joseph was blessed above all the lands—*for the precious things of heaven, for the dew*—that dew be found there at all times—*and for the deep that coucheth beneath* (33:13)—this shows that it is amply watered by springs.

And for the precious things of the fruits of the sun (33:14): This shows that the land of Joseph was exposed to the sun, and there are no fruits in the world better or sweeter than those that see the sun; and just as the land was exposed to the sun, so was it exposed to the moon, as it is said, *and for the precious things of the yield of the moons* (33:14).

And for the tops of the ancient mountains—this shows that the mountains of the territory of Joseph are older than the mountains of the Sanctuary, and that the mountains of the Sanctuary are older than the mountains of the Land of Israel—*and for the precious things of the everlasting hills* (33:15)—this shows that the patriarchs and matriarchs are called mountains and hills, as it is said, *I will get me to the mountain of myrrh, and to the hill of frankincense* (Song 4:6).[1]

And for the precious things of the earth and the fullness thereof (33:16). This shows that the land of Joseph was full and lacked no blessing. R. Simeon ben Yoḥai says: If a man anchors his ship in the portion of Joseph, he will need nothing else.

And the good will of Him that dwelt in the bush—Joseph performed the will of Him who revealed Himself to Moses in the (burning) bush—*let the blessing come upon the head of Joseph*—he was first to come to Egypt, and he will come first in the future—*and upon the crown (nĕzir) of the head of him that is prince among his brethren* (33:16)—upon him who was removed far away by his brothers and made a Nazirite (*nazir*).[2]

His firstling bullock, majesty (hadar) is his—this shows that Moses was given splendor (*hod*) while Joshua was given majesty (*hadar*), for had Joshua been given splendor, the world would not have been able to resist him[3]—*and his horns are the horns of the wild ox* (33:17): The strength of the bullock is great, but his horns are not comely, while the horns of the wild ox are comely, but his strength is not great; Joshua was accordingly given the strength of the bullock but the horns of the wild ox.

With them he shall gore the peoples, (all of them) (33:17): But did Joshua conquer all the nations? Did he not conquer only thirty-one kingdoms? This shows that the kingdoms and dominions he conquered had extended from one end of the world to the other.

All of them, even the ends of the earth (33:17): But did Joshua conquer all the lands? Did he not conquer only a small part of them? But all the kingdoms that he subjugated were (large) kingdoms and dominions. R. Judah says: Were the thirty-one kings that he subjugated all in the Land of Israel? Rather, the custom at that time was the same as that followed currently in Rome, where any king or ruler who has not purchased palaces and villas in Rome says, "I have accomplished nothing." So also any king or ruler who had not acquired palaces and villas in the Land of Israel would say, "I have accomplished nothing."[4]

And they are the ten thousands of Ephraim (33:17): Since we would not know explicitly how much wealth was possessed by the Canaanites, Scripture informs us elsewhere, *And Adoni-bezek said, "Threescore and ten kings, having their thumbs and their great toes cut off, gathered food under my table"* (Judg. 1:7). Is this not a matter of inference from the minor to the major? If Adoni-bezek (alone), who was not even fit to be numbered among the kings of Canaan, had threescore and ten kings gathering food under his table, just imagine how much wealth was possessed by (all) the Canaanites!

And they are the thousands of Manasseh (33:17): Since we would not know explicitly how many Canaanites Joshua had slain, Scripture informs us elsewhere, *Now Zebah and Zalmunna were in Karkor, and their hosts with them, about fifteen thousand men, all that were left of all the host of the children of the east; for there fell a hundred and twenty thousand men* (Judg. 8:10). This comes to a total of one hundred and thirty-five thousand, which fulfills that which is said, *And they are the ten thousands of Ephraim, and they are the thousands of Manasseh.*[5]

Pisḳa 354

And of Zebulun he said (33:18): Why is this stated? Because elsewhere it is said, *And from among his brethren he took five men, and presented them unto Pharaoh* (Gen. 47:2), but their names are not specified. Zebulun was one of them.[1]

Rejoice, Zebulun, in thy going out (33:18): This shows that Zebulun was an agent for his brothers. He would buy (goods) from his brothers and sell them to Gentiles, and would buy from Gentiles and sell to his brothers.

And Issachar, in thy tents (33:18): This shows that the Tribe of Issachar was outstanding in Torah,[2] as it is said, *And the children of Issachar, men that had understanding of the times* (1 Chron. 12:33). And similarly we find that his father praised him, as it is said, *For he saw a resting place that it was good* (Gen. 49:15). Another interpretation: *And Issachar, in thy tents*—this shows that it would have been appropriate for the Chosen House to be built in the portion of Issachar.[3]

They shall call peoples unto the mountain (33:19): Hence you conclude that the nations and kingdoms would gather together and come to see the goods available in the Land of Israel, and would say, "Since we have taken the trouble to come here, let us see what kind of goods the Jews have to offer." They would then go up to Jerusalem and observe the people of Israel worshiping only one God and eating only one kind of food, whereas among the nations, the god of one nation is not the god of another, and the food of one nation is not the food of another. So they would say, "There is no better nation for us to cling to than this." (Hence, *They shall call peoples unto the mountain.*)[4] And whence do you learn that the nations would not budge from there until they became proselytes and offered sacrifices and burnt offerings? From what the verse goes on to say, *There shall they offer sacrifices of righteousness* (33:19).[5]

For they shall suck the abundance of the seas (33:19): Two take away abundantly and give abundantly, and these are the sea and the government. The sea gives abundantly and takes away abundantly. The government gives abundantly and takes away abundantly.

Another interpretation: *For they shall suck the abundance of the seas*: This refers to the bay of Haifa, which has treasures hidden away for the righteous in the future.[6] Whence do you learn that whenever a ship is lost in the Great (Mediterranean) Sea with a treasure of silver, gold, precious stones, pearls, glassware, and all other kinds of precious cargo, the Great Sea spews it up into the bay of Haifa, where it is hidden away for the righteous in the future? From the verse, *For they shall suck the abundance of the seas.* R. Jose said: Once, as I was walking from Chezib to Tyre, I came across an old man. I asked him, "How do you make your living?" He replied, "From the *ḥillazon.*"[7] I asked him, "Is that still available?" He replied, "By heaven, there is a place in the sea which is surrounded by mountains and encircled by venomous spiders. And no man goes there but that he is bitten by the spiders and dies, and (his corpse) rots there." I said, "It is clear that it is hidden away for the righteous in the future."

And the hidden treasures of the sand (33:19): *Treasures* refers to the *ḥillazon, hidden* refers to the *ṭariṯ,*[8] *sand* refers to glassware. The Tribe of Zebulun complained to God, saying, "Master of the universe, Thou hast given my brothers the land, and to me Thou hast given the sea.[9] To my brothers Thou hast given fields and vineyards, and to me Thou hast given the *ḥillazon*!" God replied, "In the end I shall make them dependent upon you because of the *ḥillazon.*" Said Zebulun, "Master of the universe, how will I know this?" God replied, "You shall have a sign of it in that anyone who steals from you will not profit from his goods at all."[10]

Pisḳa 355

And of Gad he said (33:20): Why is this stated? Because elsewhere it is said, *And from among his brethren he took five men* (Gen. 47:2), but their names are not specified. Gad was one of them.[1]

Blessed be He that enlargeth Gad—this shows that the territory of Gad widens toward the east—*he dwelleth as a lioness*—this shows that he is next to the border, for anyone who is next to the border is compared to lions—*and teareth the arm, yea, the crown of the head* (33:20)—*teareth the arm,* in the past; *the crown of the head,* in the future.

And he chose a first part for himself (33:21): He was at the head at first, and he will come at the head in the future.

For there a portion of a ruler was reserved (33:21): This refers to the burial plot of Moses which was in the portion of Gad. But did not Moses die in the portion of Reuben, as it is said, *Get thee up into this mountain of Abarim, unto Mount Nebo* (32:49), and Nebo is in the portion of Reuben, as it is said, *And the children of Reuben built Heshbon, and Elealeh, and Kiriathaim; and Nebo and Baal-meon* (Num. 32:37–38)? What then does *For there a portion of a ruler was reserved* mean? It means that Moses was carried upon the wings of the Shekinah four miles from the portion of Reuben to the portion of Gad, while the ministering angels mourned for him, saying, "May he come in peace and rest upon his bier!" This[2] is one of the things which were created at twilight before the (first) Sabbath, and they are: the rainbow, the manna, the well (in the wilderness), writing and writing instruments, the (stone) tablets, the mouth of (Balaam's) ass, the mouth of the earth, the burial place of Moses, the cave in which Moses and Elijah stood, and Aaron's staff with its (carved) almonds and blossoms. Some say, also Adam's clothes; others say, also garments[3] and the noxious spirits. R. Josiah says in the name of his father: The ram (sacrificed in Isaac's stead) and the *šamir*[4] were also among them. R. Nehemiah says: Fire and the she-mule were also among them.[5] R. Judah says: Also the tongs,[6] as the saying puts it, "Tongs are made with (the use of) tongs, so how were the first tongs made?" Therefore it must have been created.[7] They said to him, "It could have been cast in a mold and cut out of it, therefore it was not created."[8]

And there came the heads of the people (33:21): Moses made the Torah *tawim*.[9] Another interpretation: This shows that in the future Moses will enter at the head of every group—at the head of the group of Bible scholars, at the head of the group of Mishnah scholars, at the head of the group of Talmud scholars—and take his reward with each one of them,[10] as it is said, *Therefore will I divide him a portion among the great, and he shall divide the spoil with the mighty* (Isa. 53:12).

He executed the righteousness of the Lord (33:21): What righteousness did Moses perform for Israel? Is it not true that all during those forty years that Israel was in the wilderness a well sprang up for them, manna came down for them, pheasants were available for them, and the clouds of glory encompassed them? Rather, this refers to what Moses said, *If there be among you a needy man* (15:7).[11]

He executed the righteousness of the Lord: This shows that righteousness is kept under the throne of glory together with justice, as it is said, *Thus saith the Lord: Keep ye justice, and do righteousness* (Isa. 56:1).

And of Dan he said (33:21): Why is this stated? Because elsewhere it is said, *And from among his brethren he took five men* (Gen. 47:2), but their names are not specified. Dan was one of them.

Dan is a lion's whelp—this shows that Dan is next to the border, for anyone who is next to the border is likened to lions—*that leapeth forth from Bashan* (33:21): Just as a stream spurts forth from one place and then divides itself into two channels, so the Tribe of Dan takes a portion for itself in two places, as it is said, *And the border of the children of Dan was too strait for them; so the children of Dan went up and fought* (Josh. 19:47).

And of Naphtali he said (33:23): Why is this stated? Because elsewhere it is said, *And from among his brethren he took five men* (Gen. 47:2), but their names are not specified. Naphtali was one of them.

O Naphtali, satisfied with favor—this shows that Naphtali was happy with his portion, with the sea, the fish, and the ships (that were his)—*and full with the blessing of the Lord* (33:23): This refers to the valley of Gennesaret. Rabbi (Judah the Prince) says: This refers to the court of Tiberias, of which it is written, *He will fulfill the desire of them that fear Him* (Ps. 145:19).

(Possess thou) the sea—this refers to the lake of Sofne[12]—*and the south* (33:23)—this refers to the lake of Tiberias. *Possess thou*—this shows that he took possession of the entire strip of his portion in the south.

And of Asher he said (33:24): Why is this stated? Because elsewhere it is said, *And from among his brethren he took five men* (Gen. 47:2), but their names are not specified. Asher was one of them.

Blessed be Asher above sons—there was none among the (fathers of the) Tribes as blessed with sons as was Asher—*let him be favored of his brethren* (33:24)—he favored his brothers with omphakinon oil[13] and with *ḳibla᾽ot,*[14] and they favored him with produce.

Another interpretation: *Let him be favored of his brethren*: When Reuben perpetrated that (foul) deed,[15] Asher went and told his brothers about it, but they rebuked him, saying, "Is that how you talk about our eldest brother?" When Reuben admitted the deed, however, they were reconciled with Asher. Hence it is said, *Let him be favored of his brethren.*

Another interpretation: *Let him be favored of his brethren*: When the Tribes were comparing their pedigrees, this one said, "The right to serve as Levites should be mine," while that one said, "The right to serve as Levites should be mine." Asher then said to them, "If Scripture begins the pedigree with Reuben, the right to serve as Levites should belong to me; if Scripture begins with Benjamin, the right to serve as Levites should belong to the Tribe of Levi." He thus pacified his brothers, hence it is said, *Let him be favored of his brethren.*[16]

Another interpretation: *Let him be favored of his brethren*—there is none among the lands that observes the law of the Sabbatical year as does the land of Asher—*and let him dip his foot in oil* (33:24): This shows that the land of Asher gushed forth oil like a fountain. It happened once that the people of Laodicea had a shortage[17] of oil. So they appointed a deputy and told him, "Go and purchase for us one hundred myriad (*zuz*) worth of oil." He went to Tyre and said to the people there, "I need one hundred myriad (*zuz*) worth of oil." They replied, "Go to Gush Halab."[18] He went to Gush Halab and said to the people there, "I need one hundred myriad (*zuz*) worth of oil." They replied, "Go to a certain man." He went to the man's house, but did not find him there, and was told, "He is in the field." The deputy went off and found him breaking the ground under his olive trees. He said to him, "I need one hundred myriad (*zuz*) worth of oil." The man replied, "Wait until I finish with my olive trees." When he finished with his olive trees, he took his tools and slowly walked to the deputy, whereat the latter thought, "Can this fellow really have one hundred myriad (*zuz*) worth of oil? It seems that the Jews have made sport with me." When the man arrived at his house, he called his maidservant and said to her, "Come and wash our feet." She filled a basin with oil and washed their feet, thus fulfilling what is said, *And let him dip his foot in oil.* The man then set bread before the deputy, and they ate and drank. After they had eaten and drunk, the man arose and measured out for him a hundred myriad (*zuz*) worth of oil. Then he asked him, "Would you like to have more?" The deputy replied, "I have no more money." The man said to him, "Take it anyway, and I will come with you and collect my money." He then arose and measured out eighteen more myriad (*zuz*) worth of oil. It is said that the man left no camel or ass in the Land of Israel that he did not hire (to carry the oil). The people of Laodicea recognized him, came three miles out to meet him, and praised him with lavish praise. He said to them, "Do not lavish your praise upon me, but rather upon this man, for all of this is his, and furthermore, I owe him for eighteen myriad (*zuz*) worth of oil," thus fulfilling what is said, *There is that pretendeth himself rich, yet hath nothing; there is that pretendeth himself poor, yet hath great wealth* (Prov. 13:7).[19]

Iron and brass shall be thy bars—this shows that the land of Asher served as the bar of the Land of Israel[20]—*and as thy days, so shall thy strength (dob̲ʾek̲a) be* (33:25)—this shows that all the lands stream (*dob̲ʾot̲*) their money to the Land of Israel, as it is said, *And Joseph gathered up all the money,* etc. (Gen. 47:14).

There is none like unto God, O Jeshurun (33:26): Israel says, *There is none like unto God,* and the holy spirit responds, *O Jeshurun.*[21] Israel says, *Who is like unto thee, O Lord, among the mighty?* (Exod. 15:11), and the holy spirit responds, *Happy art thou, O Israel, who is like unto thee?* (33:29). Israel says, *Hear, O Israel, the Lord our God, the Lord is one* (6:4), and the holy spirit responds, *And who is like Thy people Israel, a nation one in the earth* (1 Chron. 17:21). Israel says, *As an apple-tree among the trees of the wood, (so is my Beloved)* (Song 2:3), and the holy spirit responds, *As a lily among thorns, (so is my love)* (Song 2:2). Israel says, *This is my God, and I will glorify Him* (Exod. 15:2), and the holy spirit responds, *The people which I formed for Myself* (Isa. 43:21). Israel says, *For Thou art the glory of their strength* (Ps. 89:18), and the holy spirit responds, *Israel, in whom I will be glorified* (Isa. 49:3).

Who rideth upon the heavens as thy help—when Israel is upright and performs the will of God, He *rideth upon the heavens as thy help,* but when they do not perform His will—*and in His excellency on the skies* (33:26)—if one dare say such a thing. *And in His excellency on the skies*: All of the people of Israel gathered around Moses and said to him, "Our master Moses, tell us, what is the glory (of God) really like on high?" He replied, "You can surmise what the glory (of God) is like on high from the appearance of the lower heavens." A parable: To what may this be likened? To a man who said, "I wish to behold the glory of the king." He was told, "Go to the capital city and you will see him." He went there and saw a curtain set with precious stones and pearls and spread out at the entrance of the city. He could not take his eyes off of it, until he collapsed in a swoon. They then said to him, "If you could not take your eyes off of a curtain set with precious stones and pearls and spread out at the entrance of the city, until you collapsed in a swoon, how much more so had you entered the city (and beheld the glory of the king)." Hence it is said, *And in His excellency on the skies.*

Pisḳa 356

The eternal God is a dwelling place (mĕʿonah) (33:27): Three Scrolls (of Torah) were found in the Temple Court:[1] one read here *mĕʿon* (instead of *mĕʿonah*), another spelled (the feminine singular pronoun) *hiʾ*[2] (instead of the more common *huʾ* for both genders), and a third used the word *zaʿăṭuṭim* (for the common *nĕʿarim,* "young men"). The Sages rejected the first reading here and upheld the other two Scrolls, which read *mĕʿonah.* They found that one Scroll spelled *hiʾ* in nine places, while the other two spelled *hiʾ* in eleven places, and rejected the former and upheld the latter. They found one Scroll using *zaʿăṭuṭe* in *And he sent the young men of Israel* (Exod. 24:5) and in *And upon the nobles of the children of Israel* (Exod. 24:11), while the other two used *naʿăre,* and rejected the former and upheld the latter.

And underneath are the everlasting arms—this shows that the Land of Israel is the force which upholds the earth—*and He thrust out the enemy from before thee*—those who fled to Asia—*and said, "Destroy"* (33:27)—those who dwell in the Land of Israel.

And Israel dwelleth in safety (33:28): "Safety" means security,[3] as it is said, *And they shall dwell in safety in the wilderness* (Ezek. 34:25).

(The fountain of Jacob) alone (33:28): Not like the "alone" spoken of by Moses, *the Lord alone did lead him* (32:12), nor like the "alone" spoken of by Jeremiah, *I sat alone because of Thy hand* (Jer. 15:17), but like the "alone" spoken of by that wicked one (Balaam), *Lo, it is a people that shall dwell alone* (Num. 23:9).

The fountain of Jacob—with the blessing with which their father Jacob had blessed them, as it is said, *But God will be with you* (Gen. 48:21)—*in a land of corn and wine*—with the blessing with which their father Isaac had blessed them, as it is said, *So God give thee of the dew of heaven* (Gen. 27:28)—*yea, his heavens drop down dew* (33:28)—as it is said, *Drop down, ye heavens, from above* (Isa. 45:8).

Happy art thou, O Israel, who is like unto thee? (33:29): Israel says, *Who is like unto Thee, O Lord, among the mighty?* (Exod. 15:11), and the holy spirit responds, *Happy art thou, O Israel. Happy art thou, O Israel*: All Israel gathered together before Moses and said to him, "Our master Moses, tell us what good things the Holy One, blessed be He, has in store for us in the future." He replied, "I do not know what to tell you. Happy are you with that which is prepared for you." A parable: A man gave his son into the care of a tutor. The tutor took the boy around, showing him things, and telling him, "All of these trees will be yours. All of these vines will be yours. All of these olive trees will be yours." When he wearied of showing him all these things, he said to him, "I do not know what more to say to you. Happy are you with all that which is prepared for you." So too did Moses say to Israel, "I do not know what to tell you. Happy are you with that which is prepared for you," *Oh how abundant is Thy goodness, which Thou hast laid up for them that fear Thee* (Ps. 31:20).

Happy art thou, O Israel, who is like unto thee? A people saved by the Lord—a people whose salvation depends entirely upon the Shekinah, *O Israel, thou art saved by the Lord with an everlasting salvation* (Is. 45:17)—*the shield of thy help*—as it is said, *The God who is my rock, in Him I take refuge* (2 Sam. 22:3)—*and that is the sword of thy excellency* (33:29): The Holy One, blessed be He, said to Moses, "Moses, in the future I shall give back to Israel the same ornaments that I took from them at (Mount) Horeb," as it is said, *And the children of Israel stripped themselves of their ornaments from Mount Horeb onward* (Exod. 33:6);[4] "I have sworn an oath that I shall give them back to them in the future," as it is said, *As I live, saith the Lord, thou shalt surely clothe thee with them all as with an ornament, and gird thyself with them like a bride* (Isa. 49:18).

And thine enemies shall dwindle away (wĕ-yiḳḳaḥăšu) before thee (33:29): When Israel is prosperous, the nations of the world flatter (*mĕkaḥăšim*) them and act as if they were brothers. Thus Esau said to Jacob, *I have enough, my brother, let that which thou hast be thine* to Jacob, *I have enough, my brother, let that which thou hast be thine* (Gen. 33:9), and Hiram said to Solomon, *What cities are these, which thou hast given me, my brother?* (1 Kings 9:13).

And thou shalt tread upon their high places (33:29): As it is said, *Joshua called for all the men of Israel, and said unto the chiefs of the men of war that went with him, "Come near, put your feet upon the necks of these kings." And they came near, and put their feet upon the necks of them* (Josh. 10:24).

Pisḳa 357

And Moses went up from the plains of Moab (34:1): It is an elevation for him and not a degradation.[1] *From the plains of Moab*—this shows that the Holy One, blessed be He, showed him the line of kings that was to be descended from Ruth the Moabitess, namely David and his progeny.

Unto Mount Nebo, to the top of Pisgah (34:1): Just as the branch (*pisgah*) is separated from the (grape) cluster yet is not really separated, so the burial place of Moses is separated from the mountain, yet is not really separated, since the valley is between them.[2]

Over against Jericho (34:1): This shows that God showed Moses the line of prophets that was to arise from Rahab the harlot.[3]

And the Lord showed him all the land—this shows that He first showed him the Land of Israel inhabited in peace, and then showed him oppressors in possession of it—*even Gilead* (34:1): This shows that He showed him the Temple established in peace, and then showed to him destroyers demolishing it. "Gilead" means the Temple, as it is said, *Thou art Gilead unto Me, the head of Lebanon* (Jer. 22:6).[4]

As far as Dan (34:1): This shows that God first showed Moses the land of Dan inhabited in peace, and then showed him oppressors in possession of it. Another interpretation: *As far as Dan*: This shows that He first showed him the Tribe of Dan worshiping idols, as it is said, *And the children of Dan set up for themselves the graven image* (Judg. 18:30), and then showed him the redeemer of Israel who was to arise from that Tribe in the future. And who was this man? Samson son of Manoah.

And all Naphtali (34:2): This indicates that God showed to Moses the land of Naphtali inhabited in peace, and then showed him oppressors in possession of it. Another interpretation: This indicates that He showed him Barak son of Abinoam who waged war against Sisera and the hosts who were with him, (since) here Scripture says, *And all Naphtali,* while of Barak it says, *And she sent and called Barak the son of Abinoam out of Kadesh-Naphtali* (Judg. 4:6).

And the land of Ephraim (and Manasseh) (34:2): This indicates that He showed him the land of Ephraim inhabited in peace, and then showed him oppressors in possession of it. Another interpretation: *And the land of Ephraim*: This indicates that He showed him Joshua son of Nun waging war against the Canaanites, (since) here Scripture says, *And the land of Ephraim,* and elsewhere it says, *Of the Tribe of Ephraim, Hoshea the son of Nun* (Num. 13:8). *And Manasseh*: This indicates that He showed him the land of Manasseh inhabited in peace, and then showed him oppressors in possession of it. Another interpretation: *And Manasseh*: This indicates that He showed him Gideon the son of Joash, who waged war against Midian and Amalek. Another interpretation: Since Ephraim was the youngest, Scripture placed him next to the older, as it is said (of Gideon), *Behold, my family is the poorest in Manasseh* (Judg. 6:15).

And all the land of Judah (34:2): This indicates that He showed him the land of Judah inhabited in peace, and then showed him oppressors in possession of it. Another interpretation: *And all the land of Judah*: This indicates that He showed him David reigning as king, (since) here Scripture says, *And all the land of Judah,* and elsewhere it says, *Howbeit the Lord, the God of Israel, chose me out of all the house of my father to be king over all Israel for ever: (For he hath chosen Judah to be prince)* (1 Chron. 28:4).

As far as the hinder sea (34:2): This indicates that He showed him the entire West inhabited in peace, and then showed him oppressors in possession of it. Another interpretation: *As far as the hinder sea*: Read not *As far as the hinder sea (yam)* but "As far as the hinder day (*yom*)"—this indicates that He showed him the entire world, from the day of creation to the resurrection of the dead.

And the South (34:3): This indicates that God showed to Moses the south inhabited in peace, and then showed him oppressors in possession of it. Another interpretation: *And the South*: This indicates that He showed him the cave of Machpelah in which the patriarchs are buried, (since) here Scripture says *And the South,* and elsewhere it says, *And they went up into the South, and came unto Hebron*[5] (Num. 13:22).

And the Plain (34:3): This indicates that He showed him Solomon son of David making vessels for the Temple, (since) here Scripture says *And the Plain,* and elsewhere it says, *In the plain of the Jordan did the king cast them* (1 Kings 7:46).

Even the valley of Jericho (34:3): This indicates that He showed him Gog and all his multitude who were destined to fall in the valley of Jericho. Another interpretation: Just as the valley is so clear that one (can see it) as it is and a field of barley (in it) as it is,[6] so did He show him the entire world in the valley of Jericho.

The city of palm trees (34:3): This indicates that He showed him the Garden of Eden, with the righteous strolling about in it, for they are compared to palm trees, as it is said, *The righteous shall flourish like the palm tree* (Ps. 92:13). Another interpretation: This indicates that He showed him Gehenna, which is near by its side, and which is narrow at the top and wide at the bottom, as it is said, *Yea, He hath allured thee out of distress into a broad place, where there is no straitness* (Job 36:16).[7]

As far as Zoar (34:3): This refers to the oppressors[8] of Israel, such as the constables employed by the government, who are destined to perish with it.

And the Lord said unto him: "This is the land" (34:4): He said to him, "The patriarchs, they received only My oath, whereas you, *I have caused thee to see it with thine own eyes* (34:4)."

But thou shalt not go over thither (34:4): Here Scripture says, *But thou shalt not go over thither,* and elsewhere it says, *But thou shalt not go thither* (32:52).[9] What then does *But thou shalt not go over thither* imply? Said Moses, "If I may not enter it alive, let me enter it dead." Replied God, "*But thou shalt not go thither.*" Said Moses, "If I may not enter it as a king, let me enter it as a commoner. If I cannot enter it alive, let me enter it dead." Replied God, "*But thou shalt not go over thither,* neither as a king nor as a commoner, neither alive nor dead."

So Moses . . . died there (34:5): Is it possible that Moses died and yet himself wrote *So Moses died there?* Rather, Moses wrote everything until this point, and from here on Joshua wrote the rest. R. Meir objected: Scripture says, *And Moses wrote this Torah* (31:9); is it possible that Moses would have given the Torah while it lacked even a single letter? Rather, this shows that Moses wrote what the Holy One, blessed be He, told him to write, just as it is said (of Jeremiah), *Then Baruch answered them: "He (Jeremiah) pronounced all these words unto me with his mouth, (and I wrote them with ink in the book)"* (Jer. 36:18).[10] R. Eliezer says: A heavenly voice went forth from within the camp for twelve miles in every direction proclaiming, "Moses is dead," as is evident[11] from the verse, "Woe! Moses is dead."[12] Whence do we learn that forgiveness went forth from the grave of Moses to the graves of the patriarchs? From (the use of the same adverb *there*) in this verse, *So Moses died there,* and in the verse, *There they buried Abraham and Sarah his wife* (Gen. 49:31). Others say: Moses never died, and he stands and serves on high, as is shown by the use of the same adverb *there* in this verse and in the verse, *And he was there with the Lord* (Exod. 34:28).[13]

The servant of the Lord (34:5): Scripture speaks in praise of Moses and not in deprecation of him,[14] for we find that the early prophets were called "servants," as it is said, *For the Lord God will do nothing but He revealeth His counsel unto His servants the prophets* (Amos 3:7).

According to the word of the Lord (34:5): When God takes the soul of the righteous, He takes it from them with gentleness. To what may this be likened? To the parable of a bailee who was so trustworthy that everyone in the city deposited his goods with him. When the bailor himself would come to claim his deposit, the bailee would take it out and hand it to him, since the bailee knew where it was. But when the bailor had to send his son, his servant, or his messenger (to the bailee for his deposit), he had to turn everything upside down, since he did not know where it was. Thus also, when God takes the soul of the righteous, He takes it with gentleness, but when he takes the souls of the wicked, He does so through merciless and cruel angels, so that they would drag their souls along, as it is said, *Therefore a cruel angel shall be sent against him* (Prov. 17:11), and, *Their soul perisheth in youth* (Job. 36:14).

And he was buried in the valley (34:6): Since Scripture says *in the valley,* why does it go on to say, *in the land of Moab* (34:6)? Or since it says *in the land of Moab,* why does it say *in the valley?* To inform you that Moses died in the portion of Reuben and was buried in the field possessed by Gad.[15]

And no man knoweth of his sepulcher (unto this day) (34:6): Some say: Even Moses himself does not know the place of his sepulcher, as it is said, *And no man knoweth of his sepulcher,* and "man" always refers to Moses, as it is said, *Now the man Moses was very meek* (Num. 12:3). The imperial house of Caesar once sent two commissioners with orders, "Go and find the sepulcher of Moses." They climbed up above and saw the bier down below, but when they went down below, they saw it up above. They then split up, half of them going up and half going down, but those above saw the bier below, while those below saw it above. Hence Scripture says, *And no man knoweth of his sepulcher (unto this day).*[16]

And Moses was a hundred and twenty years old (when he died) (34:7): He was one of four who died at the age of one hundred and twenty, and these were Moses, Hillel the Elder, Rabban Johanan ben Zakkai, and R. ʿAḳiba. Moses was in Egypt for forty years and in Midian for forty years, and led Israel for forty years. Hillel the Elder came up from Babylonia when he was forty years old, served the Sages for forty years, and led Israel for forty years. Rabban Johanan ben Zakkai was a merchant for forty years, served the Sages for forty years, and led Israel for forty years. R. ʿAḳiba began to study Torah when he was forty, served the Sages for forty years, and led Israel for forty years.[17] There are six pairs of persons who lived the same number of years: Rebekah and Kohath, Levi and Amram, Joseph and Joshua, Samuel and Solomon, Moses and Hillel the Elder, Rabban Johanan ben Zakkai and R. ʿAḳiba.[18]

His eye was not dim—this proves that the eyes of the dead turn dim—*nor his natural force abated* (34:7): R. Eliezer ben Jacob says: Read not *nor his natural force abated* but "even now his natural force is still not abated," for if anyone should touch the flesh of Moses, its natural force would spring out in all directions.[19]

And the children of Israel wept for Moses—this implies, for (at least) one day—*so the days*—the plural implies (at least) two days—*of weeping in the mourning for Moses were ended* (34:8)—thus totaling three days. Why then does Scripture say (at the beginning of this verse), *(And the children of Israel wept for Moses . . .) thirty days?*[20] This indicates that they wept for him thirty days prior to his death. And whence do we learn that the period of Naziriteship is also thirty days? From the fact that Scripture says here *the days of* and says also elsewhere *the days of* (Num. 6:4) (in referring to the Nazirite). Just as *the days of* stated here means thirty days, so *the days of* there means thirty days.

And Joshua the son of Nun was full of the spirit of wisdom—how so?—*for Moses had laid his hands upon him; and the children of Israel hearkened unto him*—there is no hearkening greater than this—*and did as the Lord commanded Moses* (34:9): Yet his fear was not yet upon them, as it is said, *On that day the Lord magnified Joshua in the sight of all Israel, (and they feared him, as they feared Moses)* (Josh. 4:14). Only then did his fear come upon them.

And there hath not arisen a prophet since in Israel like unto Moses (34:10): None has arisen in Israel, but one has arisen among the nations. And who was he? Balaam son of Beor. Yet there is a difference between the prophecy of Moses and that of Balaam: Moses did not know who was speaking to him (out of the burning bush), whereas Balaam did know who was speaking to him, as it is said, *The saying of him who heareth the words of God* (Num. 24:16). Moses did not know when God would speak to him, whereas Balaam did know, as it is said, *And knoweth the knowledge of the Most High* (Num. 24:16). Moses was spoken to by God only while he was standing, as it is said, *But as for thee, stand thou here by Me, (and I will speak unto thee)* (5:28), whereas Balaam was spoken to when he was fallen down, as it is said, *Who seeth the vision of the Almighty, fallen down, yet with open eyes* (Num. 24:4).[21] To what may this be likened? To the parable of the king's butcher who knows what the king's expenses are for supplying his table.

Whom the Lord knew face to face (34:10): Why is this said? Because elsewhere it is said, *And he said, "Show me, I pray thee, Thy glory"* (Exod. 33:18). God said to Moses, "In this world, which is symbolized by 'face,' as it is said, *Thou canst not see My face* (Exod. 33:20), you may not see, but in the world to come, which is symbolized by 'back,' as it is said, *And I will take away My hand, and thou shalt see My back* (Exod. 33:23), you shall see." When did God reveal it to him? When Moses was on the verge of death. Hence you learn that the dead do see (God's glory).[22]

In all the signs and wonders, which the Lord sent him to do in the land of Egypt, to Pharaoh, and to all his servants, and to all his land—to Egypt itself, to Pharaoh personally, and to his servants personally—*and in all the mighty hand*—this refers to the plague of the first-born—*and in all the great terror* (34:11–12)—this refers to the parting of the Red Sea. R. Eleazar says: *In all the signs and the wonders*—whence do we learn that this includes also the events at Mount Sinai? From the following, *and in all the mighty hand.* And whence do we learn that this includes also the events in the wilderness? From the following, *and in all the great terror.* And whence do we learn that this includes also the breaking of the tables? From the use of "before . . . eyes" in *And broke them before your eyes* (9:17) and in *Which Moses wrought before the eyes of all Israel* (34:12).

Abbreviations

Tractates of Mishnah, Tosefta, and Talmud

Ab	ʾAḇoṯ	Ḳid	Ḳiddušin	Sanh	Sanheḏrin
Ar	ʿAraḵin	Kil	Kilʾayim	Shab	Šabbaṯ
AZ	ʿAḇoḏah Zarah	Mak	Makkoṯ	Sof	Sofĕrim
BB	Baḇa Baṯra	Meg	Mĕg̱illah	Soṭ	Soṭah
Ber	Bĕraḵoṯ	Men	Mĕnaḥoṯ	Suk	Sukkah
BM	Baḇa Mĕṣiʿa	Mid	Middoṯ	Ta	Taʿăniṯ
Ed	ʿEḏuyyoṯ	MḲ	Moʿeḏ Ḳaṭan	Tem	Tĕmurah
Er	ʿEruḇin	Ned	Nĕḏarim	Ter	Tĕrumoṯ
Giṭ	Giṭṭin	Neg	Neg̱aʿim	Uḳṣ	ʿUḳṣin
Ḥag	Ḥag̱ig̱ah	Nid	Niddah	Yad	Yaḏayim
Ḥul	Ḥullin	Par	Parah	Yeb	Yeḇamoṯ
Ker	Kĕriṯoṯ	Pe	Peʾah	Yoma	Yoma
Ket	Keṯubboṯ	Pes	Pĕsaḥim	Zeb	Zĕḇaḥim
		RH	Roš haš-Šanah		

Other Sources and Commentaries

ARN-A	ʿAḇoṯ dĕ-Rabbi Nathan, Version A
ARN-B	ʿAḇoṯ dĕ-Rabbi Nathan, Version B
B	Oxford manuscript (Neubauer 151)
EH	*ʿEmeḳ ha-Neṣiḇ,* commentary of R. Naftali Zebi Judah Berlin on *Sifre*
EJ	*Encyclopedia Judaica* (English)
F.	Louis Finkelstein, *Siphre on Deuteronomy* (New York, 1969)
Ginzberg, *Legends*	*The Legends of the Jews,* by Louis Ginsberg (Philadelphia, 1909–38)
HUCA	*Hebrew Union College Annual*
JE	*Jewish Encyclopedia*
JPS	Jewish Publication Society translation of the Bible, *The Holy Scriptures* (Philadelphia, 1917)
JQR	*The Jewish Quarterly Review*
ḲS	*Ḳiryat Sefer*
MEḴ	*Meḵilta dĕ-Rabbi Ishmael,* ed. J. Lauterbach (Philadelphia, 1949)
MT	*Midrash Tannaim,* ed. D. Hoffmann (Berlin, 1909)
MTe	*Midrash Tehillim* (Warsaw, 1865)
MhG	*Midrash hag-Gadol,* ed. S. Frisch (Jerusalem, 1975)
PAAJR	*Proceedings of the American Academy for Jewish Research*
PRE	*Pirḳe Rabbi Eliezer* (Warsaw, 1852)
R	Vatican manuscript 32 of *Sifre*
R.H.	Commentary on *Sifre* by R. Hillel ben Eliakim (12th century)
Sif	*Sifra* (Tannaitic commentary on Leviticus), ed. Weiss (reprinted New York, 1946)
TA	*Toldoṯ ʾAḏam,* commentary on *Sifre* by R. Moses of Troyes
TK	*Tosefta ki-Fshutah,* by Saul Lieberman (New York, 1955–)
Tos	Tosefta
YJS	Yale Judaica Series
YŠ	*Yalḳuṭ Šimʿoni* (Warsaw edition)

Notes

A Note on the Text and Translation

1. Important commentaries on Sifre were written by RAD (Abraham ben David of Posquières), R. Hillel, R. Meir ben Kalonymus, Toldot ʾAdam (R. Moses of Troyes), and ʿEmek ha-Nĕṣib (R. Naftali Zebi Judah Berlin); and important notes were added by Elijah Gaon of Wilna (see L. Finkelstein, "Prolegomena to the Sifre," p. 27; S. Lieberman, *Introduction to Tosefta,* p. 71; E. E. Urbach, *Baʿale hat-Tosafot,* p. 364). Parts of Sifre were translated into German by G. Kittel, *Sifre zu Deuteronomium* (Stuttgart, 1922). Following the preparation of this work, but prior to its publication, there has appeared a translation and commentary to the section of Haʾăzinu by H. W. Basser, *Midrashic Interpretations of the Song of Moses* (New York, 1984).

Introduction (1): Sifre on Deuteronomy (Sifre D.) as Part of the Genre of Tannaitic Midrash

1. See H. Z. Dimitrovsky, "Talmud and Midrash," in *Encyclopedia Britannica,* 15th ed. (1974), pp. 1006ff. He defines Midrash as "initially a philological method of interpreting the literal meaning of Biblical texts. In time it developed into a sophisticated interpretive system." See also G. Porton, "Midrash: Palestinian Jews and the Hebrew Bible in the Greco-Roman Period," *Aufstieg und Niedergang der römischen Welt* (Berlin, 1972–79), p. 128.

2. H. L. Strack, *Introduction to the Talmud and Midrash* (New York, 1959), p. 8.

3. J. N. Epstein, *Maboʾot lĕ-Sifrut hat-Tannaʾim* (Jerusalem, 1957), p. 502.

4. Isa. 34:17. See Epstein, ibid.

5. S. Lieberman, "Rabbinic Interpretation of Scripture," in his *Hellenism in Jewish Palestine* (New York, 1962), p. 48.

6. See W. Bacher, "The Origin of the Word Haggada (Agada)," *JQR, 4* (1892), 418, for a general discussion of exegesis. See Piska 48 for the usage of these terms.

7. Lieberman, "Rabbinic Interpretation," p. 53.

8. Epstein, *Maboʾot,* pp. 521ff.

9. D. Halivni, "Whoever Studies Laws," *Proceedings of the Rabbinical Assembly, 41* (1979), 303, n. 11.

10. See L. Finkelstein, *JQR, 31* (1940–41), 211ff. C. Albeck, in *Maboʾ lat-Talmudim* (Tel Aviv, 1969), p. 133, does not agree that these works can be ascribed to the Schools of R. ʿAkiba and R. Ishmael. He does concur with the view that Sifre on Numbers and the Mekilta draw from a common source and resemble each other in method and terminology, while Sifre D. and Sifra draw from another source (pp. 87ff.), and that the teachings of R. Ishmael are to be found frequently in the former group and seldom in the latter (p. 133).

11. Epstein, ibid., pp. 725ff.

12. Epstein, ibid., p. 741; S. Lieberman, *Sifre Zuṭa* (New York, 1968).

13. D. Hoffmann, ed., *Midrash Tannaim zum Deuteronomium* (Berlin, 1909).

14. According to J. Z. Lauterbach (*JE, 8,* 571), "the phrase Midrash Halacha was first employed by Nachman Krochmal in *Moreh Nebuke ha-Zeman*." The Talmud uses the phrase *Midrash Torah*.

15. See S. Lieberman, *Kiryat Sefer, 14* (1937–38), 322; D. Daube, "Rabbinic Methods of Interpretation," *HUCA, 22* (1949), 241.

16. See C. Albeck, ibid., p. 2.

17. R. Hammer, "Section 38 of Sifre Deuteronomy," *HUCA,* 50 (1979), 165.

18. Gen. Rabbah, among the oldest of the homiletic Midrashim, stems from the 5th century. See Strack, ibid., pp. 217–18. Material based upon Genesis is found in Tannaitic Midrashim. See, for example, the extensive discussion of Jacob and his children in Pisḳa 31. J. Z. Lauterbach, in *Mekilta de-Rabbi Ishmael* (Philadelphia, 1949), p. xvii, conjectures that the part of the Torah dealing with history prior to the formation of the people of Israel was not as important as the later part, and therefore was not interpreted, thus explaining the absence of a Tannaitic Midrash on Genesis and on the early part of Exodus. The Book of Jubilees, he notes, is, however, practically such an interpretation.

19. This term is used by L. Finkelstein in many of his articles.

20. Extensive discussion of this problem may be found in Epstein, ibid., pp. 505ff.; J. Z. Lauterbach, "Mishnah and Midrash," in *Rabbinic Essays* (Cincinnati, 1951), pp. 164ff.; C. Albeck, "Halakhoth and Derashoth," in *Alexander Marx Jubilee Volume,* Hebrew Section (New York, 1950), p. 1.

21. E. E. Urbach, *Tarbiz, 27* (1957), 166–82.

22. Ibid., p. 173ff. See also Urbach, "The Talmudic Sage—Character and Authority," in *Cahiers d'Histoire Mondiale, 11* (1968), 116–47.

23. "Ham-Midraš haḳ-Ḳadum wĕham-Midraš ham-Mĕʾuḥar," *Tarbiz Jubilee Volume* (Jerusalem, 1982), p. 94. In these studies based upon the Dead Sea Scrolls, A. Goldberg has posited that the early Midrash of the Second Temple period was really Mishnah, in that it represented law which stood by itself as independent tradition that did not need to be proven from the text of Scripture. Rather it was incorporated into law by being placed within the context of Scriptural passages. The type of Midrash typical of Sifre D., which attempts to prove the validity of traditions from Scripture, would represent a later development.

24. See Yaḏ 4:3.

25. D. Halivni, ibid., p. 298.

26. See Daube, ibid., on Hillel's role in formulating these norms. See also Lieberman, ibid., p. 53.

27. Albeck, ibid., Introduction, pp. 59–60. As Ginzberg has indicated, however, these laws are not necessarily from the Mishnah, but could have belonged to more ancient collections. See note 19 to part 2, below.

28. S. Lieberman says, in *ḲS, 14* (1937–38), 323, that these Midrashic works have a special place in Tannaitic literature, with their emphasis on the connection between Scripture and Oral Law, between the verse and the law. We see in them the early stages of Rabbinic creativity, simple explanations, "translations" from an ancient period, together with parables and legends of great charm. See also C. Albeck, ibid., pp. 79–143, on the entire genre.

Introduction (2): Sifre on Deuteronomy— Origin and Structure

1. Dimitrovsky, ibid., p. 1008.

2. B. Ḳid 49b, Meḡ 28b, Sanh 86a, Ḥaḡ 3a, and Shebu 41b. It is mentioned together with Sifra, the exegesis to Leviticus, and the Tosefta as one of the works that must be studied by anyone who aspires to mastery of Jewish Law.

3. *Iggeret̲ Sherira Gaʾon* (Jerusalem, 1972), p. 39; see Epstein, ibid., p. 510.

4. See Albeck, ibid., p. 104.

5. D. Hoffmann, ed., *Midrash Tannaim zum Deuteronomium*; Epstein, ibid., p. 631.

6. *Pisḳa* (pl. *pisḳaʾot̲*) is the Aramaic form of *Pasuḳ*, "Biblical verse." Finkelstein, in "Studies in the Tannaitic Midrashim," *PAAJR*, 6 (1934–35), 228, explains that this word was written at the beginning of the exposition of a verse. The divisions in the manuscripts, however, are not identical with those of the printed edition, nor are they consistent. There is no differentiation at all between many verses. There are, however, indications of the beginning and conclusion of each Biblical *sidra* ("section"). Therefore no importance should be attached to the placement of pisḳaʾot̲ other than for convenient reference.

7. This section (Niṣṣab̲im) is based almost entirely on the interpretation of Num. 27, and not on the actual verses from Deuteronomy concerning the death of Moses.

8. It should be noted, however, that neither Mek̲ilta nor Sifre on Numbers is a complete commentary on the entire Biblical Books. The Mek̲ilta starts with Exod. 12:1, continues to 23:19, then takes up 31:12–17 and 35:3 (Lauterbach, Introduction, p. xviii; and "The Arrangement and the Divisions of the Mekhilta," *HUCA*, *1* [1924], 434). Sifre on Numbers also comments only on certain sections beginning with Num. 5:1, and skips 8:5–23, 9:15–23, 10:11–28, all of chapter 13, the story of Korah, 20:1 to end of Ḥuḳḳat̲, the narrative of Balak, etc. Some of the parts skipped are repetitious or lists of places or people, but some is fascinating narrative. Lauterbach's explanation (Introduction, p. xxvii) is that the editor wanted only to deal with certain events and laws. The early part of Sifre D., of which more later, very much resembles this pattern, dealing only with certain narrative portions, skipping others, but giving a complete commentary on the legal portions.

9. Pisḳas 1–54 and 304–57 were thought to be the work of the School of R. Ishmael, and 55–303 of the School of R. ʿAḳiba. See Epstein, ibid., pp. 625ff., 644; M. D. Herr, "Sifrei," *Encyclopedia Judaica* (English), *14*, 1521–23; G. F. Moore, *Judaism* (Cambridge, Mass., 1946), *2*, 145; D. Hoffmann, "Likkute Mechilta, Collectanäen aus einer Mechilta zu Deuteronomium" (Hebrew), *Jubelschrift zum Geburtstag des Dr. I. Hildesheimer* (Berlin, 1890), pp. 1–32. See Epstein, ibid., pp. 588ff., for a discussion of the various technical terms used by the two schools, and A. J. Heschel, *The Theology of Ancient Judaism* (Hebrew) (London–New York, 1962–65), for a discussion of the theological differences between them. See also S. Lieberman, "Rabbinic Interpretation," pp. 47–82.

10. A. Goldberg, "Dĕ-be R. ʿAḳiba udĕ-be R. Ishmael bĕ-Sifre Dĕb̲arim, s. 1–54" in *Tĕʿud̲ot̲*, *3* (1983), 9–16.

11. A. Goldberg, "Lĕšonot̲ Dab̲ar ᵓAḥer Bĕ-Midrĕše ha-Halakah," in *Studies in Rabbinic Literature, Bible, and Jewish History* (Ramat-Gan, 1982), pp. 99–107.

12. *Mĕlammed̲,* R. ʿAḳiba's term, for example, occurs thirty-three times in Pis-ḳas 1–42, while *maggid̲,* Ishmael's term, is found fifteen times, mostly in the halakhic section.

13. Goldberg, "Dĕ-be," pp. 14–15.

14. Ibid., p. 10.

15. It still seems quite likely that there was a continuation of Sifre D. from the School of Ishmael which has been lost, and we see a tiny fragment of it in the Genizah find published by Schechter. See Goldberg, ibid., p. 1.

16. See Finkelstein's note to text on p. 81, line 9; S. Lieberman, *Sifre Zuṭa,* pp. 94–95.

17. See references in note 9, above.

18. I. Drazin, *Targum Onkelos to Deuteronomy* (New York, 1982), p. 6. Drazin demonstrates that this Targum drew on the Sifre (p. 9) and points to 201 parallels between them.

19. L. Ginzberg has pointed out, however, that there are places in Tannaitic Midrashim in which this phrase (*mik-kan ᵓomru*) may refer to a collection of Midrashic laws which were older than the Mishnah and from which the Mishnah itself drew its formulations. He posits that there existed earlier versions of Tannaitic Midrashim, prior to the final redaction of the Mishnah, while the Midrashim in their current form are later than the Mishnah. See his article "The Relation between the Mishna and the Mekilta," in *Studies in Memory of Moses Schorr* (New York, 1944), p. 57; see especially pp. 90–91, 94–95.

20. See note 26, below.

21. See notes to Pisḳa 31.

22. *Sefer Assaf* (Jerusalem, 1953), pp. 415–26.

23. Halivni, ibid.

24. Although the final editing was done after the completion of the Mishnah, the work was in the process of formation before the final redaction of the Mishnah and contains sections which reflect this earlier period. See D. Halivni, "Yeš Mĕb̲iᵓim Bikkurim," *Bar Ilan Annual,* 7/8 (1970), 75–76.

25. "Roman Legal Institutions," *JQR,* 35 (1944/45), 27, n. 172.

26. See Finkelstein's introduction to his edition, and his "Prolegomena to the Sifre," *PAAJR,* 3 (1931–32), 39.

Introduction (3): Interpretive Methods and Formulas

1. Daube, ibid.; Strack, *Introduction,* pp. 93–98; Lieberman, "Rabbinic Interpretation."

2. Epstein, ibid., p. 521ff.; *JE,* 12, 33; *EJ,* 8, 366.

3. Lieberman translates the term as "a comparison with the equal" ("Rabbinic Interpretation," p. 59). Originally it was a simple analogy, but later it was applied "not to analogy of content but to identity of words" (ibid., p. 61).

4. Lieberman, ibid., pp. 48–49, and *ḲS,* 14 (1937–38), 323. See also L. Finkelstein, "Midraš, Halakot̲ wĕ-Haggad̲ot̲," in *Baer Jubilee Volume* (Jerusalem, 1961), p. 47; M. Kadushin, *The Rabbinic Mind* (New York, 1952), p. 101;

S. Schechter, "The Talmud," in *Studies in Judaism, Third Series* (Philadelphia, 1924), p. 214.

5. Albeck, ibid., pp. 94–98.

6. Albeck, ibid., p. 93.

7. Lieberman, "Rabbinic Interpretation," p. 51.

8. The terms discussed above may be a shortened form of *melammed̠ šĕ, maggid̠ šĕ.*

9. Epstein, ibid., pp. 588ff. See W. Bacher, "The Origin of the Word Haggada (Agada)," *JQR, 4* (1892), 406. See Albeck, ibid., p. 94; Goldberg, ibid., p. 11.

10. See F's note to line 8, Pisḳa 240. The subject under discussion is a married woman, but the interpretation speaks about her father's house, which is not relevant here. See also Albeck, ibid., pp. 84ff.

Introduction (4): Basic Homiletic Themes and Ideas

1. E. Mihaly, "A Rabbinic Defense of the Election of Israel," *HUCA 35* (1964), 103–44.

2. R. Hammer, "Section 38 of Sifre Deuteronomy," *HUCA* 50 (1979), 165–78.

3. E. Schweid, *Homeland and a Land of Promise* (Hebrew) (Tel Aviv, 1979), pp. 37–46.

4. M. Kadushin, *Rabbinic Mind,* pp. 201ff.

Pisḳa 1

1. On Moses writing the entire Torah, see B. BB 14b, 15a; and see Pisḳa 357. See A. J. Heschel, *Theology of Ancient Judaism* (New York, 1962), 2, 219, 344–93, on the nature of the Torah and its completeness.

2. The statement seems superfluous, inasmuch as we know that Moses wrote the entire Torah. The answer is that these words indicate that he rebuked the people. The principle is stated in Sif Num. 99: the root *dbr,* "spoke," always indicates rebuke or harshness, while *ʾmr,* "said," always indicates mercy. This is an extension of the Rabbinic concept of the two qualities of God, *middat̠ had-din,* "justice," and *middat̠ raḥămim,* "mercy." See M. Kadushin, *Rabbinic Mind,* pp. 194–201. On rebuke in general, see Sif Lev. 89a–b, and B. Shab 119b. Both Targum Onkelos and Targum Jonathan include "rebuke" in their translation of Deut. 1:1. See Deut. Rabbah, ed. Lieberman (Jerusalem, 1964), pp. 1–3, where Moses is called *the* rebuker.

3. Although various explanations have been offered, including the fact that Jeremiah was considered to have written Lamentations, the fact that the verse states *Thus far* indicates that this is the conclusion of one book. See F.

4. On Solomon as author of these three books (Proverbs, Song of Solomon, and Ecclesiastes), see Song Rabbah 1:1. Cf. R. Gordis, *Koheleth: The Man and His World* (New York, 1951), pp. 39–42.

5. Rebuke can be seen in the fact that he speaks of the wicked, represented allegorically by the sun, the moon, and the sea, as engaged in an activity which carries no reward. In Eccl. Rabbah 1:5 the sun is used for the opposite purpose and represents the righteous.

6. In Deut. Rabbah 1:8 (ed. Lieberman, p. 5) a similar statement is found in the name of R. Simeon ben Yoḥai. According to B. Sanh 86a, anonymous statements in the Sifre are all his.

7. Or "all of them were rebukers and able to stand up under rebuke," so R.H.: all of them rebuked one another and were able to stand up under it, for those who did rebuke were also rebuked themselves.

8. Sif Lev. 89:1. See also F.'s note on the parallel in B. ᶜAr 16b: "R. Tarfon said: I doubt if there is anyone in this generation who is fit to rebuke others, for if one says to him, 'Remove the mote from between your eyes,' he will reply to him, 'Remove the beam from between *your* eyes.'" See Matt. 7:3 for a similar saying. The meaning is that there is no one free enough from sin to be fit to rebuke others.

9. In such a way as not to embarrass the other person (R.H.).

10. For a discussion of Johanan ben Nuri's position as one who rebuked others, see Piska 16.

11. Cf. Gen. Rabbah 51:25. Rebuke is a sign of love and leads to a good relationship, and may be repented, but not to the point of embarrassing someone (Sif Lev. 89:1).

12. Various traditions suggest how this verse should be understood. In this section three approaches may be seen:

(a) The places named are those where the Israelites had sinned, for which Moses is about to rebuke them. In MT 1:1 it is explained that "beyond the Jordan" was not a "wilderness" but was well populated. Therefore the following list of names must refer not to the places where Moses stood but to the places for which he rebuked them.

(b) Moses rebuked them at each place and on the way to it as well.

(c) These are allegorical names referring to sins and not to actual places (R. Judah). Similar lists of the people's sins appear in various versions in B. ᶜAr 15a, ARN-B 38, and ARN-A 34, where an attempt is made to reach the number 10, possibly based on the statement in Num. 14:22 that the people had tried God ten times. In ARN-A this is tied to our verse as well. Here too we have an amalgam of two themes: the ten trials and the rebukes of Moses.

13. According to R.H., this is the sin of Baal Peor, which appears later explicitly. In MT 1:1 the reading is: "He rebuked them beyond the Jordan for what they had done in the wilderness." Our text seems to have incorrectly extended this idea of "for what they had done in . . ." to these words as well, although this is inappropriate.

14. Interpreting *Suph* as *Yam Suph,* the Sea of Reeds (Red Sea).

15. In Num. 33:8–10 the list of their journeys seems to indicate that they went three steps backward in returning to the Sea. In Mek̲ Wayyissaᶜ 1(ed. Lauterbach, 2,84) this is understood as a sign of Israel's great devotion to God—they were willing to follow wherever He led them. Here it is given a negative connotation, possibly indicating that they refused to follow Moses and went their own way.

16. A separate interpretation according to MT 106 and Deut. Rabbah (ed. Lieberman, p. 5): they did not want to enter the Red Sea, and when they did, they complained that they had left the mud and clay of making bricks in Egypt only to wallow in the mud and clay of the seabed.

17. See above, note 12. According to this, the rebukes took place during the journeys and not at the end of Moses' life. See F.'s comments.

18. A play on words: *tiphlut* ("disparaging, trifling") and *Tophel.* In MT (p. 2) this interpretation is strengthened by adding that Laban refers to the manna which was white (*laban*) in appearance.

19. Note that here and in the subsequent interpretation God is the speaker. Perhaps these sections are part of an interpretation referring to the ten trials for which God rebuked Israel. It is certainly inappropriate in the mouth of Moses.

20. Adam. In both instances God's favor is taken as something to complain about.

21. See Sif Lev. Mĕṣoraᶜ 5:8 (72:D) and Sif Num. 98. Cf. L. Ginzberg, *The Legends of the Jews* (Philadelphia, 1909–38), 3, 255.

22. Since Scripture says, *And the Lord heard* (Num. 12:2) (R.H.).

23. *Di-Zahab* is read as *day zahab,* "the gold is enough," i.e., the sin of the golden calf was sufficient to establish their guilt and to make it impossible for God to overlook what they had done. All else pales in comparison with this sin.

24. *Watrah* means "sufficient" (*day*), and also "to overlook." See S. Lieberman, *Tosefta Kifšuṭah* (New York, 1955–), 7, 588; *ḲS, 14* (1937–38), 330; J. Goldin, *The Song of the Sea* (New Haven, 1971), p. 178, understands it as "a colloquial expression," such as "it's hardly worth it," or "this could be overlooked." See also Kutscher, *Lĕšonenu 32* (1967–68), 116.

25. *Day-zahab.* See above, note 23. R. Simeon's parable is another interpretation of *Di-Zahab,* and not part of the main discussion.

26. In contrast to R. Simeon, R. Benaiah praises Israel for the gold given to the Tabernacle.

27. The word for Ark cover is *kapporet̲,* which means also "atonement."

28. See above, note 12. Cf. ARN-A 34 for a list of the sins at each place, and ARN-B 38.

29. "Ben Dormaskit"—"son of the woman from Damascus."

30. Or "of the School (*be*) of Rabbi"; MT 1:1. According to Ginzberg, *JE, 3,* 52, it is a "title of learning (bestowed) upon scholars who were the sons of scholars, or upon members of the family of the patriarch." See also Rashi to B. Ḥul 11b.

31. R. Judah must have interpreted all the place-names in the same allegorical manner as Tophel is interpreted above. R. Jose, on the other hand, contends that the allegorical nature of the names indicates that they were given to these places after the events that occurred in them, in order to commemorate them, but that they represent actual places.

32. He divides the word Hadrach into two, *ḥad,* "sharp," that is, critical or exacting, and *rak̲,* "soft." This method of interpretation, *noṭariḳon,* is described in detail by S. Lieberman, "Rabbinic Interpretation," p. 69.

33. If Hadrach is an actual place, so is Damascus, and Damascus is not God's resting place, which is Jerusalem.

34. R. Jose replies with an interpretation indicating that Jerusalem will expand as far as Damascus, i.e., it is a real place. "R. Jose replied" has been added.

35. Which contradicts the idea of reaching as far as Damascus.

36. Pesiḳta de-Rab Kahana 20:7, end of *Ranni ᶜĂḳarah* (ed. Mandelbaum, p. 316) and Song Rabbah 7:5. It can both expand and reach Damascus. Our text has some confusion concerning the identity of the speakers. See *Revue de Qumran, 41* (1982), 97ff.; Haim Milikovsky suggests that "Whence do we learn" is not R. Jose's reply, but the continuation of R. Judah's response, wherein he attempts

to interpret all of the verse messianically. See also G. Vermès, *Scripture and Tradition in Judaism* (Leiden, 1961), pp. 43–49, on earlier belief that Damascus was to be "the seat of the eschatological Sanctuary . . . and the place of the Messiah's coming," which was later reconciled with traditional belief concerning Jerusalem in passages such as this. Text has "he said" before "How do I explain."

Piska 2

1. I.e., from Sinai to the border of the Land of Israel. See Num. 33:16, which is paraphrased here.

2. *Resting-place* is taken to mean the Land of Israel. Note that in Piska 1 it was identified with Jerusalem.

3. R. Judah interprets a day as a journey, i.e., one day's journey (*EH*).

4. There are three figures, three, eleven, and forty, all purporting to be the traveling time from Sinai to the Land of Israel. How can they all be right?

5. Since R. Judah identifies *resting-place* with Shiloh (Piska 66), F. suggests reading "Rabbi" (i.e., R. Judah the Prince).

6. Connecting the two sentences in Exod. 13:4–5: you will go forth and enter the land this day, immediately. On the idea that Israel was not worthy for even one day, see Mek De-pisha 16, which states that they were taken out of Egypt even though they rebelled against God. Concerning their rebelliousness even at the Sea, see Piska 1.

7. He spoke to them in the eleventh month, near his death; they mourned him for thirty days (Deut. 34:8), and entered the land with Joshua on *the tenth day of the first month* (Josh. 4:19) (see below). TA suggests that the basis is the unusual Hebrew form *ʿashte ʿaśar,* which could be read *šěte ʿaśar,* "twelve." Finkelstein, in the *Harvard Theological Review, 16* (1923), 40, suggests that this could be meant against those sects that counted thirteen months, as in the Book of Jubilees.

8. R. Benaiah's statement is an expansion of the first interpretation that the year has twelve months. Before Solomon we learned it from Moses.

9. See Tos Soṭ 11:6–7; B. Soṭ 13b or b. In Josh. 1:11 we read *For within three days ye are to pass over this Jordan.* The Tosefta concludes: "Now go out and count back thirty-three days, and you will find that Moses died on the seventh of Adar."

10. The sentence is missing in the editions and is supplied by F. See Lieberman, *ḲS, 14* (1937–38), 330. See Gen. Rabbah 54:3 on rebuke and peace.

11. An example which seems inappropriate, since this is a blessing and not a rebuke.

12. *Ḳal wa-ḥomer,* inference from the minor to the major; *gězeroṯ šawoṯ,* analogy based on verbal congruities.

13. *Kělal u-pěraṭ.* All these are technical terms used in the interpretation of the Torah. The intent seems to be to include all of the Torah as well as its official interpretation in that which issued from Moses. See Sif Lev. Bě-ḥuḳḳoṯay, end, where R. ʿAḳiba states that at Sinai Moses was given "the Torah, its laws, its details, and its explanations."

14. It may be that this Midrash was originally concerned with the question of the relation of the Ten Commandments to the rest of the Torah. If so, this would

be part of the Jewish insistence, against early Christianity, that the Ten Commandments are not to be regarded as the only part of the Torah still valid. It should be noted that the phrase "these words" appears in Exod. 19:6 in the description of the giving of the Ten Commandments, and the term "words" is itself the descriptive name of the Ten Commandments (Exod. 20:1). See B. Ber 12a, P. Ber 1:8, and Meḵ Neziḳin 1. Cf. L. Ginzberg, *Commentary to the Yerushalmi, 1,* 166. Vatican 32 (R) reads, "Did Moses prophesy only the Ten Commandments?" F.'s reading is taken from Midrash hag-Gadol.

Piska 3

1. Ginzberg suggests "when they returned" (*šaḇu*) for "again" (*šuḇ*). See F.'s notes.

2. Literally "because the king is able (*kašer*)." The appropriateness of the parable is difficult to understand. The similarity lies in the fact that the rebuke of the lieutenant, like that of Moses, comes after the king has demonstrated his abilities and not before.

3. The word "otherwise," missing in F., is taken from R.

4. He gave you bread before, but that is no reason to trouble him now. So Lieberman, *KS, 14* (1937–38), 327. *Kašer* is understood as "able and enterprising." The king has demonstrated his ability—he brought the ovens with him for use in extraordinary circumstances. There is no need to bother him now. This rebuke does not cause the army to question the king's ability since it was already demonstrated. So also Moses' rebuke comes at a time when they cannot question his ability since they have won the battle.

5. Rashi points out that Ashtaroth appears in Gen. 14:5, where it seems to have been a fortified stronghold. R reads "*In Ashtaroth, at Edrei*: which was the royal capital."

Piska 4

1. See Piska 27. Cf. Exod. Rabbah 1:33. According to the Sages, this was not merely a reading of the Torah but the binding of the people to it by means of an oath.

2. The word *saying* is treated here, as always, as implying something additional.

Piska 5

1. *Haḳ-Ḳodeš*; variant reading, "the Holy One, blessed be He."

2. In each case the word *raḇ*, "long enough," is taken to mean "gain"—something Israel has gained at the mountain, emphasized by the word *laḵem*, "for you." Even the last interpretation, which may also be a play on the words *raḇ* and *ra*ᶜ ("bad"), interprets the verse in a positive sense for Israel—leaving the mountain will also be beneficial for them. This last phrase is missing in R.

Piska 6

1. Mentioned in Judg. 1:16–17.

2. Samuel Klein (*Tarbiz, 1* [1929], 143) explains the location as follows: Arad

and Hormah were in the southeastern wilderness of Judah. Ammon, Moab, and Mount Seir were in the east and southeast. The plain was south of the Dead Sea. The lowland of Lod and the lowland in the south, as well as the mountain of the king, are terms borrowed from Sheḇi 9:2 and Tos Sheḇi 7:7. Klein explains the mountain of the king as the name of a mountain in the Betar region upon which a fortress, Bet Melek, was built, although later on the term was used in a broader sense for the mountain in the north of Judea, from Beth-El to Caẹsarea (*Tarbiz, 1* [1929], 141).

3. The "Chosen House" refers to the Sanctuary in Jerusalem.

4. The parable is explained in Ezek. 17:12, "The king of Babylon came to Jerusalem and took the king thereof."

5. Isa. 10:32 refers specifically to Zion and Jerusalem. See also Sif Num. 134, and see Piska 28. On Lebanon as a metaphor for the Temple, see G. Vermès, *Scripture and Tradition,* 33ff.

6. Therefore it is called great. The relationship to Israel makes it special. See Gen. Rabbah 16:1.

7. In Hebrew *pĕraṯ/mafriḏ*; the two words have the same two letters, *pe* and *reš,* while the third letter is similar in sound, *t* and *d.*

Piska 7

1. A formula borrowed from legal terminology for acceptable testimony. Cf. Sanh 4:5. This has been corrected by F. from R's reading *ʾomer,* probably an error of *reš* for *daleṯ.*

2. Since no mention is made of fighting but only of taking possession. The Midrash emphasizes the gift that God is giving them—all they need is a compass.

Piska 8

1. Indicating that there was an oath to each one of the fathers: why then mention each name again? See F., *JQR, 31* (1940/41), 255.

2. A second answer to the question.

3. In Midrash Tannaim the reading is "he improved it, saying, 'What am I to do? I was given it only as it was.'" Ordinarily improvements belong to the owner of the property but when in this case the owner, God, says, "the land I swore to Abraham, Isaac, and Jacob," He is giving Israel title both to the land and to the improvements made by each one of the patriarchs.

4. The paragraph illustrates a common method of Rabbinic interpretation, in which each part of the Scriptural verse refers to a different matter.

5. Rabbi understands it as referring to the rights to the land which belonged to the returnees from Babylonia. F. interprets this in the context of Rabbi's position that the holiness of the land was not binding on parts which the returnees had not conquered, such as Beth-Shean. See B. Ḥul 7a.

Piska 9

1. See Piska 5. It is customary for the Sifre to repeat the identical interpretation whenever the same word or phrase appears in Scripture.

2. The burden of the consequences of judging your actions is too great.

3. 1 sela[c] = 2 common shekel = 1 Temple shekel; 1 common shekel = 2 denar; 100 denar = 1 mina.

4. Judges usually are free to act as they wish. A judge in Israel, however, be he Moses or Solomon, is required to follow the Torah, to be just and not capricious. He cannot determine the punishment by his own whim. Even the prescribed mode of execution cannot be changed by him, and any misjudgment is considered as serious as a capital crime. That is the burden which Moses cannot bear, and not merely the task of judging. Cf. Sif Lev. Ḳĕdošim 3:6 (88:3).

5. Thus the judge's life is forfeit for despoiling a person of money. See B. Sanh 7a: "A judge who unjustly takes the possessions of one and gives them to another, the Holy One . . . takes from him life" (Soncino translation).

Piska 10

1. The phrase *hinneḵem hay-yom* is cut off from the rest of the verse and understood as "You are the day," you are like the day, i.e., something which has eternal existence.

2. I.e., from this verse mentioning the stars. See Deut. Rabbah 1:4, "Just as the stars are one course upon another, so is Israel." Originally this may have been connected to Ps. 16:11. See below, note 4.

3. Seven stars, i.e., planets, were known, hence seven groups of the righteous (F.). It may also be a play on words—*śoḇa*[c], "satiety," and *šeḇa*[c], "seven." See L. Ginzberg, *Legends*, 5, 30, n.85.

4. *Śoḇa*[c] *śĕmaḥoṯ*, *"fullness of joys"* (Ps. 16:11), is read as *šeḇa*[c] *śĕmaḥoṯ*, "seven joys." Cf. P. Ḥag 2:1, and Lev. Rabbah 30:2, where this interpretation is explicit.

5. Cf. Piska 47, where Hos. 14:7 is quoted in similar context. The verse in Zechariah likens the lampstand to an olive tree, while the verse in Hosea likens the righteous person to an olive tree; hence the righteous is like the lampstand. On the shining faces of the righteous, see M. Smith, "The Image of God," *Bulletin of the John Rylands Library*, 40 (1958), 497ff.

Piska 11

1. The implication is, "Why do you give me so little to live on?" In place of Gen. 22:17, R has Gen. 26:4 and 13:16.

2. Cf. Sif Num. 84: Moses said, "I am flesh and blood, and there is a limit to my own blessings." In Deut. Rabbah 1:17 (ed. Lieberman, p. 16) a similar parable is cited concerning a king's gift to his legions.

Piska 12

1. The root in Hebrew is the same, *ṭrḥ*. After the verse R reads "I am speaking not on my own—what I am saying comes from the mouth of the Holiness."

2. The form of this homily is often repeated: the interpretation is cited, explained, and then repeated. According to Tos Sanh 6:4, it was legal to demand additional judges before the verdict was reached (see Lieberman, *ḴS, 14*, 331). According to Alon, these were citizens who acted "as judges in private matters, when called upon to try the case by the parties to the dispute." G. Alon, *Jews, Judaism, and the Classical World* (Jerusalem, 1977), p. 389, n. 47.

3. An ʾ*apiḳoros* is one who scoffed at the Sages; see, e.g., B. Sanh 89b (F.).

4. F. suggests that the verse may be inappropriate. On is also Egypt (Gen. 41:50—*priest of On*). R has "it being well known that his wife counseled him."

5. *Roněnim*; MT and Berlin manuscript have *diněnin,* i.e., those who delight in trials (*dinim*). See Lieberman, *ḲS, 14,* 331.

6. In MT the example is more extreme: they would expend a larger sum to get a smaller one.

7. In Hebrew, *riḇ,* "strife," also means a lawsuit.

Pisḳa 13

1. See Sif Num. 92, ARN-A 28. The "mosaic-like" man has many facets: he knows Midrash, halaḵah, aggaḏah, and Tosefta. The phrase does not appear in R.

2. Arios is mentioned again in Tos BM 3:11. He was a Gentile who had been converted to Judaism. See M. D. Herr, "The Historical Significance of the Dialogues between Jewish Sages and Roman Dignitaries," *Scripta Hierosolymitana, 22* (1971), 149.

3. The next word in the verse.

4. It was the custom of judges to wrap themselves up in their cloaks when trying a case (B. Shab 10a).

5. See S. Lieberman, *Sifre Zuṭa* (New York, 1968), pp. 85–88. The Naśiʾ (president of the Sanhedrin) did not have to consult the people about the judges, hence they used to complain. See Alon, *Jews,* p. 415, n. 118, for an entirely different view.

6. This may reflect the struggle between the Naśiʾ and the *Beṯ-Din* (court) over powers of ordination, with Moses representing the Naśiʾ. See Sanh 1:3; B. Sanh 19a. Cf. H. Mantel, *Studies in the History of the Sanhedrin* (Cambridge, Mass., 1961), p. 248; Alon, *Jews,* p. 414.

7. The Hebrew word for "obey" and "be safe" is the same, *šmr.*

8. I.e., the people's leaders are responsible when the people sin.

Pisḳa 14

1. Literally "under the heels of your feet."

2. The word "answered," ʿ*nh,* is interpreted as "to prompt," i.e., to urge one to do something. For this usage, see Meḵ Ba-ḥoḏeš, p. 223, B. Ber 45a.

Pisḳa 15

1. This is based on a combination of Exod. 18:21 and Deut. 1:13. In the former, four qualities are mentioned: *able men, such as fear God, men of truth, hating unjust gain*; in the latter, three more. According to Exod. 18:25, he found only one: *able men.* In our verse, Deut. 1:15, two, *wise men and full of knowledge* are mentioned. The tradition here is in truncated form; see Deut. Rabbah 1:7, and MT.

2. The captain served the full complement of one unit plus the overflow, so long as the overflow did not reach the size of a complete unit, when it would have been entitled to its own captain.

Piska 16

1. See ʾAḇ 1:1; Meḵ Pisḥa 6. Each case is unique and requires full attention, even though it resembles previous cases.

2. See Piska 1. See also B. Hor 10a, where the reason for the appointment is discussed. See also Alon, *Jews,* p. 400, n. 72, for a different view of this incident.

3. Or "did not attend to them." In any case the point is that they did not attempt to exercise the authority given them.

4. See Bacher, *ʾAggaḏoṯ hat-Tannaʾim* (Berlin and Jerusalem, 1922–28), *1*, part 2, p. 97, n. 3. R. Gamaliel wished to discourage contentious argumentation among his pupils. The proctors were supposed to be present in a prominent way and maintain order and discipline.

5. R reads "you have informed the community."

6. R. Ishmael interprets the verse as demanding justice only for *your brethren,* i.e., fellow-Jews. It should be noted, however, that Ishmael had been incarcerated in Rome as a youth (B. Giṭ 58a). This interpretation is found also in a slightly different version in B. BḲ 113a. In both places objections are raised against it.

7. Regardless of the outcome: he emphasizes the last part of the verse, *and judge righteously.* So MhG and MT. The problem of deceiving a Gentile is dealt with in Tos BḲ 10:15, Sif Deut. 344, and P. BḲ 4:3, and in all these cases it is condemned. So too in B. BḲ 113a, where R. ʿAḳiba forbids it on the ground of the duty to sanctify God's name. Cf. *Shiṭṭah Měḳubbeṣeṯ,* ad loc.

8. Tos Ter 1:11.

9. *Ger,* "a resident (stranger)," or later "proselyte," is derived from the verb *gur,* "to reside." Here the word is taken fancifully to derive from *ʾāgar,* "to gather, to store up."

Piska 17

1. Probably from *ḳěroḇaʾ*, one who leads prayers, composes poems. So Lieberman, *ḲS, 14* (1937/38), 332. The list refers to those whose outward qualities are appealing.

2. This is Hoffmann's reading in place of "lent me money," *hilwani mamon,* which, as F. points out, would explain the gloss found in some mss., "understands all languages." The author teaches that one whose qualifications are based on wealth, power, or status will not be a good judge.

3. See Alon, *Jews,* p. 394.

4. See Sif Lev. Ḳěḏošim 89:1, where the same conclusion is drawn from the verse *Thou shalt not respect the person of the poor* (Lev. 19:15).

5. See B. Sanh 6b. While F. considers this a marginal gloss, Goldberg has shown that there is no reason to doubt the authenticity of this section, *Teʿuḏoṯ, 3* (1983), 12.

6. Arbitration does not determine guilt or innocence and is therefore in contradiction to the rule of law and justice. F. understands the difference of opinion on this matter to have originated in the practice of compromise, which began during the period when it was forbidden by the Romans to judge by Jewish law. When this practice continued later, many opposed it.

7. Usual translation: *The covetous (boṣeʿa) vaunteth himself.*

8. Since arbitration is based on the judge's feelings and not on the role of law, it will result in the loser resenting his loss and doubting God's justice.

9. F. identifies the pupil with Eleazar the Priest. However, this may be simply a general reference to the Sages who would have deduced the verdict by their rules of interpretation. Albeck suggests that the original reading was "that women will be able to judge," but it was changed out of respect for Moses. Cf. C. Albeck, *Mabo*ʾ *lat-Talmudim* (Tel Aviv, 1969), p. 127.

Piska 18

1. These are enumerated in Sanh 4:1: "Both civil and capital cases demand inquiry and examination, as it is written, *Ye shall have one manner of law* (Lev. 24:22). What is the difference between civil and capital cases? Civil suits (are tried) by three, capital cases by twenty three. Civil suits may be opened either for acquittal or condemnation: capital charges must be opened for acquittal, but not for condemnation. Civil suits may be decided by a majority of one, either for acquittal or condemnation, whereas capital charges are decided by a majority of one for acquittal, but (at least) two for condemnation. In monetary cases the decision may be reversed both for acquittal and for condemnation, whilst in capital charges the verdict may be reversed for acquittal only, but not for condemnation. In monetary cases all may argue for or against the defendant, whilst in capital charges anyone may argue in his favor, but not against him. In civil suits he who has argued for condemnation may then argue for acquittal, and vice versa, whereas in capital charges one who has argued for condemnation may subsequently argue for acquittal, but not vice versa.

"Civil suits are tried by day and concluded at night. But capital charges must be tried by day and concluded by day. Civil suits can be concluded on the same day, whether for acquittal or condemnation; capital charges may be concluded on the same day with a favorable verdict, but only on the morrow with an unfavorable verdict. Therefore trials are not held on the eve of a Sabbath or festival. In civil suits and in cases of cleanness and uncleanness we begin with (the opinion of) the most eminent (of the judges), whereas in capital charges we commence with (the opinion of) those on the side (benches).

"All are eligible to try civil suits, but not all are eligible to try capital charges, only priests, Levites, and Israelites (laymen) with whom priests can enter into marriage relationship" (Soncino translation).

2. He is reminding them of past victories in order to assure them of their ability to deal with future problems.

3. The reference is to the entire verse.

Piska 20

1. See Sif Num. 136.

2. In proper order and not in confusion.

3. See Sif Num. 2 (p. 79).

4. This interpretation emphasizes the purpose of the spies to aid in the conquest of the land.

Pisḳa 21

1. Literally "Place," a Rabbinic term indicating that He is the "Place" or Preserver of the world, but the world is not His "place." God is eternal, not so the world. See Gen. Rabbah 68:11.

2. Since the Sifre understands Deuteronomy to be a work of rebuke (see Pisḳa 1), what place is there for praise?

3. Presumably A did not go through with the trial when he saw that B did not oppose it (so the reading of the Vilna Gaon). Thus Moses was not really pleased, but cooperated so that they would withdraw their request to send spies to the land. See Num. Rabbah, Šĕlaḥ, 16:6, where God agrees to the people's request, so that they should not say that the land is in fact a poor one, and that therefore God does not want them to view it. Instead of "in order to take my money" R has "for his own money."

4. The list of spies in Num. 13:4–15 does not include anyone from the Tribe of Levi. The number twelve was achieved by counting Joseph as two Tribes, Ephraim and Manasseh.

Pisḳa 22

1. Rahab was thought to have been the ancestress of a line of prophets. See Ginzberg, *Legends*, 6, 171, n. 12. See Sif Num. 78.

2. B. Ket̲ 10b. This was long before Horeb (i.e., Sinai) became a holy mountain.

3. From all four directions; based on the word *"it"* (*ʾot̲ah*), its entire arc (*EH*).

Pisḳa 23

1. They had come not to consume produce but to preserve it and display it; therefore they should have acted with greater respect. See Pisḳa 20.

2. See end of Pisḳa 37. Height is taken as a sign of better quality.

3. The words *and said,* which seem superfluous, are taken to imply that only Joshua and Caleb said it, not all the spies (cf. Num. 14:6–9).

Pisḳa 24

1. They spoke quietly, in secret, in their tents, and not in public.

Pisḳa 26

1. This whole paragraph seems to be a gloss and not an original part of the work. F. Heinemann, *Scripta Hierosolymitana,* 22 (1971), 120, n. 77, disagrees, and considers this a Tannaitic proem form, beginning with a verse from the Writings.

2. See Shebi̲ 4:7.

3. In B. Sanh 107a we find the term *paga* ("unripe") applied to Bathsheba. She would have been appropriate for David, but was "unripe."

4. Cf. Lieberman, *JQR,* 35 (1944), 36: "The criminal was often led to the execution with the *corpus delicti* hanging on his neck." Perhaps that is what is meant here. See Lev. Rabbah 31:4 and Sif Num. 137. The version in Sif Num. has two women, one who did commit adultery and one who did not, thus corresponding to

Moses and David. See the comprehensive discussion in S. Lieberman, *Greek in Jewish Palestine* (New York, 1942), p. 162.

5. Cf. Num. 20:2ff. Moses was commanded to speak to the rock so that it would produce water miraculously. Instead he struck it. This is understood to have brought about the punishment of Moses.

6. "Doomed," literally "slew." See Num. 20:13, 20:24, Deut. 33:8. Actually Miriam died before this incident, but her death is connected with it here because the well ran dry, at least temporarily, when she died. See MhG, Num. 20:2. This entire homily is here only because the verse quoted above mentions the waters of contention.

7. Following the reading of fragments from the Genizah cited by S. Lieberman, "Ten Words," in *Texts and Studies* (New York, 1974), p. 8: *škn* is to give a gift, ἀποχή, a receipt.

8. *Ḥinnom,* literally "free." This is connected to the word *wa-ʾeṯḥannen, "and I besought."* Moses did not claim a reward for his good deeds, but asked only for a favor. R reads "could have suspended [judgment of] all sins." For this meaning of *tlh,* see Soṭ 3:4.

9. Cf. Deut. Rabbah 2:1: "No creature has any claim upon its Creator." The idea that it is God's compassion and grace rather than our merits upon which we must depend is found in Dan. 9:8 and is quoted in the daily prayers, as well as in the concluding service of the Day of Atonement. In Christianity this became the doctrine of grace; cf. Rom. 3:19ff. For a contrasting view, see ʾAḇ 2:16, 3:19, and 4:11. See E. P. Sanders's discussion of this in *Paul and Palestinian Judaism* (Philadelphia, 1977), pp. 144–47.

10. Thirteen terms for prayer are actually listed here. MT adds that beseeching is the term closest to God and connects it with David through Ps. 51:3, *Be gracious (ḥanneni) unto me.* See also Deut. Rabbah 2:1.

11. G. Alon, in *Toldoṯ hay-Yehuḏim bĕ-Ereṣ Yiśraʾel* (Jerusalem, 1975), *1,* 84, points out that Caesarea was made a colony as a reward for helping the Roman army, and was therefore exempt from paying the head-tax.

12. The bracketed passage seems to be another gloss inserted into the text.

13. Cf. Sif Num. 105; *leʾmor,* "saying," thus is understood as *li ʾemor,* "tell me."

14. See B. Ber 60b; Meḵ Širaṯa (2, 28); Exod. Rabbah 3:6; Sif Num., p. 180; Gen. Rabbah 12:15 and 33, 21:7; Midrash hag-Gadol Deut. 59. In Exod. 22:8 and 22:27, *ʾelohim* is often rendered "judges" (Targum Onqelos). On the concepts of the qualities of mercy and justice, see G. F. Moore, *Judaism, 1,* 386–400; M. Kadushin, *The Theology of Seder Eliyahu* (New York, 1932), pp. 108–18, 163–65; idem, *Rabbinic Mind,* pp. 194–201.

Pisḳa 27

1. The verb *haḥellota* ("you began") is from the root *ḥll* which means "to open, to break," including to break a vow.

2. God said *"let Me alone,"* implying that if Moses would not let Him alone, He would not be able to destroy the people. God thus invites Moses' intervention. See Exod. Rabbah 42:9 for a similar thought: "Did Moses actually seize hold of God?" It is compared to a king who is about to strike his son and calls out, "Let

me be, and I will strike him," knowing that the son's teacher will overhear it and will come to plead for him.

3. "Greatness" always means spiritual greatness (F.). Others connect it with God's graciousness. Cf. Sif Num. 134. "Basic statement" (*binyan ʾab̲*) is a technical term of Rabbinic interpretation of Scripture, indicating the verse upon which a standard rule is based.

Pisḳa 28

1. The first servant shows his contempt for the king's decree by indicating how easy it is for him to fulfill it. The second pleads against it, showing how precious is the thing he is giving up because of his desire to fulfill his master's word. So Moses' repeated pleading is not a sign of contempt for God but a demonstration of his full obedience.

2. See Pisḳa 6.

Pisḳa 29

1. A play on words: *hit̲ʿabber* can mean either "to become angry" or "to become pregnant."

2. See Deut. Rabbah (ed. Lieberman, p. 43) on Moses pleading in vain for his life.

3. A play on words: *rab̲* may mean a human master (= teacher) or the divine Master (= God). F. suggests that there may have been two interpretations here, one suggesting that unlike man God has no one who can release Him of His vow that Moses will not enter the land, the other that Moses must listen to his Master, God.

4. *Rab̲ lĕḵa* is taken to mean "you are a master," i.e., an example for others.

5. Apparently another gloss.

6. See Lieberman, *ḲS, 14,* 329, and references given there. Lieberman and F. agree that the interpretation here is based on the word *way-yit̲ʿabber, was wroth*; see B. Sanh 31b.

7. B. Ber 32b.

8. Tos Ber 3:15; P. Ber 4:5; B. Ber 30a. F. suggests that this is based on the next part of the verse, *and lift up thine eyes westward.*

9. Sif Num. (p. 179), with slight variation.

10. Sif Num., chap. 1.

11. Joshua; the interpretation is based on the seemingly superfluous pronoun *he* (E.H).

Pisḳa 30

1. Based on the conclusion of the verse, *over against Beth-peor.*

2. The next verse, *And now, O Israel, hearken unto the statutes* (4:1), indicates that they have been forgiven their sin (*EH*). The interpretation of 4:1 which follows should be considered the proof of the forgiveness and thus the end of this interpretation, as it is in MhG.

Piska 31

1. Why was this commandment addressed specifically to the progeny of Israel (Jacob's alternate name), and not to the progeny of all three patriarchs?

2. Not so much the fear itself as the result of his anxiety, the possibility of his posterity resembling Esau and Ishmael in their actions—see the conclusion of the story (Exod. 19:8), where his children declare their loyalty to God.

3. I.e., Ishmael, from Abraham, and Esau, from Isaac.

4. F. and others believe that this bracketed passage is a gloss. It is found in Tos Soṭ 6:6 and elsewhere. Here it certainly interrupts the main argument, which continues with the paragraph beginning with "Ishmael issued from Abraham," further on.

5. In Gen. Rabbah 43:13, *making sport* is interpreted by R. Ishmael as idolatry, while R. Eleazar takes it to mean bloodshed, and R. ʿAḳiba states that it refers to sexual misconduct. In Tos Soṭ the tradition is the same as here.

6. Isaac and Ishmael.

7. Possibly deriving *Miṣriṯ, "the Egyptian,"* from *ṣarar,* "to show enmity"; so R.H.

8. I.e., it would not be enough for them. See Tos Soṭ 6:6 and Lieberman's notes, p. 672. R. Simeon says that according to ʿAḳiba, Moses was questioning God's ability to provide enough, while he, Simeon, interprets it to mean that they would have complained no matter what the amount. See Sif Num. 95 (p. 95), where Simeon's statement is much clearer: "They were looking for an excuse to break away from God."

9. The use of this verse as proof for the correctness of R. Simeon's interpretation is unclear. In Tos Soṭ it is used once to explain R. ʿAḳiba's interpretation, and again as part of R. Simeon's.

10. I.e., "You claim the merit of the commandments, but you do not fulfill them." In Tos Soṭ, R. Simeon points out that the prophet is actually referring to the violation of the Noachide commandments: they do not observe even these, much less those specifically imposed upon Israel. The version given here is severely truncated and thus presents many difficulties. R. Simeon ascribes a virtuous claim to the people, even though they do not practice what they say. R. ʿAḳiba is more severe: their claim in itself is obnoxious.

11. The inclusion of the day of Gedaliah's death as a fast day, while the other fasts are all connected with the destruction of the Temple, shows that his assassination was as weighty a matter as the destruction of the Temple itself.

12. See B. RH 18b, P. RH 4:8, Tos Soṭ 6:6, and Lieberman's note (p. 675).

13. The verse *then shall the Lord be my God* is understood as Jacob's plea that God rest His name upon him—i.e., "let the Lord be my God"—by granting that his progeny be worthy. It is not a conditional part of a vow, but a prayer that God grant him this favor.

14. The emphasis is upon the word "me," i.e., something special that Jacob had requested concerning the relationship between God and himself. Cf. MhG Gen. 28:21: "*My,* meaning that He should rest His name upon me."

15. I.e., there were twelve worthy sons, and not eleven worthy and one unworthy.

16. Reuben was not with them when they sat down to eat, since Gen. 37:29

says, *When Reuben returned.* This can be explained only by assuming that he was fasting in repentance.

17. Moses' blessing indicates that Reuben's repentance had been accepted and he would not be subjected to punishment in afterlife. See Piska 347, comment on 33:5.

18. Literally "dispute," meaning, are you divided, not wholehearted, in regard to the worship of God? See Ginzberg, *Legends,* 2, 140.

19. Taking the words *bowed down* in the sense of giving thanks, and *bed's head* in the sense of the issue of the bed. "Jacob's bed was perfect, in that all the children born to him were righteous" (Lev. Rabbah 36:5). See also MhG Gen., p. 814.

20. Two variant interpretations of the verse are given here, after which the main Midrash concludes with God's reply to Jacob.

21. Reading *miṭṭah* ("bed") as *maṭṭeh* ("tribe"), i.e., "he bowed (in thanks) for the head of the tribe (Reuben)." See Peshiṭta and LXX to Gen. 47:31, Targum Jonathan, the Peshiṭta, and LXX to Amos 3:12.

22. The presence here of this phrase, which is not found in the Bible, probably explains its inclusion in the recitation of the Shemaʿ.

23. This same expression, "all your days," is used in the first paragraph of this chapter. Its repetition here brings the story to a proper stylistic conclusion.

24. According to F. this reflects the ancient rule which was changed in the Mishnaic period and is cited in Ber 2:3 as the individual opinion of R. Jose. According to the Mishnah, one need not hear the Shemaʿ as he recites it. The story in Tos Ber 2:13 indicates that ʿAḳiba and his colleagues recited it aloud except in times of danger. See Lieberman's notes to Tos, p. 21. See also Deut. Rabbah, ed. Lieberman, p. 63.

25. If there is only one God, He must also be our God, there being no other. The word for "our God," seemingly superfluous, must therefore add something new to the meaning of the Shemaʿ. See Piska 8 for another example of this. The verses cited here offer examples of words which are seemingly superfluous, but actually indicate the unique closeness of God to Israel.

26. Emphasizing the possessive *our.* This is similar to the interpretation given above to Jacob's use of *my*.

27. I.e., another solution to the seeming redundancy. Both parts of the verse are needed, since each refers to a different matter. Only MhG, however, has "over us."

Piska 32

1. A similar interpretation is found in Mek̲ 20:6 and B. Soṭ 31a, where two verses are contrasted: *unto the thousandth generation of them that love Me and keep My commandments* (5:10) and *for them that love Him and keep His commandments to the thousandth generation* (7:9). *Keep My commandments* is taken as referring to those who perform out of fear, and they follow the expression "thousandth generation," whereas those who love God and are rewarded precede it.

2. Another verse is presented here which is interpreted as meaning that fear is an inferior motive, since one who serves out of fear does so as does a slave, who would cease his service if the master were to lose his power and be in need of him.

3. *Maṣriḵo*; see Piska 354 for this usage. R.H. interprets it to mean "when B (the master) forces him to work."

4. In MT 25 and P. Ber 9:7 this is said to mean that both are important: love, so that one should not hate God, and fear, so that one should not rebel. Since the verse about fear (10:20) is followed almost immediately by one about love, *Thou shalt love the Lord, thy God* (11:1), this may be a fragment of a homily contrasting the two verses and showing how both motivations are needed and can co-exist.

5. Having shown that the verse cannot refer to actual making of souls, the homily interprets it as indicating something else: Abraham "made" them in that he converted them—"A convert is like a newborn child" (B. Yeḇ 22a).

6. The word *lĕḇaḇḵa* ("thy heart") is spelled with two letters *beṯ,* which is taken to indicate the two parts of the heart, i.e., the two Inclinations. See Ber. 9:5.

7. Dividing the word into two parts, *leḇ bĕḵa,* "heart in you." This method of interpretation was used also at the end of Piska 1 and is described by Lieberman in *Hellenism in Jewish Palestine,* pp. 69ff.

8. One's trust in God must be complete and wholehearted. See Piska 31 and Deut. Rabbah, ed. Lieberman, p. 70: "Your heart should not be divided, rather perform the commandments for their own sakes with a perfect heart."

9. The verse from Psalms is quoted because like the verse under consideration it indicates the willingness to give up one's life for God. R. Simeon's interpretation of that verse is a dissenting one.

10. "Might" in the sense of wealth, as interpreted above. Since wealth is thus already implied in *With all thy soul,* "might" must mean here something else. R. ʿAkiba uses a play on words: *middah* ("measure" or "quality") is similar in sound to *mĕʾoḏ* ("might") and indicates that one must be willing to accept whatever measure God decrees, even if it carries suffering or punishment. See B. Ber. 61b, where R. ʿAkiba's martyrdom is described, during which he invoked this verse in explanation of the commandment he was fulfilling by his acceptance of death.

11. In times of both joy and sorrow David "called upon the name of the Lord," i.e., acknowledged and accepted God's decrees.

12. Following the reading of Meḵ (2, 277). The Sifre D text here reads, "for the good, how much more so for punishment," which is inappropriate and illogical. Its presence may possibly be accounted for by the influence of the repeated use of "all the more so" (*ḳal wa-ḥomer*) in this passage.

13. This is the homiletic rendition of Job's speech to his wife. It takes the verse (Job 2:10) as a positive command: Speak like one of those impious women of the generation of the flood, for, as unworthy as they were, they accepted God's decree of punishment; we, the worthy, should do no less. For an entirely different view of the generation of the flood, see B. Sanh 107b, 108a, and Num. Rabbah 21:23.

14. The meaning is unclear: perhaps the covenant to grant them the land arises out of the covenant to chastise them; Or, just as the land is assured to them, so is punishment which brings reward. In MT 94:3 the reading is "because of them, the covenant was made with the children of Israel."

15. *Wisdom* is Torah. *Musar* (from the same root as *yĕsurim,* "sufferings"), here translated as "chastisement," is usually translated as "instruction." The same applies to the following proof verses.

16. The verse is from a section concerning the sufferings of exile which will come upon the people.

17. R. ʿAḳiba alone gives meaning to Eliezer's suffering, for instead of praising him, he expounds upon the benefits of chastisements.

18. We assume that he had been taught by his father. Nevertheless he sinned and atoned only after chastisement. Thus this passage proves that suffering can bring results which even learning cannot attain.

19. *Friend* (ʾohăḇi), literally "he who loves Me."

20. On Isaac's willingness to be sacrificed, see Lev. Rabbah 2:10 and the references and discussion in Shalom Spiegel's classic book *The Last Trial* (New York, 1967).

21. Another play on the word *mĕʾoḏ*. Here it is connected with *moḏeh*, "thankful."

Pisḳa 33

1. *Diyategma*, "edict," is law only after it is displayed in the public place of the city. See S. Lieberman, *Texts and Studies*, p. 62.

2. The connection is by no means clear. Lieberman (*ḲS*, *14*, 330) thinks that an entire section is missing here and that therefore any attempt to conjecture a connection is futile. It has been suggested that the word *ʿal* ("upon") suggests the language of a vow as seen from Neḏ 5:4 and 6:6.

Pisḳa 34

1. See B. Ḳid 30a. The root *šnn*, "teach," means also "to sharpen," as in the verse from Psalms.

2. *Šinnun*, a technical term for recitation of those parts of the Torah which must be recited daily.

3. *Ḳĕširah*, literally "tying," the technical term for the sections of the Torah contained in the phylacteries which are tied to one's head and arm.

4. This section attempts to determine, by logic and by comparison of the verses contained in the Shemaʿ and in the phylacteries, which verses should be in the Shemaʿ. The academic nature of the discussion is apparent.

5. Note that at one time the Ten Commandments were included in the recitation, and possibly also in phylacteries. See the discussion above, Pisḳa 2, note 14.

6. Logic might lead us to an incorrect conclusion, hence the verse specifies *them*, not others.

7. *Ki-fĕloni*. These were some teachers of whom the Sages did not approve, and to whom they referred only as "So-and-so." See Lieberman, *ḲS*, *14*, 333.

8. At no time should you not be busy with them. This opinion is found in MTe 1:17; ṬAZ 1:20; Sif Lev. 86:1 (ʾAḥăre, 13). In B. Men 99b this is repeated, but is disputed by those who say that the verse "is not an obligation or a commandment, but a blessing," i.e., not that one may not ever cease studying, but that if he is blessed, he will not. See also Soṭ 9:16 (24:3). See S. Lieberman, *Greek in Jewish Palestine*, pp. 20–28, for a discussion of the knowledge of Greek culture among the Rabbis.

9. ARN-B 35.

10. Cf. Ber 1:3; B. Ber 11a; i.e., not whenever you stand or recline, but at the normal times for doing so. The text may be corrupt, with the words *talmuḏ loʾmar* standing before *when thou risest up*, which would force us to regard the

quotation as both the answer and the question. The correct structure is two questions followed by the answer. See *EH*.

11. This conversation occurred in the evening. R. Ishmael did not want it to be thought that one must recline in the evening to recite the Shemaʿ, as Shammai taught, so he stood up. R. Eleazar followed Shammai's practice. See Ber 1:3; Tos Ber 1:4. R. Ishmael could have remained reclining, but this might have been misinterpreted. See Yelamdenu, *Waʾetḫnannen,* 35 (101:2, ed. Gruenhut). Lieberman points out, however, that the original version as reflected in manuscripts has the Shammaite, R. Eleazar, act first, followed by the Hillelite, R. Ishmael, who acts in protest. See *TK,* Ber, p. 4.

Piska 35

1. See Piska 34 and notes thereto. This Piska is the reverse of Piska 34, but follows the very same structure.

2. Singular, not plural "signs." See B. Sanh 4b and Mek, *1,* 151. This Piska reflects R. Ishmael's opinion.

3. The two singulars total two frontlets; the plural must total at least two frontlets, hence four in all.

4. Singular, therefore separate scrolls within a single case.

5. See B. Men 37b. It was unusual for the phylactery of the arm to be exposed.

6. Leprosy is marked on a spot free of hair by one mark, the appearance of white hairs. A spot where there is both hair and flesh, or between the eyebrows, is marked unclean by yellow hairs among the hair as well.

Piska 36

1. *U-kĕtabtam.* In B. Shab 103b the word is divided into *u-ketab tam,* "perfect writing."

2. In each case the two letters are graphically very similar.

3. And not as proper lines of poetry. The reference is to the Song of the Sea (Exod. 15).

4. See Sof 1:9.

5. The stones of the house, rather than a scroll to be affixed to the house door.

6. Referring to the stones to be set up when crossing the Jordan. See B. Men 34a for this entire Piska.

7. See Sif Num. 124.

8. Here two are specified, indicating that elsewhere the word refers to only one door-post.

9. A play on words.

10. According to Lieberman (*KS, 14,* 327), the correct reading is *silkot,* the water-pipes used for sanitation in the city.

11. A type of public bathhouse.

12. See P. Yoma 38c (1:5); MSh 3:8.

13. Tos Ber, end.

14. Since the fringes are four in number, we have a total of seven commandments. See Men 3, end; Lieberman, *TK,* Zĕraʿim, p. 125, n. 117. Circumcision thus becomes the eighth; it also takes place on the eighth day after birth.

15. A play on words: *Tirṣah* (Tirzah) and *rĕṣuyah* ("desirable").

Piska 37

1. The verse says that they are not the same, but it does not indicate which is better. Several proofs are then offered to demonstrate that the verse does indeed praise the Land of Israel.

2. The text cites Gen. 35:27, but almost the same identification of Mamre or Kiriath-Arba with Hebron is found in Gen. 23:2–4 (or possibly Gen. 23:19), which is much more appropriate, indicating as it does that Hebron was good only for burial. If Gen. 35:27 is correct, it would refer to the following verse 29, where Isaac's burial is mentioned.

3. Since Hebron was built seven years earlier, we know that it was more important. If the worst of the Land of Israel is more important than the best of Egypt, the comparison in the verse is obviously in favor of the Land of Israel.

4. The fact of its being built earlier.

5. Therefore the dates would mean nothing.

6. He built all these cities for his sons. See Num. Rabbah 16:13.

7. He built Hebron first for Canaan and then Zoan for Mizraim (Egypt). See Yalkuṭ Prov. 943. In B. Ket̲ 112b the verse is interpreted to mean not that Hebron was seven years older but that it was seven times more beautiful.

8. I.e., the fact that it was older is clear proof that it was also more beautiful.

9. A play on two words from the same root. Jewish Publication Society (henceforth JPS) version: *Playing in his habitable earth.*

10. The verse *Her king and her princes are among the nations, Torah is no more* (Lam. 2:9) is incorrectly divided here in order to support this interpretation. See the end of Piska 305 for another such example.

11. He did not dare imply that his land was superior.

12. This is the second proof that the Scriptural comparisons between the Land of Israel and other lands are always favorable to the former.

13. R. Simeon's statement is another comment on the verse from 2 Kings and is not part of the main discussion.

14. A third proof of the same proposition.

15. *Ḥăwilaʾot̲*; F. relates this to the Latin *villa.* The interpretation may be connected with the word *ṣib̲ʾot̲* (*goodliest heritage*), which ordinarily means an army, here probably a castle or fortified dwelling.

16. See Piska 353 for the entire homily of R. Judah.

17. Another interpretation of the verse from Jeremiah; *ṣĕb̲i* means "deer."

18. See also Exod. Rabbah 32:2.

19. Literally "in the horn, the son of fat." This is another proof of the superiority of the Land of Israel.

20. Variant reading: *ʾi,* "if."

21. Textus receptus omits *of the house.*

Piska 38

1. Literally "drinks." The reference is to the two types of watering: Egypt's, by the Nile which rises and falls, and Israel's, by the rains as well as by streams. Although the Biblical intent may have been to indicate how dependent Israel is on God's personal and immediate supervision, the homily emphasizes the superiority of Israel over Egypt, thus continuing the theme of the preceding Piska. The rest

of this verse and the following one describe the process of watering the Egyptian land. For a detailed analysis of this Piska, see R. Hammer, *HUCA,* 50 (1979), 165ff.

2. Possibly another view of the subject: there is rain in Egypt, but it is only supplemental and unimportant, while Israel has two important sources of water, rain and streams.

3. So Yalkuṭ Deut. 857.

4. Or "in his (the king's) service," so F.

5. See the parallel in B. Ḳid 32b. Rashi explains that "Rabbi" here means a highly honored person, and not, as usual, R. Judah the Prince.

6. Returning to the discussion of the beginning of the verse in Piska 37, where the statement *The land whither thou goest . . . is not as the land of Egypt* is interpreted as praising Israel over Egypt, in that if Egypt is the best of all lands, how much better is Israel.

7. Describing the Land of Israel. The verse shows that Egypt is indeed an excellent land—it is like the garden of the Lord, thus sustaining the original interpretation. This is a well-known formula of reasoning:

Step 1. "You say," a statement;

Step 2. The statement is questioned;

Step 3. "Scripture states," confirming the statement in Step 1, and thus preventing one from lapsing into the error of Step 2.

8. In each instance, the analogy is between a wonderful place—Egypt—and an even better one—Israel—thus heightening the praise of the Land of Israel. The manuscripts read "Or is the contrast with the unpleasant and the superior aspects."

9. When the plagues had devastated Egypt.

10. Stressing the word *whence,* i.e., as it was when you were there.

11. During the years that Jacob was in Egypt there was plenty there. This is explicit in Tos Soṭ 10:9 (p. 216). See also B. Sanh 39b, ARN-B 11.

12. Joseph promised to sustain his brothers after Jacob's death by using a phrase similar to that used in Gen. 45:11, where famine is expressly mentioned. The assumption is that both before and after Jacob's sojourn in Egypt there was famine there. See Gen. Rabbah 95 (1233) for other versions of Jacob's blessing.

13. *Ḳidduš haš-šem,* literally "sanctification of the (Holy) Name."

14. According to Tos Soṭ 10:9, R. Jose was the author of the following statement: "When Jacob our father died, the famine returned, as it is said, *Now therefore, fear ye not—I will sustain you and your little ones.* Here Scripture says *sustain,* and elsehwere (Gen. 45:11) it also says *sustain.* Just as sustenance here refers to a time of famine, so sustenance there refers to a time of famine." In our text only the latter part of the statement is cited, although the subsequent discussion is obviously based upon a full statement, such as that in Tos.

15. Interpreting the verbs in disregard of the negative *lo*ʾ, "not."

16. This idea is typical of R. Simeon ben Yoḥai (see Mek̲ Bĕ-šallaḥ, 1, 171). In all such instances his preference for having others engage in physical labor, so that the scholar could devote his full time to study, is clear—an idea which was not accepted by other scholars. On "merit" see Sanders, *Paul,* pp. 180ff.

17. According to Mek̲ Bĕ-šallaḥ, *1,* 171–72, the Canaanites destroyed everything, so that the Israelites would not get it. The forty years were spent in replant-

ing, rebuilding, etc. Thus this period was interpreted as a mark of favor to Israel rather than as a punishment, as the Torah views it.

18. Now that the land was fruitful because of the Israelites, might not the Canaanites enjoy it themselves?

19. A return to the interpretation of the previous verse (11:10), repeating the interpretation of the words *From whence you came out,* in order to show that Egypt was blessed while Israel was there.

20. That is to say, in comparing the Land of Israel with Egypt, the Torah indicates that the former was even better than an excellent land, as Egypt was while the Israelites were there.

21. Although the same Hebrew word is used, *heḳiš,* it has two meanings: above, it was "to contrast"; here, it is "to compare." Both are from the idea of finding the connection between the verses. See Lieberman, *Hellenism in Jewish Palestine,* pp. 60–61.

22. That is to say, to live there in perpetuity, not only temporarily.

23. Therefore the latter was *not* the purpose of the verse. How one could interpret this verse as comparing the two lands when it says expressly *not as the land of Egypt,* is difficult to understand. We may have here an example, not altogether rare, of the homily continuing to use a formula for its stylistic and rhythmic effect even when usage and meaning are not appropriate, thus continuing an effective style of interpreting, almost as one would continue to repeat a refrain in a poem. Unless one examines the text carefully, the problem is hardly noticed and the intended meaning is conveyed, especially if the interpretation is given orally in the fashion in which many such homilies may have originated.

Pisḳa 39

1. The mention of valleys and hills serves an additional purpose—to call attention to the variety of taste in their produce.

2. The amount of ground which can be sown with a *kor* measure of seed.

3. JPS version: *countries.*

4. The word *lands* in Ezekiel is taken as referring to the Land of Israel itself, although usually it is referred to as *land* in the singular. The interpretation that there are many different types of land in it is actually a second explanation of the verse from Ezekiel, the first being that of R. Simeon to the effect that because of its hills it contains several "lands," i.e., many times more land than other countries.

5. I.e., the separate mention of hills and valleys. Another interpretation is added: each hill and valley produces different fruit.

6. The 12 different mentions of *land,* indicating one land for each Tribe.

7. Probably Banyas in the Golan.

8. Either indicating that the valley would thus be turned into a mire or swamp (F.) or that it would be filled with so much dirt that not enough water would remain (*TA*).

9. After an interpretation which shows how one might misunderstand a Scriptural verse and be led to downgrade the blessings of the Land of Israel, a series of other such instances is attached.

10. A similar procedure is used at the beginning of Pisḳa 38. Here the verse from Zechariah is taken to indicate that fields, being exposed, receive rain, but

perhaps not other parts "folded up" into hills. The verse from Deuteronomy indicates that it will receive water, and in all places. This same device is used in the several following interpretations.

11. Taking *mayim* (*water*) as a plural or as a contrast to rain, i.e., irrigation water.

12. Another explanation concerning dew, not another interpretation of the same afore-cited verse.

Piska 40

1. *Kibĕyakol,* a formula introducing an idea which could be considered incompatible with the Lord's dignity, justice, mercy, etc.

2. The verse refers to the Temple.

3. The root *drš* means both "to care for" and "to require." The interpretation here uses the latter meaning.

4. *ʾOtah*—omitted in the JPS version for stylistic reasons. See Ḥal 2:1.

5. Using another meaning of *drš*—"exposition or study of Torah" (as in the word *midraš*). Two sets of verses are cited to demonstrate that study of Torah was a requirement for Israel and will lead to possession of the land.

6. In P. Ber 9:3 this interpretation appears with the additional phrase "and separate their tithes as they should" to explain the meaning of being obedient to God's will. This connects it with the line above and with the reference to tithes in the second paragraph of this Piska.

7. This is another interpretation of the application of the two verses. In B. RH 17b it appears as an interpretation of the verse from Deuteronomy alone. In P. RH 1:3 it is given in the name of R. Simeon ben Yoḥai and is not connected with these verses at all.

8. A separate homily on the theme of the connection between the withholding of rain and the sin of failure to separate offerings. See RH 1:3.

9. As F. points out, this reflects the view of R. Meir that all is decided on New Year's Day and is sealed on the Day of Atonement, while R. Judah taught that the decree is finalized at different times, for rain on the Festival of Tabernacles. See Tos RH 1:13. This represents God's own limitation on His powers.

10. That is, that God has the power to bless produce already stored.

11. This parable illustrates the idea above, that God can both bless and curse the people, according as they may deserve.

12. The Torah is called "tree of life," therefore this verse can be understood as tying together and contrasting the sword and the scroll. For the parallel, see Lev. Rabbah 35.

Piska 41

1. The verb "hearken" (*šamaʿ*) in Hebrew means "to listen" and implies that the next step is "to study."

2. Exod. 13:1.

3. Lev. 1:1ff.

4. Lev. 27:32.

5. Lev. 23:10.

6. Lev. 8:26.

7. Lev. 23:17.
8. Exod. 25:30.
9. Inferred either from the plural of *commandments* or from the emphatic *hearken diligently.*
10. Lev. 19:9.
11. Num. 18:25.
12. Num. 18:8.
13. Lev. 25:1ff. Again, the fact that Scripture speaks of *My commandments* indicates that it refers to all of them, regardless of when or where to be observed—all must be studied.
14. The interpretation stresses that each additional part of the Scriptural verse refers to another group of commandments that we might not have otherwise included. As frequently happens, only the first part of a verse is written out, but the rest of it is implied—a kind of shorthand frequently employed, much as we might today refer to a verse by number only.
15. A discussion is inserted here of Deut. 5:1, already quoted above, which continues until the next part of Deut. 11:13 is quoted later on.
16. JPS version: *As the tongue of fire devoureth the stubble, and as the chaff is consumed in the flame*; but grammatically the sentence may be understood in either way.
17. B Ḳid 40b. On Bet ᶜAris, see *Tarbiz, 1* (1929), 2nd section, 132, where Epstein identifies this as a place near Lod.
18. The quotations from Deuteronomy discuss study of Torah and indicate a more magnificent reward than that promised in Psalms for performance, thus proving the statement that study is more important than performance. See Sanders, *Paul,* pp. 217ff.
19. F. explains this verse to mean that even if you learn it from a lesser teacher, it is as if it comes from God.
20. So King James version. JPS version: *composed in collections.*
21. Interpreting *Bath-rabbim* ("daughter of multitudes") as *beth-rabbim* ("house of teachers") or Rabbinic academy.
22. Since Elijah is mentioned in connection with Damascus, the reference to Damascus in Song 7:5 is understood as a reference to him.
23. See B. Ned 62a.
24. The root *ᶜbd* encompasses both ideas of "service" and "work" (or "performance"). In the verses from Deuteronomy and Genesis the root is here understood to refer to service by study of Torah and not by physical work or performance.
25. The view that Adam had done no physical work prior to his fall is found in ARN-B, chap. 21. See Ginzberg, *Legends, 5,* 92, n. 54, where it is pointed out that the opposite view is also found there.
26. Literally "of divided heart"; while offering a particular sacrifice, the priest's intention should coincide with the original purpose and nature of the sacrifice. Cf. Zeḇ 4:6, B. Zeḇ 46b–47a.
27. In 6:5 the command is addressed to an individual (*thy*), while in 11:13 it is addressed to the people (*your*).
28. A second explanation of why the command was repeated.

Piska 42

1. The homily emphasizes God's personal concern for the welfare of the people

of Israel and the Land of Israel. The same idea and the same phrases are found in the Passover Haggadah and in Meḵ Pisḥa (*I*, 53). See B. Ta 2a. J. Goldin, "Not by Means of an Angel and not by Means of a Messenger," in *Religions in Antiquity* (ed. J. Neusner, Leiden, 1968), p. 423, points out that until now Moses has been speaking, and that versions such as the Samaritan read, "You shall give." Therefore the Sifre stresses the legitimacy of the Masoretic reading.

2. According to B. Ta 10a, God Himself attends to the watering of the Land of Israel, but sends a messenger to give water to other lands. The verse from Job is understood to indicate this, in that *earth* is taken to mean the Land of Israel, while *fields* is taken to refer to other lands, where God *sendeth waters*, i.e., has His messenger do the work of watering. See Pisḳa 38 where this idea is spelled out.

3. In the days of the good queen Salome Alexandra (reigned 76–67 B.C.E.) and her brother Simeon ben Sheṭaḥ rain fell as a reward for their piety. The tradition in Sif Lev. Bĕ-ḥuḳḳoṯay 1, is the same as here. In B. Ta 22b–23a we are told that rain fell only on Wednesday and Sabbath eves. Both sources state that grapes grew thereafter to unusual size. See also B. Pes 112b. In Sifra (ibid.), however, the story follows the interpretation that "its time" means Sabbath eve (Friday night). Since people did not go abroad that night, the rain did not interfere with them. The story of Shelomziyyon is simply an illustration of rain as a blessing, not of the time indicated by *in its season*. Sifre has shortened the section and has thus yielded the strange concept that *in its season* means all week.

4. Reading *ʾayyeh* for *hăre* ("behold"), as F. suggests. Should people say, "We have performed the commandments, yet received no reward," the answer would be, "If you had performed them properly, you would have been rewarded with rain; since no rain has fallen, it follows that you did not perform the commandments properly." It is possible that the story about Queen Shelomziyyon originally concluded as it does in the other sources (above, note 3) with "until wheat kernels became as large as kidneys, barley kernels as large as olive pits, and lentils as large as gold denars." The Sages kept samples of the unusually large produce for future generations to see, in order to demonstrate to the people the blessing for piety and the punishment for wickedness. If that is so, the question here is, why did they keep the samples? The answer is, in order to refute those who say that God does not reward obedience, and to show how great the reward for it can be. The translation of the preceding question ("Why is this emphasized?") would then be, "Why did they do this?"

5. The blessing of rain which makes the earth fruitful.

6. In what follows, *yoreh* is connected with the various meanings of the root *yrh*, the first being "to instruct."

7. Connecting it with the next meaning of *yrh*, "to shoot (an arrow)."

8. Another meaning of *yrh*, "to saturate." See B. Ta 6a.

9. These rains must come at the times specified, not earlier. If they come earlier, they are not considered as the rain of blessing meant here. "When they come in their time, they are a blessing to the world" (R.H.). See B. Ta 6a, Lev. Rabbah 35:12.

10. A second interpretation of the verse from Leviticus. The crops will grow so rapidly that one agricultural process will be continuous with the other.

11. King James and JPS versions: *upon my branch*. Possibly the verse is here

interpreted to mean that both the *root* (= seed) and the harvest are in existence at the same time.

12. The passage appears in B. Ber. 35b, where it is said, "Act according to them (the words of Torah) in the usual manner," i.e., the Torah expects you to live a normal life, including study and work. Abbaye comments there: "Many have followed the advice of R. Ishmael, and it has worked well; others have followed R. Simeon ben Yoḥai, and have not been successful."

13. A play on the word *daḇʾeḵa* (*thy strength,* 33:25), here interpreted as "overflow." The money in other lands will flow into the Land of Israel in exchange for food which will be plentiful there. See Lev. Rabbah 35:11.

14. Hebrew *tiroš,* literally fresh grape juice not yet fermented into wine.

15. Hebrew *yiṣhar,* literally freshly pressed and not yet clarified oil.

Pisḳa 43

1. You will not have to go far away in order to graze your cattle, because your fields will produce enough food to feed your cattle as well as yourselves.

2. I.e., that your cattle will eat up all that is in your fields, leaving nothing for yourselves, which is not a blessing at all.

3. This indicates that you will have enough food left for yourselves, so that the entire verse must have been intended as a blessing.

4. The spaces between the sections of your fields will provide enough fodder for your animals. This is a separate interpretation, not in contradiction with the one above.

5. This is another of R. Simeon's ideas: necessary labor in the fields will be reduced, so that one will have more free time to study. See Pisḳa 42.

6. The two terms—*ḥaṣir* (*grass*) and *ʿeśeḇ* (*herb*)—are practically synonymous. Since man does not eat grass, *herb* must mean a plant useful to man in some other way, namely, to make linen cloth. Both you and your animals will be supplied from your fields. The verse expresses the same idea: flax will be eaten by animals and will also be useful to man. See YŠ, Prov. 948.

7. Perhaps meaning that *thou shalt eat* implies that your eating well is connected with your beast's eating well. The verse from Proverbs indicates that a person who cares for his beast is righteous: hence if your animal eats well, this is a sign that you are righteous and will be rewarded for it.

8. From the young that will be produced by your beasts. Even the young ones will be sufficient to provide for you.

9. The streams and waters that were already there made them feel that they did not need God, whose blessing to the world is rain. See the versions in Meḵ, *2,* 13 and Tos Soṭ 3:6.

10. A possible reference to sexual sins; a play on the word *maʿăyanoṯ* ("fountains"), which is similar to *ʿayin* ("eye"). See Meḵ dĕ-Šhirata, 2, where the reading is, "They cast their eye upon what lies below," i.e., the maidenhead. See Goldin, *Song of the Sea,* ad loc.

11. The Hebrew verb for "dwelling" and "sitting" is the same, *yšḇ*.

12. The verse describing their "dwelling," i.e., eating their fill, is followed by the verses describing their rebellion against God.

13. The Hebrew root for "hospitality" and "foot" is the same, *rgl.*

14. The Hebrew root for "to water" and "to drink" is the same, *šḳh.* Thus the prosperity of the plain of Jordan is connected with the sin committed by Lot's daughters.

15. This is a separate interpretation of the source of the wine, which is added here because it is based on the same verse. The original idea is then carried on further in the following homilies.

16. See B. Mak 24a; Lam. Rabbah 5.

17. See Jer. 26:20, where Uriah is reported to have prophesied the same things as Jeremiah.

18. Emphasizing the seriousness of neglect of study—even David, pious man though he was, was led astray in this manner. For other interpretations of the verse, see Tos AZ 4:3, and YŠ, Sam. 139.

19. The Hebrew *ʾaḥer,* "other," and *ʾaḥer,* "to postpone, to delay," are derivatives of the same root.

20. Literally "others," singular *ʾaḥer,* used in reference to the learned Elisha ben Abuyah who lapsed into heresy (B. Ḥag̃ 14b).

21. Usually translated: *to call upon the name of the Lord.*

22. See Gen. Rabbah 23, and Mek̲, 2, 240.

23. Hebrew *ʿayyarot̲,* presumably a Syriac loanword meaning "vengeances." The fact that Scripture calls idols *gods,* and does not list them under their individual names, indicates that God is lenient toward idol worship. Were all the names to be listed, it would indicate punishment, and no amount of vengeance would suffice to cover all those guilty of idolatry. Mek̲ reads *ʿorot̲* ("hides") suggesting that there is not enough parchment in the world to write upon it all the individual names of pagan deities. See also S. Lieberman, "Palestine in the 3rd and 4th Centuries," *JQR,* 37 (1946), 31.

24. See above, note 19.

25. In Hebrew *ʾElohim,* "God" or "god," is grammatically a plural noun.

26. A homily on the verse from Exodus (see Mek̲ Nezik̲in 17). Had they not called the golden calf "god," indicating that they still worshiped the true God, they would have been destroyed forthwith.

27. In other sources, R. Simeon ben Yoḥai (see F.).

28. According to R. Simeon, the verse means that if one associates the worship of the true God with that of idols, he is liable to extirpation (*karet̲*). He stresses the last part of the verse. See B. Sanh 63a, and Mek̲ de-R. Simeon 22:19.

29. The text here reads *other gods,* referring to the verse from Deuteronomy; other sources, however, refer to the verse from Exodus. The point is that according to the alternative views, the plural suffix in *ʾElohim* indicates not that Israel worshiped both the true God and the golden calf, but that they made several golden calves.

30. A continuation of the homily above, "you worship them, you do not worship Me," as recognized by R.H.

31. See B. Soṭ 9a.

32. Hebrew *meb̲iʾ*; Sif Lev. Bĕ-ḥuk̲k̲ot̲ay 5 (112d) reads *mob̲il* ("have borne"), a play on the Biblical term *yĕb̲ulah* ("her fruit").

33. Thus exile is the most severe of all possible punishments, since a horrible mode of death is less a cause for mourning than a comfortable captivity in exile.

34. Possibly referring to the Babylonian exile. This statement seems to belong

after the comment about the generation of the flood. The author may be suggesting that if in the case of Israel God was actually so long-suffering, even though He had said *quickly,* it was to be expected that He would be equally patient with the generation of the flood, who had not been told that they would be punished *quickly.* E.H. connects this with Ezek. 38, which deals with the wars of Gog and Magog.

35. Rashi (ad loc.) interprets this to mean that the commandments of phylacteries, mezuzah, etc., referred to in Deut. 11:18, would be observed in exile so that they might not be forgotten. Nahmanides disagrees, on the ground that these commandments apply to all places whatsoever, and regards this verse as a reminder to observe them also in exile. R.H. remarks that Sifre, in contradiction to the established custom, seems to call for observance in exile even of such laws as those of heave offering and tithe, so that they might not be forgotten. See P. Shebi 6:1; Ḳid 1:9; P. Ḳid 1:9, on this same question. Sifre seems to imply that these commandments were actually intended to be observed only in the Land of Israel, and that observance of them elsewhere is a matter of practice. See also Pisḳas 44 and 59.

36. Not found in any of the sources.

Pisḳa 44

1. That they are to be observed outside of the Land of Israel as well as within it. This is based upon the connection with the previous verse, *And ye perish quickly from the good land which the Lord giveth you* (11:17). This verse (11:18) is taken as ordaining that when one has gone into exile, he should study Torah and wear phylacteries. From these two particulars the general command is then deduced to observe all personal commandments outside of the Land of Israel. See P. Shebi 6:1, where this is so stated. The legal formulation of this rule, without the proof verses, is found in the Mishnah, Ḳid 1:9.

2. *Binyan ʾab.* See ARN-A, chap. 37. This is one of the seven hermeneutic rules ascribed to Hillel, used to deduce from two Scriptural passages something which is applicable to other passages as well.

3. See Lev. 19:23ff., prohibiting the fruit of a tree produced during the first three years.

4. The mixing of different seeds, etc.

5. The new grain crop which may not be eaten before the ceremony of the *ʿomer.* See Lev. 23:10–14.

6. These exceptions are based upon oral tradition. See B. Ḳid 37a.

Pisḳa 45

1. In B. Ḳid 30a the word *śamtem* (*shall ye lay up*) is divided into two, *sam tam,* "perfect remedy." Here, too, there may be a play on words, *sam ha-ḥayyim,* "elixir of life." *Sam* means generally a medicine or drug.

2. Apply Torah, which is compared to bread or water, to your enemy, i.e., to the Inclination to evil, and you will defeat him. See B. AZ 5b, MTe 119.7 (*YJS,* 2, 256).

Pisḳa 46

1. The Hebrew word *bĕneḵem* may mean either generally "your children" or

specifically "your male children." See B. Ḳid 30a. In P. Ber 1:3, it is pointed out that women are not obligated but are permitted to study Torah and to wear phylacteries.

2. This verse, not R. Jose's interpretation, is the source. See Tos Ḥag̅ 1:2, Sif Zuṭa Bĕ-šallaḥ 38.

3. This is not a Scriptural verse but a negative paraphrase based upon the principle which follows.

Pisḳa 47

1. See B. Sanh 90b on the problem of the Biblical basis for the resurrection of the dead. See also Moore, *Judaism,* 2, 379ff.; Kadushin, *Rabbinic Mind,* pp. 361ff.

2. An interpretation of the verse, *In your presence is fullness* (*śoḇa*ᶜ) *of joy* (Ps. 16:11), where *śoḇa*ᶜ is read *šeḇa*ᶜ ("seven"). See Pisḳa 10.

3. Based on the interpretation of the verse in Judges, to the effect that there were seven groups of the righteous, one higher than the other. See also Lev. Rabbah 30:2, and P. Ḥag̅ 2:1. "Ascents" refers to levels.

4. Another interpretation of Psalm 121:1.

5. He divides the Hebrew *le-ma*ᶜ*ălot̲* into *l* (the letter *lamed̲* = 30) and *ma*ᶜ*ălot̲,* "levels." Rabbi doubles it to 60 on the basis of the plural form.

6. *Ṣĕd̲aḳah,* "alms," is from the same root as *ṣaddiḳ,* "righteous man."

7. Returning to the interpretation of Dan. 12:3. Perhaps they are like the stars, even if they do not do God's will. However, since in this verse they by definition do His will (*turn the many to righteousness*), it is likely that this is a comment originally based on a verse such as Gen. 22:17, 15:5, where Abraham's descendants are described as being like the stars. The conclusion is that this reward will come only when they do His will.

8. Possibly people would have lived forever, were it not for sin. See Eccl. Rabbah 1:4.

9. The verse is understood as saying first that there is a finite number to the children of Israel, and then that they cannot be counted. They are limited in number when they disobey, and unlimited when they do obey. Instead of "One Scriptural verse . . ."—which is F.'s emendation—R has "Similarly Scripture states." No emendation is needed here, since this is a continuation of the paragraph ending with "*dust in threshing,*" which was interrupted by "Another interpretation." It continues the same theme: the contrast between when Israel do God's will and when they do not.

10. Another solution to the contradiction in the verse. See B. Yoma 22b; Num. Rabbah 2:18.

Pisḳa 48

1. The usual translation is "obey," but the Hebrew root *šm*ᶜ means literally "to listen," which is understood here to refer to studying. See Pisḳa 41, where this verse is interpreted to mean that one is obligated to study even when he cannot fulfill the commandments.

2. I.e., studied.

3. Literally "his *sela*ᶜ (a coin worth two common shekels)."

4. ʾ*bd* can also mean "to lose." The word is used throughout this passage in both senses. The proof verses from Proverbs speak of "wisdom," which is interpreted as meaning Torah.

5. The Roman *as,* 1/24 of a denar.

6. The parable elaborates on the theme of studying a lesson and going over it again and again.

7. In Yalḳuṭ Prov. 945 the reading is simpler: "If one says, 'Tomorrow I shall study, tomorrow I shall review . . .' " Perhaps the text here should read, "Today I will not (reading ʾ*eni* for ʾ*ăni*) study, tomorrow I will study," etc.

8. See ARN-A 24, where several elements of this section are found in a different arrangement ascribed to Elisha ben Abuyah. Literally "by way of tradition (*bĕ-ḳabbalah*)," a Rabbinic term for the Prophets and the Writings. Lieberman has suggested that this may reflect the idea that the writers of these books "received" their tradition orally. See Finkelstein, *New Light from the Prophets* (London, 1969), p. 136, n. 17.

9. The statement may mean that the beginning student is hungry for every bit of instruction. In YŠ, Prov. 961 the reading is "this is a disciple who did not learn in his youth."

10. See ARN-A 40.

11. *Ḥărisim,* possibly read *ḥăsidim,* as in R, Midrash Samuel 1, and P. Ber 9, end. Some accept the alternate meaning of *ḥărisim,* "suns," and see in it a reference to the Essenes, who are said to have recited their morning prayers at the appearance of the rising sun. See F. Perles, *JQR,* 17 (1926–27), 405.

12. *Ye* = all of Israel.

13. In Midrash Psalms 1:18 this proof-verse is used to include proselytes as well. See also Sif Lev. ʾAḥăre Moṯ 13:13; B. Sanh 59a.

14. The text is difficult. The translation here is based on the parallels in YŠ ʿEḳeḇ 873, and MhG. The sense seems to be that those who were of common origin did indeed save the Torah. Their "word"—their teachings and interpretations—was as valuable as the observance of Torah by the whole nation of Israel.

15. The extant text here contains some additional words which were probably misread by copyists. A similar discussion in Tos ʿEḏ 1:1 uses the verse in Amos to point out that interpretations of Torah differed one from the other, as in the case of Hillel and Shammai, and discusses those who attempt to secure rulings made to their own liking. Here the meaning is that the verse refers to people who go from one legal authority to another in order to get an appropriate answer, but find none qualified to supply it.

16. Commenting on the same verse in Amos, as is clear from the version in B. Shab 138b.

17. The verse says neither simply "a commandment" nor "the commandment" but *all this commandment,* meaning that one is never quit of the duty to study, since he must learn everything, including all interpretations. Midrash means interpretation of the Biblical text, either legal or narrative, probably the older, short interpretations to explain the text. Halaḵah means rules passed on by oral tradition. Haggaḏah consists of sayings or stories of nonlegal nature not connected to the text. F. states that these are three types of learning subsumed under the title Mishnah, the equivalent of Midrash or Biblical exposition (*Baer Jubilee Volume* [Jerusalem, 1960], pp. 28–35). See also Pisḳa 306, note 40, and B. Ḳid 44a.

18. Going back to the discussion above of *it is your life.* One must study every Scriptural lesson, thus causing God to rejoice.

19. The seemingly superfluous *even Mine* must be interpreted as referring to an additional father, the One in heaven.

20. He has kept them, in the sense of keeping them in his memory and not forgetting them. See the discussion in Piska 41.

21. See Piska 41.

22. I.e., the Torah. See ʾAḇ 3:18 on improper use of the Torah for worldly purposes, and the comment on this in ARN-B 27, which is the same as this one. See Dan. 5:2–3 on Belshazzar's profaning the Temple vessels which had been consecrated for exclusive Temple use.

Piska 49

1. JPS and Authorized versions: *on.*

2. Rabbinic tradition calls upon man to imitate God by living in accordance with His qualities of mercy and justice, not those of punishment. See Mek̲ Bĕšallaḥ, Širah, 3; P. Pe 1:1. And see Goldin, *Song of the Sea,* p. 114; Schechter, *Some Aspects of Rabbinic Theology* (New York, 1936), pp. 199ff.

3. See Piska 26 on God's dispensing of grace as free gifts (*ḥinnam*).

4. The devout man (*ḥasiḏ*) is zealous in his performance of commandments and willing to dispense with his legal rights. On the meaning of *ḥasiḏ,* see S. Schechter, *Studies in Judaism* (Philadelphia, 1958), pp. 123ff.

5. Some readings have "expounders of *rĕšumoṯ.*" Lauterbach, in *JQR, 1* (1910–11), 291ff., 503ff., considers them to be "Palestinian teachers . . . (who) developed their method of allegorical interpretation independent of external influences" (p. 305). He translates the following sentence here "Learn to understand and interpret correctly what Scripture says about Him, for in this way thou canst recognize the Holy One" (p. 304).

Piska 50

1. Perhaps rather R. Eliezer ben Jacob, who is mentioned immediately below, since R. Jacob was not a contemporary of R. Eleazar ben Azariah (F.).

2. Making certain that the land should not become desolate, so that wild beasts would not multiply.

3. Compare Piska 25, above. "Numerous" in Hebrew means also "strong."

4. *Thou* (7:1) is singular, while *yourselves* (11:23) is plural, indicating all of you together.

5. This is taken to mean that the Amorite nation by itself was mightier than all Israel.

Piska 51

1. Even places not specifically designated may be conquered. This may refer to the inclusion of these places for such commandments as dough offering, P. Ḥal 2:5, 58:1,2.

2. This question is discussed in Piska 44. The commandments meant here

may be the agricultural ones, as in the subsequent discussion. Alternatively, the discussion here may cover all commandments, and the subsequent discussion may cover a different subject: where do the rules governing agricultural produce apply?

3. The verse repeats the word twice, once in regard to foreign lands that they may conquer, and once specifically in regard to the borders of the Land of Israel.

4. I.e., the Land of Israel.

5. See B. Giṭ 8a for a discussion of the exact boundaries of the Land of Israel. Cf. also Maimonides' *Code, VII,* III, *i,* 2–9 (*YJS, 21,* 98–101).

6. And may be conquered.

7. I.e., is not your property.

8. Attaching the last word of the verse to the words under discussion.

9. Perhaps referring to islands (as in B. Giṭ 8a) or else to the control of the sea.

10. The verse says *hay-yam hag-gaḏol u-gĕḇul* rather than *gĕḇul yam hag-gaḏol,* therefore the implication is that there are two possible boundaries, the one which is given them, and the other if they conquer it. The Great Sea is the Mediterranean.

11. Referring to the Sabbatical year. See Sheḇi 6:1. The connection with the discussion and with the quoted verses is unclear. According to various sources (P. Sheḇi 6:1, Ḳid. 1:9) the holiness of the Land ceased after the first exile. The returnees voluntarily accepted this holiness again, therefore only the places they occupied come under the obligation of commandments connected with the Land of Israel.

12. This list appears in other sources as well: Tos Sheḇi 4; P. Sheḇi 6, 36c (see Tos Ḳid, ad loc.). Most interestingly, the text, with minor changes, has been found in the mosaic inscription in the synagogue at Reḥob. J. Sussman, in his Hebrew articles in *Tarbiz, 43* (1974), 88–158, and *45* (1976), 213–57, has analyzed it in detail. A translation of the inscription and a general discussion in English may be found in his "The Inscription in the Synagogue at Reḥob," in *Ancient Synagogues Revealed,* ed. L. Levine (Jerusalem, 1981), pp. 146–59. The list goes from southwest to north, northeast, southeast, and southwest, with details only along the northern border. As Sussman notes, "the intention of the baraita was primarily to delineate this short border segment on the edge of the dense Jewish settlement in the Galilee, and to define precisely the limits of the land as denoted in Sheḇi 6. Hence what we have here is plainly a halaḵic baraita . . . rather than an early historical-geographical document" (p. 149). For further discussion, as well as a detailed map, see Pinhas Neʾeman, *Tĕḥume ʾEreṣ Yiśraʾel lĕ-fi Sifruṯ ḤaZaL* (Jerusalem, 1978), and the Hebrew articles by R. Frankel, I. Finkelstein, and R. Zadok, in *Cathedra, 27* (1983), 39ff.

Pisḳa 52

1. See Goldin, *Song of the Sea,* p. 224, note on *Awe and terror.*

2. See Sifre Num. 157, Meḵ Širaṯa, chap. 9; Goldin, *Song of the Sea,* p. 214.

3. See Goldin, *Song of the Sea,* p. 53, on Rabbinic resentment toward Solomon's marriage.

4. Meḵ dĕ-Pisḥa 12.

Piska 53

1. The passage concerns the end of 30:19 rather than 11:26. Why does 30:19 say *choose life?* So that you will not think that either choice is legitimate. The idea of setting before the children of Israel both blessing and curse appears also here and thus enables the editor to set it forth at this point.

2. The word *ʾaḥărit̲*, "end" (or "future"—so JPS version) also indicates a reward (and is so rendered in the King James version).

3. Either interpreting this as meaning the wicked when they suffer, or possibly reading *ʿošḳim*, "oppressors," for *ʿăšuḳim*, "oppressed."

4. *Tomik̲*, literally "graspest."

5. Once Ps. 16:5 is mentioned, the interpretation of the following verses is also included.

Piska 54

1. The word *lifted up* (*śeʾet̲*) is from the same root as *yiśśaʾ* in the phrase *yiśśaʾ b̲ĕrak̲ah*, "receive a blessing."

2. A sarcastic comment: these interpretations of yours are not deep secrets revealed only to you—they are stated explicitly in the text.

3. Part paraphrase and part quotation from Deut. 11:27–28.

4. Each will receive the appropriate consequence of his conduct, good or evil.

5. This third example lacks any interpretation. Probably it was something to the effect that the just man will be rewarded with good and the evil man will be punished, to which R. Eliezer replies: This is obvious from Prov. 16:4. See B. Ḥag̱ 14a for this particular meaning of "whisper" (*laḥaš*).

6. See Piska 2.

7. See Piska 43.

8. See Sif Num. 111 (p. 116) and parallels. In other sources this idea is attached to more appropriate Scriptural verses. It should be noted that the form and quality of sections in the Sifre vary greatly. This section, for example, is poorly developed in comparison with the preceding ones and includes many statements based on other verses borrowed for use here.

Piska 55

1. See B. Bek̲ 5a, Mek̲ de-R. Simeon 13:11 (p. 42), where this interpretation is applied to Exod. 13:11 and refers to the commandment of the first-born.

2. The singular *blessing* implies one blessing at a time, not all of them together.

3. The technical term used is *kĕlal u-fĕraṭ*. This is one of the seven principles of hermeneutics formulated by Hillel and one of the thirteen formulated by R. Ishmael.

4. The reference is to the two groups, six tribes on each of the mountains. Both groups responded "Amen" to all the pronouncements of the Levites who stood below. See Soṭ 7:5 for a complete description of the ceremony.

Piska 56

1. See B. Soṭ 33b, where the entire section is found, as well as Tos Soṭ 21:3.

2. The word *mab̲oʾ*, "going down," means literally "coming" and is therefore

interpreted here as "rising." From the point of view of the Canaanites, the Israelites were in the east, where the sun rises, while the Israelites arriving from the desert thought of themselves as being in the west.

3. In Deut. 11:29 they added the words "which is Shechem," since the latter place is sacred to them.

4. R. Eliezer disagrees with the previous interpretation. He attempts to show that the points of reference in the verse do not fit the location of the mountains in Samaria. According to P. Soṭ 7, 21:3, he held that they erected artificial mounds of earth where they were and called them Gerizim and Ebal. See Tos Soṭ 8:7 for an opposing opinion.

5. See Gen. 34:2.

6. He agrees that the verse does not fit the mountains that we know, but says that the intent of the verse is only to describe the path which they were to take.

Piska 58

1. See Piska 48.

2. *Midrašot*, i.e., laws learned through interpretation of the Scriptural text, such as those we find in the Sifre. This interpretation of such terms is to be found in many places in Tannaitic literature. They include the various forms of Rabbinic teaching. See Sif Num. 46:4, 85:4, 99:3, 112:3.

Piska 59

1. See note 2 to Piska 58.

2. The verse first speaks of performing all the laws, then speaks of the Land of Israel, but then refers to *ʾădamah*, which means land in general and not the Land of Israel alone. This method of deduction is associated with R. ʿAkiba. The same idea is presented in Piska 44, in a different manner associated with R. Ishmael (F.).

3. B. Ḳid. 37a. *ʿOrlah* is the fruit of newly planted trees in the first three years, which was forbidden to be eaten (Lev. 19:23–25). Diverse kinds (*kilʾayim*) refers to planting of mixed seeds together in the same field, mixed breeding of animals, making cloth of mixed stuffs, etc., all of which is forbidden (Lev. 19:19). New crops (*ḥadaš*) denotes the consumption of new crops before the waving of the sheaf of *ʿomer*, likewise prohibited (Lev. 23:10–14).

Piska 60

1. Literally "with a destroying ye shall destroy," indicating that this must be done as many times as needed.

2. *Their gods* is actually the subject of the verb *served*, which appears before it in the Hebrew text. The interpretation here is based on the exact order of the Hebrew words, literally "to dispossess them, their gods."

3. The Canaanites'.

4. In Deut. 7:5 and elsewhere we are commanded to destroy the trees, whereas according to R. Jose's interpretation here the trees themselves were not worshiped as a divinity. See AZ 3:5, B. AZ 45a.

5. R. ʿAkiba differs from R. Jose in his interpretation of the verse: it does not signify that these themselves are not gods, but that idols are always located there.

Piska 61

1. See AZ 3:7 for a fuller text.

2. The full text in the Mishnah refers to a tree which has been trimmed in order to worship branches which will then sprout. These must be cut off, but the rest of the tree is permitted.

3. I.e., removed the idol.

4. Used for idol worship. This section precedes the other in the Mishnah.

5. See B. AZ 45b, 46a, where examples are given of changing the names of places used for idolatry in order to show how detestable they were: thus the title "all seeing eye" was changed to "eye of a thorn," and "house of revelation" to "house of concealment." Cf. Tos AZ 6(7)4. R. ʿAḳiba believed that the meaning of the verse was not what R. Eliezer said it was, since that idea was expressed elsewhere.

6. See Tos Mak 5(4):8.

7. F. suggests that this is a prohibition issued following the destruction of the Temple: Jews were not to remove any of the debris from the site, thus compounding its destruction.

Piska 62

1. I.e., seek out the proper location by inquiring of a prophet.

2. Whether that is the right place or not.

3. To compensate for the loss of land needed for the Temple compound. See Ginzberg, *Legends,* 3, 75, and Piska 352 (and notes to both).

4. Until the plot of land was taken over for the Temple.

5. R has "They benefited from it for four hundred and forty years." The tradition that Jethro's descendants benefited from the land during the hundreds of years before the building of the Temple is found in many places including ARN-A 35 (104) (*YJS, 10,* 145) and Sif Num. 81 (p. 77).

6. The parallel source in ARN-A 35 reads as follows: "One verse says, *The place which the Lord shall choose in one of thy Tribes* (Deut. 12:14), and another verse says, *Out of all your Tribes* (12:5). *In one of thy Tribes* refers to the Tribes of Judah and Benjamin; *Out of all your Tribes* refers to Jerusalem, in which all Israel share. What was contained in the portion of Judah? The Temple Mount, the Temple treasuries, and the Temple courts. And what was contained in the portion of Benjamin? The Sanctuary, the Porch, and the chamber of the Holy of Holies. And a triangular strip extended (from the portion of Judah into the portion of Benjamin), and upon it was the altar built. Benjamin was found worthy and was made host for the Almighty, as it is said (concerning Benjamin), *And He dwelleth between his shoulders* (33:12). Said Joshua at that time: 'I know that the Temple is to be set up on the border between Judah and Benjamin; I shall go (therefore) and prepare the pasture of Jericho.'" (Goldin's translation, *YJS, 10,* 144–45).

7. Literally "in the limits" (*bag-gĕḇulim*), i.e., everywhere, not only in the Temple. Instead of "Chosen House" all the texts have "the holy language." F., following Elijah Gaon, assumes that this was the result of an incorrect reading of an abbreviation.

8. What is the point of specifying the Temple if the blessing (including the Ineffable Name) is to be recited everywhere? The answer is that the Name itself (the Tetragrammaton) was pronounced only in the Temple. Elsewhere the substitute

Adonay ("Lord") was used. There were differing traditions concerning the source of this statement in the Bible, although the practice was accepted by all. Exod. 20:21, used here to prove that the blessing was recited everywhere, is quoted in Meḵ Baḥodeš 11 (p. 287) as referring to the Temple. The verse in Deuteronomy is used here to prove that the Name itself was used only in the Temple, while in Sif Num., pp. 43, 48, and B. Soṭ 38a, the verse from Num. 6:27 is used for this purpose.

Piska 63

1. Perhaps the Torah permits but does not require these to be offered on the festival day. Not so, for the verse proves otherwise.

2. In Lev. 23:38, as interpreted above. In all the sources the verse cited throughout is Num. 29:39. F. follows Elijah Gaon's reading.

3. This is the answer to the question posed at the beginning of this Piska.

4. That they must be brought on the festival day.

5. Cf. Exod. 22:28, Deut. 23:22.

6. *Seasons* is the plural, implying all the festivals.

7. See Sif Lev., ʾEmor 12:10 and P. RH 1:1 (56:2), where this entire passage is found. From there it is obvious that this ruling is based on the interpretation of the verse in Leviticus, and has been inserted here because the verse in Deuteronomy plays a role in this homily.

8. Tos Beḵ 7:1.

Piska 64

1. Within the curtained area of the Holy of Holies. See Zeḇ 5:5–6.

2. See Yoma 1:1. The wife was often referred to as "one's house" because of her central role in the family.

Piska 65

1. In the wilderness Israel had the Tabernacle and brought sacrifices nowhere else. In the Holy Land they sacrificed for years both at the various altars and at a central shrine, as explained below and in B. Zeḇ 112b and Tos Zeḇ 14:4–8.

2. See Tos Zeḇ 13:15, B. Zeḇ 117a.

3. In Meḡ 1:10 there is a discussion concerning the individual's own altar and the communal altar. The general principle enunciated there is that whatever is vowed or pledged may be offered on the private altar.

4. There was a tradition that only burnt offerings and peace offerings were brought on the altars. See Sif Lev. 84:1, *ʾAḥăre moṯ* 1:6.

Piska 66

1. For how long will the present situation continue?

2. R. Simeon's identification was traditional. See Piska 1, above. Here, however, it is inappropriate, as R. Judah points out, since the more permanent expression, "possessing," must apply to the permanent place, Jerusalem.

Piska 67

1. Although the last part of verse 10 does not appear in the text, clearly that

is what is under discussion. The Temple will be built after you have rest, i.e., once your enemies have been destroyed, which in turn comes after the appointment of a king. See B. Sanh 20b and Tos Sanh 4:5. The order is: appoint a king, destroy the Amalekites, and then build the Temple.

2. In the Hebrew the same root (*šam*) is used for both, indicating to the commentator that there were two areas called "there."

3. See Pisḳa 64. The higher sacrifices must be eaten within the priestly section of the Sanctuary. So-called lesser sacrifices might be eaten within the precinct of Jerusalem.

Pisḳa 68

1. In 12:6; why repeat it again in verse 11? See Pisḳa 63.

2. According to Rabbi, the former refers to the sanctuary which was set up at Shiloh, the latter to Jerusalem.

Pisḳa 69

1. Pisḳa 64, note 1.

2. Literally "this Levite"; the term occurs also in 12:18, 14:27, 29. These verses are taken to indicate the various places from which he may draw support.

Pisḳa 70

1. The phrase *take heed* is to be taken as a warning against an action that is prohibited elsewhere in Scripture. See B. Zeḇ 106a, P. Kil 8:1 (31b).

2. See Zeḇ 4:5. The sacrifices offered to the Temple by non-Jews do not involve the same restrictions as those offered by Jews.

3. Derived from verse 27 (F.)

4. 1 Kings 18:23. Elijah's is an extreme case, since he offered sacrifices outside the Temple when it was still in existence and therefore violated a prohibition. See Lev. Rabbah 22:9, B. Zeḇ 90b. Nevertheless, as an established prophet (see B. Sanh 89b), he was to be obeyed.

5. See Pisḳa 62.

6. The negative, as above (12:13), and the positive, here.

Pisḳa 71

1. The permission to eat flesh not slaughtered as a sacrifice is stated elsewhere (Deut. 12:20; see Pisḳa 75). Therefore this verse must refer to something else, namely to an animal which was dedicated but was subsequently found unfit to be offered. See Lev. 27:28, Beḵ 2:2.

2. Sif Lev. Bĕ-ḥuḳḳotay 4:1, B. Beḵ 6a. An imperfect animal may be redeemed only when the imperfection is permanent; otherwise it may be offered later, after the imperfection has corrected itself.

3. See B. Beḵ 15a, Tos Beḵ 2:3.

4. The prohibitions apply only before the slaughtering.

5. See Exod. 13:13. Cf. Beḵ 2:2 on the question of which animals are or are not to be included.

6. According to the School of Hillel, nonpriests may be invited to share in its flesh; see B. Bek̲ 32b.

7. *Gĕzerah šawah.* An analogy between similar phrases in two Scriptural passages is preferred to a logical inference, since the latter might be disproved logically.

8. The comparison is to the firstling which is blemished.

9. Concerning animals slaughtered for profane consumption. R includes the phrase *the unclean and the clean* from the same verse. Since 12:15 includes *and the clean,* this verse (12:22) too must be understood as if it then said, "and the clean," i.e., from the entire statement, with *as one*(12:22) adding that they may both eat from the same dish. The form may be influenced by a more appropriate usage elsewhere (see next note).

10. This appears in Pisḳa 75 concerning the firstling, and is simply copied here (F.).

11. The gazelle and the hart are wild animals and therefore exempted from priestly gifts and from the firstling offering. See B. Bek̲ 15a.

12. The fat of the gazelle and of the hart is permitted, but not that of the dedicated blemished animals (B. Bek̲ 15a).

13. In B. Ker 4b it is stated that there are five negative commandments concerning blood. Here we are told that even though stated more than once, it is the same single prohibition.

14. See B. Pes 22a; benefit does not include use as food or drink.

15. Make fit to be defiled; see B. Pes 22b.

Pisḳa 72

1. It is a question not of ability, as might be deduced from the literal meaning of the Hebrew *tuk̲al* ("mayest"), but of being forbidden to do so.

2. Another form of the same Hebrew verb is used here, *yok̲lu.*

3. That it may not be eaten outside of Jerusalem.

4. The fuller version in B. Mak 19b specifies that this applies equally when the eater is unclean and when the produce is unclean.

5. See B. Mak 16b, Tos Mak 4.4.

6. A comparison is made in B. Mak 16b with Deut. 26:12, where the poor man's tithe is mentioned and the same phrase *within thy gates* is used.

7. See Pisḳa 67.

8. Deut. 26:5–10.

9. And is liable to a flogging. See B. Mak 17a for the entire section.

10. Not liable to being cut off (R.H.).

11. A sacrifice rejectable in consequence of an improper intention in the mind of the officiating priest.

Pisḳa 73

1. So Elijah Gaon of Vilna.

2. Which separated the partitions of the Temple, as they did the partitions of the Tabernacle.

Pisḳa 74

1. See Pisḳa 73, note 2.

2. See Piska 107, where this prohibition refers both to Shiloh and to Jerusalem.

3. Instead of "wherever you find the term Levite" R has "support this Levite."

4. You must support the Levite even when there is no tithe due him, but in the Diaspora he is no different from any other poor man (R.H.).

Piska 75

1. See Mek Dĕ-Pisḥa 12, where Exod. 34:24 is mentioned.

2. If it does not refer to the territory of the seven Canaanite nations mentioned elsewhere.

3. R. Ishmael understands from this verse that before this they were not permitted to eat such meat, while R. ʿAkiba insists that the verse tells us only how to eat it, and no more. See also B. BB 60b.

4. See B. Ḥul 84a, Tos ʿAr 4:26.

5. Perhaps offered as good advice, rather than as a binding rule.

6. See B. Ḳid 57b. *Ḥullin,* i.e., nonsacrificial meat, may be slaughtered only outside the Temple and not within it, hence you may slaughter it not for sacrifice only when *the place* (i.e., the Sanctuary) is far away from you, i.e., when you are not within it or near it.

7. The clean and unclean may eat together (F.).

8. See Piska 71; Lev. 7:31–32.

9. Lev. 3:4.

10. See B. Ḥul 28a, where it is stated that this verse, instead of setting down the rule for hart and gazelle, merely indicates that these beasts are subject to the same rule as disqualified consecrated domestic animals, and consequently must be slaughtered ritually. In other words, this verse is not a new rule but a reference to another, covering, rule; it does not prescribe, but must be understood from other verses.

11. B. Yoma 75b. The rule for fowl is not in the Torah but was given orally to Moses.

Piska 76

1. Since Moses is speaking of it now, one might think that they were still continuing in that practice. See L. Ginzberg, *An Unknown Jewish Sect* (New York, 1976), p. 13. According to this "sect," the eating of blood was forbidden since the time of Noah.

2. Why, then, emphasize this one by *only be steadfast?* On the traditional number of commandments, see B. Mak 23b. Here the figure three hundred is a round one, since a specific figure did not exist during Tannaitic times (F.).

3. Or "simplest" in that it is easy to observe and costs nothing. See Mak 3:15, where it is stated that man has a natural aversion to blood, thus rendering this a commandment which everyone would be eager to observe.

4. See B. Shab 130a (ascribed to R. Simeon ben Eleazar), referring to the persecution by the emperor Hadrian during the Bar Kokhba rebellion. For "is performed in public," the Talmud reads "is firmly observed." "In public" implies proudly. This may have some connection with the idea that public desecration of any commandment was eventually forbidden, B. AZ 74a. See also Mek Šabbata 1, which reads "have been retained by them." This saying reflects the change in

attitude toward martyrdom which took place in the generation following the Hadrianic edicts. See M. D. Herr, "Persecution and Martyrdom in Hadrian's Days," in *Scripta Hierosolymitana,* 23 (1972), 122, n. 134.

5. See B. Sanh 56a, Tos AZ 8:4ff. The captive woman was permitted only to those who were commanded to conquer the Land of Israel, i.e., that particular generation of Israelites, even though she had been prohibited to all the children of Noah. On the Noachide laws, see Moore, *Judaism, 1,* 274; Ginzberg, *Legends, 1,* 70.

6. An animal slaughtered in any manner deviating from that prescribed by Jewish law.

7. See Exod. 12:9. One is forbidden to eat of the Paschal lamb if it is boiled rather than roasted, but there is no commandment against the cooking itself.

8. Logic cannot establish the rule, hence the verse is needed to do so.

Piska 77

1. In Deut. 12:5–6 (*EH*).

2. *Be᾿er hag-Golah,* located southward in the Hall of the Diaspora (Mid 5:4, ʿEr 10:14).

3. That these, too, are such as were brought from outside the Land; they were not. See B. Tem 21a–b, where R. ʿAḳiba teaches that on the basis of Deut. 14:23, firstlings were not to be brought from outside the Land. This is found in Piska 106. See also Ḥal 4:11.

4. See Tem 3:5. They can pasture anywhere until a defect appears, after which they are eaten, whereas the blemished sin and guilt offerings must be sold and replaced with unblemished ones, and unblemished ones must be offered at the Temple.

5. In the singular. See B. Beḵ 56b.

6. *Only* is taken as excluding someone, in this case the orphan.

Piska 78

1. See B. Pes 77a, Tos Zeḇ 4:1. If one is unfit, the other may not be offered.

2. Blood is dashed against the altar, flesh is cast onto the altar.

3. See B. Ḥul 90a.

4. The Hebrew word *dam* ("blood") is here in the singular.

5. B. Naz 25a. A substitute for it was not permitted, but if it was offered, both animals would then be considered consecrated.

Piska 79

1. See Tos Sheḳ 2:1. R. Ishmael is concerned not with what men think but only with what is pleasing to God. R. ʿAḳiba is concerned with both (F.). R reads "R. Ishmael, however, says: *Good and right* in the sight of heaven and *good* in the sight of man; similarly Scripture says, *So shalt thou find . . . favor,* etc."

Piska 80

1. See Piska 55.

2. You are not confined to their houses and cities, but may build new settlements anywhere in the Holy Land.

3. The verse places this one commandment on an equal footing with all the commandments together.

4. See Tos AZ 4:4; B. Ket 110b, 111a, on the subject of leaving the Holy Land.

Piska 81

1. Variously interpreted as wide trousers (by Hoffmann) or helmet (by Jastrow).

2. See B. Sanh 61a, AZ 51a–b. One is liable only for worshiping an idol in the same way as God is worshiped or in the way in which that idol is usually worshiped. Other ways of such worship are also forbidden, but one is not liable for them. One is also forbidden to worship God in the same ways as idols are worshiped.

Piska 82

1. Meaning that every positive commandment implies a negative commandment, forbidding the violation of the positive commandment.

2. Zeb 8:10, Tos Zeb 8:5. The conclusion of the Baraita, which does not appear in our text, discusses cases of not adding or not diminishing. The section quoted here is not pertinent to the discussion.

3. Tos Suk 2:8. There are to be in them no more and no less than the four statutory species.

Piska 83

1. The false prophet will naturally pattern himself after the greatest true prophet, Moses. It has been suggested that this Piska would fit more appropriately with the description of the true prophet (see F.'s note).

2. Sif Num. 103.

Piska 84

1. B. Sanh 90a. See Lieberman, *KS, 14,* 328: God permits this for a while; nevertheless, you must not join them.

2. They performed miracles when they were true prophets. F., in "Improved Readings in the Sifre," *PAAJR, 4* (1932–33), 43, sees in this a reference to the question of the authenticity of the miracles ascribed to the Christian Savior.

3. Jer. 28:1. See Ginzberg, *Legends, 6,* 389; P. Sanh 11:7 (30b).

4. Perhaps meaning that he is not to be put to death.

5. His previous prophecies, prior to his apostasy, need not be suspect. See Lieberman, *KS, 14,* 334; Tos Bek 3:32.

Piska 85

1. This reading is F.'s reconstruction on the basis of logic. The manuscript (R) reading is: "*and His commandments shall ye keep*—this is a positive commandment—*and unto His voice shall ye hearken*—in order to apply a negative commandment to the voice of His prophets."

Piska 86

1. B. Sanh 67a. See Ginzberg, *Unknown Sect,* p. 150: stoning was also specified by the laws of that sect.

2. See B. Sanh 90a. If he suggests only partial abandonment of a commandment, he is exempt. But if that commandment is the interdict of idolatry itself, he is liable.

Piska 87

1. B. Sanh 27b. Since Deut. 26:16 goes on to say, *Every man shall be put to death for his own sin,* the first part of the verse must indicate something else, namely that fathers and sons may not testify against each other.

2. The son of your father or of your mother, even if by another wife or a previous husband, respectively.

Piska 88

1. See B. Sanh 61b.

Piska 89

1. Be helpful to him. None of the verses of the Torah commanding you to treat someone well apply to one who attempts to lead you into idolatry.

2. This is an exception to the general rule that once declared innocent, a person may not be later declared guilty; but if first declared guilty, he may be later cleared. See B. Sanh 33b.

3. *Miṣwah,* i.e., it is proper that it be done in this way; but if not, it may be done otherwise. See D. Halivni, *Mĕḳorot̲, Našim* (Tel Aviv, 1968), p. 274.

Piska 90

1. See Piska 149. The Hebrew word is in the singular in Lev. 20:27.

2. See Piska 86.

Piska 91

1. B. Sanh 99a.

2. Tos Sanh 10:3; Sanh 7:6. Those guilty of embracing, etc., are not to be put to death.

Piska 92

1. See P. Soṭ 9:1 (23:2). You must act if you know, but you need not go out and investigate.

2. Sanh 1:5. See Tos Sanh 14:1.

3. Since *cities* is in the plural, the possibility of condemning two exists, since the word *one* defines only the minimum. See Tos Sanh 14:1, where the statement is made that the condemned city never existed and was only a theoretical construct.

4. B. BḲ 82b. Jerusalem was not apportioned to a particular Tribe, indicating that it was not intended to be a populated city like all the others, i.e., merely a place of residence, but had a special status. See also B. Sanh 112b, ARN-A 35.

Piska 93

1. A Scriptural word (*men*) includes only the group specifically mentioned and is intended to exclude others (women and minors).

2. The word *bĕliyaʿal* is divided into two words and is read *bĕli ʿol,* "without a yoke." On this method, known as *noṭariḳon,* see Lieberman, *Hellenism in Jewish Palestine,* pp. 69–70.

3. See Sanh 1:5. This might endanger the security of the country.

4. The general principle in Jewish law is that before a person is condemned for an offense, a warning must have been given to him against that offense before the offense took place. In Sif Num. 113 this requirement in the case of idolatry, a weighty violation, is used to infer that such a warning is required for all commandments. See *Talmudic Encyclopedia,* 11, 291. The word *saying* is usually viewed as indicating some sort of required statement, and not simply as an indication of a quotation.

5. *Gĕzerah šawah,* a method of interpretation involving "a comparison of equals." In this case the fact that the same word appears in both verses permits an analogy between them. See Lieberman, *Hellenism in Jewish Palestine,* pp. 58–63.

6. *Ḥăḳirot,* "examinations," refers to the official fixed set of questions that were put to all witnesses. *Bĕdiḳot,* "cross-examinations," indicates other questions that may be added but which have less weight in disqualifying a witness. See B. Sanh 40a. The questions were: in what year of the Jubilee, in what year, in what month, on which day of the month, on what day, at what hour, at what place?

7. The idea that proselytes and slaves are included in the number needed to condemn a city is contradicted in other sources cited by F., P. Sanh 10:7 (29:3), and a manuscript reading in Tos Sanh 14:2. It is not clear what the interpretation here is based on. The manuscripts have here *If it be truth, and the thing certain* instead of *That such an abomination,* etc. This amendment is the Vilna Gaon's.

Piska 94

1. *Hakkeh takkeh.* The repetition of the verb is taken to indicate that he must be smitten in any way possible. See B. Sanh 95b. For a similar usage, see B. BM 31b. The method of execution depended on the severity of the offense.

2. So Lieberman in *Tarbiz,* 3 (1932), 466. I.e., even if he has repented and therefore been forgiven by God, he must be punished by the court. F. amends the text to read, "even if he has escaped your hand, he will not escape Mine."

3. Tos Sanh 14:3 states that children may not be slain. This opinion is contradicted by R. Eliezer and defended by R. ʿAḳiba, who sees in this an instance of God's mercy. Abba Ḥanan's opinion here seems to confirm the latter view.

4. See Sanh 10:5, B. Sanh 112a. The men of the caravan may be counted as inhabitants of the city, and if they, together with the citizens who did not succumb, constitute a majority, the city is saved.

5. Tos Sanh 14:6.

6. B. Sanh 112a, however, adds that these too are to be destroyed, because it was these possessions that caused their righteous owners to reside in such a wicked place.

Piska 95

1. This is R. ʿAkiba's opinion as found in B. Sanh 45b and elsewhere. R. Ishmael, on the other hand, states that if there is no broad place, the city cannot be declared condemned.

2. Sanh 10:6. The specific citation from the Mishnah follows an insert which F. considers to be from another source. The Mishnah forbids the destruction of objects belonging to heaven, but neither are they to be used.

3. Man-made objects only are subject to destruction, hence wood cut from the soil is to be destroyed, but those trees that are growing, as well as other natural objects, are not "thereof," i.e., are not connected to the man-made city. So too Scriptures are permitted since they belong to heaven. This contradicts the other opinion (see note 2, above) which saves them but forbids their use.

4. See Sanh 10:6, Tos Sanh 14:5. R. Eliezer states that unless everything can be burned, nothing is to be burned. B. Sanh 113a.

5. Sanh 10:6. The story of Hiel who rebuilt Jericho indicates that he knew it was prohibited. One is punished only if he was aware that his act is expressly prohibited by God.

Piska 96

1. In Sanh 10:6, R. Jose the Galilean prohibits this but R. ʿAkiba permits it. *ʿEmek han-Naṣib* suggests that the citation is not complete, and is meant merely to refer to the Mishnah.

2. In this way one redeems the forbidden objects, and all the other objects may then be used as well. See AZ 3:9.

3. The relationship of God with His people Israel is one of mercy. There are other instances in which it is indicated that God's quality of mercy is dominant in His relationship with the entire world. See Gen. Rabbah 49:25 on Abraham's plea to save wicked cities, where he argues that if God requires merciless justice, He will not be able to permit the world to exist.

4. See Tos BK 9:30. The importance of mercy is stressed in such sources as B. Yeb 79a and B. Beṣ 32b, where mercy, together with humility and deeds of loving-kindness, is mentioned as one of the three distinguishing marks of the people of Israel.

5. See Sanders, *Paul,* p. 195; Schechter, *Some Aspects,* pp. 170ff.

6. See Piska 79, where the interpretation is more appropriate, since there one is asked to listen to some specific commandments.

7. The reference is to a longer version of this interpretation found above, in Piska 79, where R. ʿAkiba says that the verse means "in the sight of men."

8. R. Meir's opinion is found in his name in ARN-A 39. In ʾAb 3:18, it is quoted in the name of R. ʿAkiba.

9. This verse illustrates R. Judah's opinion that there are times when you are indeed God's children and times when you are not. See B. Kid 36a and Sif Num. 112.

10. He has created His people, one united group on earth. See B. Yeb 13b, 14a.

11. The cutting which is forbidden is only that performed as an idolatrous rite.

12. The legal question is, if one causes several kinds of baldness, is he liable only once, or individually for each kind? See Sif Lev. ᵓEmor 1:1.

13. See Piska 93, note 5. The two verses are connected so that what applies to one applies to the other as well.

Piṣḳa 97

1. Your election as a chosen people is the result of your holiness.

2. *Thee* (*beḵa*) is in the singular and is therefore interpreted to mean that each individual Israelite, and not only the people as a whole, is more precious than *all peoples*.

3. That the Israelites are more precious than the patriarchs, who were no longer living when this statement was made.

Piṣḳa 98

1. B. Ḥul 60b, where it is described as an animal with two backs and two spinal columns.

2. See Sif Lev. Mĕṣoraᶜ 1:12; B. Ḥul 63b and 139b, where these discussions are cited at length. This section, which is not part of the original Sifre (F.), quotes only part of the detailed discussions on this subject.

3. See B. Ḥul 63a–b.

4. There is such a list in Deut. 14 as well as in Lev. 11, and certain species are mentioned in only one of the two. In B. Ḥul 63b, Rabbi (Judah the Prince) explains that although some of the names of birds refer to the same species, they are all mentioned so as "not to give skeptics cause for criticism," i.e., since they are known by various names, it would be unwise to omit any of them.

Piṣḳa 99

1. According to Beḵ 5:3, the Sages permit such an animal to be eaten once it has acquired another defect not deliberately inflicted by its owner.

Piṣḳa 100

1. See Piṣḳa 103, and B. Ḥul 63b.

Piṣḳa 101

1. A difficult section. The translation follows R.H. Animals unfit for offering on the altar are also forbidden to laymen.

2. I.e., permit their use as food. According to Sif Lev. Wayyiḳraᵓ 2:7, some animals which have been used for forbidden purposes are unfit for sacrificial use. The Sifre here is asking whether this principle should be applied also to using them as food. The answer is that the specific enumeration in 14:4 is superfluous, since the general characteristics are given in 14:6, thus indicating that they may indeed be eaten. See also B. Ḳid 57b.

3. This list of animals that may not be offered is taken from Tem 6:1 and obviously includes animals that cannot be eaten. Once the list was used, all of it

was included even though inapplicable (F.). *Kilʾayim* ("hybrid") is a mixture, the offspring of a he-goat and a ewe.

4. Thus indicating that they are permitted.

5. See Epstein, *Maḇoʾ*, p. 232, who disagrees with F.'s reading and prefers the accepted text: ". . . cleanness, I still do not know whether or not to include an unclean animal that was suckled by a clean animal," etc. See B. Tem 31a.

6. *ʾOṯah* (literally "it"), indicating the entire animal and not a part of it.

7. The positive commandment indicates those animals which may be eaten. To this must be added the prohibition of those animals which may not be eaten.

Piska 102

1. Moses could not have known so much about nondomestic animals; hence this legislation indicates that the Torah is of divine origin, containing information received by Moses directly from God. See B. Ḥul 60b.

Piska 103

1. The ceremony involved is that of cleansing the leper from ritual uncleanness. One of the birds is slaughtered but may not be eaten.

2. Since it too is involved in a ritual act (22:6), even though it is clean. The slaughtered bird is also clean.

3. *All* includes the released mother-bird.

4. See Lev. 14:4.

5. In B. Ḳid 57a this verse is taken in the same way: of all clean birds one may eat, including the released mother-bird; but these are the birds of which one may not eat, including the slaughtered bird. A conclusion probably based on seemingly superfluous words in the Biblical text.

6. See the discussion in Sif Lev. Šĕmini 5:1, where the authority quoted is R. Ishmael and not R. Simeon. A. Goldberg suggests that R. Simeon's statement is not a separate teaching but his version of R. ʿAḳiba's teaching, while the version ascribed to R. ʿAḳiba both here and in Sif is the version of R. Judah, who was the transmitter of the Sif. See *Sefer ha-Zikkaron le ha-Raḇ Nissim* (Jerusalem, 1985).

7. Sif Lev. Šĕmini 5:5: *ben ha-hadayah,* another species of hawk.

8. See Piska 100.

9. Ḥul 3:6 and Tos Ḥul 3(4):22.

Piska 104

1. Scripture does not say just *that dieth of itself,* but adds *any thing,* which is seemingly superfluous, and is therefore taken to include those torn by beasts of prey.

2. Which is assumed to refer both to the preceding *stranger* and to the following *foreigner.*

3. In B. Pes 21b this is cited in the name of R. Meir.

4. R. Judah sees here two separate rules, one applying only to the resident alien and the other only to the foreigner. See B. Pes 21b.

5. Why is it mentioned in three places (Exod. 23:19, 34:26; Deut. 14:21)? A more complete version of this discussion is to be found in Meḵ Kaspa 5 (3, 187).

6. Each mention excludes one of these categories. Ḥul 8:4.

7. See Ḥul 8:4 and B. Ḥul 116a, which state that this ruling of R. Jose's was actually followed.

8. The section in brackets does not appear in manuscripts, but was added by F. from other commentators, such as Elijah Gaon, on the basis of Meḵ and Ḥul.

Piska 105

1. See Sif Lev. Bĕ-ḥuḳḳoṯay 12:13 (115b), where this opinion is stated in the name of R. ʿAḳiba. See also Ter 1:5, B. RH 8a and 12b. According to Tos Beḵ 7:1, R. ʿAḳiba taught that one may tithe from one year for another. See F.'s note.

2. The tithe which was brought to Jerusalem and consumed there. See Deut. 14:22–29. This tithe was set aside in the first, second, fourth, and fifth years of each septennial cycle.

3. The Hebrew verb *tithe* is repeated (literally "tithing thou shalt tithe"). See references in note 1, above.

4. Emphasizing *all*—seed of animals as well as of plants.

5. *Šĕ-hu bĕ-ʿămoḏ wĕ-ʿaśśer,* literally "that it is under the category of 'rise up and tithe.'" Lev. 27:32 states, *Whatsoever passeth under the rod,* which could indicate that only those animals which pass before the owner have to be tithed. From *Thou shalt surely tithe* the Rabbis conclude that this is not the case, but that a person is obligated to set aside one tenth of all his animals. See Sif Lev. Bĕ-ḥuḳḳoṯay 13:1, where this same opinion is quoted in the name of R. ʿAḳiba.

6. But not used for human food.

7. *Isatis,* used as a dye. See Lieberman, *TK,* p. 242, to Tos Ma 3:16.

8. Only that which is eaten is subject to tithing.

9. Which are animal, and not agricultural, products.

10. *Hišrišu.* R. Hillel reads "one-third grown" (*šališ*). See Ma 1:3 and P. Ma 49:1.

11. For the identification of these plants, see the notes in Y. Felix, *Marʾoṯ ham-Mishnah, Zĕra ʿim* (Jerusalem, 1967).

12. Apparently varieties of carob trees grown in these two places in Palestine.

13. According to Ma 1:5 this applies only when the produce is brought to the market place. In Tos Ma 2:2 it is the opinion of R. Eliezer, with which the Sages disagree.

14. P. Pe 1:6 and B. BM 88a. These were stores set up by a wealthy priest to sell items used in sacrifices. They followed their own interpretation and left the tithing to the farmers who raised the produce.

Piska 106

1. Based on this verse. See Tos Sanh 3:5.

2. Tem 3:5 states that the first-born and tithe may not be brought from outside the Land, but if brought, they may be offered.

3. In B. Tem 21b the reading is "ben Azzai."

4. Offerings of greater sanctity—for example, the burnt offering—had to be sacrificed in a special place and manner; lesser sacrifices—such as the firstling—could be consumed anywhere within the walls of Jerusalem. See Zeḇ 5:4–8.

5. Ben Zoma wishes to prove that there is no difference between the law of the firstling and that of second tithe in regard to where it may be eaten. Since there

is a difference in regard to the time limit, i.e., the firstling must be eaten over a period of two days (B. Tem 21b and B. Zeb̲ 56b, 57a, based on Num. 18:18), while second tithe may be eaten at any time, one might incorrectly infer that there is also a difference in the place of eating. The verse, however, is seen as explicitly excluding this. Logic is insufficient, so a Scriptural verse is needed. Thus R. ʿAḳiba uses the verse to exclude the firstling from outside the Land, while Ben Zoma uses it to exclude the firstling outside the wall.

6. After the destruction of the Temple.

7. In which point second tithe differs from the firstling and could therefore be consumed when there is no Temple.

8. That the second tithe may not be brought while the Temple is not in existence.

9. R. Ishmael uses the verse to prove that second tithe may be eaten only when the Temple is in existence. Again the use of logic alone is insufficient.

10. As unfit for offering.

11. Which may not be offered.

12. Just as the second tithe mentioned in the verse may be brought even the next year (see B. Tem 21b), so the firstling may be offered in the next year. This is the fourth interpretation of the verse.

13. As did Ben Zoma.

14. Tosafot̲ suggest that going to Jerusalem and witnessing the rites there inspires one to learn and to revere God (B. BB 21a). See Sif Num. 5 (p. 8).

15. Probably referring to the study of Torah. See Pisḳa 43.

Pisḳa 107

1. For whatever reason, no matter how small the amount to be carried; R.H., but *EH.* understands this to refer to distance, i.e., what if the distance is actually small, but nevertheless is too difficult? See B. Mak 19b.

2. A poor man may be unable to afford the expense of transporting produce to Jerusalem.

3. There are also circumstances in which even a man blessed by God, i.e., wealthy, might not be able to convey the produce to Jerusalem. He too may sell it and come to Jerusalem with the money realized from the sale.

4. Hebrew *kesef,* literally "silver."

5. Sif Lev. Bĕ-ḥuḳḳot̲ay 12:1.

6. Meaning money in the form of coins that can be held in the palm of the hand.

7. Logical inference could lead to an incorrect conclusion; therefore the literal wording of the verse must be followed, to the effect that any coins are acceptable.

8. Deriving the word not from *ṣrr,* "to bind," but from *ṣwr,* "to fashion, to delineate."

9. A kind of token which was not minted like a regular coin (Greek ἄσημος, "uncoined metal"). See B. BM 47b.

10. MSh 1:2, Tos MSh 1:5. The coins may not be where one cannot get at them, as at the bottom of a pit.

11. Literally "the House of Eternity."

12. MSh 3:10 and Tos MSh 2:17; against R. Judah's view that it must be buried, the Sages permit it to be redeemed.

13. MSh 3:9.

14. In the singular.

15. MSh 1:7.

16. MSh 1:3.

17. Thus indicating that tithe money may be used only to purchase animals for sacrifices and not for profane consumption, such as a wedding feast. See P. MSh 1:3, where those who purchase an animal for peace offerings are obviously preferred over those who purchase one for their own consumption. This section of Sifre seems to reflect a more stringent position than that of the Mishnah on this question.

18. Burnt offerings are mentioned in 27:6 and peace offerings in 27:7; rejoicing is mentioned only in 27:7.

Piska 108

1. The fact that he has nothing of his own causes the Torah to ordain these gifts for him. See Piska 69.

Piska 109

1. See Piska 302, from which this was taken (F.).

2. The question is, how do we know which festival marks the end of the yearly tithing season? See P. MSh 5:5, Jubilees 22.

3. See MSh 5:6, where it is stated that this means the first day of Passover. In MSh 5:10, however, the last day is mentioned for the declaration of tithes. F. suggests that Sifre is speaking here of the conclusion of the period of cleaning out the past tithes, while the Mishnah speaks of the beginning of it. Alternately, this may reflect a different opinion.

4. The fact that 26:12 designates the third year as the year of tithing is taken to indicate that there is also a year which is not liable to tithing, which must be the seventh year.

5. The passage here is difficult, since it has just been stated that *no* tithe is required in the seventh year. It probably refers, however, to any year, i.e., only one tithe must be set aside in any year, as indicated by the singular *of tithing* (not "tithings"). See Piska 302, which gives the same interpretation to 26:12 and obviously refers to the third year and not to the seventh. It may have been erroneously applied here. Possibly the meaning here is that one extra tithe, that of the poor man, is added in that year, and not two.

6. For which removal and confession are required. The reference is to 26:12.

7. Possibly "an unclean state."

8. Only the poor man's tithe may be eaten in a state of uncleanness and may be set aside out of unclean produce. See F.'s note.

9. Out of the third year's produce, not the fourth year's.

10. The first tithe was given to the Levite, while the second was taken by the owner to Jerusalem and was consumed there. Since only one additional tithe was to be set aside in each year, which one of the two was to be eliminated in the year of the poor man's tithe? Since the Levite is mentioned in the next verse, the conclusion

is that he always receives his (first) tithe. Therefore it must be the second tithe which was eliminated in the third and sixth years of each septennate.

11. R. Eliezer argues that first tithe may never be postponed, and that there is no need to cite Deut. 14:29, as does R. Judah, since Num. 18:21 may be used to prove the same point.

Piska 110

1. I.e., that they are to receive this tithe even if they have sufficient means to take care of themselves.

2. At this suggestion, since in a similar case, that of taking raiment in pledge, we do indeed interpret it to mean whether the pledger is rich or poor, as stated in Tos B.M. 10:10 and parallels, and in Piska 281.

3. Referring to gleanings, etc. The inference is that what applies to gleanings applies also to the poor man's tithe, and only those who are poor are eligible.

4. I.e., are Gentiles.

5. Pe 8:5. See also Tos Pe 4:2.

6. Everything possible must be done to prevent the poor from leaving the Land of Israel. No matter how much has to be given to him to sustain him, it should be given, even if the possibility exists that he could sustain himself in another land. So the Gaon of Vilna. Others (including Maimonides) take it to mean that the poor man's tithe may not be permitted to leave the Holy Land.

7. According to P. Pe 8:8 the words *thy gates* were understood to include Jerusalem, i.e., to forbid the poor to leave the city in order to sustain themselves elsewhere rather than to receive tithe. See also Tos Pe 8:11. See Ket 13:11, on leaving Israel or Jerusalem.

Piska 111

1. Is it done at the end of the seventh year or at the beginning, which is the end of the cycle of crop growth?

2. 31:10 concludes with *in the feast of Tabernacles,* which is taken to mean the end of the seventh year and the beginning of the eighth. See B. Soṭ 41a.

3. Following MhG to this verse: the verse speaks of two releases, one of land and one of lent money. When release of land is in force, money also must be released. Hence the dispersion after (so R. Hillel) or during the Second Temple period, when there is no release of land, there is neither release of money. See B. Giṭ 36a.

4. Deut. 15:12. In the case of the slave the counting is not uniform, since he must be freed after serving six years no matter when his servitude began.

5. That of the Hebrew slave or that of land.

6. The release of loans, to be performed even when the law of Jubilee is not in force.

7. The release of loans. The text is difficult; see Mek de-R. Simeon 21:2 for a variant reading.

8. Deut. 15:1 and 15:9, to prevent one from coming to the wrong conclusion.

9. Before Israel entered the Holy Land.

10. In the future tense, connecting two kinds of release. See note 3, above.

11. According to Tos Ḳid 1:12 this was an exception to the general rule that if an ordinance was not practiced in the wilderness, it need not be practiced outside

of the Land of Israel. Both release of loans and freeing of Hebrew slaves were practiced only after Israel had entered the Land, but are nevertheless obligatory everywhere. See end of Piska 112, and B. Ḳid 38b.

Piska 112

1. Shebi 10:8.

2. Literally "the word (*dĕbar*) of the release"; the creditor must recite the formula of release in any case, even though the debtor may refuse to take advantage of it.

3. But the Sabbatical year does not. See Sif Lev. Bĕ-har 2:6. Verses prove the point which could not be logically determined otherwise. The verse concerning the Sabbatical year, 15:2, makes no mention of slaves; on the other hand, it does describe loans, while Lev. 25:13 does not.

4. According to Shebi 10:1, both wages and store debts can be regarded as equivalent to loans. Therefore the same laws apply to all.

5. Gentiles who are not part of the covenant community.

6. See Piska 111, note 11.

Piska 113

1. This is an abbreviated version of Shebi 10:2: "A loan secured by a pledge, and one the bonds of which have been handed over to a court, are not canceled."

2. Shebi 10:3–4.

3. The *prosbul* was devised in order to circumvent the law canceling loans in the Sabbatical year, when the realities of commerce made such cancellation impractical. See B. Giṭ 36a–b.

Piska 114

1. The contradictory verses apply to different situations.

Piska 115

1. See B. Ber 40a and Suk 46b.

Piska 116

1. MT uses instead Deut. 7:14, *Thou shalt be blessed above all peoples,* which seems preferable, since it precedes 15:6 while 28:3 comes much later, but not necessarily so, since the Midrash literature views the Bible as a single entity.

2. The concluding part of the verse, not quoted in the Hebrew text, shows that once he had ruled over others but now he is ruled by others.

3. Since 13:7 defines *thy brother* as *the son of thy mother,* the implication is that *thy brother* refers to a son by the same father. In Piska 87 *thy brother, the son of thy mother* is explained as *thy brother* = one on your father's side, *the son of thy mother* = one on your mother's side.

4. Literally "one."

5. In other sources it is stated that one must still give him a small sum, such as is given to any other needy person. See B. BḲ 9a and Tos Pe 4:8.

6. Literally "opening thou shalt open."

7. Tos Pe 4:12.

8. Literally "which is wanting to him."

9. Tos Pe 4:10, which reads "an elderly man" for "a guest."

Piska 117

1. See Piska 93.

2. See Tos Pe 4:20.

3. See Piska 111.

4. Since one might think that this continues the list of what should not be done, we are told specifically that the needy person is permitted, perhaps encouraged, to cry out when you do him this injustice.

5. Literally "and he cry not"; he is not commanded to cry out.

6. The sin of failing to give to the poor remains a sin before God, whether the poor man cries out or not.

7. Implying that before it is considered a sin the poor man must cry out.

8. Literally "giving thou shalt give." See Piska 116, note 5.

9. An abbreviated quotation from Shek 5:6, where this chamber is spoken of. God-fearing people put their charitable contributions there secretly, so that the "poor of good families might sustain themselves from it secretly," and avoid embarrassment.

10. Literally "word."

11. Tos Pe 4:17. Even a kind word is a contribution to charity.

Piska 118

1. See Piska 114.

2. The extra word *saying* is interpreted as meaning to give advice.

3. See Tos Pe 4:10. This follows what was said in Piska 116 in commenting on *in that which he wanteth.* In the Tosefta that verse follows this interpretation. See also Lieberman, in *KS, 14,* 328, for an alternate reading.

4. The Sages were anxious that Jews should not be sold as slaves to Gentiles, but should remain in the community, guarded by the laws of Judaism against mistreatment.

5. B. Kid 18a.

6. See Mek Nězikin 3 (*3, 22*).

7. According to B. Kid 17b, the two verses are interpreted as follows: since Exod. 21:2 says *he shall serve* without adding "thee" (Rashi), this indicates that there is someone else to be served. But since Deut. 15:12 says *serve thee,* it limits the right to be served to someone who has "thy" powers, namely the son, but not an heir or a brother. See also P. Kid 1:2 and Mek Nězikin 3.

8. The comment is sarcastic: how can you tell from the verse who it is that is to be served? The word "whispering," is used also for pronouncing a magical incantation, thus implying: what possible way, natural or supernatural, do you have of knowing this?

9. See B. Kid 12a and Exod. 21:9–10.

10. If such a field has been consecrated, it can be redeemed either by the father or by the son.

11. B. Ḳid 16b, where the implication is that the two halves of the verse are seemingly repetitious: why say that he is to go free in the seventh year when it has just been stated that he must serve six years? Hence something more must be implied: the first half refers to the runaway slave, the second to the slave who is ill.

12. In Mek̲ Nĕziḳin 2 this conclusion is based upon the words *he shall serve,* i.e., the six years are meant for one who is physically able to work; if he was sick for a while, he need not serve longer to make up for his illness.

Pisḳa 119

1. Since this follows the command that the Hebrew slave is to be freed after six years of servitude.

2. The repetition covers others as well as the one who has served six years. B. Ḳid 16b cites only the second and third quotations. Here only the third quotation is cited exactly as found in the Hebrew Biblical text. The second is slightly inaccurate and the first is not in the Bible (and is therefore set in roman type within quotation marks). See also P. Ḳid 1:2.

3. Literally "furnishing thou shalt furnish," repeating the verb.

4. See B. Ḳid 17a, where the reading is, "Whence do we learn that everything is included? From the verse, *Of that wherewith the Lord thy God hath blessed thee* (15:14)." Blessing is visible in those things which grow and increase.

5. B. Ḳid 17b. See also B. BM 31b, where the remark is made that others do not interpret these repetitions of words as implying some special laws, and maintain that "Scripture uses language similar to the language of (ordinary) men," an idea identified with R. Ishmael, while the method used here is that of R. ʿAḳiba. See A. J. Heschel, *Theology of Ancient Judaism, 1,* 3ff.

6. There are certain minimums, as stated in B. Ḳid 17a, but one must add to them according to the blessing received.

Pisḳa 120

1. Mek̲ Pisḥa 13, end.

2. See Pisḳas 121–22.

Pisḳa 121

1. Literally "saying shall say," repeating the verb.

2. See Mek̲ Nĕziḳin 2.

3. See B. Ḳid 22a. In P. Ḳid 1:2 (49:4) this is based upon the repetition of the verb: "There are two requirements to say, one at the end of the six years, and one at the beginning of the seventh."

4. The missing section is supplied on the basis of similar passages. See Pisḳa 137, for example. Two verses cover similar topics, but one would be insufficient without the other. *I love my master* clearly indicates the slave's attitude. This verse is understood to indicate that the master also loves him, possibly because it states that it is well with him there. Other versions which reach the same conclusion are concerned only with the verse in Deuteronomy. See Mek̲ Nĕziḳin 2, P. Ḳid 1:2 (49:4), and B. Ḳid 22a.

Piska 122

1. See Tos Ḥal 1:1, where the word indicates wheat.

2. In B. Ḳid 21b the reading is, "thus including anything that can be taken in hand." See also P. Ḳid 1:2 and Mek̲ Nĕziḳin 2.

3. See P. Ḳid 1:2 and Mek̲ Nĕziḳin 2.

4. P. Ḳid 1:2. The traditional law is more inclusive than the written Torah would appear to be.

5. Ḥul 6:6. In Tos Ḥul 6:11 the reading is, "anything that comes from the dust and absorbs, and (in which) things that grow can be used for covering."

6. Giṭ 2:4. See Tos Giṭ 2:4, where it is explained that since a book is characterized as separate from the ground, anything which is connected to the ground may not be used.

7. See Mek̲ Nĕziḳin 2 (3, 14). Door and doorpost are compared: just as the doorpost is always upright, so a door must be in an upright position.

8. See P. Ḳid 1:2 (59:4).

9. Or "to consult with the sellers," as in Mek̲ Nĕziḳin 2. Since the court had sold him, they must be aware of what happens thereafter to him. P. Ḳid 1:2 explains that *unto the judges* refers to a slave sold by the court, while *or unto the doorpost* refers to one who had sold himself. The Hebrew here for "God" often means "judges."

10. The ear-lobe is not subject to blemish that would render a priest unfit for his priestly function.

11. See B. Ḳid 21b and Mek̲ Nĕziḳin 2. The interpretation refers to *through his ear* (15:17): which part of the ear is meant? If the ear-lobe, there would be no reason to refrain from doing this to a priest; therefore this must refer to a part of the ear itself.

12. Mek̲ Nĕzikin 2.

13. Inexact citation—*And the priest shall put it upon the tip of the right ear of him that is to be cleansed* (Lev. 14:14); referring to a leper.

14. Literally "in (or, at) his ear."

15. B. Ḳid 22b, where the specific wording of the verse is discussed: "If it were said, 'his ear into the door,' without *through,* I would have said that one must pierce the door opposite his ear," meaning that the ear itself would not be pierced at all.

16. *ʿOlam,* "for ever" (literally "world") is interpreted as "the existence of the master." See Mek̲ Nĕziḳin 2, where *proclaim liberty* (Lev. 25:10) is used to prove that the slave must be freed in the Jubilee year even if he is a slave "forever."

17. After the death of the master.

18. B. Ḳid 17b. In the case of the Hebrew slave whose ear has been pierced the verse says *thy bondman,* which is taken to indicate that after the master's death he is free. However, during his six years of service this conclusion does not apply, and the master's male heir inherits the right to the remainder of the slave's term of servitude. See Piska 118.

19. To a Hebrew slave sold by the court.

20. Exod. 21:6, where the case is that of a slave who has sold himself.

21. See Deut. 15:13.

22. *ʿEb̲ed̲,* masculine, thus excluding the female slave.

Piska 123

1. Based on the term *double.* Although this part of the verse is missing in the text, it is found in the parallel passages in B. Ḳid 15a and P. Ḳid 1:2. Mek̠ Nĕziḳin 1 holds the opposite view, that both labor only during the day, based on Lev. 25:40.

2. In MhG this statement is applied both to this verse and to 14:29; in both a monetary loss may be involved.

Piska 124

1. See Bek̠ 4:1, where verse 20 is the proof-text.

2. This is the opinion of R. ʿAḳiba, as stated in Bek̠ 2:9.

3. This entire paragraph is omitted by Elijah Gaon since it seems to be a repetition of the first paragraph. Also the use of the verse *All the firstling males* to prove a point concerning consecrated offerings seems inappropriate. Perhaps the word *all* is seen as superfluous and pointing to the other offerings as well.

4. Selected words from this verse are used here to reach this conclusion. In other words, one cannot reach it by logical inference alone, therefore the verse itself is required to make the desired decision.

5. The reference in Lev. 27:26 is to declaring an object or an animal devoted or consecrated to the Temple. The verse states that this may not be done in the case of a firstling, since *it is the Lord's.*

6. This passage from ʿAr 8:7 interprets the discussion, and is regarded by F. as a secondary note inserted from the margins.

7. The first-born is already consecrated and may not be offered as another type of sacrifice, but the owner may consecrate it by offering the value of his own satisfaction if someone pays him to have the firstling given to the son of his daughter or the son of his sister, as prescribed in ʿAr 8:6.

8. That it may not be sheared or used for work. So F. Others (Elijah Gaon) take this as a continuation of the immediately preceding discussion of the consecration of the value of one's satisfaction.

9. But not if consecrated for the repair of the Temple.

10. See above, note 4.

11. The reading in B. Bek̠ 9b is "with one belonging to you and to others," i.e., one owned in partnership with others.

12. In B. Bek̠ 9b the verse is quoted in full, *Thou shalt do no work,* etc.

Piska 125

1. Two days in a row, the last day of its first year, and the next day, which is the first day of its second year. See also B. Bek̠ 27b. In Sif Num. 118 (p. 140) this view is attributed to R. Tarfon at Jabneh and derives from Num. 18:18, which is interpreted as comparing the first-born to the wave-breast offering, which is eaten over a period of two days and one night. The verse from Deuteronomy seems to strengthen this, rather than to be the source of it.

Piska 126

1. The word *kol* ("all" or "any") is taken to include those born with blemishes.

2. This is part of a list found in Bek̲ 6:12 and based in part on Lev. 22:22. See the discussion in B. Bek̲ 41a.

3. Animals blemished in the manner described above, as specified in the Mishnah.

4. That is, that animals so blemished may be slaughtered and consumed elsewhere, but may not be offered as a first-born sacrifice.

5. Which may be slaughtered elsewhere because of their blemish.

6. See Pisḳa 95.

7. For punishment; but actually even half this amount is forbidden by the Torah (so F.). See B. Yoma 74a, where this is the position of R. Johanan, as opposed to R. Simeon ben Laḳish, who thought that half the minimum is permitted according to the Torah.

8. These were considered idolatrous practices. See B. Ḥul 41b.

9. Ḥul 2:9.

10. See B. Ḥul 27a, where this rule is derived from a play on the words *wĕ-šaḥaṭ* (*and he shall slaughter* [Lev. 1:5]) and *šaḥ*, the organ that bends down (= the neck).

11. Food is susceptible to uncleanliness only if moist.

12. B. Pes 16a.

13. Since these types of blood do not flood out as water. See B. Pes 16a.

14. This entire section within brackets is not part of the original text.

Pisḳa 127

1. See Mek̲ Pisḥa 2 (pp. 19–20). Passover and spring are to be kept together; therefore the year is to be adjusted to the season by adding a month prior to the month in which Passover is to come. The word *šamor* here is taken to mean not "observe" but "preserve."

2. Lev. 23:1–44.

3. Num. 9:1–14. The reference is to the special regulations governing the Passover sacrifice.

4. See Sif Num. 66, where this last sentence is prefaced by "Another interpretation." This is a separate explanation of why the festivals are discussed in three different places.

5. In Sif Num. 66 the reading is, "to ask about the matter and to expound it." See Tos Meg̲ 4:5, where it is said that one should inquire into, and study, the laws of the festivals prior to their arrival. The idea is that Moses repeated the pertinent laws at each festival, teaching Israel to study them each year at the time when they observe them. This may be a continuation and explication of "when they were due to be observed," in which case the formula "another interpretation" is superfluous here.

Pisḳa 128

1. Usually translated: *keep,* literally "do," indicating performance in a specific manner.

2. See Mek̲ Pisḥa 11 (*1,* 83). The Passover sacrifice must be slaughtered specifically for that purpose, otherwise it is not ritually valid; other acts, not part of the ritual, do not involve the same requirements.

3. *Košarot*, taken as a description of the month, i.e., the month that is appropriate for it.

4. B. Ber 9a. They were freed from slavery at night, but did not leave until the next morning.

Piska 129

1. The Paschal lamb.

2. The words do not refer to the Passover sacrifice, but are intended to show that all of these are brought of *ḥullin*, that is, of animals that do not belong to second tithe. So Men 7:6. See the subsequent discussion in B. Men 82a, where it is pointed out that the Paschal lamb must have been of *ḥullin*, since there was no second tithe in Egypt.

Piska 130

1. The Passover sacrifice may be eaten at any time after noon, and R. Judah takes this verse to mean that one may not eat leaven from the moment that one is permitted to eat the sacrifice. See Tos Pes 1:8. The same rule, but derived from a different verse, is found in Mek Pisḥa 17 (*1*, 147).

2. See B. Pes 28a for a detailed discussion of the reasoning behind this dispute.

3. *Ḥaluṭ*, a kind of rich bread made by stirring flour in hot water.

4. *ʾĂšišah*, a kind of pressed cake or pancake. See B. Pes 36b.

5. *Paṯ hadraʾah*, bread made out of flour of the second course. See B. Pes 37a, where the reading is "except with coarse bread," which is preferable.

6. The unleavened bread need not be made of inferior flour as long as it is unleavened.

7. Which are too luxurious, being closer to cake than to bread.

8. *ʿOni* in *leḥem ʿoni* (*the bread of affliction*) could be understood as meaning coarse poor man's bread, or as "bread commemorating affliction," indicating the suffering of the people who had eaten this bread. The latter is R. Simeon's interpretation.

9. Haste means confusion. See Mek Pisḥa 7 (*1*, 52), where the opposite interpretation is given to the verse in Exodus.

10. Ber 1:5, Tos Ber 1:10. The reference is to the inclusion of a mention of the Exodus in the prayer following the evening Shemaʿ. See Lieberman, *TK*, Zĕraʿim, *1*, 12. See also H. A. Fischel, *Rabbinic Literature and Greco-Roman Philosophy* (Leiden, 1975), p. 159, nn. 200, 202, who sees in this the influence of the Epicurean school, which taught constant repetition of the basics of its belief.

Piska 131

1. That is, leaven belonging to Gentiles. This method of interpretation is common in the Sifre: from a negative which is limited, it infers a positive. The emphasis here is on *thee*.

2. See P. Pes 2:2, B. Pes. 5b. Leaven dedicated to Temple repairs.

3. So David Hoffmann.

4. Pes 3:7.

5. A date is larger than an olive. According to the Talmud (B. Beṣ 7b), this

refers to removing leaven, but both agree that in regard to eating, anything the size of an olive is prohibited. The dispute concerns the fact that the verse in Exodus mentions these two actions separately, which the School of Shammai takes to mean that each one involves a different minimum.

6. Beṣ 1:1.

7. This interpretation takes the verse to refer to the festive offering accompanying the Passover sacrifice, and uses the interpretation of Lev. 7:16 found in Sifra (ad loc.). The words *until the morning* must thus mean the morning of the third day, i.e., the second day of the festival. The Talmud (B. Pes 70a) indicates that this is opposed to Ben Tema's view that the Passover sacrifice may be consumed only until the second morning. It also differs from the interpretation above, where the sacrifice referred to is understood to be the Passover lamb (F.).

Piska 132

1. The word *bĕ-ʾaḥad* (*within one*) is understood to mean "for one," i.e., for one individual, which is improper, since the Passover offering is a community offering. This view is found in the Mishnah (Pes 8:7). See also P. Pes 8:7 (36:1) and B. Pes 91a.

2. All of it must be consumed.

3. According to the Mishnah (Pes. 7:6), if the majority were unclean, it was sacrificed in uncleanness. If only a minority was unclean, those who were clean sacrificed on Passover, and those who were unclean waited until the second Passover in the following month. See Lieberman, *TK,* Pes 6:2 (p. 583).

4. In uncleanness because of one. This is a matter of dispute. See Tos Pes 6:2, B. Pes 79b and 80a.

5. B. Pes 91a has, "when all Israel enter through one gate." When there is only one proper place for sacrifices, one may not slaughter at a private altar; but at the time when private altars were permitted, before the Temple was built and when there was no central sanctuary at Shiloh, it was permitted to offer sacrifices at these altars.

6. Only then is it forbidden.

Piska 133

1. Rather than interpreting all three phrases, *at even, at the going down of the sun, at the season that thou camest forth,* as referring to the time of slaughtering, R. Eliezer takes each phrase as referring to a different step in the process of the Passover offering. The season of coming out means the daytime, since the Israelites left Egypt after dawn according to Exod. 12:22, as interpreted in Mek Pisḥa 13 (p. 100). See Mek Pisḥa 9 (p. 74). See Piska 128.

2. See B. Ber 9a, where this is cited in the name of R. Joshua.

3. This is the view of R. Simeon ben Yoḥai, Mek Pisḥa 5 (p. 42), who holds that the Israelites left Egypt in the afternoon, agreeing with Rabbi (Judah the Prince), who taught that "When did the Israelites leave Egypt? Later than at six hours, as it is said, *And it came to pass in the middle part of that day* (Exod. 12:51)."

Piska 134

1. This is opposed to Tos Pes 7:2, which states "It is not to be returned in

pieces." F. and others amend the text to conform with the Tosefta, but Lieberman thinks there is no justification for this. Rather, the Sifre disagrees with the Tosefta and presents R. Judah's opinion, as based on his interpretation that the Passover lamb must be roasted at sundown (Deut. 16:6). If it is the eve of the Sabbath, and it is necessary to cut the lamb into pieces, to be returned later to the fire, this must be done before the onset of the Sabbath, i.e., before sundown.

2. See B. Pes 95b. According to Rashi this refers only to the first night of Passover. Tos holds that it means the entire festival. Sif Num. 151 (p. 196) seems to favor the latter interpretation, by holding that all the pilgrim festivals required one to remain in Jerusalem.

3. P. Bek̲ 2:3 (65:1). MhG Deut. 16:7 makes it clear that whenever you bring something to the Sanctuary, you must remain in Jerusalem overnight and return home only the next day. This is derived from the verse, *And thou shalt turn in the morning.*

4. Known also as the second Passover, the 14th of the following month, Iyar, when those who were unable to offer the Passover lamb at the right time must offer it instead.

5. Before the counting of the *ʿomer* on the second night of Passover, only the old crop may be used. Therefore on that first day, called here the seventh, the old crop must be used, but on the other six days one may eat from the new crop. In Mek̲ Pisḥa 8 it is understood as meaning six days when eaten from the new crop, but seven days when the old crop is also used.

Pisḳa 135

1. Taking *ʿăṣeret̲* (*solemn assembly*) to mean "closed up" or "shut up," as in Sif Num. 141 (p. 196).

2. These contrasting verses are found in B. Pes 68b. Another possibility is that Rabbi's comment refers to Lev. 23:36, which contains both terms, *holy convocation* and *unto you: On the eighth day shall be a holy convocation unto you; and ye shall bring an offering made by fire unto the Lord; it is a day of solemn assembly.* F. refers to Lev. 23:15. In any case, part of the day is the Lord's (study) and part yours (eating and drinking). R reads ". . . the entire day; therefore Scripture says, *A solemn assembly to the Lord thy God.* How so? . . ."

3. There is no such explicit interdict in the Torah. How then can we learn it by way of interpretation?

4. Another word-play on *ʿăṣeret̲,* "closed up" or "restrained."

5. The fact that the verse distinguishes between the seventh day and the other six indicates that there must be some distinction between them in regard to this matter of work (restraint). What the difference is, is for the Sages to decide.

6. There are several discussions of the question whether work is permitted on the intermediate days of festivals. See Mek̲ Pisḥa 9 and B. Ḥag̃ 18a. It is not clear whether these Baraitas forbid all work or only certain types of work. From the conclusion of the Sifre and from the discussion in the Sifra (ʾEmor 12:5; 102a), the latter alternative would seem to be true. The Sifra introduces the two concepts, *mĕlak̲ah* and *mĕleket̲ ʿăb̲od̲ah,* "work" and "work of labor"; the former is less inclusive and is forbidden on the intermediate days, but not the latter, which is the equivalent of *kol mĕlak̲ah,* "all work," in the Sifre.

Piska 136

1. B. Men 65b and Sif Lev. ʾEmor 12:3. *Unto thee* indicates that you, i.e., the court, has the power to determine the reckoning, probably by proclaiming the new month and thereby determining the date of Passover (so Rashi). This is contrary to the Boethusian position (B. Men 65b) that the counting must always begin on Saturday night.

2. B. Men 65b, based on the plural of *you,* i.e., each one of you—each person is commanded to count the *ʿomer*.

3. Meaning either that the entire field must contain only unharvested corn at the time when the procedure begins, or, as Tos Men 10:33 suggests, that the *ʿomer* is to be brought only from the standing corn.

4. Sif Lev. ʾEmor 10:3 (p. 100b).

5. The Jewish twenty-four hours begin at sunset.

6. See B. Men 66a and Sif Lev. ʾEmor 12:6.

Piska 137

1. Since the verse in Exodus is subject to such misinterpretation, our verse clarifies the issue: the festival is to be kept under all conditions—whether you have a harvest or not, whether you have a field or not, *thou shalt keep the Feast of Weeks.*

2. See Men 7:6, and Piska 129 and notes thereto. Here, too, the verse indicates that the offering is obligatory, and all obligatory offerings must come out of unconsecrated money.

3. Possibly indicating that it may be brought out of any of your blessings, which includes second tithe. According to Ḥag̱ 1:3, the School of Hillel held that for this sacrifice money out of second tithe may be used, and it may be added to other money in order to offer a larger animal than that which is required. The School of Shammai disagrees. See also B. Ḥag̱ 7b, Tos Ḥag̱ 1:4, and Lieberman, *TK,* p. 1279ff.

Piska 138

1. Deut. 27:7 reads: *And thou shalt sacrifice peace offerings, and shalt eat there; and thou shalt rejoice before the Lord thy God.*

2. Found anonymously in Tos Ḥag̱ 1:4. See also B. Ḥag̱ 6b.

3. Peace offering, as explained above.

4. Based on Exod. 5:1, *That they may hold a feast unto Me.* So P. Ḥag̱ 1:2.

5. This is explicit in the verse under discussion.

Piska 139

1. In the comments of Tosafoṯ to Ḥag̱, a different version of this statement is cited: "(Does this mean that) everything observed on the Festival of Weeks is to be observed also on Passover, or are the things observed on the Festival of Weeks not to be observed then? Hence the verse states, *and thou shalt observe,* etc." There are also other versions in which Passover is mentioned. This leads to the possibility that this otherwise difficult passage may be based on the fact that there are two verses with the term "observe," this one in connection with the Festival of Weeks and the one above (16:3) concerning Passover. The question was: From these verses

are we to conclude by way of analogy that the practices cited for one festival are to be performed also on the others? The answer is, the words *these statutes* show that these particular statutes are to be performed on this festival alone.

Piskạ 140

1. I.e., that it is to be observed "in the name of heaven," for a holy purpose dedicated to God. See B. Suk 9a: "Just as the name of heaven rests on the festival offering, so does it rest upon the booth, as it is said, *On the fifteenth day of this seventh month is the Feast of Tabernacles for seven days unto the Lord* (Lev. 23:34)." See also Sif Lev. ʾEmor 12:3, where the distinction is made between the offering, which is God's, and the booth, which is man's. RABD, however, interprets this as meaning building a booth on the Temple Mount.

2. Usually translated: *thou shalt keep.*

3. In Suk 1:1 we are told that the School of Shammai forbade an old booth, while the School of Hillel permitted it. However, both permitted one made for the festival, no matter when. The Gaon of Vilna emends this to read, "and not only one already made (for some other purpose)."

4. So B. Suk 11b. There is no connection between this and the rule concerning an old booth, in which Sifre reflects the view of Shammai. See F.'s article in *Assaf Jubilee Volume,* p. 415.

5. Which would thus belong to all of them; hence each one would, as it were, have to "borrow" it from all the others (Rashi).

6. Attributed to R. Ishmael in Pesiḳta Zuṭraṯa. See Piskạ 135, where it is indicated that the intermediate days were also subject to regulations concerning forbidden work.

7. Agriculture does not demand work at those times (early spring and late summer).

8. See B. RH 14a for a slightly different version. F. speculates that this interpretation may have been based on Num. 18:27. According to R. Hillel, R. ʿAḳiba takes the view that anything raised on rainwater belongs to the past year, while anything using well water is tithed as produce of the next year. The actual reading in R is "R. ʿAḳiba, however, says: Since the products of the threshing floor and the winepress are nourished by all types of water, they are therefore tithed as produce of the next year." This may, however, be the result of the scribe having shortened the text by leaving out the middle section, either because everyone knew it or by mistake.

Piskạ 141

1. With the several types of offerings for rejoicing in the festival, as above, in Piskạ 138.

Piskạ 142

1. See B. Ḥag̱ 9a. If one failed to bring the festival offering on the first day, when it is due, he may bring it on any other day during the festival, but not later.

2. That one will be blessed only in the same type of produce or animal that has been offered.

3. *Altogether* (*ʾak,* literally "but, only") is taken to exclude something—in this case, the last night of the festival. The same reasoning is found in B. Pes 71a and P. Ḥag 1:4 in regard to Passover, where the reading is "the last" in place of "the first" night. The Gaon of Vilna suggests changing the reading here accordingly.

4. An alternate version of the rule in Piska 141. Again, *ʾak* excludes.

Piska 143

1. One may not appear at any time one chooses to fulfill the commandment; it must be at the appointed festival season. See Mek Kaspa 4.

2. The Hebrew for "foot" is *regel,* the same word as for "(pilgrimage) festival," while the word for "step" is *paʿam,* the same word as for "time"; thus the identification of the two is strengthened by the verse in Isaiah.

3. See B. Ḥag 4b, showing that blind persons are exempt.

4. Ḥag 1:1, without citing this verse.

5. Literally "feet," i.e., the child must come on his own feet. See above, note 2.

6. Literally "at the face of," taken here as "to face" or "to turn," a play on words.

7. Connecting all the holidays in this order.

8. To offer the sacrifice at its appointed time. See B. RH 4a.

9. Possibly a later addition, since it has no connection with the comment that follows (F.). The Gaon of Vilna emends this to "of sacrifice."

10. A silver coin = ⅙ of a denar. R. reads "one silver mĕʿah."

11. I.e., the festival offering. See Ḥag 1:2.

12. The Mishnah quoted above is therefore only the minimum amount, which should be adjusted for wealthier individuals. See Ḥag 1:5.

Piska 144

1. See B. Sanh 16b, Tos Sanh 3:10.

2. See B. Sanh 16b, where R. Judah's comment follows the discussion of Tribes and cities. Rashi takes it to refer to the great Sanhedrin, which outranked all other courts, but Tos understands it to mean the Prince (*Naśiʾ*), on the basis of the Sifre. F. explains that the verse may be interpreted to mean that Moses (*thou*) is told that he is to head the seventy judges whom he is to appoint.

3. In MhG this verse comes at the conclusion of a section discussing the need to have officers whenever you have judges, otherwise law and justice cannot be performed. Its purpose here is unclear.

4. Tos Sanh 3:10.

5. Although this was so, capital cases were in fact almost exclusively tried by the great Sanhedrin, according to Alon, *Jews,* pp. 104, 107. R. adds here: "R. Eliezer ben Shammuʿa says: If there is an officer, there is a judge; if there is no officer, there is no judge. *Judges (šofṭim) and officers*: they are called judges, officers, elders, and judges (*dayyanim*)."

6. These were not special courts for specific adjudication but regular courts with general jurisdiction. See Alon, *Jews,* p. 382, n. 29.

7. See Piska 17 and notes thereto.

8. See F. in *PAAJR,* 4 (1932–33), 45. He will die only when he can no longer

teach justice (*EH*). See, however, Mek̠ Kaspa 3 (III, 173), which reads: "Whosoever takes money and perverts judgment will not leave this world before the light of his eyes will be diminished." Some such negative statement seems called for here as well, especially since both of these "another interpretation" sections are based upon Mek̠. See A. Goldberg, "Lĕšonot̠ Dab̠ar ʾAḥer, p. 101. Goldberg demonstrates that the phrase "another interpretation" frequently introduces the opinion of the opposing school. In the case of Sifre D., which reflects the legal opinions of R. ʿAḳiba, it brings in the opinion of R. Ishmael.

9. Possibly "capital cases" as opposed to monetary ones.

10. Referring to seating in the academy. F. suggests that this refers to the status of the upper and lower classes, in accordance with R. Ishmael's view.

11. B. Sanh 33b, citing a different verse, Exod. 23:7. There we learn that this applies when another witness comes forth to testify for or against him after the trial. See Pisḳa 89. Here the word "righteousness" (*ṣedeḳ*) may be taken the first time as "to justify," and therefore, once a person has been justified, i.e., freed, he cannot be tried again. The second time it is taken as "justice," therefore, if an innocent man has been convicted, justice will be served by reopening his case.

12. See F., in *Assaf Jubilee Volume,* p. 422.

Pisḳa 145

1. The Greek term for an arcade, either open or roofed over, with seats for academic discussions.

2. See *EH*. Meaning altars which were used before the Temple was built.

3. The verse speaks of planting in the very wide sense of suffering the existence of an Asherah.

4. Which has such a tree inside it.

5. So R.

Pisḳa 146

1. R. reads "an Asherah and an idol."

Pisḳa 147

1. See B. Zeb̠ 36a–b. This was not the place designated for slaughtering sacrifices.

2. The order, based on regularity, is spelled out in Zeb̠ 10:1. See B. Pes 58b.

3. See Tem 6:1.

4. And all these are equally abominable.

5. The offspring of a ewe and a goat.

6. I.e., a priest. See Sif Lev. ʾEmor 8:5, B. Bek̠ 45b, and Bek̠, chap. 7, on similar blemishes in most animals. This one, however, which might be taken to mean bestiality, is not mentioned. This may mean that if the priest was a victim of depravity, he is not disqualified.

Pisḳa 148

1. The present Hebrew text cites 19:15 (with the variant *šĕnayim* for *šĕne*). In the text of the Sifre many Biblical verses are incorrectly cited, because originally

only the initial word or words were written down, and the additional words were supplied by later copyists, frequently incorrectly. This must have happened here also, because only if the verse quoted is connected with *if there be found* (as in 17:2) does it make sense to say that *if there be found* requires two or three witnesses.

2. The question is, why are the words *thy gates* found in 17:2? The answer is that otherwise one might have thought that the execution of the transgressor (17:5) is to take place at the court, a common meaning of the word "gates." Since here it obviously means "your dwelling place," so too in 17:5 it must mean "your dwelling place" and not the court.

3. 13:16.

4. The inhabitants are executed by the sword, but the verse concerning stoning (17:5) is taken to refer only to those who led them astray.

5. See B. Sanh 111b.

6. All these epithets are applied also to those judges who pervert the law. See Sif Lev. Ḳĕḏošim 8 (91:1).

7. These, too, appear in Sifra.

8. The one who does evil and breaks the covenant, leading others astray.

9. Another case of confused quotation.

10. See Pisḳa 43, and the references there.

11. See B. Meg̃ 9b, where it is stated that the Septuagint has changed the wording of Deut. 4:19 to avoid misinterpreting the verse to mean that idolatry was permitted to Gentiles. See Rashi.

12. Taking "unto them" as referring to the Gentile nations.

13. A play on the words *dibbarti* ("spoke") and *dibroṯ* ("commandments").

14. That is actually the subject of Jeremiah's discourse.

15. See Ginzberg, *Legends*, 6, 314.

Pisḳa 149

1. See Pisḳa 93 and notes thereto.

2. See Pisḳa 148 and notes thereto.

3. See B. Sanh 43a.

4. R adds "so that their stoning is their death."

Pisḳa 150

1. See B. Sanh 33b, 34a, and Sanh 5:4. Disciples of the wise watched the proceedings.

Pisḳa 151

1. See Sanh 6:4, Sif Num. 114. The witnesses must personally act as executioners. See Pisḳa 306, where this law is used for ʾaggaḏic interpretations.

Pisḳa 152

1. A play on the words *yippaleʾ* in this verse and *muflaʾ* ("an expert or distinguished judge"). See Hor 1:4, B. Sanh 87a.

2. In B. Sanh 87a the word is *yoʿeṣ*, "adviser," one who is qualified to give expert opinions on such matters as intercalation of the year.

3. Rashi says: "the laws of Moses given at Sinai"; P. Sanh 11:3 has "ʾaggadah."

4. *Din,* meaning logical learning as opposed to laws learned by tradition.

5. Of gonorrhea; instead of "blood of birth" (*yoledet*), manuscript R has *yaldut,* i.e., virginal blood, in accord with P. Sanh 11:3 (30:1). See Epstein, *Mabo*ʾ, p. 122. R adds the distinction between those (deliberately) slain and those to be exiled (who would die by accident).

6. The valuation of persons for pledges to the Temple.

7. Num. 5:12ff.

8. Deut. 21:1–9.

9. Lev. 14:1ff.

10. Lev. 19:9.

11. Deut. 24:19.

12. Deut. 26:12, where the term *thy gates* appears in this connection.

13. In B. Sanh 86a this refers to disputes among the elders. If one elder disagrees with all the others, he is considered a rebel. See also Tos Sanh 7:1. The great court took a vote and thus determined the law if there was no previous tradition for such cases.

Piska 153

1. See Sanh 11:4 and Piska 154, where it is stated that this court did not have the authority to impose the death penalty.

2. See Alon, *Toldot,* p. 118, and Ginzberg, *Unknown Sect,* p. 119. Priests were recommended for a criminal case and required for the high court.

3. If the judge had been related to the litigants by marriage, but was no longer so at the time of the trial, he may participate. This is a second interpretation of the verse. See B. Sanh 28b.

4. This is a reference to the interpretation of *In those days.* Do not succumb to nostalgia for the former judges. See also, B. RH 25b, and Tos RH 2:3.

Piska 154

1. See Piska 153, and notes thereto; P. Hor 1:1 (45:4).

2. This is so in regard to capital cases. In other matters, however, Rabbinic ordinances were regarded as even more important. See Sanh 11:3, B. Sanh 87a.

3. Song Rabbah 1:3. See, however, P. Hor 1:1, where the opposite view is found: obey them only when they say that right is right and left is left.

Piska 155

1. See B. Sanh 89b. He is liable only when he himself does his deed, or when others do so on his instructions.

2. He must hear the rule from the Sanhedrin itself.

3. See Sif Num. 39 (p. 42).

4. See Piska 153.

5. B. Sanh 52b.

Piska 156

1. This stock interpretation is used frequently, sometimes more appropriately

than at other times; see, for example, Piskas 170 and 297. Frequently the Sifre attaches a standard interpretation to a word and then uses it consistently, even when it is unnecessary or inappropriate.

2. See B. Sanh 20b. R. Judah believed that this was God's wish, but the people did it prematurely and presumptuously. R. Nehorai thought that God merely responded to their complaints.

Piska 157

1. Based upon the Hebrew, which repeats the verb "set" (literally "Thou shalt with a setting set").

2. See Sanh, end of chapter 2; Tos Sanh 4:2. The latter is cited in full in R.

3. Literally "a foreign man."

4. Who was the grandson of Herod and thus partly of Edomite origin.

5. Soṭ 7:8, B. Soṭ 41b. Alon (*Jews,* pp. 4, 23, 32, 39, 86) discusses this section. He sees the ordinance against a ruling queen as antedating Salome, who was nevertheless accepted as queen. Similarly the Sages ignored this section in the case of Agrippa, but applied it to Herod.

Piska 158

1. For his cavalry, but not for his own personal use. B. Sanh 21b, Tos Sanh 4:5.

2. See B. Sanh 21b for a fuller version of the text.

3. The people are prohibited from returning to Egypt, but sin can cause this to happen. Certainly, then, sin can cause them to be exiled to other lands.

Piska 159

1. Sanh 2:4, Tos Sanh 4:5, B. Sanh 21a.

2. See Exod. Rabbah 6:2 (*Wa-ʾeraʾ*), where R. Judah's opinion is refuted.

3. Wife of King David, who was the epitome of virtue. Nevertheless, he may not marry more than eighteen of them.

4. See MT to this passage. This may be a generalization about David, who did not use gold, etc., for himself, while Solomon did.

Piska 160

1. B. Sanh 21b. Each king must have his own copy.

2. *Mišneh,* hence the following identification with Mišneh Torah, the alternate title of the Book of Deuteronomy.

3. A play on words: *Mišneh* is derived from the root *šnh,* "to change." It will change its form of writing. See Tos Sanh 4:7. Either Ezra changed it or it was that way, changed and changed back (B. Sanh 21b). Some disagree and say that it was never changed. See Ginzberg, *Unknown Sect,* p. 214, on the mistaken notion that this means a change in the Torah itself; the discussion deals only with the change of writing from the ancient Hebrew script to the Babylonian script.

4. Deut. 31:10ff.

5. *Sefer,* the usual meaning of the word when used for copies of Scripture.

6. Read out and checked for errors before three courts of priests, Levites, and common Israelites (see Tos Sanh 4:7).

7. See Piska 48.

Piska 161

1. Tos Sanh 4:7. R adds that he must read therein whenever he has time.

2. *Mora*ʾ. Some read *marʾeh,* "sight," which could mean that seeing the Scroll leads to various levels of learning, with the end in mind of true *yirʾah,* "reverence." Some (the Gaon of Vilna) read *talmud,* "learning," instead. F. (*Sefer Asaf* [Jerusalem, 1953], pp. 419–20) indicates that this is the teaching of the School of Shammai, who held that fear, rather than love, was the basis of religious conduct.

3. Sanh 2:4 (but only the first part).

4. BB 6:7.

Piska 162

1. The text here is difficult. R.H. suggests that the meaning is "he should be warned not to disdain his brethren—he need not be warned not to disdain God." However, the usual meaning of *wĕ-lo*ʾ is "and not." Others read *hekdeš,* "he may take certain things from consecrated offerings." Pardo, referring to 2 Chron. 17:6, *And his head was lifted up in the ways of the Lord,* suggests that the meaning is that he should not imitate people, but should pursue God's ways. Elijah Gaon of Vilna reads ʾ*Akum,* "heathens," instead of *hekdeš.*

2. *Parnasim.* See Alon, *Jews,* p. 449.

Piska 163

1. Who therefore may not serve.

2. See Sif Num. 119, where they are enumerated, including such things as the firstling. There are twelve of them in the Temple and twelve outside of it.

Piska 164

1. Those that settled on the other side of the Jordan. See Sif Zuṭa to Num. 18:24. Others say that it refers to the three nations not conquered at once, the Kenites, the Kenezites, and the Kadmonites (Gen. 15:19).

2. The text reads "five," but F. and others have suggested "nine," on the assumption that this also refers to the Tribes.

Piska 165

1. The word *due* (*mišpaṭ*) means also "legal trial." See B. Ḥul 130b, where this matter is in dispute, and Ben Betherah objects to it.

2. Ḥul 10:1—they are not liable. This is another instance where the Sifre demonstrates that logic alone could lead to an incorrect conclusion, but the verse prevents it.

3. B. Ḥul 136b. Even though *ṭĕrefah* ("unfit meat") could be used by the priest as feed for his own animals, it is not his due.

4. Ḥul 10:4. See also B. Ḥul 134a. "Sacrificed" is understood as "slaughtered."

5. Ḥul 10:1. The shoulder, cheeks, and maw were to be given to the priest everywhere, even after the destruction of the Temple.

6. See Deut. 26:1.

7. I.e., first fleece.

8. Only when there are five or more shorn animals. B. Ḥul 11b.

9. Since logic could lead to the wrong conclusion, there is an extra verse which indicates both in the Land and outside of it.

10. Ḥul, end of chap. 10.

11. On this interpretation of the act of Phinehas, see B. Ḥul 134b; Ginzberg, *Legends,* 6, 138, n. 801. See also Lauterbach, in *JQR, 1* (1910–11), 291–333, 503, 531 (they were allegorical interpreters of the law [p. 509]).

12. Usually translated: *wrought judgment.* The Hebrew root *pll* has both meanings.

13. He pierced them both through the belly.

Pisḳa 166

1. Ter 2:4.

2. Variously explained as goat hair, which is not usually sheared or used, or as wool that was not sheared but came off when the animal was washed.

3. Ḥul 11:1; above, Pisḳa 165.

4. B. Ḥul 11b.

5. B. Ḥul 138b.

6. Ḥul 11:1, Tos Ḥul 10:5.

7. A coin equal to two common shekels.

8. Ḥul 11:1, Tos Ḥul 10:5. *Give* and *gift* are from the same root.

9. Since "first" implies at least one more (F.).

10. Since *sheep* is plural, it must be at least two more.

11. See Tos Ḥul 10:4, B. Ḥul 137a. R. ʿAḳiba, following his usual interpretive methods, breaks the verse into sections and reaches the final number through adding the sum of the parts together.

Pisḳa 167

1. See Pisḳa 155.

2. R.H. explains that this refers to the priestly blessing.

Pisḳa 168

1. The verse is interpreted as referring to the priests, who are of Levite descent, and not to the other Levites, whose livelihood comes from the tithes which they receive.

2. Hence specifying priests who do serve (Rashi).

3. See B. BḲ 109b.

4. R omits "does not."

5. *Mĕ-ʾaḥad̲,* translated literally; usually translated: *any.*

6. B. Suk 55b.

Piska 169

1. Zeḇ 2:1.

2. I.e., equal. See Suk 5:7. The Gaon of Vilna believed that the latter part of the sentence was a simple repetition and eliminated it.

3. *Mimkaraw,* usually translated "his due," but here understood as meaning "sold."

4. Tos Shab 56b. They agreed that each group will get its own weeks of service, in addition to the festival offerings themselves.

Piska 170

1. See B. Shab 78a.

Piska 171

1. The wording indicates that the warning is addressed not only to the individual but also to the court, which must be vigilant to prevent this (*EH*).

2. The text cites Lev. 20:4, which does not use the term "passing." See Sif Lev., Ḳĕḏošim 10:3, where the subject is "passing," as opposed to putting the child into the fire.

3. Sanh 7:7, Tos Sanh 10:4.

4. Tos Shab 7:4. Divining rods were used in deciding what to do or not to do.

5. MT, p. 109, line 30.

6. Lev. 20:2.

7. Perhaps R. Judah's comment is to Lev. 18:21 (cited above), where fire is not mentioned. He then interprets this verse as referring to a different ceremony mentioned in Jeremiah. This entire section is missing in R.

8. Connecting *mĕʿonen* ("soothsayer") with *ʿayin* ("eye")—both words are derived from the same root. He sees things that the eyes do not see. See Tos Shab 7:14; Lieberman, *TK,* p. 97, and B. Sanh 65b.

9. Connecting *meʿonen* with *ʿonoṯ,* "seasons."

10. B. Sanh 65b: "pull them now, so they will not be bad."

11. Literally "those who hold the eyes."

12. See B. Sanh 65b, Tos Shab 7:13. He does not want to repay a debt at certain times, or sees bad omens in things that happen to him.

13. Sanh 7:11. Merely creating an illusion that one is doing something does not constitute forbidden magic.

Piska 172

1. *Piṯom* (Greek *pythōn*), ventriloquist or necromancer. See Sanh 7:7.

2. Sanh 7:7. One who transmits a spirit's message in his own words.

3. B. Sanh 65b.

Piska 173

1. B. Mak 24a.

2. Applying the word *kol* ("soever," literally "any") to the act, as well as to the actor.

3. Tos AZ 8:6.

4. Emphasizing the future tense of the Hebrew "thou shalt be": only under certain circumstances will you be wholehearted.

Piska 174

1. Literally "hath not given thee."

2. Taking the verse against its grammatical meaning and separating *given thee* from *hath not*: "God has not done so—He has given you (Torah), but you do not observe it." This sentence is not found in most manuscripts, including R.

Piska 175

1. And not like Jews, although they are Jews.

2. See B. Yeb 90b and B. Sanh 90a. Strictly speaking, Elijah should not have offered a sacrifice outside of the Temple in Jerusalem.

Piska 176

1. See Mek Ba-ḥodeš 9.

2. Or "they anticipated My will." R reads "they wanted to understand."

3. *Mĕturgĕman,* the aide who repeats the words of the teacher in a loud voice. The prophet must speak directly and not through an intermediary (Gaon of Vilna, E.H.).

Piska 177

1. Jonah 1:2.

2. 1 Kings 20:35. R reads "permits," i.e., allows what the other prophet has forbidden.

3. See 1 Kings 13:26; Ginzberg, *Legends,* 6, 221, n. 133, and 345, n. 10.

4. 1 Kings 22:24; Sanh 11:5, and Tos Sanh 14:15.

5. Jer. 28:1.

6. Sanh 11:6. Even if his teaching is in agreement with the Torah, he is liable to death because he ascribes it to an idol.

Piska 178

1. See Piska 155.

2. These words are not found in the Bible. The Gaon of Vilna suggests they are based on Jer. 27:22.

Piska 179

1. See Piska 80. These verses have been placed here by F. following Elijah Gaon. R reverses the position of the verses.

Piska 180

1. See Sif Num. 159, Tos Mak 3:8.

2. Perhaps meaning that if he kills someone in the city of refuge, he need not

leave it, but may move to another neighborhood. See Sif Num. 160. E.H. explains this as meaning that a new arrival may not be sent to another city of refuge on the ground that this city already shelters too many slayers.

Piska 181

1. *Dĕbar,* literally "word."
2. The part in parentheses is taken from Mak 2:8 and Tos Mak 3:8. The text here quotes only the beginning and assumes that the reader will fill in the rest.
3. Whether related to the slayer by blood or not.
4. Where he would not be outraged and want to kill the slayer; e.g., one brother slaying another, or a father slaying a son. See P. Mak 2:5, and Mak 2:5.
5. Num. 35:6, 11, 15.
6. R reads "There shall be his going down."
7. Deut. 19:4–5.
8. As the verse demonstrates, *neighbor* indicates one who was not hated. Had he been hated, there would have been an element of premeditation, and the charge would have been deliberate murder.

Piska 182

1. In such a case he need not go into exile. See Mak 2:2.
2. Mak 2:2. These are actions he must perform, such as punishing a wayward child. If the child happens to die, the father need not go into exile. See B. Mak 8b. Note how the emphasis has changed in the Rabbinic decisions from who *may* go into exile and be safe, to who *must* go into exile because, although he is not guilty of premeditated murder, he is guilty of negligence.

Piska 183

1. Tos Mak 2:1.
2. There is a disagreement concerning the interpretation of the word *wood.* Rabbi Judah the Prince maintains that it always refers to the tree, while the Sages take it to mean here the wood of the axe hewing the tree. See Mak 2:1, 4; Tos Mak 2:11.
3. See B. Mak 8a.
4. If he reaches one of them, he may not be sent to another one. See Piska 180.
5. Both here and in Sif Num. 160 the actions of the blood avenger are taken to be obligatory—he must pursue, and in certain cases he must kill the slayer. See also B. Sanh 45b.
6. See Piska 171, and notes thereto.

Piska 184

1. Without the "if" the verse becomes a promise, conditional on the performance of His will. In this Piska two doctrines are enunciated: the reward for the performance of good deeds and the merit of the fathers. See S. Schechter, "The Zachuth of the Fathers," in his *Some Aspects,* pp. 170–98. Schechter published also

a fragment in *JQR, 16* (1904), 452, in which these two ideas are brought in and the merit of one's deeds is said to be the only one which is operative. He sees this as an argument against the view expressed here.

2. See Sanders, *Paul,* p. 195. Merit is used here in the sense of "for the sake of."

Piska 185

1. R. Nehorai uses *three* in verse 19:2, *three* in 19:7, *three* in 19:9, and the word *more* for another three, making twelve. R. Saul includes the word *these* for another three, making fifteen. A similar count is used in the Passover Haggadah to count the number of plagues. In P. Mak 2 (end) the two Rabbis are reversed.

Piska 186/87

1. As above, Piskas 171 and 183.

2. Minor does not mean unimportant, but rather one which requires no great expenditure. See ARN-A, chap. 28.

3. The reading in R is closer to the statement as found in Piska 235 (the repetition of the first two verses at the end may be a scribal error): "If he transgresses *Thou shalt love thy neighbor as thyself* and *That thy brother may live with thee,* he will eventually transgress *Thou shalt not take vengeance, nor bear any grudge, Thou shalt not hate thy brother in thy heart, Thou shalt love thy neighbor as thyself,* and, *That thy brother may live with thee,* until he ends up shedding blood."

4. The last part of the quotation is not in the Hebrew text, but is required as an introduction to what follows. See Mak 2:6, Sif Num. 160.

5. *That he may die* is interpreted as not connected to *the avenger of blood,* but as a separate command: in any case he must die.

Piska 188

1. Following Lieberman, *TK, 5,* 1337. For the law to apply, the plot must be yours alone. If you give it to one who has no right to it, i.e., a fetus up to thirty days old, you may sell it without violating the law. F. suggests omitting "does not," which cannot be sustained. See also S. Lieberman, *Texts and Studies,* p. 522, and Tos Oh 16:12.

2. See B. Ket 23b. This opinion is disputed, however, and one witness is usually enough.

3. B. Yeb 122b. See Ginzberg, *Unknown Sect,* pp. 119–20, for a discussion of the need for two witnesses in Rabbinic law and in the laws of that sect.

4. B. Ket 87b. In cases where two witnesses would make the defendant liable to pay, one witness makes him liable to swear.

5. Tos Shebu 5:4. F. changes the reading to "capital cases" rather than "monetary cases" and explains: if he cannot join another witness in order to prove his own guilt in capital cases, but can by himself cause himself to be required to swear, i.e., when he acknowledges a monetary claim partially, surely a witness, who could join another witness to prove him guilty in capital cases, can by himself cause him to be required to take an oath. The conclusion here is that logical deduction will not be able to prove that one takes an oath on the basis of one witness, but the verse proves it.

6. Mak 1:9. The term *at the mouth* is emphasized: at the witnesses' own spoken word, and in no other manner.

7. Not to seclude herself with the other man.

8. That she did indeed seclude herself with him. See Soṭ 1:1, where R. Joshua, however, requires two witnesses.

9. That she had secluded herself; so Lieberman, *TK,* p. 610. This is based on R. Joshua's opinion as stated above. See Soṭ 6:3. Drinking the bitter waters is required only when there are no witnesses that she had actually been defiled. If there is even one witness (called here "latter testimony"), she does not undergo the ordeal of drinking the waters but is forbidden to her husband. Since this may go against logic, it is specifically stated in Scripture.

Pisḳa 189

1. Instead of *ʿaberah,* "transgression," R has *ʿabo zr,* i.e., *ʿabodah zarah,* "idolatry," which is appropriate for the verses cited.

2. *Against him* is taken to mean "against the witness himself." See B. Mak 5a, where this is cited as the view of R. Ishmael.

3. Mak 1:4, where the entire matter is discussed. The Hebrew text here quotes only the first part; the remainder is added from the Mishnah.

4. Witnesses were not regarded as false if they gave false evidence, but only if others could prove that they could not have seen the event or were not there at all. See Mishnah, ed. Albeck (Jerusalem, 1959), *4* (*Nĕziḳin*), 215.

Pisḳa 190

1. Rather, not Deut. 19:15 but Num. 11:26. Since Deut. 19:17 uses the masculine form of *two* and has just been interpreted to include women as well, a clarification is added, as in P. Yoma 6:1 (43:2), where three verses are cited, including Deut. 17:6 (on witnesses) and Num. 11:26 (on the two men who remained in the camp)—both refer to men and not to women. Then the question is asked about Deut. 19:17, where *two* obviously cannot be limited to men.

2. B. BḲ 112b, Sanh 19a; meaning that the owner of the ox, or of the slave, or of whoever or whatever has caused injury to the plaintiff, must be there.

3. See notes to Pisḳa 153.

4. See Pisḳa 93, and notes thereto.

5. See Tos Ket 2:1.

6. From the fact that the verse has additional clauses.

7. One may declare them unfit in a chain-like succession, one after the other. See Mak 1:5.

8. Supplied by F. and others, but missing in the Hebrew text.

9. But before it has been carried out. This is based on the word *purposed.* See Maimonides' *Code,* XIV, II, x, 2 (*YJS, 3,* 102–03); Mak 1:6.

10. See B. Sanh 90a.

11. In the case of a woman who seizes a man by his secret parts.

12. Literally "there"; apparently this was originally a comment on the other verse, and the wording has not been changed here (F.). See B. BḲ 84a.

13. The statement in Exodus is interpreted in the Talmud as prescribing a

monetary fine. From then on all repetitions of it are taken to mean monetary compensation.

14. By a tour de force R. Jose joins the initial words of 20:1 to the last verse of chap. 19.

15. B. Soṭ 44b. See Pisḳa 198. This section is not found in R and other manuscripts.

16. This is a quotation from Mek̲ Bĕ-šallaḥ 2, which is quoted here only in part, as if it were a mere reference.

17. This type of war was one for expansion or gain, as opposed to Joshua's war or a defensive war. See Sanh 1:3, B. Sanh 16a. See also Soṭ 8:7, where a distinction is made between commanded wars, like that of Joshua, and obligatory wars for self-defense.

18. Therefore it is a nonobligatory war. The war against the seven nations or against Amalek was a war against God's enemies as well.

19. The exodus was seen as a surety for the future as well: "It will be no different in the future . . . clearly, for the Tannaim history is a preview of that future which arrives with the end of time" (Goldin, *Song of the Sea,* p. 14).

Pisḳa 191

1. According to B. Soṭ 42a, the priest must recite to them the pertinent war regulations at the boundary of the Holy Land. In Tos Soṭ 7:18 we are told that he must also recite them at the battlefield. There are thus two recitals, one at the boundary, where they are to be told under what conditions they may go on, and another at the battlefield. See Lieberman, *TK,* p. 687. Thus 20:2 refers to the first recital and 20:3 to the second.

Pisḳa 192

1. Meaning that unfit persons are to be told to go home, so that progress in building up the cities should not stop. Soṭ 8:5. This section is not found in several manuscripts.

2. Since there are many such legitimate reasons for leaving the ranks, he will not be embarrassed by charges of cowardice.

3. I.e., urine. See B. Soṭ 42b and Soṭ 8:1, where these various terms are connected to parts of the verse, as below in the Sifre text proper.

4. See B. Soṭ 42b.

5. Soṭ 8:1. The last sentence is added from there and from MT.

Pisḳa 193

1. The widow of a brother who has died childless must be formally released from the obligation of marrying the surviving brother, if he refuses to wed her (Deut. 25:5ff.). See Pisḳa 196. This section is not found in several manuscripts.

2. That is, their own instructions, not those recited by the priest.

3. See B. Soṭ 43a; above, Pisḳa 191.

Pisḳa 194

1. Literally "who," meaning "whosoever." See B. Soṭ 43a. It does not matter who built it—the new owner is exempt.

2. Who may not be excused from battle.

3. See Tos Soṭ 7:22, where more details are given. His presence in battle will have a dire effect, resulting in defeat.

4. In the series of curses: *Thou shalt betroth a wife, and another man shall lie with her* (so Lieberman). See Tos Soṭ 7:22; F. refers to Deut. 20:7.

Piska 195

1. B. Soṭ 43b. See Piska 194, note 1.

2. So Elijah Gaon. B. Soṭ 43b has "even of other types." The text reads literally "of the five species."

3. And not trees, etc.

4. To make it take root and grow as an independent plant.

5. See Piska 194.

Piska 196

1. His brother has died childless, hence he must return and either marry the widow or release her to marry another man. This section is found in Soṭ 8:2. Another version appears in Tos Soṭ 7:19. See also Lieberman, *TK*, pp. 690–91.

2. A descendant of the Gibeonites. See B. Yeb 78b, Josh. 9:27. All these marriages are deemed improper and to be eschewed.

Piska 197

1. See Piska 193.

2. This is the interpretation of R. Jose the Galilean in Soṭ 8:5. The sinner is fearful not of war but of the consequence of sin, which is death.

3. And is not physically able to serve. This is F.'s reconstruction of the text based on Piska 190. See his article in *PAAJR, 3* (1931), 39. S. Lieberman, in *KS, 14* (1937–38), 328, disagrees and restores the reading *baʿal mem,* i.e., "forty years old." Such a man was too old to fight. See B. Shab151b.

4. All might become fearful and leave. See Piska 194, note 3.

Piska 198

1. Soṭ 8:7. See Piska 190.

Piska 199

1. The specific Biblical statement is taken to exclude anything else. Here only actual combat is discussed, and no other means of defeating an enemy.

2. Num. 6:26.

3. On the importance of peace, see Sif Num. 42, Deut. Rabbah 5:12, Lev. Rabbah 9:9.

Piska 200

1. Although they were to be destroyed, under such peaceful surrender they may be spared. See Rashi, ad loc.

2. Num. 31:17–18. The Midianite women were killed, but not the female children.

3. See MhG to this verse. The meaning is: since we learn the rule governing female children by reasoning, the explicit term *little ones* here must indicate something that we could not have learned by reasoning, i.e., male children. Thus male and female children are to be spared.

4. *But* implies an exception from the rule.

5. And should be destroyed.

Piska 201

1. See B. Sanh 67a. Note, however, that individuals from the seven nations who are in one of the cities which make peace are to be spared. See Piska 200.

2. Which also refers to the Canaanite nations—their goods need not be destroyed; on the contrary, they are prepared for you. See Piska 38.

3. Even though they are not mentioned here. See Deut. 7:1. According to Rabbinic tradition, they left and went to live in Africa. See Lev. Rabbah, 17:5.

Piska 202

1. See Tos Soṭ 8:7, B. Soṭ 35b. The stones in the Jordan had the Torah inscribed on them. The nations could read it, and if they decided to repent, they would not be considered part of the seven nations.

Piska 203

1. Tos ʿEr 3:7. Laying it later would indicate a deliberate intention to fight on the Sabbath. This way there is a possibility that the war may be concluded before the Sabbath. On the question of warfare on the Sabbath, see further on.

2. Tos ʿEr 3:7. See also B. Shab 19a and P. Shab 1:4. Both this rule and the law concerning siege reflect the views of Shammai. See F., *Assaf Jubilee Volume,* pp. 415–18. This entire section is found only in MhG.

3. The question is read as a statement: "For man *is* the tree of the field."

Piska 204

1. Which no longer bear fruit. See B. BK 91b.

2. It may be cut down first. All the manuscripts read "If eventually we are going to include unfruitful trees."

3. B. BK 92b quotes only the initial word from the verse as proof.

4. So F. Perhaps for crossing moats filled with water.

5. Both are machines for hurling missiles.

6. See Piska 203, note 1.

Piska 205

1. See B. Soṭ 45b. This applies only when such occurrences are rare.

2. Soṭ 9:9, Tos Soṭ 14. This was at the time of R. Johanan ben Zakkai (end of the Second Temple period). See Lieberman, *TK,* p. 750.

3. See Soṭ 9:9. In Josephus, *Ant.,* XX, 6, he is called a robber.

4. B. Soṭ 45b. "Hence it has nothing to do with a quasi-chthonic sacrifice to appease the spirit" of the murdered man, as was the common custom (S. Lieberman, *Texts and Studies,* p. 514).

5. So B. Soṭ 45b. This refers back to the statement concerning the place where the corpse is found. R. Eleazar says that even if the corpse is found floating on water, hidden under stones, etc., the heifer's neck must be broken.

6. In other words, if you insist that this rule applies to slaying by the sword, why not insist on all the other conditions stated in the verse? B. Soṭ 45b records the answer: *slain* is repeated several times (21:1–3), while the other conditions are not.

7. So R. Eleazar. See P. Soṭ 9:2.

8. See B. Sanh 14b, where R. Simeon cites only the word *elders,* which is clearer. The Mishnah also speaks of only three.

9. Soṭ 9:3, based on different ideas about where in the body the measurement should begin. See also Soṭ 9:4. The verse indicates that the measurement should be from the body, as found at the end of the discussion there.

10. B. Soṭ 45b, Tos Soṭ 9:1. See Lieberman, *TK,* p. 715.

Piska 206

1. This is found also in P. Soṭ 23:1.

2. This is in opposition to Soṭ 9:1. It may be an addition, or it may refer to the fact that Jerusalem did not bring a heifer, as stated above and in Soṭ 9:2.

3. B. RH 10a., Par 1:1.

4. It must be a heifer, and it must be part of the herd (F.).

5. This explains the specific functions of the priests and the elders. It belongs more appropriately in Piska 209 and is not found in several manuscripts.

6. Sif Num. 123, B. Soṭ 46a.

Piska 207

1. See B. Soṭ 46b for a fuller version.

2. Exod. 13:13, concerning the firstling of an ass.

3. As explained at the beginning of this Piska.

Piska 208

1. See Piska 163.

2. A difficult passage. Elijah Gaon reads: "The priestly blessing may be pronounced by blemished Levites." See B. Ta 27a, and E.H. According to F. (*Assaf Jubilee Volume,* p. 420), this is the ruling of Shammai, against the Mishnah (Meḡ 4:7), which holds that only blemishes on the Levite's hands render him unfit. Shammai holds that all blemishes do so.

3. B. Sanh 34b.

Piska 209

1. In the interpretation of Deut. 21:2, concerning the number of elders or judges.

Piska 210

1. See Soṭ 9:6, B. Soṭ 38b.

2. See B. Ker 26a, which states that the rite atones for all blood shed from the Exodus on, and that the Day of Atonement does not atone for this case of bloodshed, and the ritual must be performed even after the Day of Atonement.

3. See Tos Soṭ 9:2.

Piska 211

1. See notes to Piska 190.

2. Since the Hebrew word *ʿal* "upon" might be misunderstood, the more common word *kĕ-negeḏ* ("against") is used.

3. See B. Soṭ 35b, and Piska 200.

4. B. Ḳid 31b. This limits it to the moment when she is captured, and not at some later time (*EH*).

5. The Hebrew *ʾešeṯ* may be taken as hinting at *ʾešeṯ ʾiš,* "a married woman."

Piska 212

1. "Doing" is in fact not used in the verse for the head, but shaving does imply action on her part.

2. See B. Yeḇ 48a.

Piska 213

1. Although Scripture seems to indicate removal of poor garments, the homily takes it the opposite way, as if she was captured in alluring and enticing garments. The garments are then removed so that she becomes less attractive.

2. See Tos Yeḇ 6:8 and B. Yeḇ 48b; D. Halivni, *Mĕḳoroṯ, Našim,* p. 55.

3. This section is not found in R and other manuscripts.

4. E.H. She cannot be acquired by you except by "going in unto her." Other women could be married by payment of money or by contract.

Piska 214

1. Literally "the house of her gods."

2. See above, the beginning of this Piska.

3. This part does not appear in R and other manuscripts.

Piska 215

1. R.H. and *EH* do not have this final sentence. Without it, the meaning is that these women do not yet have legal marital status, and therefore their children do not have the status of heirs spoken of here. F. includes it, meaning that they do have that status. See B. Ḳid 68b, B. Yeḇ 22a.

2. See B. Beḵ 47b; Beḵ 6:1. R. Simeon holds that birth by Caesarean section is to be considered normal. In R and other manuscripts the Piska begins with the next paragraph.

3. Both forms are used in this verse, a redundancy which is taken to imply additional meaning.

4. See B. Yeḇ 23a, Ḳid 68a. The phrase is taken there to mean that God does not take such a thing into consideration as far as the law is concerned, but the marriage is "hated" because it is not desirable—it is prohibited before the fact but legal after the fact; for example, the marriage of a priest to a divorcée.

5. Therefore the only ones excluded are those who have no legal status, even after the fact. See the beginning of this Pisḳa. Both Hebrew words cited come from the same root *hayah,* "to be, to have."

6. The Hebrew *banim* ("children," literally "sons") is masculine.

7. One whose sex is uncertain. See B. BB. 127a.

Pisḳa 216

1. See B. BB 113b.

2. Not merely in this case, but in all cases. See B. Beḵ 46b; Beḵ 8:1.

Pisḳa 217

1. B. Ḳid 74a, 78b; BB 127b. The Sages may have rejected the idea that he is to be believed without examination even concerning the first-born.

2. I.e., twice as much as any other one, rather than two-thirds of the entire estate.

3. See B. BB 122b.

4. Since the just cited phrase from 21:16 mentioning the other sons is seemingly superfluous, it must indicate something additional, namely that he receives a portion in proportion to his brothers, rather than to the entire estate (TA).

5. In Deut. 21:17.

6. The word translated "right" is *mišpaṭ,* which means also "judgment."

Pisḳa 218

1. That is, he may be declared rebellious only from the moment that he ceases being a minor, i.e., when he reaches the age of thirteen years and a day, at which time he is physiologically fully mature. See Sanh 8:1, B. Sanh 68b.

2. Repeated in verse 20.

3. So R.H. and F., from the Greek *mōros,* "a fool." Dr. Leon Nemoy suggests that *šoṭeh* ("fool") should be read *śoṭeh,* one who deviates from right behavior.

4. Since "teaches himself" is the alternate meaning of *moreh* (*rebellious*), this could be an interpretation of that word, and not of the preceding word *stubborn* (*sorer*). Lieberman in *ḲS, 14* (1937–38), 335, suggests reading *sor,* similar to *śeʾor,* one who permits himself to lead a different, i.e., immoral, life.

5. See B. Sanh 72a; he will eventually waste all of his father's wealth, which will lead him to robbery and murder. See Pisḳa 220, note 4.

6. B. Sanh 35b.

7. Each word is taken as referring to a different matter and not merely as a repetition.

8. See B. Soṭ 25a, Sanh 88a. This entire section is not found in R.

9. In verse 18 and in verse 20.

10. B. Sanh 71a.

Piska 219

1. Since the verse places the two on the same level, they must be equal in worth. See Sanh 8:3–4.

2. Sanh 8:3–4. Each phrase is taken literally and seriously, in such a way as to exclude many who might otherwise have been declared rebellious.

Piska 220

1. According to Sif Lev. ʾĔmor 19:3 and Sif Num. 114, he is to be stoned by the witnesses in the presence of the entire community.

2. See Piska 148.

3. One-third of a Roman *as,* or about three ounces.

4. See B. Sanh 72a, P. Sanh 8:7. Although his disobedience now has brought him to crimes which by themselves seem trivial and certainly would not justify the death penalty were they not connected to his rebellion against his parents, the Torah foresees that he will waste his inheritance and rob and kill in order to satisfy his fancy. Let him be executed now before he reaches that stage.

Piska 221

1. One of the most prominent early Sages (first century B.C.E.).

2. On the charge of witchcraft.

3. See Sanh 6:4. On this incident, see S. Baron, *A Social and Religious History of the Jews* (New York, 1952), 2, 21, and Alon, *Jews,* pp. 120–21.

4. B. Sanh 45b.

5. False witnesses who testified against other witnesses. When false witnesses are put to death, their bodies are not afterwards hanged. See B. Sanh 46a.

6. Literally "with a burying thou shalt bury him," from which the conclusion is drawn that both the corpse and the tree are to be buried.

7. Sanh 6:4, B. Sanh 46b.

8. Sanh 6:3, Tos Sanh 9:6. This section is not found in R and other manuscripts.

Piska 222

1. The Piska begins with an addition, not from the original Sifre, interpreting the verses in Exodus which deal with a similar law about assisting another person with his animals. See Mek dĕ-Kaspa 2.

2. It might be taken to mean near enough to touch.

3. Thus indicating close enough to see clearly.

4. Two-fifteenths of a mile.

5. Perhaps meaning that the enemy too may be an Israelite, and one must resist the temptation to hate him, since he is your brother. See B. BM 32b, where a similar expression is used. Both there and in Mek dĕ-Kaspa to Exod. 23:5 there is a dispute as to the identity of the enemy. R. Josiah says it is a heathen, but others refer it to proselytes, apostates, or simply a person with whom one has a quarrel.

6. Not when the owner himself has let them loose.

7. BM 2:9

8. A priest is forbidden to defile himself by contact with the dead (Lev. 21:1–4).

9. The owner of the strayed beast.

10. B. BM 30a. Since the words *and hide thyself* are placed far from the word *not,* they can also be taken to be meant positively, i.e., at certain times you may *hide thyself.*

11. So Lieberman, *ḲS, 14* (1937–38), 335. Others read, "he need not care for it"—if he brings it to a place where the owner can see it, he is no longer responsible (R.H.). See B. BḲ 57a, Tos BM 2:23.

Piska 223

1. BM 2:7, B. BM 28a. A play on words, "require" and "examine" both deriving from *drš.*

2. See Tos BM 2:28, B. BḲ 81b. R reads "but you need not restore yourself to him," the meaning of which is unclear.

Piska 224

1. See BM 2:8.

2. The verse is not in the Hebrew text, but is obviously being interpreted here. See BM 2:5.

3. *And so shalt thou do with every lost thing of thy brother's which he hath lost, and thou hast found* (22:3).

4. The smallest copper coin.

5. B. BM 27a; there, however, R. Judah excludes anything worth less than a *pĕruṭah.* F. believes that Sifre has the correct text.

Piska 225

1. See Piska 222, and notes thereto.

2. BM 2:10.

3. See Piska 222.

4. BM 2:10. The owner may not take advantage of this commandment.

5. One must help the owner, but if the owner does nothing, one is under no obligation to help him.

6. *Help him* (*ᶜimmo,* literally "with him") is taken to mean, provided that he is as healthy as you are, in which case he too must assist you. If he refuses, you are not obligated to *help him.* Not so, of course, if the owner is incapacitated by age or illness.

Piska 226

1. B. Naz 59a.

Piska 227

1. B. Ḥul 139b. This excludes domestic birds.

2. B. Ḥul 139b. This excludes wells, caves, etc.

3. Ḥul 12:3.

4. One might think that for such a sacred purpose an exception would be made, but this commandment is of such importance that taking the birds is always forbidden and would be considered a transgression. See Ḥul 12:5 and Tos Ḥul 10:16.

Pisḳa 228

1. *Šem-mardu.* But possibly *mardu,* the name of a bird (B. Ḥul 62b).

2. See B. BM 25b. The interpretation of *dereḵ,* "way," as indicating something permitted is found in B. Ber 11a in regard to the recitation of the Shemaʿ: "A 'way' is optional." See also Pisḳa 34.

3. See B. Ḥul 139a.

4. The entire section within brackets is a fragment probably taken from a marginal gloss.

5. See B. Ḥul 140a, Ḥul 12:2, Tos Ḥul 10:9. The male partridge was believed to join the female in brooding, hence the view that it too must be released.

6. The Roman *as,* 1/24 of a denar.

7. Ḥul 12:4–5. The Hebrew text quotes only the beginning of this Mishnaic passage, and points to the rest with the notation "etc."

Pisḳa 229

1. *House* is taken to mean any structure, and not only a residential one.

2. See Pisḳa 194, where these same terms are used.

3. See Mid 4:6; even though it is neither a dwelling place nor a storage place.

4. *ʾUlam,* the structure leading to the interior of the Temple Hall, which did not have the full walled characteristic of a building. See Mid 4:7.

5. Where there is a walk-way. On the higher place, see Mak 2:1.

6. B. Shab 32b. According to the school of R. Ishmael, the victim is called *he who falls* because he is actually deserving of the punishment of falling. Nevertheless, the owner who has caused him to fall is also guilty of failing to build a parapet, and deserves punishment for it.

7. B. BḴ 51a, where this is part of a longer discussion. The victim must fall down from the roof before the owner is liable for failing to build a parapet.

8. B. Suk 3a, P. Ma 3:7.

9. A symbolic act extending the Sabbath limit of movement, etc.

10. Extending their boundaries in order to consider them as one city. See B. Suk 3a.

11. See B. BM 87b, 88a. *Ṭeḇel,* produce from which tithe has not yet been taken, is not liable to it until it has been brought into a house. This tiny house, however, is not considered a house that makes produce liable for tithes.

12. See B. BB 11a. Usually, if one owns an entrance, he also owns four square cubits in front of it.

13. B. Suk 3a. Building such a structure does not require one to dwell in it, as would a normal house. See Pisḳa 194. This section does not appear in R and is probably a gloss.

Pisḳa 230

1. Deut. 22:9.

2. R.H. thinks that Lev. 5:15 is meant. Others believe it to be Deut. 23:18.

3. Referring to the following sentence in verse 9, *lest the fulness of the seed . . . be forfeited (tiḳdaš)*. The Hebrew root *ḳdš*, "to be holy," is used also in the sense of "to be forbidden for profane use, to be declared taboo, to be forfeited." This applies also to the derivatives of the same root used in Lev. 5:15 and Deut. 23:18. Hence "holiness" is used here in this prohibitory sense.

4. Kil 7:7, Tos Kil 4:2. The Mishnah reads the word *tašriš*, "rooted," as *tašliš*, "grown a third."

5. Tos Kil 4:12. See Lieberman, *TK*, p. 645.

6. From the list of cases which are not liable.

7. The sowing must be deliberate (Kil 5:7); therefore the wind-blown seed is not excluded from the list and is not liable.

8. Kil 5:8, where the reasoning of the Sages is quoted: if it is not a common practice, i.e., if it is not something desirable and useful, it is not prohibited.

9. Since Scripture says *thy vineyard*, which might imply that the prohibition covers only your sowing in your own vineyard.

10. The stress is on the words *with two kinds of seeds*, i.e., you may not sow two kinds of seeds anywhere. See P. Kil 7:4 (30d).

11. Possibly in the sense that the verse in Leviticus sets forth the law governing a field, while this verse indicates that vineyards are also included in the prohibition.

12. This section, which does not appear in R, is probably a gloss.

Piska 231

1. Kil 8:3,6. They may not be permitted to do any sort of work together. One who violates this rule is liable to forty lashes.

2. Kil 8:3.

3. So Jastrow and Albeck. See Kil 8:4. This is the opinion of R. Meir in Tos Kil 5:4, which differs from that of the Mishnah.

Piska 232

1. See Kil 9:8, Sif Lev. Ḳĕdošim 89:2.

2. Tos Kil 5:21. See Lieberman, *TK*, p. 661.

3. Or hold it behind him, as in the case of the seller who demonstrates it to a buyer. See B. Yeḇ 4b, Kil 9:10.

4. See Kil 9:9. Both strips are tied to the leather strap, each strip going in a different direction.

5. See Kil 9:10. One kind of cloth is attached to the basket, and the other kind to the sack, and the two containers are kept together. They may not be carried together on one's back (so Albeck).

6. Kil 9:9. This section is not in R and other manuscripts.

Piska 233

1. To indicate that in the case of the positive commandment of *twisted cords* (fringes) one may mingle two seeds. See B. Yeḇ 4a.

2. See Meḵ Ba-ḥoḏeš 7.

Pisḳa 234

1. See Sif Num. 115 and B. Men 41b. It is unclear which part of the fringe is under discussion. See Rashi and R. Tam, ad loc.

2. B. Men 39a. The length of the fringes must be as described above measuring from the root of them, but if one is frayed later on, it is still valid.

3. Τηβέννα, similar to a toga. See S. Krauss, *Talmudische Archäologie* (Leipzig, 1910–12), *1*, 605, n. 541, on the entire passage.

4. Latin fibulatorium.

5. Greek νεϱβικά.

6. See Kil 9:7, BB 5:11, where they are called thick cloaks.

7. Brundisian cloak. See Krauss, *Talmudische Archäologie, 1*, 211, 213.

8. A kind of linen cloak, probably not suitable to be worn as a garment. This rule follows the School of Shammai (B. ᶜEd 4:10). See F., in *Assaf Jubilee Volume*, p. 419.

9. Σάγος, a soldier's coarse blanket.

10. *Maᶜăforeṯ,* a covering protecting one's clothing from dust (*ᶜafar*).

Pisḳa 235

1. B. Keṯ 45b. If one slanders his wife, he is liable to a flogging, but only if he had had intercourse with her. Another version of this rule is that he is liable in either case, but is subject to a fine only if he had had intercourse with her.

2. Added by F.

3. See Pisḳa 186/187, and notes thereto.

4. F. repeats Lev. 19:18 here, but it does not appear in R.

5. See P. Keṯ 4:4.

6. The word *this,* here as elsewhere (Meḵ Dĕ-Pisḥa 2), shows that one is pointing to something. Therefore she must be present.

7. If he is telling the truth and wishes to prove that she was not a virgin, he must bring such witnesses (*EH*).

8. Added from the margin and incorrect in many respects (F.). In B. Keṯ 44b, 45a it is stated that if the witnesses come forth after the marriage, i.e., from her husband's or father-in-law's house, she is to be stoned at the door of her father's house, but if the witnesses come from her father's house, she is to be stoned at the gate of the city.

9. Literally "evil tongue." This section is not in R and other manuscripts.

10. B. Keṯ 54a: "Look at the plant that you have grown!"

11. This is the opinion of R. Eliezer ben Jacob (B. Keṯ 46a). The Rabbis, however, interpret these words symbolically: bring witnesses and make the matter as clear as if the stained garment itself had been shown. See Pisḳa 237.

12. Although both parents must bring her out, only the father may speak.

13. B. Keṯ 56b.

Pisḳa 236

1. B. BḲ. 46b.

2. See Pisḳa 241.

Piska 237

1. According to him, the Torah is speaking here not of the actual garment (the public exhibition of which would be unseemly), but of clear verbal evidence (B. Ket 46a, Mek Nĕziḳin 6).

2. That is to say, the stained garment itself is to be exhibited as evidence.

Piska 238

1. Usually translated: *fine him.*

2. See B. Bek 50b, Tos Ket 13:3, on Tyrian coins.

3. See Ket 4:1, B. Ket 14a.

4. He has tarnished her reputation. See Ket 3:4, where this expression refers to a rapist (Deut. 22:29).

5. All his days he must be married to her, but if the marriage is childless, he may arrange for a divorce at his death, so that she would not be obligated to marry his brother.

Piska 239

1. Which implies any procedure.

2. See Piska 235.

3. Or vice versa, as the answer indicates. This section uses abbreviated language. See Ket 4:3.

4. Literally "a commandment," but not absolutely required if not possible.

Piska 240

1. The word *all* is not in the Masoretic text. It may have been put in here under the influence of an interpretation which understood the verse as speaking of all of the elders.

2. Concerning a priest's daughter.

3. The text reads "stated there . . . so here." This makes no sense, because here it is clear, while there it is not. Probably the statement was copied from the comment on the verse in Leviticus as it appears in Sif Lev. ʾEmor 1:15. See also B. Sanh 50a.

Piska 241

1. Legally, for the purpose of betrothal. Ḳid 1:1.

2. The reference is to necrophilia. See B. BB 3b. See also B. Sanh 66b, where the verse is taken to refer to gratifying one's lust on a part of a woman's body other than her sex organ (*EH*).

3. A second paramour is also to be put to death. See B. Sanh 66b. Some take it to refer to their child, as specified in the name of R. Johanan, B. ʿAr 7a.

Piska 242

1. B. Sanh 66b.

2. See Piska 148.

3. Literally "upon the word," after verbal warning.

4. The man who holds her may not be executed in the same manner, since he did not lie with her. See Sanh 7:9.

Pisḳa 243

1. Sanh 8:7, B. Sanh 73a. The would-be rapist may be lawfully slain by anyone who sees him in the act, in order to save his victim. The same applies to one who is about to commit murder or homosexual rape, as indicated here.

2. See Sanh 8:7. One may not slay the aggressor in these other cases without a trial in court.

3. Tos Sanh 11:11. In this case her cry was meant not to save herself but to save the rapist's life.

Pisḳa 244

1. Since we can deduce this by reason, why is it stated specifically in Exod. 22:15?

2. So F.

3. In both verses, and not merely in the case of rape. See B. Keṯ 38a.

4. See B. Yeḇ 60a–b. One who has accidentally ruptured her hymen with some sharp object.

5. Even if she is the victim of an accident, she is no longer considered a virgin. See Tos Keṯ 3:5; Lieberman, *TK,* p. 225. In this interpretation the same word in the verse is used to derive the second meaning. This is found frequently in the Sifre. The method seems to be this: according to one interpretation, I would understand that the only possible meaning is A. What about meaning B? Answer: the same word also implies meaning B.

6. *Naʿărah,* a girl between the ages of twelve years plus one day and twelve years and six months plus one day. See B. Keṯ 38a. R and other manuscripts, however, read "*Damsel* is stated here, and *damsel* is stated in the case of seduction." The reference could be to Deut. 22:23.

7. *Bog̅ereṯ,* older than a damsel.

8. Or the rule, and make him liable for a *bog̅ereṯ* as well, by paying damages to her, since *naʿărah* is stated explicitly twice, for both cases (F.).

Pisḳa 245

1. See Pisḳa 238 and Keṯ 3:4–5.

2. Keṯ 3:6, P. Keṯ 3 (27:2–3), in the name of Jose the Galilean. R reads "Eleazar" instead of "Eliezer." See Epstein, *Maḇoʾ,* p. 66. See also F., in *Assaf Jubilee Volume,* p. 423.

Pisḳa 246

1. Yeḇ 11:1.

Pisḳa 247

1. Added by the Gaon of Vilna. It is the second part of the Hebrew phrase translated *crushed.*

2. Literally "of the sun," from the moment he first saw the sun. See B. Yeḇ 75a. The vineyard was the site of the academy.

3. To health and to virility.

4. This is the definition given by medical practitioners. See B. Yeḇ 9b.

5. Ḳid 4:1, Tos Ḳid 5:6; Lieberman, *TK,* p. 963. The Sages did not regard proselytes as a separate group.

Piska 248

1. Yeḇ 4:13, B. Yeḇ 49a.

2. *Kareṯ,* divine punishment, such as premature death, lack of issue, etc.

3. The Mishnah accepts Simeon the Yemenite's definition. See Lev. 18:6 on prohibited marriages.

Piska 249

1. Only the males are excluded, on the basis of the fact that the Hebrew words are in the masculine gender, Yeḇ 8:3. Historically speaking, it should be noted that the great-grandmother of King David was a Moabitess, and Naamah, Solomon's wife, was an Ammonitess. Thus the Sages had good reason to assume that females must be and should be exempted.

2. In B. Yeḇ 77a this is taught in the name of R. Simeon. The other Sages agree on the law but differ on the source of it.

3. See B. Yeḇ 76b, where a similar argument is fancifully described as a discussion between Doeg and Abner. The argument here seems to be that of R. Judah, justifying the need for the masculine form (F.).

4. A difficult clause, possibly extraneous (F.).

5. Probably the correct reading should be: "If Scripture states *for ever,* why add *the tenth generation?*"

6. See Lieberman, *Hellenism in Jewish Palestine,* p. 61.

7. Deut. 23:3, concerning the bastard.

Piska 250

1. Literally "on account of the (spoken) word (*ʿal dĕḇar*)," taken here to refer to the spoken advice of Balak.

2. *Noy*; possibly read *gĕnay,* "reproach" (Yalḳuṭ, and some other manuscripts).

3. The difference between this and the preceding is unclear. It may be two separate interpretations, or a repetition of the same interpretation.

Piska 251

1. In the case of an escaped slave. The Hebrew word is the same in both verses.

Piska 253

1. The masculine *banim* is again interpreted here as "sons" rather than as "children." Thus, according to R. Simeon, only males are excluded unto the third generation, while females are acceptable immediately. See Yeḇ 8:3.

2. On the ground that this phrase, seemingly superfluous, must add something to the term *children.*

3. Referring to the Moabites and the Ammonites. See Piska 249.

4. Matters of logical deduction, such as the principle of inference from the minor to the major, may be questioned and refuted, but a rule passed down as a tradition through the generations must be accepted. See B. Yeb 77b.

5. In B. Yeb 78a the discussion concerns the time of the giving of the Torah. We are not discussing the generations from then on, but rules for all time.

6. This story is in the context of the question, does the child follow the mother or the father, and attempts to show that it follows the mother. See B. Yeb 78a, P. Yeb 8:2. In Tos Ḳid 5:4, R. ʿAḳiba states that none of this applies any longer, since Sennacherib has totally mixed all the nations, therefore there are no longer any Ammonites, Moabites, Egyptians, etc., in the Biblical sense, and all are acceptable immediately.

Piska 254

1. In mass formation (R.H.).

2. The term usually refers to sexual misconduct.

3. On the exile of the Shekinah, see Gen. Rabbah 19:7, Num. Rabbah 12:6. See also R. Hammer, "The God of Suffering," *Conservative Judaism* (Fall–Winter, 1976–77), p. 34.

4. Literally "word."

Piska 255

1. The Temple itself; see B. Pes 68a. The Levitical camp is the Temple Mount.

Piska 256

1. Zab 2:3.

2. He may not come in until after sunset; a flux does not prevent him from coming in, since during that period of time it has no effect. F. would read *zibho,* "his sacrifice," instead of *zibato,* "his flux."

Piska 257

1. *Yad,* usually translated "place."

2. Usually translated: *monument.*

3. Elijah Gaon reads "not in the camp." F. suggests "not sitting," referring to the oriental position when urinating.

4. F. changes this to *not standing.* See above, note 3. See also Tos Meg 3:25, Lieberman, *TK,* p. 1205.

5. Toward the Temple, the dwelling of God. This is said of those who are in Galilee, north of Jerusalem. See B. BB 61b.

Piska 258

1. P. Ber 6:4.

2. Because of the unpleasant odor.

3. B. Sanh 21b. Such places are not fit for holy objects.
4. Ber 9:5.
5. See Piska 254.

Piska 259

1. Giṭ 4:6, B. Giṭ 43b, 45a.
2. Ger 3:4.
3. So F. Some read, "and not in the city itself."
4. This whole Piska is taken as referring to a resident alien. According to ARN-A 35 (*YJS, 10,* 143), he may not reside in Jerusalem.
5. See BM 4:8.

Piska 260

1. In other words, one might reason that a warning against one of the two would have been sufficient. The answer is that both are mentioned in order to prevent wrong deductions.
2. Unclear. Probably a fragment of a marginal reference.

Piska 261

1. Tos Tem 4:6. The lamb may not be offered on the altar.
2. The question is, does this apply to hire for any sexual services, or for only those which are totally forbidden. See Tos Tem 4:6.
3. Tem 6:3.
4. The animal received in exchange for the dog.
5. Not the one at the Temple in Jerusalem.
6. I.e., the red heifer which was not a usual sacrifice, and whose ritual was conducted on the Mount of Olives. See B. Tem. 30b.
7. B. Tem 30b. Gold given for these purposes could not be used to make decorations for the Temple.
8. Such as a pigeon. See Tem 6:4, B. Tem 30b.
9. B. Tem 29b.

Piska 262

1. The verse is understood to mean that one is forbidden to pay interest. See Rashi, ad loc.
2. See Mek Dĕ-Kaspa 1.
3. Asking the borrower to perform a service is also prohibited as a form of interest. BM 5:6, Tos BM 6:17.

Piska 264

1. They may be required since they are mandatory, unlike vows and freewill offerings.
2. See Piska 41.
3. See B. RH 5b. The sacrifice is still acceptable. See also B. RH 6a.

Piska 265

1. B. Ḥul 2a, Tos Ḥul 2:17, where the wording of R. Judah's statement is: "Even better is one who brings his sheep to the Temple Court, places his hands on it, and slaughters it." The names of the Rabbis are reversed in some versions: Lev. Rabbah 37:1; P. Ned 1:1.

2. Vowing and paying, and vowing and not paying.

3. Vowing and not paying, and not vowing at all.

4. *Tišmor,* literally "watch, care for."

Piska 266

1. Literally "forever." R.H.: even before the work is completed, before the grapes are plucked from the vine. See B. BM 87b.

2. BM 7:4.

3. *Bĕ-nafšeka,* literally "with your life," i.e., the value of your person.

4. Thereafter you may eat. The Mishnah (BM 7:4) records that permission was given to laborers to eat while walking from row to row, thus saving the employer's time.

Piska 267

1. See B. BM 87b. See above, Piska 266.

Piska 268

1. *Taketh* is understood as meaning taking by way of payment of money. *Marrieth* is literally "has intercourse with," which is another way of contracting marriage.

2. See B. Ḳid 4b. Without the specific verse, it would not have been possible to deduce this by logical reasoning.

Piska 269

1. Giṭ 9:10, B. Giṭ 90a. See Piska 254, note 2.

2. Therefore, anything whatever that he finds unseemly.

3. I.e., her husband.

4. I.e., other men, who were forbidden to her because she was married.

5. She may be divorced for any of these reasons and may then remarry.

6. Giṭ 3:1. Here, as in other places, the text cites the Mishnah as if it were a Biblical verse, without writing it out in full, thus directing the reader to consult the Mishnah itself. The passage referred to deals with several persons bearing the same name as the one on the bill of divorcement.

7. See B. Giṭ 19a, where these terms are defined.

8. *Sefer,* literally "letter, document, scroll," later "book."

9. Tos Giṭ 7:3.

10. *Kĕritut,* literally "cutting off."

11. Tos Giṭ 7:3.

12. Giṭ 9:1, Tos Giṭ 7:1.

13. Tos Giṭ 7:1 adds, "to marry any man except So-and-so."

14. The Mishnah rules that he must hand her the bill once more without adding "except So-and-so."

15. Tos Giṭ 9:1.

16. The law of levirate marriage obligates the childless widow to marry her brother-in-law, who in this case is So-and-so himself.

17. Hence no conditions may be attached to it.

18. The Talmud (B. Giṭ 83a) explains this more fully: the case is that of So-and-so who is a priest. If the woman's divorced husband dies, as a widow she may marry this priest, but as a divorcée she may not. If the divorce makes her unfit to marry a priest, should not the former marriage (and widowhood) forbid her to marry all other men? The absurdity of this logic shows that the condition imposed on the divorce formula cannot stand.

19. Since she has violated the condition attached to the divorce, she is still a married woman and therefore an adulteress. In the Talmud (B. Giṭ 83a) this argument also is ascribed to R. ʿAḳiba.

20. Giṭ 8:1.

21. Quotations from Giṯ 8:1–2. See note 6, above.

Pisḳa 270

1. B. Giṭ 90b. He is *another* (i.e., different) in that the first husband had no way of knowing of her deficiency when he married her.

2. That she may not remarry her first husband.

3. We could have included the widow by way of logical interpretation.

4. We might have thought that this made the widow a special case, since it would not apply to a divorcée.

5. I.e., one who behaved promiscuously after her divorce, and not only one who was divorced and remarried.

6. And did not remarry.

7. Yeḇ 10:1.

8. *Niśuʾim,* the second and final stage of marriage.

9. *ʾErusim,* the first stage of marriage, which also requires a writ of divorce to dissolve it.

10. That is, after the marriage has been consummated, following the rite of matrimony. B. Yeḇ 11b.

11. After having been warned by her husband not to do so. She too is forbidden to her husband.

12. A verse from the Prophets supporting the rule that a woman who had remarried may not return to her first husband.

13. The Hebrew word is spelled *hwʾ* ("he, it, that") but is read as if spelled *hyʾ* ("she").

Pisḳa 271

1. B. Soṭ 44a. All these are cases of transgression. The Talmud emphasizes the words *his wife*—one proper for him to marry. The Gibeonites, who deceived Joshua (see Josh., chap. 9), were condemned to be hewers of wood and drawers of water, and were regarded as unfit to intermarry with Jews.

2. See Pisḳa 193.

3. Deut. 20:6–7.

4. In regard to business, this applies only in the case of a new wife. Other individuals are obligated to help.

Piska 272

1. See BM 9:13, where this verse is used regarding all things used in the preparation of food; Tos BM 10:11.

Piska 273

1. The phrase is taken to mean that there must be witnesses to the theft. In Mek Něziķin 5 this stipulation is repeated, and the requirement for witnesses to the selling also is added.

2. Literally "treat him tyrannically," interpreted here as "make use of his forced labor."

3. See Piska 155, and notes thereto.

Piska 274

1. See Tos Neḡ 3:1. The patient must not pluck out the white hairs, which constitute evidence, even after the priest has examined him.

2. See Tos Neḡ 3:1. You need not cease your normal activity for fear that it might affect the scab. See also Tos Shab 133a.

Piska 275

1. That is, malicious slander or gossip. Miriam is consistently seen as the prototype of the slanderer. See Num., chap. 12, and Ginzberg, *Legends, 3,* 255ff.

2. For the siring of proper children. According to Sif Num. 99, Miriam's complaint was that Moses avoided marital relations with his wedded wife.

3. See Piska 1.

4. See Ginzberg, *Legends, 6,* 92. This has no connection with the matter of slander, but is a separate matter, giving honor to Miriam. R reads "Everything is ascribed (to Miriam) in order to show you," etc., i.e., the verse mentions Miriam and speaks of the exodus from Egypt because of the important role and honor accorded her.

Piska 276

1. That one may not enter the debtor's house in order to seize a pledge, as stated at the end of the verse.

2. See also B. BM 115a, where permission is given to enter in the case of fees due for various things.

3. The word *without* in the next verse is connected to the end of this verse.

Piska 277

1. The Hebrew reads literally "And if he be a man, poor"; if one stops at the comma, the resulting meaning is any man, poor or rich.

2. The cause of the poor is more urgent in the sight of God.

3. B. BM 114b.

4. Perhaps it is the emphatic *surely restore* (literally "with a restoring thou shalt restore") that is taken to indicate this. See B. BM 114b.

5. Greek σάγος, a coarse woolen blanket used also as a sleeping mat.

Piska 278

1. Tos BM 10:3.

2. R reads "five."

3. Not in R.

4. See Piska 277. See Mek de-R. Simeon ben Yohai, 22:21. The reason is that the poor have no one to turn to but God.

5. Possibly (a) not to oppress, and (b) not to defer paying the laborer his hire.

6. See B. BM 111b for a more detailed discussion.

7. B. BM 111b. R and other manuscripts, however, have "but not in Jerusalem." This could be an instance of repeating an interpretation connected to a word even when it has no meaning in the new context. See Piska 259.

Piska 279

1. BM 9:11.

2. When the employer has given the laborer his wages in the form of an order to someone else (a storekeeper or a money-changer), he is not liable. See Sif Lev. Ḳĕdošim 2:9, BM 9:11.

3. *Setteth his heart,* literally "bears his life." See B. BM 112a for examples of risking life.

4. "If so" does not fit. It may have been assimilated from its appearance in the next paragraph.

5. *Lest he cry,* literally "and he not cry."

Piska 280

1. Rather, at the end of this same verse. See B. Sanh 27b for a fuller discussion.

Piska 281

1. *Ger,* usually translated "stranger." In Rabbinic literature the term is understood as meaning a proselyte, not a stranger. See Kadushin, *Rabbinic Mind,* pp. 290–93, for a discussion of this concept and the change from the Biblical to the Rabbinic meaning.

2. See B. Yeb 61a; a rich woman in Jerusalem during Titus's siege of the city.

3. Related to him (wife, etc.).

Piska 282

1. Pe 2:7, Tos Pe 1:8. In these cases, the owner is not liable for not leaving forgotten sheaves.

2. Pe 4:6.

3. Pe 5:7.

Piska 283

1. P. Pe 6:4. Obviously one sheaf could not feed three kinds of needy people.

2. Pe 6:5. Dropped grapes belong to the poor.

3. Pe 6:10, stored in the ground.

4. "The right of the poor" refers to his right to take gleanings and corner crop. These are taken from the standing corn but not from the sheaf. See Tos Pe 3:6–7; Lieberman, *TK,* p. 168.

5. Standing corn which has not been forgotten can "save" the sheaf and other standing corn from coming under the law of forgotten sheaves. According to Pe 6:8 even one stalk not forgotten "saves" the others.

6. Since the reasoning could have led to an incorrect conclusion, the version had to specify that standing corn is included in the law of forgotten sheaves.

7. Pe 6:3.

8. Since Scripture says *it,* in the singular.

9. Pe 6:6. The "etc." indicates that the rest of the Mishnah is to be cited.

10. Pe 5:2.

11. Pe 4:11. It belongs to the poor; therefore, if the owner wishes to take it from him, he must bring legal evidence for his claim.

12. This conclusion is drawn from the word *yihyeh* ("shall be").

13. The last part of the verse, not found in the text, is the basis for this rule. See Sif Lev. Way-yikra᾿ 12:13, Tos Pe 3:8; Lieberman, *TK,* p. 170.

14. Lieberman, *TK,* p. 170, states that this may reflect a custom of leaving money for the poor to find. Here the loser earns the same merit even for doing it unintentionally. See Piska 252.

Piska 284

1. Literally "the earlier ones,"indicating a custom which existed formerly.

2. By beating them, rather than gathering the olives one by one directly from the tree (F.); thus many olives would remain on the tree for the poor.

3. Pe 7:2.

4. Of the forgotten sheaf. This part of the Mishnah in parentheses does not appear in the text, but seems to be the part referred to, since only there is the matter of beating mentioned. See Lieberman, *TK,* p. 171. See also Piska 283 and 269, for other examples of such abbreviated quoting of the Mishnah.

5. A play on words: *tĕfa᾿er* ("go over the boughs") and *titpa᾿er* ("lord it").

6. Pe 5:6.

7. *Again,* literally "after thee." Do not return to take up these things, because they are "after you," that is to say, now they belong to the poor. B. Ḥul 131a. See Piska 285.

8. See Piska 283; Pe 3:6.

Piska 285

1. *ʿOlĕlot,* small single bunches of grapes, rather than ripe clusters (see below); these are defective growths. The Scriptural word translated "glean" (*tĕʿolel*) is derived from the same root.

2. Pe 7:7.

3. See Pisḳa 284, note 7.
4. Pe 7:8.
5. See Pisḳas 284 and 283.

Pisḳa 286

1. All manuscripts read ". . . strife. Similarly Scripture says, *Then both the men, between whom the controversy is, shall stand* (19:17). What causes the (wicked) man," etc. This reading thus cites two additional verses concerning strife, Gen. 13:7 and Deut. 19:17, and then concludes with a comment on the original verse.

2. Since this verse is so close, it is taken as an example of a case when the guilty party is to be beaten.

3. But not for acts which can be rectified. Tos Mak 5(4):16.

4. Mak 3:13.

5. MT reads: "and not as others do—that while the culprit is being beaten, the judge is busy with something else."

6. Tos Mak 5(4):17. B. Mak 13b cites this as the teaching of R. ʿAḳiba.

7. See B. Mak 22b.

8. In R and in the Talmud, "comes close to forty." See B. Mak 22b, and MT ad loc.

9. Where is the extra (fortieth) lash to be applied, since the thirty-nine lashes were divided one-third in the front and two-thirds in the back? See Mak 3:10.

10. The singular *him* is emphasized, which can only mean the particular culprit.

11. Of thirty-nine as prescribed by the Torah.

12. See Mak 3:11. The court may estimate the number of lashes that the culprit will be able to bear without danger to his life.

13. *ʿAl,* literally "in addition to," whether more or less.

14. Mak 3:14.

15. The beating is to be stopped.

16. Mak 3:15. This second interpretation does not appear in any of the manuscripts. F. has added it from MhG.

17. See Sanders, *Paul,* p. 179. Sins against God are more easily atoned for than those against man.

18. See Sanders, *Paul,* p. 123. God's mercy is greater than His severity in judgment.

19. In the Mishnah (Mak 3:15) this statement of R. Simeon is connected with the reasoning that if a man's life may be taken for even one transgression, how much more is it true that his life will be granted to him for performing even one commandment.

20. Bĕ-Rebbi (*ben Rabbi,* "son of a Rabbi") is a "title of learning . . . conferred especially upon scholars who were the sons of scholars, or upon members of the family of the patriarch" (Ginzberg, *JE, 3,* 52). See Rashi to B. Ḥul 11b.

21. Mak 3:15.

Pisḳa 287

1. See B. BM 88b, and the subsequent discussion. The owner may make a stipulation with the laborer that he is not to eat of the produce he is working with.

Muzzling is not the pertinent action; it is the permission to eat or not to eat of the produce.

2. B. BM 91b. R. Jose reasons that this is so because one must work like the ox, which uses all its four limbs, but the Rabbis disagree. Tos BM 8:7 offers a longer version.

Piska 288

1. If one brother dies before the other is born, the latter is not required to marry the widow, since he has never "dwelt together" with his deceased brother.
2. Yeb 2:1.
3. The text quotes only part of the Mishnah.
4. See B. Yeb 17b, where the case of Jacob is cited to show that fathers, and not mothers, establish the relationship of brotherhood.
5. Except of course the one surviving brother—otherwise there would be no case.
6. The interpretation must be based on the words *of them* (R.H.), implying that at least one survives.
7. Yeb 3:10.
8. Marking the surviving brother's refusal to marry the widow (25:7ff.).
9. *Ben,* usually translated "child," but understood here as a male child.
10. This problem is discussed in B. BB 115a in connection with the laws of inheritance, based on Num. 27:8. It may be inappropriate here. It is possible to take it as indicating that his own child is dead, but he has grandchildren. See Maimonides' *Code,* IV, III, i, 3 (*YJS, 19,* 265).
11. B. Yeb 22b.
12. Only *ḥăliṣah* may be performed, not levirate marriage, as above. Here either one is permitted.
13. See Tos Yeb 7:2; Lieberman, *TK,* p. 60, to Yeb 5:1; B. Ḳid 14a. The bill of divorcement makes her forbidden, but does not release her from the obligation of *ḥăliṣah.* This must still be performed before she can marry again.
14. Yeb 6:1. Even if one of them did not know what the circumstances were when they had intercourse, the conditions have been fulfilled.
15. The words *unto her* indicate that there are some women whom he may not take in levirate marriage.
16. Yeb 1:1.

Piska 289

1. Yeb 4:5, 2:8. Perhaps based on reading the beginning of the sentence as "and it shall be that the eldest (surviving) brother shall cause to give birth."
2. The Hebrew phrase usually translated *shall succeed in the name* means literally "shall stand upon the name." B. Yeb 24a argues that this indicates not that the child must necessarily bear the deceased brother's (the child's uncle's) name, but rather that the child is to inherit the deceased's property, and may bear any name that his real father may prefer (cf. F.'s note ad loc., and see below, end of this Piska).
3. *That is dead* seems to be superfluous, hence it must add something to the

rule, to wit, that if the second brother too dies, the duty devolves upon the third brother.

4. The women permitted are those not forbidden by the Torah, i.e., by God.

5. Usually translated: *he will not perform the duty of a husband's brother unto me.*

6. Not sterile, as above, but not yet having given birth (F.).

7. Thus including a barren, elderly, or minor widow. R reads "that Scripture includes something else."

8. Yeḇ 11:2, although not in the same language. Tos Yeḇ 12:2.

9. See Tos Yeḇ 12:2, which, as suggested by Lieberman, should read, "do not perform *ḥăliṣah* and do not contract levirate marriage."

Piska 290

1. The opposite opinion is stated in B. MḲ 21a. See Albeck, *Maḇoʾ lat-Talmuḏim,* p. 129.

Piska 291

1. She may not seclude herself with him when the judges are not present. The phrase "with spittle that is visible to the elders" does not appear in most manuscripts.

2. It does not say "his shoe" specifically. See however, Yeḇ 12:2, which specifies his shoe.

3. See Yeḇ 12:1. This probably refers to the location of the straps of the shoe. But it may also mean cases where the leg has been amputated at the knee.

4. Hence there must be some distance between the two faces.

5. Yeḇ 12:3.

6. In connection with the curses. See Soṭ 7:2.

7. See above. In Yeḇ 12:3 these actions appear together.

8. It is the removal of the shoe that validates the ceremony.

9. This sentence is found in some manuscripts. The meaning seems to be that the ceremony of *ḥăliṣah* should be performed in such a way as to resemble levirate marriage, which includes intercourse.

10. See B. Ḳid 14a; Yeḇ 101b, in the name of R. Samuel ben Judah, a third generation Babylonian Amora. This ruling may reflect the generally antiproselyte position of the School of Shammai. See L. Finkelstein, "Hašpaʿaṯ Beṯ Šammay," *Sefer Asaf,* p. 421.

11. See Yeḇ, end of chap. 12; Tos Yeḇ 12:15.

Piska 292

1. See Piska 286. Here too the verse in all the manuscripts is 19:17.

2. *ʾAḥiw,* usually translated "another."

3. See BḲ 8:3 and B. BḲ 88a (slaves are not subject to family relationships), cited in the name of R. Judah; the Sages, however, say: They are brothers as far as the commandments are concerned.

4. B. BḲ 28a: "excluding an officer of the court," who is not liable to a fine for an offense caused while he is carrying out the court's orders. The Talmud thus interprets this law not literally, as imposing a monetary fine. See Piska 293.

5. So the Hebrew text, which does not have *him,* usually added by translators.

Pisḳa 293

1. This rule is sometimes interpreted as referring to a "pursuer" (*rodef*), whom one may slay in order to save his intended victim, thus "saving" the pursuer from becoming a murderer. Others, such as R. ʿAḳiba, interpret it as an actual case of "causing disgrace" (*bošet*) (F.).

2. In the case of false witnesses (*zomĕmim*).

3. Monetary payment, i.e., payment of damages for disgrace is under discussion here.

Pisḳa 294

1. Each is half of the other. When the weights get too small through wear, they may not be used, since the result is deceptive. See B. BM 52b, Tos BM 3:17.

2. You must destroy it.

3. Originally two *ḳab,* later three *ḳab.*

4. When it is supposed to have only three.

5. One may not keep a deceptive measure even for strictly private use. Even if there is no intention to use it for others or to defraud them, it is forbidden. See B. BB 89b, 90a.

6. BB 5:11.

7. One might think that this is permitted to him, but it is not, because it is not *just.* So most manuscripts. See B. BB 88a.

8. Usually translated: *just weight.*

9. Greek ἀγορανόμος (P. BB 5:11), an official responsible for checking weights and measures.

10. See BB 5:12.

11. The bracketed words are not in the Biblical text.

Pisḳa 295

1. BM 4:11, Tos BM 3:26.

2. A tressis is a coin worth three Roman ases. See the discussion in B. BM 60a. No matter how innocent it may seem, one must avoid deception.

3. See Pisḳa 148, where the same list appears. In R the order in this Pisḳa is the same as there.

Pisḳa 296

1. Sif Lev. Bĕ-ḥuḳḳotay, beginning.

2. I.e., all the nations have heard and trembled, but not Amalek. Elijah Gaon places this reference at the "time of redemption," below.

3. Perhaps in accord with the statement which follows, in the sense that God set them up to punish Israel.

4. See Meḳ ʿĂmaleḳ 1.

5. F. suggests that this is only a segment of the full statement in Pesiḳta *Zakor,* where these verses are contrasted: when Amalek wages war against God, He will destroy them; otherwise it is your responsibility.

Piska 297

1. See Piskas 196 and 57. You must first conquer the land, and that will earn you the merit of living in it.

2. See Sif Lev. Way-yikra᾿ 13:4. The ᶜ*omer* was brought out of wheat and barley. On the seven species, see Deut. 8:8, quoted below. R reads "perhaps just as there wheat," etc.

3. B. Men 84a,b. See Bik 1:3, 10, which states that only the seven species may be brought as first fruits.

4. A medium-size olive of good quality, fit for storage.

5. Based on the phrase *of thy land,* i.e., it must belong to the rightful owner. See D. Halivni, "Yeš Mĕbi᾿im Bikkurim," *Bar Ilan Annual,* 7/8 (1970), 74.

6. Added from Bik 1:2 (which derives it from a verse in Exodus). There this verse is quoted also before, so that "same reason" may mean "the same as already stated" (Halivni, ibid.). In these cases the land is not rightfully theirs.

7. Bik 1:6. There are times when only one or the other may be done, but from Pentecost to Tabernacles both may be done.

8. Bik 1:1–2. Again the Mishnah is added to the Sifre. The two used different verses. See note 6, above.

Piska 298

1. See Piska 153, where this verse is applied more fittingly to a judge.

Piska 299

1. Bik 1:9.

2. See Bik 1:4. The proselyte must bring first fruits but need not make the declaration. Maimonides, however, states that he must make the declaration, since proselytes are regarded the same as Abraham's descendants (*Code,* VII, VI, iv, 3 [*YJS, 21,* 303–04]).

3. Bik 1:10. There the reasoning is that that part of the Land of Israel is not termed "a land flowing with milk and honey." See P. Bik 1:2, where both reasons are discussed. See also Piska 301.

Piska 300

1. Bik 3:8.

2. Bik 2:4.

3. Tos Shek 3:24, based on the same verse. Only when the Temple is in existence are first fruits obligatory.

4. Bik 1:8, where this is based on Exod. 23:19. See Halivni, "Yeš Mĕbi᾿im Bikkurim," *Bar Ilan Annual,* 7/8 (1970), p. 79.

Piska 301

1. *We-ᶜanita,* usually translated "speak."

2. The verse refers to the blessings and curses pronounced by the Levites upon Mount Gerizim and Mount Ebel, respectively.

3. Bik 3:7.

4. The priest read it, and the man repeated it.

5. This meaning of *ʿanah,* "to respond to someone else's prompting," is found above, in Piska 14. See the notes there.

6. He assumed that he would not survive. If the Aramean is Jacob, the following is a separate interpretation. Possibly the Aramean is Laban, as he is in the Passover Haggadah, but we are told here that Jacob knew that Laban meant to destroy him.

7. The same interpretation as in the Haggadah. Hoffmann (MT) believes that these are two separate interpretations, and that this one is of later date.

8. The initials of the Hebrew words for these plagues.

9. Therefore *this place* must mean not the land but the Temple.

10. Why mention the Temple as well as the whole land?

11. Above, Piska 300.

12. *Behold* (*hinneh*) is connected with rejoicing: "R. Jonathan says: . . . *Behold* always means rejoicing" (Sif Num. 119). See also Sif Num. 117.

13. R. reads "of His own," i.e., all the produce is really the property of God.

14. Bik 3:1.

15. Bik 1:5.

16. Bik 3:4, Tos Bik 2:10: When the procession reached the Temple Court, the Levites sang *I will extol Thee, O Lord, for Thou hast raised me up* (Ps. 30:2). "This psalm was sung at all times of thanksgiving and acknowledgment of the mercies of the Lord" (Lieberman, *TK,* p. 850).

17. The word *house* is frequently interpreted as referring to a man's wife.

18. MSh 5:14. See Piska 299, note 2.

Piska 302

1. *At the end of every seven years . . . in the feast of Tabernacles* (31:10), referring to the gathering of Israel to hear the reading of the Torah. See Piska 109. Actually the word "end," *keṣ,* appears only in 31:10, while in 26:12 the word is *tekalleh,* literally "hast completed." The implied meaning, however, is the same.

2. MSh 5:6.

3. See Piska 109, and the discussion there. R reads "On the eve of the first day."

4. The first tithe was due to the Levites and was given each year. The second tithe, consumed by the owner in Jerusalem, was given in the first, second, fourth, and fifth years. The poor man's tithe was given in the third and sixth years. Thus, in addition to the regular (first) tithe, another one was given each year, but two additional ones were not given in the same year. See *JE,* under *Tithe,* and Albeck's introductions to the Mishnah tractates Ter, Ma, and MSh. See also Rashi ad loc., and above, Piska 109.

5. Since it speaks here of the third year of the septennate, when the additional poor man's tithe is due. R reads "that Scripture adds here . . ."

Piska 303

1. Pe 8:5. See also Tos Pe 4:11.

2. See Piska 110, and notes thereto.

3. The fruit of the fourth year was permitted for consumption (that of the first

three years was forbidden), but on the same terms of redemption as second tithe. See BM 4:8.

4. MSh 5:9.

5. MSh 5:11.

6. MSh 5:11.

7. MSh 5:12.

8. MSh 5:12.

9. MSh 5:13. This is a condensation. In MSh and in R the blessing is described as children, dew and rain, offspring of cattle, and fruit which is toothsome.

Piska 304

1. This is the blessing recited upon hearing bad news, especially of a death. See Ber 9:2.

2. *Chief* (*ʾalluf*) refers to God. See B. Ḥag̃ 16a. In MT Way-yelek̠ (p. 178) and MhG to Deut. 31:14, the interpretation is followed by a series of conversations in which Moses pleads for his life but is rebuffed. God plays no favorites. See Ginzberg, *Legends, 3,* 441ff. The story which follows here is independent. See F. ad loc.

3. The translation follows R, while F.'s printed text includes the verse, *And the Lord said unto Moses: Take thee Joshua the son of Nun* (Num. 27:18), which interrupts the flow of ideas. *Take thee* is the reply which would have to be understood and which comes at the beginning of the next Piska. Our text is similar to Sifre Zuṭa 27:16 (320): "*That the congregation of the Lord be not as sheep which have no shepherd.* Moses said to God: Lord of the world, You did not bring Israel out of Egypt . . . so that they would have no leaders, but so that they would have leaders, as it is said, *And he said, 'I saw all Israel scattered upon the mountains as sheep that have no shepherd'*" (1 Kings 22:17). Moses requests that a leader be appointed, so that the people will not be like lost sheep, as described in the verses from the Song of Solomon and 1 Kings. God replies that Joshua will be their leader, and that they will not be abandoned.

Piska 305

1. The Piska continues with another interpretation of the verse from Numbers cited as God's answer to Moses. Much of this Piska seems to be connected with the section in Numbers dealing with the appointment of Joshua (Num. 27:18) and with God's original announcement to Moses that he was to die (Num. 27:13). It was inserted here because the subject of Moses' death has been raised (Deut. 31:14).

2. *Ḳaḥ lĕk̠a,* literally "take for yourself," here interpreted to mean "someone like yourself."

3. Literally "man-like" or "masculine," i.e., potent, powerful, or heroic.

4. Another interpretation of Num. 27:18.

5. *Lĕḳiḥah,* "acquisition"; cf. *ḳĕḥeh,* "acquire, purchase," in ARN-A 8, which is here quoted. The act of acquisition is completed by the purchaser taking hold with his hand of the acquired object.

6. The conversation in Piska 304 continues here. Moses requested a leader to replace him; God tells him to appoint Joshua and now instructs him exactly how to go about it. See ARN-A 17, Sif Num. 140 (p. 186).

7. *Turgĕman,* not a translator but a spokesman, who loudly repeats to the public the words of the teacher. Having an official "proclaimer" is a sign of Joshua's newly acquired authority. Targum Onqelos refers to Aaron as Moses' *mĕturgeman* in Exod. 7:1. On Joshua's appointment, see Ginzberg, *Legends, 3,* 399.

8. In Sif Num. 140 Moses raises him from the ground and has him sit next to him.

9. Aaron's son's .

10. They are "kids" as opposed to grown animals. See Yelammedenu Way-yelek̲ 2 (161b), Song Rabbah 1:8. Based on the verse *Go . . . by the footsteps of the flock and feed thy kids beside the shepherds' tents* (Song 1:8). See ARN-A 17, Exod. Rabbah 2:4, Song Rabbah 1:8. See also note 11, below. In Yelammedenu Way-yelek̲ 2 this verse from Hosea is used to prove that Israel is called a child, and the verse *Withhold not correction from the child* (Prov. 23:13) is inserted to instruct Joshua that he must be firm with them, since one should be firm with a beloved child.

11. The interpretation is that of the last part of Song 1:8. *Miškĕnot̲ ha-roʿim* is rendered here as *ʾohăle roʿim,* "tents of the shepherds," as was recognized by the Vilna Gaon and by early commentators. In Song Rabbah 1:8, *ha-roʿim* is interpreted as *ha-raʿim,* "the evil ones," referring to Sihon and Og. Here, however, it may mean the burial place of the fathers, Hebron. See *ʿEmek̲ han-Nĕṣib̲,* p. 390. Since the verse from Song of Solomon is in the second person, it is likely that the interpretation was also in the second person. That the homily is based on that verse is quite clear from the fact that the following story, which cites the verse, has no justification for being here unless seen as another interpretation or an illustrative interpretation of a previously cited verse. The interpretation is: "feed your kids"—remember that the people I am giving you is young, treat them all kindly "beside the shepherds' tents," and do what I cannot do—take them into the land itself. See also ARN-A 17, where the verse from Song of Solomon is cited and followed by the same story as that cited here concerning the daughter of Nak̲dimon. In Mek̲ Širat̲a 10 (2, 76) the verse is interpreted to mean that the sons ("kids") would enter the land, but not the parents ("goats").

12. The legendary wealth of Nak̲dimon is described in B. Ket̲ 66b–67a. R speaks only of her father, not her entire family.

13. This verse is interpreted to mean that the three gifts obtained through the merit of the three leaders ceased when Moses died, therefore Israel had no more satisfaction. Thus we read in Tos Soṭ 11:10 (ed. Lieberman, p. 220, version B): "When Moses died, all three were removed and did not return, as it is said, *And I cut off the three shepherds in one month.*" See also Song Rabbah 4:13.

14. The verse in the printed editions is, *The noblest of the people are gathered together, the people of the God of Abraham* (Ps. 47:10), which is totally inappropriate to the context and puzzling to all the commentators. It may be that the words *nobles of the people* in Num. 21:18 were confused with *noblest of the people* in Ps. 47:10. The practice of citing verses by a few words, sometimes not even the ones important for the interpretation, has led to more than one substitution of an incorrect verse containing the same or similar words. Here the sense is that the well (Num. 21:18) was connected with all the leaders, not only Miriam, through whose merit it was obtained, since their merit brought it back after her death. This leads to the idea expressed here, that only with the death of Moses was Israel deprived of the three

miraculous gifts. Nevertheless Num. 21:18 appears in Song Rabbah 4:13 and may be taken to mean that all three were gathered together in the same year.

15. Reading *mattanah* in place of *miṣwah*. Yalḳuṭ reads simply *mik-kol,* "of everything." *Zeraʿ A*ḇ*raham* suggests *mik-kol ṭo*ḇ*ah,* "of all good things." This is the explanation of the statement made above, that Israel had no more satisfaction, the reason being that all the gifts were taken away.

16. Since Aaron's death has been mentioned here, a famous homily, found in many places (Yelammedenu Ḥuḳḳaṯ 22, Num. Rabbah Ḥuḳḳaṯ 12:20), is inserted. See Ginzberg, *Legends, 3,* 475ff. The homily does not seem to be in place here, however, and interrupts the main story of Moses' plea for a leader to succeed him, the appointment of Joshua, the death of Moses, and Joshua's mourning for his master. The words "When Aaron died" are found in the Yalḳuṭ.

17. I.e., at the time Moses was to die, returning to the main theme and following Moses' conversation with Joshua. See Ginzberg, *Legends, 3,* 475ff.

18. The version in ARN-A 12 adds that God Himself took the soul of Moses and deposited it under His throne.

19. Reading *bĕ-merer* ("bitterly") for *bĕ-mereḏ* ("rebelliously"), as in Esther Rabbah 3.

20. I.e., do not mourn so bitterly—he has his reward.

21. The verse actually goes on to say, *And this people will rise up, and go astray*; but here *will rise up* is applied to Moses, to mean that he will arise from the dead.

Pisḳa 306

1. Israel is taken here literally as the Tribes of the kingdom of Israel, as opposed to the Tribes of the kingdom of Judah.

2. The same term *ḳilḳĕlu,* "corrupted," is used here, but is followed by the preposition *bĕ,* to indicate that the prophets were "corrupted" by Israel. The meaning is not that the prophets were actually corrupted, but that they had no effect and were subject to popular contempt.

3. By making them the object of idolatrous worship, they corrupted them. Therefore the heavens, being themselves involved, albeit involuntarily, could not act as objective witnesses.

4. By itself, and not together with heaven, as above.

5. Scripture goes on to say, *How long wilt thou sleep, O sluggard* (Prov. 6:9), indicating that he has still not changed his ways. R. Simeon comments on the verses in Proverbs independently both of the foregoing comments of R. Meir and of what follows.

6. Witnesses who will testify against Israel. God's quality of mercy is then revealed in His willingness to destroy them.

7. Literally "He says." This section uses the present tense after the introductory future tense of "will say," thus forming a dramatic dialogue. See B. AZ 2a ff., for another example of Rabbinic dialogue and dramatization.

8. My name as a sinner still exists.

9. R reads "Your (i.e., God's) name."

10. An unclear reference, perhaps connected with the names of the children in Hos. 1:6ff.

11. MT has: "on condition that he not move him away."

12. Heaven represents the Presence, and one cannot escape from under its wings, nor can one leave the earth. There is no place for Israel to escape to, where it would be possible to defy God unnoticed.

13. F. suggests omitting "saying to Him: Master of the universe," so that it is the compiler, and not Israel, who is saying, "I do not know," etc. These words would thus be a later addition to preserve the style of dialogue, as above.

14. Or "about him," as in some versions. Elijah Gaon amends, "until he said, 'To whom am I to complain? To the heavens, as it is said, *Give ear.* . . .'"

15. Who else is left, since I have complained to everyone else to no effect?

16. In the sense of adding to and making more and better than before. MT reads "improved."

17. The wicked are too many, and the world is diminished by them.

18. Since heaven and earth are the witnesses called upon in Deut. 32:1, they must therefore be the first to punish Israel.

19. See also B. AZ 25a, where miracles such as these are discussed.

20. The question is, why did Isaiah use an expression opposite of that used by Moses. Three different reasons are given. The expression *samak̲ lĕ-dab̲ar,* translated here "added," is most appropriate for the last interpretation, since it means "gave support to." It does not appear in the first interpretation, as cited in Yalḳuṭ Isa. 387.

21. The meaning is unclear. Perhaps it is that by switching the verbs but keeping the singular for the earth and the plural for the heavens, Isaiah gave support to Moses' concept of which of the two was the greater.

22. Had Moses said this and had Isaiah not supplemented it.

23. Their testimony would thus be different, and therefore inadmissible.

24. Literally "from."

25. The previous interpretation dealt with the content of the commandments. This one deals with the place from which they were given. Some came from heaven, i.e., from Sinai, others were given at various times through Moses on earth.

26. The *song* is the Torah. See Hoffmann's commentary to MT, p. 183. This section does not appear in R, which continues with "Because he said . . . ."

27. In MT Hoffmann reads "disproves," which is supported by several Sifre manuscripts (see F.). Hoffmann explains it thus: Even if heaven and earth continue to yield rain and produce, thus indicating Israel's innocence, the Torah can prove their guilt. The current reading, however, can be understood as follows: Since the verse indicates that the testimony of the song (Torah) is binding, why did Moses hasten to call two other witnesses? The Israelites could deny having received the Torah, and Moses would not be there to contradict them. Heaven and earth, however, will remain forever and can support the fact that Israel did indeed receive the Torah.

28. Phoenician, meaning to change money into smaller coins (F.).

29. MT explains that it is difficult on a journey to carry many small things, but easier to carry them all together in a large package, which can be broken up as needed. It is easier to remember the Torah when it is organized systematically, but when teaching it, the details should be dispensed in small units. R reads "Like drops of rain, not like large drops of rain, but like small drops of rain."

30. Investigate the smallest details. In the manuscripts the name which follows is Jacob ben Ḥaninah.

31. *Śeʿirim* may mean either "small rain drops" or "goats." The latter meaning is far more common.

32. *Kfr,* which means "to atone," but literally "to cover." This Pisḳa is thus fond of double meanings: *ʿrf,* "change" and "break"; *śeʿirim,* "goats," and "raindrops"; *kfr,* "cover" and "atone." See below, note 41, for another possible meaning.

33. On the theme of ascension to heaven and the dangers involved in it, see G. Scholem, *Jewish Gnosticism, Merkaba Mysticism, and Talmudic Tradition* (New York, 1960), especially chap. 8.

34. *Tizzal* ("drop") is here taken as derived from *zol* ("low price"). As difficult as learning may be, teach it freely to others, as if it were inexpensive to acquire. Another play on words. See ʾAb 6:4.

35. A figure mentioned in Pe 8:7 as a reasonable normal price.

36. MhG says, "Study (or, repeat) and you will attain your learning," i.e., your learning will be stored in you. This may be compared to the saying in ʾAḇ 2:8 that R. Johanan ben Zakkai likened his pupil Eliezer ben Hyrkcanus to a "cistern which loses no water," and R. Eleazar ben ʿArak to an "overflowing fountain," with the preference for the latter.

37. The same Hebrew root *nzl,* "to distill," appears in the first part of 32:2 and in this verse from Proverbs.

38. See above, in the name of R. Nehemiah.

39. See note in MT, p. 252, where the suggestion is made that this was the market place near Hebron (ʾElone Mamreʾ), which was known as the largest of all markets. See Gen. Rabbah 47, end, and P. AZ 1:4 (39:4).

40. Equal, respectively, to 10,000 and 20,000 common shekels.

41. Possibly the name of a small domestic animal (see F.). This homily is best read as a continuation of the one above. It refers to both parts of the verse and interprets *śeʿir* as a demon, and *raḇiḇ* as a pet animal: when you begin to study, Torah is so difficult that it attacks you like a demon; after you learn a little, it becomes as tame as a pet ewe that follows after you.

42. F. (see above, Pisḳa 48, note 17) takes Talmud here as meaning Midrash. These three, Midrash, Halaḵah, and Haggaḏah, are three types of Mishnah.

43. People develop under the influence of Torah with different emphases. Each quality here is good and indicates the emphasis revealed by the person. As is frequent in Rabbinic literature, the *ḥasiḏ* ("pious") is the most desirable personality, since he goes beyond the requirements of strict observance of the law.

44. In verse 43, Elijah's servant sees no sign of rain.

45. *Parnas*; such officials were, according to Alon, to be "not the heads of cities and communities, but spiritual leaders" (*Jews,* p. 413, n. 113).

46. B. BB 25a, in the name of R. Judah. R. Simai was a late teacher, at the end of the Tannaitic period. See Tos Shab 12:14.

47. Possibly meaning here a sheep. See above, note 41. In the Talmud (above, note 46) the reading is "which brings up showers and causes the grass to grow." The reading here is preferable, since the destructive image of scratching furrows in the soil would be more in accord with the earlier description.

48. F.'s text is corrected according to MT. The manuscripts read "the north wind is pleasant in the summer and pleasant in the rainy season; the east wind is always pleasant; the west wind is always harsh."

49. Literally "man." The word *ʾaḏam* is derived from *ʾaḏamah,* "earth"; cf.

Gen. 3:19, *Till thou return unto the earth, for out of it wast thou taken,* and Gen. 2:7 for the description of man as composed of both earth and breath of God. See B. Sanh 91a; E. E. Urbach, *ḤaZaL* (Jerusalem, 1971), pp. 190ff.; Goldin, *Song of the Sea,* p. 104.

50. Amended partially in accord with Elijah Gaon. See also Yalḳuṭ Maḳiri to Psalms, p. 137, where the phrase "this refers to the body" is missing. The printed text reads, "*and to the earth to judge His people*—this refers to the body. Who can judge with Him?" Perhaps read, "*and to the earth to judge His people (la-dun ʿammo)*—(read *ʿimmo,* 'to judge with it',)" meaning that the soul is to be judged with the body (see manuscript ה), referring to the idea that the body and the soul are to be brought together for judgment, as in B. Sanh 91:a.

51. The reference is to the main verse, Deut. 32:2, which has been interpreted as referring to winds.

52. Twenty-one Hebrew words in 32:1–3 precede *the Lord.*

53. Or "seven times as cautious." See B. Ḥul 91b, where the opposite view is presented: in the Shemaʿ declaration Israel utters God's name after two words, which indicates Israel's superiority to the angels who utter it after three words. F. points out that in certain versions of the Sanctification, twenty-one words do precede the name of God, under the influence of this interpretation.

54. Until the specific item has been mentioned and thus proclaimed sacred. Sif Lev. 2:4 (p. 42) has a variant version in the name of R. Simeon: "If concerning that which will be sanctified in the future the Torah says, 'Do not mention the name of Heaven except after mentioning the sacrifice,' how much more," etc.

55. The formula with which the service is begun. See also Meḵ Dĕ-Pisḥa 16.

56. When I proclaim His name, you must respond by ascribing greatness to Him.

57. In B. Ber 53b this saying is connected with R. Jose's statement, "Greater is he who answers Amen than he who pronounces the blessing." Although it is not in the text here, it clearly belongs there. See the comment of TA. The meaning is that the one who completes the blessing earns the greater merit in this case as in warfare. In MhG the statement is, "The way of heaven is the same as the way of the earth. . . ."

58. "Ascribe ye" is plural, hence there must be a minimum of three persons present.

59. In the Shemaʿ this is said after "the Lord is one." After hearing God's name, this is the response. The reference could also be to the ritual in the Temple on the Day of Atonement, when this was said by the people after the High Priest had pronounced the Ineffable Name itself and not the usual substitutes. See Yoma 3:8 and B. Ta 16b.

60. This is the Hebrew version of the Aramaic response in the Kaddish prayer. The custom of this response was not followed in later times.

61. Missing from the text, but essential to the exposition.

62. The interpretation is that when Israel cried out to God in Egypt, the result was to bring greatness unto Him. The sanctification of God's name comes from acts which demonstrate His power and cause people to acknowledge Him.

63. See Num. 21:26ff.; the reference is to the war against Sihon.

64. Probably added to bring this in line with the previous interpretations. Actually the answer to the question "Whence do we learn" lies in the verses from

Exodus and Joshua dealing with the Red Sea, the Jordan, and the Arnon. These interpretations are connected not by the verse in Deuteronomy but by the idea of the sanctification of God's name.

65. The concept of "sanctification of the Name" (*Ḳidduš haš-Šem*) here signifies not martyrdom but sanctifying God through the demonstration of His redemptive powers. Martyrdom was a Hellenistic ideal which was accepted in Judaism only after the Hadrianic persecution. So M. D. Herr, "Persecution," p. 107.

Piska 307

1. See Lieberman, *TK,* Pĕsaḥim, p. 583, bottom.

2. A play on words: *ʾĕmunah* ("faithfulness") and *heʾĕmin* ("believed").

3. *Raʾuy.* Note that in the Hebrew the same root *rʾh* is used in each of the preceding queries.

4. He keeps the reward of the righteous and the punishment of the wicked and dispenses them in the world-to-come. So TA.

5. One hundred shekels.

6. Paying the reward of a good deed in full immediately, and punishing later.

7. The preceding verses deal with the wicked, *even our enemies* (Deut. 32:31). See P. Pe 1:1.

8. See P. Pe 1:1. Cf. Sanders, *Paul,* pp. 127ff.

9. B. Ta 11a, where punishment is connected with *a God of faithfulness* and reward with *and without iniquity.* It is possible that in our text the words *and without iniquity,* which appear at the beginning of the following section, also belong within this section. See also P. Pe 1:1 (16:2), where the reason is added that this is meant to give a perfect reward or punishment in the world-to-come.

10. So apparently understood here. The verse is usually translated *He sealeth up the hand of every man, that all men whom He hath made may know it.*

11. Usually translated: *That thou mayest be justified when thou speakest.* See B. Ta 11a.

12. On this story and martyrdom in general, see L. Finkelstein, "The Ten Martyrs," in *Essays and Studies in Memory of Linda R. Miller* (New York, 1938), pp. 29–55.

13. See B. AZ 18a for the entire story. He had violated Hadrian's decree against teaching Torah. Families of political prisoners were also executed.

14. B. AZ 18a reads "to be consigned to a brothel." The Sifre is using polite language.

15. Or "called to mind." The Berlin manuscript uses the masculine form of the verb "recited," making the father recite these verses.

16. A Gentile "philosopher," a member of the governor's council, speaks thus to the governor and is threatened with death, which he accepts as earning him a place with the Jews. So S. Lieberman in his article "Rĕḏifoṯ Daṯ Yiśraʾel," in *Baron Jubilee Volume* (Jerusalem, 1975), p. 218. See Lieberman, *TK,* Yoma, p. 755, n. 14, on R. Ḥaninah's teaching of the Ineffable Name at the time of Hadrian's persecution. R. Ḥaninah was the only Sage to defy consistently the Hadrianic decrees, according to Herr, "Persecution," p. 115. Other Sages, including R. ʿAḳiba, may have supported the revolt, but did not publicly defy the decrees, an act which would

have led to martyrdom. On the title ἔπαρχος, the prefect who sat in judgment in criminal cases, see S. Lieberman, *Texts and Studies,* p. 67.

17. Moses, having pleaded with God on behalf of Israel and having been shown God's attributes, is asked to explain God's treatment of human beings in His aspect as judge.

18. Literally "I tell you not that He justifies the innocent and punishes the guilty." F., following Elijah Gaon, suggests that this is euphemistic language for "justifies the guilty and punishes the innocent," meaning "I assure you that not only does God not do this, but. . . ."

19. See Pisḳa 347. Merit and guilt are not exchanged one for the other, but a person is appropriately rewarded or punished for each one of his deeds.

Pisḳa 308

1. See Pisḳa 96. R. Judah connects *No* with *His children* and reads, *Is corruption His? His children's is no blemish.* This ingenious method permits R. Judah to turn Biblical condemnation of the people of Israel into praise. F. suggests that he does this because in his view (see Pisḳa 96) they are "children" only when they are good; therefore, since they are called here "children," they must have been without blemish at the time.

2. A continuation of R. Meir's comment.

3. Perhaps originally "Herodes," transposed in order to avoid connection with the disliked King Herod (F.).

4. This is a variant interpretation of the same verse, *Is corruption His? (šiḥeṯ lo loʾ).* Abba Hedoros understood it to mean "(Israel) has corrupted itself with every 'No,'" (that is, by violating every negative ordinance in the Torah).

5. That corruption is not His, i.e., that corruption does not affect God. This is another interpretation of the same verse, *Is corruption His?* See MhG, ad loc. TA, however, takes it as a continuation of the preceding paragraph, the question being, why was God so patient in permitting Israel to sin so much before punishing them? The answer is, in order not to give the wicked an excuse, etc.

6. The text uses the reflexive form, "we bring trouble upon ourselves before Him." This is in order to avoid using blasphemous language (F.).

7. The sinner is the one who really suffers, so those who believe that they can cause suffering to God by these misdeeds are mistaken. The parable is not exact, but the main idea is clear.

8. Or "with a hollow reed (*ʾoḇ*)." This is suggested by Hoffmann in MT.

9. He discards the staff. MhG has: "he cuts it into small chips and casts them into the fire."

10. See Pisḳa 296. Both verses use the same terms, "crooked" and "perverse."

Pisḳa 309

1. Greek βουλευτής.

2. Greek ὑπατικός.

3. Literally "in the future to come," i.e., after the resurrection of the dead. See S. Lieberman, *Šěḳiʿin* (Jerusalem, 1939), p. 81; Goldin, *Song of the Sea,* p. 65.

4. Wisdom is often interpreted as meaning Torah.

5. In Exod. Rabbah 24:1 the same statement is connected with *O foolish people and unwise,* which is to be preferred.

6. Not something received from someone else and therefore taken for granted, but something created by God himself.

7. See B. Pes 87b, where a fourth acquisition is mentioned, heaven and earth.

8. See Meḵ Širata 9, on this passage. Goldin translates *ḳinyan* as "masterpiece" (*Song of the Sea,* pp. 228–29). There, however, the word appears by itself, while here the expression is *ḳinyan lam-Maḳom,* which seems to indicate the idea of a special and precious acquisition by God. See Piska 312 for another parable which seems to have a similar theme—the continued special relationship of God to Israel, even after destruction of the Temple and defeat.

9. Referring to Jerusalem; it is *established* in the sense of having among the population men capable of interpreting and putting into practice the ordinances of the Torah.

10. *Kawwin,* a word-play on *yeḵonĕneḵa,* "established thee."

11. *Kĕnunim,* another word-play.

12. See B. Ḥul 56b. Had the chambers not been in the right place, you would not be established, i.e., exist.

Piska 310

1. Referring to the prophet Elijah.

2. I.e., not simply old people but the members of the council (the Sanhedrin).

3. B reads "in the future."

4. Literally "generation, generations"; "generations," being a plural, means at least two, hence the total is three generations. It is interpreted thus in the name of Rabbi (Judah the Prince) in B. Sanh 99a, where other authorities offer varying opinions about the length of the Messianic reign which will precede the world-to-come. See also Pesiḳta Zaḵor, p. 53; Meḵ Bĕ-šallaḥ 2.

Piska 311

1. "Harshness," *middaṯ ʾaḵzariyyuṯ,* is another term for the more common *middaṯ had-din,* the measure of justice which is opposed to the measure of mercy, *middaṯ-raḥămim.* See Meḵ Širata 3, and Goldin, *Song of the Sea,* p. 120. According to Seder Eliyyahu Zuṭa 25, Abraham's proclamation of the one God brought about God's acting by the measure of mercy toward mankind. See also Gen. Rabbah 39, on the blessings Abraham brought to the world. See also ARN-A 32, ARN-B 36.

2. Probably based on the next part of the verse, when *He separated the children of men* (32:8).

3. Deriving *yaṣṣeḇ* ("He set") not from the root *nṣb* ("to set") but from *yṣb* ("to stand up"); see Lev. Rabbah 12:2. Here it may mean "to stop." God looks into the future and sees that they alone will be worthy. See Sanders, *Paul,* p. 92.

4. In MhG the reading is, "as it is said, *According to the number of the children of Israel* (32:8)." This reading is found also in various manuscripts. On God's search for a worthy nation, see B. AZ 2b.

5. Ezek. 32:21 speaks of them as being in "the netherworld."

6. A reference to proselytes who share in Israel's inheritance.

7. See Num. Rabbah 9:14.
8. Emphasizing the plural *borders.*
9. So MhG and several manuscripts.

Piska 312

1. See Piska 31.
2. According to Eugene Mihaly, in "A Rabbinic Defense of the Election of Israel," pp. 103–44, this entire section is a refutation of Christian polemics concerning Israel's election or rejection by God. The point here is that the election began with Jacob, not with Abraham, and therefore does not include Abraham's other offspring. It belongs exclusively to the descendants of Jacob, i.e., Israel. See especially Mihaly's summary, p. 126. Compare also the parable in Mark 12.
3. Possibly because the verse in the original Hebrew could be understood in either one of two ways, that the Lord chose Jacob or that Jacob chose the Lord. According to Mihaly, however (ibid., p. 125), the assumption here, which is not made explicit, is that even after the sin of the golden calf Israel remained the chosen of God, and the specific ritual commandments were part of the eternal covenant.
4. Mihaly (ibid., p. 321) sees this as the conclusion of the argument against Christianity, in which Christianity claims that the current situation—i.e., the destruction of the Temple, the failure of the Bar Kokhba rebellion, and the suffering in its wake—indicates God's rejection. The answer is that this is a rebuke and not a rejection, and that Jacob need only choose God for the Messianic redemption to come.
5. Possibly referring to the three words *sĕgullah* ("treasure") (Deut. 14:2), *ḥebel, goral* (Josh. 19:10). See F.'s note.

Piska 313

1. In this case the king represents Abraham, who attempted to recruit converts to God's cause. When they abandoned him at the time of Nimrod's persecution, God (the Valiant Man) helped him. So TA.
2. *Yĕbonĕnehu* ("cared for him") is read here as if derived from the root *byn* ("to understand"), i.e., God made him wise or understanding.
3. See Tos ʿAr 1:10, Mek Ba-ḥodĕs 9; Ginzberg, *Legends,* 6, 38. In Mek this is based on the verse, *and stand afar off* (Exod. 20:15). The connection to our verse is not clear. B does not have it, but instead states that they understood the implications of each pronouncement (i.e., each of the Ten Commandments) and were not troubled by the thunder and the lightning.
4. *Maṣuy,* literally "found," a word-play on *yimṣaʾehu* ("He found him"). The word is read as if vocalized *yamṣiʾehu* ("provided") which may have been a variant reading. See J. Goldin, "From Text to Interpretation," *Prooftexts,* 3 (1983), 167–68.
5. A reference to the encampment described in Num. 2.
6. See Zech. 6:1.
7. *Ham-molikeka*—possibly a word-play on *malkut,* "kingdom."

Piska 315

1. Usually translated: *did lead him.*

2. The heavenly beings that protect and rule the various nations of the world.

3. The verses prove that there are such "princes" ruling the nations.

4. *ʿAṯiḏ* here and below may mean simply "the future," but it may also mean the age-to-come (*ʿaṯiḏ la-ḇoʾ*). See Goldin, *Song of the Sea*, pp. 65, 128.

5. Usually translated: *was.*

6. *Naḥaṯ ruaḥ,* a word-play on *yanḥennu,* "shall lead him."

7. See B. Keṯ 111b.

Piska 316

1. See Piska 37, end.

2. See P. Pe 7:4. The incident occurred in Siknin.

3. P. Pe 7:4.

Piska 317

1. Deut. 26:2.

2. That is, wisdom (Prov. 8:1) = Torah.

3. The interpretation seems connected with the word "field," which appears in both verses. The meaning here is unclear. The following interpretation as the four kingdoms is connected with this verse in MT.

4. Interpreted as future: "He will make him suck honey. . . ."

5. A small coin (1/8 of an *ʾissar*).

6. Greek ὑπατικός.

7. Greek ἡγεμών. See F. and his references for all these officeholders.

8. Greek χιλίαρχος, commander of a thousand.

9. Latin *beneficiarii,* personal servants to commanding officers.

10. *Ben šinnayim,* a word-play on *běne Bašan,* "the breed of Bashan." See B. Giṭ 57b and Lieberman, *Texts and Studies,* p. 528, for other uses of this interpretation. B has "those who understand among them," while this reading (*ben šinnayim*) is in MhG and in some manuscripts.

11. Greek σύγκλητος.

12. Interpreted as referring to the future: "you will drink." The Roman oppressors will very soon lose their power, and their riches will be enjoyed by the people of Israel.

13. See B. Keṯ 111b for another version of these tales. Turnip (*lefeṯ*) is not of the wheat family, but seems to be used here as an example of how large a plant can grow in the Land of Israel.

14. Greek πίθος. See B. Keṯ 111b.

Piska 318

1. See Piska 43.

2. Evidently a marginal comment, in Aramaic, explaining that the entire comment has not been reproduced here but can be found earlier (see Piska 43, comment of R. Jose son of the Damascene woman).

3. See Piska 43. F., in *JQR, 31* (1940/41), 222, suggests that the copyist did not consider what he was writing here as part of Sifre on Deuteronomy, but thought that it was a separate work which had been attached to the Sifre.

4. See above, notes 2–3.

5. *Karšinah,* "horse-bean."

6. The people had forsaken God (Deut. 32:15), therefore He has forsaken them, as indicated in the several verses cited. The same Hebrew root *(ntš)* is used.

7. R. Dostai's understanding of the verse (like that of the English versions) is that the word "contemned" belongs to the following phrase and therefore has God for object, and not to the first phrase where it would have Israel as object. This is the way that the traditional marks of cantillation (*ṭeᶜamim*) take it.

8. A play on words: *śeᶜarum* ("dreaded") and *śeᶜar* ("hair").

9. Another play on words, reading *šeᶜarum* ("evaluated them") for *śeᶜarum.*

Piska 319

1. In MhG the version is " 'You made Me feel like a male who wishes to give birth but is unable to do so.' If a woman sits on the birth-stool, is she not troubled, as it is said, *Pangs (ṣirim) have taken hold upon me, as the pangs of a woman in travail* (Isa. 21:3)?" Note the word-play *ṣirim* ("pangs" and *Ṣur* ("Rock"). B reads ". . . does she have strength? As Scripture says, . . . *there is not strength. . . .*"

2. A difficult statement. Elijah Gaon reads, "You forgot the deeds of your fathers." Meir Friedmann suggests reading, "You caused Me to forget the merit of your fathers." The cited verse from Isaiah suggests that this is an attempt to interpret the word "rock" in this verse also as referring to Abraham.

3. *Mattišim,* taking *teši* ("unmindful") as derived from the root *tšš* ("to weaken").

4. *Ḥil.* This Piska is replete with alternate meanings given to words derived from similar roots.

5. The body is full of cavities and channels which enable a person to live. MhG adds: "If one impinges upon another, you cannot survive." See Piska 309.

6. See Piska 31.

7. The text cites *I am the Lord thy God, who brought thee out of the land of Egypt* (Exod. 20:2). However, the idea requires a verse which indicates the uniqueness of the relationship.

8. *Ḥullin,* literally "profane," the opposite of sanctified. The nations will have power over you (so B).

9. Interpreted to mean, "makes the mighty unsanctified (= weak)."

Piska 320

1. See F. in *PAAJR, 3* (1931–32), 39.

2. See Piska 86. R. Meir's view is that Israel's relationship with God is at all times that of children with their Father, and is not dependent upon their good actions.

3. See Piskas 313 and 317. B reads "sell" for "deliver."

4. The text reads "I will know what their end will be." MT (p. 196) reads "I will deliver them to the kingdoms, who will trouble them . . . to let them know what their end will be."

5. "Inverted" and "overturned" are both from the same root as *forward.*

6. See Piska 319.

7. Changing only the vocalization of the word.

8. *Hablehem,* usually translated "vanities."

9. A reflection, such as in water. See B. AZ 47a.

10. So Lieberman, in *JQR, 36* (1945/46), 355; i.e., the "socii populi Romani," from whom the auxiliary troops were drafted. Roman troops ejected the natives from their homes. Lieberman notes: "The text is probably of the beginning of the third century."

11. Possibly Tunis.

12. Possibly Britain.

13. Possibly connected to the next part of the verse, as in B. Yeb 63b. "For there is none," etc. is not in B, and has been taken from MhG.

14. *Nabal,* the same word translated above as "vile." Alon (*Jews,* p. 361, n. 26) suggests that this is the term for Samaritans as found in Patristic literature.

15. MhG quotes here 2 Sam 22:9, *Smoke arose up in His nostril.*

Piska 321

1. *ʾAsuf,* from the root *ʾsf,* "to gather."

2. *ʾAspeh,* here derived from *suf,* "to end, to conclude."

3. *Yĕkallu.* These dire prophecies are here reinterpreted to indicate not God's wrath but His intention to bring an end to suffering and preserve Israel.

4. *ʾĂkalleh,* i.e., the arrows will be consumed.

5. So Jastrow, *A Dictionary of the . . . Talmud* (New York-Berlin-London, 1926), p. 890 (under *nzz*).

6. A tradition says that *keṭeb* was a spirit. A description of it is found in Midrash on Psalms 91:3 (*YJS, 13, 2,* 102–03). See also Num. Rabbah 12:3.

7. See F. in *PAAJR, 3* (1932–33), 51. *Mĕriri,* "bitter," is read *merir,* "drips saliva."

8. See A. Perles, "Peruš šĕne maʾămarim bĕ-Sifre," in *Bet Talmud, 1* (1881), 114–15.

9. So too Hoffmann in MT. So as to make it seem that he was not circumcised.

10. See P. Ta 3:6 (66:4).

11. This verse is also quoted as part of the proof of this idea in B. BḲ 60b. The same admonition appears in Ruth Rabbah 1:4, in the discussion of Elimelech's leaving the Land of Israel and of the circumstances under which it is permitted to do so.

12. *Watrah*; see Piska 1, note 21, and the references given there.

13. So King James version. The word is usually translated 'from his youth up." The word *baḥur* appears in various places, and while it usually means "youth," the homily takes it in the sense of "chosen."

14. Another example of a word interpreted not in its usual meaning but with some specific religious connotation.

15. The latter part of the verse tells us that these men were *brought captive to Babylon*; how then can they be described as mighty warriors? B reads "captivity" for "exile."

16. I.e., discussion of Torah.

17. Reading not *ḥaraš,* "craftsman," but *ḥoreš,* "silencers."

18. See B. Giṭ 88a, "once he closes, they should not open the discussion again." See also P. Sanh 1:2 (19:1).

Piska 322

1. Making *ʾafheyhem* ("I would make an end of them") into a portmanteau word: *ʿappi* ("My anger"), *ʾayyeh* ("where"), *hem* ("are they").

2. The following verse (32:27) begins with the same word, *lule,* leading the author to bring in other verses which begin with it.

3. Another verse beginning with *lule.*

4. A difficult sentence. Perhaps read as in B, "What caused Me to be angry with them? The enemy's provocation."

5. Deriving *ʾaḡur* not from the verb *gur,* "to dread," but from the verb *ʾaḡar,* "to gather."

6. *Mĕḡuram,* usually translated "dwelling," deriving the word from the verb *gur,* "to sojourn."

7. *Ṣaremo* ("their adversaries") is read as *ṣaraṯam* ("their trouble").

8. Literally *Arabia,* in Hebrew *ʿaraḇ,* from the same root as *maʿăraḇ,* "the west."

9. B reads "Tribes."

10. Referring to the next two verses (32:29–30): *If they were wise, they would understand this. They would discern their latter end. How should one chase a thousand, and two put ten thousand to flight?*

11. See Piska 343, where this is discussed in greater detail. See also B. AZ 2b.

12. Referring to Bar Kokhbah's revolt. See F.

13. An officer in command of ten horsemen.

14. The victory of the Romans was seen as willed by God. See Herr, "Persecution," p. 120.

Piska 323

1. Both here and further on *yaśkilu* ("be wise") is connected with *histaklu* ("to look") because of the similarity of sound.

2. Based on Gen. 49:28, *And this is it that their father spoke unto them* (so Hoffmann). The words *latter end* appear both in Gen. 49:1 and at the end of Deut. 32:29.

3. The verse 32:30 is read here as "For their Rock had not given them over." The reference is obscure.

4. *Ḳeri,* Greek καιρός.

5. This is the opposite of the previous interpretation. Here God does both give them over and deliver them.

6. Inserted by F., see *PAAJR,* 6 (1935), 214.

7. *Hisgir,* usually translated "shut him up."

8. *Toḳef,* "superior strength" (so Goldin, *Song of the Sea,* p. 108).

9. See B. Sanh 29a.

10. R. Judah takes the particle *ki* ("for") as indicating a question: Is Israel's vine that of Sodom, i.e., corrupt? The answer is, No.

11. *Riʾšon,* here connected with *roš* ("gall").

12. *Ḥamtem,* a word-play on *ḥamaṯ,* "venom." In B this section follows R. Nehemiah's interpretation below.

13. And not of Adam. Spiritually the heathen nations are not descendants of Adam, as evidenced by their treatment of Israel. The great sufferings of the post-Bar-Kokhba period are evidently reflected in R. Nehemiah's sayings.

Pisḳa 324

1. Same as "laid up." MhG has *kos ᶜamus,* "a cup which is filled."

2. Perhaps read, "One might think that it is empty; therefore Scripture says, *with foaming wine* (Ps. 75:9)," as in Midrash to Psalms ad loc. (*YJS, 13, 2,* 10). The entire verse, Ps. 75:9, reads: *For in the hand of the Lord there is a cup, with foaming wine, full of mixture, and He poureth out of the same; surely the dregs thereof, all the wicked of the earth shall drain them, and drink them.*

3. Perhaps that it will not be drunk from until later. See MhG, where the interpretation consists of a mixture of verses from Deuteronomy and Psalms.

4. See ARN-A 40; MhG; and Tos Pe 1:1–3, on things which are rewarded or punished in this world or the next. See also S. Schechter's essay, "The Doctrine of Divine Retribution in Rabbinical Literature," in his *Studies in Judaism,* pp. 105–22.

Pisḳa 325

1. Or "not as it is said"; so MhG. The verse is a negative illustration, since it concerns the use of a messenger. See the Passover Haggadah, ed. L. Goldsmith (Jerusalem, 1969), p. 44, and comments thereto. See also the comment in Pisḳa 323 to verse 30, where the punishment to Israel is not inflicted directly by God Himself.

2. Israel's. See Pisḳa 43, end.

3. The emphasis is upon the haste with which this occurs.

4. So in MhG, and not Jer. 1:8, as mistakenly cited in the editions. Both verses begin with the same words.

Pisḳa 326

1. *His people* refers to the Gentile nations, in contrast to the second half of the verse which refers to *His servants,* meaning Israel.

2. Both *stay* and *power* are represented in the Hebrew original by the same word *yaḏ,* literally "hand."

Pisḳa 327

1. See notes to Pisḳa 317, above.

Pisḳa 328

1. Three kinds of allowances given to Roman soldiers: victuals (especially fish), money awarded on special occasions, and money to purchase salt.

2. So King James version; JPS version: *him.*

3. The word *wyᶜzrkm,* although vocalized by the Masoretes as a plural (*let them help you*), is spelled as a singular ("let him help you").

4. The preceding verse, *Where are their gods?* (32:37). According to R. Nehemiah, this is what Titus said, referring to the God of Israel.

5. The full story appears in ARN-B 7; ARN-A 2; B. Giṭ 56b. See also Alon, *Jews*, p. 253. Herr ("Persecution," pp. 118–19) shows that this legend is concerned more with Hadrian than with Titus. The two were often confused, following the defeat of Bar Kokhba. Here this story is in the brief original version, which was elaborated elsewhere.

6. Probably Titus implied that *they*, i.e., Moses and Aaron, ate the sacrifices they commanded and thus deceived the people.

7. The interpretation of R. Nehemiah ends here with this comment. Titus came into the Sanctuary and challenged God, thus desecrating His name. For this he was to be punished soon enough.

Piska 329

1. B reads "There is no authority in heaven."

2. See B. Sanh 91b: "*I kill, and I make alive* speak of the same person and in that order." See also above, Piska 306.

3. See Ginzberg, *Legends*, 5, 419, n. 11, concerning the merit of the fathers.

Piska 330

1. So MhG, MT, and ed. Friedmann. F. reads: "by a spoken word alone, and only with an oath." On the creation of the world by God's word, see ARN-A 31 (*YJS*, 10, 125, and n. 2).

2. Ps. 106:24 reads, *They believed not His word.* See Ginzberg, *Unknown Sect*, p. 121, n. 60, on objections to swearing. God's oath was not initiated by Him, but was caused by the wicked.

3. So the editions. Others quote Ps. 106:27: *And that He would cast out their seed among the nations.*

4. Human power is limited. A human ruler cannot always collect what is due him, but God can.

Piska 331

1. The same Hebrew word *barak* is used for both *glittering* and "lightning."

2. That is, Samaritans.

Piska 332

1. *Purᶜanuṯ*, a word-play on *parᶜoṯ*, "long-haired." Calamities will be counted beginning with the heads of the enemy, i.e., their earliest known ancestors.

2. A play on words: *purᶜanuṯ* ("calamity") and *parᶜoh* ("Pharaoh").

Piska 333

1. Taking *harninu*, "sing," as meaning crying in distress, as in Lam. 2:19. Cf. Midrash to Psalms 99:1 (*YJS*, 13, 2, 144).

2. See Piska 315, note 4. This Piska contains many such references to the

future. Messianic events lurk behind the entire interpretation. See also Goldin, *Song of the Sea,* p. 218 and p. 66.

3. The term "inhabitants of Sela" was understood as referring to the dead and thus to the ancestors at the time of resurrection. This may be based on the meaning of *selaᶜ*, "rock," those who dwell within the rocks or the earth. See Yalḳuṭ Makiri to Isa. 42:11.

4. By their martyr's death they become saints. See Midrash to Psalms 79:4 (*YJS, 13,* 2, 46), "Once judgment was executed upon them, they became saints."

5. MhG adds, "unto the souls of Israel." See also B. Ber 62b.

6. Usually translated: *ransom.*

7. Are their iniquities completely done away with (*prḳ*) or merely borne (*nś*ᵓ)? The word *forgiven* in Isa. 33:24 could mean "tolerated." Mihaly, *HUCA, 35* (1964), 124, translates "either the land atones for its inhabitant's sins, or it makes them suffer their sins."

Pisḳa 334

1. Greek διάδοχος. See Pisḳa 27, end.

2. That is to say, humble.

Pisḳa 335

1. See Ḥag̃ 1, end. Many of the Rabbinic laws, regarded as teachings of Torah, have only the slightest connection with the Scriptural text.

Pisḳa 336

1. See B. Sanh 99b and Sif Num. 112. She wished to be converted, but the patriarch would not accept her. She therefore sought any connection with the family, even if only with Esau's son. She herself was of royal descent.

2. "Tents" was taken to mean places of Torah study. See B. Ber 16a.

3. See Pe 1:1.

Pisḳa 337

1. See Ginzberg, *Legends,* 6, 151.

2. *ᶜEṣem,* "selfsame," is understood as meaning at the very height of the day. *ᶜEṣem* means something clear, as the day is clear. See Meḵ Dĕ-Pisḥa 14.

Pisḳa 338

1. See B. BB 17a, where these three and the three patriarchs are described as having died by God's hand and not by the hand of the angel of death. On the other hand, many Midrashim ascribe their death to the sin of the water (Num. 20). See Pisḳa 26.

2. See Pisḳa 357. B reads "He showed him three kings who were to issue from Rahab the harlot."

Piska 339

1. The emphasis is on *a man,* i.e., any man whatsoever.

2. See ARN-A 12 (*YJS, 10,* 65), Sif Num. 136; i.e., every man must die, without exception.

Piska 340

1. Speaking to the rock to produce water (Num. 20.8); instead Moses struck the rock with his rod, thus disobeying God's command.

2. The connection is unclear. Some versions close with verse 52, *For thou shalt see the land afar off.* B reads "Whence do we learn that Moses did not depart from this world until he troubled (?)*ṣarah* the Holy One, blessed be He? From the verse," etc.

Piska 341

1. See Piska 357.

Piska 342

1. The word *wĕ-zoʾṯ* ("and this") appears in both places and thus connects them. See Pesiḳta de-Rab Kahana, ed. Mandelbaum (New York, 1962), p. 437.

2. Based on the conjunction *and,* showing that something had preceded the blessing.

3. *Kĕ-day.* A Genizah fragment (*Bate Midrašoṯ, 11* [1980], 121) has *raʾuy,* "fitting, appropriate."

4. Since Samuel is involved, it is assumed that Elkanah is referred to here. See ARN-B 37 for this list of men of God.

5. See 2 Chron. 12:15: *in the histories of Shemaiah the prophet and of Iddo the seer.*

6. Tos Sanh 14:15.

Piska 343

1. S. Lieberman, in "Roman Legal Institutions," *JQR, 35* (1944/45), 27, points out that this is a description of the actual opening speech of a public advocate at that time.

2. This example may be a later addition, since it does not follow the pattern of praise—petition—praise.

3. Finkelstein (*New Light,* pp. 37ff.) claims that this is the earliest form of the *ʿAmiḏah* prayer, prior to the return from the exile. The phrase "Who releases the captives" does not appear in our version as a separate paragraph. B has it after "the sick," which is the order in the prayer. "We give thanks unto Thee" may be not part of the prayer but the command to the congregation to prostrate themselves before God. See also Sanders, *Paul,* p. 64.

4. Meaning the Latin language; Seir is another name for Edom, and Edom is regularly used as an alias for Rome.

5. Usually translated "myriads holy," but here interpreted as a place-name.

6. See Meḵ Yiṯro Ba-ḥoḏeš 5; B. AZ 2b; Sanders, *Paul,* p. 87, on the election of Israel.

7. In Mek̲ the reply is in the first person, "The very heritage which our forefather has left us was," etc.

8. One child was the forefather of the children of Ammon; see above, note 6.

9. See Pisḳa 322.

10. 1 *kor* = 2 *let̲ek̲* = 30 *sĕʾah.*

11. *Parak̲,* the same verb used above for casting off God's commands. See B. Sanh 59a on the Noachide commandments.

12. He came from having offered the Torah to the other nations.

13. After the fall of Rome (Edom), Israel (Jacob) will rule, and there will be no other power in between (F.). This is the symbolism of Jacob's clutching Esau's (Edom's) heel. Such a statement would seem appropriate to the period of Persian incursions against Rome and to the time prior to Christianity's ascent, i.e., during the third century.

14. The parable seems connected with Gen. 25:27. God wanted to give the Torah to Israel. In order to do this, He searched for a reason that everyone could see. Jacob's blameless family life provided the reason.

15. By painting the body or dyeing the hair. Although usually disapproved of, here this is seen as an attempt to please. B reads "He proclaimed himself and his sorrow."

16. See Pisḳa 31.

17. See Mek̲ ʿAmaleḳ 2, 162 (ed. Lauterbach) for another version.

18. *From* indicates that only some of the myriads holy are meant, not all.

19. *Wĕ-ʾat̲ah* (*and He came*) is read here as *wĕ-ʾot̲ hu* ("and He is an [outstanding] mark") (cf. *PRE,* Ba-ḥod̲eš, 108a). *The myriads holy* is understood as referring to the angels.

20. Usually translated: *Therefore do the maidens love thee.* Here *ʿălamot̲* ("maidens") is read as *ʿal mawet̲* ("unto death").

21. The last verse in the Masoretic text ends with "altogether lovely." Here only the first part of each verse is quoted, and the reader is expected to fill in the rest. On this interpretation of the Song of Songs, see G. Cohen, "The Song of Songs and the Jewish Religious Mentality," in *Friedland Lectures, 1960–1966* (New York, 1966), pp. 1–22. See Mek̲ Bĕ-šallaḥ 3; Song Rabbah 5:9; Goldin, *Song of the Sea,* pp. 116–17.

22. See E. E. Urbach, "The Talmudic Sage," p. 132. The Sages constituted "a class apart," who could be easily recognized.

23. The Torah, like fire, is too powerful to be borne. The laws (*dat̲*) given with it, i.e., the ways of ordinary life and work with which it must be combined, make it possible for the Torah to be followed (*TA*). B. Beṣ 25b interprets the same verse thus: had the Torah not been given to Israel, no nation could have withstood them, since they are the boldest of all the nations. The discipline of the Torah is intended to modify the fiery ways of Israel.

Pisḳa 344

1. A reflection of the problems during the time of the Hadrianic persecution as perceived by the following generation, which saw in martyrdom an ideal. See Herr, "Persecution," p. 122.

2. See Pisḳa 16, and notes thereto; B.BḲ 113a, P. BḲ 4:3.

3. Possibly a scribal error for Jamnia (Yabneh). See Finkelstein, "Studies in Tannaitic Midrashim," *PAAJR*, 6 (1934–35), 215. According to Herr ("The Historical Significance of the Dialogues," pp. 132–33), there were "discussions about the granting of some partial official recognition to the status of R. Gamaliel of Jabneh," which led to the visit of these officials to his academy. They approved the proposal of recognition, except for the discrimination against Gentiles, which led to R. Gamaliel's prohibition of stolen Gentile property. It is strange, however, that this prohibition is not mentioned here. Another possibility, suggested by A. J. Baumgarten, in "The ʿAḳiban Opposition," *HUCA*, 50 (1979), 196, n. 61, is that the correct reading is "R. Simeon ben Gamaliel at Usha," meaning R. Simeon ben Gamaliel II, after the Bar Kokhba rebellion, when the Romans were investigating the patriarchate as part of the "process of making that renewed commitment" to that institution, which had, after all, failed to prevent the revolt. Lieberman views this story in connection with the fact that "Jewish courts existed in the diaspora after the destruction of the Second Temple. These courts were recognized by the government . . . they were supposed to judge according to Jewish law. It is therefore natural to expect that the Roman government in Syria was interested in the fairness of Jewish civil law. A delegation was accordingly sent to the authoritative academy in Palestine to learn something about Jewish law." Since such courts were primarily concerned with internal Jewish affairs, the fact that Gentiles were discriminated against would not have been of primary concern to the delegation, which could legitimately feel that there was no "moral obligation to reveal these unfair laws to the government" (S. Lieberman, "Achievements and Aspirations of Modern Jewish Scholarship," *American Academy for Jewish Research, Jubilee Volume,* [Jerusalem, 1980], pp. 375–76). Lieberman believes that this visit took place before the Hadrianic persecution, when the Rabbis trusted the Romans and had a more positive attitude toward Rome (such as is found in B. Shab 33b), and that the detail of the officials disguising themselves, which does not appear in parallel sources, is not part of the original tradition (ibid., p. 373, n. 14).

4. See L. Finkelstein, "Midraš, Halaḵoṯ wĕ-Haggaḏoṯ," *Baer Jubilee Volume* (Jerusalem, 1961), pp. 28ff. Mishnah includes also Midrash. "Midrash" here refers to the early single short explanations (ibid., p. 32). "Halaḵah" refers to oral traditions. The original order of study was first Bible, then simple explanation (Midrash), then traditions (halaḵoṯ), followed by haggadoṯ. See also Pisḳa 306 and 48.

5. B. BḲ 38a. Other sources conclude that as a result both kinds of stolen property were forbidden.

6. See B. Shab 33b. They die in place of Israel (F.).

7. See Pisḳa 313.

Pisḳa 345

1. God Himself does not need the house; it is meant only to house the Ark, and therefore serves only the people of Israel.

2. Alon (*Jews*, p. 454, n. 48) sees here an attempt to counteract the tendency to "restrict Torah to the world of the rich and 'great.' "

3. I.e., is forbidden to them. See B. Sanh 59a, where the opposite view is found.

4. This interpretation rejects the previous one.

Piska 346

1. The president of the Sanhedrin has the right to appoint the elders without the approval of the people. See S. Lieberman, *Sifre Zuta,* p. 88. B, however, reads "When the Holy One, blessed be He, seats. . . ."

2. Probably it is then that there will be a king in Jeshurun.

3. The conclusion does not seem to fit the parable. More likely it is connected with the proof-verse, i.e., when all the Tribes are together, like the ships, God is king, i.e., the heavenly palace can stand. The parable may have been inserted here and thus interrupts the text, which should read: ". . . *upon the earth* (Amos 9:6). Thus is it also with Israel: when they do," etc.

4. The text reads euphemistically "He is glorious."

Piska 347

1. Reuben persuaded his brothers not to slay Joseph (Gen. 37:22), but committed a grave sin by lying with Bilhah, his father's concubine (Gen. 35:22).

2. *Ṣelaᶜ*, "side," is understood as "rib," i.e., woman, referring to the affair of Bath-sheba (2 Sam. 11). *Har,* "hill," represents the hill of the Temple. Perhaps the breech David had made to allow the people into the city atoned for his sin. See B. Sanh 101b.

3. See Piska 31. The Sages disagree: God does not treat guilt and innocence capriciously; each action is treated appropriately, either with justice or with mercy (so Sanders, *Paul,* p. 128).

4. See B. Shab 55b; Gen. Rabbah 96; Ginzberg, *Legends, 1,* 415. Reuben moved his mother's bed into Jacob's tent in place of Bilhah's.

5. Not in B. This is taken from MhG.

Piska 348

1. See Piska 347, note 1.

2. See P. Soṭ 17:3, where a different verse is quoted.

3. Since Exod. 13:19 indicates that Judah's body, as well as the bodies of all his brothers, was brought out of Egypt, the phrase *Bring him unto his people* must mean something else, unique to Judah.

4. In the cave of Machpelah. Jacob is to be buried there, but not others who will die subsequently. B has "Rabbi (Judah the Prince)" instead of "R. Meir."

5. P. Ket 1:5, Giṭ 5:6; Ginzberg, *Legends, 5,* 372.

6. The blessing of Moses contains no reference to Simeon, but the Sages, on the basis of Judg. 1:3, included this Tribe in the blessing. See Ginzberg, *Legends, 6,* 155, n. 923. In a Genizah fragment (*Bate Midrašot, 11,* 122) we find the following addition: "Why did Moses not bless the Tribe of Simeon? Because he continued to hold that deed against them (Num. 25:1ff.)." It goes on to say that the word *hear* in Deut. 33:7 refers to Simeon, on the basis of Gen. 29:33: *"Because the Lord hath heard that I am hated, He hath therefore given me this son also." And she called his name Simeon.* See also Pesikta to the blessing of Moses.

7. See Midrash on Psalms 90:3 (*YJS, 13, 2,* 86–87).

Piska 349

1. Why is Levi singled out for this blessing?

2. Sinned and had to regain their status.

3. The text here has "the word of the Lord."

4. Perhaps read, "Thus Levi is blessed, but not Simeon."

5. In the giving of tithes. Elijah Gaon reads, "who did gracious things for Thy children."

6. Yet Aaron, too, was punished for this affair. See Num. 20:12.

Piska 350

1. Is it possible that some Levites worshiped the golden calf and were therefore slain by the loyal Levites? According to this section and to B. Yoma 66b, they did not. The "father" referred to is a grandfather on the mother's side. Since tribal status is determined by the father, this grandfather need not have been a Levite, but could be from the other Tribes. The same would apply to uncles on the mother's side and to a daughter's child.

2. B omits "in the wilderness."

3. See Num. 13–14.

Piska 351

1. See Num. 19.

2. To be offered when the body of a murdered person is found near a city. See Deut. 21.

3. See Num 5:11ff.

4. *Negaᶜ*, literally "plague."

5. Apparently reading *Toroteka* ("Thy Torahs," as in the Samaritan version) instead of *Toratĕka* ("Thy Torah") (F.).

6. Variously identified as a corruption of Quintus, Quietus, or Atticus. Cf. Jastrow, *A Dictionary*, p. 13. But see the next note.

7. This view is contradicted by R. ᶜAkiba (Sif Lev. Bĕ-ḥukkotay 8, end), who holds that only one Torah was given, together with the methods of interpretation which permitted one to expound its text. See Finkelstein's discussion of this in *New Light*, pp. 815ff. See also M. D. Herr, "The Historical Significance of the Dialogues," pp. 129–30. The general is probably Marcus Antonius Julianus, procurator of Jordan at the time when the Temple was destroyed in 70 C.E.

8. Lev. 16:13. See also Yoma 5:1 for a description of the ceremony of the incense.

Piska 352

1. See Piska 308.

2. Num. 16.

3. 2 Chron. 26:16ff. A king of Judah, he attempted to burn incense upon the altar. He contracted leprosy and had to live out his life shut up away from all others.

4. On "beloved" in the sense of "favorite," see Goldin, *Song of the Sea*, p. 156. See ARN-B 43, where Jerusalem appears in place of the Temple. See B. Zeb 118b; Gen. Rabbah 2.

5. He foresaw it in a vision of the future.

6. Gen. Rabbah 56, to the verse, connects each section to another verse where a similar word appears and which indicates that it exists (Deut. 16:16), is destroyed (Lam. 5:18), and will be rebuilt (Ps. 102:17).

7. Here, too, as in the previous instance, Gen. Rabbah 65:23 connects the phrases to other verses: Num. 28:2, Mic. 3:12, and Ps. 133:3.

8. See Gen. Rabbah 69:17: the verses are Ps. 69:36, Lam. 5:17, and Ps. 147:13.

9. Josh. 15:9, 11.

10. Num. 34:11, 12, etc.

11. Literally, "the head of a *tor*," either the Aramaic "ox" or the Hebrew "dove." See B. Yoma 12a; ARN-A 35 (*YJS, 10,* 144–45). The Holy of Holies was in the portion of Benjamin, while most of the rest of the Temple was in the territory of Judah.

12. The presence of God.

13. The meeting place of the Sanhedrin.

14. See ARN-A 35 (*YJS, 10,* 145), Sif Num. 78.

15. As compensation to Benjamin for the land that they gave up for the Temple.

16. See B. Tem 16a, Josh. 15:17. Jabez was thought to have been a great scholar.

17. See Sif Num. 42.

18. Although F. considers these two sections within brackets as not part of Sifre, they are found in B and in other sources.

19. Or, "Why did Benjamin merit?" See Sanders, *Paul,* p. 189.

20. Jacob. God will dwell with Benjamin since Jacob was so close to him.

Piska 353

1. See Song Rabbah 4:15, where the verse is connected with the patriarchs.

2. In the sense of being deprived. He was sold as a slave and thus deprived of the good things of life.

3. *Hod* is the quality of superhuman splendor. In Exod. Rabbah 47:6 the rays emanating from Moses' face are called rays of *hod* which come from God. Joshua's military might combined with such splendor would have been totally irresistible. See a similar comment at the end of Piska 343.

4. See Piska 37. They were not all kings of the Land of Israel, but kings who had some holdings there.

5. The numbers being understood as referring to slain Canaanites.

Piska 354

1. This is in accord with the idea that those whose names are repeated in Deuteronomy were presented to Pharaoh. See B. BK 92a; Gen. Rabbah 95.

2. The tent was frequently taken to mean the place where Torah is studied. See Gen. Rabbah 63, where Jacob's being a man "who dwelt in tents" is interpreted as meaning that he was a student in two houses of study.

3. Since they were outstanding students of Torah (F.).

4. Not in the text, but understood.

5. Unlike many interpretations in these Piskas, this one seems to reflect an earlier, pre-destruction, period of time.

6. This coastal area is nearest to the Tribe of Zebulun. See S. Klein, in *Kiṯbe ha-ʾUniḇersiṭah, 1* (1923), plate 5. The bay of Haifa was regarded as a separate "sea."

7. B. Sanh 91a. The sea snail from which the purple dye for the ritual fringes was derived.

8. A kind of fish used for pickling.

9. See Gen. 49:13.

10. B reads "who takes it from you without payment will have no blessing from his dealings."

Piska 355

1. See Piska 354, note 1.

2. The bier of Moses. See ARN-B 37; Ginzberg, *Legends, 5,* 109, n. 99.

3. Either Joseph's garments or more likely Adam's. See Gen. Rabbah 20.

4. Ginzberg, *Legends, 1,* 34; the legendary worm that cut the stones for the Temple in Jerusalem, since no iron tool was to be used on them.

5. Perhaps because it is sterile.

6. Since one could not create tools without other tools, the tongs were considered a miraculous gift of God. See Tos ʿEr 8:23; ʾAḇ 5:6; B. Pes 54a.

7. See Lieberman, *TK,* p. 469.

8. It need not have been created in a miraculous fashion.

9. Either "letters" or "marks." Variant reading, "from *alef* to *taw,*" i.e., "in its entirety" (see *TA,* and ed. Friedmann). The latter interpretation is based upon the spelling of the Hebrew word *wyṯʾ* (*and there came*), which ends with the letters *taw* and *alef.*

10. Moses, as the deliverer of Torah, will be rewarded with all those who study Torah and subjects derived from it.

11. There was nothing Moses could provide for them in the way of righteousness (*ṣĕḏaḳah,* a term used also for "charity") or fulfillment of their needs, since God had already provided them with everything they needed. But Moses did lay down the basis for the future care of the needy. Note that in Piska 305 Moses is credited with causing the well, etc., to be on hand. That is not mentioned here.

12. Or Sokne; see Tos Beḵ 7:4.

13. Greek term for olive oil made from unripe olives.

14. The word appears also in Tos Neḡ 83:3, where it seems to refer to a kind of fowl (F.).

15. Gen 35:22. See Piska 31.

16. The tenth son, like the tithe of the crop, belongs to God. Counted by seniority, beginning with Reuben, the tenth son is Asher; counted in inverse order, beginning with the youngest, Benjamin, the tenth is Levi. Asher magnanimously ceded the honor to Levi.

17. See Lieberman, *JQR, 35* (1944/45), 7.

18. Piska 316. See also Lieberman, *JQR, 35* (1944/45), 38.

19. See B. Men 85b.

20. It was situated on the border, thus barring enemies from entering.

21. So Elijah Gaon. The text here has "God of Jeshurun." MhG has *ʾellaʾ,* "except Jeshurun."

Piska 356

1. See P. Ta 4:2.

2. In ARN-A 34 (*YJS*, 10, 139–40) eleven instances are cited where the feminine pronoun is spelled *hiʾ*. See also Sof 6:4 for a slightly different version.

3. See Piska 352.

4. At the time of the revelation there were crowns upon their heads. These were taken away when they sinned (B. Shab 88a). This is a play on words: *ḥereb̲* ("sword") and *Ḥoreb̲*.

Piska 357

1. See Piska 338.

2. The trunk of the vine with grape clusters is separated from the branch. Here the valley connects the mountain and the grave. See Ibn Ezra to 34:6.

3. Tos Meḡ 14b. The line includes Jeremiah. Rahab lived in Jericho. See Josh. 6:22–23.

4. See Piska 28. The oppressors have been identified by Alon, in *The Jews in Their Land in the Talmudic Age* (Jerusalem, 1980), p. 62, as "none other than the *conductores*, Gentile or Jew, who squeezed the heavy taxes out of the tenant-farmers, and sometimes pushed them right out of their own land—all, of course, in close cooperation with the government, whose purposes they served so well."

5. Hebron is the site of the cave of Machpelah.

6. Based on the reading of Elijah Gaon. The words "can see it" are not in the text. See Mek̲, end of Bĕ-šallaḥ.

7. Probably to be attached to the next part of 34:3, where *Ṣoʿar* (the city of Zoar) is interpreted as *ṣar*, "narrow." So MhG.

8. Deriving *Ṣoʿar* as from *ṣoʿar*, "trouble, pain."

9. In Hebrew *go over* is *taʿăb̲or*, literally "pass over," while *go* is *tab̲oʾ*, "come." See Piska 341.

10. See B. BB 15a. See A. Heschel, *Theology of Ancient Judaism*. The book contains a discussion of the differences between the schools of ʿAkiba and Ishmael on the question of the Torah's nature and the importance of its concluding verses.

11. Greek σημαλέον. See F. in *PAAJR*, 6 (1934–35), 215–16.

12. Reading not *and (Moses) died (way-yamat̲)* but "Woe! (Moses) is dead" (*way met̲*).

13. This contradicts the idea expressed in Piskas 304 and 305.

14. "Servant" is a positive, not a negative, term. See Piska 27.

15. See Piska 354.

16. See Ginzberg, *Legends*, 6, 163, 410.

17. See B. RH 31b, Sanh 41a, ARN-A 6.

18. See Gen. Rabbah, end of Wayḥi.

19. Ginzberg, *Legends*, 6, 164.

20. See B. MK 27b.

21. In Lev. Rabbah 1:13 and Num. Rabbah, beginning of Balak, comparisons are made between the prophets of Israel and those of the nations, and specifically between Moses and Balaam. Moses sees more clearly than any prophet. Balaam and the other non-Israelite prophets used their prophecy to destroy others, while the Israelite prophets invoked the quality of mercy. In this passage there seems to be

an attempt to give credit to Balaam but at the same time to downgrade him. He is close to God and knowledgeable of Him, but only in the way that a servant is of his human master.

22. "Scripture says, *for a man shall not see Me and live* (Exod. 32:20)—in their lives they do not see Me, but in their deaths they do see Me" (Sif Lev. Wayyikra' 2:12). See ARN-A 25.

Biblical Passages Cited

Genesis

1:9 78
1:10 78
1:14 136, 302–303
2:6 89
2:7 310
2:15 85
2:18 25, 162
3:12 25
3:24 82
4:5 327
4:7 97
4:26 92
6:7 338
7:11 90
7:12 89
7:13 346
8:21 98
9:15 354
10:6 70
10:19 32
11:1 325
11:1–3 90
11:4 90
11:8 90
11:9 317
12:1 319
12:10 317
13:7 276, 283
13:10 74, 90
13:16 46
13:17 33
14:22–23 70
15:7 319
15:18–19 128
16:12 352
18:2 74
18:3 50
19:33 90
19:36 352
20:18 300
21:9 55, 56
21:10 56
21:25 29
21:27 29
21:33 33
22:2 319
22:10 62
22:14 52, 365
22:17 35, 310
23:2–4 70
23:3 319
24:7 319
25:21 48
25:22 328
25:26 353
25:27 318, 345, 353
26:4 46, 144
26:12 33, 75
26:24 50
26:27 29
26:29 26
26:31 29
26:33 26
27:22 352
27:27 365
27:28 79, 377
27:40 352
28:14 99
28:17 365
28:20 57
28:21 57
29:31 300
30:27 75
32:11 50, 62
33:9 333, 377–378
33:19 33
34:25 361, 362
35:5 361
35:19 366
35:22 57

36:12 345
36:22 345
37:25 57
38:21 258
39:5 75
41:43 27
45:25 45, 73, 322
47:2 370, 372, 373
47:6 74
47:7 75
47:14 88, 375
47:31 58
48:7 366
48:17 67
48:21 377
48:22 228
49:1 29
49:1–8 58
49:3 29
49:4 360
49:7 362
49:10 366
49:15 370
49:27 366
49:28 350
49:31 381
50:5 361
50:21 75

Exodus

1:5 344
1:16 290
1:22 290
2:21 31, 50
2:23–24 48, 309
3:1 44
3:10 49–50, 337
4:2–3 348
5:1 136
6:12 49
11:7 174
12:7 68
12:15 177
12:41 346
13:2 63
13:4–5 28
13:5 291
13:7 175
13:9 66
13:11 63
13:19 361
14:14 214
15:1 109, 212
15:2 328, 354, 359, 375
15:11 375, 377
15:14 286, 342
16:3 25
17:4 49
17:14–15 287
19:4 321
19:12 320
20:8 242
20:12 345
20:13 211, 352
20:19 302, 355
20:21 118
21:2 164
21:5 166, 168
21:6 167
21:10 225
21:19 245
21:24 211
22:8 49
22:15 249, 250
22:19 93
22:23 94
22:27 49
23:4 233
23:5 233, 235
23:12 241
23:16 178
23:19 287, 288
23:25 81
23:27 110
23:29 106
23:30 106
24:1 316
24:5 376
24:7 302, 328, 329, 356, 357
24:11 376
25:2 55
25:17 26
31:14 242

32:4	329
32:6	89, 90, 325
32:8	89, 92, 93, 325
32:11	48
32:26–27	363
32:26–28	362
32:32	356
33:6	377
33:18	383
33:20	383
33:23	383
34:6	49, 105
34:23	58
34:24	110
34:28	38, 305, 381

Leviticus

1:2	308
1:4	61
1:9	132
1:12	132
1:13	133
3:2	129
6:16	364
7:16	175, 260
7:31–32	124
11:2	146
11:13	148
11:14	149
13:2	223
13:4	335
14:4	148, 237
14:14	167, 282
17:13	167
18:3	74
18:4	64
18:5	278
18:16	242
18:21	199
18:22	327
18:28	76
18:29	278
19:10	157
19:13	207, 270, 271
19:16	139
19:17	207, 244
19:18	139, 206, 207, 244
19:19	240, 242
20:10	244
20:27	188, 231, 247, 248
21:5	145
21:9	247
23:15	178
23:15–16	178
23:17	287
23:34	181
23:37	118
23:38	119
23:40	180
23:41	181
23:42	180
25:36	207, 244, 259
25:37	259
26:3–4	86
26:5	87
26:16	94
26:19	94
26:20	94–95
26:26	81
26:43	61
27:26	169
27:30	151

Numbers

1:51	91
2:17	257
5:13	209
5:23	68
6:4	382
6:27	118
10:29	367
10:30	367
10:33	28
10:35	320
11:16	84, 316, 358
11:22	56
11:23	56
11:28	332
12:7	50
12:8	136
12:13	49
13:8	379

13:16 344
13:21 45, 73, 322
13:22 45, 70, 73, 322, 379
13:30 45, 73, 322
14:4 328
14:24 51
14:34 28
15:38 65, 243
15:41 328
16:1 36
17:13 339
18:21 157
18:27 152
19:14 347
20:10 53, 363
20:12 348
21:14 332
21:18 296
23:9 376
23:10 340
24:4 383
24:16 383
25:1 25
25:4 358
25:7 197
25:8 197
25:11 362
25:14 362, 363
27:5 42
27:14 47, 348
27:15–16 49
27:17 294
27:18 294
27:21 295
28:4 339
28:9 242
29:3–4 286
29:35 177
29:39 119
31:6 109
33:3 173
34:6 108
35:23 335
35:25 207
36:8 242
36:9 242

Deuteronomy

1:1 23, 24, 25, 26, 30
1:2 27
1:3 30
1:4 30, 31
1:5 31
1:6 31
1:7 31, 32
1:8 33
1:9 34
1:10 34, 77
1:11 35, 36, 136
1:12 36
1:13 28, 37
1:14 38, 112
1:15 38, 39
1:15–16 38
1:16 39, 40
1:17 40, 41
1:18 42
1:19 42
1:20 42, 43
1:21 28, 43
1:22 43
1:23 44
1:24 44
1:25 45
1:26 45
1:27 45
1:28 46
1:29 46
1:30 46
1:31 321
3:9 71
3:11 109
3:23 46, 48
3:24 49, 52
3:25 52
3:26–27 53
3:27 54, 72
3:28 54
3:29 55
4:1 55
4:9 101
4:19 187
4:24 106
4:26 297

4:44 334
4:48 71
5:1 82, 83
5:12 242
5:19 303
5:20 43
5:28 383
6:4 55, 58, 84, 310, 375
6:5 59, 62, 85
6:6 62, 66
6:7 63, 64, 65
6:8 65, 66
6:8–9 67
6:9 68, 69
6:10–11 218
6:11 75
7:1 107
7:12 69
7:26 116
8:3 104
8:5 60, 61
8:7 43, 61, 77, 78
8:8 77, 280
8:9 71, 77
8:10 77, 81
8:12–13 89
8:12–14 325–326
8:14 89
8:15 320
8:16 111
8:19 103
9:1 46
9:7 349
9:8 349
9:9 38, 305
9:14 50
9:17 383
9:25 48
9:26 48
10:20 59
10:22 290, 318
11:9 70, 73, 77
11:10 73, 74
11:11 76, 77, 78
11:12 77, 79, 80
11:13 82, 84, 85, 100
11:13–14 86
11:14 86, 87
11:15 88, 89
11:15–16 89
11:17 82, 93, 94, 95, 96, 300
11:17–18 96
11:18 97
11:19 84, 98
11:19–21 79
11:20 68
11:21 84, 98
11:22 100, 105, 106
11:23 106, 107
11:24 107
11:25 109, 110
11:26 110, 111
11:28 112
11:29 112
11:30 113, 114
11:31–32 134
12:1 114
12:2 115, 116
12:3 116, 184
12:3–4 116
12:5 117, 118, 123
12:5–6 118
12:6 119
12:8 120
12:9 120
12:10 121
12:10–11 121
12:11 122
12:13 122
12:14 117, 122, 123, 125
12:15 123, 124
12:16 124, 125
12:17 125, 126, 127, 153, 185
12:18 127
12:20 128
12:21 128, 129, 130
12:22 124, 129
12:23 130, 278
12:24 131
12:26 131, 133
12:27 132, 133
12:28 133, 134
12:29 134, 204
12:31 135

13:1	136	15:6	161
13:2	136, 137	15:7	161, 373
13:3–4	137	15:8	162
13:4	137	15:9	159, 162, 163, 271
13:6	137, 138, 209	15:10	163
13:7	138, 139	15:11	160, 163
13:8	139	15:12	164, 165
13:9	139	15:13	165
13:10	139, 140, 156	15:13–14	164
13:11	138, 140	15:14	165
13:12	140, 141	15:15	165, 166
13:13	141	15:16	166
13:14	141, 162	15:17	166, 167, 168
13:15	141, 142, 187, 210	15:18	168
13:16	140, 142	15:19	168, 169
13:17	143	15:19–20	168
13:18	143, 144	15:20	153, 171
13:19	144	15:21	171
14:1	144	15:23	171
14:2	145, 318	16:1	172, 173
14:3	146, 149	16:2	172, 173, 174
14:4–5	146, 147	16:3	174
14:5	147	16:4	175
14:6	145, 147	16:5	175, 185
14:7	148	16:6	176
14:7–8	148	16:7	176
14:11	148, 238	16:8	177
14:12	148, 149	16:9	178
14:13	146, 149	16:10	178, 179
14:14–15	149	16:11	179
14:15–17	149	16:12	179
14:19	149	16:13	180
14:20	149	16:14	181
14:21	149, 150	16:15	181
14:22	150	16:16	110, 182
14:23	151, 152, 154	16:17	182
14:24	154	16:18	183
14:25	154	16:19	183, 272
14:26	154, 155	16:20	184
14:27	156	16:21	184
14:28	156, 157	16:22	185
14:29	157, 158	17:1	185, 186, 259
15:1	156, 158	17:2	186
15:1–2	158	17:3	187
15:2	160	17:4	141, 187, 188, 210
15:3	160	17:5	188
15:4	160, 163	17:6	188
15:5	161	17:7	189, 301

17:8	189, 190, 323, 365	19:12	207
17:9	190	19:12–13	207
17:10	190	19:14	207
17:11	190	19:15	208, 210
17:12	191	19:16	209
17:13	140	19:17	210
17:14	191	19:18	210, 211
17:15	191	19:19	211
17:16	192	19:21	211, 212, 284
17:17	193	20:1	212
17:18	73, 193	20:2	212
17:19	193, 194	20:3	212, 213
17:20	195	20:4	214
18:1	195	20:4–7	214
18:2	195	20:5	214
18:3	196	20:6	215
18:4	197	20:7	216
18:5	198	20:8	214, 216
18:6	198	20:9	216
18:7	198	20:10	217, 254
18:8	198, 199	20:11	217
18:9	199	20:12	217
18:10	199, 200	20:13	218
18:11	201	20:14	218
18:12	201	20:15	218
18:13	201	20:16	218
18:14	201	20:17	218
18:14–15	202	20:18	219
18:15	202	20:19	219
18:16	202	20:20	220
18:17	195	21:1	220
18:17–18	202	21:2	220, 221
18:18	202	21:3	221
18:19	202	21:4	221–222, 305
18:20	203	21:5	222, 363
18:21	203	21:6	223
18:22	203	21:7	220, 223
19:1	134, 203	21:8	230
19:2	204	21:9	223
19:3	204	21:10	224
19:4	204, 205	21:11	224
19:5	205	21:12	224
19:6	204, 206	21:13	225
19:7	206	21:14	225, 226
19:8	206	21:15	226, 227
19:9	206	21:16	227, 228
19:10	206	21:17	228, 229
19:11	206, 207	21:18	229, 230

21:19	230
21:20	230, 231
21:21	231
21:22	229, 231
21:23	232, 233
22:1	233, 234
22:2	234
22:3	234, 235
22:4	233, 235, 236
22:5	236
22:6	236, 237, 238
22:7	237, 238, 345–346
22:8	238, 239
22:9	240
22:10	240, 241
22:11	241
22:11–12	242
22:12	243
22:13	243
22:14	244
22:15	244
22:15–16	245
22:16–17	245
22:17	245
22:18	246
22:19	246
22:20	246, 247
22:21	247
22:22	245, 247, 248
22:23–24	248
22:24	248
22:25	248
22:26	248, 249
22:27	249
22:28	249, 250
22:29	250, 251
23:1	251
23:2	251
23:3	252, 253
23:4	252, 253
23:5	253
23:5–6	254
23:7	254
23:8	254
23:9	255
23:10	255
23:11	256
23:12	256
23:13	257
23:14	257
23:14–15	257
23:15	255, 257
23:16	257
23:17	254, 258
23:18	258
23:19	259
23:20	259, 260
23:21	260
23:22	182, 260, 261
23:23	261
23:24	261
23:25	261, 262
23:26	262
24:1	167, 262–265
24:1–2	263, 264
24:2	265
24:3	266
24:4	266, 267
24:5	267
24:6	267, 268
24:7	268
24:8	268
24:9	269
24:10	269
24:11	269
24:12	269, 270
24:13	270
24:14	270, 271
24:15	163, 270, 271
24:16	138, 142, 272
24:17	157, 272
24:19	272–276
24:20	274, 275
24:21	275
25:1	276, 283
25:2	276, 277
25:3	277
25:4	278
25:5	279, 280
25:6	280, 281
25:7	281, 283
25:8	282
25:9	282, 283
25:10	282, 283
25:11	283, 284
25:12	211, 284

25:13	284
25:14	285
25:15	285, 286
25:16	286
25:17	286
25:18	287
25:19	286, 287
26:1	287
26:2	287, 288
26:3	288, 289
26:4	119, 289
26:5	290
26:7	290
26:9	290, 291
26:10	291
26:11	288, 291
26:12	156, 291, 292
26:13	292, 293
26:14	293
26:15	293
27:6–7	155
27:7	119, 122, 179
27:8	68
27:12–13	113
27:14	290
27:15	283
27:20	360
28:3	81, 161
28:5	81
28:6	81
28:8	81
28:12	300
28:14	187
28:16	81
28:17	81
28:19	81
28:20	81
28:23	95
28:30	215, 216
28:48	87
29:9	104, 357
29:27	95
30:19	110, 298, 303
31:1	343
31:7	54, 295
31:9	23, 380
31:10	158
31:14	293
31:16	297
31:19	303
31:20	89, 325
31:21	303
32:1	297, 300, 301
32:2	29, 79, 303, 304
32:3	308
32:4	310
32:5	313
32:6	314, 315
32:7	316
32:8	316, 317
32:9	318
32:10	319, 320
32:11	321
32:12	321, 322
32:13	322, 323
32:14	329
32:15	23, 325, 326
32:16	327, 376
32:17	327
32:18	328
32:19	329
32:20	329
32:21	330
32:22	330
32:23	94, 330, 331
32:24	331
32:24–25	349
32:25	331, 332
32:26	332
32:27	333, 334
32:28	334
32:29	334
32:30	334, 335
32:31	335
32:32	335
32:33	336
32:34	311, 336
32:35	337, 338
32:36	338
32:37	339
32:38	339
32:39	340
32:40	340, 341
32:41	341
32:42	342
32:43	342, 343

32:44 101, 343, 344
32:46 344
32:47 104, 345
32:48 346
32:49 72, 346, 347
32:50 347
32:51 348
32:52 348, 380
33:1 349, 350, 351
33:2 321, 351–355
33:3 356
33:4 104, 357
33:5 351, 358
33:5–6 359
33:6 58, 340, 360
33:6–7 360
33:7 360, 361
33:8 362, 363
33:9 363
33:10 363, 364
33:12 364, 365
33:14 368
33:15 369
33:16 369
33:17 369, 370
33:18 370
33:19 370, 371
33:20 372
33:21 372, 373
33:23 373
33:24 373, 374
33:25 88, 375
33:26 351, 375
33:27 376
33:28 376, 377
33:29 375, 377, 378
34:1 378
34:2 378, 379
34:3 379, 380
34:4 348, 380
34:5 380, 381
34:6 381
34:7 382
34:8 382
34:9 382
34:10 383
34:11–12 383
34:12 383
39:42 341

Joshua

1:8 87
2:1 109
2:10 309
2:16 44
4:14 383
4:19 29
5:1 109, 309
6:26 143
7:5–8:10 55
7:9 46
10:12–14 302
10:24 378
15:8 366
15:15 72
15:49 72
15:63 125
17:5 319
19:9 319
19:47 373
24:15 29
24:21–22 29
24:22 297
24:29 51

Judges

1:3 361
1:7 161, 370
1:16 367
4:6 379
5:4 353
5:26 67
5:31 35, 98, 99
6:3–4 88
6:15 379
6:37 137
6:40 137
8:10 370
15:19 51
18:30 378
19:6 31
21:3 213

1 Samuel

2:27 350
3:10 51
4:17 216
8:7 191
8:20 191
9:6 350
9:18–19 42
12:3–5 29–30
14:24 31, 50
15:12 256
16:1 42
16:6 42
16:7 42
17:14 344
25:18 197
25:29 357
26:10–11 63
26:19 92, 138

2 Samuel

1:1 219
2:30 110
6:12 75
7:1–2 121
7:19 347
12:13 48
12:25 364
16:13 359
19:25 224
20:1 329
22:1 110
22:3 377
22:7 48
22:27 314
23:1 23
23:2 23
23:6 23
24:18 117
24:24 367

1 Kings

2:1 30
3:9 34, 51
3:13 195
3:14 195
4:7 28
4:19 28
5:2 323
5:3 323
5:10–11 34
5:26 34
6:1 366
7:46 380
8:20 357
8:21 357
8:48 54
9:3 79
9:13 333, 378
10:27 193
11:1 110
11:13 51
11:27 360
12:22 350
13:1 350
14:24 327
15:13 327
16:34 143
18:28 144
18:45 306
19:8 28
19:15 85
20:28 351
21:25 138
22:17 294

2 Kings

2:5 64
2:12 64, 316
4:9 350
5:16 63
5:17 110
5:20 63
12:25 33
13:7 99
13:14 64
14:9 32
17:13 297
18:32 71
19:3 328

19:34 50
19:35 337
20:1 53
21:16 362
22:20 362
24:16 332

Isaiah

1:2 302
1:3 298, 314
1:4 313
1:9 333
1:18 32, 53
1:19–20 82
2:2 52
2:2–3 27
2:3 52, 73, 323, 365
2:6 326
2:7–8 326
3:9 313
3:10 337
3:11 337
3:25 360
5:1 73, 364
5:3–4 297
5:19 338
5:24 83
6:2 305
6:3 308
7:21 197
8:2 91
8:23 96
10:10 327
10:34 32, 52
14:2 342
15:11 338
20:3 51
21:13 333
22:12 297
22:20 51
22:22 332
24:22 338
25:6 336
26:6 182, 338
27:9 322
29:10 84
30:4 70
30:17 100
30:20 316
30:21 316
33:24 343
34:6 341, 342
37:19 92
38:2 53
40:4 299
41:8 50, 62
42:11 342
43:3–4 343
43:6 321
43:7 106
43:12 359
43:21 375
44:6 340
44:25 342
45:8 377
45:17 377
48:13 66
49:3 375
49:5 50
49:18 377
49:22 321
50:1 299
51:1–2 328
53:12 373
54:13 346
55:1 103
55:10 78
55:12 342
56:1 373
59:2 201
61:5 87
62:2 299
62:8–9 88
63:11 84
65:6 337
65:8 88
65:17 298
65:22 100
66:22 99

Jeremiah

1:5 202

2:13	326
2:21	335
2:27	225
3:1	266, 299
3:12	106
3:19	72
4:22	313
4:31	328
5:22	301
6:11	332
6:16	298
6:18	298
6:19	298
7:16	48
7:17–18	297
7:34	350
8:7	298
8:23	342
9:11–12	83
10:16	319
11:5	329, 330
11:13	331
11:15	364
12:7	326, 364
14:16	331
14:18	331
14:21	327
15:2	95
15:17	376
16:18	337
17:12	78
19:5	187
22:6	32, 52, 378
22:10	95
22:18	92
22:19	95
27:16	203
28:13	326
28:16	209
29:11	111
29:23	303
30:4	23
30:5–7	23
30:6	328
30:11	338
30:18	27
31:6	73
31:12	89
31:13	350
31:21	96
32:14	58
32:19	312
32:27	58
34:18	200
36:18	68, 380–381
51:7	336
51:64	23, 350
52:33	95

Ezekiel

4:4–6	356–357
5:5	77
5:16	331
7:15	331
8:10	298
8:12	332
8:16	327, 332
16:25	298
16:48–49	325
16:48–50	90
17:3	32
18:5	278
18:9	278
21:36–37	314
23:34	337
32:29	317
32:30	317
32:33	317
33:7–9	38
33:24	56
33:25–26	56
33:31	313
34:25	365, 376
34:26	87
36:7	341
37:9	308
37:25	50
39:17	341
39:18	341
39:20	341
41:7	27
44:5	344
46:11	286
48:1–7	128

48:2 322
48:6 322
48:7 322

Hosea

2:1 100, 144
2:16 320
2:19 299
2:23–25 301
4:1 83
4:6 83
4:13 298
6:2 340
9:10 320
9:14 349
11:1 295
11:9 299
12:1 297
12:12 298
14:3 303
14:5–6 349
14:6 79
14:7 98
14:7–8 349
14:12 200

Joel

1:2–4 349
2:23 87
2:24 88
2:25 349
3:5 105, 106
4:2 343
4:18 91
4:19 343
4:20–21 343

Amos

1:1 23
1:3 333
1:6 333
1:9 333
2:4 83
2:9 107
3:7 51, 381
4:1 23, 349
5:3 100
5:8 93
6:4 323, 326
6:6 323, 326
6:7 326
6:13 334
7:17 95, 329
8:12 104
9:6 144, 358
9:13 349

Micah

1:2 303
3:2–3 349
5:1 366
5:6 79
5:14 353
6:2 298
6:5 253
6:14 81
6:40 269
7:1 336
7:5 293
7:18–20 349

Nahum

2:5 35, 98

Habakkuk

1:8 338
1:14 298
3:3 321, 352
3:6 317
3:9 33

Haggai

1:9 81
2:19 81
2:23 51

Zechariah

2:12 321
4:3 35
4:10 79
6:1 330
8:4 92
8:16 41
8:19 56
9:1 26, 27
10:1 78
10:4 315
11:8 296
14:9 59

Malachi

2:6 296
2:11 297
3:5 303
3:6 300
3:23 351

Psalms

10:3 41
11:7 106, 311
12:1 69
14:1 330
15:1 35
15:1–5 278
16:5 111
16:6 319
16:6–7 111
19:5–6 301
19:8 103
19:9 103
19:11 103
22:21 320
24:3 35, 52
26:11 201
29:3–4 354
29:3–9 329
29:7 355
29:8 79
29:11 354
31:20 311, 337, 377
32:8 111
34:14 112
37:25 364
41:13 201
44:23 59, 355
45:1 35, 98
45:6 63
48:7 328
49:8 340
49:8–9 340
50:2 354
50:4 307
50:6 300
50:7 58–59
51:6 48, 312
55:16 333
62:12 243
65:5 35
65:11 86
68:7 173
68:14 166
68:19 106
72:5 316
72:16 322
73:6 46
75:9 336
78:54 315
78:60 326
78:67–68 366
79:1–3 343
80:2 84, 354
80:14 324
82:6 307, 329
82:7 307, 329
84:2 364
84:5 35
85:14 270
89:18 375
90:1 350
92:13 380
94:1 354
94:12 61
95:10 55
103:20 332, 360
104:14 89
104:32 80
105:44–45 80, 84
106:7 25

106:20 298
106:23 333, 339
106:26 340–341
106:30 48, 197, 339
106:35 298
116:3–4 60
116:12–13 60
116:16 50
119:64 83
119:140 102
119:164 69
121:1 98, 361
121:4 79
123:1 359
124:2 333
125:2 330
127:4 63
127:5 63
132:1–5 117
132:6 366
132:14 27, 121
133:3 365
135:4 145, 318
137:5–6 96
138:4 353
139:21 341
140:14 34
141:2 85
141:6 47
145:8 106
145:19 373
149:1 351
149:4 351
150:1 351

Proverbs

1:2 61
1:8 303
1:9 103, 304
2:4 100
3:4 134
3:12 60
3:15 103
3:16 105
3:18 100, 105
4:2 96, 303
4:8 304
4:9 103, 105, 304
4:13 303
4:18 111
4:19 111
4:22 102, 105, 305
5:15 306
5:15–16 102
5:16 306
5:17 64
6:6–8 298
6:22 64
6:23 61
6:27–29 358
7:3 63
7:4 63
7:9 139
7:26 305
8:10 303
8:14 334
8:22 70, 315
8:22–23 324
8:23 70
8:26 70
8:31 71
8:33 303
9:8 24
10:5 101
11:31 112
12:10 89
13:7 375
13:11 101
14:4 89
15:3 79
15:23 104
16:4 106, 112
17:11 381
17:14 41
17:17 319
18:21 112
18:23 46–47
20:4 101
22:22 34
22:28 275
23:5 104
23:15 105
23:20–21 231
23:23 83

24:20	111
24:30–31	101
25:1	61
25:21–22	98
25:25	102
26:22	45
27:7	102
27:11	105
30:1	333
31:14	102

Job

1:6	310
1:18–19	326
1:21	60
2:3	51
2:4	61
2:9	60
2:10	60
4:21	315
5:10	86
5:23	107
12:5–6	90
12:6	90
12:8	298
12:10	79
12:16	354
15:18–19	360
15:27	326
20:27	299
21:9	325
21:9–13	89
21:14–15	89
25:2	217
28:4	90
28:5	325
28:5–8	90
28:17	101
29:19	87
36:14	381
36:16	380
37:6	78
37:7	312
37:11–12	78
38:7	310
38:10–11	301

Song of Songs

1:2	103
1:3	103, 355
1:8	295
2:2	375
2:3	375
2:8	321
4:6	369
5:9	355
5:10–16	355
6:1	355
6:3	355
6:4	69
6:8	318
6:10	35, 98
7:5	27, 84
8:8	294

Ruth

3:13	63

Lamentations

2:9	71
4:11	94
5:17–18	91

Ecclesiastes

1:1	23, 24
1:4	100
1:5	300
1:5–7	24
4:1	111
4:5	111
4:9	294, 319
4:12	294, 319
5:1	315
5:4	261
5:8	86
5:9	86
7:8	111
7:10	190, 210, 289
7:29	310
9:12	239

10:8 102
11:4 101
12:11 84

Esther

1:6 91
3:13 28

Daniel

3:26 51
3:32–33 310
6:11 85
6:21 51, 85
6:27–28 310
7:9 106
10:13 321–322
10:20 321
10:21 322
12:3 35, 98, 99
12:7 338

Ezra

4:1 341
7:10 1

Nehemiah

8:11 39
12:24 350

1 Chronicles

2:55 118
5:1–2 228–229
5:6 360
12:33 370
17:21 375
17:27 31
21:17 356
21:25 118, 367
22:14 193
28:4 379
29:23 121

2 Chronicles

3:1 117
6:14 351
6:26 54
6:28 351
6:32 54
6:34 54
6:41 352
18:31 362
19:6 41
19:11 39, 183
25:7 351
28:8–11 213
28:15 213
29:7 93
29:11 64
33:1 61
33:10–13 62
33:13 362
33:16 297
36:23 365

Rabbinic Sources

Mishnah

ʿĂḇoḏah Zarah

3:5	421
3:7	422
3:9	431

ʾAḇoṯ

1:1	397
2:8	492
2:16	400
3:18	418, 431
3:19	400
4:11	400
5:6	511
6:4	492

ʿĂraḵin

8:6	442
8:7	442

Baḇa Baṯra

5:11	471, 485
5:12	485
6:7	454

Baḇa Ḳamma

8:3	484

Baḇa Mĕṣiʿa

2:5	468
2:7	468
2:8	468
2:9	467
2:10	468
4:8	476
4:11	485
5:6	476
7:4	477
9:11	480
9:13	479

Bĕḵoroṯ

2:2	424
2:9	442
4:1	442
5:3	432
6:1	465
6:12	443
7	450
8:1	466

Bĕraḵoṯ

1:3	405, 406
1:5	444
2:3	403
9:2	488
9:5	404, 476

Beṣah

1:1	445

Bikkurim

1:1–2	486
1:2	486
1:3	486
1:4	486
1:5	487
1:6	486
1:8	486
1:9	486
1:10	486
2:4	486
3:1	487
3:4	487
3:7	486
3:8	486

ʿEruḇin

10:14 427

Giṭṭin

2:4 441
3:1 477
4:6 476
5:6 508
8:1 478
8:1–2 478
9:1 477
9:10 477

Ḥăḡiḡah

1:1 449
1:2 449
1:3 447
1:5 449
1 (end) 504

Ḥallah

4:11 427

Horayoṯ

1:4 451

Ḥullin

2:9 443
3:6 433
6:6 441
8:4 433, 434
10:1 454, 455
10:4 455
10 (end) 455
11:1 455
12:2 469
12:3 468
12:4–5 469
12:5 469

Keṯubboṯ

3:4 472
3:4–5 473
3:6 473
4:1 472
4:3 472
13:11 437

Ḳiddušin

1:1 472
1:9 415
1:9 419
4:1 474

Kilʾayim

5:7 470
5:8 470
7:7 470
8:3 470
8:4 470
8:6 470
9:7 471
9:8 470
9:9 470
9:10 470

Maʿăśēroṯ

1:3 434
1:5 434

Maʿăśer Šeni

1:2 435
1:3 436
1:7 436
3:8 406
3:9 436
3:10 436
5:6 436, 487
5:9 488
5:10 436
5:11 488
5:12 488
5:13 488
5:14 487

Makkoṯ

1:4 460
1:5 460
1:6 460

1:9 460
2:1 469
2:2 458
2:4 458
2:5 458
2:6 459
2:8 458
3:10 482
3:11 482
3:13 482
3:14 482
3:15 426, 482

Mĕḡillah

1:10 423
4:7 464

Mĕnaḥoṯ

3 (end) 406
7:6 444, 447

Middoṯ

4:6 469
4:7 469
5:4 427

Nĕḏarim

5:4 405
6:6 405

Parah

1:1 464

Pe᾿ah

1:1 504
2:7 480
3:6 481
4:6 480
4:11 481
5:2 481
5:6 481
5:7 480
6:3 481
6:5 481
6:6 481
6:8 481
6:10 481
7:2 481
7:7 481
8:5 437, 487
8:7 492

Pĕsaḥim

3:7 444
7:6 445
8:7 445

Roš haš-Šanah

1:3 410

Sanhedrin

1:3 396, 461
1:5 429, 430
2:4 454
2 (end) 453
4:1 398
4:5 394
5:4 451
6:3 467
6:4 451, 467
7:6 429
7:7 456
7:9 473
7:11 456
8:1 466
8:3–4 467
8:7 473
10:5 430
10:6 431
11:3 452
11:4 452
11:5 457
11:6 457

Šĕḇiʿit

4:7 399
6:1 419
10:1 438
10:2 438
10:3–4 438
10:8 438

Šĕḳalim

5:6 439

Soferim

1:9 406
6:4 512

Soṭah

1:1 460
3:4 400
6:3 460
7:2 484
7:5 420
7:8 453
8:1 461
8:2 462
8:5 461, 462
8:7 461, 462
9:1 464
9:2 464
9:3 464
9:4 464
9:6 465
9:9 463

Sukkah

1:1 448
5:7 456

Tĕmurah

3:5 427, 434
6:1 432, 450
6:3 476
6:4 476

Tĕrumoṯ

1:5 434
2:4 455

Yĕḇamoṯ

1:1 483
2:1 483
2:8 483
3:10 483
4:5 483
4:13 474
5:1 483
6:1 483
8:3 474
10:1 478
11:1 473
11:2 484
12:1 484
12:2 484
12:3 484
12 (end) 484

Yoma

1:1 423
3:8 493
5:1 509

Zaḇim

2:3 475

Zĕbaḥim

2:1 456
4:5 424
4:6 411
5:4–8 434
5:5–6 423
8:10 428
10:1 450

Babylonian Talmud

ʿAḇoḏah Zarah

2a ff. 490
2b 496, 501, 505
5b 415
18a 494
25a 491
45a 421
45b 422
46a 422
47a 500
51a–b 428
74a 426

ᶜArakin

7a 472
15a 390
16b 390

Baḇa Baṯra

3b 472
11a 469
14b 389
15a 389, 512
17a 504
21a 435
25a 492
60b 426
61b 475
88a 485
89b 485
90a 485
113b 466
115a 483
122b 466
127a 446
127b 466

Baḇa Ḳamma

4:3 397
10:15 397
9a 438
28a 484
38a 507
46b 471
51a 469
57a 468
60b 500
81b 468
82b 429
84a 460
88a 484
91b 463
92a 510
92b 463
109b 455
112b 460
113a 397, 506

Baḇa Měṣiᶜa

24a 414, 456
25b 469
27a 468
28a 468
30a 468
31b 430
32b 467
47b 435
52b 485
60a 485
87b 469, 477
88a 434, 469
88b 482
91b 483
111b 480
112a 480
114b 480
115a 479

Běḵoroṯ

5a 420
6a 424
9b 442
15a 424, 425
27b 442
32b 425
41a 443
45b 450
46b 466
47b 465
50b 472
56b 427

Běraḵoṯ

4:5 401
9a 444, 445
11a 405, 469
16a 504
30a 401
32b 401
35b 413
40a 438
45a 396
53b 493
60b 400

61b 404
62b 504

Beṣah

7b 444
25b 506
32b 431

ʿEduyyoṯ

4:10 471

Giṭṭin

8a 419
19a 477
36a 437
36a–b 438
43b 476
45a 476
56b 503
57b 498
58a 397
83a 478
88a 500
90a 477
90b 478

Ḥăḡiḡah

3a 387
4b 449
6b 447
7b 447
9a 448
14a 420
14b 414
16a 488
18a 446

Horayoṯ

10a 397

Ḥullin

2a 477
7a 394
11b 391, 455, 482
27a 443
28a 426
41b 443
56b 496
60b 432, 433
62b 469
63a–b 432
63b 432
84a 426
90a 427
91b 493
116a 434
130b 454
131a 481
134a 455
134b 455
136b 454
137a 455
138b 455
139a 469
139b 432, 468
140a 469

Kĕriṯoṯ

4b 425
26a 465

Keṯubboṯ

10b 399
14a 472
23b 459
38a 473
44b 471
45a 471
45b 471
46a 471, 472
54a 471
56b 471
66b–67a 489
87b 459
110b 428
111a 428
111b 498
112b 407

Ḳiddušin

1:2 (49:4) 440

4b 477
12a 439
14a 483, 484
15a 442
16b 440
17a 440
17b 439, 440, 441
18a 439
21b 441
22a 440
22b 441
30a 405, 415
31b 440, 465
32b 408
36a 431
37a 415, 421
38b 438
40b 411
44a 417
49b 387
57a 433
57b 426, 433
68a 466
68b 465
74a 466
78b 466

Makkot̲

5a 460
8a 458
8b 458
13b 482
16b 425
17a 425
19b 435
22b 482
23b 426

Mĕḡillah

9b 451
28b 387

Mĕnaḥot̲

34a 406
37b 406
39a 471
41b 471
65b 447
66a 447
82a 444
84a 486
84b 486
85b 511
99b 405

Moᶜed̲ Ḳaṭan

21a 484
27b 512

Nazir

25a 427
59a 468

Nĕd̲arim

62a 411

Pĕsaḥim

5b 444
16a 443
21b 433
22a 425
22b 425
28a 444
36b 444
37a 444
54a 511
58b 450
68a 475
68b 446
70a 445
71a 449
77a 427
79b 445
80a 445
87b 496
91a 445
95b 446
112b 412

Roš haš-Šanah

4a 449

5b 476
6a 476
8a 434
10a 464
12b 434
14a 448
17b 410
18b 402
25b 452
31b 512

Šabbaṯ

19a 463
32b 469
33b 507
55b 508
78a 456
88a 512
119b 389
130a 426
138b 417
151b 462

Sanhedrin

4b 406
6b 397
7a 395
10a 396
14b 464
16a 461
16b 449
19a 396, 460
20b 424, 453
21a 453
21b 453, 476
27b 429, 480
28b 452
29a 501
31b 401
33b 429, 450, 451
34a 451
34b 464
35b 466
39b 408
40a 430
41a 512
43a 451
45b 431, 458, 467
46a 467
46b 467
50a 472
52b 452
56a 427
59a 417, 506, 507
61a 428
61b 429
63a 414
65b 456
66b 472
67a 429, 463
68b 466
71a 466
72a 466, 467
73a 473
86a 387, 390, 452
87a 451, 452
88a 466
89b 424, 452
90a 428, 429, 457, 460
90b 416
91a 493, 511
91b 503
95b 430
99a 429, 496
99b 504
101b 508
103b 406
107a 399
107b 404
108a 404
111b 451
112a 430
112b 429
113a 431

Šĕḇuʿot

41b 387

Soṭah

9a 414
13a 392
25a 466
31a 403
33b 420

35b	465
38a	423
38b	465
41a	437
41b	453
42a	461
42b	461
43a	461
43b	462
44a	478
44b	461
45b	463, 464
46a	464
46b	464

Sukkah

3a	469
9a	448
11b	448
46b	438
55b	455

Taʿănit̲

2a	412
6a	412
10a	412
11a	494
16b	493
22b–23a	412
27a	464

Tĕmurah

16a	510
21a–b	427
21b	434, 435
29b	476
30b	476
31a	433

Yĕb̲amot̲

4a	470
4b	470
9b	474
11b	478
13b	431
14a	431
17b	483
22a	404, 465
22b	483
23a	466
24a	483
48a	465
48b	465
49a	474
60a–b	473
61a	480
63b	500
75a	474
76b	474
77a	474
77b	475
78a	475
78b	462
79a	431
90b	457
101b	484
122b	459

Yoma

12a	510
22b	416
66b	509
74a	443
75b	426

Zĕb̲aḥim

36a–b	450
46b–47a	411
56b	435
57a	435
90b	424
106a	424
112b	423
117a	423
118b	509

Palestinian Talmud

ʿAb̲od̲ah Zarah

1:4	492

Baḇa Baṯra

5:11 458

Baḇa Ḳamma

4:3 506

Bĕḵoroṯ

2:3 446

Bĕraḵoṯ

1:3 415
6:4 475
9:3 410
9:7 404
9 (end) 417

Bikkurim

1:2 486

Ḥăḡiḡah

1:2 447
1:4 449
2:1 395, 416

Ḥallah

2:5 418

Horayoṯ

1:1 452

Keṯubboṯ

1:5 508
3 473
4:4 471

Ḳiddušin

1:2 439, 440, 441, 442
1:9 415

Kil'ayim

7:4 470
8:1 424

Maʿăśer Šeni

1:3 436
5:5 436

Maʿăśĕroṯ

3:7 469
49:1 434

Makkoṯ

2:5 458
2 (end) 459

Nĕḏarim

1:1 447

Pe'ah

1:1 494
1:6 434
6:4 481
7:4 498
8:8 437

Pĕsaḥim

2:2 444
8:7 445

Roš haš-Šanah

1:1 423
1:3 410
4:8 402

Šabbaṯ

1:4 463

Sanhedrin

1:2 500
8:7 467
10:7 430
11:3 452
11:7 428

Šebi‘it

6:1 415, 419

Soṭah

7:3 421
9:1 429
9:2 464
9:16 405
17:3 508
23:1 464

Ta‘ănit

3:6 500
4:2 512

Yĕbamot

8:2 475

Yoma

1:5 406
6:1 460

Tosefta

‘Abodah Zarah

1:20 405
4:3 414
4:4 428
6 (7):4 422
8:4 ff. 427
8:6 457

‘Arakin

1:10 497
4:26 426

Baba Ḳamma

9:30 431

Baba Meṣi‘a

2:23 468
2:28 468
3:11 396
3:17 485
3:26 485
6:17 476
8:7 483
10:3 480
10:10 437
10:11 479

Bĕkorot

2:3 424
3:32 428
7:1 423, 434
7:4 511

Bĕrakot

1:4 406
1:10 444
2:13 403
3:15 401
end 406

Bikkurim

2:10 487

‘Eduyyot

1:1 417

‘Erubin

3:7 463
8:23 511

Giṭṭin

2:4 441
7:1 477
7:3 477
9:1 478

Ḥăgigah

1:4 447
1:12 416

Ḥallah

1:1 441

Ḥullin

2:17 477
3 (3):22 433
6:11 441
10:4 455
10:5 455
10:9 469
10:16 469

Keṯubboṯ

2:1 460
3:5 473
13:3 472

Ḳiddušin

1:12 437
5:4 475
5:6 474

Kilʾayim

4:2 470
4:12 470
5:4 470
5:21 470

Maʿăśer Šeni

1:5 435
2:17 436

Maʿăśěroṯ

2:2 434
3:16 434

Makkoṯ

2:1 458
2:11 458
3:8 457, 458
5 (4):8 422
5 (4):16 482
5 (4):17 482

Měḡillah

3:25 475
4:5 443

14b 512

Měnaḥoṯ

10:33 447

Něḡaʿim

3:1 479
83:3 511

ʾŎhaloṯ

16:12 459

Peʾah

1:1–3 502
1:8 480
3:6–7 481
3:8 481
4:2 437
4:8 438
4:10 439
4:11 487
4:12 439
4:17 439
4:20 439
8:11 437

Pěsaḥim

1:8 444
6:2 445
7:2 445

Roš haš-Šanah

1:13 410
2:3 452

Šabbaṯ

7:4 456
7:13 456
7:14 456
12:14 492
56b 456
133a 479

Sanhedrin

3:5 434
3:10 449
4:2 453
4:5 424, 453
4:7 453, 454
6:4 395
7:1 452
9:6 467
10:3 429
10:4 456
11:11 473
14:1 429
14:2 430
14:3 430
14:5 431
14:6 430
14:15 457, 505

Šĕbiʿit

4:11 419

Šebuʿot

5:4 459

Šĕkalim

2:1 427
3:24 486

Soṭah

3:6 413
6:6 402
7:18 461
7:19 462
7:22 462
8:7 421, 463
9:1 464
9:2 465
10:9 408
11:6–7 392
11:10 489
14 463
21:3 420

Sukkah

2:8 428

Tĕmurah

4:6 476

Tĕrumot

1:11 397

Yĕbamot

6:8 465
7:2 483
12:2 484
12:15 484

Zĕbaḥim

4:1 427
8:5 428
13:15 423
14:4–8 423

Midrashim

Mekilta dĕ-Rabbi Ishmael

ʿĂmaleḳ

1 485
2 506

Ba-Ḥodeš

4 396
5 505
6 414
7 470
9 497
10 404
11 423

Bĕ-šallah

1 408

2	461, 496
3	506
end	512

Dĕ-Kaspa

1	476
2	467
3	450
4	449
5	433

Dĕ-Pisḥa

2	443, 471
5	445
6	397
7	412, 444
8	446
9	445, 446
11	443
12	419, 426
13	440, 445
14	504
16	392, 493
17	406, 444

Nĕziḳin

1	442
2	440, 441
3	439
5	479
6	472
17	414

Šabbaṯa

1	426

Širaṯa

2	413
3	400, 496
9	419, 496
10	489

Wayyissaʿ

1	390

Meḵilta dĕ-Rabbi Simeon

13:11	420
20:6	403
21:2	437
22:19	414
22:21	480

Sifra

ʾAḥăre Moṯ

1:6	423
13:10	405
13:13	417

Bĕ-har

2:6	438

Bĕ-ḥuḳḳoṯay

beginning	485
1	412
4:1	424
5	414
8:11	392
8 (end)	509
12:1	435
12:13	434
13:1	434

ʾEmor

1:1	432
1:15	472
8:5	450
10:3	447
12:3	447, 448
12:5	446
12:6	447
12:10	423
19:3	467

Ḳĕḏošim

2:9	480
3:6	395

4:8 389, 390, 397
10:3 456
89:2 470
91:1 451

Mĕṣora'

1:12 432
5:8 391

Šĕmini

5:1 433
15:5 433

Way-yiḳra'

2:4 493
2:7 432
2:12 513
12:13 481
13:4 486

Sifre on Numbers

1 401
5 435
39 423, 452
42 510
43 423
66 443
78 399, 510
81 422
82 398
84 395
92 396
95 402
98 391
99 389, 479
103 428
105 400
111 420
112 431, 504
113 430
114 451, 467
115 471
117 487
118 442
119 454, 487
123 464
124 406
134 394, 401
136 398, 505
137 399
140 488, 489
141 446
151 446
157 419
159 457
160 458, 459
179 401
180 400

Sifre Zuṭa on Numbers

15:28 416
18:24 454
27:16 488

Other Midrashim

'Aḇoṯ dĕ-Rabbi Nathan, Version A

2 503
6 512
8 488
12 490, 505
17 488, 489
24 417
25 513
28 396, 459
31 503
32 496
34 390, 391, 512
35 422, 429, 476, 510
37 415
39 431
40 417, 502

'Aḇoṯ dĕ-Rabbi Nathan, Version B

7 503
11 408
21 411
27 418
35 405
36 496

37	505, 511
38	390, 391
43	509
213	509

Genesis Rabbah

2	509
12:15	400
12:33	400
16:1	394
19:7	475
20	511
21:7	400
23	414
39	496
43:13	402
49:25	431
51:25	390
54:3	392
56	510
63	510
65:23	510
68:11	399
69:17	510
95	408, 510
96	508
100	512

Exodus Rabbah

1:33	393
2:4	489
3:6	400
6:2	453
24:1	496
32:2	407
42:9	400
47:6	510

Leviticus Rabbah

1:13	512
2:10	405
9:9	462
12:2	496
17:5	463
22:9	424
30:2	395, 416
31:4	399
35	410
35:11	413
35:12	412
36:5	403
37:1	477

Numbers Rabbah

2:18	416
9:14	497
12:3	500
12:6	475
12:20	490
16:6	399
16:13	407
20:1	512
21:23	404

Deuteronomy Rabbah

1:10	396
1:14	395
2:1	400
5:12	462

Deuteronomy Rabbah (ed. Lieberman)

pp. 1–3	389
5	390
16	395
43	401
63	403

Song Rabbah

1:1	389
1:3	452
1:8	489
4:13	489, 490
4:15	510
5:9	506

Ruth Rabbah

1:4	500

Lamentations Rabbah

5 414

Ecclesiastes Rabbah

1:4 416
1:5 389

Esther Rabbah

3 490

Midrash on Psalms

1:17 405
1:18 417
75:9 502
79:4 504
90:3 508
91:3 500
94:2 404
99:1 503
106:4 390
119:7 417

Midrash Samuel

1 417

Seder Eliyyahu Zuṭa

25 496

Yalḳuṭ Šimʿoni

Deuteronomy

857 408

ʿEḳeb

873 417

Samuel

139 414

Isaiah

387 491

Proverbs

943 407
945 417
948 413

Midrash hag-Gadol

Genesis

28:21 402
814 403

Numbers

20:2 400

Deuteronomy

59 400

Yelammedenu

Ḥuḳḳaṯ

22 490

Wa-ʾeṯḥannan

35 406

Way-yeleḵ

2 489

Pĕsiḵta Dĕ-Raḇ Kahanā

p. 52 485
53 496
437 505

Rabbinic Authorities

Abba Ḥanan, 142, 146
Abba Hedoros, 313, 364
Abba Jose ben Ḥanan, 28
Abba Kohen ben Dalya, 28
Abba Saul, 205
ᶜAkiba, 1, 2, 6, 8, 11, 24, 55, 56, 60, 61, 83, 91, 99, 102, 115, 116, 119, 122, 128, 132, 134, 135, 137, 140, 143, 148, 150, 152, 154, 176, 180, 197, 200, 216, 220, 221, 224, 225, 246, 264, 265, 275, 283, 285, 293, 301, 305, 325, 382, 392, 397

Benaiah, 8, 26, 28, 29, 301, 305
Ben Azzai, 132
Ben Bag-Bag, 155
Ben Zoma, 174

Dostai b. Judah, 305, 315, 327, 329

Eleazar, 220
Eleazar b. ᶜArak, 194
Eleazar b. Azariah, 24, 61, 65, 91, 106, 128, 174, 254, 264, 265, 266, 274, 325
Eleazar b. Ḥananiah, 285
Eleazar b. Mattithiah, 176
Eleazar b. R. Simon, 75, 220
Eleazar b. Shammua, 134
Eleazar ha-Ḳappar, 129
Eleazar Ḥismah, 39, 262
Eleazar of Modiᶜin, 82
Eliezer, 59, 61, 66, 74, 93, 97, 113, 115, 116, 131, 132, 146, 167, 171, 176, 180, 201, 209, 221, 224, 225, 232, 238, 240, 251, 259, 264, 275, 283, 285, 293, 381
Eliezer b. Jacob, 53, 60, 85, 107, 114, 136, 157, 165, 184, 205, 215, 236, 243, 246, 289, 382
Eliezer b. R. Zadok, 105
Eliezer son of Jose the Galilean, 112, 113, 187, 304, 317–318, 336, 347

Gamaliel, 24, 39, 74, 91, 117, 131, 144, 260, 274, 325, 363–364, 397

Ḥananiah b. Aḥi, 134
Ḥananiah b. Gamaliel, 131, 195, 242, 277, 359
Ḥanina b. Antigonus, 93

Ḥanina b. Teradion, 312
Ḥanina of Ṭibʿin, 335
Hillel, 8, 160, 162, 382; School of, 175, 182, 197, 243, 263

Isaac, 66, 68, 93
Ishmael, 2, 5, 6, 8, 11, 39–40, 65, 68, 87, 101, 117, 128, 133, 134, 144, 153, 154, 167, 169, 177, 200, 219, 226, 239, 244, 245, 274, 283, 307
Ishmael son of R. Joḥanan b. Barokah, 251

Jacob, 106
Jacob be-R. Hanilai, 304
Joḥanan b. Barokah, 268
Joḥanan b. Nuri, 24, 39, 390
Joḥanan b. Zakkai, 212, 295, 382
Joḥanan the Sandal-maker, 134
Jonathan, 134, 225, 226
Jose, 37, 75, 92, 152, 175, 176, 208, 231, 308, 323, 338, 371
Jose b. ʿAkiba, 98
Jose b. Dormaskit, 26, 27, 90
Jose b. ham-Meshullam, 77–78
Jose b. Ḥanina, 26
Jose b. Kippar, 266
Jose b. R. Judah, 60, 167, 207, 220, 271, 278, 285, 345
Jose the Galilean, 83, 115, 125, 137, 150, 159, 162, 179, 180, 210, 211, 216, 264, 265, 273, 289, 291
Jose the net-maker, 67
Joshua, 53, 61, 71, 91, 132, 134, 200, 252, 325, 347
Joshua b. Korḥah, 96, 100, 111, 125
Josiah, 62, 146, 229, 238, 241, 372
Judah, 25, 26, 27, 28, 31, 67, 72, 102, 113, 118, 120, 121, 122, 123, 130, 132, 140, 144, 150, 154, 157, 162, 170, 174, 175, 176, 183, 185, 186, 191, 193, 196, 200, 205, 206, 208, 211, 212, 221, 228, 230, 243, 245, 249, 251, 252, 253, 255, 266, 268, 272, 273, 277, 281, 283, 284, 288, 290, 292, 300, 313, 315, 323, 328, 329, 334, 339, 361, 366, 369, 372
Judah b. Baba, 88
Judah b. Betherah, 134, 230, 233, 264, 288, 302
Judah the Prince, 4, 8, 33, 62, 86, 88, 93, 99, 122, 128, 167, 177, 205, 207, 239, 259, 278, 284, 292, 304, 312, 331, 345, 365

Mattiah b. Ḥeresh, 134
Meir, 6, 60, 62, 91, 144, 167, 230, 241, 273, 275, 297, 306, 313, 315, 328, 329, 343, 361, 366, 380

Nathan, 67, 86, 294
Nathan b. R. Joseph, 60
Nehemiah, 61, 295, 300, 304, 328, 334, 335, 336, 339, 372
Nehorai, 191, 206, 308

Saul, 206
Shammai, 219; School of, 175, 182, 197, 243, 263
Simai, 307
Simeon, 6, 26, 43, 44, 47, 118, 120, 121, 122, 124, 125, 130, 138, 149, 151, 165, 170, 174, 176, 177, 180, 182, 186, 193, 201, 221, 254, 255, 256, 260, 272, 276, 277, 278, 289
Simeon b. Azzai, 59, 130
Simeon b. Eleazar, 298
Simeon b. Gamaliel, 37, 41, 46, 93, 130, 183, 360
Simeon b. Ḥalafta, 315, 324
Simeon b. Judah, 150–151, 315
Simeon b. Menasya, 59, 99, 102, 105
Simeon b. Yoḥai, 2, 35, 55, 56, 61, 70, 71, 75, 77, 81, 82, 87, 88, 96, 98, 99, 101, 102, 293, 308, 358, 369, 390
Simeon b. Zoma, 152
Simeon the Yemenite, 252

Tarfon, 24, 61, 83, 264, 283, 390

Yudan be-Rabbi, 167

Zadok, 74
Zeᶜera, 229

General Index

Aaron: where doomed 47, 347–348; death of 295, 296; pillar of cloud disappears after his death 296; assumes priesthood 311; pleads for mercy 339; death of not caused by sin 346–347; sin of 363; staff created miraculously 372

Abraham, 319; merit of 18, 19; rebukes Abimelech 29; blessing of, to Israel 35; God's promise to 46; servant of God 50; son is idol-worshiper 55; bound by only one commandment 56; inherits Land 56; causes God to be beloved by mankind 59; loves God 62; binds his inclination by oath 63; serves angels disguised as Arabs 74; sacrifice of son not intended by God 187; mediates God's harshness 316–317; endured sufferings 317; father of unworthy children 318, 353; brings God's reign to world 319; brought to Land 319; gives God anything 319; soul of 319–320; cannot save Ishmael 340; beloved by gentiles 345; known as "beloved" 364; has vision of Temple 365

Abrech: meaning of 27

Academy: supervisors of 39

Achzib: border of Land 108

Adam, 391; foolish ways 25; death decreed 335, 411; led astray by serpent 336; died as result of disobedience 347; clothes created at twilight 372

Adultery: forgiveness of 229; one suspected of 363

Age: four die at *120* 382

Aggadah: study of 104; expounders of 106; leads to knowledge of God 106, 306, 307; definition 417

Agnitus: Roman general 363

Agrippa: wept upon hearing Deut. *17* 192

Ahab, 326; considered poor leader 294

Ahaz, 326

ʿAkiba: receives rebuke 24; comforts R. Eliezer on deathbed 61; comforts companions over destruction of Temple 91, 92; causes Torah not to be forgotten 104; dies at *120* 382; martyrdom 404

Allegorical interpretation, 391, 418

Alms. *See* Charity

Alphabet: mistakes in writing of 67–68

Altars: when permitted 120; permitted in Land until Shiloh 120–121

Amalek: command to destroy 121; remembrance of 286–287; slew those who strayed from God 287

Amen: response to blessing 309; Israel did not respond to prophets 329–330

Ammonites, 253; plot to make Israel sin 254; prohibited forever 254; offered Torah 352

Amos: rebukes Israel 23; comforts after castigating 349

Amoz: called "man of God" 351

Analogy, 124, 141, 145, 159, 199, 210, 235, 253, 263

Ancestors' attitude toward idols 327

Angel of Death seeks Moses 296

Angels: mention God's name with Israel 310; defend Moses 347

Anger, 94

Animals: marks showing that they are permitted 145–146; those that can be eaten 146; permitted for food 147; clean and unclean 147, 148; which die by themselves 149; consecrated 169, 170; congenitally blemished 185; used for abominable

Animals (*continued*)
things 186; when lost 233–234; helping lift 236
Animal tithe, 151; only from animals of same year 150
Ant: man must learn from 298
Apikoros: definition of 396
Aramean woman: children of as God's enemies 200
Arbitration: attitudes toward 41, 397, 398
Arios, 37, 396
Ark of God: brings blessings 75; houses broken tablets 75
Asael: power of 110
Asher: appears before Pharaoh 373; blessed with most sons 374; has abundant oil 374; observes Sabbatical laws 374; pacifies brothers 394; produces omphakinon oil 374; rebuked for revealing Reuben's deed 374
Asherah: cutting down 115; three kinds of 116; forbidden 184; uprooting 184
Ashtaroth: fortified and mighty 30–31
Assault, laws of 249
Assembly of the Lord: maimed may not enter 251–252; four assemblies 252; bastard may not enter 252
Atonement, 223; not by money 340
Authority: none in heaven 340; two in heaven 340

Babel. *See* Tower of Babel
Babylonian exiles: given Land 33, 108, 394
Balaam, 253, 376; assures nations world not being destroyed 354; compared to Moses 383
Baldness: prohibition from causing 144–145
Barak: Moses has vision of 379
Barbaria, 330
Base fellows: entice city to worship idols 141
Bastard: definitions of 252; rules for 253
Battle: priest speaks before 212, 213, 214; supplying water and food for 214; those who may return from 214, 215, 216
Beasts: return of to owner 234, 235; biting people 331
Beating. *See* Lashing
Beloved six 364
Belshazzar: uprooted from world 105
Benedictions, eighteen: ordained by early prophets 352; order of 352
Benjamin: favored and beloved of God 364; likened to beast of forest 366; Shekinah dwells in portion of 366, 367, 368; born in Land of Israel 368; not involved in selling Joseph 368; took care of Jacob 368
Benjamin the Egyptian proselyte, 255
Bestiality, 147
Bet Aris, 83, 411
Bet Ilias: market at 306
Beth-Shean, 394
Bilhah, 359
Birds: clean 146, 149, 238; permitted 148, 149; distinguishing marks not stated 149; of prey unclean 149; for vows 259
Bird's nest: rules of 148, 236, 237, 238; commandment of, easy 238
Bitter waters: not used when there are witnesses 209
Blasphemer: hanging of 232
Blessing, 111–112; of field 86; of God in synagogue 308. *See also* Priestly blessing
Blessings and curses, 113
Blood: prohibition on eating 124; poured on earth only 125; compared to water 125, 171; eating of before Torah given 130; prohibition of as least of commandments 130, 131; casting of 132; sprinkling of 136; covering of 167; pouring of 171; types of 171–172, 189; may not be eaten 278
Blood avenger: duty of 204, 205, 207
Boaz: binds inclination 62
Body: found in field 220–221
Booth, 180
Border: enlargement of 128

Borders: of Land of Israel 366, 419
Brotherhood: praise of 254; not applied to slaves 284
Brothers: childless 279
Burnt offerings: rules of 127; method of offering 132–133; called "rejoicing" 155

Caesarea, 306; made Roman colony 400
Caesarean section, 226
Calamity: God brings upon nations 338; comes from God swiftly 341
Camp: conduct within 256–257; making of, holy 257
Canaanites: build Land for Israel, not for selves 76; steeped in idolatry 115; sacrifice children and parents 135; warned against abomination 201; reason for exile 256; wealth of 369–370; number slain 370
Capital cases, 42
Captains: appointment 39
Captured woman, 224–226
Cattle, feeding 88
Chamber of Hewn Stone: Torah dispensed from 189
Chamber of Secrets: for giving charity 163
Chambers: man made up of 315
Charity, 182; extended as loan 162; obligation to 163; method of giving 163–164
Charmer, 200
Chastisement: preciousness of 60, 61, 62
Child: of doubtful parentage 226
Childlessness, 279
Children: cannot testify against parents 138
Chosen House, 293. *See also* Temple
Christianity: its claims refuted 18; attitude to commandments 393
Circumcision: praised by David 69
Cistern of the Diaspora, 132
Cities of refuge: location 204; number 206; slayers proceed to 207
Civil cases, 42
Cloud: pillar of 137
Coins: used for second tithe 154, 155; denominations 395
Commandments: observance outside Land 20; performed out of love 59; must be learned 82; observed before entering Land 82; observed after entering Land 82; questioning reward of 86; observance in exile 96, 415; dependent on Land 97, 115; in conquered lands 107–108; lands not applied to 108; where observed 114; those given when entering Land 121; accepted with joy 130; lives sacrificed for 130; light one also precious 134, 136, 144, 161; transgressions of minor lead to transgressions of major 206, 244; easy and weighty 238; with monetary loss 286; given in heaven and earth 303; earn reward now and in world to come 345–346; for sake of Israel 357. *See also* Ten Commandments
Common sayings, 32
Compartment of Temple: sacrifices consumed within 119; peace offerings brought within 122
Condemned city, 141; destruction of 142; broad place of 143; not rebuilt 143; sanctified objects in 143
Consecrated animals: substitution of 133; unfit 146
Consecrated offerings, 169; where offered 131; of greater and lesser sanctity 152
Corner crop, 189, 261, 272, 275, 292, 303; observed after settlement 82; not liable to tithe 157
Court of law: participation of priests and Levites in 190; location of 281
Covenant: at Horeb, Moab, Gerizim, and Ebal 150; members of 157
Co-wives: forbidden 280
Cruelty of leaders 336
Cup: from which all generations have drunk 336
Curse: earned by evildoing 112

Damages: unintentional 284

Damascus, 391; meaning of 26, 27; to be included in Jerusalem 27
Dan: likened to lion 373; next to border 373; portion of, in two places 373; presented to Pharaoh 373; worships idols 378
Daniel, 309
Daughters: not to be taught Torah 98; father may betroth minor 245
David, 311; speaks words of rebuke 23; rebukes Solomon just before death 30; areas conquered by 33; wants transgression hidden 47; begs God for grace 48; rebuked for sin 48; called "servant of God" 50; serves God no matter what 60; surrounded by commandments 69; ceased studying Torah 92; disobeyed Torah 108; always inquired of prophet 117, 118; maintained army 193; righteousness of 344; called "man of God" 350; opens with praise of God 351; gives life for Israel 356; guilt and merit 359; slew Goliath 361; Moses prayed for 361; takes money from Tribes to buy site of Temple 367
Dead: honor of 232
Dead Sea: coins cast into 144
Death: for transgression of Torah but not of Scribes 190; at hands of heaven 203; decreed for all men 347
Death penalty: by Jerusalem court 190
Debir: different names of 72; fought over by four kingdoms 72
Dedicated animals: when blemished 259
Deeds: not outweighed by suffering 60; dependent on learning 83; performed for their own sake 105
Deer: compared to Israel 72
Demons: actions of 327; possession by 331
Deuteronomy: read by king 193
Dew, 78–79
Disciples: called "children" 64; should study little by little 101; misinterpret if slothful 101–102; at onset of learning 102; one should cling to 106; distinguishing marks 355–356; can always return to Torah 358
Disgrace: must be intentional 284
Dispersion: generation of 316, 317
Divination: by staff 199–200; by fox 200
Divorce: writing bill of 167, 264; ground for 263–264; conditional 264–265; delivery of 265; rules of 266
Doorposts: writing upon 68; laws of 69
Dough offering, 79, 292

Edomites: confront Israel with sword 254
Egypt: inferior to Israel 70; planting of 73; watering of 73, 74; blessed because of Israelites 75; those who came up from 108; spoils of 166; departure from 173; prohibition of returning to 192; God shines forth 354
Egyptians, 254
Elders: appointed over community 84
Eleazar, 294–295; dressed in Aaron's garments 348
Eliezer, R.: comforted by ʿAkiba at death 61
Eliezer ben Dinai, 220
Elijah: coming of 84–85; offerings at Mt. Carmel 122; disobeyed Torah in emergency 202; termed "man of God" 350; will prophesy near coming of "the day" 351
Elkanah: termed "man of God" 350
Enchanter: definitions of 200
Enosh: flood at time of 92–93
Enticement, 138
Ephraim: Moses sees future of 379
Ephrath: identified with Beth-lehem 366; located in portion of Benjamin 366
Esau, 333; Jacob fears that Reuben will join 29; referred to as "fire" 83; unworthy 318; honored father 345; children of refuse Torah 352; slain by Judah 361; flatters Jacob 377
Essenes, 417

Eternal House, 289. *See also* Temple.
Eunuch: need not perform levirate marriage 281; widow of does not require levirate marriage 281
Euphrates: descriptions of 32
Evildoers: remove from Israel 138, 189, 191, 207, 223, 231, 247, 268
Evil spirits, 321
Examinations: in addition to investigations 187
Execution: performed by witnesses and others 189; by strangulation 191, 203, 268; manner of 211; hanging following 231, 232; by stoning 232; testimony of relatives 272
Exile, 332; of Ten Tribes 95; weighed against all other punishments 95; will come immediately 95; of Two Tribes 95–96; does not come immediately 96; observance of commandments in 96; as punishment of manslayer 205; not for one who killed from hatred 206
Exodus: haste at departure 174; story of recited at night 174; in daytime in defiance of Egyptians 346
Ezekiel: hostage for Israel 356–357
Ezra: caused Torah to be established 104

Famine, 331
Fasts: four 56–57
Father in heaven, 105
Fathers: merit of 206, 458; cannot save children 340
Favor: asked of God 48
Fear: inferior motive for observance of Torah 59; of God by prophets 202; of God 403–404
Festival of Tabernacles: offering of 181; why last 182
Festival of Weeks: observed even if no harvest 178–179; observance of 180; shorter because of work season 180
Festival offering, 173, 175
Festivals, 172; offerings of 118; working on 177; commandments of 179; each with its own statutes 179–180
Firstborn, 132; before entering Land 82; splitting of ear 146; laws of 227–228; plague of 383
First fleece: laws concerning 197
First fruits, 119, 323; forbidden to laymen 125; where consumed 125; declaration of 126; consumption of 153; liability for 287–288; when brought 288; declaration of 126, 288, 289, 290; basket for 289; brought when altar exists 289; vessel for 289; waving of 289; where brought 289; not brought by proselytes or slaves 289, 291; not from Transjordan 289, 291; set down twice 291
Firstling: laws of 123–124, 168, 169, 170; eaten after sprinkling of blood 126; forbidden to laymen 126; where consumed 126, 152–153; only from Land 152; rules of 152; how offered 153; when consumed 171; blemished 171
First tithe, 125
Five nations: territory of 291
Flood, generation of 311, 316; is vile 60; is lustful 90; extension granted to 95; quenched like sparks 317; generation of rebels 89, 325, 404
Forefathers: deeds of 337; bones brought out of Egypt 361
Forgiveness: granted Israel 55
Forgotten sheaves, 189, 261, 292, 303; after settlement of Land 82; not liable to tithe 157; laws of 272–273; when considered forgotten 274–275; of grapes 275
Four kingdoms, 320, 324; will enslave Israel 329; Israel delivered to 338
Fowl: species of 146
Free gifts: granted by God 106
Friend: acquiring 294
Fringes: laws about 243
Fruit trees: lack of yield a punishment 94
Future: dialogue of God and Israel 298ff.; when God will judge 311; Israel will hear from God 316; of Israel 320; redemption in 321; Israel

Future (*continued*)
will inherit world 322; pleasure for Israel in this world 322; when Israel will inherit oppressors' possessions 324; Israel will taunt nations 339; nations will praise Israel 342; Song refers to 343; God will punish nations 353

Gad: appears before Pharaoh 372; to be first in future 372; Moses buried in portion of 372; territory of 372
Gamaliel, R.: rebukes ʿAkiba 24; serves guests 74; and Roman officials 356
Garden of Eden: seen by Moses 380
Garment: returning of 235
Gates: place of judgment 186, 188
Gehenna: descent of wicked into 343; seen by Moses 380
Gentile: deceiving 397
Gideon: seen by Moses 379
Girgashites, 218
Gleanings, 189, 261, 272, 292, 303; after settlement of Land 82; not liable to tithe 157
God: nature of 19, 21; troubled by golden calf 26; does not hate Israel 45; promise to Abraham not hyperbole 46; will perform miracles for Israel when they go to Land 46; qualities of 49, 81, 389; servants of 50; ways not those of men 51–52; angry with Moses 53; asks Moses to be example for judges 53; promises Moses world to come 53; rests name upon Israel 58; is God of all the world 59; love and fear of 59; service with all one's heart and soul 59; how to love and recognize 62; serves man 74; feeds all 74; cares for all lands 79; concern is for Israel 79; power of blessing 81; rewards those who study most 83; knowledge of 84; provides rain 86; Israel does will of 87; rebellion against 89; and generation of flood 89; and people of Sodom 90; provides for those who do His will 91; causes flood at time of Enosh 93; castigates Israel for not appreciating prosperity 94; commands observance of commandments in exile 96; calls for repentance 96; changed order of world 100; man should imitate 105–106; merciful and gracious 105–106; cleaving to 106; knowledge of through aggadah 106; will drive out nations 106; chastises David for neglecting conquest of Jerusalem 108; guards Israel's possessions 110; places two paths before Israel 110; awe of 137; cleaving to 137; falsifying His words 138; claim on Israel because of Exodus 138, 140; fear of 154, 194; busy with those who are busy with Him 182; being whole-hearted with 201; considerate of His creatures' honor 212–213; with people in time of trouble 212, 214; has pity on tree and fruit 219; makes two utterances at once 243; is truthful judge 293; commands Moses concerning Joshua 294; delivers Israel to nations 295; eulogizes Adam 296; mourns at death of Moses 297; destroys witnesses against Israel 298; will forgive Israel 298–299; will not divorce Israel 299; rebuffed by, but not rebuffing Israel 299–300; accused Israel of changing character 300–301; calls Song to testify against Israel 303; name of not to be taken in vain 308; actions perfect 310; artist 310; no complaints possible about His work 310–311; keeps trust 311; three acquisitions of 315; harshness 316; will speak to Israel in future 316; assigns areas to nations 317; chooses Jacob 318; reigned only in heaven until Abraham 319; reveals self from four directions 321; feels as if in birthpangs 328; rests name upon Israel 328; wants to do good things for Israel 328; will remove presence 329; anger of 332; will deliver Israel to enemies 335; will take vengeance

337; regrets when He judges Israel 338; rejoices when He judges nations 338; will not forgive desecration of His name 339; arguments against 340; creates world with word, not oath 340; always collects His due 341; ways not those of humans 341; guides Moses 347; refuses Moses' request to go on living 347; refuses Moses' request to enter Land 348, 380; Moses, David, Solomon start with praise of 351; characteristics when giving Torah 352, 353, 354; shines forth four times 354; recognizable 354; loves Israel most 356; loves Israel differently 356, 357; name praised 358; is God when Israel is witness 359; glorious when acknowledged 359; called "Beloved" 364; dwells in Jerusalem always 365; praise of God and Israel for each other 375; description of His glory 376; will return to Israel ornaments taken away at Sinai 377; shows Moses all 378–380; takes souls of righteous and wicked 381; glory of seen by Moses 383; personal concern for Israel 411–412

God's name: desecration not forgiven 339

Gods, other: why termed "other" 92, 93; worship of 93; must be dispossessed 115

Gog and Magog: God will shine in time of 354

Golden calf, 391; worst sin of Israel 26; gold of Ark cover atones for 26; gold of Tabernacle atones for 26; many images of made 93

Good deeds: compared to prayer 54; Joshua commanded to 54

Goodness: reward of 112

Government: takes and gives abundantly 371

Grace: said when three persons are present 308; of God 400, 418

Grapes: definition of bunch 275

Great Assembly: sayings of 39

Greek culture: Rabbis' attitude toward 405

Guilt, 239

Guilt offerings, 132; where and how offered 126–127

Gush Halab: oil of 323

Haifa: treasures hidden in bay of 371

Halakah, 1, 16, 189, 306, 307; study of 104; circumvents Scripture 167; rules of 417

Ḥaliṣah: laws 279ff.; ceremony 282; shoes used for 282, 283; when valid 282, 283

Hall of Hewn Stones: located in portion of Judah 366

Hanan: children of did not tithe 152

Hananiah, Mishael, and Azariah: sanctify God's name 310

Hananiah ben Azzur: false prophet 137; prophesied that not said to him 203

Hananiah ben Teradion: martyrdom 312

Hanging: Roman practice 232; body not to hang overnight 232–233; different rules of for men and women 233

Hanukkah, 156, 288, 291

Harlotry: 258–259

Ḥasid, 418

Heart: undivided toward God 59

Heathens: power over heavenly bodies 137

Heave offerings, 125; from Israel alone 79; after settlement of Land 82; eating of 129; in condemned city 143

Hebrew bondwoman: ear not pierced 168

Hebrew slave: laws different for male and female 164; attainment of freedom 164; treatment conditioned by Egyptian slavery 165–166; piercing of ear 166; who rejects freedom 166, 167; serves master's son 167

Hebron, 70, 407

Heifer, 189; breaking neck of discontinued 220; conditions for 220; not brought by Jerusalem 221; number of judges required 221; neck of, how

Heifer (*continued*)
broken 222; ceremony of 223; atones for shedding of blood 305
Helping others, 233
Heretics, 330, 341; one should not learn from 102
Herodian doves, 143
Heshbon fortified, 30
Hezekiah: teaches Torah to all Israel 61–62, 64
Hiding one's self rather than helping 234, 235
Hillazon, 371
Hillel: died at age *120* 382. *See also* School of Hillel
Hiram, 378
Holiness: Israel must attain 145
Holiness (God): dictates to Moses 31, 34, 42, 46
Holy: permitted things prohibited to Israel 150
Holy Name: Passover sacrifice to 173
Holy of Holies: Titus tears curtain 339
Holy Scriptures in condemned city 143
Holy tongue: ḥaliṣah performed in 283; declaration of first fruits made in 290
Horeb: ornaments taken from Israel at 377
Hosea: comforts after using harsh words 349
Hospitality: not observed in Sodom 90
House of study: attendance at on holy days 177

Iddo: violated his words 203; called "man of God" 350
Idleness condemned 31
Idol(s): offerings to for which one is liable 135; kind of worship forbidden 141; abomination to Patriarchs 185; called "parents" 225; Jews have many 327
Idolater: causes five things 187; five names of 187
Idolatry, 162; destruction demanded 116; results from separation from Torah 92; in time of Enosh 92–93; association of God's name with 93; great number of idols 93; denies Torah 112; Canaanites steeped in 115; hills where practiced not to be destroyed 115; on mountains, hills, and trees 115; destruction of commanded only in Israel 116; three types of houses of 116; use of stone pillars and asherah 116; no benefit from objects of 143–144; caused God's anger 144; animals used for 147; execution by sword for 186; Israel worships things of no benefit 327
Imitation of God, 105–106
Incense, 364
Inclination to evil, 59, 92, 97, 98; bound by oaths 62–63; Torah speaks against 233, 235
Inclination to good, 59
Infidelity, suspicion of 209
Inheritance, laws of 228–229
Inquiries: seven questions in 187; difference from examinations 187–188
Intercourse, sexual: normal and abnormal 246; execution for illicit 248; establishes marriage 262, 263
Interest: laws of 259–260; advanced and delayed 260
Interpretation of Torah: technical terms of 114, 392, 401, 404, 409, 415, 420, 421
Isaac, 319; rebukes and makes peace 29; quarrels with Ishmael 56; binds himself on altar 62; brings blessing to Gerar 75; has unworthy descendants 318, 353; cannot save Esau 340; envisioned Temple 365; blessing 377; willing to be sacrificed 405
Isaiah: adds interpretations to Moses' words 302
Ishmael, 318
Ishmael, R.: interprets Torah symbolically 245
Ishmaelites: offered Torah 352
Israel: importance 17ff.; rebuked by Moses 24; rebelled at sea 25; sin prevents entering land 28; rebuked only

after overthrow of Sihon and Og 30; eternal as stars 34; accuses Moses of plotting 36; called "litigious" 36; troublemakers and skeptics 36; anxious to have judges 38; called endearing names 38; arrogance 43; demands spies 43; God cannot hate 45; hates God 45; punished after incident of spies 45; God perceives penitence of 55; God's name rests upon 58–59; receives three gifts through suffering 61; precious because of commandments 69; decked in commandments 69; desirable to God 69; pacified when leaving Egypt 70; receives God's reward when good 81–82, 87, 375; disregards God's good gifts 94; will be punished 94; to be exiled 96; to observe commandments in exile 96; changed deeds 100; numbering of 100; need not fear beasts 107; seven nations mightier than 107; fear of 109; no one can stand against 109; content with portion 111; abandons traditions and worships idols 139; when called "children of God" 144, 313; must be holy 145; each one of more precious than nations 145; welfare of 180; those who curse it curse themselves 254; distinguishable in Egypt 290; ruled by four kingdoms 294; scattered after Moses died 296; witnesses against 297; gets rain when fulfills God's will 300; should not change character 300–301; punished by those who witness against it 301; did not fulfill commandments concerning heaven 302; did not fulfill commandments concerning earth 303; symbolized by stars 310; called people of God 313; self-corrupted 313; cause of disgrace of 314; repaid measure for measure 314; precious to God 315; will hear from God in future 316; only nation worthy of Torah 317; actions at pronouncement of Ten Commandments 320; found in wilderness and taken to Sinai by God 320; perceives God's pronouncements 320; no nation will rule 321; protected from evil spirits 321; set apart 321; will have pleasure in future 322; will not have idolaters 322; will inherit the world 322; will inherit oppressors' possessions 324; backslides after miracles 328; God's children 329; not trustworthy 329; will never cease 330; worships insubstantial things 330; not helped by nations in time of trouble 333; flattered by nations in its prosperity 333, 377; inconquerable if Torah observed 334; voided good counsel 334, 335; its punishment will not be renewed 337; suffering of not immediate 338; benefits from Abraham 342; God will redeem in future while nations rage 342; being slain by nations serves as expiation 343; deserving of Moses' blessing 350; needs of 351; accepted Torah with details 353; asked by nations about God 354–355; prepared to die for God 355; loved by God 356; betrothed to God 357; though sinful, accepts yoke of Torah 357; called "beloved" 364; called upon to build Temple 364–365; gifts during years in wilderness 373; God and Israel praise each other 375; inquires of Moses concerning God's glory 375–376; salvation depends upon Shekinah 377; weeps for Moses 382. *See also* Land of Israel

Israelite woman: holy and pure 225

Israel-Land: *See* Land of Israel

Issachar: outstanding in Torah 370

Jabneh: court of 190; vineyard in 251

Jacob, 333; attitude toward 18, 19; rebukes sons just before death 29; called "servant of God" 50; merited Shema[c] 55–58; learns of Reuben's sin and repentance 57; vow of 57; reproves sons 58; thanks God for

Jacob (*continued*)
mercies 62; brings blessing to Laban 75; brings blessing to Pharaoh 75; commands sons when near death 112; expected to perish in Aram 290; goes to Egypt 290; all children of worthy 318, 353; chosen by God 318; chose God 319; received reward of all Patriarchs 319; advises people to accept kingdom of heaven 334; observed all of Torah 345; blessing 350, 377; has vision of Temple 365; would lean upon Benjamin 368; flattered by Esau 377
Jebusites, 108
Jehoiachin: life of in exile 95
Jehoiakim: fate of corpse 95
Jehoshaphat, 362; poor leader 294
Jehu, 326
Jeremiah, 376; author of two Scrolls 23; speaks rebuke 23; responds "Amen" to himself 330; speaks harshly, then comforts 349–350
Jericho: strong as all other cities together 109; pasture of for Jethro 117–118; not to be rebuilt 143
Jeroboam, 326, 366–367
Jerusalem, 118, 120, 122, 258, 331, 380; expands to Damascus 27; called "resting place" 27, 121; destruction of 56, 57; David did not conquer first 108; Judah not permitted to drive out inhabitants 125; chosen by God 127; cannot be a city condemned for idolatry 141; second tithe consumed in 153; home of house of Nebalta 158; chamber of secrets in 163; staying overnight in on Passover 177; need not bring heifer 221; scholars of 229; supplies idol molds to world 327; nations come to 370–371
Jethro: tells Moses qualities of judges 38; descendants benefit from pasture of Jericho 117, 367
Job: "called servant of God" 51; serves God no matter what 60; satiety brought suffering 326
Joel: speaks harshly, then comforts 349
Joḥanan ben Zakkai: meeting with daughter of Nakdimon 295; dies at *120* 382
Jonah: suppressed prophecy 203
Jordan River, 309; Israel rebuked for deeds beyond 24
Jose: incident with oil 323
Joseph: wisdom of 27; brings blessing to Potiphar 75; right of primogeniture 229; righteousness of 344; Reuben's actions concerning 359; land of blessed 368; mountains of older than Sanctuary 368–369; first to go to Egypt and will be first in future 369; performed God's will 369
Joshua, 107; rebukes Israel just before death 29; speaks in favor of Land 45; called "servant of God" 51; must accompany people to Land 54–55; elevated to leadership 294; weeps at death of Moses 297; chosen 332; gains authority 344; righteousness 344; apportioned Land 366; conquests 369; given strength and beauty 369; quality of majesty 369; slays many Canaanites 370; Moses has vision of 379; writes conclusion of Torah 380; fear of 382–383
Josiah, 362
Journey: places described 32
Journey in wilderness: duration of 27, 28
Jubilee year, 300, 303; observed after settlement of Land 82; releases slaves 159; does not release loans 159, 239
Judah: admits sin 360; causes Reuben to repent 360; would be buried with patriarchs 361; Moses sees history of 379
Judah, R.: incident with honey in jar 323; school of 391
Judges: burden of 34; must be exact in decisions 34; appointed by Moses 37; characteristics 37; must be known to Tribes 37; women not eligible 37; wrapped in cloaks 37; bear guilt of people 37–38; fortunate to be ap-

pointed over Israel 38; to be held in honor 38–39; must exercise authority 39; not to be appointed by favoritism 40–41; not to respect persons 41; not to fear 41; appointment of for cities and Tribes 183; must not show favoritism 183; must not pervert justice 183–184; experts 189; qualifications 190, 210; responsibilities 395

Judgment: deliberation in 39; in future 299; according to deeds 316

Justice: between Jews and non-Jews 39–40; measure of on high 312

King: command to appoint 121, 192; Israel demands 191; may not multiply horses for self 192; not a Gentile 192; not from outside Land 192; rules concerning 192; may not have more than eighteen wives 193; may not multiply own riches 193; should not be led astray by wives 193; writes own Torah 193; common man equal to in Torah 194; should keep Torah with him 194; special rights 194; must observe Torah 195

Kingdoms, four. *See* Four kingdoms

Kings: Joshua subjects thirty-one 369

Korah, 311

Laban: considered destroyer of Jacob 290

Laborer: right to eat of produce 261, 262

Land of Israel, 270, 330; merit of 19; will expand 27; "called resting place" 28; to be possessed without weapons 33; higher than all lands 45, 75; earned through suffering 61; most precious 70; superior to Egypt 70; lacks nothing 71; Torah dwells in 71; compared to deer 72; fruits of 72–73, 77; praised by Scripture 72, 76; all kingdoms want place in 72, 369; contrasted with best of Egypt 73; how watered and planted 73, 74; blessed because of Israelites 75; built up by Canaanites 76; duty of coming to 76; retained only if Israel obeys God 76; contains many lands 77; watering of 78; all other lands cared for by God because of 79; given as reward for studying Torah 79; offerings taken from 79; others will purchase its produce 88; defining boundaries of 107; must be conquered first 107; borders 108; possession as reward for entering 112; dwelling in as reward 114; possessed because of merit 114; altars permitted after entering 120; profane meat permitted in after arrival 128; as reward for going in to dispossess inhabitants 134; Sages weep when leaving 134; duty of dwelling in equivalent to all commandments 134–135; poor not to be taken out of 158; inhabitants of take precedence 161; polluted by idolatry 187; highest land 190, 322; possession of 191; obligation of first fleece 196; obligation of first fruits 196; one enters as reward for performance 199; prophet must come from 202; possession of 287; saved by God for Israel alone 317; has most digestible fruits 322; oppressors in possession of 324; makes expiation for dwellers 343; Moses sees 347, 419; money streams to 375; upholds earth 376; holiness ceased after first exile 419

Landmark: removal of 207, 208

Languages: four used by God in giving Torah 352

Laodicea, 345; sent to purchase oil in Gush Halab 374, 375

Lashing: punishment by 276–277

Leaders: give lives for Israel 356

Learning: not dependent on deeds 83

Leaven: when prohibited 174; may not be eaten after sixth hour 174; nullification of 175; size of prohibited amount 175

Lebanon: refers to king 32; refers to Temple 32, 394; means "sanctuary" 52, 53

Leper: cleansing of 189, 237, 238
Leprosy: various plagues of 268–269
Levi: not among the spies 44; repays debt concerning Shechem 362; helps God 362; not guilty of idolatry 363; makes Israel acceptable to God 364
Levirate marriage: laws of 279ff.; exclusions from 281
Levites, 198; administer lashing 39; pronounce blessings and curses 113; given gifts 122; received various portions 127–128; not responsible in Diaspora 128; supported during Sabbatical and Jubilee years 128; receive gifts 155–156; may take portion 157; rights 195; tithe 292; brothers fight over right to be 374
Levitical camp, 256
Limbs: of animals forbidden 130
Loaf: descends with cudgel from heaven 82
Locusts: clean and unclean 149
Lost article: returned if worth one peruṭah 235
Lot's daughters: sin because of satiety 90
Love: cause for observing commandments 59; cause for study of Torah 85; makes others love God 99; of neighbor, but not of one who inclines to idolatry 139; of God 404
Lulab̲: not to be added to 136; must belong to individual 180

Machpelah: Moses envisions 379
Man: likened to angels and beasts 307; created to be righteous 310
Man of God: title given to ten men 350–351
Manasseh, 326, 362
Manna: disparaged by Israel 25; for Israel alone 320
Manslayer: definition of 204, 205; need not wander from city to city 205
Marriage: by money 262, 263; by intercourse 263; by document 263
Martania, 330
Martha, daughter of Boethus: riches of 272
Measure for measure, 287, 326
Meat: profane consumption of 128–129; prohibition of with milk 131, 150
Mercy, 49, 389, 431; indicated by name "Lord" 49; Hezekiah begs 53; Moses begs 53; for those who show mercy 144; should not be withheld 162; felt by Israel for nations 335
Merit: brought by the meritorious 239; fathers', causes Israel to multiply 144
Messiah, 392; sharp toward nations 26–27; time of 33, 64, 98, 334, 365; Exodus remembered in days of 174; generation of 316; three generations preceding rebel 326; God will shine in time of 354
Methods of interpretation: taught by Moses 30
Mĕzuzah, 68, 69; required 239
Micah: speaks harshly, then comforts 349; called "man of God" 350–351
Midrash, 1, 3, 4, 8; must be studied 104. *See also* Tannaitic midrashim
Midrash Tannaim, 5
Minor: definition of 182
Minor to major, inference from, 59, 64, 65, 71, 72, 74, 75, 99, 100, 110, 123, 126, 127, 138, 148, 159, 184, 192, 219, 250, 254, 255, 269, 274, 278, 286, 308, 313, 329, 344
Miriam: punished for slander 25, 26, 269; place where doomed 47; Moses asks if God will heal 49; spoke against Moses for his benefit 269; went before banners 269; death 295; well disappears at death 296; did not die because of sin 346–347; sin of questioned 363
Mishnah, 1, 2, 7, 306, 324
Mixed seeds: prohibited in Land and elsewhere 97
Mnemonic for Ten Plagues 290
Moabites, 253; plot against Israel 254; prohibited forever 254; offered the Torah 352

Molech: prohibition against sacrificing children to 199
Monetary compensation, 211
Months: number of 392
Moses: attitude of Sifre toward 19; author of Torah 23; rebukes all Israel 24; challenged to provide sustenance for children 25; rebukes Israel before death 29; rebukes Israel after overthrow of Sihon and Og 30; teaches methods of interpreting Torah 30; speaks God's word, not his own 31; wants to go to Land even if only after death 31; gives land to the people 33; his acts described 34; reluctant to sit as judge 34; adds his blessing to Abraham's 35–36; accused of plotting 36; feels rejected by the people 38; taught humility by God 41–42; tells Israel of Land 43; asks to have transgression recorded 47; fears being accused of falsifying Torah 47; place where doomed 47; transgression 47; begs God for favor 48; begs mercy 48ff., 53; asks God for favor after defeat of Sihon and Og 49; asks three things of God 49; called "servant of God" 50; prays for Israel's forgiveness 50; vows not to leave Jethro 50; demonstrates preciousness of God's word to him 52; asked to be example for judges 53; attempts to claim part of Israel 54; learning from 84; defines what may be conquered 107; equal to all Israel 109; explains why wicked prosper 111; commands rules of ritual slaughtering 130; example for prophets 136; not a hunter or an archer 148; receives festival laws at Sinai 172; teaches laws of festivals at each one 172; lover of peace 217; asks who will succeed him 293–294; lifts up and fortifies Joshua 294, 295; saddened that son is not leader 294; wanted to bring people to Land 295; death 295, 380; after his death Israel has no satisfaction 295; all gifts disappear after his death 296; accused by Israel at time of Aaron's death 296; sought by angel of death 296–297; assured of world to come 297; close to heaven 302; called two witnesses against Israel 303; suffered for Torah 305; went among angels 305; brings witness against Israel 307; mentions God after uttering twenty-one words 308; describes God's justice to Israel 312–313; tells Israel to think of God's goodness 314; pleads for mercy for Israel 339; grateful to Israel for observing Torah 344–345; greatest of all 345; Israel does not want him to die 346; did not die because of sin 346–347; questions why he must die 347; sees kings and prophets, future 347; sees whole world 347; desired same death as Aaron 347–348; caused Israel not to sanctify God 348; enveloped in God's wings 348; pleads to be permitted to enter Land 348; speaks harsh words, then comforts 349; called "man of God" 350; continues Jacob's blessing 350; deserving of blessing Israel 350; blessed Israel close to death 351; opened blessing with praise of God 351; gives life for Israel 356; prayed for Tribe of Judah 360; prayed for Simeon 361; prayed for David 361; prayed for house of David 361–362; splendor of 369; carried after death by God to burial place 372; buried in portion of Gad 372, 381; dies in portion of Reuben 372, 381; will sit at head of scholars 373; describes God's glory 376; tells Israel about future 377; sees kings who descend from Ruth 378; burial place 378; sees prophets descended from Rahab 378; foresees all of future 378, 379, 380; has vision of Garden of Eden and Gehenna 380; begs to be brought to Israel even if after death 380; wrote Torah 380, 389; writes end of Torah at God's

Moses (*continued*)
dictation 380–381; death proclaimed by heavenly voice 381; never died, but serves on high 381; mysterious sepulcher 381–382; body of after death 382; died at *120* 382; mourned before and after death 382; compared to Balaam 383; sees glory of God when on verge of death 383

Mountain: Israel commanded to leave 31

Mt. Abiram: four names of 346–347

Mt. Gerizim and Mt. Ebal: blessings and curses upon 112; location of 113

Mt. Hermon: four names 71; fought over by four kingdoms 71

Mt. Nebo: three names 72; fought over by three kingdoms 72

Mt. Sinai, 383; rebellion after 329

Naaman: fears to take soil without permission 110

Nakdimon ben Gorion, 295

Name of God: letters of may not be erased 117; pronounced only in Temple 118

Naphtali: presented to Pharaoh 373; happy with portion 373; Moses has vision of 378–379

Nations: voided Noachide commandments 18, 334–335; rejoice while Israel suffers 94; should not be imitated 135; do not abandon traditions 139; each Israelite more precious than 145; idolatrous worship 187; may learn their ways for understanding 199; Israel inherits their portions and adds to them 203–204; are inheritance for the worthy 317; Gehenna their portion 317; God gives each an area 317; have double Israel's portion 318; estrange themselves from Israel 333; flatter Israel when it is prosperous 333, 337; cruel to Israel 335; punishment will be renewed 337; punishment includes deeds of ancestors 342; praise Israel in future 342; inquire of Israel concerning God 354–355; want to become proselytes 371. *See also* Seven nations

Naziriteship: lasts thirty days 382

Nebalta: family in Jerusalem 158, 292

Ne<u>b</u>elah: no liability for unless eaten 131

Nebuchadnezzar, 336

Necromancer: definition 201

Needy: alone eligible for poor man's tithe 157; Israel needy only when failing to do God's will 160; of own city have precedence 161; obligation to support 161

Nehemiah, R.: interprets verses as referring to cruelty of nations 336, 339

New Produce: observed within Land and outside 97; observed outside Land 115

New Year's Day, 157; rain decreed on 80; blessing decided upon 80

Nisbis, 134

Noachide commandments: taken away from nations 18; governing consumption of animal limbs 130, 131; cast off by nations 353; given Israel 353

Noah: enters Ark in defiance of people 346

Notarikon, 430

Observance, methods of 133

Officers, appointment of 183

Og, might of 30

Olive trees, beating of 274–275

Omer: observed after entering Land 82

Onkelos, Targum of. *See* Targum Onkelos

Oppressors: Moses sees Israel's 380

ʿOrlah, law of: observed in Land and outside 97, 115

Parables: one entertains all without discrimination 26; concerning sin of golden calf 26; king asked to supply troops with white bread 30; king gives field to servant who improves it 33; guardian adds gift to those king gives his son 35; tutor shows king's son everything belonging to him 43; trial permitted when selling animal 44; woman paraded in arena for eating Sabbatical figs 47; king's son injured when carriage overturns 47; man cannot repay loan to king 47–48; king grants colony status to city following defeat of enemies 48–49; king forbids servants to drink wine 52; king forbids son to enter bedchamber 54; beautiful room first built of two 70; proper way to entice a woman into betrothal 71; king gives one noble manservants but favors another 73–74; king keeps keys to storehouse 81; king instructs son on behavior in banquet house, but son disgraces himself 93; robber enters field and owner does not object 96; king sends wife away but instructs her to wear jewelry 96; king strikes son, then bandages him 97; king gives servant bird intended for son and cautions him to guard it 101; two brothers inherit money 101; king favors friends at banquet 111; person stands at crossing of smooth and thorny paths 111; king's unworthy son 294; king entrusts son to tutor 299; king's depraved son 300; king entrusts son to two deputies 300; man goes to Caesarea with sum of money 306; one who is crucified 313; one who insults a senator 314; one who insults his father 314; one who inherits fields then buys one of his own 315; king takes field from dishonest tenants 318; king deserted by all but one person 319; man puts yoke on calf 326; owner sells slave to be delivered in future 335; animals laden with produce 353; giving gifts to favorites 353; king's son taken into captivity 358; man builds palace on two ships 358; king visits children 359; two men borrow from king 362; king's youngest son sad because king stays with elder brothers 367; youngest son takes care of king 368; one wishes king's glory, but swoons at lesser sights 376; tutor tells man's son what will belong to him 377; bailee with whom goods are deposited 381; king's butcher 383

Paradise, 34

Parapet, 238–239

Passover, 157; time of conclusion of tithes 156; not a work season 180

Passover sacrifice: when one is liable for 131; application of blood 133; slaughter must be for that purpose 172, 173; brought from sheep and goats 173; needed for expiation 173; consumed at evening 175; for single individual 175–176; offered in uncleanness 176; on private altar 176; on Sabbath 176

Patriarchs: each improves Land 33; each worthy 33; each Israelite more precious than 145; favor pillars 185; reject idols 186; and Matriarchs called "mountains and hills" 369; did not attain to Moses' visions 380

Peace: brought by rebuke 29; greatness of 217; conditions for making 217; suing for 219; not to be achieved from strife 276, 283

Peace offerings, 323; laws of 126; called "rejoicing" 155, 179; when offered 182

Pentecost, 288

Performance of Torah, 86, 114; compared to study of 83

Pharaoh, 336; daughter favored by Solomon 110; first to enslave Israel 342

Phinehas: equal in worth to all others 109; reward 196–197; pleads for mercy 339

Phylacteries, 405; sections of 63, 64, 65; and Ten Commandments 65, 66; placement of 66, 67; writing of 67–68; compared to Torah 97; incumbent upon person 97; not dependent

Phylacteries (*continued*)
upon Land 97; not worn in bathhouse or tannery 257
Pilgrimage offering, 182
Pilgrim festivals, 156
Pillars: forbidden 185; favored by patriarchs 185
Place: name for God 399
Plagues, 365; come from evil talk 269; Miriam punished with 269. *See also* Ten Plagues
Plague-spots: rules of 222–223
Planets: seven (seven stars) 395
Plants: grow to large size 324
Platana, 134
Pledge: what may not be taken as 267–268; seizure of 269, 270; not to be kept overnight 270
Plowing: prohibited with yoked ox and ass 240–241
Poor: amount due them 157–158; sustained in Land 158; result of not doing God's will 163; proper treatment of 275; help given to 292
Poor man's tithe, 125
Prayer: ten terms for 48; individual and group 50; more efficacious than good deeds 53–54; directed toward Israel and Jerusalem 54; called "service" 85; precedes blessing 350
Priestly blessing, 198; how performed in Temple and outside 118; may not be added to 136; given only by unblemished 222
Priests: warned to be wholehearted in service 85; not singled out for Torah study 104; claim dues through judge 196; dues to described 196; portion of, 197, 198; stand while ministering 198; watches of 198; when qualified 289; wealth 364
Profane animals: rules on slaughtering 129
Proper conduct: taught by Torah 128
Prophets: inquired concerning place of Temple 117; voice of God 137; definition 202; determination of true prophet 203; called "father" 316; learn from Moses to speak comfort after harsh words 349
Prophets, false, 136; Hananiah ben Azzur an example 137; execution 138, 140; how they entice 141; when to be put to death 202–203
Prosbul, 161
Proselytes, 136, 196; included in population of idolatrous city 142; damsel 246; Egyptian 255; not to be oppressed 271; justice to may not be perverted 272; not liable for gleanings if converted after harvest 272; exempt from levirate marriage 281–282; court of 283; need not bring first fruits 289, 291
Prosperity not as beneficial as chastisement 60. *See also* Satiety
Proverb, popular, 45
Punishment: measure of 60; five types 94; from God's nostril 330; of nations 337; of Israel will not be renewed 337

Qualities of God, 81, 400, 418

Rachel: died in portion of Benjamin 366
Rahab, 309; holy spirit rests upon 44; fears Israel 109; prophets issue from 347
Rain: as means of punishment 80, 94; from Sabbath eve to Sabbath eve 86; given by God 86; season 86–87; why called "former rain" 86–87; blessing from west 307; harmful from south 307
Ram sacrificed for Isaac created miraculously 372
Rape, 250, 251; homosexual 249; liability for 249
Rapist: when liable 248; execution of 248
Rebellion: caused by satiety 325
Rebellious elder forgiven 230
Rebellious son: laws of 230–231; dies innocent 231
Rebuke, 389, 390; prophecies of 23; in Deuteronomy 23; methods 24; of Is-

rael for sins 24, 25; brings peace 29; administered just before death 29; will cease after comfort 350
Redemption: of blemished animals 123; future 337
Red heifer, 363
Red Sea, 166, 383, 390
Regulations: always fresh 114
Rejoicing: refers to peace offerings 119, 122, 179; offering on Festival of Tabernacles 181
Release: of debts 158–159, 160; of land only in Land 158, 159
Repentance: God calls Israel to 96; of inhabitants of Canaan 218
Resident alien: animals permitted to 149, 150
Responses: to blessings 308–309
Resurrection: taught in Torah 98; deduced from Scripture 307, 308; four assurances of 340; foreseen by Moses 379
Reuben: rebuked by Jacob 29; sins and repents 57, 58, 360; fasts to repent 57–58; God reconciled to by other Tribes 359; will live in world to come 359; admits sin 360; did not actually sin 360; Asher tells about deed of 374
Revolt in Judea, 334
Reward: for commandments 86, 286; for not transgressing 278; overcoming temptations 278; in this world and world to come 345
Reward and punishment, 311–312, 360; by rain 80, 94
Righteous: seven groups of in paradise 34; resemble seven things 35; gravity of assassination of 57; slain for God's sake 59; bring blessing 75; faces will shine 98; will greet the Shekinah 98; no hatred among 99; compared to stars 99; endure for all eternity 99, 100; world created for 99, 100; suffer 111; possessions of in condemned city 142; quietude beneficial 231; drunkenness bad 231; world enlarged because of 300; have dominion over world 302; man created to be 310; take nothing due them in this world 311; deeds 337; not rewarded here 337; souls kept in God's treasury 357; treasures hidden away for 371; how God takes souls 381
Righteous courts: examples 184
Righteousness: kept under throne of glory 373
Ritual fringe: number of strands may not be added to 136
Ritual slaughter: details of commanded 130; of fowls, rabbinic 130
Roman government: hangs people alive 232
Rome: everyone wants place in 72, 369; visited by Sages 91, 325

Šaʿăṭnez: laws of 241–242
Sabbath: spirits questioned on 201; siege to be laid no less than three days prior 219; setting out to sea before 219
Sabbatical year, 303; unripe figs of 47; observed after settlement of Land 82; borders of Land in respect of 108; releases loans 159; does not release slaves 159; observed most in Asher 374
Sacred pole: uprooting 116
Sacrifice: of children 187
Sacrifices: cause appeasement 61; observed before entering Land 82; on festivals 118, 119; of greater and lesser sanctity 124; rules 185
Sadducees: refutation of 211
Sages: one should cling to 106
Samaria, 327
Samaritans: falsify Torah 113
Šamir: created at twilight 372
Samson: seen by Moses 378
Samuel: rebukes Israel before death 29; taught humility by God 42; called "man of God" 350
Sanctification: threefold 308
Sanctification of God's name: achieved

Sanctification of God's name (*continued*) by punishing Pharaoh 309; as purpose of going to Egypt 309; as purpose of miracles 309–310
Sanctified objects: saved from condemned city 143
Sanhedrin, 84; tries capital cases 183
Satiety causes rebellion 89–90, 325
Saul: mighty as all others together 110
Saying: meaning of 49
School of Hillel: teaching concerning Shema^c 65
School of Shammai: teaching concerning Shema^c 65
Scribes' ordinances, 190
Scroll: descends from heaven 82; read by king and corrected by priests and Levites 193, 194
Scroll of pottery, 104
Sea: gives and takes in abundance 371
Second tithe: money of 125; in condemned city 143; may not be taken from one year to the next 150; rules 152; where consumed 152–153; defilement 154–155
Seduction, 250, 251
Seeds: diverse kinds of forbidden 240
Selfsame day: interpretations of phrase 346
Seminal discharge, 256
Sennacherib, 336; did not disparage Land 71
Sepphoris, 323; liṭra of 324
Sepulcher of Moses, 381–382
Servants: those called "servants of God" 50; early prophets called 381
Seven nations: will be driven out 106; mightier than Israel 107
Seven species, 287–288
Seventh year: produce not liable to tithing 156
Seven weeks: counting of 178
Shammai, School of. *See* School of Shammai
Shaphan: caused Torah to be established 104
Sheaf: harvesting and counting 178
Shekinah, 377; wings of 59; righteous will greet 98; idolatry causes departure of 187; kept away by iniquities 201; camp of 256; departs from world 256; driven away by unchastity 257; inescapable 299; dwells in Benjamin's portion 366; carried Moses' body 372
Shelomziyyon, 86, 412
Shema^c, 5, 6, 7; origins of 58; recited aloud 58; sections of recited 63; story of R. Ishmael reciting 65; when recited 65; where not to be recited 257; assures world to come 343; recited aloud 403
Shemaiah: called "man of God" 350
Shiḥin, 324
Shiloh: 122, 127, 289; chosen by God 154; God's name dwells in 174
Showbread: observed after entering Land 82
Sidon, 134
Sifre: origin and structure 4ff.; interpretive methods and formulas 8ff.; homiletic themes 15ff.
Sihon, might of 30
Siknin, honey of 322
Simeon: did not make up for sin of Shechem, but added to it 362
Simeon bar Yoḥai: concept of study 408, 413
Simeon ben Shetah: hanged women in Ashkelon 232
Sin: forgiveness of 60; causing others to 254; God will punish 353
Sin offerings, 132; sprinkling of blood 126; where offered 126
Sisera, 336, 379
Slander, 256
Slave: release of 158; given to purchaser's son 164; Hebrew slave to be sold only to Israelite 164; if ill need not make up time 164; purchase only a Hebrew one 164; returning runaway 164; helping when freed 164–165; contrasted to hireling 168; labors day and night 168; freed if sold to heathen or outsider 257; condition of

half-slave 268; need not bring first fruits 289; when freed need not bring first fruits 291
Sodom, 311, 316; eliminated hospitality 90; rebelled out of satiety 90, 325; to be eradicated 90; fire 317; vine of 336
Sodomy, 258, 327
Sofne, lake of 373
Solomon, 323, 333, 378; author of three Scrolls 24, 389; exactitude in judgment 34; merit of, dependent on David 51; precedes needs of Israel with praise of God 351; was beloved 364; seen by Moses making vessels 380
Son, stubborn and rebellious. *See* Stubborn and rebellious son
Song, greatness of 343
Soothsayer, definitions of 200
Sorcerer, definitions of 200
Soul: origin of 307; precious 340
Species, seven. *See* Seven species
Spies, 399; arrogance of 44; demand for displeases God 44
Spring, 172
Stealing of persons, 268
Stoning, 248; number of stones used in 188; man must be naked at, but woman not 233; of woman not a virgin 247
Strangulation: method of execution if not otherwise specified 247
Stubborn and rebellious son: laws over 229ff.; result of marriage to captive woman, 229; judged by actions 229; may be forgiven 229–230
Study, 114; relation to performance 83; called "service" 85, 86
Sufferings, 316; value of 60; appease more than sacrifices 61; due to preciousness of Israel 317; of Israel not immediate 338
Sword descends from heaven, 82

Tabernacle, 292; altars forbidden after its erection 120
Tabernacle festival, 156, 288; not a work season 180
Tablets: inscribed with word of God 355; created at twilight 372; breaking of 383
Talmud, 306, 324
Tannaitic midrashim, 3, 8
Targum Onkelos, 7
Teacher: called "father" 64
Tebel, 125
Teḥina ben Perishah, 220
Temple (in Jerusalem), 290; called "Lebanon" 32; does not require mĕzzuzot 69; created before all else 70; highest and best of temples 73; service 85; ruins 91; will be rebuilt 92; destruction of not to be forgotten 96; built in territory of Judah and Benjamin 117; destruction caused by following heathens 117; prohibition of chipping stones from 117; "My name" refers to 118; money for raised from all Tribes 118, 123; building of commanded 121; two areas for holier and lesser sacrifices 121; tithes and firstlings to be consumed whether Temple stands or not 153; place chosen by God 154; God's name dwells in 174; higher than Land of Israel 190; vows to 261; repair 261; is God's acquisition 315; highest place 323, 365; people rebelled after building 329; purpose to house Ark 357; called "beloved" 364; First and Second 365; built in portion of Benjamin 366; main building in Joseph's portion 366; section of in Judah 366; envisioned by Moses 378. *See also* Compartment of Temple
Temple Mount, 295; called "mountain" 52; trees forbidden upon 184; three courts of 189; may not be entered while carrying staff or purse 257
Temple service: swearing by 24
Ten Commandments: 63–64, 187, 320, 392–393; not in phylacteries 65, 66; in Shemaʿ and phylacteries 405

Ten Plagues: as "hand" 51; mnemonic for 290

Ten Tribes: exile of 95; time of 323; satiety of causes exile 326

Thanksgiving offerings: laws of 126

Throne of glory, 373

Tiberias: court 373; lake 373

Tithes, 119, 132, 303, 487; due from Israel alone 79; of animals, observed before entering Land 82; of Israel, observed after settlement 82; grain and animal 122; unclean 125; laws 126; of cattle 132; application of blood 133; not taken from one year for next 150; products liable for 151, 152; of corn 152; sometimes turned into money 154; number of each year 156, 157; declaration may be said in any language 292; one per year 292; removed on last day of Passover 292. *See also* First tithe; Second tithe

Tithing: leads to study 154; confession of 292, 293

Titus: wicked 339; accuses Moses of misleading the people 339

Tomorrow: when God will bring redemption to Israel 298, 299, 316, 324, 337, 342

Tongs: creation of 372

Torah, 323–324; earned by suffering 61; uses common language 65; created before all else 70; dwells in Israel 71; reward for observing 82; guide to knowledge of God 84; leads to coming of Elijah 84; study of out of love 85; speaks of normal things 87; time for study 87; separation from causes idolatry 92; called "good' 96; compared to elixir of life 97; masters inclination to evil 97; study of incumbent upon person 97; study of not dependent upon Land 97; contains doctrine of resurrection 98; taught to sons, but not daughters 98; as difficult to acquire as silver 100; as easy to lose as glass to destroy 100; called "tree" 100; created for glory of Israel 100; endures for all eternity 100; to be studied more than once 100; likened to water 102–103; likened to wine, ointment, honey 103; should be learned gradually and retained 103; both easy and difficult parts must be studied 104; would have been forgotten but for great leaders 104; all are equal in regard to 104, 194; to be both studied and performed 105; to be studied for its own sake 105; world created with 105; one should feel as if receiving it 106; acknowledgment of is denial of idolatry 112; merit of learning 134; words of always spoken publicly 139; proof of its coming from heaven 148; not above God 194; metaphorical interpretation of 196; abrogated for needs of hour 202; made void 202; given from heaven 302; words of 303; compared to rain and dew 304; assembled into general rules 304, 306; atones for sins 305; brings life 305; lack of fulfillment of brings death 305; learning 306; types of men who study it 306; Israel fails to gain wisdom from 314–315; God's acquisition of 315; only Israel worthy of 317; rules of interpreting 324; men mighty in 332, 360; one must direct self to 344; contains nothing vain 345; God comes to give 352; God offers to nations who question its worth 352; given to Jacob because his children worthy 353; called "strength" 354; God shines forth when giving 354; likened to fire 355; attained because of merits of forefathers 357; betrothed to Israel 357–358; Israel's inheritance 358; two given to Israel 363–364; Issachar outstanding in 370; three Scrolls of in Temple 376; writing of last eight verses 380–381. *See also* Interpretation of Torah

Tower of Babel, 311; men of rebel out of satiety 90, 325; people scattered 317

Tree: source of life 219; may be cut down for siege 219; used for hanging 232
Trees: fruitful and unfruitful 220
Trial: all stand before God's 210
Trials: ten trials of God 26
Tribes (of Israel): given twelve lands 77. *See also* Ten Tribes
Twilight: things created at, before first Sabbath 372
Two loaves: observed after entering Land 82
Tyre, 374
Tyrian silver, 246

Unleavened bread: definition of 174; time of eating 174; called "bread of affliction" 174; eaten for seven days 177
Usha: story of Rabban Gamaliel 356
Utterances: spoken simultaneously by God 242–243

Vengeance: of God 342
Vineyards: prohibition of diverse seeds in 240
Violence: of nations against Israel 342–343
Violent men, 315
Virgin, 267, 332; laws concerning 249, 250
Virginity: changed rules concerning 244–245, 246; accidental loss of 250

Wages: prohibitions of withholding 270; when may be collected 271
War: men without limb not obligated to serve in 211; but all commanded to serve in defensive 212; nonobligatory 212, 217, 224; destruction of cities 218; execution of captured males 218; spoils 218; voluntary 219; rules 255–256; newly married man exempted 267; supplies 267
Water: comparison of in Israel and in Egypt 407ff.
Weights: rules of honest 284, 285; cleaning of 285
Wicked: represented by sun, moon, and sea 24; receive no reward 24; prosperity of 111; cause world to be straitened 300; rewarded in this world for minor commandments 311; take nothing due them in this world 311; deeds of 337; not punished here 337; God takes souls 381
Widow: garment not to be taken as pledge 272
Wife: referred to as "household" 119–120; laws concerning beloved and hated 226–227. *See also* Co-wives
Wilderness: Israel rebuked for sins in 24, 25; people of rebel out of satiety 325
Winds: witness against Israel 307; four 307
Wine: great quantities in future 325
Wisdom: definition of the wise 37; nations' not to be studied 64
Witnesses: examination 141–142; inquiry 142; two or three required 186; claim ignorance 188; condemning person to death 188; contradicting one another 188; must participate in execution 189; two required in monetary and capital cases 208; for woman to remarry 208; for oath 209; when considered false 209; false 210; tested 210; false, execution of 211; must be first to lay hands upon guilty man 301
Women: may not be judges 37; litigation with men 40; included in those addressed by prophets 136; not included in festival appearance at Jerusalem 182; not to be appointed leaders of community 192; two witnesses required in cases concerning 208; cannot act as witnesses 210; hanged with back to people 233; nakedness of considered illicit 233; not to be stoned naked 233; may not wear men's garments 236; may not carry arms 236; may not speak in man's stead 245; Ammonite and Moabite may be accepted 253; how

Women (*continued*)
acquired in marriage 262, 263; care for reputation of 272
Word: goes forth from God 355
Workman: not to be oppressed 270
World: all in it remains constant 300–301
World to come, 64, 98, 359; earned through suffering 61; bestowed by Torah 105; Moses assured of 297; good things of, 316; how to be assured of 343

Year: number of months 28, 29; intercalation 172

Zebulun: presented to Pharaoh 370; agent for brothers 370
Zechariah: God's witness 91–92
Zelophehad, daughters of: Moses unable to solve case of 42